FINANCE AND GOVERNMENT UNDER
MARIA THERESIA
1740–1780

TO ALAN BULLOCK,
LORD BULLOCK OF LEAFIELD

Founding Master of St Catherine's College
Oxford

Finance and Government under Maria Theresia 1740–1780

P. G. M. DICKSON

In two volumes

VOLUME I
SOCIETY AND GOVERNMENT

CLARENDON PRESS · OXFORD

1987

Oxford University Press, Walton Street, Oxford OX2 6DP

Oxford New York Toronto Melbourne Auckland
Delhi Bombay Calcutta Madras Karachi
Petaling Jaya Singapore Hong Kong Tokyo
Nairobi Dar es Salaam Cape Town

Associated companies in Beirut Berlin Ibadan Nicosia

OXFORD is a trade mark of Oxford University Press

Published in the United States
by Oxford University Press, New York

British Library Cataloguing in Publication Data
Dickson, P. G. M.
Finance and government under Maria Theresia,
1740–1780.
1. Austria—History—Maria Theresia,
1740–1780   2. Hungary—History—
1683–1848
I. Title
943.6'03   DB70
ISBN 0–19–822570–9 Vol. 1
ISBN 0–19–822882–1 Vol. 2

Library of Congress Cataloging in Publication Data
Dickson, P. G. M. (Peter George Muir)
Finance and government under Maria Theresia, 1740–1780.
Includes indexes.
Bibliography: v. 2, p.
Contents: v. 1. Society and government—v. 2. Finance and credit.
1. Finance, Public—Austria—History—18th century.
2. Austria—Politics and government—1740–1780.
3. Social structure—Austria—History—18th century.
4. Maria Theresia, Empress of Austria, 1717–1780.
I. Title
HJ1059.D52 1987 336.436 87–1614
ISBN 0–19–822570–9 (v. 1)
ISBN 0–19–822882–1 (v. 2)

Set by Promenade Graphics Ltd, Cheltenham
Printed in Great Britain
at the University Printing House, Oxford
by David Stanford
Printer to the University

PREFACE AND ACKNOWLEDGEMENTS

THE idea of writing a book about eighteenth-century Austrian finance was first suggested to me by Professor J. S. Bromley over twenty-five years ago. I began work seriously on the subject in 1965. The delay in bringing the study to completion is partly due to its extension to cover society and government, partly to its intrinsic difficulties, which are reviewed in Ch. 1. It is hoped that the results presented, though inevitably containing much that is speculative and uncertain, will throw new light on a period which is both famous and, in many respects, puzzling and obscure.

A number of institutions generously supported the research for this book. The American Philosophical Society and the Twenty-Seven Foundation made initial grants, and the British Academy and the Houblon–Norman Fund subsequent ones. The Leathersellers' Company provided additional funds at an important juncture. The British Academy and the Twenty-Seven Foundation have contributed subsidies towards the costs of publication. I should like to express my gratitude to all these bodies, and to those in them with whom I corresponded. My university made several financial grants, and conceded sabbatical leave. My college gave additional dispensation from duties, at a time when it was most needed. I thank them both, and hope that this book will repay, in small part, my debt to them.

The late Dame Lucy Sutherland encouraged the earlier stages of research, and expressed characteristic interest in it. I honour her memory. My greatest single debt has been to the Founding Master of St Catherine's College, Lord Bullock of Leafield, the most striking of whose many qualities is to have retained a steady dedication to academic work, and patronage of those engaged in it, during a career notable for practical achievement. My debt to Professor Derek Beales is second only to this. He has, over a friendship of eleven years, provided illuminating criticism, unfailing encouragement, and most generous communication of his discoveries of new sources for the period. Dr T. C. W. Blanning supported, at short notice, an application to the British Academy for a subsidy towards the cost of publication. Dr R. J. W. Evans helped generously about sources and problems. Friedrich Graf von Hatzfeldt kindly provided a photograph of his ancestor Friedrich Anton Graf von Hatzfeld. I am grateful to Dr S. Anand and Dr A. B. Tayler for instruction about sinking funds and growth rates, and to Dr L. Auer, Mr J. Cowan, Dr José Harris, Dr G. A. Holmes, Professor J. J. McCusker, Dr D. M. Melcalf, Mr H. G. Pitt, Professor J. M. Price, Mr T. J. Reed, Dr J. M. G. Rogister, Dr Karl Schulz, Mr J. Ch. Simopoulos, Mrs Joan Spencer, Dr J. W. Stoye, and Professor C. H. Wilson for advice and information.

Libraries and archives have been consistently helpful. I have sometimes felt that my demands on the Bodleian Library were excessive, but the staff, at all levels, have taken them in their stride. The remarkable collections of the British Library proved indispensable, and, in Vienna, those of the Österreichische Nationalbibliothek and the Wiener Stadt- und Landesbibliothek. Thanks are above all due to the staff of the archives in Austria, Belgium, England, France, and Hungary, which will be found listed at the end of the book. The convention of impersonality traditionally applies to such acknowledgements. It would be unfair not break it in the instance of the Hofkammerarchiv in Vienna, where the Director, Hofrat Dr Walter Winkelbauer, and his staff, not only gave advice and friendship during a series of visits, but, in a protracted correspondence, often involving difficult orders for microfilms and photocopies, showed uniform qualities of helpfulness and accuracy. Their service embodies the long Austrian tradition of respect for learning and scholarship.

The technical work involved in completing this book has been difficult. I wish to thank Mrs Rosemary Dawe and Mrs C. Fitzharris for research assistance, and the staff of the Cartography Department of the Oxford School of Geography for preparing the map and Figures. The first draft of half the book was typed by the secretaries of the Modern History Faculty Office, and I am grateful for their willingness in this rebarbative task. The process of completion, and of rewriting and retyping, since that stage, has been lengthy. The burden has fallen on Mrs Susan Seville and, most extensively, on Mrs Patricia Wallace, who continued with it at a time when circumstances made this difficult for her. I express my thanks to them both for their conscientiousness and professional skill. Lastly, Dr Leofranc Holford-Strevens of the Oxford University Press copy-edited the text with immense flair and patience, suggested many improvements, and saved me from many errors. I am much in his debt.

St Catherine's College   P. G. M. DICKSON
August 1986

CONTENTS

VOLUME I
SOCIETY AND GOVERNMENT

VOLUME II
FINANCE AND CREDIT

PLATES

VOLUME I

Between pages 236 and 237

1. Count Friedrich Wilhelm Haugwitz, President of the *Directorium in Publicis et Cameralibus* 1749–61. Bildarchiv, Österreichische Nationalbibliothek.
2. (*a*) Count Johann Fries, Court Banker. Bildarchiv, Österreichische Nationalbibliothek.
   (*b*) Count Johann Fries's palace on Josefsplatz (now Palais Pallavicini). Bildarchiv, Österreichische Nationalbibliothek.
3. Count Friedrich August Harrach (d. 1749), last sole Chancellor of Bohemia. Bildarchiv, Österreichische Nationalbibliothek.
4. Count, later Prince, Wenzel Anton Kaunitz, *Hof- und Staatskanzler* 1753–92. Bildarchiv, Österreichische Nationalbibliothek.

VOLUME II

Between pages 208 and 209

1. Count Ludwig Friedrich Zinzendorf, President of the *Hofrechenkammer* 1762–73. Bildarchiv, Österreichische Nationalbibliothek.
2. Count Leopold Kollowrat, President of the *Hofkammer* 1771–82. Bildarchiv, Österreichische Nationalbibliothek.
3. Count Friedrich Anton Hatzfeld, President of the *Hofkammer* 1765–71, Directing Minister in the *Staatsrat* 1771–93. By kind permission of Friedrich Graf von Hatzfeldt.
4. The State Inventory of 1763, Finanz- und Hofkammerarchiv, Vienna.

FIGURES IN VOLUME I

MAP

TABLES IN VOLUME I

An asterisk after a number indicates that the table appears at the end of the volume. All moneys in the tables are in Austrian florins unless otherwise stated. A dash (—) denotes 'nil'; two dots (. .) denote that the data may exist but have not been found.

ABBREVIATIONS

ADB	*Allgemeine Deutsche Biographie*
AGR	Archives générales du Royaume, Brussels
AKÖG	See *AÖG*
AÖG	*Archiv für österreichische Geschichte* (before 1866 *Archiv für Kunde österreichischer Geschichts-Quellen*)
ASRAB	*Annales de la société royale d'archéologie de Bruxelles*
AVA	Allgemeines Verwaltungsarchiv, Vienna
ČČH	*Český časopis historický*
FA	Familien-Archiv
f	Dutch florins
fl.	Austrian florins, or gulden, see ii, App. F; 'fl. ex.' means Belgian florins of exchange and 'fl. Brab.' current florins of Brabant
HGBL	K. Bosl (ed.), *Handbuch der Geschichte der böhmischen Länder* (4 vols., Stuttgart 1967–74)
HHSA	Haus-, Hof- und Staatsarchiv, Vienna
HKA	Hofkammerarchiv, Vienna
Hs	Handschrift
KA	Kriegsarchiv, Vienna
L.	Lire
m.	million; e.g. 30m. = 30,000,000
MIÖG	*Mitteilungen des Instituts für österreichische Geschichtsforschung*
MÖSA	*Mitteilungen des österreichischen Staatsarchivs*
NDB	*Neue Deutsche Biographie*
NÖLA	Niederösterreichisches Landesarchiv
OS	Old Style
ÖZV	T. Fellner, H. Kretschmayr, *et al.* (eds.), *Die österreichische Zentralverwaltung* (1909–71); for details see Bibliography. Vols. are cited by their year of publication.
PRO	Public Record Office, London
SP	State Papers

SSMSGA	*Schriften der historisch-statistischen Section der k. k. mährisch-schlesischen Gesellschaft zur Beförderung des Ackerbaues, der Natur- und Landeskunde*[1]
VSWG	*Vierteljahrschrift für Sozial- und Wirtschaftsgeschichte*
WSLA	Wiener Stadt- und Landesarchiv

[1] (30 vols., Brünn 1851–95). There is a history of this Society, which dated from 1770, and in revised form from 1811, by the editor of this series, C. Ritter d'Elvert, *SSMSGA* 20 (1870).

DATES AND NOMENCLATURE

DATES are normally given New Style. The few Old Style dates have the suffix OS. The usage 'Maria Theresia' is preferred in this book to the more common 'Maria Theresa', and the more logical 'Mary Theresa' of the British Library catalogue. The empress's husband is, however, referred to as Francis Stephen rather than Franz Stephan. 'Belgian', 'Belgium' are sometimes used instead of 'Austrian Netherlands'. The currency is called 'florins' rather than the equivalent 'gulden'. All sums noted during the research for this book were recorded net of kreuzer, of which there were 60 to the gulden. Given the amount of work involved, this procedure, rather than accurate rounding, seems permissible. Its effect in several of the tables is to make the totals slightly larger than the sum of the constituent items. In proper names, 'von' is omitted in titles of *Freiherr*, or baron, and upwards, unless reproducing the style of the records, as in ii, Ch. 10. The forms of surname in the Austrian and Bohemian lands are the German or Germanized one found in the sources. Hungarian surnames are retained in Hungarian spelling. For place-names, besides the usual English versions (Austria, Prague, Vienna, etc.), the sources are largely followed. This gives results which are not entirely consistent. 'Pressburg', for example, is preferred to the Hungarian 'Pozsony', but the names of most Hungarian towns are given in their Hungarian form. In contrast, most towns in the Bohemian lands appear in their German version. 'Styria' has been preferred to 'Steiermark', and 'Carinthia' to 'Kärnten', but 'Krain' is used, not 'Carniola', and, in a Hungarian context, 'Siebenbürgen', not 'Transylvania'.

In untranslated quotations, the original spelling and punctuation are retained.

I

Introduction

THIS book is concerned with society, government, and public finance in the Austrian Monarchy during the reign of its last purely Habsburg ruler, the great reforming empress Maria Theresia. No systematic exposition of these subjects has so far been available in English, and many aspects of them are unstudied in any language. It was at first intended to confine the book to finance, and to investigate this as far as possible from existing work, largely in German, with some supplementary resort to archival sources. This intention proved unrealistic, largely because of the insufficiency of the literature, discussed below. It also became apparent that finance was so closely connected with the structure and functions of government that exposition of the former without the latter would be, if not meaningless, unsatisfactory. The social background, too, seemed increasingly in need of separate discussion.

After an introduction surveying the literature, the first Part of Volume I discusses population, social structure and selected social groups: the church, the nobility, the peasantry, and Austrian and Belgian bankers. The second Part of Volume I is concerned with government, and with the changes in it over the period. As will be seen from the text, and has long been recognized in outline, the history of Austrian government in this period is, to a significant degree, that of attempts to recast existing fiscal systems so as to permit the deployment of greater military power, defensive and offensive. The concentration of central authority, and the diminution of the influence of the Estates, which this involved, fit plausibly, if not completely, with the thesis of a general European trend from about 1660 towards the bureaucratic organization of larger and more systematically trained armed forces.[1] The development of Austrian

---

[1] W. H. McNeill, *The Pursuit of Power* (Oxford 1983). The concept of a 'Military Revolution' in Europe in the period 1500–1800 overlaps with McNeill's thesis, though not coinciding with it. See the exposition by M. Duffy in id. (ed.), *The Military Revolution and the State 1500–1800* (Exeter Studies in History 1, Exeter U. 1980). The usage 'the Austrian Monarchy' is explained in the next chapter.

public finance against this social and institutional background is the subject of Volume II. Many areas of government activity are omitted, or accorded only limited space. Codification of the law, policy towards industry and trade, policy towards the church, military administration and reform, to take only examples, all had financial overtones, but are not treated systematically. The often imperfect and provisional nature of the conclusions presented will also be apparent, as is argued later in this chapter. The attention of the reader, who is faced with a long book, should be drawn to the reviews of findings at the end of i, Chs. 5, 7, 8, 11, and 13 and of ii, Chs. 1, 8, and 10. The numerous tables also offer a short-cut for the statistically minded to many of the conclusions suggested.

An introductory chapter may appropriately include a short survey of the scope and sufficiency of the literature bearing on the subject. The character and range of the manuscript sources, and the difficulties in using them, will also be briefly described. The exposition attempts to explain why a combination of factors often makes it difficult to reach satisfactorily rigorous conclusions about many of the subjects treated in this book. It then sketches some of the ways in which the text modifies the frequently used description of the period as one of Enlightened Absolutism.

In the last twenty-five years, the Austrian Monarchy has become the focus of increasing academic attention, much of it directed from outside Austria itself. To take examples only, in former lands of the Monarchy, the Hungarian Academy of Sciences has been responsible for the important journal *Acta Historica* and the monographs in the series *Studia Historica*, and the National Commission of Hungarian Historians has published nine volumes of *Études historiques*.[2] The Czechoslovak Academy of Sciences has sponsored *Historica*, an equivalent journal for the history of the Bohemian lands.[3] The contributions in all these are largely in Western languages. In Munich, the Collegium Carolinum has published a journal and an important series of monographs, besides the standard *Handbuch*

---

[2] *Acta Historica Academiae Scientiarum Hungaricae* (Budapest 1951–); *Studia Historica Ac. Scient. Hung.* (Budapest 1951–); Commission nationale des historiens hongrois, *Études historiques* (Budapest 1960); *Nouvelles Études historiques* (Budapest 1965); *Études historiques* (Budapest 1970); *Études historiques hongroises 1975* and *1980*. Titles cited in full in this chapter are subsequently abbreviated.

[3] Československá akademie věd, *Historica. Historical Sciences in Czechoslovakia* (Prague 1959–).

der Geschichte der böhmischen Länder, while the Ungarisches Institut there is responsible for the *Ungarn-Jahrbuch*, a journal for the history of the Hungarian lands.[4] It is a strong feature of these German publications that they draw on the literature in Eastern European languages. In the United States, the *Austrian History Yearbook*, initiated by Professor R. J. Rath in 1965, has provided both focus and impetus for the growing body of American scholarship, much of which also uses the Eastern European literature.[5] In England, the late C. A. Macartney surveyed *The Habsburg Empire 1790–1918*, while in France, Victor Tapié published his attractive *Monarchie et peuples du Danube* in the series L'histoire sans frontières.[6]

General works apart, however, the distribution of historical literature in recent years has been uneven. The weight of it has fallen on the period since 1848, as can be seen from the contents of the journals referred to, and from the titles of monographs. This tendency, observable for other European countries as well, is indicated by the choice of period for the recent important co-operative work in four

---

[4] Collegium Carolinum, Munich, *Bohemia, Zeitschr. f. Gesch. u. Kultur d. böhm. Länder* (Munich 1960–); *Handbuch der Geschichte der böhmischen Länder* (Stuttgart 1967–74). For the monograph series see n. 13 below. Ungarisches Institut, Munich, *Ungarn-Jahrbuch. Zeitschrift für die Kunde Ungarns und verwandte Gebiete* (Mainz 1969–). The Collegium Carolinum was established in 1956 for the study of the Czech lands and the history of their past and present inhabitants. There are other important historical institutions in Munich. The publications series of the Osteuropa-Institut includes Glassl's study of Galicia, see n. 41 below. Its journal *Jahrbücher für Geschichte Osteuropas* (n.s. 1953–) is largely devoted to Russian history. The Südost-Institut publishes a monograph series, and also the journal *Südostforschungen*, whose scope is Balkan history, sometimes including Hungary. The Südostdeutsche Historische Kommission has sponsored in its 'Buichreihe' the studies by Jordan, K. Müller, and Schuller, see the Bibliography.

[5] American Committee to promote Studies of the History of the Habsburg Monarchy, *Austrian History Yearbook* (Rice U., Tex., 1965–78, then Center for Austrian Studies, Minnesota U., 1979–). An *Austrian History Newsletter* preceded it from 1960, see Professor Rath's introduction to vol. I. The East European Monographs publ. by Columbia UP for the *East European Quarterly* are another important American series.

[6] C. A. Macartney, *The Habsburg Empire 1790–1918* (1969, repr. with corrections 1971); Victor-L. Tapié, *Monarchie et peuples du Danube* (1969), tr. as *The Rise and Fall of the Habsburg Monarchy* (1971). These authors were specialists in the Hungarian and Czech literature respectively. Tapié includes some references to MS sources. J. Miskolczy, *Ungarn in der Habsburger Monarchie* (Wiener Studien 5, Vienna and Munich 1959) mostly deals with the period after 1780, and is rather general. Robert A. Kann has written *A History of the Habsburg Empire 1526–1918* (California UP 1974); cf. the rev. by R. J. W. Evans, *EHR* xci (1976) 383–6.

volumes sponsored by the Austrian Academy of Sciences, *Die Habsburger Monarchie 1848–1918*.[7] The period between the treaties of Westphalia and the revolutions of 1848 has attracted less attention, and the monographs written about it in the nineteenth and early twentieth centuries have remained relatively predominant. An important exception is the recent brilliant study by Dr R. J. W. Evans, *The Making of the Habsburg Monarchy 1550–1700*, a pioneer work using difficult and scattered sources, and exploiting the literature in Czech and Hungarian, as well as German.[8] The finances of Austria under Leopold I have also been studied by Professor Jean Bérenger, and there have been recent welcome reassessments of Leopold I, Joseph I, and Prince Eugene by Spielman, Ingrao, and McKay.[9] It is none the less true that for much of the period referred to, and in particular for the century after 1740, the researcher is largely dependent on the older literature, though there are important recent contributions, some of them noticed below. The adequacy of the literature in Western languages, principally German, for the subjects investigated in this book must now be briefly reviewed.

Austrian society in this period has been insufficiently studied. Older works are few in number, and there is little Austrian equivalent to the extensive modern debate about English, French, or American eighteenth-century population and social structure. Gürtler's pioneering, but in many respects unsatisfactory, monograph on Austrian population 1753–90, published in 1909, is still usually referred to as the standard work on this subject.[10] The damaging criticisms later made of it by Grossmann are usually over-

---

[7] Österreichische Akademie der Wissenschaften, *Die Habsburger Monarchie 1848–1918* (Vienna 1973–9). This beautifully produced work includes chapters by American, Austrian, Czech, and Hungarian historians.

[8] R. J. W. Evans, *The Making of the Habsburg Monarchy 1550–1700. An Interpretation* (Oxford 1979).

[9] Jean Bérenger, *Finances et absolutisme autrichien dans la seconde moitié du XVIIème siècle* (1975); John P. Spielman, *Leopold I of Austria* (1977); Charles Ingrao, *In Quest and Crisis: Emperor Joseph I and the Habsburg Monarchy* (West Lafayette, Ind., 1979); Derek McKay, *Prince Eugene of Savoy* (1977). The books by Spielman and McKay are in the series *Men in Office*, ed. Professor Ragnhild Hatton.

[10] A. Gürtler, *Die Volkszählungen Maria Theresias und Josef II. 1753–1790* (Innsbruck 1909). One aspect of social development, the growth of industry and trade, has been much more fully studied than others, but falls only marginally within the scope of this book. See the monographs by Hassinger, Klíma, Otruba, and K. Přibram, listed in the Bibliography.

looked.[11] In some compensation, Galician society in the 1770s has been studied in detail by A. J. Brawer, while the great Hungarian demographer Gusztáv Thirring published in French and German in the 1930s the main conclusions of his work on the Hungarian census of 1784–7, which appeared in Hungarian in 1938.[12] Most recently, the Bohemian nobility have been the subject of an important book by Dr Hassenpflug-Elzholz.[13] Government, understandably in an Austrian context, has attracted much more attention. Here, the great von Arneth blazed a trail in his magisterial *Geschichte Maria Theresia's*, though inevitably leaving many obscurities and loose ends.[14] Some of these were taken care of by Hock and Bidermann's study of the *Staatsrat*, and by Adolf Beer's subsequent monograph on financial administration.[15] The important documents for the period 1740–80 published by the Kommission für neuere Geschichte Österreichs in 1907, 1925 and 1934, and the constitutional history based on them by Friedrich Walter, which appeared in 1938, greatly increased knowledge of Theresian central government, and revealed the extent to which it was preoccupied with financial issues.[16] In doing so, they paradoxically increased the obscurity surrounding local government, and the role

[11] H. Grossmann, 'Die Anfänge und geschichtliche Entwicklung der amtlichen Statistik in Österreich', *Statistische Monatschrift*, n.s. 21 (1916), 331–423. Grossmann also exposed flaws in two articles published by J. Vincenz Goehlert in 1855 which are often cited, and which Gürtler had accepted; see Ch. 2.

[12] A. J. Brawer, *Galizien wie es an Österreich kam* (Leipzig and Vienna 1910); G. Thirring, 'Les recensements de la population en Hongrie sous Joseph II (1784–1787)', *J. de la Soc. hong. de statistique*, 9 (1931) 201–47; id., 'Contributions aux questions de source et de méthode de la statistique historique hongroise', ibid. 12 (1934) 11–39; id., 'Die Bevölkerung Ungarns zur Zeit Josephs II. Die Hauptergebnisse der Zählungen von 1784–1787', ibid. 16 (1938) 160–81.

[13] Eila Hassenpflug-Elzholz, *Böhmen und die böhmischen Stände in der Zeit des beginnenden Zentralismus* (Veröffentlichungen des Collegium Carolinum 30, Munich and Vienna 1982).

[14] A. Ritter von Arneth, *Gesch. Maria Theresia's* (Vienna 1863–79), esp. iv, chs. 1–3, vii, chs. 1, 6, 7, ix, chs. 11–14, x, chs. 3–5 (on Galicia, Hungary and Siebenbürgen). Most of these chapters dealt with financial questions too. Arneth, who constructed the history of the period virtually single-handed, relied heavily for internal affairs on the dispatches of the Venetian ambassadors, supplemented by the imperial family's letters and memoranda.

[15] C. von Hock and H. I. Bidermann. *Der österreichische Staatsrath. Eine geschichtliche Studie* (Vienna 1879); A. Beer, 'Die Finanzverwaltung Oesterreichs 1749–1816', *MIÖG* 15 (1894), 237–366.

[16] The vols. are part of the series 'Die österreichische Zentralverwaltung' which goes up to 1867, see Bibliography.

of the Estates, which remained the object of scattered, and not always intelligible, special studies.[17]

Central and local royal government have not attracted much attention from Austrian scholars since Walter, one important area apart. This is the history of state policy towards the Catholic church, or Josephinism. The massive collection of documents on this subject for the period between 1760 and 1850 published by Maass in 1953–61 has since been supplemented by the important monographs of Professor Klingenstein on the censorship, and Dr Hersche on Late Jansenism.[18] Maass later published a slim volume pushing the origins of the movement backwards, and to some extent changing his first interpretation of it.[19] Interesting though these works are, however, they throw little or no light on the church as a great landowning and administrative institution, and are therefore of only marginal use for the present book. A further and very important aspect of the history of the period is the size, organization, and supply of the army. In neither the general nor the specialist literature is this wholly clarified.[20]

Lastly, public finance under Maria Theresia, in some ways the most difficult of the subjects investigated here, is poorly treated in the literature. The pioneering study by Hauer is a hotchpotch.[21] Arneth and his friend Hock provided only partial information, and tended to misinterpret what they provided.[22] Adolf Beer's monograph on finanical administration, already referred to, made an important contribution to the history of the period 1760–80.[23] Its sequel on government credit, published a year later, was markedly less successful.[24] Beer did not discuss, in either of these works, the difficult question of state revenue and expenditure. In partial com-

[17] For example, the works of Egger on Tyrol, d'Elvert on Moravia, Ilwof on Styria, Thiel on Inner Austria, are hard to grasp. An exception is Hassinger's essay of 1967 on the Austrian Estates, drawn on in Ch. 11.
[18] F. Maass, *Der Josephinismus. Quellen zu seiner Geschichte in Österreich 1760–1850* (Font. Rer. Aust. 71–5, Vienna 1953–61); G. Klingenstein, *Staatsverwaltung und kirchliche Autorität im 18. Jahrhundert. Das Problem der Zensur in der theresianischen Reform* (Munich 1970); P. Hersche, *Der Spätjansenismus in Österreich* (Vienna 1977).
[19] F. Maass, *Der Frühjosephinismus* (Vienna 1969).
[20] See ii, App. A.
[21] J. Ritter v. Hauer, *Beiträge zur Geschichte der österr. Finanzen* (Vienna 1848).
[22] See ii, App. C.
[23] See n. 15 above.
[24] A. Beer, 'Die Staatsschulden und die Ordnung des Staatshaushaltes unter Maria Theresia', *AÖG* 82 (1895) 1–135, repr. Vienna 1972.

pensation, he later published a substantial essay, largely based on manuscript sources, on financial developments under Charles VI.[25] This rather pointedly ignored the earlier massive study by Baron Franz Mensi of Austrian finance in the years 1701–40. Mensi's work, though not free of defects, remains indispensable, and throws much light on the subsequent period.[26] He later published a substantial monograph on Styrian direct taxation before 1740, as well as some general articles on financial history.[27] The documents on government referred to above provide important additional information about financial policy and organization, though not much in the way of statistics. More recently, the late Professor Hanns Leo Mikoletzky wrote a number of essays about the emperor Francis Stephen as businessman and financier, as well as some on different aspects of Austrian finance.[28] There have also been a handful of special studies and unpublished theses by other authors.[29] The topic of government finance as a whole in the years 1740–80 has, however, not been re-examined.

A feature of the literature discussed, whether on society, government, or finance, is that it is centralist and Germanist. The Bohemian lands were until very recently treated as integral to those of Austria, and indeed the late Friedrich Walter considered this integration one of Maria Theresia's most important achievements. Developments in the Hungarian lands tend to be treated in outline, if at all, and the biases against Hungary of eighteenth- and nineteenth-century Austrian administrators are fully apparent in the historiography. The Austrian Netherlands and Italy are, like Hungary,

---

[25] Id., 'Finanzlage beim Regierungs-Antritt Carl VI.', in KA, *Österreichischer Erbfolgekrieg 1740–1748* Vienna 1896–1914) i. 199–295. Despite the title, this essay, which is of varying quality, covers the whole reign.

[26] F. Freiherr von Mensi, *Die Finanzen Oesterreichs 1701 bis 1740* (Vienna 1890). There is a distinctly grudging reference to Mensi's book in a footnote to the first page of Beer, 'Finanzlage'.

[27] Mensi, *Gesch. der direkten Steuern in Steiermark bis zum Regierungsantritt Maria Theresias* (Forsch. zur Verfassungs- u. Verwaltungsges. der Steiermark 7, 9, 10, 11, Graz and Vienna 1910–36); arts. 'Finanzgeschichte', 'Papiergeld', and 'Staatsschuld' in E. Mischler and J. Ulbrich (eds.), *Österreichisches Staatswörterbuch* (2nd edn. rev., Vienna 1905–9). Mensi retired from state service in 1910, and devoted himself to research in Styrian archives.

[28] A convenient *locus* for Mikoletzky's findings on the emperor is his short book *Kaiser Franz I. Stephan und der Ursprung des habsburgisch-lothringischen Familienvermögens* (Vienna 1961). For his other publications see the Bibliography.

[29] The history of the Vienna Bourse by Baltzarek, and the unpublished theses of Gross, Janetschek, Marhringer, and Zwanowetz, are examples.

largely neglected, and, when mentioned, referred to almost as foreign countries. The acquisition of a rudimentary reading knowledge of Czech and Hungarian led, in the first instance, to the unsurprising discovery of equal and opposite prejudice in historians writing in those languages. In the modern Communist history books, the standardizing and centralizing Maria Theresia rules in the name of Enlightened Absolutism, giving short shrift to Czech and Magyar susceptibilities. This is a lineal development from the nationalist histories of the nineteenth century. But the literature, older and newer, in these languages also yields much information for the subjects studied. To take only leading examples, the work of Placht and Kárníková is important for the history and structure of population in the Bohemian lands.[30] Thirring's book on the Josephine census in Hungary amplifies his earlier French and German articles.[31] The later studies by Danyi and Dávid, and by Pápai and others, sensibly add to Hungarian demographic history.[32] Bílek's work on monastic dissolutions in the Bohemian lands contributes, though obscurely, to the history of the church there.[33] The lengthy article on the abolition of the *Directorium* published by Prokeš in Czech in 1926 uses sources later destroyed, and was inadequately exploited by Friedrich Walter.[34] Rieger's two substantial volumes on the Circle institution in Bohemia are an important, though far from lucid, contribution to the understanding of provincial government.[35] Ember's rare book on the Hungarian Council of Lieuten-

---

[30] L. Kárníková, *Vývoj obyvatelstva v českých zemích 1754–1914*, i (Prague 1965), a posthumously publ. work; O. Placht, *Lidnatost a společenská skladba českého státu v 16.–18. století* (Prague 1957). (For translations of Czech and Hungarian titles see Bibliography.)

[31] G. Thirring, *Magyarország népessége II. József korában* (Budapest 1938).

[32] D. Danyi and Z. Dávid, *Az első magyarországi népszámlálás (1784–1787)* (Budapest 1960), a printed version of the returns, with an introduction; B. Pápai, 'Magyarország népe a feudalizmus megerősödési és bomlása idején (1711–1867)', in J. Kovácics (ed.), *Magyarország történeti demográfiája* (Budapest 1963) 143–219.

[33] T. V. Bílek, *Statky a jmění kolejí jesuitských, klášterů, kostelů, bratrstev a jiných ústavů v království Českém od císaře Josefa II. zrušených* (Prague 1893).

[34] J. Prokeš, 'Boj o Haugvicovo "Directorium in publicis et cameralibus" r. 1761', *Věstník Král. české společnosti nauk*, tř. 1 (1926), no. IV. I am indebted to Professor D. E. D. Beales for providing me with a copy of this article, which is extensively drawn on in Ch. 9.

[35] B. Rieger, *Zřízení krajské v Čechách* (Prague 1889–92). This author is not to be confused with J. A. S. von Riegger, for whose important late-18th-c. collections of Bohemian docs. see Bibliography.

ancy and Felhő and Vörös's scholarly catalogue of the latter's archive, are essential reference works. The recent impressive survey of the Hungarian Chamber by Dr István Nagy overlaps the areas between government and finance.[36] Also in finance, Eckhart's old, but still unsuperseded, book on Austrian economic policy towards Hungary contains valuable statistics of government revenue and expenditure.[37] Pekař, though difficult to grasp, is still the standard authority for the development of the Contribution in Bohemia.[38] The modern works by Czech historians comprising the series 'Edice berních katastrů českých, moravských a slezských' have added to this an enormous amount of detailed information about the Contribution, not only in Bohemia, but in Moravia and Silesia as well, and in doing so have provided material for the social, as well as financial, history of the period.[39]

Some important and helpful new work has also appeared in German, French, Italian, and English. The second volume of the *Handbuch der Geschichte der böhmischen Länder*, published by the Collegium Carolinum in 1974, is a monument of exact scholarship, which makes the absence of a comparable series for the Austrian and Hungarian lands the more regrettable. It covers the period from the late fifteenth century to 1848.[40] Horst Glassl's study of Austrian rule in Galicia 1772–90 adds considerably to knowledge of the

[36] Gy. Ember, *A M. kir. helytartótanács ügyintézésének története 1724–1848* (Budapest 1940); I. Felhő and A. Vörös (eds.), *A helytartótanácsi levéltár* (Budapest 1961); I. Nagy, *A magyar kamara 1686–1848* (Budapest 1971).

[37] F. Eckhart, *A bécsi udvar gazdasági politikája Magyarországon Mária Terézia korában* (Budapest 1922).

[38] J. Pekař, 'České katastry 1654–1789'. *ČČH* 19 (1913), 20 (1914), and 22 (1916); repr. photomechanically with addns., corrs., and index (Prague 1932). The journal version is used here for reasons of availability.

[39] In order of date, the vols. are J. Radimský and M. Trantírek (eds.), *Tereziánský katastr moravský* (Prague 1962); A. Chalupa et al. (eds.), *Tereziánský katastr český* (Prague 1964–70); J. Brzobohatý and S. Drkal (eds.), *Karolínský katastr slezský* (Prague 1972–3).

[40] Stuttgart 1974, publ. earlier in parts. K. and M. Uhlirz, *Handbuch der Geschichte Österreichs und seiner Nachbarländer Böhmen und Ungarn* (Graz, Vienna, and Leipzig 1927–39) has been revised, to 1526 only, as M. Uhlirz, *Handbuch der Geschichte Österreich-Ungarns*, i (Sudöstdeutsche Historische Kommission, Graz, Vienna, and Cologne, 1963). The original text is outdated for the period studied here. For the Hungarian lands, see the immensely learned bibliography by D. Kosáry, *Bevezetés a magyar történelem forrásaiba és irodalmába* (Hung. Acad. of Sciences, Budapest 1951–8) and the rev. edn., *Bevezetés Magyarország történetenek forrásaiba és irodalmába*, i (Budapest 1970).

relatively neglected 1770s.[41] The important analysis of the Bohemian nobility by Dr Hassenpflug-Elzholz has already been mentioned. In a different area, the monograph by Professor Philippe Moureaux on economic aspects of Belgian government in this period is a model of its kind, and provides a valuable perspective for developments in Austria.[42] Professor Felloni's magisterial study of the foreign investments of Genoa, a republic with close Austrian financial ties, is essential for the subject of Austrian external borrowing.[43] Lastly, the initial publications arising from Professor Beales's important reappraisal of the life and times of Joseph II have thrown much light in dark corners.[44]

Without the work of these and other scholars, the present inquiry could not have proceeded. However, although the secondary literature is extensive, and treats some aspects of the subject thoroughly, it leaves others only partially examined or not examined at all. It also contains many mistakes and misconceptions. This raises a general issue. The preface to C. A. Macartney's history retails Alfred Pribram's remark that he had given up trying to write the history of the Monarchy, because he did not know fourteen languages.[45] The anecdote is in danger of being widely circulated, and confirms a traditional belief that all the answers are already in print, if they could only be read. In the limited context of the present study, this belief has been found to be incorrect. The real difficulty is the absence of systematic investigation of manuscript sources by historians of the period. This makes it difficult, or impossible, to proceed by making a synthesis from reliable monographs. Such investigation, secondly, when undertaken, encounters considerable difficulties. These include the sheer bulk of the original

[41] H. Glassl, *Das österreichische Einrichtungswerk in Galizien (1772–1790)* (Veröffentlichungen des Osteuropa-Institutes München 41, Wiesbaden 1975). A further important recent monograph is R. Kutschera, *Landtag und Gubernium in Siebenbürgen 1688–1869* (Cologne and Vienna 1985).

[42] P. Moureaux, *Les préoccupations statistiques du gouvernement des Pays-Bas autrichiens* (Brussels 1971).

[43] G. Felloni, *Gli investimenti finanziari genovesi in Europa tra il Seicento e la Restaurazione* (Milan 1971). I am grateful to Professor Felloni for giving me a copy of his book.

[44] D. E. D. Beales, 'The False Joseph II', *Hist. J.* 18 (1975) 467–95; 'Writing a Life of Joseph II: the Problem of his Education', in G. Klingenstein *et al.* (eds.), *Biographie und Geschichtswissenshaft* (Wiener Beiträge zur Gesch. der Neuzeit 6, Vienna 1979) 183–207; 'Joseph II's "Rêveries" ', *MIÖG* 33 (1980) 142–60.

[45] Macartney, p. xi, a remark made to him by Pribram about 1925.

materials, their arrangement and character, the important gaps in them, their handwriting and language, and, above all, their inter-pretation. These points deserve fuller exposition.

Austrian government in the eighteenth century produced a large, and growing, mass of paper, with much duplication, whose arrange-ment paid little heed to the requirements of modern investigators. Information is fragmented by subject, and often by geographical area, as well as being housed in different archives. It is therefore easy to form a partial, misleading view. A further characteristic of this mass of material is that much of it is necessarily trivial, and yields no general conclusions. An avalanche of unsystematic detail was inherent in government procedures, and increased as the scope of government developed. This partly explains the repetitive cen-tral search, born of exasperation, for greater clarity and less scrib-bling. The censuses of population, the prolonged attempts to construct a rational system of finance accounts, the attention lavished on the records of the new *Staatsrat*, the publication of elab-orate and beautifully indexed collections of government decrees, the careful regulation of Hungarian business from the 1770s, are instances of this.[46] Building on these achievements, government records achieved a new standard of clarity and completeness under Joseph II.[47]

A paradoxical complement to the problem of archival extent and division is that of gaps and losses. Ferocious and unsystematic prun-ing of records by nineteenth-century Austrian officials meant that swathes of material had been lost by 1914.[48] Cession of documents to Hungary after 1867 and to Czechoslovakia after 1918 represented transfer, not loss, and is less significant for research in this period than the destruction of the *Justiz-Palast* in Vienna by fire on

---

[46] See Chs. 2, 11, and ii, Ch. 3 for these developments.

[47] The *Handbilletten-Protokoll*, Puechberg's revised finance accounts, and the chronological and analytical volumes of government decrees, are examples.

[48] Thus the *Akten*, or main council documents, of the *Hofkriegsrat* are scanty in this period, owing to 19th-c. 'Skartirung', i.e. destruction of documents (information from the staff). In the former archive of the Ministry of the Interior, 2,190 fascicles of documents were reduced to 310 by 'Skartirung' in the years 1806–26: *Inventar des allgemeinen Archivs des Ministeriums des Innern* (Inventare österreichischer staat-licher Archive 1, Vienna 1909). The vicissitudes of storage of the records of the *Hof-kammer*, as described by Friedrich Walter, make it difficult to understand how they survived at all, let alone could be as full as they are, *Inventar des Wiener Hofkam-merarchivs* (Invent. österr. st. Archive 7, Vienna 1951), introd.; though deliberate destruction is not mentioned.

15 July 1927. The building housed among other records the remainder, after nineteenth-century pruning, of those of the former Bohemian and Austrian Chancellery, which had in turn inherited those of Haugwitz's *Directorium* of 1749. Many of these were burnt, and what was left, now in the Allgemeines Verwaltungsarchiv, is only partially usable.[49] The wide extent of the Chancellery's responsibilities, including the oversight of the Contribution, extensive correspondence with the local Estates, the records of the censuses of population, and of births, deaths, and marriages, and the registration of sundry financial information, makes this especially unfortunate. So does the destruction of material about the nobility in the former legal records. Further loss occurred by military action during the Second World War, including the burning of most of the *Akten* (though not the register, or *Protokoll*, and the indexes to it) of the *Staatsrat* created in 1760.[50]

The investigator's first problem is not the extent of materials, their arrangement, or the gaps in them, but their handwriting. The German hands of this period are less difficult than those of the seventeenth century or earlier, and become clearer from the 1750s. They are none the less a significant obstacle to volume of reading, and may even have been so to contemporaries. The problem is compounded for the English reader by the baroque style of the documents, and their copious inclusion of jargon and technicalities. This leads logically to the last, and most important, problem raised here, that of interpretation. The question most frequently asked in this research has been 'what does this mean?' In answering it, in the frequent absence of guidance from other records or secondary studies,

[49] The archive was the Staatsarchiv des Innern und der Justiz. The bulk of the records of the pre-1749 Bohemian chancellery had, however, already been transferred to Czechoslovakia after the First World War. Much *Hofkammer* material, mostly relating to the years before 1749 or after 1780, was also transferred, Walter, *Inventar*, pp. xxxii-xxxiii. The records of the Hungarian Chancellery were transferred to Hungary after 1867, and formed, together with those of the Council of Lieutenancy and Chamber, the core of the National Archive (*Országos Levéltár*) of 1875.

[50] Anna Coreth, 'Das Schicksal des k.k. Kabinettsarchivs seit 1945', *MÖSA* 11 (1958) 514-25. For the *Protokoll* and the indexes to it see Ch. 11. The *Staatsratsakten* were never systematically consulted by historians before they were destroyed. Arneth did not use them much, and the Theresian period in Hock–Bidermann, *Staatsrath*, is superficially dealt with. The immediacy of the *Akten* is brought out by Ember's pre-war extracts from them about policy towards Hungary, which he published in 1959-60; see the Bibliography.

reasonable inference, and speculation, have had to be used more often than could ideally be wished. The effect of the difficulties described here, taken together, has been to import into the text a distinct measure of reserve about the quality and sufficiency of many of the conclusions presented. It will be found that the literature and original sources are repeatedly criticized as unsatisfactory for one reason or another, and that the conclusions drawn from them are provisional. This does not, it is hoped, invalidate what is put forward, much of which is based on primary material. It does, however, invest it with a penumbra of uncertainty which would not be expected in a study of English or French, or American history in this period. The Monarchy, in short, was found to resemble the Cheshire Cat, now visible in great detail, now fading from view.[51] This general characteristic may not necessarily be true only of this period. It clearly holds for the reign of Joseph II, which is badly in need of reappraisal; and could be argued to hold for much of the subsequent period up to 1848, or even later.

In conclusion, while an extended summary of the remainder of the book would not be appropriate in an introductory chapter, some general points can usefully be made. It will be found that the evidence presented to some extent confirms traditional views of the reign of Maria Theresia, and in other respects qualifies them. The personal determination of the young empress to restore her position in the early years of her reign, and the central role of Count Friedrich Wilhelm Haugwitz in helping her to do so, are documented. The assertion of the power of the Crown against internal vested interests such as the Estates or the church is described in detail. Similarly, Maria Theresia's resolution to keep up a large standing army after the peace of 1763, and to ensure that Austrian debts were serviced, and the external ones repaid, however harsh the implications for levels of taxation, is brought out by the sources. There are numerous illustrations of the empress's belief in her God-given authority, and her autocratic treatment of those who contested it, especially in fiscal matters. On the other side of the account, many of the standard theses are shown to need modification.

---

[51] The sheer unintelligibility of much of the internal history of the Monarchy, and the defects of the literature, are seldom mentioned by historians, as though it would be tactless to do so. A notable modern exception is Professor Klingenstein's demolition of some of Professor E. Winter's more absurd views about Josephinism; see n. 18 above.

Many contradictions and hesitations appear when the record is studied at a detailed level. To take examples only, Haugwitz and the empress were hostile to the feudal classes entrenched in the Estates, but in practice conciliated them, and recognized the need for doing so. The Seven Years War increased the financial importance of the Estates, and necessitated further concessions to them. In 1767, a monopoly bank directed by the Estates was actually, though only briefly, approved by the Crown. Under the pressure of events, the empress also found herself having to conciliate Jews and Protestants, two groups she notoriously detested, in order to secure their financial services. Again, while the power of the state undoubtedly increased during the period, there is much evidence that government showed a progressive tendency after 1763 to become bogged down in detail, to lose the power of decision, and to substitute argument for action. It also has to be recognized that the reforms of central authority in 1747–9 and 1761–3, while impressive in scope, were to a large extent less the deliberate and far-sighted assertion of fundamental principles of government than desperate expedients provoked by the justified fear of total political collapse. Further, this nightmare, most strongly experienced in 1741, was not altogether removed, and recurred during the Bohemian famine of 1771–2, the Bohemian peasant revolt of 1775, and to some extent even in the Bavarian War of 1778–9. Reinforcing this theme, it is clear from the evidence that the unsuccessful Seven Years War created fiscal pressures and social problems which were not removed by 1780. It was not for nothing that the empress referred at the end of her life to the Austrian Netherlands as 'le seul pays heureux . . . ces peuples contribuent plus que nos pays allemands, exténués et mécontents!'[52] At the same time, population growth was beginning to lead to a faster increase of the poorer classes in the Bohemian lands, Galicia, and Hungary by the 1780s, hence to exacerbate existing social tensions.[53]

These and other aspects of the period, for example, the recurrent almost Utopian belief in the imposition of total fiscal, political, or economic systems, of which the young Joseph II as co-regent merely devised extreme versions, are brought out in the chapters

---

[52] Arneth (ed.), *Mar. Ther. Kinder und Freunde*, i. 1, Maria Theresia to Joseph II, 22 July 1780.
[53] See Ch. 2.

which follow. Partly, no doubt, because the historian, like a chameleon, is coloured by his sources, the arguments of the book reinforce the interpretation of Enlightened Absolutism in this period as primarily concerned with the assertion of fiscal and military power, rather than the welfare of subjects. This assertion, in turn, was often surprisingly unrealistic or hit-and-miss in character. That does not invalidate the conventional descriptions of Austrian Enlightened Absolutism, which draw heavily on the significantly different reign of Joseph II. They do suggest, however, that the concept, brilliantly invented by Wilhelm Roscher in 1847, may only be of continued service if detailed studies reveal the difficulties, contradictions, and hardships, and the differing and often passionately opposed arguments and philosophies, which such general labels inevitably conceal.[54]

---

[54] Roscher suggested that the history of absolute monarchy could be divided into three phases, confessional, courtly, and enlightened, with as their respective mottoes 'cuius regio, eius religio', 'l'État, c'est moi', and 'le roi, c'est le premier serviteur de l'État'. He first developed this argument in his 'Umrisse zur Naturlehre der drei Staatsformen', *Allgemeine Zeitschrift für Geschichte*, 7 (Berlin 1847) 451. It appeared later in his *Geschichte der National-Oekonomik in Deutschland* (Munich 1874), 380–1. I am grateful to Professor Beales for help on this point.

PART ONE

SOCIETY

2

Population

AT the death of Maria Theresia on 29 November 1780, the lands of the Austrian Monarchy stretched irregularly across Europe from the Balkans to the North Sea. Their names and areas, as subsequently defined by the great statistician Baron Czoernig, are shown in Table 2.1. Austrian Silesia represented the fraction of territory left after Prussian seizure of the remainder in 1740–1, confirmed by treaty in 1742, 1745, and 1748. In 1748, the duchy of Milan had been pared for the benefit of the kingdom of Sardinia, and Parma and Piacenza lost to Don Philip of Spain. (East) Galicia (1772–4), the Bukovina (1775), the small Innviertel carved out of Bavaria (1779) were compensating gains. The larger entity of which these lands formed part was usually referred to in this period as 'the Austrian Monarchy', or simply 'the Monarchy', though 'the Archhouse' (*das Erzhaus*) was also often employed.[1] The English referred to the House of Austria or to Austria.[2] As elected rulers of the Holy Roman Empire ('the German Empire', 'the Empire') the

---

[1] Sometimes in the same document: see the royal decree for Baron Bartenstein dated 12 May 1753, which refers both to the 'Ertzhaus' and the 'Oesterreichische Monarchie', *Khev.-Metsch*, 12 May 1753, n. 140. *Land* is wherever possible translated by 'land', without a capital letter, rather than by 'province', which in its German form *Provinz* was increasingly used towards the end of the 18th c., and has centralizing overtones. There is a good summary of the differing nomenclatures for Austria in E. Zöllner, 'Formen und Wandlungen des Österreichbegriffes', in *Historica. Festgabe für Friedrich Engel-Janosi* (Vienna etc. 1965) 63–89, where the usage 'Monarchia Austriaca' is shown to have occurred as early as 1711. This was before the Pragmatic Sanction of 19 Apr. 1713, stipulating the integrality of the Habsburg lands.

[2] For example PRO SP 80/188, Newcastle to Robert Keith in Vienna, 21 Jan. 1752 OS 'the Low Countries have ever been looked upon, as the Cement of Union, between the Maritime Powers, and the House of Austria', one of many instances from that period. By 1779 Sir Robert Keith was using 'Austria', e.g. PRO SP 80/221, Keith to Stormont 4 Dec. 1779, 'the commencement of the unnatural Alliance between Austria and France'. English nomenclature for Maria Theresia was 'the Queen of Hungary' until 1745, thereafter 'the Empress Queen' until her death.

Habsburgs had an imperial title too.[3] The Circles in Table 2.1 are the Circles of this Empire. The Bohemian lands were formally within the Empire, but were not part of its Circle organization. The Hungarian and Italian lands were outside the Empire, but within the Monarchy. The overlap in title and territory between the Austrian Monarchy and the German Empire has often understandably confused historians, who have spoken of the Austrian Empire and the Habsburg Empire in this period, and designated Austrian officers of state as imperial when they were not. Kaunitz, for instance, is often referred to as Imperial Chancellor, a position in fact held by the Elector Archbishop of Mainz. Kaunitz himself emphasized, or exaggerated, this point when he told Stormont in 1764 that he knew the Emperor Francis Stephen's views, though he had not the honour to serve him.[4]

It is convenient to call the lands within the Austrian and Swabian Circles of the Holy Roman Empire 'the Austrian lands' of the Monarchy, though this usage was not employed at the time. They were defined separately or in groups as Austria below the Enns or Lower Austria, and Austria above the Enns, or Upper Austria; Inner Austria, comprising Styria, Carinthia, Krain, Görz-Gradisca, Trieste and the *Litorale* (Austria's eastern share of Istria, the larger remainder belonging to Venice); Tyrol; and Further Austria (*Vorderösterreich, die Vorlande*), comprising the Breisgau, Swabian Austria, and Vorarlberg. Tyrol and Further Austria together were often, confusingly, also called Upper Austria. The definition of 'Lower Austria' was more extensive in the past, and was not invariable even in this period.[5] Collectively, the Austrian lands and those

---

[3] Not, however, from Maria Theresia's accession until the election of her husband Francis Stephen as emperor on 13 Sept. 1745. In the interim, institutions such as the *Hofkammer*, which before her reign were 'imperial', were styled 'royal', and thereafter, though not invariably, 'imperial-royal', (*kaiserlich-königlich*). The kingdoms referred to were those of Hungary and Bohemia. E. Holzmair, 'Maria Theresia als Trägerin "männlicher" Titel', *MIÖG* 72 (1964) 122–34 shows that on commemorative medals in 1741 and 1743 she was shown as 'Rex' in Hungary and Bohemia respectively, and that among her other male titles the commonest was 'Archidux'.

[4] PRO SP 80/200, Stormont to Sandwich, 17 Jan. 1764.

[5] Under Maximilian I (1493–1519), Tyrol and Further Austria comprised 'Upper Austria' and the remaining Austrian lands 'Lower Austria'. From 1565 'Inner Austria' (a term in fact not encountered till in the 17th c.) was detached from 'Lower Austria'. The latter then came to mean either Austria above and Austria below the Enns, or just the latter. The changing definitions are a fruitful source of confusion. Cf. also the excellent description in Evans, *Making of the Habsburg Monarchy*,

TABLE 2.1. *Geographical area of the Habsburg lands, 1780*

Territory	Area (Aust. sq. mil.)	Territory	Area (Aust. sq. mil.)
Austrian Circle		*Bohemian Crown*	
Lower Austria	344.49	Bohemia	902.85
Upper Austria	204.47	Moravia	386.29
Styria	390.19	Silesia	89.45
Carinthia	180.26	*Subtotal*	*1,378.59*
Krain	180.57		
Görz-Gradisca	48.31	Galicia	1,420.50
Trieste	1.63	Bukovina	181.69
Istria	30.00		
Fiume	6.00	Milan and Mantua, with	
Tyrol	335.80	principalities of Castiglione	
Vorarlberg	45.20	and Sabbioneta	124.60
Subtotal	*1,766.92*	*Hungarian Crown*	
Swabian Circle		Hungary	3,627.13
Further Austria	49.50	Croatia-Slavonia	329.00
		Siebenbürgen	954.27
Burgundian Circle		Military Frontier	682.00
Austrian Netherlands	479.00	*Subtotal*	*5,592.40*
Upper Rhenish Circle			
County of Falkenstein	200.00		

Total Habsburg lands   11,095.20

Source: Carl Freiherr von Czoernig, *Statistisches Handbüchlein für die Oester-reichische Monarchie* (Vienna 1861) 41.
1 Austrian sq. mil. = 22.22 English sq. mil. or 57.56 sq. km. The areas of Upper Austria, Krain, Görz-Gradisca, Tyrol, and Vorarlberg, which later changed, are stated by Czoernig as they were in 1780. Vorarlberg, though contiguous to Tyrol, and within the Austrian, not the Swabian Circle, was formally part of Further Austria, see text. Somewhat larger areas for the Bohemian and Austrian lands, but smaller ones for the Hungarian lands, are given in Joseph Marx Freiherr von Liechtenstern, *Skizze einer statistischen Schilderung des Oestreichischen Staats* (Vienna 1800) 5-9; id., *Grundlinien einer Statistik des österreichischen Kaiserthums* (new edn. Vienna 1817) 16. The figures in the second book are different from those in the first. The county of Falkenstein, near Worms, inherited by Francis Stephen of Lorraine, was detached from all other Austrian territories.
Bohemia, Galicia (formally 'Galicia and Lodomeria'), Hungary, and Croatia-Slavonia were kingdoms. Siebenbürgen was a Grand Principality (*Grossfürstentum*) from 1765, before that a Principality. Moravia was a Margravate (*Markgraftum*). Upper and Lower Austria were Archduchies. Silesia, Styria, Carinthia, and Krain, were dukedoms. Tyrol and Görz-Gradisca were 'beprinced counties' ('gefürstete Grafschaften'). Gradisca was acquired when Prince Eggenberg's line lapsed in 1717, and the two counties are usually treated as an entity in this period.

of the Bohemian Crown were spoken of as 'the Hereditary Lands' (*die Erbländer*), or, again confusingly, 'the German Hereditary lands'. By employing a suitable number of adjectives, all the lands could be described as hereditary, Count Ludwig Zinzendorf in 1763, for instance, referring to 'the entire German, Hungarian, Netherlands and Italian hereditary lands'.[6] In 1804 the Monarchy became the 'Austrian Imperial State' (*Österreichischer Kaiserstaat*), the Holy Roman Empire being dissolved in 1806; 'the Austrian Monarchy' was, nevertheless, frequently used until 1867. From November 1868 it was 'the Austrian-Hungarian Monarchy' (or Empire, interchangeably), then simply Austria-Hungary. From 1867 it was conventional to distinguish the Hungarian lands as 'Transleithanian' and the remainder as 'Cisleithanian', the Austrian lands forming within the latter the so-called Alpine lands. Most recently, 'the Habsburg Monarchy' has become common in both the English and German literature.[7]

The size of the population of the central lands of the Monarchy in the early eighteenth century was disputed at the time, and is still uncertain. Population in the Bohemian lands certainly fell drastically during the Thirty Years War, Placht's estimates that Bohemia declined from 1.7m. to 0.93m. inhabitants and Moravia from 0.8m. to 0.6m in the years between 1615 and the early 1650s being generally accepted. This is, however, in contrast to earlier estimates that the population of Bohemia alone was over 3m. in the early seventeenth century and the fall correspondingly steeper.[8] The population of the Bohemian and Austrian lands has been recently put at

158–62 (Austrian lands), 195–6 (Bohemian lands). He correctly stresses the obscurity of frontiers in the Austrian lands, especially in Further Austria, and the presence of enclaves, including those belonging to foreign bishops and other lords.

[6] HHSA Nachl. Zinz., Hs. 19, fo. 401, 'den gesamten sowohl Teutschen, als Hungarischen, Niederländischen und Welschen Erblanden'. Cf. 'die gesammte k.k. böhmische, österreichische, hungarische und Siebenbürgen Erblande', coinage contract with Baron Fries 30 Jun. 1766, cit. C. Peez and J. Raudnitz, *Gesch. des Maria-Theresien-Thalers* (Vienna 1898) 49. Many other examples could be given.

[7] Nineteenth-century usage is outlined in Zöllner. 'Kaiserlich-königlich' after 1868 referred to the Austrian empire and Hungarian kingdom.

[8] Placht, *Lidnatost a společenská skladba*, 39, 117. He computes that Silesia may have approached 1.5m. inhabitants in 1615; no estimate is available for the 1650s. The higher figure of over 3m. for Bohemia is repeated by Macartney, 35, evidently from R. J. Kerner, *Bohemia in the Eighteenth Century* (New York 1932) 14. The estimates for 1615 in Placht, 38–9 total 3,802,279 not 3,864,794 as there stated, but this does not affect his rounded total of 4m.

6–7m. in the late seventeenth century, and was presumably recovering.[9] Hungarian and Transylvanian population, which is discussed later, is similarly disputed, earlier estimates that it was less than 3m. in 1720 having been revised upwards.[10] Contemporaries were quite unsure of the position. Mensi cites guesses of equal date in the early eighteenth century that the inhabitants of the Bohemian and Austrian lands numbered 4.15m. and 6.5m.[11] Another source at this time implies a population of no less than 16m. for the same area, including over 4m. in Bohemia and over 3m. in Silesia.[12] The Bohemian official Jan Bořek in 1705 more modestly computed Bohemian inhabitants aged 11 years and over as 1.1m., perhaps implying 2m. in all.[13] Another guess, in the 1730s, was that the number of *taxpayers* in the Bohemian and Austrian lands was 4.6m.[14] Working from the published confessional registers of the archdiocese of Prague, Placht has reconstructed the population of Bohemia at decennial intervals from 1672, when on this basis it numbered 1,267,241, to 1722, when it numbered 2,160,776. He estimates the population of Moravia and Silesia at the later date as 900,000 and 1m. respectively, making a total around 1720 of 4,160,776 for the Bohemian lands.[15]

---

[9] *HGBL* ii. 349. No authority is cited; however, the cue for n. 6, which refers to Placht as authority, is missing, and may be intended there. Placht's figures are compatible with a population approaching 4m. in the Bohemian lands by 1700. A population of 2.1m. in 1700 in the area of the present Austrian Republic is suggested by K. Klein, 'Die Bevölkerung Österreichs vom Beginn des 16. bis zur Mitte des 18. Jahrhunderts', in H. Helczmanovski (ed.), *Beiträge zur Bevölkerungs- und Sozialgeschichte Österreichs* (Munich 1973) 105. Allowing for subsequent alterations of territory, this could probably be increased to at least 2.5m. for the then Austrian lands.

[10] See p. 34.

[11] Mensi, *Die Finanzen Oesterreichs*, 116 n. The higher estimate included Tyrol and Further Austria.

[12] HKA Hs. 650, Miscellanea Cameralia I, fo. 200, 'Eigentliche Entwurff Wievill Stadt Marckt-Fleckhen Schlosser und Dörffer, wie auch Unterthannen In dennen Kayen. Erb Landten . . . Sich befünden', undated but probably 1699.

[13] J. Pekař, 'Prvé sčítání obyvatelstva v Čechách', *ČČH* 20 (1914) 330–3. Pekař's manipulation of the data is not quite accurate, but this does not substantially affect his conclusions.

[14] Id. *ČČH* 19 (1913) 161 n. Pekař treats the undated MS as from 1734–5. A similar computation, with a similar title, in HKA Hs. 648, puts numbers at 4.9m. It is undated, but with proposals of 1719.

[15] Placht, 289–320, esp. 316 and 320. The table on p. 316 has, however, slipped, and the later totals are in the wrong rows. Furthermore, the apparent total of 2,995,255 for 1722 is a misprinted version of the 1,955,255 for 1712. The figure of 1,970,378 should be in the previous column, headed 'lay census of 1754'.

Despite some earlier efforts to get at the facts, starting with an attempted fiscal census by Leopold I in 1695, systematic collection of Austrian population data did not begin until after the War of the Austrian Succession. It was first mooted in 1753, and at Count Haugwitz's insistence introduced into the Bohemian and Austrian lands in 1754. The two proposals of 1753 were initially for an annual count by the clergy of all Christians, then for a secular census. Those of 1754 at first envisaged an annual census under lay control, then modified this (16 February 1754) to a triennial one under both lay and clerical control.[16] The influences here are uncertain. There was much interest in demography at this time. Swedish registration of baptisms, marriages, and deaths, introduced in the 1730s, was centrally recorded from 1749. A bill for an annual census of England and Wales passed the House of Commons in May 1753, though subsequently rejected in the Lords. Dr Webster of the Tolbooth Church in Edinburgh carried out the first census of Scottish population in 1755, at the request of Lord President Dundas.[17] In a more narrowly German context, the Prussian demographer Johann Süssmilch (1706–67), whose important theoretical work on demography was first published in 1741, is unlikely to have influenced this census, though he may have affected some of its successors. The young Saxon cameralist Johann Heinrich Justi (1720–71) published in 1754 a scheme for a register of population, which he claimed to have drawn up in October 1752, when he was working in Vienna. (In 1750 he was tutor to Haugwitz's son.) He printed more elaborate schemes for censuses of persons and occupations in 1759–60, this time in Prussia. The former French official

---

[16] Gürtler, *Volkszählungen*, 1–8: 13 Oct. 1753 (clerical census), 27 Oct. 1753 (lay census in Lower Austria), 7 Jan. 1754 (lay census, general), 16 Feb. 1754 (clerical and lay authorities each to take a triennial census and check these against each other to reach a final result). Gürtler partly drew on [J. V. Goehlert], 'Die Ergebnisse der Volkszählungen', *Sb. d. k. Akad. d. Wiss.* 14 (1854) 52–73; id. 'Die Bevölkerungsverhältnisse Österreichs', ibid. 15 (1855) 52–9. Gürtler's book, though useful, is based on state decrees, and secondary literature, and is not definitive. Its faults, and Goehlert's, are attacked by Grossmann, *Stat. Monatschrift*, n.s. 21 (1916), 331–423. Gürtler's reply (ibid. 673–5) is quite unconvincing. For Leopold I's census of 1695 see Grossmann, 336, 422. Its scope and effectiveness are not known.

[17] E. Heckscher, 'Swedish Population Trends before the Industrial Revolution', *Ec. HR*, 2nd ser. 2 (1950); M. Drake, 'The Census 1801–1891', in E. A. Wrigley (ed.), *Nineteenth-century Society. Essays in the Use of Quantitative Methods for the Study of Social Data* (CUP 1972), ch. 1; H. Hamilton, *An Economic History of Scotland in the Eighteenth Century* (Oxford 1963) 1–2.

Benoît-Marie Dupuy presented the government of the Austrian
Netherlands in February 1752 with an extremely wide-ranging proposal for a census of persons, occupations, and production there.
This may have attracted attention in Vienna.[18] The more general
context of the Austrian census must be Haugwitz's tax reforms
from 1748, which explain, for instance, the decree (2 March 1754)
ordering a count of houses, on which the Contribution was partly
based; and the simultaneous rebuilding of the army, which made it
desirable to know what human resources were available for it. The
tax, army, and census projects in turn were only the most important
in a series of reforms which marked the early years of the *Directorium* (1749–56).[19]

The scope of the first census or 'description of souls' ('Seelen-
beschreibung') in 1754 was relatively modest. It asked for returns
divided between town and countryside, by age in five groups, by
sex, and by marital status. The numbers of Jews and of houses were
also to be returned.[20] A further census in 1761 listed large and small
towns, markets, and villages, and attempted to estimate population
from this. It arrived at much lower figures than those of 1754.[21] In
April and May 1762, apparently in reaction, a much more
ambitious scheme was introduced, perhaps at the suggestion of
Count Ludwig Zinzendorf, the statistically conscious president of

[18] Süssmilch, *Die göttliche Ordnung in den Veränderungen des menschlichen
Geschlecht's, . . . erwiesen* (Berlin 1741, further edns. 1756, 1761, 1775, 1787),
worked from large samples of parish register entries to establish a 'natural' rate of
growth of population. For Justi see Gürtler, 4–5 and tables IX–XI. In Aug. 1750
Count Haugwitz proposed Justi, who was then tutor to his son, as professor of
cameral studies in the Collegium Theresianum, H. Haussheer, *Verwaltungseinheit
und Ressorttrennung* (Berlin 1953) 81. Justi subsequently became a royal mines councillor (*Bergrat*) in Hungary, leaving in 1754. For Dupuy, see Moureaux, 141–4.

[19] See ii. 31–5. See Gürtler, 10 for the decree of 2 Mar. 1754. The idea of statistical
investigation for economic purposes was common to the Austrian cameralists
Becher, Hörnigk, Schroeder *et al.* in the 17th c. Schroeder favoured a population census, general statistics, and a bank. Partial censuses were carried out in Austria under
Charles VI, for example of Trieste in 1735, Grossmann, 338 n. Manufacturing tables
were ordered in Bohemia by decree of 7 June 1749, ibid. 419. G. Otruba, 'Die älteste
Manufakturs- und Gewerbe-Statistik Böhmens', *Bohemia*, 5 (1964) 161–241 discusses the subject and prints the Bohemian tables of 1756, 1766, and 1788.

[20] See Table 2.2* for this census, and the incomplete versions of it printed by
Goehlert and Gürtler. There is a survey by C. Durdik in H. Helczmanovszki (ed.),
Beiträge, 225–67. For the data over a long period see K. Klein, 'Österreichs Bevölkerung 1754–1869', *Mitt. der Österr. Geographischen Gesellschaft*, 113 (1971) 34–62,
which takes as its area the territory of the present Austrian Republic.

[21] Gürtler, 13–14 and Grossman, 372–4 including his table XIII showing the census results. These are reproduced in Table 2.2*.

the new *Hofrechenkammer*, and his zealous official Mathias Puech-berg. The census, or listing of souls ('Seelenconscription'), which was to be taken annually, sought the numbers not only of towns, villages, houses, and families, and of population by age, sex, and marital status, as in 1754, but also of lordships, monasteries, clergy, nobles, officials, burgesses and craftsmen, and poor in almshouses. Jews were returned separately, in practice only in the Bohemian lands.[22] The information was to be collected by each lordship, and returned to the Circle offices, which would summarize it and send it to the provincial government. Participation by the clergy continued. They were to take returns of those able to confess and of those confessing, and to keep an accurate record of births, deaths, and marriages. In December 1763 similar returns of births, deaths, and marriages, and of immigrants and emigrants, were required from the lay authorities. Despite its ambitious scope, this census, too, proved to be far from perfect when delivered.[23]

The results of the 'enlarged' censuses from 1762 were of great general interest. Among other things, they supplied the central government with statistics of ecclesiastical personnel and religious houses that assisted its growing control over the church. But they were not closely enough focused to be of real help to the army in its task of post-war reform. It was this military influence which in future determined the form of the census. Lacy and Joseph II

[22] Grossmann, 375, 24 Apr. and 22 May 1762; Gürtler, 15 and table III. Grossmann, table XIII prints a fuller and more accurate version of the census. The suggestion that Zinzendorf and Puechberg may have influenced its form is guess-work. Puechberg was working on the State Inventory in 1762–3, see ii. 82–3. In the summary volume to this (HKA Hs. 243) he included a section (fos. 177–91) showing, for each land, revenue by type, mineral production, volume of trade, and the results of the 1754 census of population. Justi's Prussian tables of 1760 (Gürtler, Table IX) bear some, though not a close, resemblance to the Austrian census. Maria Theresia's order of 26 Jan. 1762 to Count Rudolf Chotek to prepare an Instruction for the Bohemian and Austrian Chancellery urged him to draw up a yearly account of the inhabitants of each province, also of agricultural and industrial production, and of imports and exports. These would form a mirror in which everything could be observed, ÖZV (1934) 125–6.

[23] Gürtler, 15–16, 22–3. There is a fuller account in Grossmann, 375 ff., and especially p. 383, where the criticisms in the *Staatsrat* in 1763 of the census of 1762, which was delivered by Count Chotek on 12 Nov. 1763 with an apologetic covering note, are discussed. Both Borié, a *Staatsrat* councillor, and Kaunitz developed an interest in population and statistics in this period. Kaunitz's protégé Zinzendorf was their mentor, and inspired further orders to Chotek in 1768 to compile statistical tables of population and production, see ÖZV (1934) 275–9, 11 Feb. and 28 Oct. 1768, also Pettenegg, *Zinzendorf*, 121.

wanted to create recruiting-districts on the Prussian model. These were first proposed at the end of 1765, and the plan for them circulated in the *Hofkriegsrat* in April 1766. They were not officially introduced until March 1771, when the Austrian and Bohemian lands, excluding Tyrol and Further Austria, were divided into regimental areas, each subdivided by company. In Bohemia, for instance, there were fifteen recruiting-districts, largely identical with the Circles there, and each assigned to a named regiment. In advance of this measure, a patent of 10 March 1770 instituted a new form of census, whose primary aim was declared to be to maintain the army without the abuses in recruiting experienced during the recent war. The honeyed initial phrases about leaving merchants and artisans free to trade, and peasants to cultivate, however, concealed a more brutal intention, the listing of the entire male population so as to determine how many members of it aged 18 to 40 years were available for the army. The declaration that long annual leave (on the Prussian model) would make military service acceptable may not have consoled those affected. The census, still described as a listing ('Conscriptio') of souls, aimed to count towns, markets, and villages; and, within these, houses (which were all now to be numbered) and their inhabitants. Women were entered *en bloc* by the civil authorities. Men were divided into two basic categories. The first comprised, in a lump, clergy, nobles, foreigners, 'Honoratiores', royal officials, members of commercial trades with their sons and apprentices, and settled peasants and their heirs. All these were to be exempt from peacetime service. The second category comprised those liable to be called up, who were classed by age in subgroups from 18 to 40 years, and checked for height and health. Male children aged from 1 to 17 were also registered. So were draught animals, divided by age and height. The operation proceeded by way of an annual military census, followed by an annual inspection to verify it, and quarterly returns by lordships and clergy to the Circle offices. The dual approach was to provide control, hence greater reliability.[24]

[24] Joseph II proposed recruiting-districts in late 1765, see Table 9.5* below. The whole subject requires closer investigation. There is a rather hazy account in Edith Kotasek, *Feldmarshall Graf Lacy. Ein Leben für Österreichs Heer* (Horn 1956) 79–127. Gürtler, 28–37 shows by quoting from government decrees the scope and mechanism of the census, introduced by patent dated 10 Mar. 1770, and at pp. 42–3 documents the formal introduction of recruiting districts by patent dated 14 Mar. 1771.

This ambitious operation must have aroused fundamental resentment. It was no wonder that the patent of 1770 threatened those who fled from the conscription with two years on fortress-building. It imposed on the members of the population a form of military servitude, for example incapacity to leave the place where they were militarily registered without their lords' consent, which contrasted notably with government efforts at the same time to relax the burden of feudal servitude. The census also failed to realize its aims. A string of regulations from 1771 attempted to define which artisans, which classes of workers on the land, were exempt from call-up.[25] These indicated that the system was not working well, and in 1777 a new and much more elaborate census was introduced, whose basic categories and procedures lasted until 1848. It was to be effective from 1 November 1777. It had some of the breadth of the returns of the 1760s, but was more closely tailored to military needs. Population was grouped by household, by sex, by marital status, by religion (in so far as Jews continued to be returned separately), and by a number of social categories, which are discussed below, some of which derived from the census of 1770. The census was built up from lordship returns based on printed forms [*Hausbogen*], to be retained and kept up to date by each household. Circle commissaries were to distribute these forms, and to compile local, then Circle, summaries from them by the end of January each year. Army officers and clerks would subsequently make a tour of inspection to verify the summaries. All returns were in duplicate, one copy civil, one for the army. This meant that at top level the census summaries came to the Bohemian and Austrian Chancellery and to the *Hofkriegsrat* respectively. In spite of defects, this new census surpassed all previous ones in thoroughness and accuracy. In scope and method it perhaps provided a partial model for the subsequent Josephine land-tax.[26]

Before 1784 the censuses described only affected the Bohemian

---

[25] Gürtler, 40–2.

[26] Ibid. 52–65. According to Kotasek, 128 a new form of census was ordered on 12 Nov. 1775. The evidence for the initial dating of the new system is conflicting. From 1779, each household was to record all changes in the population under its roof, including births, deaths, and marriages, in the family record (*Familienbogen*) which it was obliged to keep, Gürtler, 98, citing a patent of 5 July 1779. The actual working of these arrangements, and a map showing how Circles, regimental districts, and civil districts based on parishes, corresponded with each other, would be helpful, but is lacking.

and Austrian lands and Galicia. Tyrol and Further Austria were excluded from the military census until 1785 and 1789 respectively. Meanwhile, attempts were made to get at the population of the Hungarian lands. Puechberg included estimates of this in the summary volume of the State Inventory in 1763, basing himself on tax returns and the number of towns. The results, however, were far too low.[27] In 1768, a series of *Tabellae Inpopulationis* were introduced into Hungary, whose principal intention was to elicit the religious composition of the population, and to keep track of births, deaths, and marriages there. The context here must be the general Austrian interest in population in general, and the colonization of Hungary in particular, after the Seven Years War. The initial instruction, to sheriffs, was obeyed only slowly, and an attempt in 1769 to correct this by using the dioceses failed. Half the counties made returns in 1771, the parish clergy doing the basic work. Much fuller returns were made in 1772, and from 1774 there was an annual census, which the clergy took and the county officials summarized. The Council of Lieutenancy compiled national totals. The *Tabellae* omitted nobles and serving soldiers.[28] They were a useful advance on Puechberg's round-number guesses of 1763, but still underestimated the population. The last *conscriptio animarum* (as they were also called) was probably made in 1783. Revision of the series was planned in 1784, but was overtaken by events when Joseph II carried through the first, and until 1850 the last, complete census of the population, including nobles, of Hungary and Siebenbürgen (1784–7). The Military Frontier was not included, though estimates were made for it. Serving soldiers, as with the Austrian censuses, were also excluded. The census was carried out under army supervision, with the help of county officials. Its form was identical with that in the Bohemian and Austrian lands and, likewise, was in German not Latin.[29]

---

[27] For the results, see n. 40.

[28] E. Fügedi, 'A 18. századi lélekösszeírások története', *Demográfia*, 9.3 (1966) 366–80.

[29] Thirring, *J. de la soc. hong. de statistique*, 9 (1931) 201–47; ibid. 12 (1934) 11–39. The second of these articles includes a general and undated account of the 'Conscriptiones Animarum' of 'the end of Maria Theresia's reign'. The results of the Josephine census begun in 1784 were presented to Joseph II on 4 Apr. 1786, and then revised in 1786–7. The initial work met with bitter resistance from the county assemblies, the introduction of German-style military arrangements being feared as the next step, A. Geisler, *Skizzen aus den Karakter und Handlungen Josephs des Zweiten* (Halle 1783–90) vi. 76–7, Nov. 1784.

It is not without interest, and cannot be coincidence, that in 1769, the year after the *Tabellae* for Hungary were introduced, a royal instruction instituted an annual census in the duchies of Milan and Mantua, the first results showing a population of nearly 1.3m. persons. The census, carried out by the clergy, listed 'souls in communion', children, clergy, and births, deaths, and marriages, with appropriate subheadings. This scheme resembled the Hungarian one, though it was less complex. The results are complete for the years 1768–98.[30] No census of the population of the Austrian Netherlands appears to have been carried out in this period, despite the projects of Dupuy and others, but modern regional studies suggest a considerable increase in it. For 1784, the population has been calculated as 2,273,000 persons.[31]

The scope and method of the censuses of population in the central lands of the Monarchy in this period are clear in outline, even if much of the detail, particularly of the system of army recruitment, remains obscure. Interpretation of the results, however, raises considerable difficulties, as can be seen from examining Table 2.2*. This shows the results available in the literature, adding to them from a MS source the figures for the (civil) census of 1790, when, however, no count was made in Inner Austria. Some general features of the table should first be noted. The data are of the legal or registered population, which was usually somewhat higher than the actual population, but, judging from the results for the Bohemian lands in the 1780s, not significantly so.[32] Larger variations occurred earlier, especially in 1754 and 1762. The incompleteness

---

[30] F. Valsecchi in *Storia di Milano*, xii (1959) 532: 1,107,728 persons in 1770, including 70,193 in the city of Milan. For Mantua, see K. J. Beloch, *Bevölkerungsgeschichte Italiens*, ii (Berlin 1939) 301: 183,151 inhabitants in 1770. I owe this reference to Dr G. A. Holmes. M. Romani, 'Il movimento demografico in Lombardia dal 1750 al 1850', *Economia e storia*, 2 (1955) 412–52 is concerned with rates of change, and gives little information about total population and its structure.

[31] J. A. van Houtte *et al.* (eds.), *Algemene geschiedenis der Nederlanden*, viii (Utrecht 1955) 265. In the relevant vols. vii–ix (1979–81) of the revised *Algemene geschiedenis* there is no section on Belgian population before 1800. The estimate for 1784 is repeated in E. H. Kossmann, *The Low Countries 1780–1940* (Oxford 1978) 48. There is an outline of the 18th-c. position ibid. 16.

[32] The difference in Bohemia was less than 0.5%, and in Moravia lower still, see notes to 1780–9 in the table. Registered population, at least from 1770, excluded serving soldiers, Gürtler, 70, 91. It included those from a given locality who were absent, because working elsewhere. In their place of work they were not *counted* but were entered as 'inland foreigners', i.e. migrants, ibid.

of the data, except in the Bohemian lands, between 1762 and 1780 is evident. There is little doubt that further archival research would turn up many of the missing figures. Enough are available to arrive at an approximate total for the Hereditary Lands in 1768, on the eve of the acquisition of Galicia. The figure for 1771 in Bohemia is an average between higher and lower estimates, and is recognizably out of trend with the series for the 1760s. For the 1780s, the results, which except for 1790 are those of the military census, are more nearly complete; as noted above, however, Tyrol was excluded until 1785, and Further Austria until 1789. The area of Tyrol was also defined differently at different dates. Alternative civil census figures are available for the Bohemian lands in the 1780s, and for all lands in 1789. The divergence from the military series is not great; but uniformity was only achieved in 1804.

The data raise awkward, and at present not wholly soluble, problems of interpretation. The ground is probably firmest for the 1780s. The figures here show that the population of the Austrian lands increased very slowly under Joseph II, by an annual average of 0.21%. This concealed an actual fall in the population of Inner Austria at the end of the reign, owing to severe epidemic disease. In 1790, presumably in deference to this situation, no census was taken there. In 1793 Styria had 816,345 inhabitants, Carinthia 293,646, Krain 416,755, all below the levels of 1787.[33] At the opposite extreme, Galician population grew at an annual average of 2.2%. In between came the Bohemian lands, where the annual average of 1.06% conceals the somewhat faster growth of Bohemia itself (1.12%), and the more rapid increase in the industrial districts of northern Bohemia and Moravia. These general results are consistent with other characteristics of the constituent populations, which are discussed below.[34]

In the pre-Josephine period, the figures are not only more sparsely available, but suffer from two breaks in series, in 1762 and 1770, and from alternative subtotals often differing widely from

[33] AVA Hofkanzlei 498, Böhmen, no. 120, a badly burnt table dated Aug. 1796, giving the census results of 1794 in Inner Austria, and including the 1793 totals.

[34] See Ch. 3. The rates of growth referred to can be envisaged as a trend-line drawn through scattered data-points (I am grateful to my colleague Dr S. Anand for explaining this technique). The rates of growth computed by J. V. Goehlert in 1854 for the Bohemian and Austrian lands 1754–1800 are broadly similar, but he miscalculated his figure for Upper Austria, 'Ergebnisse', 62.

each other. Such problems are no doubt endemic in early demo-graphic history. On the face of the record, population fell sharply during the Seven Years War, as contemporaries themselves believed, recovering slowly thereafter in the Austrian lands, more quickly in Bohemia, where acceptance of the lay data implies rapid growth to a peak in 1771, cut back by the famine of 1771 and 1772 to lower levels for the rest of the decade. This may be correct, but there was much uncertainty at the time about how large given populations were; and the clerical count was usually, though not invariably, larger than the lay one. The divergence between the results of the first three censuses are bewildering, and the Austrian official Goehlert's unsubstantiated statement in 1854 that the first 'deserves the fullest trust' cannot necessarily be accepted, especially as his transcription of it was itself defective.

Given the uncertainty of the data, it is not without interest to look at the results set out in Table 2.3, obtained by extrapolation backwards from the populations of the 1780s in the Bohemian and Austrian lands, at their then rates of growth, to four earlier dates: 1768, 1762, 1754, and 1740. The census results of 1789 and 1780 are added for comparison in the first two rows of the table. The census totals before 1780 are the highest figures that can be got out of the earlier census data. A figure of 1m. is added to the population of the Bohemian lands in 1740 to take account of Silesia, most of which passed to Prussia in 1741.[35] These figures, whose schematic and hypothetical nature will be appreciated, suggest that the Bohe-mian lands took two decades to recover the population lost to Prus-sia in the first Silesian war, and as a result were less populous than the Austrian lands until the reign of Joseph II, having been equal to them initially. This is not implausible, and the orders of magnitude above may be approximately right. Extrapolation, however, con-ceals fluctuations, and it is hard to believe that the third Silesian war (the Seven Years War) did not result in some loss of population, as even the highest census data suggest.

The census figures at present available are in fact consistent with three possible developments of Austrian/Bohemian population over

[35] G. Hanke's statement, *HGBL* ii. 478, that Silesian population was 2m. fl. in 1740, that of the Bohemian lands 4.8m., seems unacceptably high for Silesia. H. Fechner, *Wirtschaftsges. der preuss. Provinz Schlesien . . . 1741–1806* (Breslau 1907) 730–1 suggests just under 1m. inhabitants in 1740.

TABLE 2.3. *Estimated population of the Bohemian and Austrian lands*

	Austrian lands	Bohemian lands	Total	
			Extrapolation	Census
1789	4,291,668	4,463,543	—	8,755,211
1780	4,184,738[a]	3,995,548	—	8,180,286
1768	4,072,059	3,556,814	7,628,873	—
1762	3,999,225	3,337,664	7,336,889	6,607,487
1754	3,904,134	3,066,322	6,970,456	6,939,047
1740	3,743,134	3,643,470	7,386,604	—

[a] Including estimates for Tyrol and Further Austria, see Table 2.2*. Rates of growth in 1780s were 1.06% Bohemian lands; Austrian lands (excl. 1790) 0.30%.

the period 1754–90. First, that it grew uniformly from a total of about 7m. in 1754 to one of about 8.75m. in 1789. Second, that its initial base was lower, and its initial growth-rate faster, levelling out to the rates and totals of the 1780s. Third, that it was higher initially, but fell during the Seven Years War, recovered in the 1760s at an accelerated rate, but suffered a Malthusian check in the Bohemian lands, and especially in Bohemia itself, during the famine of 1771 and 1772. This pattern has been forcefully argued for Bohemia by Dr Kárníková.[36] The difficulty in accepting it is that the very rapid increase of population in Bohemia in the 1760s evident from the lay censuses is less evident if the earlier years (1762, 1763) are excluded, less still if the clerical totals are used. The Bohemian data are consistent with a population of around 2m. (Placht) having been maintained for half a century (1720–70), then being savagely cut back, and recovering by accelerated growth, in turn made possible by increasing industrialization.[37] Further elucidation of these difficulties must depend on central and local archival research.

In the Hungarian lands, the Josephine census of 1784–7 revealed, in its final version, a legal civil population of 8,560,160 persons, a present one, once emigrants were subtracted and foreigners added,

---

[36] Kárníková, *Vývoj obyvatelstva*, 20–8. This important posthumous study draws heavily on the data printed by F. Dvořáček, 'Soupisy obyvatelstva v Čechách, na Moravě a ve Slezsku v letech 1754–1921', *Českoslov. statist. věstník*, 5–7 (1924–6). For the famine see p. 128; ii. 196–7.

[37] See pp. 45–7, 50–2.

of 8,555,832.[38] To this, perhaps 260,000 troops and 700,000 inhabitants of the Military Frontier may be added, to give a total of 9,516,000.[39] This was far bigger than previous inquiries had suggested. Puechberg's estimate in 1763 was of 2,872,000 persons in Hungary and Siebenbürgen.[40] The *Tabellae Inpopulationis* from the 1770s revealed higher totals for the population, excluding nobles, but even these were too low, that of 1777 showing 3,650,158 persons in the counties covered (six are missing) compared with 4,647,840 in the same area in 1787.[41] The *Conscriptio* of (?) 1782 printed by Marczali gives only 5,732,621 persons in Hungary and Croatia.[42] Throughout Maria Theresia's reign, therefore, the human resources of the Hungarian lands were underestimated.

In the modern literature, too, the earlier population of Hungary was initially set at too small a figure. Ignác Acsády's computation in 1896 of a population of 2,582,598 in Hungary and Siebenbürgen in 1720–1 was based on the land-tax inquiries in Hungary of 1715 and 1720, extensively supplemented by estimates from other material. Thirring in 1938 accepted Acsády's results, and they have recently (1969) been reprinted by Király, together with Thirring's for 1787, to show 'the Population of Hungary' in the eighteenth century. It seems clear, however, from the work of Zoltán Dávid in 1957 and

[38] Thirring, *M. Népessége*, 34 and his article of 1938. His book, which is of modest size, analyses the census results in extensive tables, and maps based on them. An appendix prints the leading official documents, most in German or Latin. Danyi–Dávid, *Az első magyarországi népszamlálás* give even more detail, printing among other things the names of lords in a majority of the localities. In a number of respects, however, their book is less easy to use than Thirring's.

[39] Thirring, loc. cit. He does not explain his estimate for the Military Frontier, which receives some confirmation from HKA Hs 735 item d, 'Summarium uber die Population . . . inclusive Gallizien und Hungarn', [1785].

[40] See p. 29 above. The figure of 2,872,000 was composed as follows (HKA Hs. 243, fos. 178–80): *Hungary, Croatia, Slavonia*, men 600,000, women 650,000, children under 15 years 650,000, Jews 20,000, total 1,920,000; *Banat of Temesvár*, 70,000, 90,000, 90,000, 2,000, 252,000; *Siebenbürgen*, 200,000 250,000, 250,000, —, 700,000. As there was no Conscription, it was explained, the results were derived from area, the number of towns, the amount of Contribution paid. They were nearer to fantasy. The sex-ratio was interestingly misstated: there was in fact a surplus of males in all these areas.

[41] D. Danyi, 'Az 1777. évi lélek összeírása' *Történeti statisztikai évkönyv*, I (1960) 175.

[42] H. Marczali, *Magyarország története II. József korában* (Budapest 1885–8) ii. 533, 'results of the Hungarian Conscriptio'. Marczali was a master of the unanchored document, and gives no hint of the provenance or date. Danyi, 167 says it is for 1782; Thirring, *M. Népessége*, 4 points out that the summary of this *Conscriptio* in the Hungarian State Archives actually gives a total of only 5,651,116 persons.

TABLE 2.4. *Estimated population of the Hungarian lands*

	Hungary	Croatia	Siebenbürgen	Total
1787	6,467,829	647,017	1,440,986	8,555,832
1768	5,353,680	535,561	1,192,761	7,082,002
1762	5,043,408	504,523	1,123,635	6,671,566
1754	4,657,503	465,918	1,037,655	6,161,079
1740	4,051,855	405,332	902,724	5,359,911

Béla Pápai in 1963 that Acsády's estimate of population for 1720–1 is too low, and that the implied rates of eighteenth-century growth are therefore too high. Pápai substitutes an estimated population for Hungary, Siebenbürgen, and the Military Frontier of 4.1m.–4.2m. in 1720, implying a growth rate to 1787 of 1% per annum, of which 1m. may have been by immigration. The latter figure derives from Dávid, who estimates that there were 350,000–400,000 German immigrants, from 1720 to 1787, with as many Romanians and 200,000 of other nationalities.[43]

On this basis, the population of Hungary, Croatia and Sieben-bürgen can be extrapolated from 1787, see Table 2.4.[44] If these results are joined to those for the Austrian and Bohemian lands, and including Galicia, the estimated civil population, excluding that of the Military Frontier, is as shown in Table 2.5. These figures indicate perhaps 12m. persons in the central lands of the Monarchy at the beginning of Maria Theresia's reign, reduced by 1m. by the loss to Prussia of most of Silesia in 1741–2, but with natural growth restoring the former number, within a reduced area, by 1754. Population was already 16% above its original level by 1768, and from 1772 the acquisition of teeming, if poverty-stricken, Galicia, gave it a further boost. By the close of Joseph II's reign, Austria's population comfortably exceeded 20m., and if the Military Frontier

[43] See the important study by Pápai, in Kovácsics (ed.), *Magyarország tört. demog.*, esp. pp. 147–50, where the work of Acsády and Dávid is discussed. For Thirring's acceptance of Acsády's figures see *M. Népessége*, 35–6. B. Király, *Hungary in the Late Eighteenth Century* (Columbia UP 1969), app. B repeats them, and partly garbles Thirring's figures.

[44] The computation is from the actual population of 1787, rather than from the slightly higher legal one. It omits the army and the population of the Military Frontier. A uniform rate of growth of 1% per annum is assumed, of which part, totalling 1m. by 1787, was due to immigration. The population of Siebenbürgen has been estimated in the literature at 1m. in 1761, alternatively at 1,295,795 in 1767, I. Bakács in Kovácsics, 135.

TABLE 2.5. *Estimated population of the central lands of the Monarchy*

	Austrian lands		Bohemian lands		Hungarian lands		Galicia		Total
	(000s)	%	(000s)	%	(000s)	%	(000s)	%	
1787	4,354	21.0	4,383	21.1	8,555	41.3	3,435	16.6	20.727
1768	4,072	27.7	3,556	24.2	7,082	48.1	—		14,710
1762	3,999	28.6	3,337	23.8	6,671	47.6	—		14,007
1754	3,904	29.7	3,066	23.3	6,161	46.9	—		13,131
1740	3,743	29.4	3,643	28.6	5,359	42.0	—		12,745

is added approached 22m., not markedly short of that of its nominal
ally France, with 26m., to which it had been markedly inferior in
1740. Within the total, the population of the Hungarian lands was
the largest throughout, even if for most of the period it was not
known to be. It was, however, consistently balanced by the combined populations of the Bohemian and Austrian lands. Rates of
growth of population varied, Upper, Lower, and Inner Austria,
officially the Catholic heartland of the Monarchy, showing an
obstinate tendency to increase more slowly than the Bohemian and
Hungarian lands and Galicia, with their suspect Protestant and Jewish minorities. The populationist dream of most contemporaries,
including Joseph II himself, was thus realized, but like other
realized dreams proved to have disadvantages.[45]

Conclusions about total population over a period of fifty years
drawn from insecure and incomplete statistics, and with generous

---

[45] ' . . . je considère comme premier objet . . . la population, c'est à dire la conser-
vation et augmentation des sujets', Joseph II's memoir of 1765 printed in Arneth,
Mar. Ther. und Jos. II. iii. 344. A large population, observed Joseph, defended itself
better and generated more revenue. The basic study for population policy, essentially
one of settlement in the Banat of Temesvár and the neighbouring county of Bács, is
still K. Schünemann, *Österreichs Bevölkerungspolitik unter Maria Theresia*, i (Berlin
[1935]), no second volume publ. The section on the level of population in 1760 is
impressionistic and unconvincing, but the remainder of the book is closely based on
original records. Colonizing policy was at its height 1760–72, when *c.* 11,000 families
were settled in the Banat and 'Batschka'. About 2,000 more were placed on cameral
estates. In all this represented *c.* 52,000 persons, p. 372. The wave of immigration in
the European famine years 1770–2 seems to have bankrupted the scheme, though it
continued on a voluntary basis. For the period before 1740 see J. Kallbrunner, *Das
kaiserliche Banat*, i (Munich 1958), and Sonja Jordan, *Die kaiserliche Wirtschaftspolitik im Banat im 18. Jahrhundert* (Munich 1967).

use of estimation, must be regarded with caution. They offer a hypothetical structure, to be tested by further investigation. They also provide a framework for the examination of other characteristics of population, and of social groupings, in the next chapter. This one concludes by briefly considering some of the population data given by eighteenth-century publicists, including those in the Monarchy's employ.

A string of figures from these sources is published by Gürtler, still the most widely-cited authority, in table I of his book, showing 'the population of Austria in the time of Maria Theresia and Joseph II'. Two examples from it, for 1780 and 1789, will be considered first. The figures for 1780 are taken by Gürtler from an Austrian school textbook of 1781, the *Erdbeschreibung zum Gebrauche der studierenden Jugend*, perhaps by Ignaz de Luca, subsequently professor of statistics at Vienna University.[46] Those for 1789 are one of four variants for this year published by de Luca. The correspondence of these figures with the military census of 1780, and with the military and civil censuses of 1789, drawn on in Table 2.2*, is shown in Table 2.6. Those given by Josiah Dornford in his translation (1790) of Pütter's *Germanic Empire* are added for the sake of further comparison.[47] Dornford set the population of Hungary at 3,170,000, a figure he apparently derived from the *Wiener Taschenkalender* for 1786.[48] As an approximation, several of the unofficial figures are acceptable. Others, especially for the Bohemian lands and Upper and Lower Austria, do not inspire confidence. Dornford comes off worst, partly because he took his information from different dates as well as sources. Many similar examples could be given from other writers. It must follow that publicists' statements

---

[46] Gürtler, 116. Ignaz de Luca (1746–99), initially a protégé of Sonnenfels, was professor of politics at the Lyceum in Linz, 1771–80, and at Innsbruck University, 1780–3; in retirement 1784–91; professor of statistics in Vienna from 1794 to his death. Quarrelsome, and suspected of favouring the French Revolution, he was a prolific author on geographical and statistical, and latterly legal, subjects. The correspondence of his figures with archival ones seems not to have been tested.

[47] J. Dornford, *The historical Developement of the . . . Germanic Empire. By John Stephen Pütter . . . translated from the German, with Notes, and a comparative view of the Revenues, Population, Forces, & c. of the respective Territories* (1790) iii, app. Dornford's statistics are carefully compiled, but are a historian's nightmare, since they all derive from secondary sources, and none can be accepted without verification. They are not in Pütter's original text.

[48] He gives no source; Gürtler, table I n. 11, states the calendar's Hungarian total.

about population, as about much else in this period, were hit-or-miss in character, and must be treated with reserve.[49]

This conclusion is relevant to the data about Austrian population in *August Ludwig Schlözer's Briefwechsel* (1776–82). Schlözer, professor at Göttingen, compulsive editor and publicist, general thorn in the flesh of the European establishment, collected social and economic statistics from a wide network of correspondents, with uncritical zeal. He believed himself to be the first to draw attention to Austria's reservoir of men.[50] Printing an undated estimate of Austrian population, probably from 1774, he observed,

As far as I know these are the first figures of this kind ever printed. In the countless lists of the populations of our European states, the mighty Habsburg has hitherto been lacking . . . [The figures show] a terrifying [*fürchterlich*] Power, far the largest in Europe after France and Russia.

His total of 15.4m., including only 3.4m. for Hungary, cannot be taken seriously.[51] Two subsequent statements deserve closer attention. They purport to show the results of the military census of 1771 and of a census of all the Austrian lands in 1772, including the Netherlands and 'the Italian states'.[52] The year 1771 is important, because it marked the introduction of the new military census, whose results are partly missing, partly controverted.[53] A census in

---

[49] Macartney, *Habsburg Empire*, 37 takes the figures from Gürtler, table I for 1779 as applicable to 1780. These, figures, which are all in round numbers, also diverge from the census results; for instance Upper and Lower Austria are put at 1,800,000 persons, and so on. De Luca may have been officially misled, or encouraged, into bigger population figures. Geisler, xii. 73 claimed that de Luca's figures showed that population increased by more than a quarter between 1780 and 1786. The true increase seems to be under one-tenth.

[50] A. L. Schlözer, *Briefwechsel meist statistischen Inhalts* (Göttingen 1775); *August Ludwig Schlözer's . . . Briefwechsel meist historischen und politischen Inhalts* (4th edn., Göttingen 1780–2); *Stats-Anzeigen gesammelt . . . von August Ludwig Schlözer* (Göttingen 1782–9). This immense corpus of official, semi-official, and purporting-to-be-official papers and statistics has been freely exploited by historians, but experience cautions against uncritical acceptance of anything in it. August Schlözer (1735–1809) was professor at Göttingen from 1769 until his death.

[51] *Schlözer's Briefwechsel*, i. 1 (n.d.).

[52] *Briefwechsel*, xvi. 239 (1771), 'Haupt Summarium der Seelenbeschreibung . . . von J. 1771'; ibid. 237–41, 'Haupt Summarium der Seelen Beschreibung . . . von J. 1772 in allen Kaiserl. Königlichen Erblanden teils militariter, teils nicht militariter conscribiret'. Gürtler, table IV reproduces the results for 1771 (but puts Moravia at 1,455,758 instead of 1,465,758) and in table V accurately prints Schlözer's figures for 1772, omitting, however, Italy and the Austrian Netherlands.

[53] For the difficulties of the evidence see Table 2.2*.

TABLE 2.6. *Population estimates and census figures, 1780 and 1789*

	1780		1789			
	Erdbeschreibung	Military Census	Dornford	De Luca	Military Census	Civil Census
Bohemia	2,265,867	2,550,609	2,226,000	2,922,000	2,868,478	2,852,465
Moravia } Silesia }	1,385,113	1,449,939	1,137,000	1,532,000	1,595,065	1,588,651
Lower Austria } Upper Austria }	1,682,395	1,569,914	1,685,000	{ 1,268,000 620,000	1,637,153	{ 1,012,864 622,593
Styria	800,000	807,164	760,000	760,000	800,500	..
Carinthia	289,507	292,256	290,000	295,000	287,944	..
Krain	383,170	401,887	400,000	440,000	405,526	..
Görz-Gradisca	114,365	115,305	115,000	120,000	119,974	118,569
Galicia	2,580,796	2,775,394	2,800,000	3,147,000	3,395,847	3,393,466

Sources: see p. 37.

TABLE 2.7. *A. L. Schlözer's figures for Austrian population,*
1771–2

	1771	1772
Bohemian lands	4,192,579	3,882,970
Austrian lands (military census)	3,146,336	—
Austrian lands (military and civil censuses)	—	3,799,022
Hungarian lands	—	7,398,177
Austrian Netherlands	—	4,003,762
'Italian states'	—	2,218,718
Total		21,302,649

all lands in 1772 is a surprise, and contrary to other evidence. Schlözer's population figures are summarized in Table 2.7. This would indeed have denoted a 'terrifying might', especially as he soon afterwards reported the population of Galicia in 1773 as 3,888,946, nearly double its true size.[54]

Schlözer's figures cannot be dismissed out of hand. The Bohemian lands' total of 3,882,970 for 1772 does not agree badly with the 3,681,234 of the military census of 1773. The combined Austrian lands' total of 3,799,022 in 1772 is not radically different from the projection above of 4,072,000 for 1768. Similarly, a Hungarian lands' total of 7,398,177 for 1772 is of the same order as the projection of 7,082,000 for 1768. None the less, some of the totals and much of the detail are suspect. The figures for the Belgian and Italian lands are much too large, and no Belgian census is known to have occurred anyway. Tiny Slavonia is credited with a population of 2,219,300, 'Unter Oesterreich' (a term little used by Austrians) with one of 1,667,127. This is not reassuring. The same data for 1772 are included in a long despatch by the Venetian ambassador in Vienna, discovered by Professor Beales. This included inflated figures for Austrian revenue and expenditure. The ambassador and Schlözer must have had access to a common, misleading source. Whether it was the product of Austrian 'disinformation' cannot at present be determined.[55]

---

[54] Schlözer, *Briefwechsel*, 240.
[55] For this MS see ii, App. C.

3

Social structure

ENOUGH has been said in the previous chapter about the difficulties of tracing the main demographic contours of the period. This chapter turns to some subordinate statistical characteristics of the population, beginning with those in Table 3.1*. Here, as with the larger figures, much uncertainty surrounds the data, and they must be treated with caution.[1] The first column shows relatively little change in the proportion of the youthful male population of the Austrian and Bohemian lands and Galicia between 1754 and 1785, if account is taken of the fact that the later census category included those up to eighteen years old. In Upper and Lower Austria, the proportion fell. Galician population was conspicuously young. These results are consistent with the lower rates of growth in the Austrias, and especially Inner Austria, suggested earlier, and the faster rates in the Bohemian lands and, particularly, Galicia. The implications of the age-structure of 1754 for the preceding thirty years of population history are uncertain. Density of population, taking the position in 1785 (col.2), was highest in Moravia-Silesia, Bohemia, and Upper and Lower Austria, all over 50 inhabitants per square kilometre. Inner Austria and Galicia, two structurally very different areas, had much lower densities, 28–40 per sq. km. Poverty-stricken Carinthia, with 28.5, had the least. It is shown later that Hungary, with an average of thirty-one persons per sq. km., had regions which fell below ten. In contrast, if the population of the Austrian Netherlands is taken as 2.4m. in 1785, and that of the duchies of Milan and Mantua as 1.32m., densities per sq. km. there were 87.2 and 184.4 respectively. The central lands of the Monarchy were thus relatively sparsely settled; its Belgian and, especially, Italian wings had densities among the highest in Europe. However, averages conceal regional diversity. Thus, in the Bohe-

---

[1] cf. Table 3.1* nn.

mian lands, the districts of northern Bohemia and Moravia contiguous to Prussian Silesia had populations approaching 70 per sq.
km. in 1789, thanks to the rapid growth of industry over the preceding decades. The agricultural south of these lands barely
exceeded 40 per sq. km.[2] Col. 3 indicates an average family size
higher in Inner Austria (over five persons, and in Carinthia over six)
than in the other lands, except in Galicia, where it was just over five.
The proportion of married men in the adult male population (col. 4)
was, predictably, highest in Galicia, lowest in Carinthia. The data in
cols. 5–7, though of unsatisfactorily late date, indicate high birth-
rates in the Bohemian lands and in Galicia, markedly lower ones in
Inner Austria, especially Carinthia. Lower Austria had a high birth-
rate but more deaths than births. This was due to the demographic
influence of Vienna, discussed below. The proportion of illegitimate
births in 1787–92 was modest, save in Lower Austria (9.04%),
Styria (10.05%), and Carinthia (13.5%), in contrast to the high
rates which developed by the 1840s. A further characteristic of this
area was that throughout the period females exceeded males, save in
Galicia, where the reverse was true.[3]

The attempts of Austrian census-takers from 1762 to assign the
population of the Bohemian and Austrian lands and later of Galicia,
to occupational categories afford another opportunity to get at the
social structure of the Monarchy. Table 3.2* gives the numbers
returned at different dates of clergy, male nobles, officials and dignitaries, Jews, burgesses and industrial workers, peasants, and cottars.
The results for 1846 are given for comparison where relevant. These
figures, like the rest, must be treated with caution, and only broad-

---

[2] Kárníková, 51, an average in Bohemia in 1789 of 54.8 persons per sq. km. but in
Bunzlau and Bidschow Circles densities of 68.2 and 64.8. In southern Bohemia, density was 43.7 sq. km. in 1790, ead. 56 n. In 1764 the Circles of Bidschow, Bunzlau,
Königgrätz, and Leitmeritz had an average density of 48 persons per sq. km., the rest
of Bohemia one of 32.4; in northern (industrialized) Moravia the figure was 42.8, in
the rest of Moravia 35.6, ead. 42–3.

[3] For Styria, Straka has demonstrated that in 1754 marriage was late, 60–70% of
males aged 20–40 and 40–50% of women over 50 being unmarried in two of the four
Circles examined. However, in the mainly Slovenian Marburg Circle population
structure was younger, and rates of increase twice as fast. See M. Straka, 'Die Seelen-
zählung des Jahres 1754 in der Steiermark', Zeitschr. des historischen Vereines für.
Steiermark, 51 (1960) 95–117. For the illegitimacy figures, see Goehlert, 'Bevölkerungsverhältnisse', table II. In 1785 the overall sex-ratio in the Bohemian and Austrian lands was 1,059 (Christian) females per 1,000 males, in Galicia 985 per 1,000,
calc. from HKA Hs. 735, item b.

brush conclusions are possible from them. The rubric 'clergy' (*Geistliche*) included all regular and secular Catholic, Protestant, and Greek Orthodox clergy, but not Jewish rabbis. The figures for 1781 in the Bohemian and Austrian lands are not much larger (23,282) than in 1762 (22,132), but overall clerical numbers had taken a leap upward with the acquisition of Galicia in 1772. Under Joseph II, numbers declined, presumably in consequence of the monastic dissolutions, and fell further in the ensuing half-century, at a time when total population greatly increased.[4] 'Nobles' (*Adelige*) (col. 2) meant all male nobles irrespective of age. In Galicia, however, the census included only adult males, making estimation necessary in order to reach comparable results. This rubric of the census clearly involved difficulties, the numbers recorded in 1762 being in several instances higher than in 1781. The relatively stable noble population of Galicia over the whole period to 1846 also arouses misgiving. These reservations apart, nobles appear to have comprised a tiny minority of the population, despite their social importance, in all areas save Galicia, where, reflecting the social structure of the kingdom of Poland, they were numerous.[5]

The category (col. 3) of 'officials and dignitaries' (*Beamte und Honoratiores*) included non-noble civil servants, a restriction of some significance since all the top administrators were nobles; town magistrates, but not those making a living from industry; senior officials on private lordships; and members of the legal and medical professions. The members of other professions, and the army of subordinate private officials, who were included in 1762, were

---

[4] In interpreting what the census rubrics meant, the official expositions of 1777 and later, reproduced in Gürtler, *Volkszählungen*, are relied on. The census of 1762 distinguished 7,001 secular priests, 12,364 monks and 2,771 nuns. In 1781 'Geistliche' are entered *en bloc* in the census summary. For further discussion of the clerical statistics see the next chapter.

[5] The census figures for male (adult) Galician nobles were 30,805 (1781), 31,175 (1783), 30,698 (1784), 31,066 (1785), 29,000 (*sic*, 1790), 29,779 (1846). In Table 3.2* it is assumed that they comprised 60% of the male nobility. The repetitive nature of the figures, and the round number in 1790, suggest that counting Galician nobles was, like counting the Jewish population there, fraught with problems. For the assertion that only adult male nobles were listed see Brawer, *Galizien* 18, 22. It seems plausible, though corroboration would be welcome. H. Roos, in his important study 'Ständewesen und parlamentarische Verfassung in Polen (1505–1772)', in Gerhard, *Ständische Vertretungen*, 312 n. states that the Galician censuses from 1774 revealed 31,000 'heads of families', hence *c.* 140,000 nobles in all. This is repeated in Glassl, *Einrichtungswerk*, 93.

consigned elsewhere.[6] Although the rubric is unsatisfactorily ample, the increase in those within it during Joseph II's reign, especially in Galicia, is striking. So is the further increase by 1846, though by then the legal and medical professions would have expanded. In col. 4, 'Jews' included all Jews of both sexes and all ages. The first data here are from the census of 1754, that of 1762 only showing 28,394 Jews in Bohemia and none elsewhere. The Jewish population of the Bohemian and Austrian lands was largely confined to the former, though the early censuses omit the small Jewish populations of Vienna and Trieste.[7] The acquisition of Galicia meant a decisive increase in Jewish population, no doubt increasing the case for a policy of Jewish toleration.[8]

The three categories of 'burgesses and industrial workers', 'peasants', and 'cottars and others' are shown in cols. 5–7. The rubric for the first was 'burgesses in towns and industrial workers in the countryside' (*Bürger in Städten, auch Professionisten auf dem Lande*). The explanation defined this as those owning a burgess's (*bürgerlich*) house in a town, or who either in town or in the countryside, whether owning such a house or not, engaged in industrial activity by way of manufacture, factory work, salt- or ore-mining, or with hammers. Minor or ancillary activity, 'as is often the case with weaving', was, however, excluded.[9] Peasants (*Bauern*) were defined as those who had enough land, owned or farmed, to constitute them whole, three-quarter-, half-, or quarter-peasants. The

[6] The census rubric about *Honoratiores* (Gürtler, 78) speaks of 'public offices, like those of doctors of medicine and law, procurators, notaries, etc'. Here, as elsewhere, there must have been great difficulty in classification. However, as Thirring states, *M. Népessége*, 63, teachers and clergy were put under other rubrics, and an equivalence to the 19th-c. 'liberal professions' is not observable. Macartney, *Habsburg Empire*, 50 n. takes an opposite view. In 1762 the census shows 7,421 royal officials, 1,494 Estates officials, 11,669 town and lordship officials. Most of these would have later been put in the 'other forms of occupation' category of the census, discussed below. For further details of the 1762 figs. see Table 11.2.

[7] Vienna had 518 resident Jews in 1782, see below. A census of the city of Trieste, apparently without the suburbs, dated 1758, in HKA Hs. 736, item 14, shows 221 Jews of all ages and both sexes. Another census of 1775 there gives 404 Jews.

[8] Glassl 190–1 in his excellent account of Galician Jewry, shows the difficulties in counting the Jewish population.

[9] *Professionisten* applied both to industrial workers, as here, and to blacksmiths, butchers, shoemakers, tailors, and other craftsmen. In the jargon of the time, the former were commercial trades and the latter police trades (*Kommerzialgewerbe, Polizeigewerbe*). The subject is fully discussed in K. Přibram's classic study, *Geschichte der österreichischen Gewerbepolitik von 1740 bis 1860*, i. *1740 bis 1798* (Leipzig 1907); see pp. 37–9, 135 for commercial and police trades.

thorny issue of what this meant was passed over in silence, and was presumably referred to local knowledge. In Galicia, only whole peasants were entered.[10] The next column of the census, not included in the table, recorded the next heirs, including children under eighteen, of those in the two preceding categories.[11] Lastly, the rubric 'Cottars and others' was very much an inclusive residual one. Its full title was 'cottars, owners of small gardens, serfs in mines, and others in provincial employments' (*Häusler, Gärtler, Bergholden und sonst bei Provinzial Beschäftigungen*). This was expanded as all married men 'such as cottars (*Häusler*), small gardeners (*Gärtler*), wine-growers (*Winzer*), day-labourers (*Taglöhner*), etc.' not included in the preceding rubrics. Then, all widowers who had children, minor household and lordship officials, married or not, those engaged in mining, shipping, road-building, forestry, married or not, those over forty years, those less than five feet three inches tall, all cripples, all sons of non-noble officials, and all sons of Greek and Protestant clergy.[12]

In Table 3.3, an attempt is made to assess the relative importance of these three rather disparate social groups. Adult heirs are estimated, and added to the two groups of peasants, and of burgesses and industrial workers (cols. 2 and 4). These populations are then compared with that of adult males.[13] Col. 3 of the table understates the numbers of cottars and others, since unmarried cottars and smallholders, together with day-labourers, orphans, and others, were included not here, but in the next census column, tersely headed 'usable for other state necessities'.[14] In 1785, this column

---

[10] According to Brawer, 23, though he adds 'or at least half' to 'whole'. For 'whole' etc. peasants see Ch. 6 below.

[11] *Vorstehende Bürger und Bauern Gewerbs-Nachfolger oder nächste Erben* were defined as the legitimate sons or sons-in-law of those in the two preceding categories. Heirs were to be the eldest or youngest child, according to the prevailing custom.

[12] Gürtler, 80: 1 *Schuh* 5 *Zoll*, the minimum military height, was equivalent to 5 feet 3.3 inches. The title of this rubric is taken from the 1785 military census. Gürtler, 67 has 'Keuschler, Bergholden, Weinzötl.' It is not clear which miners came under this rubric and which under the industrial one above.

[13] For the technique used see Table 3.1*. The alternative method of dividing total families by total peasant etc. families gives similar results. For heirs, cf. p. 119.

[14] 'Zu anderen Staatsnotdürften anwendbar'. The next category again was 'children', *Nachwachs* (in the census usually *Nachwuchs*). The explanation stated that 'both these rubrics have the same rules (*Grundsätze*) and differ from each other only in that the first contains men of 18 to 40 years, the second those aged 1–17, in two subdivisions', i.e. 1–12 and 13–17, Gürtler, 80–1. It included single sons of those in the preceding category [of cottars, etc.], single orphans, day-labourers, etc., and sons of peasants and craftsmen not designated as their heirs.

TABLE 3.3. *Peasants, cottars, and industrial workers, excluding Hungarian lands (1785 census)*

	1 Adult male Christian population	2 Peasants and adult male heirs	3 (2) as % of (1)	4 Cottars and others	5 (4) as % of (1)	6 Burgesses and industrial workers, and their adult male heirs	7 (6) as % of (1)
Bohemia	776,788	175,731	22.62	413,117	53.18	130,919	16.85
Moravia and Silesia	433,546	132,886	30.65	209,840	48.40	49,370	11.39
Upper and Lower Austria	526,303	144,539	27.46	246,316	46.80	67,734	12.87
Styria	249,159	85,860	34.43	129,698	52.05	16,418	6.59
Carinthia	98,456	43,559	44.24	44,489	45.19	6,542	6.64
Krain and Görz-Gradisca	152,903	89,109	58.28	47,008	30.74	5,037	3.29
Galicia	807,528	217,658	26.95	527,029	65.26	27,068	3.35
Total	3,044,683	889,262	29.21	1,635,497	53.72	303,088	9.95

Source: The 1785 census summary, see Table 3.1*.

contained an undifferentiated 168,963 persons. This reservation apart, peasants as an occupational group appear from the table as most numerous in the Bohemian lands (308,617), followed by Inner Austria (218,528), Galicia (217,658), and Upper and Lower Austria (144,539). As a proportion of the male population, however, they were most important in Inner Austria, especially in Krain. The low proportion in Galicia, it must be recalled, is artificial, since only half or whole peasants were included in the census there. Reference to the numbers of Galician cottars in 1790 (Table 3.2*) shows that the authorities must have changed their definition, since the total of peasants shoots up, and that of cottars is reduced.

Col. 3 of Table 3.3 shows, as much other evidence suggests, that, making due allowance for the imprecision of the rubric, small proprietors and landless labourers comprised a large part of the adult labour-force in all the lands of the Monarchy. It is noticeable that the proportion of this group to the combined population of this group and peasants was over 70% in Bohemia, about 70% in Moravia-Silesia, over 70% in Upper and Lower Austria. In Styria it approached 70%, in Carinthia only 60%. If the census is to be believed, it was increasing faster than that of peasants in the decade 1780–90. As a complement to this agrarian pattern, industrial workers appear most prominently in Bohemia, [Lower] Austria, and Moravia, confirming other evidence of the industrial development of these areas.

The elements of both uncertainty and artificiality in these conclusions will be appreciated. The labour-force was drawn from children and young persons as well as from adults, and the tables exclude female labour completely. Hence the absolute numbers given are too low. In Bohemia in 1788 the official statistics listed 435,641 persons engaged in manufacturing industry, including 313,842 spinners, of whom 234,008 span in flax and hemp, 51,087 in wool, 28,747 in cotton. By 1797, total numbers returned were 555,074, of whom 354,308 were spinners. Production concentrated in Bunzlau, Leitmeritz, Königgrätz, Bidschow, and Czaslau Circles and in Prague, in descending order. The manufacturing population in 1788 comprised 15.3% of the total population, but in these Circles must have approached half.[15] In Lower Austria, the

---

[15] Otruba, *Bohemia*, 5 (1964) 161–241. As appendices, Otruba published the officially compiled manufacturing tables of 1756, 1766, and 1788. The summary of numbers for 1797 at p. 165 has 555,074 spinners; this should be 354,308. An

census figures reflect the rapid development of the registered industrial population under Joseph II from 94,094 in 1783 to 120,614 in
1785 and 182,473 in 1790. In 1785, 81,756 of these, in 1790, 119,906,
were spinners.[16]

A further qualification to Table 3.3 is that workers in forestry,
shipbuilding and at least some sectors of mining were excluded from
the industrial rubric and consigned to that for cottars and others.
Construction is nowhere mentioned, but may also have been subsumed under this rubric, which must therefore have contained a
substantial minority of industrial workers.[17] The statistics, therefore, give a first approximation to the structure of society, but leave
considerable areas of uncertainty. It is probable, however, that a
more exact count extended to the whole population would not
greatly alter the social *proportions* indicated here.

The implication of the census data is that urban population in the
Bohemian and Austrian lands was relatively modest in size under
Maria Theresia. This is confirmed for the earlier part of the period
by the census of 1754, which distinguished between the (Christian)
population living 'in towns and markets' and in the countryside (the
heading was 'Plattes Land'). Bohemia had 380,783 urban dwellers,
19.6% of the population there. In Moravia, the figure was 106,905
(12.3%), in Silesia 32,213 (20.9%), in Lower Austria 214,746
(23.1%), in Upper Austria 49,118 (11.4%), in Styria 34,803
(5.0%), in Carinthia 33,891 (12.5%), in Krain 75,607 (21.9%) and
in Görz-Gradisca 15,864 (15.5%).[18] Numbers and proportions for

extended commentary is offered in id., 'Anfänge und Verbreitung der böhmischen
Manufakturen bis zum Beginn des 19. Jahrhunderts', ibid. 6 (1965) 230–331. The
rapid growth of Bohemian industry, especially, textiles, at the end of Maria Theresia's reign is also shown in Klíma, *Manufakturní obdobi v Čechách* (Prague 1955),
app., table 1; 63,257 masters, journeymen, apprentices, helpers, in 1777, and
141,383 spinners; in 1782, 84,628 and 209,198. Only full-time spinners appear to be
included.

[16] H. Hassinger, 'Der Stand der Manufakturen in den deutschen Erbländern der
Habsburgermonarchie am Ende des 18. Jahrhunderts', in F. Lütge (ed.), *Die wirtschaftliche Situation in Deutschland und Österreich um die Wende vom 18. zum 19.
Jahrhundert* (Stuttgart 1964) 147. The numbers registered in 1762 were only
19,733; in 1775, 36,130, ibid.

[17] In Dec. 1772 an official report refers to 10,000 *Bergbau* personnel in Bohemia, Dvořáček, *Československ. statist. věstník*, 5 (1924) 290 n.

[18] The figures are from AVA Hofkanzlei, Karton 497, Böhmen, 'Summarium
über die eingelangte Seelen und Häuser Conscriptiones de Anno 1754'. These data
were not published by Goehlert or Grossmann. The category 'Städte und Märkte' is
of course unsatisfactorily imprecise.

TABLE 3.4. *Number of towns and markets in 1762 census*

	Towns		Markets
	Larger	Smaller	
Bohemia	35	209	288
Moravia	12	69	182
Silesia	4	18	3
Lower Austria	5	34	211
Upper Austria	4	8	74
Styria	5	16	91
Carinthia	4	8	26
Krain	2	13	13
Görz-Gradisca	1	2	0
Total	72	377	888

Bohemia and Lower Austria are pulled up by the inclusion of Prague (50,797) in the first, and Vienna (175,403) in the second.

The census of 1762 divided towns into 'larger' and 'smaller', both undefined. The distribution of these is shown in Table 3.4.[19] 'Larger' towns were thus more common in the Bohemian lands. Some areas here were also more densely urban than provincial averages suggest. Grossman shows that the proportion of 'town and market'-dwellers in Moravia in 1754 varied considerably between the six Circles. It was as low as 7.67% in Znaym Circle, as high as 22.64% in the relatively industrialized Iglau Circle.[20] The fairly high provincial average for Silesia in 1754 suggests that there, too, some areas had much higher densities. Surprisingly, Krain also had a relatively high proportion of urban population in 1754, second only to Lower Austria.[21] Despite the existence of some larger towns, and some more urbanized districts, however, the evidence points to average town size being small. Dr Kárníková analyses the 263 towns and markets in the Moravian census of 1762 and shows

---

[19] Grossmann, table XIII. The distinction between larger and smaller towns was ignored by Goehlert and Gürtler.

[20] Grossmann, table VIII.

[21] Division by the number of towns and markets gives Krain an average town population of 2,700. This figure is relatively so high as to lead to suspicion of the data. However, a number of statistics for Krain given earlier show that it differed in social structure from Styria and Carinthia. The 1754 census does not distinguish Trieste and the *Litorale*, which may have been included with Krain.

that 91 (34.6%) had up to 500 inhabitants, 93 (35.4%) 501–1,000, 62 (23.5%) 1,001–2,000, and 17 (6.5%) over 2,000 inhabitants. Thus 70% of towns had 1,000 inhabitants or fewer. By 1791, in the same towns, this proportion had fallen to 46.8%, and towns of more than 1,000 inhabitants formed 53.2% of the total. Despite this, urban population in Moravia did not increase in proportion to the whole, and the connection between its growth and that of industry is, she suggests, tenuous.[22] Taking some absolute numbers, in 1762 Olmütz had a population of 13,962 persons and Brünn one of 13,119 (19,559 in 1791). Iglau had 7,128, Znaym 3,461 in 1762. Trieste in 1754 numbered 10,001 persons, 5,780 in the town, 4,221 in the suburbs. In 1775 there were 10,664 in the town and perhaps 18,500 in all.[23] Over the whole period 1762–85 the number of towns and markets in the Bohemian and Austrian lands, excluding Tyrol and Further Austria, remained fairly stable, 449 towns and 888 markets being listed in 1762, 471 and 949 in 1785. The stock of houses increased by 56.4%, from 759,633 in 1762 to 1,188,114 in 1785, perhaps suspiciously in line with a low-case estimate of population growth (56.7%) in the same period.[24] Dornford offers from publicists' figures a number of estimates for urban populations in the 1780s. He credits Brünn with 13,000 inhabitants, Görz with 9,000, Graz with 35,000, Innsbruck with 8,205, Klagenfurt with 7,000, Laibach with 9,500, Linz with 15,200, Olmütz with 11,000, Prague with 80,000, Trieste with 14,000, Troppau with 8,000, and Vienna with 206,000. The estimates for Prague and Vienna are tolerably close, as is shown next. Graz is too high, Klagenfurt too low. The others are perhaps correct to within 50% either way.[25] The 'home town' of up to 15,000 inhabitants identified by Professor Mack Walker as an important nursery of German culture in the south and south-west of the Empire seems, on this admittedly unsatisfactory evidence, not to have been an

[22] Kárníková, 33–4 nn.
[23] Ead. 46 n. (Brünn); Grossmann, 365, Trieste in 1754; ibid. table XVII, other Moravian towns in 1762; HKA Hs. 736, item 14, censuses of Trieste for 1758 and 1775, apparently excluding the suburbs. The town–suburb proportion of 1754 is used to estimate the total population of 1775.
[24] The numbers of houses are recorded in the censuses published by Grossmann (for 1762) and Goehlert (for 1780–9); see Table 2.2 nn. for sources. The low population figure for 1762 is 4,789,116 and for the same area in 1785, 7,506,255.
[25] Dornford, loc. cit. Cf. Klein, 'Österreichs Bevölkerung' 55, Graz had 29,382 inhabitants in 1782 and Klagenfurt 10,291.

important feature of the Austrian-Bohemian scene.[26] In Galicia, as Glassl shows, the case was worse still, the towns there being small, badly built, poor, and under the control of a weak burgess class, itself exposed to Jewish competition and oppressed by local lords.[27] All towns in this period divided into a minority of royal ones supervised by the Crown, and subject ones where lords lay or spiritual had jurisdiction, though these might have more, or less, independence.[28] The general conclusion that Austria in this period lacked a substantial urban bourgeoisie able to stand up to royal or lordly pressures, or to provide capital and enterprise for trade and industry, harmonizes with many observations and complaints made at the time.[29]

Most towns were small; Prague and Vienna were large. Prague was the only town other than Vienna returned under 'chief town' in 1754; the other lands left this space blank. Prague's population, as noted, was put in at 50,797. In 1768 it was entered as 54,294. Both figures must be too low, since in 1771, with the new census, it leapt to 77,577 legal, and 74,874 actual. This in turn may have exaggerated, since the legal population in 1780 was only 70,214. In 1786 it was 72,874, in 1790, 73,780. In 1771, Prague comprised five towns, Old, New, *Kleinseite* or Malá Strana, Jewish Town, and Hradčany, the quarter under the dominant royal castle on the left bank of the Vltava. From 1784 the census subsumed Jewish Town under Old Town. Jewish Town in 1771 had 266 houses. In 1780, 1,690 families lived there. In 1784 the census returned the number of resident Jews for the first time, 7,901. At that date the city contained 1,401 clergy, 618 nobles, 705 officials and dignitaries, 3,366 burgesses and craftworkers, 1,789 heirs to these, 10,704 cottars, gardeners, and labourers. The city contained at least thirty-one

[26] M. Walker, *German Home Towns. Community, State and General Estate 1648–1871* (Ithaca, NY, 1971).
[27] Glassl, 148–59, 'Städte und Bürger'.
[28] Riegger, *Materialien*, viii. 1–52, xii. 131–85 prints an 'Entwurf einer Statistik von Böhmen', undated, but written during the Seven Years War, which divides Bohemian towns into 27 royal, 8 royal *Leibgedinge* (rent-paying), 61 private *Schutzstädte*, which acknowledged a lord but could choose their own councillors, and (unquantified) subject towns (*unterthänige Städte*), whose members were *leibeigen*, unable to dispose of property or choose a representative without their lord's consent. In Moravia the royal towns were Brünn, Gaya, Hradisch, Iglau, Neustadt, Olmütz, Znaim; d'Elvert, 'Finanz-Geschichte', 575. For the 18 royal towns in Lower Austria see ii. 193 below.
[29] For examples see K. Přibram, 175, 182–7, 199.

cotton factories. Twenty years earlier, in 1766, 2,283 industrial
workers were listed, 592 of whom were wool-spinners and 564 cot-
ton-spinners. Prague, like Vienna, was a killer. The average birth-
rate in the years 1786–90 was 39.3 per thousand, the death-rate 40.6
per thousand. The city must have grown by immigration.[30]

The population of Vienna was entered in the census of 1754 as
175,403, of whom 54,477 were in the inner city and 120,926 in the
ten suburbs. In 1764 an apparently more authentic report from the
Lower Austrian *Regierung* lowered the population to 155,342
'including the suburbs'. In 1777 there were 1,340 houses in the inner
city, 3,774 in the nineteen suburbs, indicating the remorseless
growth of the latter. By 1783 the city had a legal population of
205,780 persons, an actual one of 202,729. At that date, it contained
5,519 foreigners and 7,401 persons from other lands of the
Monarchy. Of the recorded natives, 191,935 were Christian and 518
Jewish. There were 2,514 nobles, 3,080 officials and dignitaries,
5,942 burgesses and craftworkers, 2,779 next heirs of these, 36,555
cottars, gardeners, and labourers. Not all these figures are necessarily convincing; for example 8,300 officials alone were recorded in
1764, and the figure for burgesses and craftmen also looks too low.
The extended cottar and labourer class is, however, plausible. There
is much evidence that the teeming population of Vienna was poor.
Birth-rates were high, death-rates higher: in 1782 they were
respectively 46.3 per thousand and 54.1 per thousand. Various
forms of lung disease, not smallpox, were the main killer, and this
pattern appears to hold for the early part of Maria Theresia's reign
too. Nicolai ascribed the death-rate, which he believed to be the
highest in Europe, even London and Paris only having rates of 40
per thousand or so, to gluttony, drunkenness, and over-indulgence
in sex. Illegitimacy, according to him, was kept down by illness and
venereal disease. This picture of Catholic debauchery was perhaps
agreeable to a Prussian rationalist. In view of the fact that 45% of all
deaths comprised infants of one year or less, however, overcrowd-

---

[30] Kárníková 59–60, Prague population and birth and death rates; Dvořáček, *Českoslov. statist. věstník*, 7 (1926), tables 92–9 on Prague in the later 18th c. especially
92 for 1771 and 84 for social structure in 1784; Riegger, *Materialien*, vi. 703–18, vii.
40–69, 'Verzeichnis einiger Baumwollspinnereyen [und] Fabricken . . . in Prag' (evidently 1787); most were small. For industrial workers in 1766, see the 'General Auf-
nahm und Manufacturs Tabelle des Königreichs Böheimb Pro Anno 1776' in HKA
Hs. 736, item 2. Macartney, *Habsburg Empire*, 109 says there were 'about 40,000'
Jews in Bohemia in 1780, 'most of them concentrated in Prague'.

ing, bad sanitation, and poor maternity care seem more probable causes.[31]

It would be justifiable to conclude from the preceding discussion that the social composition of the Monarchy was drastically altered by the acquisition of Galicia, with its fast rate of demographic increase, young age-structure, predominance of males, and large noble and Jewish populations. However, from the Hungarian census of 1784–7 it appears that the Hungarian lands resembled Galicia socially in a number of ways (Table 3.5). Here, too, as in Galicia, males exceeded females in nearly all areas, except in the towns. The proportion of population aged under eighteen years was 41.8% overall, but there were area differences, Hungary having 42.2%, Siebenbürgen 38.2%, Croatia—whose population was nearly as youthful as Galicia's, and must have been increasing nearly as swiftly—46.02%.[32] Average density of population was low, at 29 persons per sq. km., in comparison with the remainder of the central lands of the Monarchy. This average, however, concealed variation not only between lands but within them. Croatia, with 39 per sq. km., was relatively more densely populated than Hungary, with 31 per sq. km., and Siebenbürgen, with 24 per sq. km. and continued to be so until 1870. Slavonia, however, with 28 per sq. km., was much less populous. Within Hungary, the more densely settled west and north-west had from 35 to (in places) over 60 persons per sq. km., the Hungarian plain 20–30, the north-west and the eastern half of Siebenbürgen 10–20 per sq. km. Máramaros county in

[31] Ten suburbs of Vienna are shown in a map of 1748. The population in 1754, and the number of houses in 1777, are from Grossmann, 367–8. The population in 1764 is given in HKA Hs. 713, fos. 786–7, 'N. Ö. Seelen-Beschreibung Ao 1764'. The census results of 1783 are reproduced in Geisler, iv. 271–3, and confirm the extracts from them in [Georg] Friedrich Nicolai, *Beschreibung einer Reise durch Deutschland und die Schweiz im Jahre 1781* (Berlin and Stettin 1783–7) iii. 181. Neither author gives nos. of clergy. Appendices V/1–2 of Nicolai's volume extract the annually published lists of births and deaths as far back as 1753. The figures of 9,392 births and 10,974 deaths in 1782 give the ratios cited. At pp. 187–203 he discusses causes of death. For lung disease and infant mortality see HKA Hs. 735, item *b*, return of 25 June 1786, and the (unreliable) statistics of baptisms and deaths printed in the *Wienerisches Diarium* from 1743.

[32] Thirring, M. *Népessége*, 69–79, but raising his estimates of the youthful population, which are based only on the 'children 1–17' columns in the census. The higher estimates agree better with the presumed rate of growth of population, and are to some extent confirmed by the 41.8% proportion of children aged 1–15 in the *Tabella Inpopulationis* of 1777, Danyi, 175.

TABLE 3.5. *Social indicators and groups in the Hungarian lands, 1787*

	Adult males	% of males under 18 years	% of males over 18 married	Persons per sq. km	Family size (persons)	Females per 1,000 males			Clergy	Male Nobles	Officials and Dignitaries	Jews
						Counties	Royal towns	Total				
Hungary	1,958,376	42.2	66.0	31	5.17	966	1,065	971	11,735	155,519	3,792	80,783
Siebenbürgen	467,084	38.2	63.0	24	4.99	955	1,154	964	5,224	32,316	771	2,092
Croatia	183,558	46.02	71.7	39	8.01	944	1,045	949	1,528	9,782	438	111
Total	2,609,018	41.8	66.8	29	5.28	962	1,076	968	18,487	197,617	5,001	82,986

Source: Thirring, M. *Népéssage*, 24–7 and map (population per sq. km.); 29–31 (family size); 36–8 and map (sex-ratios); 39–40 (marriage); 41–3 (age distribution); 45–54 and map (Jews); 57–60 and map (nobles), 60–3 (clergy). The data for Hungary and Croatia are from the final revision of 1787, for Siebenbürgen for 1785–6. Male nobles include boys.
'Adult males' includes Jews. The proportions of males under 18 years are higher than Thirring's, see n. 32.

Hungary had only 9 per sq. km. Household size was much higher in Croatia, with its *zadruga* or extended household economy, than elsewhere.[33] The crude birth-rate in Hungary in 1777, not shown in the table, has been computed from the *Tabella* of 1777 as 55 per thousand, the death-rate as 41.2 per thousand.[34] The first of these sounds implausibly high, and further evidence is required, but very high birth- and death-rates were common in eastern Europe in this period, and later, and the figures may be in the right direction.

Turning to social groupings, clergy of all kinds are shown as relatively more important (1.1% of adult males) in Siebenbürgen than in Hungary (0.6%) or Croatia (0.8%). Nobles were numerous, the male noble population exceeding that of Galicia four times. Nobles formed 4.7% of the total male population of Hungary, 4.4% of that of Siebenbürgen, 2.9% of that of Croatia. Here, too, averages conceal regional differences. In the west and north-west of Hungary, nobles formed 10–15% of male population in Pozsony (Pressburg) and Veszprém counties, only 2–4% in neighbouring Bars, Hont, Nyitra. In Borsod (central) and Máramaros (north-east) counties they formed 15–17%. Szabolcs and Szatmár counties, neighbouring to Máramaros, had 10–15%. In Siebenbürgen, nobles formed up to 10% in Udvarhely county, only 2–3% in neighbouring Három-szék.[35] This situation had long existed. Pápai has shown that nobles comprised 3.2% of taxpaying households in 1715–20, but in the lower *Dunántúl* 1.6%, and in the north-east 11.9%.[36] Again, nobles comprised 3.8% of the population in 1787 of the Royal Free Towns, but 8.5% in Kolozsvár, 14.5% in Komárom, 12.2% in Zágráb.[37] Jews were prominent in Hungary, and were the object of special fiscal policies. They were much less important in Siebenbürgen, and in Croatia, on the face of the evidence, barely existed. They were a country-dwelling, not an urban clan; thus in 1787 Pressburg had 237, Pest 94, Buda 26.[38]

A further resemblance to Galicia in the Hungarian lands was the

[33] Thirring's map of densities (ibid.) brings out these points strikingly. The north-west–south-west divide was earlier emphasized by H. Marczali, *Hungary in the Eighteenth Century* (Cambridge 1910) 33–5.
[34] Danyi, 182.
[35] Thirring, 60, map.
[36] Pápai, 154.
[37] Thirring, *M. Népessége*, 60.
[38] Ibid. 45–54; the map shows the Jewish population concentrating west of a line drawn south-west–north-west across Hungary.

relative unimportance of industrial population and the corresponding importance of the classes of peasants and cottars, implying a
predominantly agrarian structure of society (Table 3.6). It is noticeable, however, that in contrast to Galicia, and to the Bohemian and
Austrian lands except Krain, the numbers of cottars and others were
equalled, and in Siebenbürgen and Croatia exceeded, by those of
peasants. Cottars and others were only 32–37% of the adult male
population, compared with 45–53% elsewhere. Peasant society
varied in density, peasants comprising between 40% and 50% of the
population in Árva county in the north, and in Bács-Bodrog, and
the government-settled counties of Temes and Krassó, in the south.
Siebenbürgen also had a high ratio of peasants, 40–50% of population in Szeben and Fogaras counties, and 30–40% overall. The
importance of the peasantry, and the somewhat lesser importance of
cottars, are in line with evidence that in the course of the eighteenth
century the class of cottars, at first relatively unimportant, was
growing faster than that of peasants, as lords' allodial agriculture
developed, but by the 1780s was still not on a footing of equality
with it. The tax returns of 1715–20 indicate that 74.2% of the
population were peasant serfs, and only 10.9% cottars, though in
the lower *Dunántúl* cottars were already 36% of the population.
Over the next half-century, as the area under cultivation expanded,
the cottar population increased tenfold, and by 1775 controlled
one-seventh of all peasant arable. Peasant numbers also expanded,
but not so quickly. By Joseph II's reign the former seven-to-one
predominance of peasants over cottars was more like two or three to
one. Cottars, however, did not finally outstrip the peasantry until
after 1828.[39]

Agrarian predominance conforms to the evidence that Austrian
policy aimed at keeping Hungary as an agricultural market for Austrian manufactures. It is nevertheless worth noting that absolute
numbers of 'burgesses and industrial workers' in Hungary were not
negligible (125,206), and that they were proportionately higher
than in Siebenbürgen or Croatia. Again, they concentrated in a relatively small number of counties in the north-west (Hont, Moson,
Pozsony, Sopron) though with pockets elsewhere. Thirring calcu-
lates that more than two-thirds of burgesses and industrial workers
were in the counties; however in certain towns, headed by Debrecen,

[39] Pápai, 154–8, 201–4.

TABLE 3.6. *Peasants, cottars, and industrial workers in the Hungarian lands, 1787*

	1 Adult male population	2 Peasants and adult male heirs	3 (2) as % of (1)	4 Cottars and others	5 (4) as % of (1)	6 Burgesses and industrial workers and their adult male heirs	7 (6) as % of (1)
Hungary	1,958,376	696,115	35.5	734,184	37.5	125,206	6.4
Siebenbürgen	467,084	202,180	43.2	159,260	34.1	18,928	4.1
Croatia	183,558	90,504	49.3	59,086	32.2	6,554	3.6
Total	2,609,018	988,799	37.90	952,530	36.5	150,688	5.8

Source: Thirring, *M. Népessége*, 76–9 and 69–76 for absolute numbers of peasants and cottars, and of burgesses in towns and industrial workers in the countryside.

Buda, Brassó, Pozsony (Pressburg), where they were most numerous, they formed from 14.8% (Pest) to 27.8% (Debrecen) of the population. An inquiry in 1782 revealed 37,788 industrial and handicraft workers (17,074 masters, 14,612 journeymen, 6,102 apprentices) in 43 Hungarian towns, as well as 2,209 trading merchants.[40]

Despite these qualifications, the general impression that urban life in the Hungarian lands was relatively little developed is amply borne out by the evidence. Town life was only of much importance in the north-west. The census of 1787 listed 68 principal towns in Hungary and Croatia, and 9 more in Siebenbürgen. Of these, 52 in Hungary and Croatia, and 9 in Siebenbürgen, were Royal Free Towns, and 16 were episcopal or mining towns. In general they had 2,000 to 8,000 inhabitants. Only eight Hungarian and Croatian towns in 1787 had more than 15,000 people: Debrecen (29,778), Eger (17,083), Pest (24,297), Buda (26,532), Pozsony or Pressburg (28,502), Szabadka (20,708), Szeged (21,749), Szelmecbánya (18,926).[41] Pápai demonstrates that 56% of inhabitants lived in villages containing under 500 persons, and 84% in ones containing under 1,000 persons. Even so, this represented some move away from the hamlet society of the 1720s.[42]

---

[40] Thirring, *M. Népessége*, 71–4. The cotton-factory at Sassin, first established by the emperor Francis Stephen, claimed in 1785 to give employment to 5,000 domestic spinners and weavers; see the table summarizing the *Staatsrat's* findings in F. Eckhart, *A bécsi udvar gazdaságpolitikája Magyarországon 1780–1815* (Budapest 1958) 135–42.

[41] Thirring, 84, 117, actual (rather than legally registered) inhabitants.

[42] Pápai, 165–6. For the Royal Free Towns see also p. 290 below.

4

The wealth of the church

THIS chapter and the next two examine the wealth and structure of leading sections of society, beginning with the church, and going on to the nobility, middle classes, and peasantry. Certain general social characteristics are described in conclusion. Each of these subjects furnishes ample scope for a monograph on its own, and the emphasis here is deliberately selective. In Chs. 7 and 8, more detailed consideration is given to a specialist section of the middle classes, the bankers and financiers who oiled the wheels of government credit.

The intellectual forces bearing on government policy towards the Catholic church have been the object of an extensive literature, which in recent years has pushed back the beginnings of Josephinism, perhaps definable as an Austrian Gallicanism shaped by Jansenist and rationalist influences, before the Seven Years War.[1] This complex and still only partially intelligible subject lies outside the scope of the present discussion, though a good deal of evidence for the toughness of government fiscal attitudes towards the church will be presented in later chapters. The religious structure of the Austrian Monarchy in this period, and in particular the wealth and organization of the Catholic church, are much less clear in the literature, and attention will be concentrated on them. The Monarchy was officially, indeed ostentatiously, Catholic, and this appearance of orthodoxy must actually have been strengthened by Prussia's acquisition in 1740–2 of most of Silesia, with its substantial Protestant population. Grudging concessions were made

---

[1] For a recent review of the literature see Klingenstein, *Staatsverwaltung*. Hersche, *Spätjansenismus* throws new light on personalities, and demolishes a number of myths. One of the stranger aspects of the literature is that the origins of the term 'Josephinism' itself have not been investigated. It seems reasonably clear from the documents in Maass, *Josephinismus*, v, that it orginated in the 1830s, at a time when 'Protestantismus', 'Katholicismus', 'Jesuitismus', 'Febronianismus', were also much used. See ibid. 565 (18 Feb. 1840) for Metternich's reference to 'ce que l'on entend, par le joséphinisme', apparently the first such reference in this volume.

to the Protestants of Hungary at the Diet of 1681, and to those of Siebenbürgen, where they outnumbered Catholics, in 1691. There was a relatively small, but to the government irritating, Lutheran population in Upper Austria, Styria, and Carinthia, able to put 12,000 signatures on a petition, according to the Prussian envoy Baron Fürst in 1755. Kaunitz put their numbers as high as 40,000. When their grievances came to a head in 1751, a Court Commission, including the royal confessors, was summoned to study the problem.[2] As a result of its deliberations, at least 2,700 of these Protestants were removed and settled in Siebenbürgen in the period preceding the Seven Years War.[3] Riegger asserted that in 1788 there were 34,335 Calvinists and 10,466 Lutherans in Bohemia.[4] In Moravia there were perhaps half as many.[5] Altogether, 73,000 Protestants registered under the Toleration Patent of 1781; and by 1789, 156,000.[6] Besides these Protestants, there was an undisclosed number of Deists, whom Joseph II tried to deport to Siebenbürgen in 1783.[7] The census of 1781 disclosed 66,815 Jews in the Bohemian lands, only 847 in the Austrian lands. The same pattern of Jewish settlement, with lower numbers, was observable in 1754.[8]

In Galicia, the reports of the first Austrian governor, Count Pergen, show a predominant Catholic church in open rivalry with the Greek Uniat church. The Greek Orthodox population was small. Pergen thought the Greek Uniat church included two-thirds of the Christian population. There were seven Catholic and four Greek United bishops, only three and two of these respectively being resident. The Catholic church was rich, its upper ranks permeated by nobles. The Greek Uniat church had some well-off bishops, but was on average poor. Its priests were married, ignorant, and often

---

[2] *Fürst (1755)*, 42; Maass, *Frühjosephinismus*, ch. I(3), 'Die Mission Manzador'. For wider proposals for ecclesiastical reform arising from this episode, see ii, Ch. 1, n. 104.

[3] Schünemann, *Bevölkerungspolitik*, 100, 2,724 persons 1752–6. By 1762, 1,836 had died.

[4] Riegger, *Materialien*, x (1790) 128.

[5] This is an inference from the other figures referred to in the text.

[6] *HGBL* ii. 389 n. 22 states that as a result of the Toleration Patent 80,000 Protestants registered, 73,000 of them in the Bohemian lands. Hock–Bidermann, 351 n. show 73,722 Protestants registered in the non-Hungarian central lands in Oct. 1782, increasing by stages to 156,865 in Dec. 1788.

[7] P. von Mitrofanov, *Joseph II* (Vienna and Leipzig 1910) 725. The attempt at deportation failed, and on 8 July 1783 caning was decided on instead.

[8] See Table 3.1*.

drunken. There was a sizeable regular clergy, mostly Catholic.[9] A considerable Jewish population lived in Galicia. The Austrian census of 1773 put it at 224,181 persons. The statistics fell thereafter, probably because of Jewish failure to register owing to fear of expulsion.[10] Lastly, according to Thirring's reconstruction, Hungary and Croatia in 1787 had 4,472,973 Catholics (of whom about one-sixth were Uniats), 619,811 Lutherans, 980,172 Calvinists, 962,939 Greek Orthodox, and 80,783 Jews. Catholics and Uniats thus formed 62.8% of the Christian population, Greek Orthodox 13.5%, Lutherans and Calvinists combined 22.5%. His calculations did not cover Siebenbürgen, where the Josephine census merely distinguished 2,092 Jews.[11] The general picture was thus one of (enforced) Catholic obedience in the Austrian lands; Protestant and Jewish minorities in the Bohemian lands; a populous, though poor, Greek Uniat church, and a numerous Jewry, in Galicia; influential Greek Orthodox and Protestant congregations in Hungary and Croatia; a Jewish minority in Hungary itself.

Some information can be added to this from other, less accessible, sources. Marczali prints, without a date, the results of a *Conscriptio Animarum* in Hungary, which may be that of 1782.[12] This shows that 'Acatholici', the term used for Calvinists and Lutherans combined, were most numerous in the areas of Buda in the centre of Hungary, Debrecen in the east, and Kassa in the north. Pressburg, and Pécs (Fünfkirchen, in Baranya county in the south-west) followed, but were subsidiary. Greek Orthodox concentrated in the Banat of Temesvár, in Croatia, and around Buda, in that order. An earlier inquiry, in 1773, published in a scarce edition in 1920, shows a picture which partly, but only partly, agrees with this.[13] It

---

[9] Glassl, *Einrichtungswerk*, 113–48. According to General Hadik's return of 1774 there were 3,212 monastic inhabitants of all kinds, ibid. 136.

[10] Glassl 190–1. The Austrian government expelled to Poland Jews who could not pay their share of the tolerance tax.

[11] Thirring, *M. Népessége*, 46–7. His figures are a reconstruction from the civil censuses of 1782 and 1804. They are misleadingly stated in Király, *Hungary in the Late Eighteenth Century*, app. C, as though they derived from the Josephine census, which only divided the population into Christians and Jews.

[12] See Ch. 2, n. 42 above.

[13] *Lexicon locorum regni Hungariae populosorum anno 1773 officiose confectum. Publici juris fecit delegatio Hungarica pacem tractans* (Budapest 1920). The title is also given in Hungarian and French. The title-page of the royal order for this religious survey, dated 6 Mar. 1772, is reproduced in facsimile. The conclusions in the text are from the summary table on p. 312.

gives, among other data, the 'parishes of religion' in Hungary, divided into Catholic, Greek Orthodox, Lutheran, and Calvinist. In terms of these, the proportions between the denominations were 44.7% Catholic, 28.6% Greek Orthodox, 4% Lutheran, 22.7% Calvinist. But this computation assumes that parishes had uniform populations, hence is not plausible, though the figures may well have alarmed the government at the time. The largest concentration of Greek Orthodox parishes by far is ascribed to Bíhar county in eastern Hungary. The chief Lutheran county was Nógrád in the north-west, and the chief Calvinist ones were the contiguous northern and eastern counties of Szatmár, Bíhar, Szabolcs, and Borsod, in that order. The first two were probably covered by Debrecen in the *Conscriptio* of 1782, but Pest and Baranya counties, the other leaders then, are not ascribed large numbers in 1773. All the four counties just named were among those conceded rights of Protestant toleration at the Diet of 1681, and often somewhat inaccurately referred to as 'the counties along the Tisza'.[14]

Siebenbürgen also had a substantial, though divided, Protestant population, well-represented in the Diet, whose rights had been confirmed by the *Diploma Leopoldinum* of 4 December 1691. It was computed in 1765 from the 1759 tax-registers that there were 253,000 families paying the Contribution, of whom 57,744 (23%) were Saxon, that is Lutheran. The figure perhaps denotes 290,000 Lutherans. Another estimate, by Count Lacy in 1767, was that there were 93,135 Catholics, 230,884 Lutherans, 140,042 Calvinists, 28,647 Socinians (Unitarians), 119,230 Uniats, and 558,076 Greek Orthodox. The last group largely comprised Romanian peasants.[15] Macartney's estimate that Protestants numbered 350,000 in 1780 therefore seems too small, given the increase in

---

[14] *Corpus Juris Hungarici*, vol. for 1657–1740, 286, art. 26 of the 1681 Diet. For an example of the usage 'along the Tisza', see Arneth's account of the 1741 Diet, *Gesch. Mar. Ther.* i. 281.

[15] For 1765 see ii. 264. Lacy's statistics of 1767 are given in C. Göllner, *Die Siebenbürgische Militärgrenze . . . 1762–1851* (Munich 1974) 65 and app. 30. However, the Saxons are put there at only 130,884. This must be a misprint, since all the other figures, though wrongly attributed to 1772, are also in Geisler, *Skizzen*, vi. 126, with Saxon numbers stated as 230,365; this agrees much better with the tax data. K. Müller, *Siebenbürgische Wirtschaftspolitik unter Maria Theresia* (Munich 1961) 13 n., gives Lutheran numbers in 1766 as 93,276 and Calvinist ones as 418,866. This is clearly mistaken, as is his deduction that Hungarians comprised 41% of the population.

population by that date.[16] In Siebenbürgen the Catholic clergy was in a minority, and faced a Uniat clergy, as in Galicia. In contrast to Galicia, it faced a substantial Greek Orthodox clergy as well. Protestants were proportionally as numerous as in Hungary, and politically more important, though Lutherans and Calvinists tended to be at loggerheads. In this area of the Monarchy, Catholicism was clearly on the defensive, and felt that its supporters were oppressed, by the Saxon Lutherans in particular.[17] Outside the Hungarian lands, Protestantism was *proportionally* significant only in Austrian Silesia, to judge from statistics for marriage in 1795, a date when the Toleration Patent of 1781 had had time to take effect. Protestant marriages then comprised 14% of all marriages in Silesia, 4% in Carinthia, 2%, or a good deal less, elsewhere.[18] The Catholic church which presided over this situation has conventionally been regarded as rich, torpid, and dominated by the aristocracy. These generalizations, in origin perhaps due to Josephinist hostility to ecclesiastical pretensions, have not been extensively tested by research. Three aspects of the subject are selected here: the extent to which the church was run by aristocrats, the wealth of the Jesuit order, and the wealth of the church as a whole at the end of Maria Theresia's reign.

The *Court Calendar* throws some light, though not enough, on how far the church was dominated by aristocrats.[19] In 1740, the Archbishop of Vienna was Prince Kollonich, but of his four officials (provost etc.) and eleven canons, only three were nobles, the rest having plebeian names, including the reformer, and from 1759 head, of the Vienna theology faculty, Simon Ambrosius Stock.

[16] Macartney, *Habsburg Empire*, 107. Though his text says 350,000, his footnote makes the Protestants number 485,000, 135,000 of whom were Saxons. The last figure is not compatible with the data presented above, but the total may be.

[17] For these pressures, as defined by the governor, General Hadik, and Bishop Bajtay in 1767, see G.A. Schuller, *Samuel von Brukenthal* (Munich 1967–9) i. 197–8.

[18] AVA Hofkanzlei, Karton 498, no. 133, return to the *Directorium in Cameralibus et Publico-Politicis* of births, deaths, and marriages in the Bohemian and Austrian lands and Galicia, dated Oct. 1795. There were 2,782 marriages in Silesia, 399 of which were Protestant, while a further 56 were mixed. Bohemia had more Protestant marriages, 460, but they formed only 2.5% of all marriages. Moravia had 277 Protestant marriages. Protestant marriages numbered in all 1,519, and formed 1.4% of the total of 105,796 marriages.

[19] *Court Calendar* for the years cited in the text. Where independent verification is available, the *Calendar* has proved to be accurate.

These canons were typically doctors of both theology and philosophy. The cathedral consistory at this date had fourteen ecclesiastical councillors, largely overlapping with the canons, and 11 lay councillors. Of these twenty-five, only three can be identified as nobles. In 1775, on the other hand, of Cardinal Archbishop Migazzi's six officials and thirteen canons, six were counts, two were barons, five were 'von's. The Consistory by then had thirty-two ecclesiastical and only four lay councillors. These thirty-six, who overlapped with the canons, included six counts, three barons, five 'von's. There was also a number of priests with plebeian names. The *Calendar* unfortunately only gives the Christian names of the abbots of Lower Austrian religious houses, twenty-three in 1740, twenty-four in 1775. It is only a guess, from evidence referred to below, that they were largely of bourgeois or plebeian origin. In Bohemia in 1740, the Archbishop of Prague (1733–63) was Count Ernst Moritz Manderscheid-Blankenheim, who subsequently lost Court favour by supporting the Bavarian cause. The Bishop of Leitmeritz was Duke Moritz Adolph of Saxony, the Bishop of Königgrätz was Count Mitrowitz. The provost, dean, and suffragan bishop of Prague were all nobles. The five senior canons of Sankt Veit listed, however, were not, nor were seventeen out of nineteen abbots of leading religious houses. They had plebeian surnames. In 1779 the Archbishop of Prague was Prince Przichowsky, the Bishop of Leitmeritz Count Waldstein, the Bishop of Königgrätz Count Arco. The fourteen canons of Sankt Veit included five nobles. None of the nineteen listed abbots, including the ecclesiastical reformer Franz Stephan Rautenstrauch, abbot of Braunau, was a noble. In Moravia in 1740 the bishop, dean, and twenty-nine canons of Olmütz were conspicuously aristocratic. All the thirteen abbots given, however, had plebeian names. In 1779 the Archbishop (as the office now was) of Olmütz, was Prince Colloredo, and all the thirty-two canons were counts or barons. The sixteen abbots included one count and two barons, the remainder were not nobles. Lastly, the list in the *Court Calendar* for 1740 of twenty-nine Hungarian archbishops and bishops included a prince, seven counts, at least five members of known Hungarian magnate families, but also a number of doubtful names. The fourty-four abbots included Counts Falkenstein, Kollonich, and Lamberg, but also many apparently of humble, and often German, origin. The thirty heads of cathedral chapters at this date were mostly magnates but some were not. In 1775, no list of abbots is given in the *Calendar*. Of twenty-eight archbishops and bishops, eight were counts, two barons, the rest doubtful.

This is only a sketch from incomplete evidence. It suggests that leading sees were held by aristocrats, though not exclusively, while cathedral chapters might be solidly aristocratic (Olmütz) or largely bourgeois (Vienna in 1740). The more aristocratic tone of the Vienna chapter by 1775 is striking. The abbots of religious houses in Bohemia and Moravia, and to some extent in Hungary, appear to have risen from the ranks. This may also be true of Lower Austria. Here, perhaps, was a career open to talent, which dissolution of large numbers of houses cut off. On the other hand, perhaps more resistance would have been made to the dissolutions if the heads of houses had been members of leading magnate families like their episcopal brethren.

The second topic which will be examined is the wealth of the Society of Jesus at its dissolution. It will be seen later that the Jesuits were active investors in state bonds in the period before 1773, and also that their assets after the dissolution of the Order were partly employed in loans to Austrian and Bohemian landowners. The resources they controlled are thus of interest here. More generally, the arguments of Kaunitz and others that intellectual and capital resources were locked up by monasticism, and could be released by its reduction, seemed to be confirmed by the partial application of Jesuit property to state education in Austria and Hungary from 1774. A parallel operation, also under Kaunitz's auspices, and starting somewhat earlier, proceeded in the duchy of Milan. Here, the *Giunta Economale*, established in 1765 to survey and control church property, was credited later with dissolving 145 religious houses by 1781, and putting the proceeds, L. 12.4m. (3.3m. fl.), into new schools, parishes, and so on.[20] Both policies foreshadowed a more extensive rationalization of the Austrian church, in which its wealth would be investigated, episcopal boundaries made to

[20] Kaunitz's views on monasticism are discussed by Arneth, *Gesch. Mar. Ther.* ix, ch. 3 and are reproduced at length in Maass, *Josephinismus* i, no. 158/36 (probably 1768), and ii, pp. 6, 8–9, 144 (21 June and 2 July 1770). For the operations in Milan see Maass, introd., and Valsecchi in *Storia di Milano*, xii (1959) 365. The literature does not throw light on the returns of revenues and numbers of persons which the government ordered to be made by Austrian religious houses in 1770, reported by Stormont to Rochford 8 Dec. 1770, PRO SP 80/208. This inquiry deserves investigation. Its context was the wish to tax the church more heavily after 1763.

coincide with secular ones, and superfluous monastic houses dissolved, and their funds devoted to new facilities for the cure of souls, the programme carried through by Joseph II. This programme, especially the information about the church which it collected, is considered below.

The Jesuits have conventionally been the object of folk-belief about their wealth, but it is in fact not easy to find out how much they had. The Austrian case is no exception.[21] The Venetian ambassador reported in 1773 that the dissolved Order was rumoured to have property worth 400m. fl., an absurd figure, which Arneth correctly treated with scepticism.[22] Bílek subsequently showed that the assets of the Order in the Bohemian lands were relatively modest, yielding perhaps 350,000 fl. gross revenue.[23] Even this may be generous, since the twenty ex-Jesuit lordships in Bohemia only yielded an average of 102,000 fl. yearly in 1782–9.[24] Shortly after Bílek, Fináczy printed the substance of an official return of 5 October 1775, which put Jesuit assets in Hungary 'and the parts connected with it', here presumably Croatia and Slavonia, at 7,762,521 fl. Of this, 3,257,868 fl. comprised ecclesiastical estates, 1,637,497 fl. secular estates, 646,766 fl. town estates, 1,825,340 fl. securities and 395,050 fl. securities settled for charitable uses. The revenue was evidently valued at 25 years' pur-

---

[21] The massive study by B. Duhr, *Gesch. der Jesuiten in den Ländern deutscher Zunge* (Munich and Ratisbon 1913–28) gives much information about numbers of persons, but nothing systematic about property. The Society in Austria had considerable difficulty in making ends meet in the second half of the 17th c., Duhr, iii. 282–4. The legend of Jesuit wealth is attacked in the same author's *Jesuiten-Fabeln* (Freiburg im Breisgau 1891), ch. 11, but without much evidence of Jesuit wealth, or its absence. A complete list of Jesuit houses of all types, c.1750, with the numbers of persons in each province, is given in J. C. Harenberg, *Pragmatische Geschichte des Ordens der Jesuiten* (Halle 1760) i. 859–909. The German province had 8,749 persons, 4,291 of them priests, out of a world total of 22,589, 11,293 of them priests. In addition, there were those in the Austrian and Bohemian provinces, see below.

[22] Arneth, ix. 106.

[23] Bílek, *Statky a jmění*, 99. Bílek's book is far from easy to use, and he does not discuss the basis on which Jesuit property was valued. It is assumed here that the official valuation of 6,985,270 fl. at the end of 1777 which he cites represented 20 years' purchase of revenue.

[24] Riegger, *Archiv von Böhmen*, i, no. xix. Special considerations may have applied, however; the lordships were farmed on the Raab system, for which see p. 122.

chase, hence amounted to 310,000 fl. Of this, it was stated, 200,000 fl. would be needed for pensions and maintenance.[25]

Topf, in his unpublished Vienna dissertation on the dissolution of the Jesuit Order in Austria, reproduced from official sources a return drawn up in 1773, according to which there were 343 Jesuit colleges, seminaries, residences, and other houses in the Monarchy, of which 76 were in the Bohemian Province, 174 in the Austrian Province (which included Hungary), 18 in Tyrol and Vorarlberg, 16 in Milan, 46 in the Austrian Netherlands, 13 in Galicia. In all, about 5,600 persons were involved. These figures are higher than those given elsewhere for the Austrian Province, and therefore for total numbers, which, if that evidence is preferred, may not have exceeded 4,000 persons. Topf abdicated on the question of wealth, saying 'the enormous assets appear to have been worth 400m. fl.', with a reference to Arneth.[26] The records of the commission under *Hofrat* Kressel charged with the Jesuit dissolution do not contain estimates of the value of property.[27] However, a return from the *Hofrechenkammer* preserved in the Hofkammerarchiv, though not

---

[25] E. Fináczy, *A magyarországi közoktatás története Mária Terézia korában* (Budapest 1899–1902) ii. 272 n., official return in German dated 5 Oct. 1775. I have translated the phrases 'an geistlichen Gütern' and 'an weltlichen Gütern' as in the text, without being clear what the distinction means. The return stated that 199,248 fl. annually would be needed to maintain ex-Jesuits, or about 5m. fl. This implies 25 years' purchase.

[26] M. Topf, 'Die Aufhebung des Jesuiten-Ordens in Oesterreich 1773'. (Phil. Diss. Vienna 1929) 139 (numbers), 169–70 (property). He apparently (p. 139) did not realize that the Hungarian returns were included in those of the Austrian Province. The 1773 statistics are unreliable. There were only 1,819 Jesuits in the Austrian Province and 1,071 in the Bohemian, a total of 2,890, Duhr, iv/1. 347; Riegger, *Archiv von Böhmen*, iii. 174–6. The numbers of Jesuits in 1750, from Harenberg, loc. cit., were: Austrian Province 1,772 (101), Bohemian Province 1,239 (80), Belgian Province 542 (30), in the number of houses bracketed. Guessing 250 persons in Milan, the then total is 3,833, of whom perhaps a quarter were lay brothers. L. Szilas, 'Die österreichische Jesuitenprovinz im Jahre 1773. Eine historisch-statistische Untersuchung', *Arch. Hist. Soc. Jesu*, 47 (1978) 97–158, 297–349, shows that Jesuit numbers in the Austrian Province increased steadily from 1,257 in 1700 to a peak of 1,906 in 1767. In 1773 there were 1,845, 420 of whom were lay brothers.

[27] According to L. Pastor, *Hist. of the Popes*, xxxviii (1951) 341, Maria Theresia ordered *Hofrat* Kressel to set up a commission on 17 May 1773. Its initial reports, dated 28 May and 2 June 1773, are printed in *Khev.-Metsch*, 31 Aug. 1773, n. 218. For Kressl or Kressel see Ch. 13. The commission's other members were the Provost of St Dorothy's monastery, Ignaz Müller, and Martini and Greiner from the *Oberste Justizstelle* and Bohemian and Austrian Chancellery respectively. The Commission's papers are in HHSA Kaiser Franz Akten, Alte Signatur, nos. 75 a-c, but as far as can be seen contain no overall valuation of property. The report of 2 June advocated retention, not sale, of Jesuit property, and its administration by the *Hofkammer*.

unambiguous, throws some light on this. It is dated 20 August 1777, and lists the receipts of the Jesuit funds bureaux ('Jesuitenfondscassen') in the Bohemian and Austrian lands. No returns had been received from Galicia, but Topf's data indicate that revenue there was small. The document suggests a revenue from Jesuit property of 698,000 fl.[28] Together with 310,000 fl. in Hungary-Croatia, a total revenue of just over 1m. fl. is arrived at. In the Austrian Netherlands, a draft report of 1780 put the worth of Belgian ex-Jesuit assets as 10,548,850 fl. ex. (8,790,708 fl. Aust.). This agrees closely with Bonenfant's figure of 10,480,000 fl. for 1789.[29] In the Duchy of Milan, Jesuit property was valued at L. 9m. (3m. fl.).[30] The evidence is admittedly not conclusive. The belief of critics that the Society was busily sending its assets abroad may have had some foundation, though the accusation was investigated at the time in Austria and discredited.[31] The conclusion which appears to emerge is that rumours of Jesuit wealth were greatly exaggerated. Nor is this surprising, since the Order had traditionally been under-endowed compared with its older rivals. On the other hand, lacking substantial landed endowment, it may have paid more attention than they did to buying government bonds and other securities.

The last subject which will be examined is the wealth of the Austrian church as a whole at the end of Maria Theresia's reign. This emerges from the statistical investigations of the *Geistliche Hof-*

---

[28] HKA Hofrechenkammer A, Fsz. 58/3, no. 53 dated 20 Aug. 1777, badly damaged by damp, and partly illegible. The interpretation here is that the column headed 'according to the System, is offered' denoted expected revenue totalling 508,089 fl. However, Lower Austria was excluded, and entered in the next column as 4,722,937 fl. If this represented 20 years' purchase, total revenue was 744,235 fl., and its capital value 14,884,700 fl. According to Hock–Bidermann, 67, Jesuit property was valued at 15,415,220 fl. at the end of 1777. H. L. Mikoletzky, *Österreich. Das grosse 18. Jahrhundert* (Vienna 1967), 250 shows that the total capital of the *Jesuitenfonds* at 8 Aug. 1781 was 13,192,449 fl. Annual expenditure was 608,204 fl. Closely similar figures, apparently from the same MS source, were given by Georgine Holzknecht, *Ursprung und Herkunft der Reformideen Kaiser Josefs II. auf kirchlichem Gebiete* (Innsbruck 1914) 77. All fail to state the area which the returns covered, but it seems clear that it excluded the Hungarian lands.

[29] AGR Brussels, Cons. des Finances 8549, an incomplete and unfoliated draft of 1780. The disposition of the 5,447,849 fl. ex. realized by sales of ex-Jesuit property to the end of 1780 is given in detail. See P. Bonenfant, *La Suppression de la Compagnie de Jésus dans les Pays-Bas autrichiens (1773)* (Brussels 1925), table XVIII at end for the valuation at 24 Oct. 1789.

[30] Valsecchi, loc. cit. (see n. 20 above).

[31] Pastor, 346; all the pejorative reports were checked back to 1760, and found incorrect. His account is based on MS sources.

kommission appointed by Joseph II on 3 August 1782, which, as its returns show, worked closely with the *Hofrechenkammer*.[32] Table 4.1* attempts a summary of the voluminous data given in the two commissions' reports. It shows that 25.2% of a total church revenue of 19.2 m. fl. derived from the Bohemian lands, 40.2% from the Austrian lands including Tyrol, and 34.6% from the Hungarian lands. The commonly held view that the Bohemian lands were especially well endowed is, on this evidence, not correct. The Austrian lands, with a smaller population, had more ecclesiastical revenue. If the individual figures are divided by the population of 1789, Görz-Gradisca and Trieste emerge as the best-endowed areas (2.05 fl. per head), followed by Upper Austria (1.99 fl.), Lower Austria (1.73 fl.), Tyrol and Further Austria (1.47 fl.), and Inner Austria (1.4 fl.). Bohemia shows 1.08 fl., Moravia-Silesia 1.1 fl. The figure for Hungary is only 0.65 fl., for Galicia 0.47 fl., for Siebenbürgen a mere 0.32 fl. Thus the Austrian lands were best endowed both absolutely and per head, while the Hungarian lands and Galicia accounted for over one-third of church revenue, but had a low figure per head. The Bohemian lands come in between.[33]

Monks and nuns formed an important proportion of the (relatively small) ecclesiastical army, and the endowment and revenue of religious houses an important proportion of that of the church as a whole.[34] Dissolution of a number of these houses, and application of their revenue to the creation of new parishes, etc., was a leading feature of the Josephine reforms. This policy replaced earlier ones in which monastic wealth would have been appropriated to secular

---

[32] For the date of establishment of the *Geistliche Hofkommission*, see Hock–Bidermann, 449. Its model was the *Giunta Economale* in Milan, on which Cobenzl reported on 14 May 1782, ibid. 445. Its members were Baron Kressel (president) and *Hofräte* Haun, Heinke, and Rautenstrauch. Returns of the property, etc., of male and female religious houses had already been called for on 29 Nov. 1781, ibid. 395, and a Religious Fund was set up on 28 Feb. 1782.

[33] The evidence presented is put forward tentatively, in the surprising absence in the extensive literature about Josephinism of a definitive treatment of the structure of the Church, and the detail of the monastic dissolutions. Even the operation of valuing church property is mentioned only by Hock–Bidermann. The tables in the MS source used do not sufficiently distinguish between types of regular and secular ecclesiastical income, etc., to permit further subdivision of the data.

[34] See pp. 72–6 for estimates of clerical numbers and monastic wealth.

ends.[35] No issue involved more clearly the use of state power against a supposedly fainéant church, and the enthusiasm of the reformers is still apparent in the nineteenth-century literature, and even in that of the twentieth. To Josephinists, monastic dissolutions had a similar attraction to that of nationalization for modern socialists. But the actual facts are surprisingly hard to elicit. By the death of Joseph II, it had already become established in print that there were just over 2,000 religious houses in the Monarchy in 1780, of which 700 were subsequently dissolved.[36] Coxe in 1808 and Ranke in 1835 repeated the figures, but reversed them, stating that only 700 houses were left undissolved.[37] Beidtel correctly stated that the position was not clear, but cited a report by Count Kollowrat, dated 4 January 1792, that 413 houses had been dissolved between 1780 and 1792, and 469 remained; this excluded the Austrian Netherlands, Italy, and Hungary.[38] Ficker in 1875 claimed that 276 monasteries and 83 convents, 359 houses in all, were dissolved by Joseph II; this conclusion was adopted by Hock and Bidermann, who also, however, gave Kollowrat's figures and stated that the *Kassenbestände* (balances in the *caisse*) of the Religious Fund were 16,960,400 fl. in Nov. 1787, 18,224,200 fl. in Oct. 1788.[39] Riehl and Reinöhl, writing for the centenary of the Toleration Patent of 1781, claimed, without giving sources or details, that 738 houses were dissolved between 1770 and 1786, and 1,425 remained.

[35] See ii. 265. However, Count Karl Zinzendorf in 1783 contemplated creating government bonds secured on future monastic sales, ii. 155.

[36] The figure of 2,046 religious houses 'in the Austrian Dominions before the Reduction', and 1,143 since, implying dissolution of 903, is given by Dornford, *Historical Developement*, iii, app., p. 2. He also gives lower estimates of the number of dissolved houses. J. Pezzl, *Charakteristik Josephs II.* (Vienna 1790) 107, states that there were 2,024 religious houses and 63,000 monks and nuns 'in the Austrian states' in 1780; 700 houses were subsequently dissolved, and the numbers of religious were reduced to 27,000.

[37] W. Coxe, *Hist. of the House of Austria* (1807), Bohn's Standard Library edn. (1847) iii. 490 n.; L. von Ranke, *History of the Papacy* (1834–6), Bohn's Standard Library edn. (1848) ii. 453. Coxe also says that 36,000 monks and nuns were reduced to 2,700.

[38] I. Beidtel, *Gesch der österr. Staatsverwaltung 1748–1848*, ed. A. Huber (Innsbruck 1896, 1898) i. 223. This work, written earlier in an expanded version, was cut down and published by Huber after Beidtel's death.

[39] A. Ficker's article in *Statistische Monatschrift*, 1 (1875) is cited by Hock–Bidermann, 434 n., together with Kollowrat's figures, and those for the balances of the Religious Fund.

According to them, the Religious Fund was credited with a capital of over 17m. fl. by 1783, excluding Bohemia, Moravia, and Tyrol, and with a revenue of 2m. fl. by 1788 in the German Hereditary Lands. They asserted that the dissolutions put 40m. fl. into agriculture and industry.[40] Mitrofanov repeated Kollowrat's figures, but also stated that Joseph II dissolved 359 houses in the Hereditary Lands, and that their movable property alone was worth 18m. fl. by 1790.[41]

Riehl and Reinöhl's source for overall numbers of religious houses, and numbers dissolved, was in fact Wolf's study, published in 1871, of the dissolutions in Inner Austria. Wolf stated that his statistics were for the German Hereditary Lands and the Hungarian lands only, but did not say where they came from.[42] The subsequent monographs by Bílek in 1893 on the Bohemian lands, and by Laenen in 1905 on Belgium, clarified parts of the subject without disposing of the larger problems.[43] Laenen usefully showed how in Belgium charges tended to exceed revenue, so that the operation there was not a financial success. The very careful lists compiled by 'P.P.' in the 1890s of religious houses in the Bohemian and Austrian lands in 1782, and of those dissolved between 1782 and 1790, when totalled, show 585 monasteries in 1782 (including, however, religious houses in the archdiocese of Salzburg), of which 217 were dissolved by 1790; and 96 convents in 1782, of which 67 were dissolved by 1790. The initial figure for monasteries is somewhat higher than that in Table 4.1* (555); the figure for convents is lower (96 against 148). The numbers of dissolved houses are less

[40] A. Riehl and R. von Reinöhl, *Kaiser Joseph II. als Reformator auf kirchlichem Gebiet* (Vienna 1881) 97–8. The figure of 17m. fl. must be from Hock–Bidermann, who, however, make no qualifications about area.

[41] Mitrofanov, 692. Mitrofanov's account of the religious issue, as of others, is badly in need of amplification and revision.

[42] A. Wolf, *Die Aufhebung der Klöster in Innerösterreich 1782–1790* (Vienna 1871); also in A. Wolf and H. Zwiedineck-Südenhorst, *Österreich unter Maria Theresia, Joseph II. und Leopold II.* (Berlin 1884) 257: 2,163 houses in 1770, of which 205 were dissolved by 1784, 738 by 1786. A preliminary attempt to state the numbers of houses dissolved, and their capital worth, was made by S. Brunner in his extraordinary compilation *Die Mysterien der Aufklärung in Oesterreich 1770–1800* (Mainz 1869). His list at pp. 369–79 containing the names of about 270 houses dissolved outside the Hungarian lands 1782–90 is clearly defective.

[43] Bílek, op. cit.; J. Laenen, *Étude sur la suppression des couvents par l'empereur Joseph II dans les Pays-Bas autrichiens . . . (1783–1794)* (Antwerp 1905).

than those given by Kollowrat.[44] The relevant volume of Pastor's standard *History of the Popes* repeats Kollowrat's figure of 413 houses dissolved.[45] Mikoletzky, however, cites Mitrofanov's figure of 359 houses dissolved in the Hereditary Lands.[46] Professor Chadwick prefers Wolf's statistics, 2,163 'Monasteries in Austria' in 1773, 738 of which were dissolved by 1786.[47]

A complete resolution of these difficulties, which are not untypical of the historiography of the period, lies outside the scope of this work. However, in view of the importance of monastic houses before 1780 as landowners, taxpayers, and lenders to the Crown, some further information may be briefly adduced. The records of the *Hofrechenkammer* and *Geistliche Hofkommission* drawn on for Table 4.1* show that at the beginning of 1782 there were 2,047 religious houses in the Monarchy, 1,443 for men and 604 for women, of which 392 were in the Austrian Netherlands, 467 in Italy, 1,188 in the central lands.[48] They belonged to 37 different orders, headed by the Franciscans (268), Capuchins (198), Minorites (115), Dominicans (99), and Benedictines (88). These figures suggest that the true focus of the regular life was outside the central lands of the Monarchy, and it is not surprising that Lombardy pro-

[44] P.P., 'Verzeichnisse der in Ländern der westlichen Hälfte der österreichischen Monarchie von Kaiser Joseph II. 1782–1790 aufgehobenen Klöster', *Archivalische Zeitschrift*, n.s. 5 (1894) 234–75; 6 (1895) 229–79; 7 (1896) 46–164. Houses in existence in 1782, and dissolutions of convents 1782–90, are listed in vol. 7, apps. I–II. I have deducted 32 Hungarian monasteries from the total of 617 in 1782. Numbers of houses dissolved have to be totalled seriatim through the three volumes. P.P. criticizes the compilers of earlier lists, including Sebastian Brunner. Of Wolf's work he says 'zu bedauern ist nur, dass [es] zu kurz und fast skizzenartig abgefasst [wurde]'.

[45] *Hist. of the Popes*, xxxix (1952) 475; 413 dissolutions by 1791 'in the German-Austrian districts'.

[46] Mikoletzky, *Österreich*, 349. He says that there were previously 2,163 religious houses in the *Erbländer*, ibid.

[47] O. Chadwick, *The Popes and European Revolution* (Oxford, 1981) 251. Wolf's base date was 1770; Chadwick perhaps wanted to clear the dissolution of the Society of Jesus from the figures. Though his table shows 738 houses dissolved 'in Austria', his text says that 'in the Austrian part of the Empire more than 400 houses were abolished'. The supposed 2,163 houses in the Austrian and Hungarian lands in 1780 reappear in the posthumous third vol. of E. Tomek, *Kirchengeschichte Österreichs* (Innsbruck 1935–59), which is largely based on the secondary literature.

[48] See HHSA Nachl. Zinz., Hs. 146 B, 'Fondations', fos. 2–3. 'Italy' is not defined, but normal usage confined it to Lombardy. The number of Italian houses given is, however, surprisingly large.

vided the initial stimulus to monastic reform, as Maass has argued.[49] The total of 2,047 agrees well with the estimates already cited, but was for the whole Monarchy, not just for its central lands. The same records yield the (incomplete) details of monastic population and revenue set out in Table 4.2. The 1781 census figures include Protestant and Greek Orthodox clergy, the remaining columns only Catholic and Uniat clergy. The figures for regular clergy include all lay brothers, a sizeable minority of the regular population, and to that extent overstate the monastic clergy, though not the monastic population. Monastic revenue is understated, since it ought to include a proportion of endowments (*Stiftungen*) to say masses or for charitable purposes. These are usually given only as undifferentiated totals. These reservations apart, the table suggests that the regular clergy exceeded half the Catholic–Uniat total, but controlled only a third of church revenue. These generalizations apply with different force, however in different areas, Upper and Lower Austria in particular showing a different pattern. The clerical totals agree tolerably with the census figures for 1781 save in Hungary, where there was a large minority of Protestant pastors.

There was clearly much regional variety in regular population and wealth. Whereas Lower Austrian houses, taking monasteries and convents together, had 28 persons each, those in Upper Austria 33 and those in Hungary 31, houses in Galicia had only 9, and in Tyrol and Further Austria only 6. Average revenue was 10,644 fl. in Lower Austria, 1,397 fl. in Galicia. This makes it difficult to reach an acceptable estimate of the whole population of regular clergy, male and female. The census of 1762 listed 12,364 monks and 2,771 nuns in the Bohemian and Austrian lands excluding Tyrol and Further Austria, a total of 15,135, but this probably included 2,500 or so Jesuits. There were, in addition, 7,001 secular priests.[50] If for 1782 6,000 monks and nuns are estimated in the Bohemian lands, Inner Austrian houses are taken as having the same average population (28) as those of Lower Austria, as they had in 1762, and a guessed 1,500 are added for Siebenbürgen and Dalmatia, a total regular population of about 25,000 in the central lands before the

[49] Maass, *Josephinismus*, introduction to vol. i.
[50] See Table 3.2.*

TABLE 4.2. *Monastic population and revenue in certain lands, c.1782*

	Secular clergy	Religious	Total	Clergy, 1781 census	Monastic revenue	Total church revenue	Monastic revenue as % of church revenue
Lower Austria	1,402	3,298	4,700	6,918	1,256,010	2,761,710	45.5
Upper Austria	597	1,335	1,932	..	..	1,249,548	..
Tyrol and Further Austria	1,367	1,224	2,591	..	299,044	1,285,395	23.3
Galicia	5,128	2,409	7,537	7,629	354,945	1,579,587	22.5
Hungary	3,629	4,724	8,353	11,735[a]	1,291,137	4,606,611	28.0
Siebenbürgen	..	..	..	5,224[a]	73,928	458,816	16.1
Total	12,123	12,990	25,113	31,506	3,275,064	10,692,119	30.6

Source: for all cols. except clergy, 1781 census, HHSA Nachl. Zinz. Hs. 146 B, 'Fondations', fos. 215, 288, 307, 449–50, 465, 533; for clergy, 1781 census, HKA Hs. 735, item *b*, and Table 3.5.

[a] 1787.

dissolutions is arrived at.[51] It seems permissible to infer from this that the monastic population increased somewhat from the end of the Seven Years War, when it was perhaps 20,000 in all the central lands, to the beginning of Joseph II's reign, partly because the dissolution of the Jesuit Order was more than offset by the regular population acquired with Galicia.[52] However, it formed a somewhat lower proportion of the total population by the later period; the case for a remorseless upward trend propounded by the Josephine reformers was overdone.[53] The ratio of religious to secular clergy also fell. The census of 1762 showed, for the area it covered, 15,135 regular and 7,001 secular clergy. In 1782, the total secular and regular Catholic and Uniat clergy perhaps amounted to 40,000 persons, of whom, if the data presented here are accepted, 25,000 were religious. The proportion of the latter was 63%, compared to 68% earlier.[54]

Monastic endowments were on average modest. In Table 4.2, the revenue for each house is 4,303 fl., hence for 1,188 houses in the central lands would have been 5,111,964 fl. The average net revenue of 111 dissolved houses in August 1783 was, however, 6,735 fl., and of the 61 Inner Austrian houses for which Wolf gives details, 7,718 fl.[55] It is not implausible, therefore, that the overall

[51] About 13,000 monks and nuns are listed in Table 4.2. For Inner Austria, 127 houses each with an estimated 28 monks and nuns, give 3,556, say 3,600, persons. The census figure in 1781 for all clergy in Bohemia is 6,474, and for Moravia-Silesia 3,781, HKA Hs. 735, item *h*. Ignoring the Protestant pastors, applying the proportions of the 1760s, and deducting Jesuits, numbers are estimated for clergy, monks and nuns. The technique, whose crudity will be appreciated, gives 3,940 secular priests in the Bohemian lands in 1781, 5,204 monks and 1,100 nuns. With the other data a total of 24,100 is reached, which is rounded up to 25,000.

[52] The figure of 20,000 for 1762 is the result of adding a guessed 4,000 for Hungary and Sebenbürgen and 1,000 for Inner Austria to the 15,135 referred to in the text.

[53] If the data presented here are approximately correct, the regular population increased by a quarter between the early 1760s and early 1780s, while the population as a whole increased by over 60%.

[54] The estimate of 40,000 is reached by taking 30,911 clergy recorded in the 1781 census (Table 3.2*), adding 8,353 for Hungary (Table 4.2), and guessing 1,000 for Siebenbürgen.

[55] HHSA Nachl. Zinz., Hs. 146 B fo. 211, statement dated 26 Aug. 1783 of the property of 111 houses dissolved outside the Hungarian lands. The gross total was 17,092,131 fl., debts etc. came to 2,139,753 fl., leaving a net 14,952,378 fl. At 20 years' purchase this would represent 747,619 fl. revenue, or 6,735 fl. per house. Wolf, 161-2 has 61 houses with gross property of 12,211,076 fl., net property of 9,415,853 fl.

revenue of the 1,188 houses was 6–7m. fl. The records examined do not yield a clear picture of numbers of houses dissolved. If Kollowrat's figure in 1792 of 413 for the Bohemian and Austrian lands is authentic, 156 could be added to it for Belgium, as reported by Laenen, and 117 for Hungary, as reported by Felhő and Vörös.[56] This would give 686, to which Italian dissolutions must be added.[57] The number dissolved in the central lands was, on this basis 530, or 55% of all the religious houses there. If the religious orders controlled about one-third of church revenue, as suggested above, and over half the existing houses were dissolved, the government's Religious Fund might have been expected to have an income of 3–4m. fl. A statement of its revenue in 1790 and 1791 shows that in the German Hereditary Lands, defined there as the Bohemian-Austrian lands and Galicia, its income was in fact about 2.5m. fl.[58] It does not seem implausible to add 0.7m. fl. for the Hungarian lands, where three-quarters of all houses were dissolved.[59] If revenue is valued at 20 years' purchase, the principal of the Fund was about 65m. fl. The 17m. fl. of which Riehl and Reinöhl speak must denote the securities balances of the Fund, which did amount to 17–17.7m. fl. in 1789. These in turn may have derived from sales of movable property. At the beginning of 1789, 4.1m. fl. of this 17m. fl. was invested in (undefined) private securities, principally in

[56] Laenen, 419–22; Felhő and Vörös (eds.), *A helytartótanácsi levéltár*, 446–9. The minutes of the *Geistliche Hofcommission* in the AVA are missing for the years 1790–1804.

[57] The figure for dissolutions in Lombardy after 1780 is not given in the standard *Storia di Milano*. Wolf–Zwiedineck, 257 state that 45 monasteries and 14 convents were dissolved. As usual, they give no source. Acceptance of their figure of 59 has the pleasing (though not necessarily conclusive) effect of bringing the total of dissolved houses to 745, which is close to the 738 current in the literature. In Galicia, a policy of dissolving or merging small houses was decided on in 1774, and by 1777 the number of houses had in consequence been reduced by 27, Glassl, 136–8. Glassl does not, however, quantify the dissolutions after 1780.

[58] HKA Geistliche Domänen, rote Nr. 1, no. 440, revenue of the *Religionsfond* in 1790 and 1791. The figures for 1790 total 2,564,200 fl. and can be summarized as: Bohemian lands 1,026,226 fl. (40%); Austrian lands 1,174,036 (45.8%); Galicia and Bukovina 363,938 fl. (14.2%).

[59] If the revenue for 1790 referred to in the previous nn. was in respect of 413 dissolved houses, each had 6,208 fl. revenue, therefore 117 Hungarian houses had 726,419 fl. revenue, making a total of 3,290,619 fl., or 65,812,380 fl. at twenty years' purchase. Here, as elsewhere, the steps in the argument need further testing. Chadwick, loc. cit., says that the 'Central Fund' amounted to 60m. fl. by 1790. Mikoletzky, *Österreich*, 349 says the capital of the Religious Fund was 89m. fl. in bonds, cash, and land by the end of 1789.

the Bohemian lands and Galicia, and the rest in public securities.[60] The larger question of the total assets of the Religious Fund, and their realization, remains uninvestigated.[61]

Summarizing, it seems plausible that the figures given as early as 1790, and repeated by later commentators, of 2,000 or more religious houses in 1780, 700 or more of which were subsequently dissolved, refer to the Monarchy as a whole, including its Belgian and Italian lands, and not just to its central lands. The observable confusion in the literature about numbers and areas is partly, though only partly, due to this. If an average of twenty-one persons, the figure arrived at earlier for the central lands, is imputed to each house, there would have been 43,000 monks and nuns in all lands including the Belgian and Italian, in 1780, reduced by, say, 745 dissolutions to just over 27,000. The crudity of this estimate makes it precarious, however. The average used is itself dependent on estimates, and it is not necessarily plausible for the Austrian Netherlands or Lombardy. The number of religious houses assigned to 'Italy' in the manuscipt source is worryingly high if only Lombardy was meant by this. Further uncertainties apply to the capital and revenue of the Religious Fund. Its capital can be stated as a higher figure simply by applying a larger number of years' purchase to it; and so on. What is needed here, as with other aspects of the subject, is a systematic examination of manuscript sources, rather than continued reliance on the existing literature.

[60] HKA Geistliche Domänen, rote Nr. 1, 'Vormerkbuch über die bey den Religionsfondkassen in sämmtlichen deutschen Erbländern . . . Kassareste für das Militärjahr 1789', one of a series of such books; a printed format with written entries. The accounts have no overall total.

[61] The extent to which the monastic property of the 1780s was alienated, and if so whether such sales strengthened the very aristocratic classes whom Joseph II disliked, is not known. There are some inconclusive refs. in Hock–Bidermann, 412, 414, 428, 432.

5

The nobility

LIKE the church, the nobility is by no means easy to pin down in the literature.[1] Blum suggests that 'many, and quite possibly the majority of the noble families of the Austrian Monarchy were established in the course of the seventeenth and eighteenth centuries. After the conquest of Bohemia in 1620 a new Catholic nobility replaced the Protestant lords there'.[2] Macartney tells us that as a result of the Bohemian revolt of 1619 [sic] and its suppression, 'almost all the Czech nobility, higher and lower', perished or was driven into exile, their estates being . . . bestowed on a new set of Imperial servants'.[3] Both statements might be thought to imply an extensive granting of new noble titles, but according to Blum 'on the continent the majority of the nobility, including many of the greatest families, had no title, nor did they need them [sic]', and Macartney asserts that Maria Theresia used ennoblement 'only rarely, while her predecessors had resorted to it only in the most exceptional cases'.[4] This in turn suggests a marked contrast with Joseph II, who, according to Bruford, 'made financiers into noblemen by the dozen', at a fixed tariff.[5]

---

[1] H. G. Schenk, 'Austria', and C. A. Macartney, 'Hungary', in A. Goodwin (ed.), *The European Nobility in the Eighteenth Century* (1953), chs. 6–7 are outlines, the second more so than the first; Schenk's not unimportant mistakes were taken over by Macartney, *Habsburg Empire*. R. A. Kann, 'Aristocracy in the Eighteenth Century Habsburg Empire', and O. Odložilík, 'The Nobility of Bohemia 1620–1740', both in *East European Quarterly*, (1973) have little in the way of factual content. The detailed and careful accounts of Austrian and Bohemian families in Evans, *The Making of the Habsburg Monarchy*, chs. 5–6 are largely based on genealogical sources, in the absence of more general literature; see the author's comments at p. 171 n.

[2] J. Blum, *The End of the Old Order in Rural Europe* (Princeton UP 1978) 16.

[3] Macartney, *Habsburg Empire*, 88. The same view is expressed in Schenk, op. cit.

[4] Blum, 12; Macartney, *Habsburg Empire*, 50.

[5] W. H. Bruford, *Germany in the Eighteenth Century. The Social Background to the Literary Revival* (CUP 1935, pb. 1965) 61. Bruford's source for this statement was M. von Boehn, *Deutschland im 18. Jahrhundert* (Berlin 1921), which K. Epstein, *The Genesis of German Conservatism* (Princeton UP 1966) 677 dismisses as 'superficial and undocumented'.

The contradictory statements in the readily accessible literature can partly be clarified by recourse to more specialized studies. The important question of ennoblement has been examined in detail by Jäger-Sunstenau, who in 1963 published a painstaking statistical analysis of the creations recorded in the reference works of Megerle von Mühlfeld and Frank. The sources used are not free from defects, and the results are only for the Bohemian and Austrian lands of the Monarchy. They are none the less of great interest as the first attempt to plot the contours of the whole subject.[6] The author finds that from 1701 to 1918, 12,408 titles were assigned, of which 10,414 went to those acquiring nobility for the first time, the balance representing steps in the peerage.[7] The massive operation was thus mainly directed at new men. The commonest title granted was of plain noble (*Adel*), 7,514 cases; followed by those of knight (*Ritter*), 3,053 cases; baron (*Freiherr*), 1,563 cases; count (*Graf*), 240 cases; and prince (*Fürst*), 38 cases.[8] Of 12,130 concessions of titles of plain nobility, knight, and baron, 10,358 specify occupation; of these, 3,463 (33.4%) went to officials, 5,133 (49.5%) to army officers, 1,242 (12.0%) to traders, industrialists and bankers, and 520 (5.1%) to those engaged in the arts and sciences.[9] Among other interesting results, it emerges that statistically the earlier part (1849–84) of the era of Franz Joseph was the golden age of both knights and barons.[10]

The data for the period 1711–89 are summarized in Table 5.1.[11] Titles were thus not 'rarely' created. They were created at a rate of 24 a year by Charles VI, 36 a year by Maria Theresia, 40 a year by Joseph II. The great majority (77%) of all creations was, however, of simple nobility. The reticence Macartney asserts is observable at the top of the scale, in creations of counts and princes, though Maria Theresia was not stingy about barons. For plain nobles, knights,

---

[6] H. Jäger-Sunstenau, 'Statistik der Nobilitierungen in Österreich 1701–1918', *Österreichisches Familienarchiv. Ein genealogisches Sammelwerk*, i (Neustadt an der Aisch 1963) 3–16, drawing on J. G. Megerle von Mühlfeld, *Österreichisches Adels-Lexikon* (Vienna 1822–4) and K. F. von Frank, *Alt-Österreichisches Adels-Lexikon* (Vienna 1928).

[7] Jäger-Sunstenau, 14.

[8] Ibid.

[9] Ibid.

[10] Ibid. 7, 12. This was partly due to automatic assignment of titles to those reaching a given official rank, a concession ended in 1884.

[11] The figures derive from Jäger-Sunstenau's tables.

TABLE 5.1. *Ennoblements in Bohemian and Austrian Lands,*
1711–89

	Titles conceded of					
	Adel	Ritter	Freiherr	Graf	Fürst	Total
1711–40	573	63	45	27	5	713
1741–80	1,086	162	160	32	9	1,449
1781–89	295	28	24	12	4	363
Total	1,954	253	229	71	18	2,525

and barons, the division of creations by occupation, where this is
stated, is shown in Table 5.2. Occupation is unfortunately not given
for 37% of Charles VI's creations, or for 21% of those under his
daughter and grandson. If the assumption is made that the missing
occupations were distributed as those given, then of Charles VI's
titles, 53.9% were for officials, only 5% and 4.5% respectively for
the army and for trade and finance. Because the missing items are
most numerous, this result may be the least exact. The proportions
under his daughter, 36.4%, 35.7%, 6.7%, show officials as proportionally less important, army officers much more so. The titles for
the latter bunched during the Seven Years War. Joseph II (30.6%,
30.3%, 17.6%) was even-handed between officials and army officers, but, confirming Bruford, was more liberal towards trade and
industry. The latter had, however, developed by the 1780s, and even
here most of the titles were only ones of simple nobility.[12]

Under Maria Theresia, consistently with the pattern over the
whole period, 1,201 of the 1,449 titles assigned were to men not
formerly noble, and most of these titles were of simple nobility.[13]
Titles of count and prince, suitable for a new landowning aristocracy,
were only conceded on a small scale. An English parallel might be
the relative frequency of grants of arms, knighthoods, and baronet-
cies, and the relative infrequence of new peerages before the
Younger Pitt. Hungarian creations appear to have been modest in
number, Lehotzky's lists, which are admittedly not necessarily
complete, suggesting that Charles VI gave out thirty-seven titles of

[12] Ibid.
[13] Ibid.

TABLE 5.2. *Ennoblements by occupation*

	Officials				Army Officers				Trade, industry, finance			
	Plain noble	Knight	Baron	Total	Plain noble	Knight	Baron	Total	Plain noble	Knight	Baron	Total
1711–40	327	39	19	385	29	2	5	36	28	4	—	32
1741–80	385	95	48	528	446	10	61	517	79	13	5	97
1781–89	93	12	6	111	102	2	6	110	53	7	4	64
Total	805	146	73	1,024	577	14	72	663	160	24	9	193

Hungarian count and baron, and Maria Theresia a further thirty-four.[14]

The upshot of this analysis is that although new titles were frequent, and in a minority of cases denoted the arrival of powerful new houses, they did not call a new aristocracy into existence in this period. In seeking the characteristics of the nobility as a class, and whether it was old or new, homogeneous or heterogeneous, titled or untitled, and so on, it is therefore necessary to investigate the already established families. Unfortunately, the questions of who the controlling landed families actually were in the various parts of the Monarchy, what their wealth was, and how they were connected with each other, are far from easy to answer. As Hassinger has pointed out in an important study of the Austrian lands, it is often uncertain who the leading families were, how far those formally entitled to attend the Diets were in practice resident, what proportion of nobles owned lands in different parts of the Monarchy, and so on.[15] Genealogical works of reference and the somewhat rare studies of individual houses tend to be stronger on pedigrees than on social and economic background.[16] The whole subject would, no doubt, absorb a lifetime's work. The remainder of this chapter will pursue the limited objectives of developing some further information from the existing literature, and then presenting the results of specific additional investigations. Some general conclusions will be attempted from these data.

A start will be made with the Monarchy's Bohemian lands. The learned authors of the *Handbuch der Geschichte der böhmischen Länder* try consistently to keep the questions of landownership, leading families, and the distribution of power between Herrenstand (princes, counts, barons) and *Ritterstand* in view. Their conclusions, which are more fully stated for Bohemia than for Moravia or Silesia, may be summarized as follows. There was a progressive tendency over the whole period from the sixteenth to the eighteenth centuries for the *Herrenstand* to increase at the expense of the *Rit-*

---

[14] [A. Lehotzky], *Stemmatographia nobilium familiarum regni Hungariae* (Pressburg 1796–8), i. 167–70.

[15] H. Hassinger, 'Ständische Vertretungen in den althabsburgischen Ländern und in Salzburg', in Gerhard, *Ständische Vertretungen*, 258.

[16] For example, Fürst Karl zu Schwarzenberg, *Geschichte der reichsständischen Hauses Schwarzenberg* (Neustadt an der Aisch 1963) or the older work by Jacob Falke, *Gesch. des fürstlichen Hauses Liechtenstein* (Vienna 1868–82).

terstand. The actual numbers of the latter were, however, initially larger. Thus there were 182 *Herrenstand* taxpayers in Bohemia, from 69 families, in 1557, and 1,500 *Ritterstand* taxpayers. The balance of property between the two groups was about equal.[17] In 1619, there were 197 lords and 977 knights in Bohemia, 90 lords and 189 knights in Moravia.[18] The Bohemian revolt of 1618–20, the Thirty Years War, and the 'Iron Time' at the end of the seventeenth and beginning of the eighteenth century, associated with war and heavy taxation, drastically reduced the fortunes of the knights, only 100 of the 600 knightly families in Bohemia before 1620 surviving to 1750.[19] The tendency to concentration of landownership in the *Herrenstand* reached its peak in Bohemia in the later eighteenth century. In 1789 the declared worth of the 952 lordships and estates there was 239m. fl., of which 162m. fl. (67%) belonged to the *Herrenstand*, and the remainder to Crown, church, knights.[20]

Superimposed upon this general trend, however, was one of the rise and fall of families. Thus, 37 of the 69 *Herrenstand* families of 1557 in Bohemia had disappeared by 1615, while new *Herrenstand* families had risen in their place, among them those of Černín, Kaunitz, Kollowrat, Wratislaw.[21] The decline in the number of Bohemian knights by 1615 was less steep than it would otherwise have been because there were 311 new creations between 1520 and 1620.[22] In Moravia, 47 foreign noble families joined the 104 native ones during the Thirty Years War, but only 10 of these 47 were still landowners in 1750.[23] At that date there were 16 old noble houses, ten post-1620 ones, and, thanks to creations, 57 new ones.[24] Of 130 knightly families in Moravia before 1620, 84 vanished during the Thirty Years War.[25]

The authors of the *Handbuch* place the confiscations after the Battle of the White Mountain, referred to at the beginning of this chapter, in this general context. The numbers of those liable to

---

[17] *HGBL* ii. 243.
[18] Ibid. 265.
[19] Ibid. 358.
[20] Ibid. 486. No authority is cited, but the reference must be to the Josephine tax cadastre.
[21] Ibid. 243.
[22] Ibid.
[23] Ibid. 356.
[24] Ibid.
[25] Ibid.

confiscation are set lower than those presented in older sources. It is shown that the extent of the forfeitures is the object of often emotive controversy, and that conclusive results are not yet available. The anti-Protestant measures of 1627–8, it is argued, resulted in the emigration of only a quarter of the native nobility, rather than to its departure *en masse*. The confiscation of Wallenstein's huge estates in 1634 and, more substantively, the demographic and economic pressures exerted during the Thirty Years War, are shown to have been of equal importance in generating social change with the forfeitures after 1620. Even after these changes, three-fifths of subjects recorded in the tax-roll of 1654 in Bohemia had native lords, though there were lordly newcomers as well, for example Buquoy, Colloredo, Desfours, Gallas, Mansfeld, Trauttmansdorff, and other families.[26] The processes described, though less distinctly mapped towards the eighteenth century, suggest general cyclical change, with violent political change imposed upon it, rather than a complete break after 1620 as is often asserted. This is reminiscent of the controversies about English developments in the sixteenth and seventeenth centuries.

Against this background, some other published evidence for Silesia, Moravia, and Bohemia in the eighteenth century will be briefly discussed. Macartney tells us that 'Silesia was largely composed of tiny principalities, formerly the appanages of the very prolific ruling house of the Piasts.'[27] The editors of the *Handbuch* refer only to the relative poverty and clannishness of Silesian nobles in the seventeenth century, and to the numerous 'Germanified' Slavonic nobles of Upper Silesia.[28] Many years earlier (1901), however, Otto Hintze had produced an important study of Silesian landownership in 1740, on the eve of Frederick II's invasion.[29] Hintze showed the following pattern.[30]

(*a*) Royal Principalities (*Erb-Fürstenthümer*): (1) Breslau (with-

---

[26] Ibid. 284–90, 303, 355.

[27] Macartney, *Habsburg Empire*, 23 n. His statement about the origin of the principalities is correct, see Hintze below.

[28] *HGBL* ii. 356.

[29] O. Hintze, *Behördenorganisation und allgemeine Verwaltung in Preussen beim Regierungsantritt Friedrichs II.* (Acta Borussica 6/1, Berlin 1901) 499–500. D'Elvert, *Verfassung*, 44–52 provides additional details. C. Grünhagen, *Gesch. Schlesiens* (Gotha 1884–6), which goes up to 1740, is uninformative.

[30] Hintze, 499–500.

out the town); (2) Brieg; (3) Glogau; (4) Liegnitz; (5) Oppeln and
Ratibor; (6) Schweidnitz and Jauer; (7) Wohlau. All these, save
Ratibor, passed to Prussia under the peace treaties of 1742 and 1745.

(b) Mediate Principalities (*Mediat-Fürstenthümer*): (1) Jägerndorf, Prince Liechtenstein; (2) Münsterberg, Prince Auersperg; (3)
Neisse-Grottkau, Bishop of Breslau; (4) Oels and Bernstadt,
younger line of dukes of Württemberg; (5) Sagan, Prince Lobkowitz; (6) Teschen, Duke of Lorraine; (7) Troppau, Prince Liechtenstein. Of these, Prussia acquired (2), (4), and (5) and parts of all the
rest save (6), which was wholly retained by Austria.

(c) Free Estates Lordships (*Freie Standesherrschaften*): (1)
Beuthen, Count Henckel v. Donnersmarck; (2) Carolath-
Beuthen, Count Schönaich; (3) Militsch, Count Mahlzahn; (4)
Pless, Count Promnitz; (5) Trachenberg, Prince Hatzfeld; (6)
Wartenberg, Field Marshal Count Münnich. All these passed to
Prussia. The three groups, together with Breslau and ten other
towns, comprised the 'Status Majores' represented in the Princely
Diet.[31] Hintze also printed the names of twenty owners, three
ecclesiastical, the rest secular, of twenty-four lordships, estates
(*Güter*), and *Burglehen* which together formed the *Status Minores*
of Silesia, which were directly under the Crown, and not represented in the Diet. All these lordships were within one of the
territorial units previously described.[32] These data form an apparently satisfactory pattern of royal and aristocratic landownership
in large units. The pattern is marred only by Hintze's remark
that the church owned one-third of Silesia, which is not inferable
from the evidence he presented.[33]

Further light is cast on this subject by Brzobohatý and Drkal's
massive edition of the Caroline tax cadastres in Silesia, though the
editors do not allude to Hintze's work.[34] The admittedly defective
tax-returns of 1728 permit a weighting of the various groups of
lands just described. The revenues declared, in Silesian thaler, are
shown in Table 5.3.[35]

In money terms, the Royal Principalities were more than twice as

---

[31] Ibid. and d'Elvert, loc. cit.
[32] Hintze, 500.
[33] Ibid. 505.
[34] J. Brzobohatý and S. Drkal (eds.), *Karolínský katastr slezský* (Prague 1972–3).
[35] Based on the figures in Brzobohatý–Drkal, ii. 686–95, showing the second version of the valuation initiated in 1721.

TABLE 5.3. *Summary of cadastral returns in Silesia, 1728 (thlr. Sil.)*

	Dominical		Rustical		Towns		Total
	Revenue	%	Revenue	%	Revenue	%	
7 Royal Principalities	1,723,921	46.2	1,498,931	40.1	512,456	13.7	3,735,315
Mean	246,274		214,133				
7 Mediate Principalities	650,661	38.8	829,439	49.5	195,431	11.7	1,675,538
Mean	92,951		118,491				
6 Free Lordships	157,135	59.2	79,240	29.9	29,072	10.9	265,454
Mean	26,189		13,206				
Total	2,531,717	44.6	2,407,610	42.4	736,959	13.0	5,676,307

1 thlr. Sil. = 1⅔ fl. Aust. Apparent discrepancies in cross-totals are due to rounding.

important as the Mediate Principalities, and the latter were six times as important as the Free Lordships. Overall, the division of taxable revenue was roughly equal between lords' (dominical) and peasants' (rustical) revenue, but this average concealed different ratios within each group. Town revenue was a low, though not negligible, proportion of the whole. The figures just stated also exclude Breslau, which returned a revenue of 486,369 thlr. Together with the revenue of the *Status Minores*, the Silesian totals for 1728 become 2,561,589 dominical (41.2%), 2,448,277 rustical (39.4%), and 1,202,279 town (19.4%), or 6,212,146 thlr. in all. The second result which emerges from this work is that in the one Royal Principality and four Mediate Principalities for which the names of declaring landowners survive, the beneficial ownership of the land, as distinct from its overlordship, was intensely subdivided.[36] Average declared dominical revenue was less than 1,000 thlr. If these principalities were representative, as seems plausible, the pattern of ownership differed radically from the pattern of lordship indicated by Hintze. A certain number of more prominent families can be detected, among them Frakstein, Harasovský, Henckel von Donnersmarck, Kotulinský, Lhotský, Lichnovský, Sedlnický. Of these, Henckel von Donnersmarck has already been encountered as feudal lord of Beuthen.[37] But dominant, oligopolistic landownership is not observable. This general conclusion is in line with Ritter Carl von Grossa's statistics of 1731, according to which Silesia had the staggering number of 4,100 lordships. The relatively high number of freemen (*svobodníci*) in this MS, at 59,546 larger than the 49,232 for peasants, is also noteworthy.[38] The whole subject of landownership in Silesia, as elsewhere, is neglected, but the thesis that at Maria Theresia's accession it was numerous but poor, under the overlordship of magnates who were typically absentees, fits well with the alleged ruin of Silesian nobles during the Seven Years War, and the consequent establishment of a land bank there by Frederick II in 1769–70, which have never been satisfactorily explained in the literature.

[36] Based on the lists ibid. 700–42 for Oppeln and Ratibor (royal) and Neisse-Grotkow (Bishop of Breslau), Jägerndorf, Teschen, Troppau (mediate).

[37] The family descended from Lazarus Henckel von D., a war contractor *c*.1600, and in 1901 acquired the title of (Prussian) Prince. In 1728 Johann H. owned the *status minor* of Oderberg, with 6,482 thlr. declared revenue.

[38] Cit. Brzobohatý–Drkal, i. 52, 'svobodníci' presumably being their translation for *Freisassen*.

In Moravia, leading families in the tax-roll of 1656 included Althann, Dietrichstein, Kaunitz, Liechtenstein, Salm, Slawata, Waldstein, Würben, Žerotín.[39] These were all landowners in Bohemia too, though not always in the same line. The largest number of Moravian tax assessments at this date fell on the lands of the Liechtenstein and Dietrichstein families. Radimský has published an analysis of declared Moravian tax revenue drawn up about 1790 by the topographer F. J. Schwoye. This showed declared rustical revenue as 2,728,481 fl., and dominical revenue as 3,359,000 fl., of which 893,300 fl. (26.6%) was ecclesiastical and the rest secular. Of the latter, 369,000 fl. was declared by Prince Liechtenstein, and 155,000 fl. by Prince Dietrichstein.[40] The absolute figures here are too low. By this date, also, the Slawata lands had passed by inheritance to the Černíns of Bohemia.[41] However, the basic position had clearly not changed. It seems plausible that there was more overlap between Bohemian and Moravian landownership than between either and Silesian, though the Dietrichstein, Liechtenstein, and Lobkowitz families had Silesian estates.

A complete list of Moravian landowners in this period is unfortunately not available. However, Radimský and Trantírek have printed extensively the results of the Theresian tax cadastres of 1750 and 1754 (dominical) and 1760 and 1768 (rustical).[42] These show a declared dominical revenue in 1754 of 2,142,583 fl., and a declared rustical revenue in 1760 of 3,022,652 fl.[43] The proportions of the total are 41.5% and 58.5%, in contrast to 1790, when dominical revenue comprised 55.2% of a larger sum.[44] The Moravian returns for 1754 show that of 4,524,889 Moravian *Metzen* of cultivated and afforested land declared, 2,749,684 *Metzen* (61%) were arable and 1,403,892 *Metzen* (31.0%) woods, with meadows only 226,281 *Metzen* (5%). Of the area declared, 40% was dominical and 60% rustical. In the main types of land the results were as

[39] *HGBL* ii. 356.

[40] J. Radimský, 'Pozemkový majetek moravský na sklonku 18. století', *Vlastivědný věstník moravský*, 12/1 (1957) 15–18.

[41] *HGBL* ii. 355. The figures for 1790 must be too low: see the 1.75m. fl. church revenue in Moravia-Silesia in Table 4.1*.

[42] J. Radimský and M. Trantírek (eds.), *Tereziánský Katastr moravský* (Prague 1962).

[43] Radimský–Trantírek, 42.

[44] See Radimsky cit. n. 40.

TABLE 5.4. *Dominical and rustical land in Moravia, 1754*

	Arable		Gardens		Pasture and Meadows		Woods	
	Metzen	%	*Metzen*	%	*Metzen*	%	*Metzen*	%
Dominical	441,107	16.0	9,231	16.6	57,977	25.6	1,314,290	93.6
Rustical	2,308,577	84.0	46,216	83.4	168,304	74.4	89,602	6.4
Total	2,749,684	100.0	55,447	100.0	226,281	100.0	1,403,892	100.0

shown in Table 5.4.[45] Thus arable and meadow were mostly under peasants' control, woods under that of lords. Lordship revenue primarily derived from dominical income (brewing rights, demesne farming, etc., though the details are not given) rather than from rents or *robot* services.[46] The latter were, however, undervalued in the returns.[47] Lordship revenue was skewed towards the larger owners, as would be expected from the previous discussion. A random sample of declarations from the 422 lordships in Moravia in 1754 shows that 63% of lordships controlled only 19% of dominical revenue, while 37% controlled the remainder. Over half the total declared revenue was returned by no more than 15% of the lordships sampled.[48] If the names of owners were available, there can be no doubt that the degree of concentration found would be still higher, since multiple ownership of lordships could then be traced.[49]

For Bohemia, Dr Eila Hassenpflug-Elzholz has recently published a remarkable study in which, among many other results, she

[45] Radimský–Trantírek, 47, undated. The figures are the same as those for 1754 in d'Elvert, 'Gesch. Steuerw.', 532. Rustical arable is mistotalled in both these sources as 2,328,577 *Metzen*. One *Metze* equalled one-third of a *Joch*, or 0.191 ha.

[46] Radimský–Trantírek, 46 show that of a total declared lords' income in 1754 of 2,142,583 fl., 318,409 fl. was attributed to *robot* services, 10,324 fl. to wine rents, and 153,702 fl. to beer rents, presumably dues paid in these liquors.

[47] See pp. 120 and ii. 232.

[48] Based on a random sample of 65 lordships from the list of 1754 printed by Radimský–Trantírek as 'Dominikal 3'. The total income in the sample was 361,631 fl. Some *Güter*, as opposed to *Herrschaften*, must be in the 1754 list: the 1763 census gave only 388 lordships, ibid. 48.

[49] Names of owners are not given in the printed text but presumably were in the original source, since at p. 229 the editors identify Princes Liechtenstein and Dietrichstein and the Cardinal Bishop of Olmütz as accounting for one-third of the returns.

TABLE 5.5. *Structure of the Bohemian Noble Nation, 1741*

	1 Families	2 Of which, owning land in Boh.	3 Members of (1)	4 Minors	5 Lay adults liable to take oaths ((3) − (4) but excluding clergy)	6 Of whom, had no Boh. land	7 Dominical revenues of each group 1756
Princes	13	13	28	3	25	0	1,010,369
Counts	130	102	602	221	344	124	2,577,855
Barons	85	44	263	53	186	68	208,277
Total Herrenstand	228	159	893	277	555	192	3,796,501
Knights	303	126	1,228	363	768	427	264,182
Total	531	285	2,121	640	1,323	619	4,060,683

identifies all male members of the Bohemian noble nation (*Adelsnation*) liable to render homage to Charles Albert of Bavaria in 1741, and prints their names, together with their dominical revenues, as shown in the published cadastre of 1756, and their record of homage, or refusal of it.[50] The detail of her analysis of political groupings lies outside the scope of the present study. It is sufficient to state her main conclusions that 1,323 persons were liable to render homage, and 582 did so, 462 of them personally, 120 through proxies. The remaining 741 nobles refused. Of 132 nobles holding Bohemian provincial offices in 1741, however, 114 rendered homage, 108 of them personally. In contrast, 302 of the total of 351 Bohemian nobles holding central government offices, army commissions, etc., declared for Maria Theresia. The tie of provincial loyalties thus pulled a core of nobles towards Charles Albert, who made promises of restoring their powers. The larger core with ties to the Habsburg dynasty supported it.

For the present chapter, her analysis of the structure of the Bohemian noble nation in 1741 is more immediately relevant. Her statistical conclusions are set out in Table 5.5.

Part of the value of this display is its demonstration of the con-

---

[50] Hassenpflug-Elzholz, *Böhmen und die böhmischen Stände*. Tables 5.5 and 5.6 draw on her pp. 306, 321–29, 334–7, and 433. Col. 7 of Table 5.5 is computed from her lists at pp. 94–305.

siderable number of family members qualified to take the oaths. However, it is also shown that many qualified persons had no Bohemian land (col. 6). Their names inflated the ranks of counts, barons, and, above all, knights. From the above figures, it appears that half the noble nation in 1741 had no ties of property with Bohemia, though this might not denote indifference. Two of the landless knights, for example, were councillors of the Bohemian Chancellery in Vienna.

The figures for dominical revenue in the table indicate that income was highly skewed, princes having a quarter of the total, and barons and knights a relative pittance. Dominical revenue per adult family member qualified to take the oaths was 40,000 fl. for princely families, 7,500 fl. for those of counts, 2,120 fl. for those of barons, only 340 fl. for those of knights. However, within each social group there was also variation, for example ninety-four counts declared incomes of 1,000–10,000 fl., while thirty-seven had 10,000–19,999 fl., twenty-nine more 20,000–49,999 fl., and nine, incomes over 50,000 fl. Even among the knights, nine had 5,000 fl or more.

Dr. Hassenpflug-Elzholz's fifteen richest families are shown in Table 5.6. At the top of the income pyramid discernible came rich foreigners and rich nobles, easily headed by the gigantic Schwarzenberg estate. Counts' families were able to make an equal showing with those of princes because they typically had several lines.

A weakness of her data for the purposes of this chapter is that church members qualified to take the oaths were relatively few (44) in number, and only 31 had property in Bohemia, with a combined dominical revenue in 1756 of 365,324 fl. Even the Archbishop of Prague had no more than 55,000 fl. The estates of the Jesuits and other Orders not qualified to sit in the Estates were excluded from the homage lists, which thus underestimate the wealth of the church. Further, all female landowners are also necessarily excluded from the lists. These omissions help to explain why dominical revenue totalled only 4,426,007 fl., whereas declared dominical revenue in 1756 was 6.3m. fl., as is shown below. A further roll of Bohemian landowners, published by Riegger in the first volume (1792) of his scarce *Archiv von Böhmen*, supplements the conclusions of Dr Hassenpflug-Elzholz's study, and is in broad agreement with them. The list in question, however, which is from about 1770, only contains families owning land. Further, all the incomes

TABLE 5.6. *The fifteen richest families in Bohemia, 1741*
C = Count   P = Prince

	Rank	Declared income 1756 (rounded)
Schwarzenberg	P	329,000
Kinsky	C	165,000
Černín (Czernin)	C	156,000
Lobkowitz	P	154,000
Waldstein	C	120,000
Trauttmansdorff	C	115,000
Elector of Bavaria	P	94,000
Martinitz	C	84,000
Colloredo	C	82,000
Gallas	C	79,000
Morzin	C	74,000
Thun	C	71,000
Markgraf of Baden	P	68,000
Clary und Aldringen	C	67,000
Duchess of Savoy	P	63,000

TABLE 5.7. *Values and revenues of Bohemian lordships, c. 1770*

Owner	Families	Declared capital worth	Estimated revenue	% of total	Mean
Crown	—	8,319,500	332,780	3.3	—
3 foreigners	3	12,553,400	502,136	5.0	167,378
13 Princes	11	49,542,700	1,981,708	19.9	152,439
172 Counts	95	117,715,100	4,708,604	47.3	27,375
79 Barons	57	10,264,750	410,590	4.1	5,197
95 Knights	76	7,657,500	306,300	3.1	3,224
Subtotal		206,052,950	8,242,118	82.8	
Church		42,829,100	1,713,164	17.2	
Total	242	248,882,050	9,955,282	100.0	

in it are higher than those declared in 1756, and their total, 248m. fl., is close to the 239m. fl. shown for gross dominical property by the Josephine tax survey.

Riegger stated that his 'List of Lordships and estates according to their value' was drawn up 'about twenty years ago' by 'M.E., Royal Rectifications Vice-Registrator', and admitted that it was defective, which other evidence confirms. Its general pattern, however,

appears plausible.[51] When totalled, it shows the following distribution of landownership, apparently based, as suggested above, on
gross rather than net revenue (Table 5.7). Compared with the situation in 1741, the number of princely families had increased by one
(in 1741 the three foreign families are included under princely families), that of counts and barons was reduced, and that of knights was
considerably reduced, partly by promotion to the *Herrenstand*, as
several instances show. A minority of those listed was female: one
princess, twenty-six countesses, six baronesses, five female holders
of knights' lands. The landed revenue of the church was considerably higher than the homage lists of 1741 indicate, though well
short of the 3m. fl. imputed to Bohemia by the Josephine ecclesiastical survey discussed in the previous chapter. There was a high
concentration of income. Mean foreign and princely revenue was
five times greater than that of counts, who in turn, it appears, had
five times that of barons and nine times that of knights. Knights and
barons comprised 48% of secular owners, yet controlled only 7%
of secular revenue. At the top end of the scale, ten owners, including
the Crown, controlled 27.1% of *total* revenue, as shown in Table
5.8. This top group was a mixture of royal, clerical, foreign, Bohemian, and German interests.

If all families which controlled 50,000 fl. annual revenue or more
are extracted from Riegger's list, it appears that the leading families
of counts were those of Buquoi, Černín, Clam, Colloredo, Desfours, Harrach, Hartig, Kaiserstein, Kaunitz, Kinsky, Kollowrat,
Losi, Martinitz, Morzin, Nostitz, Paar, Pachta, Palm, Schwerts,

---

[51] Riegger, *Archiv von Böhmen*, i. 574–602, 'Verzeichniss der Herrschaften und
Güter in Böhmen, nach dem Werthe derselben, Verfasset von M. E.***, K. Rektifi-
kations-Vice-Registrator vor etwa 20 Jahren'. M. E. may have been Martin Eberle, a
member of the Bohemian *Commercial Consessus* in 1770. He took income as 4% of
declared capital worth. Subtotals are given in the list only for Crown lands and the
church, in the latter case inaccurately. This list has been drawn on more than once.
Wolf–Zwiedineck-Südenhorst, *Oesterreich unter Maria Theresia*, 192 date it to
1773. They give the capital worth results in round numbers, inaccurately for princes
(46m. fl), and the church (36m. fl), and refer to 13 princes, and 95 knightly *families*.
Kerner, *Bohemia in the Eighteenth Century*, 71 states that 'by the time of Maria
Theresia', princes were worth 465m. fl. [*sic*], foreigners 22.4m. fl. [*sic*], counts
119m. fl., barons 10.1m. fl., knights 7.5m. fl. According to him, the Bohemian
Court Calendar for 1789 showed 15 princes, 79 nobles [*sic*], 44 barons, 51 knights.
Macartney, *Habsburg Empire*, 53 conflates Kerner's statements, and applies them to
1792, when according to him there were 51 princely families [*sic*] worth 465m. fl., 79
counts worth 119m. fl., and 44 barons worth 10.1m. fl.

TABLE 5.8. *Proprietors of the ten largest revenues in Bohemia, c. 1770*

Prince Joseph Schwarzenberg-Piccolomini	577,224
Prince Ferdinand Lobkowitz	491,400
The Crown	332,780
The Society of Jesus	294,380
The Elector of Bavaria	212,076
Count Prokop Tschernin (Černín, Czernin)	189,820
Count Christian Clam	159,336
The Duchess of Savoy	152,280
Prince Johann Auersperg	150,740
Count Joseph Thun	137,640
Total	2,697,676

Spork, Sternberg, Thun, Trauttmansdorff, Waldstein, Wratislaw, Wrtby, a total of twenty-six. To these must be added the princely families of Auersperg, Clary, Dietrichstein, Fürstenberg, Liechtenstein, Lobkowitz, Löwenstein, Mannsfeld, Schwarzenberg, or thirty-five in all. All these are in the lists of families controlling 24,000 fl. revenue or more given by Dr Hassenpflug-Elzholz, with the exception of the *arriviste* financial dynasty of Palm, credited by Riegger with a Bohemian income of 112,760 fl. Co-existing with the plutocratic families of counts was, as at the earlier period, a larger number (69 families) whose wealth varied from the adequate to genteel poverty (under 5,000 fl. yearly).

It is not without interest that ten of the leading families in 1770, Černín, Kaunitz, Kinsky, Kollowrat, Lobkowitz, Nostitz, Sternberg, Waldstein, Wratislaw, Wrtby, were of Bohemian, not German, descent. The most prolific family seems to have been the Kollowrats, nine different members of whom in the two lines of Krakowsky and Liebsteinsky controlled in all 269,960 fl. revenue. Of the ninety-five families of counts, however, only twenty-five were Bohemian. The 'native' nobility flourished at the top of the scale, rather than lower down. Of fifty-seven baronial families, only sixteen (28%) were Bohemian, of seventy-six knightly ones, only twenty-two (29%). Several of these had members at both levels. Lastly, it should be noted that Macartney's statement that 'it was the fidei commissa that created the great families whose names are bound up with the history of Austria', has only a limited application here. In 1765 it was stated, without further detail, that there were sixty-one *Fideikommissen* in Bohemia, controlling 802,900 fl.

revenue.[52] For 1787, Riegger prints a list of sixty-two, controlling 1,321,271 fl. revenue. The second roll must be a revised version of the first, and shows that most of the entails were created in the seventeenth century and in the eighteenth century before 1740.[53]

The returns of Bohemian dominical and rustical revenue made for the revised tax cadastre of 1756 have been published in detail by Pekař.[54] Overall, 9,703,581 *Strich* of cultivated land were declared, 5,585,754 *Strich* (57.6%) of which was arable and gardens, 518,817 *Strich* pasture, 885,631 *Strich* meadows (together 14.5%), and 2,462,554 *Strich* (25.4%) woods. Of the area declared, 43% was dominical and 57% rustical. The division between these in the main types of land is shown in Table 5.9. In the proportion between dominical and rustical land, in the predominantly rustical control of arable and pasture, and in the overwhelmingly dominical control of woods, Bohemia thus resembled Moravia, though Bohemian lords had a relatively greater share of arable and pasture. The returns of dominical revenue show a total of 6,292,778 fl., of which 2,391,709 fl. (38%) came from agriculture, 2,732,119 fl. (43.4%) from the sale of beer, only 701,951 fl. (11.1%) from rents in cash and kind, and 466,998 fl. (7.4%) from *robot* services.[55]

The discussion now turns to the Austrian lands and Hungary. In Upper Austria, according to Grüll, gross declared dominical revenue in 1750 was 990,330 fl., of which 532,250 fl. (53.7%) belonged to members of the *Herrenstand*, 388,916 fl. (39.3%) to the church, 61,105 fl. (6.2%) to the *Ritterstand*, and a mere 8,059 fl. (0.8%) to the Crown. There were 131 declaring lordships, and 30 estates (*Güter*), denoting relatively large units of ownership.

[52] HHSA Nachl. Zinz. Hs. 157, [1765], unfoliated, under 'Böhmen'. The quotation from Macartney is from *Habsburg Empire*, 54; his view derives from Schenk's essay cit. n. 1 above.

[53] Riegger, *Archiv von Böhmen*, i. 426–32. Comparison of this list with that of lordships discussed earlier shows that several entries in the latter were defective, as Riegger stated.

[54] Pekař, 'České katastry', table X in *ČČH* 20 (1914) shows the areas declared in 1756, by Circles. A *Strich*, or half a *Joch*, was equivalent to 0.287 ha. The returns included the Egger District. The very extensive version of the cadastre published by A. Chalupa *et al.* (eds.), *Tereziánský katastr český*, iii. 484–7 gives figures for area and revenue, including variants, which are somewhat larger than those in the text, for example dominical revenue is stated as 6,299,342 fl., alternatively as 6,326,371 fl.; *robot* services are valued at 475,792 fl., and so on. These differences do not alter the general conclusions drawn here.

[55] The revenue from beer was, however, inflated by including in it part of that received by towns, see ii. 229, 231.

TABLE 5.9. *Dominical and rustical land in Bohemia, 1756*

	Arable and gardens		Pasture and meadows		Woods	
	Strich	%	Strich	%	Strich	%
Dominical	1,367,065	24.5	411,903	29.3	2,258,531	91.7
Rustical	4,218,689	75.5	992,545	70.7	204,023	8.3
Total	5,585,754	100.0	1,404,448	100.0	2,462,554	100.0

The ten biggest revenues, in florins, were declared by Kremsmüns-ter Abbey (76,604), the Bishop of Passau (72,368), Prince Karl Auersperg (57,511), Count Franz Joseph Weissenwolf (47,623), Count Ernst Starhemberg (43,824), Count Rudolf Salaburg (37,718), Prince Franz Lamberg (37,642), the Abbey of St Florian (34,441), Count Johann Ludwig Khevenhüller (27,699), and the Abbey of Lambach (25,328). These declarations, totalling 458,254 fl., formed 46.3% of the total, indicating a high degree of concentration of ownership.[56]

The literature is uninformative about the social structure of Lower Austria, perhaps the most important land of the Monarchy, and recourse must be had to manuscript sources. Here Vienna and the eighteen royal towns, which between them bore a fifth of the total Contribution, were separately assessed, and revision of the tax cadastre from 1750 was confined to dominical and rustical land. The gross revenues returned in 1754 came to 4,200,780 fl., of which 2,328,630 fl. (55.4%) was dominical and 1,872,150 fl. (44.6%) rustical.[57] Dominical income was divided into revenue from demesne operations, which accounted for only 230,745 fl., and other revenues, which accounted for 2,097,885 fl. The latter

[56] G. Grüll, 'Die Herrschaftsschichtung in Österreich ob der Enns 1750', *Mitt. des Oberösterr. Landesarchivs*, 5 (1957) 311–39. This article is by no means always easy to follow about taxation, but the figures for gross incomes seem well founded.

[57] NÖLA Hs. 1013, pt. I, fos. 34ʳ–35ᵛ, summaries of capital valuation of rustical and dominical returns 30 Apr. 1754. These have been divided by 20 years' purchase to obtain the figures in the text. The MS source, a report on taxation in Lower Aus-tria written c.1790, is referred to below as Nachricht I. See also ii, Ch. 8. H. Feigl, *Die niederösterreichische Grundherrschaft vom ausgehenden Mittelalter bis zu den theresianisch-josephinischen Reformen* (Vienna 1964) is unspecific about landowners and their economic activities. The Theresian tax-returns, a valuable potential source, have never been systematically investigated.

derived principally from *robot* and other labour services in cash and kind, valued at 619,520 fl. or 29.5% of the total, and dues and tithes in cash or kind, valued at 604,930 fl. or 28.8% of the total. A series of smaller sources made up the balance, none predominant, for example woods accounted for 143,060 fl. (6.8%), brewing rights for 79,745 fl. (3.8%) and so on.[58] It is clear from the returns that arable, pasture, and vineyard were predominantly in peasant hands. Rustical arable was declared as 904,000 *Joch*, dominical as 103,300 *Joch*, meadows as 203,000 and 46,700 *Tagwerk* respectively, vineyards as 182,000 and 11,400 *Viertel*, and so on.[59] Making all due allowance for the uncertainties of the evidence, this appears to confirm the generalization usually found in the literature that the lords of Lower Austria lived on the rents and other payments of a cultivating peasantry, rather than being themselves demesne farmers on any scale. The size of *robot* in the returns, given this situation, is puzzling, unless it was substantially rendered in money, a distinction unfortunately not made in the source.[60]

Great religious houses formed an important, if not predominant, part of the landlord class in Lower Austria, in a way not observable in the Bohemian lands or Hungary, and they played a significant role in both political and social life. The returns of 1751 for eight of these houses are summarized in Table 5.10 showing dominical revenue (only). There was clearly variation in the pattern of revenue, the abbey of Schotten, for instance, with its large Vienna estates, having a high proportion of *Grundbuch* fees, paid when land changed ownership. *Robot* would account for somewhat more if house and other services, included in the provincial totals given earlier, were added to it. The average declared revenue of nearly 20,000 fl. also conceals the fact that two houses, Klosterneuburg and Melk, accounted for over half the total. It seems probable that religious landownership was concentrated, but the evidence to demonstrate this is at present lacking.[61]

[58] Nachricht I, fo. 35ᵛ. '*Robot* in cash and kind' came to 461,560 fl. and 'Haus, Überland und Vogtdienst' to 157,960 fl. A *Joch* equalled 0.574 ha.
[59] Ibid., fo. 35. *Tagwerk* was conventionally an area workable in one day, defined (Grimm) as 0.34 ha, but there was much local variation.
[60] The MS speaks of services 'in cash or kind'. Feigl, ch. 3 takes the view both that demesne operations were extensive and that *robot* was often commuted for cash, but gives no evidence for either statement.
[61] Cf. the figure of 10,644 fl. average revenue for Lower Austrian religious houses in the 1780s, p. 73.

TABLE 5.10. *Declared dominical revenues of some Lower Austrian religious houses, 1751*

	Gross declared revenue	% from		
		Tithes	*Grundbuch*	*Robot*
Altenburg	6,257	17.7	14.7	32.6
Greillenstein	4,722	14.4	?	23.4
Heiligenkreutz	18,598	20.0	12.1	24.2
Klosterneuburg	39,191	35.4	13.5	15.8
Lilienfeld	15,717	11.3	23.5	36.9
Melk	43,757	67.5	?	10.7
Schotten	12,037	35.4	28.3	17.1
Seittenstätten	16,028	38.1	16.6	7.0
Total/average	156,307	39.0	11.7	17.6

Source: NÖLA 'Maria Theresianische Steuer-Fassionen; Fasz. 516, 455, 922, 1,193, 1,156, 1,053, 936, 1,045, in order as above.

Besides fifteen to seventeen heads of religious houses, meetings of the Lower Austrian Estates in 1762 and 1763 were attended by nineteen or twenty representatives of the aristocracy, among them members of the Auersperg, Breuner, Cavriani, Hardegg, Harrach, Herberstein, Hoyos, Kuefstein, Lamberg, Pergen, Schallenberg, Sinzendorf, Starhemberg, and Traun families, all members of the *Herrenstand*, and all counts; the president of the Estates was the *Landmarschall*, Prince Trautson.[62] These may be accepted as leading secular landowners, even though the list is not complete. Some barons attended, but a more noticeable feature is a numerous *Ritterstand* presence, twenty-eight members in 1763 for example. In contrast to the counts, who were nearly all from families long settled in Lower Austria, the barons and knights appear often to be of fairly recent origin, though more work is needed to pin this down.[63] Nor is attendance at the Estates conclusive for the pattern of landownership in Lower Austria, since 'foreign' families could, and did, have property there. A map of 1748 showing Vienna and the region six

[62] NÖLA Standische Bücher 96, fos. 14ᵛ–15ʳ (11 Aug. 1762), 68ᵛ (12 Sept. 1763), Cf. also the account of the 17th-c. position in Evans, *Making of the Habsburg Monarchy*, 176–7, though the Trautson family is there referred to as extinguished soon after 1700. Tables 13.1*–4* give more names.

[63] The discussion of Lower Austrian nobles in Hassinger, 'Ständische Vertretungen', 258 is not definitive.

Austrian miles round it, with the names of landowners, suggests a cosmopolitan mixture, Prince Lubomirsky having estates west of Vienna and Count Schönborn north of it, together with members of the Dietrichstein and Kinsky families. The Teutonic Knights, other religious orders, the Crown, the Crown's *Vicedom-Amt*, were also prominent, besides counts Hardegg, Kuefstein, and Sinzendorf.[64]

For Styria, too, the facts of landownership in this period are not easy to establish from the literature, though it is known that in 1726 there were 174 matriculated Styrian *Herrenstand* families, and a further 207 from the *Ritterstand*.[65] For an earlier date, the leading assessments under the property tax of 1696 have been published by Mensi in his far-reaching survey of Styrian direct taxation up to 1740.[66] These returns are rather early. Analysis of a tax register compiled by the Styrian Estates in 1759 enables the subject to be taken further.[67] The assessments recorded in this ledger amount to 1,037,043 fl. As the total Styrian Contribution was then 1,103,893 fl., this denotes that the numerous cases where 'stays the same' is entered in the ledger were for small sums only. There are in all 1,450 assessments, which reduce to 1,175 when multiple entries for one taxpayer are grouped. Of these 1,175 assessments, 458 were for priests, chaplains, and brotherhoods, three of the four groups into which Styrian taxpayers were traditionally divided. The remaining group, of 'lords and provincial people' (*Herren und Landleute*) was by far the most important in money terms. It attracted 717 assessments, against 339 of which tax was entered. The distribution of this tax, which amounted to 974,923 fl., is shown in Table 5.11.[68] This distribution is highly skewed. Twenty-four assessments for 10,000 fl. or more form only 7% of numbers but attract 46% of tax. At the other end of the scale, 174 assessments of under 1,000 fl., though forming 51% of numbers, attract only 5%

---

[64] *Chorographia VI milliarium Regionis circa Urbem Viennam Austriacam . . . 1748*, BL Maproom K. Top. 89 map 28.

[65] Hassinger, 261.

[66] Mensi, *Geschichte*, ii (Forschungen 9) 348, table VII.

[67] Steiermärkisches Landesarchiv II. 2. A. VI, Finanzwesen, Grundsteuer, catalogued as 'Berechnung der 1752 Steuer gegen 1759'. The title on the ledger itself is 'Berechnung über das Steier Contributions gülden Aufschlag Buch de Ao. 1759'. The entries were by Circles, and state what each assessed person was to pay in 1759, his or her tax 1752–8, and the difference between the two sums. The names have been extracted, and sorted alphabetically. The ensuing list is the source for the statements in the text. Styrian taxation is discussed in ii, Ch. 8.

[68] 'Berechnung' list.

TABLE 5.11. *Distribution of Styrian Contribution, 1759*

Tax liability	No. of assessments	% of total	Amount assessed	% of total
0–99	61	18.0	2,371	0.2
100–999	113	33.3	51,076	5.2
1,000–1,999	58	17.1	84,870	8.7
2,000–4,999	51	15.0	167,889	17.2
5,000–9,999	32	9.4	218,216	22.4
10,000–24,999	21	6.2	308,700	31.7
25,000–49,999	2	0.6	81,701	8.4
more than 50,000	1	0.3	60,099	6.2
Total	339	100.0	974,922	100.0

of tax. This in fact under-represents the proportion of very small payers, since the analysis excludes the 262 recorded assessments for priests, chaplains, and brotherhoods, whose group mean values were only 330 fl., 168 fl. and 111 fl. respectively. If these are included, 73% of assessments attract 11% of tax, while 27% of assessments attract 89% of tax. It should be noted, however, that there was a sizeable middle bracket of 141 assessments of 1,000–9,999 fl. attracting 48% of tax. The repartition of tax between lord and peasant (dominical and rustical tax) is not available, but it seems fair to assume that the biggest assessments fell on the lords with the largest revenues, hence that the distribution is a fair proxy for that of landlord revenue itself.

The social structure of assessments is shown in Table 5.12.[69] Church assessments accounted for over 40% of the tax payable, one prince and 100 counts and countesses for a further 42.8%. Compared with this, the barons, *edle Herren* and 'von's were unimportant, and had lower mean assessments, save for the *edle Herren*, whose average is pulled up by several members of the Stubenberg family, long resident in Styria.

These data are for those whose tax is recorded; the numbers of taxpayers in each group was larger. One prince, ninety-one counts, and twenty-five countesses came from fifty-six families, a proportion of persons to families of 2.1. Forty barons and twenty-four baronesses came from thirty-eight families, sixteen *edle Herren* from ten families, and seventy-four 'von's from sixty-seven families,

[69] Ibid.

TABLE 5.12. *Social structure of Styrian Contribution, 1759*

(1)	70 assessments for archbishops, bishops, religious orders	350,144
	2 assessments for the Teutonic Knights	8,642
	262 assessments for priests, chaplains, brotherhoods	62,121
	Total church assessments	420,907
	% of recorded tax	40.6
(2)	Assessments for 1 prince, 80 counts, 20 countesses	443,910
	% of recorded tax	42.8
(3)	Assessments for 32 barons (*Freiherren*), 19 baronesses	
	(*Freiinnen*), and 10 *edle Herren*	120,527
	% of recorded tax	11.6
(4)	Assessments for 49 payers with title 'von'	28,069
	% of recorded tax	2.7
(5)	Mean values of recorded assessments	
	church (excl. priests, chaplains, brotherhoods)	5,053
	count	4,404
	countess	2,677
	baron	1,649
	baroness	1,200
	edler Herr	4,494
	'von'	573

giving proportions of 1.7, 1.6, and 1.1 respectively. The total number of taxpayers was 271, of families 171, and the mean proportion 1.6. Family thus counted more as the social scale was ascended, as is to be expected. The title *Ritter* does not occur in the tax register. If the prince, the counts and the countesses, and the barons and baronesses are treated as the *Herrenstand*, the latter had 181 members from 94 families, substantially less than the 174 families matriculated in 1726.[70] This verifies Hassinger's contention that matriculation lists are not an accurate register of the resident nobility.[71] The ninety *edle Herren* and 'von's from seventy-seven families who comprised the Styrian *Ritterstand* were also substantially less numerous than the 207 families matriculated in 1726.

Two further points may be noted. Of the 717 lay assessments, 135 (18.8%) were in female names. The mean value of the sixty of these where tax is shown was 1,668 fl. Second, 251 lordships (*Herrschaften*) and 112 estates (*Güter*) are recorded in the register.

---

[70] See p. 99.
[71] Hassinger, 258.

TABLE 5.13. *Tax asessments of 10,000 fl. or more in Styria, 1759*

(1)	Mathaeus, Abbot of Admond	60,099
(2)	Eugenius, Abbot of St Lambrecht	43,687
(3)	Prince Joseph zu Schwarzenberg	38,014
(4)	Maria Henrica, Abbess of Göss	23,462
(5)	Joseph, Cathedral Provost at Seggau	21,926
(6)	Marianus, Abbot of Rhein	20,248
(7)	Georg, Herr von Stubenberg	17,003
(8)	Count Carl Cajetan von Leslie	16,135
(9)	Count Leopold von Dietrichstein	15,310
(10)	Johann Anton, Cathedral Provost at Staniz	15,248
(11)	Ernst Gottlieb, Bishop of Laybach	14,642
(12)	Rector of Jesuit College at Graz	14,443
(13)	Count Carl Adam von Breiner (*sic* for Breuner)	14,369
(14)	Count Ignaz von Attems	13,888
(15)	Count Joseph Bernhard Maria von Attems	13,863
(16)	Leopold Ernest, Bishop of Seggau	13,111
(17)	Count Franz Erwin von Schönborn	12,925
(18)	Count Franz Ludwig von Kienburg, *Landeshauptmann*	12,742
(19)	Sigismundus, Archbishop of Salzburg	12,151
(20)	Countess Maria Eleonora von Herberstein	11,921
(21)	Caspar, Prior of Stift Seitz	11,909
(22)	Laurentius Josephus, Cathedral Provost at Vorau	11,649
(23)	Countess Maria Theresia von Leslie	11,342
(24)	Count Anton von Gaissruck	10,413

The 251 lordships were controlled by 149 owners, of whom ninety-three had one, twenty-seven had two, twenty had three, two had four, six had five and one had six. The mean assessments were (fl.), 2,437, 2,473, 3,711, 3,854, 3,079, 5,747, indicating that the larger the number of lordships held in one hand, the higher its average income, hence tax, was likely to be. Estates (*Güter*), the typical landholding of those with titles of baron downwards, were much more dispersed, and poorer. Of the 112, ninety-two were in single ownership, fourteen were held in twos, six in threes, with mean assessments of only 521, 511, and 665 fl.

The predominance in Styria of great ecclesiastical and secular landowners is indicated in detail by the names of the twenty-four taxpayers assessed at 10,000 fl. or more, who divide neatly into twelve clerical and twelve lay. They are ranged in Table 5.13 in descending order of liability.[72] The abbey of Admond, which heads the list, had been the leading landowner in Styria since the Middle Ages,

---

[72] 'Berechnung' list.

even if it had by now declined from its former position. Göss, Rhein, and St Lambrecht were other important religious houses. Episcopal and cathedral estates (Seggau, Staniz, Vorau) were also prominent, as was the Archbishop of Salzburg, formally a foreign subject. The great secular taxpayers formed part of a nexus of families linked by kinship and marriage which must have effectively dominated Styrian social and political life.[73] Besides those named, there were the Inzaghi, Kazianer, Sauer, Saurau, Schrattenbach, Thürn, Trauttmansdorff, Webersperg, Wildenstein, Würmbrand, and other families, nearly all of ancient Styrian descent. Conversely, however, more than half the families of counts had small or negligible property, judging by their tax assessments. Some of these were great men with small Styrian holdings, for example Count Nádasdy, described simply as 'Hungarian Chancellor', was included only because he had a house in Radkerspurg. Others must simply have been poor, or unimportant, or both.

The areas discussed so far had a relatively restricted number of landowners, some lay, some ecclesiastical. The church had 26.6% of taxable revenue in Moravia in 1790, 17.2% of taxable revenue in Bohemia in 1770, 39.3% of taxable revenue in Upper Austria in 1750, 40.6% of taxable revenue in Styria in 1759. In Lower Austria, it seems plausible that the proportion was also about 40%, but at present this cannot be verified. Within the lordly population as a whole, the distribution of income was skewed towards large units of ownership. The only area where this applies less is Austrian Silesia. In general, the nobility examined can be defined as a concentrated or intensive one, and its members characteristically had titles, down to the knights and *edle Herren* at the base of the noble pyramid. At all levels, but typically at the lowest, there were holders of recently conferred titles. Many of these holders can have had little landed property.

In Galicia and Hungary there was, in contrast to this pattern, a diffused or extended nobility, the majority of whose members had no titles. It would be of great interest to have more precise information about the structure of the Galician nobility, a class which attracted close Austrian attention from 1772. The general characteristics of the Polish nobility of which they formed part are known in

[73] Cf. too the lists of local councillors in Ch. 13.

some detail from Roos's studies.[74] Though all nobles were in theory equal, a few magnate families were majority landowners, and controlled a very numerous gentry class through patronage and violence. Many of these dependants had little or no land. The Galician gentry, according to the first Austrian governor, Count Pergen, were uneducated, drunken, and frivolous, dominating the local diets by corruption and force. They were ostentatiously Catholic, and despised and hated other religions. Austria attempted to smarten this class up by introducing direct taxation, titles, and a national Diet.[75] This policy had only limited success. According to Pergen's statistical tables drawn up at the end of 1772, crown landed revenue in Galicia was 1,083,326 fl. and that of lords 4,910,532 fl. Royal revenue included 165,136 fl. from *robot* services, and 296,035 fl. from taverns. Lords had 1,003,037 fl. and 1,110,243 fl. respectively from these sources.[76] While these figures should probably be regarded sceptically as totals, the structure of revenue revealed by them confirms the central role of alcohol in the lordly economy noted by all observers. Brawer shows that lords here controlled on average 31% of the grain harvest in 1774, and peasants 67%. Parish lands had the balance.[77] At present the names and numbers which would add detail to this outline of Galician landownership are lacking.[78]

The Hungarian aristocracy and gentry, about which more information is available, are known from the literature to have had some of the characteristics of those of Poland. The magnates, or Second Estate, had titles, and a minority crown offices, whose holders were

[74] H. Roos, 'Polen von 1668 bis 1795' in T. Schieder (ed.), *Handbuch der europäischen Geschichte*, iv (Stuttgart 1968) 690–752; id., 'Ständewesen', in Gerhard, *Ständische Vertretungen*, 310–67. Ch. 7. 'Szlachta: The Nobleman's Paradise', of N. Davies's effervescent *God's Playground. A History of Poland* (Oxford 1981) elicits similar characteristics for the 16th c.

[75] Glassl, *Einrichtungswerk*, ch. 2, 'Der Adel'.

[76] HHSA Nachl. Zinz., Hs. 30 B, 'Finances de la Monarchie Autrichienne et de ses provinces 1758–1800', fo. 877, 'Ausschlag aus denen Tabellen, welche über die von dem Gallizischen Herren . . . Grafen von Pergen untern 22 Dec. 1772 abgefordete Fassiones verfasset wurden'. This summarizes and turns into Austrian currency (1 fl. equals 4 zł.) Pergen's table in Latin at the previous folio. A slightly different version is printed in Brawer, *Galizien*, 54–5, without totals or conversion from Polish currency, and without assigning a value to *robot* services.

[77] Brawer, 53, a detailed military return of 1774.

[78] Davies, ii. 143 says that members of the Goluchowski, Lubomirski, Potocki, Tarnowski, and Zamoyski families were leading landowners in Galicia.

designated *Barones Regni*. The nobility, or Third Estate, was un-titled, was even more numerous than its Galician counterpart, and, in contrast to the latter, and to the Catholic magnates, had a strong Protestant, mainly Calvinist, core. Noble property varied greatly in size, many nobles having little, and others none. Common owner-ship of land by groups of nobles appears to have been a marked feature of Hungarian society, as it was not in Poland. The theory that the church, magnates, and nobles owned the land, and only conceded the use of it to their peasants, was common to both areas as also in Bohemia. In Hungary, lord and peasant land was desig-nated allodial and urbarial, rather than dominical and rustical.[79]

There was a steady turnover of dominant magnate families, those of medieval origin (Báthory, Losonczi, Perényi) yielding place in the sixteenth century to those of Batthyány, Forgách, Nádasdy, Pálffy, Rákóczi, Zrínyi. Politics eliminated the last two, and ele-vated others, the eighteenth-century leaders comprising the families of Batthyány, Csáky, Erdődy, Eszterházy, Festetics, Forgách, Grassalkovich, Károly, Koháry, Szechényi, Zichy.[80] Marczali asserts from literary evidence that in the 1760s Prince Eszterházy had an income of 700,000 fl., Count Lajos Batthyány 450,000 fl., two others, unnamed, 300,000 fl., four 200,000 fl., four 150,000 fl. He adds, without giving a source, that the wealthiest families apart from the Eszterházy and Batthyány were those of Erdődy, Festetics, Grassalkovich, Koháry, Károly, Pálffy.[81] These data are repeated by Király and Macartney.[82] Marczali also gives

---

[79] This section relies chiefly on HHSA Nachl. Zinz., Hs. 156, probably by Baron (later Count) Franz Xaver Koller von Nagy-Manya, 'Gesetzmässige Verfassung des Königreichs Hungarn', written for Archduke Joseph in 1760, sections 9 and 10, 'Von denen Baronibus und Magnatibus Regni' and 'Von dem Hungarischen Adel-Stand' respectively. (Cf. Anna H. Benna, 'Der Kronprinzen-Unterricht Josefs II.', *MÖSA* 20 (1967) 115–79.) Marczali, *Hungary in the Eighteenth Century*, 103–29 and Király, *Hungary*, ch. iii also deal with the subject. Koller's insistence that the nobility formed a third estate distinct from the magnates was contrary to the prin-ciple of 'una eademque nobilitas' in István Werbőczi's *Tripartitum* of 1514, the con-stitutional bible of Hungary. The legal unity of the nobility as an estate was reaffirmed in Siebenbürgen as late as the Diet of 1791; however, small nobles were excluded from the highest offices, Kutschera, 22–3.

[80] E. Pamlényi (ed.), *A History of Hungary* (1978) 133, 187.

[81] Marczali, 112. His reference to 'Bernoulli's collection of travels', ix. 237, is wrong. The correct reference to *Johann Bernoulli's Sammlung kurzer Reisebeschrei-bungen* . . . (Berlin and Leipzig 1781–7) is ix. 286–7, x. 226. The first refers to Esterhasi (*sic*), but not to Batthyány, the second has the anonymous incomes.

[82] Király, 30 n.; Macartney, 53.

some useful, but general, information about the distribution of Hungarian landownership in 1787.[83] Lehotzky shows that 253 titles of baron and count were conferred on Hungarian families to 1780, of which 21 were assigned in the sixteenth century, 137 in the seventeenth, 95 in the eighteenth. Among the sixteenth-century recipients were members of the families of Althann, Balassa, Csáky, Csobor, Dobo, Draskovics, Erdődy, Eszterházy, Gyulay, Illésházy, István, Majláth, Nádasdy, Pálffy, Revay, all later prominent under Maria Theresia.[84]

The attempts of the government from 1715 to count and define the Hungarian nobles have been described by Illéssy.[85] The motive for this was to find out how many were very small nobles, *Armalisten*, who were not tax-exempt. After the failure of earlier attempts in 1723 and 1732, a fuller count was executed in 1754–5, though even this was palpably defective. Many nobles known as such by common fame were excluded, magnates, not called for, were included, and so on.[86] The census probably, but not certainly, included only adult males.[87] The number recorded was 32,554, of whom no less than 13,766 (42%) were *Armalisten*. Huge concentrations of the latter were shown in the counties of Borsod, Máramaros, Vas, and Zala. However deficient the data, the large proportion of *Armalisten* nobles is impressive. The continuing efforts of the Council of Lieutenancy to monitor this situation must have made all nobles nervous.[88]

Further light is thrown on the structure of Hungarian landlordship by Dr Felhő's edition of the returns in Transdanubia to the urbarial inquiry instituted in 1767.[89] In this large, and relatively

---

[83] Marczali, 35–6, from a Latin MS of 1787 giving the names of lords in 11,298 places. His summary is by class proportions (only) for areas, and does not distinguish between magnates and the church.

[84] Lehotzky, *Stemmatographia*, i. 167–70. The Draskovics family was Croatian.

[85] J. Illéssy, *Az 1754–55 évi országos nemesi összeírás* (Budapest 1902). This consists of a short introduction, followed by lists of names by counties, and an official summary at the end.

[86] Illéssy, 2–3.

[87] However, the notes to the official summary of numbers show that in some areas only heads of households were included. Cf. Table 3.5: 155,519 male nobles, 1787.

[88] Felhő-Vörös 94–5. *Armales* were properly letters conferring nobility and *Armalistae* those holding them, the *Briefadel*. In practice, the term seems to have applied to very small nobles new and old. For the etymology, see Antonius Bartal, *Glossarium mediae et infimae Latinitatis regni Hungariae* (Budapest 1901) 48.

[89] Ibolya Felhő, *Az úrbéres birtokviszonyok Magyarországon Mária Terézia korában*, i. *Dunántúl* (Budapest 1970).

TABLE 5.14. *The ten largest landowners in*
Transdanubia, 1767

	hold
Prince Miklós Eszterházy	206,821
Archduchess Christina	72,281
Prince Károly Batthyány	54,799
Heirs of Count Miklos Eszterházy	47,576
The Hungarian *Hofkammer*	38,640
Pécsvarad abbey	38,595
Archbishopric of Esztergom	37,847
Count Zsigmond Szechényi	33,674
Bishopric of Veszprém	32,385
Count Mihály Althann	27,849

well-populated, area of western Hungary, 1,150 lay lords, 88% of a total of 1,307 lords, controlled 71.5% of the land registered, and 137 ecclesiastical lords (10.5% of numbers) controlled 20.2%.[90] As this implies, very small lords were typically lay rather than ecclesiastical. Of the lay lords, 943 (82%) controlled 500 *hold* (= *Joch*) of land or less, amounting in all to 6.1% of the area. The corresponding ecclesiastical class comprised 65 lords (47.4%), controlling a mere 2% of the area. Taking lay and ecclesiastical lords together, 59.8% of numbers controlled only 1.2% of the area, and 77.2% controlled only 4.7%. At the top of the scale, 28 lords, 5 of them ecclesiastical, had 10,000 *hold* and over, and controlled 47.6% of the area.[91] Whatever reservations are expressed about the certainty of the data, this denotes a very high degree of concentration of landlordship.[92] The fact that it relates only to land occupied by a tilling peasantry suggests that if the lords' allodial (demesne) estates were included, the curve would be even more inflected. The ten leading landowners are shown in Table 5.14.[93]

In an attempt to carry the subject further, for a somewhat later period, the names of landowners given in Danyi and Dávid's edition of the Hungarian census of 1784–7 were transcribed and sorted

[90] Ibid., tables 14–19 at pp. 54–65.
[91] Ibid.
[92] J. Varga, *Typen und Probleme des bäuerlichen Grundbesitzes in Ungarn 1767–1849* (Budapest 1965), ch. 1 explains how the unit of one *hold* used for the inquiry was supposed to equal one *Joch* of 1,200 *Klafter*, but was often defined as containing 1,800 or 2,400 *Klafter*. He also points out that much land was concealed.
[93] Felhő, 32.

alphabetically, together with the number of houses against each name.[94] These data are, of course, only a proxy for the distribution of property. They relate also to lordship rather than ownership since they must cover both allodial (or lords') land and urbarial land (or peasants'). Further, the printed returns are defective, names being fully available for only 32 of the 47 Hungarian, three Slavonian and three Croatian countries and four privileged districts, at that date.[95] The total number of houses returned under the census was 1,015,394, of which the analysis below covers 616,348, or 61%. Of these, no fewer than 93,203 (15%) are listed as 'in common ownership', an expression used in the census to denote cases where 'many lords', 'several', and so on were entered in the returns. This phenomenon is particularly observable in Máramaros county in the north-east, a centre of noble landownership, as the inquiry of 1754–5 showed.[96] It is also observable in Bihar, Gömör, Nyitra, Trencsén, Zala. These were clearly centres of squireen society. As an anonymous memorialist of the 1770s observed, the wealth of Hungary tended to be judged by that of its magnates and prelates. But this was an error. Fifty landowners, themselves not rich if the extent of their possessions were considered, had the greater part of the wealth of the country. The real mass of nobles comprised about 40,000 persons, often working small estates with their own hands, or serving their equals.[97]

In the analysis which follows, the 'community' holdings are omitted. The distribution of the remaining 523,145 houses is

[94] [Danyi–Dávid (eds.)], *Az első magyarországi népszámlálás*. I am indebted to Mrs Rosemary Dawe for arranging the names alphabetically when I had transcribed them, and to Mrs Catherine Fitzharris of the Institute of Economics and Statistics for making the numerical analysis. The difficulties involved with names of lords, which were often abbreviated or ambiguously entered in the returns, are explained by the editors at pp. 22–3. They verified them as far as possible from works of reference.

[95] The 47 Hungarian counties were reduced for administrative purposes to 40 by five pairings and one threesome, but the results for each are given separately in the census. The privileged districts comprised the three Jasz-Kun enclaves, treated as one in the census, the Hajdu towns, the Szepes or Zips towns, and Fiume-Buccari. The names of landlords are available for Körös and Varasd counties in Croatia, for the Jasz-Kun districts, and for the following Hungarian counties: Árva, Baranya, Békés, Bereg, Bihar, Borsod, Csongrád, Esztergom, Gömör, Győr, Heves, Komárom, Liptó, Máramaros, Moson, Nyitra, Pest, Somogy, Sopron, Szabolcs, Szatmár, Szeverin, Torontál, Trencsén, Turóc, Vas, Veszprém, Zala, Zemplén. The census returns largely omitted the names of landlords in Siebenbürgen. For a list of noble families there see Kutschera, 26.

[96] Illéssy, op. cit.

[97] Eckhart, *A bécsi udvar Már Ter. korában*, 262–3.

TABLE 5.15. *Distribution of lordship over Hungarian houses, 1787*

Houses	No. of lords	%	No. of houses	%
1–99	927	57.7	42,542	8.1
100–999	591	36.8	159,327	30.5
1,000–1,999	49	3.0	67,553	12.9
2,000–4,999	28		85,546	16.4
5,000–9,999	9		64,176	12.3
10,000–24,999	1	2.5	10,411	2.0
25,000–49,999	1		35,433	6.7
50,000 and over	1		58,157	11.1
Total	1,607	100.0	523,145	100.0

shown in Table 5.15. Of 1,607 lords, 927 or nearly 60% controlled under 100 houses each, and 1,567 (97.5%) under 2,000. In all, these lords controlled just over half (51.5%) of the total number of houses. The forty lords with 2,000 houses or more controlled the rest. This distribution indicates a very long tail of small lords, which would become longer still if 'common ownership' numbers were included within it. The division in Hungary between allodial and urbarial land at this date is not certain, but it seems from evidence discussed later that peasant land comprised about 6.5m. *Joch* of a total cultivable area of nearly 32m. *Joch*, implying that the proportion between lords' allodial land, much of it probably uncultivated, and peasant land was much less favourable to the latter than in the areas examined so far.[98]

The names of the forty lords of 2,000 houses and over are given in Table 5.16, in descending order. This list confirms the conclusions outlined earlier, in the sense that the families named there are all in it, with those of Eszterházy (45,267 houses) and Batthyány (19,898 houses) firmly on top. It is striking, however, that apart from the Károlyis (15,532 houses), no other landowning family was in the same league, the next, those of Grassalkovich and Erdődy, controlling only 6,363 and 5,496 houses respectively. None the less, the Crown, not the Eszterházy family, was by far the largest

[98] See p. 124.

landlord in Hungary, and in the most counties.[99] The cameral estates were reinforced by those of Maria Theresia's daughter, the Archduchess Christina, wife of the *Locumtenens* till 1781, Prince Albert of Saxony. It is observable that ten ecclesiastical lords controlled nearly 19% of the houses. If the census had been taken before the monastic dissolutions, this figure would perhaps have been higher.

The large estates of the Károlyi, Harruckern, and Grassalkovich families confirm the statements in the literature that the Károlyis did well out of arranging the Peace of Szatmár (1711) ending Prince Ferenc Rákóczi's rebellion, Johann Harrucker (d. 1742), created Baron von Harruckern, did well out of Hungarian war contracts, and that the Grassalkovich, a minor noble family, established their fortunes with the long presidency of the Hungarian *Hofkammer* (1748–71) by the remarkable Count Antal Grassalkovich.[100] Apart from the Free Villages of the Jasz-Kun district, which had no lord save the king, all the secular owners in the list had titles, with one exception, Kristóf Nákó of Torontal county. The Aspremonts, the Harruckerns, and the ubiquitous Schönborns are the only names not of Hungarian or Croatian origin. The top landowners were thus mainly indigenous. This point is perhaps worth extending, since Marczali, and more recently Király, give the impression that large numbers of 'foreigners' held Hungarian land, and it is certainly the case that many German magnates possessing the right as *indigenae* to attend the Hungarian Diet were summoned to it in Maria Theresia's reign, seventy-six, for instance, in 1741.[101] Persual of the partial list of lords of houses in 1787 suggests, on the contrary, that the great majority of lords were native, not foreign. The only substantial foreign families in it other than the three mentioned above, were those of Althann, which in various lines controlled 5,365 houses,

---

[99] Baranya, Bihar, Borsod, Esztergom, Győr, Heves, Komárom (few houses in these three), Máramaros, Nyitra, Pest, Szatmár, Szeverin, Torontál, Trencén, Turóc, Varasd, Vas (few in these last four). Torontal in the Banat of Temesvár, with 12,682 houses (21.8% of the total) had, predictably, the largest numbers.

[100] For Grassalkovich and Franz Harrucker see Ch. 13.

[101] Gy. Bónis, 'Die ungarischen Stände in der ersten Hälfte des 18. Jahrhunderts', in Gerhard, *Ständische Vertretungen*, 297. *Indigena* effectively meant (Hungarian) national, and was a prior condition to ownership of land in Hungary under art. 23 of the Diet of 1715, ibid. Marczali's citation of the *Almanach von Urgarn* for 1778, which showed 247 *indigenae* among the magnates, is reproduced by Király, p. 29 n. The point is expanded in his text, pp. 28–9.

TABLE 5.16. *Lords of 2,000 or more Hungarian houses, 1787*

	No of counties	No. of houses
The Hungarian Hofkammer	21	58,157
Prince Miklos Eszterházy	13	35,433
Count Antal Károlyi	3	10,411
Bishop of Nagyvarad	1	9,613
Harruckern family and heirs	1	9,304
Free Villages (19) of Jasz-Kun District	1	7,735
Archduchess Christina	3	7,157
Archbishop of Esztergom	3	6,658
Greek cathedral chapter of Nagyvarad	1	6,464
Grassalkovich princely family	3	6,363
Count Lajos Batthyány	5	5,761
Károlyi family	4	5,121
Count József Batthyány	7	4,794
Count Fülöp Batthyany	4	4,705
Count Tivadar Batthyány	4	4,638
Count Ferenc Eszterházy	3	4,439
Nagyvarad (R.C.) cathedral chapter	2	4,330
Bishop of Veszprém	2	3,650
Koháry family	2	3,621
Archbishop of Kalocsa	1	3,540
Count János Erdődy	3	3,495
Eger cathedral chapter	4	3,343
Count Károly Eszterházy	2	3,101
Count Ferenc Balassa and Count Pál Szapáry	1	2,803
Bishop of Pécs	1	2,768
Aspremont family	4	2,749
Count György Festetics	4	2,633
Count Ferenc Koháry	1	2,629
Count Janos Pálffy	2	2,569
Count Ferenc Szechényi	5	2,537
Bishop of Eger	3	2,536
Count János Illesházy	2	2,493
Count György Keglevich	1	2,493
Schönborn family	1	2,414
Bishop of Vácz	1	2,385
Csáky family	3	2,298
Count Janos Eszterházy	3	2,294
Kristóf Nákó	1	2,186
Pécs Cathedral chapter	2	2,102
Erdődy family	4	2,001
Total		253,723

Though several of the above had houses in the Croatian counties of Körös and Varasd, none had property only there.

Brudern (1,140), Dietrichstein (1,168), Haller (584), La Motte (589), and Traun (945), though there are a number of smaller names.[102] On this evidence, admittedly not conclusive, Hungarian landownership did not resemble that of Bohemia (or Ireland) with numerous and influential settlers. The summons of foreign *indigenae* to the Diet must then be interpreted as a device for controlling it, not as an indication of the pattern of landownership.[103]

Below the top magnate families referred to earlier, leading families included those of Almásy, Balogh, Draskovich (Croatian), Hunyádi, Kiss, Nádasdy, Niczky, Orczy, Révay, Serényi, Szunyogh, Teleki, Vay, Zichy, the Vays, at least, being Protestants.[104] There were also in this subordinate group (1,000–1,999 houses) more members of the Eszterházy, Erdődy, Batthyány, and other top families, no doubt confirming their predominance. Perusal of the genealogical tables in Wurzbach also casts doubt on Marczali's contention, accepted and amplified by Király, that Hungarian magnate families intermarried extensively with Austrian and Bohemian ones under Maria Theresia.[105] This appears to be true only in a limited number of cases, of which the Batthyány, Eszterházy, and Pálffy families were the most prominent. The growing residence of Hungarian aristocrats in Vienna, exposed to the blandishments of the court, also appears to be a myth.[106] A list of nobles living there in February 1789 contains no more than eight or nine Hungarian names, mostly from the Batthyány, Eszterházy, Keglevitch, and Pálffy families. It is possible, but implausible, that numerous others

---

[102] Arneth, *Gesch. Mar. Ther.* i. 272 cites as examples of German families in Hungary those of Attems, Lobkowitz, Liechtenstein, Rottal, Schwarzenberg, Seilern, Starhemberg, Traun. None of these except Traun is in the incomplete list used for Tables 5.15 and 5.16.

[103] Cf. Arneth, 285 for the Diet's demand in 1741 that *indigenae* without Hungarian property should not be summoned to it.

[104] Ibid. iv. 52, delegation of Hungarian Protestant nobles, July, 1749. The Vays were Calvinists. The other families in this delegation were Raday (also Calvinist) and Podmaniczky, Pronay, Szirmay, all Lutheran. These are all in the list of 1787, the last most prominently.

[105] Marczali, 115 n.; Király, 29, 'the marriage of the Hungarian magnates with ambitious and luxury-loving Austrian and Bohemian aristocratic ladies'.

[106] Marczali, 119 lays emphasis on the economic ruin of Hungarian families by residence in Vienna. Király, loc. cit. says 'The Queen . . . went out of her way to lure Hungarian aristocrats to Vienna in order to bind them to her throne and court'. Macartney, *Habsburg Empire*, 55 states that 'a substantial proportion of the Hungarian magnates . . . had . . . taken to regarding Vienna as their spiritual home'.

had returned home to defend the constitution.[107] If the conclusions suggested here are correct, the integration of Hungary with the German lands was less advanced at the top of society by 1780 than is commonly asserted, and Joseph II's assault on Hungary likely to arouse a correspondingly greater resentment.

The subject of noble landownership is opened up, but far from exhausted, by the preceding discussion. The state of the evidence is clearly defective. The extent of holdings of land in several provinces by great families like those of Dietrichstein, Schönborn, or Schwarzenberg cannot at present be uncovered. The probable wealth of individual families has only been touched on.[108] Noble revenue from mines and factories has not been discussed.[109] However, certain general conclusions emerge. Landlordship differed in structure between the Bohemian and Austrian lands on the one hand, and Galicia and the Hungarian lands on the other. It was concentrated (relatively small numbers of nobles) in the first area, extended (large numbers of nobles) in the second. Ownership in all areas however, was skewed, a restricted number of large owners, including the Crown and the church, ruling the economic roost. The social and political implications of this structure are complex. In the Bohemian and Austrian lands, the assent of a relatively small number of

---

[107] Geisler, Skizze, xiv. 235.

[108] Snippets of information on this subject appear in Khev.-Metsch. Count Ferdinand Harrach, Bohemian Chancellor, acquired 800,000 fl. with his second wife, Princess Dietrichstein. Prince Hanns Auersperg married Countess Maria Schönfeld in Nov. 1746; her dowry was 2m. fl. Princess Löwenstein died on her Bohemian estates in June 1765 worth 1.25m. fl. Count Karl Joseph Palm, scion of a financial family, was reputed to be worth 4m. fl. at his death in 1769. (Khev.-Metsch, 1 Feb. 1745, 13 Nov. 1746, 4 Jun. 1765, 5 Feb. 1771.) This is, however, little more than gossip. The house of Schönborn had an estimated income of 110,000–120,000 fl. in the early 18th c., two-thirds from Hungarian and Austrian possessions, A. Schröcker, 'Besitz und Politik des Hauses Schönborn von 14. bis zum 18. Jahrhundert', MÖSA 26 (1973) 228. For the Palm family see Ch. 7. According to Count Philipp Cobenzl, Count Palm's son, also Karl Joseph, cr. a prince in 1783, dissipated his inheritance, see Cobenzl's memoirs, ed. Arneth, AÖG 67 (1886) 111–12.

[109] For some rather general facts about ownership of mines, see ii. 100. There is a summary of noble factory enterprises, which were mostly in the Bohemian lands, in Adolf Beer, 'Studien zur Gesch. der österr. Volkswirtschaft unter Maria Theresia, I. Die österreichische Industriepolitik', AÖG 81 (1894) 101–7. About a dozen noble families were involved in Bohemia in the 1760s, half this number in Moravia, much fewer elsewhere. The greatest Bohemian noble capitalist was Count Joseph Kinsky, whose Bürgstein linen-factory was a showpiece; however after 1771 government opinion increasingly moved against noble participation in industry. Cf. also H. Freudenberger, The Waldstein Woolen Mill (Boston, Mass., 1963), and Otruba, Bohemia, 6 (1965) 230–331.

leading men to fiscal changes might be expected to carry the assent
of the remainder, as could be argued to have happened with Haugwitz's reforms of 1749–56. The resistance of the same men to the
abolition of serfdom might make it politically unfeasible, as Maria
Theresia complained of the Bohemian magnates in 1777.[110] A
numerous untutored nobility not accustomed to political responsibility might prove useless for staffing local government, as in Galicia. Such a class accustomed to run its own affairs, as in Hungary,
could form a powerful obstacle to schemes of political and fiscal
change. In economic terms, oligopolistic ownership might be
expected to yield more reliable revenues from direct taxation, partly
by coercion of tenants. A skewed distribution of savings might be
expected to provide state loans more easily than one more equal,
and larger investible funds for industry, agriculture and building.
Some of these aspects will be returned to in later chapters.

[110] See p. 370.

6

Peasants and others

THE discussion now turns from the nobility to the peasantry. Some analogy between the two is apparent, for here too the evidence, while far from sufficient, points to heterogeneity between areas and within groups, to a skewed structure of incomes, and to variety of status, so that to speak of a single class, in this case a peasant class, is convenient rather than accurate. The subject must first be briefly placed in a general German setting. The older view of the peasantry of the *Reich*, including those parts of it within the Austrian Monarchy, was of a broad division along the Elbe, east of which large-scale landlord agriculture prevailed, depending on a servile peasantry rendering labour dues, and west of which peasants cultivated their land, but paid rents in cash and kind to feudal lords not themselves engaged in extensive agriculture. The distinction between the two economies was seen as one between a *Gutswirtschaft*, associated with peasant unfreedom, often called *Leibeigenschaft*; and a *Grundherrschaft* associated with peasant juridical and fiscal dependence, but relative freedom to cultivate.[1] This second type of peasant society, familiar in a French context to readers of Tocqueville's *L'Ancien Régime*, was typified in a German one by the Rhineland or Bavaria, while Mecklenburg or Pomerania represented its antithesis. The revived exploitation of labour services in the east was defined by Engels in 1882 as a 'second serfdom', a concept which has developed longevity for reasons not altogether academic.[2] Given this background, the emphasis of the historiography was on attempts by rulers to modify, or transform, peasant legal status, associated in Prussia with Stein and Hardenberg's reforms of 1807–11 and in Austria with the *robot* regulations of 1767–80 and

---

[1] There is a good exposition of this basic pattern, with modern additions to it, by G. Oestreich in Schieder (ed.), *Handbuch*, iv. 407–10.
[2] See the literature referred to ibid. 418 n. 24. The concept is not discussed in J. Blum's ambitious study, *The End of the Old Order in Rural Europe* (Princeton UP 1978), nor would it be possible to get from it a summary of the German position along the lines attempted here.

Joseph II's abolition of *Leibeigenschaft* in the Bohemian lands (1781), in Galicia (1782), and in Hungary (1785).

It was already apparent in the older literature that this picture, though by no means false, might require modification in detail. The characteristic status of the Prussian peasant was shown by Knapp in 1887 to be one of hereditary subjugation (*Erbuntertänigkeit*) rather than *Leibeigenschaft*, the status of *adscriptus glebae* in Roman law.[3] He also demonstrated the variations in serf-tenure, and the increasingly favoured position of peasants on the huge crown estates in East Prussia. Modern research shows that in Poland, as in Pomerania, the landlords denied that *Leibeigenschaft* existed, though in Poland the partitioning powers in 1772 thought fit to abolish it.[4] The emphasis of more recent studies is on the economic realities of peasant life. Juridical status affected this less than had been thought. It has been shown that *Leibeigenschaft* was not only found east of the Elbe. It flourished west of it too. The officials of the Margrave of Baden were *leibeigen* until 1764, for example.[5] And western peasants were typically *leibeigen*. In practice, however, this meant that they paid dues to a lord for exercising normal social and economic choice: sale, emigration, marriage, mortgage, inheritance, and so on. It did not mean that they were tied to the soil.[6] Peasant society in general is increasingly recognized as complex and heterogeneous.[7] There was considerable variety of peasant wealth. In the Black Forest and Württemberg, there was a substantial class of peasants which took a high line against lords' encroachments, had ample means, and effectively ran its own affairs. Marriage with 'lesser' peasants was frowned on. Similiar peasants are found in Eastern Switzerland and Tyrol. All across Germany, it has been argued, there was a minority of peasants whose holdings were worth 10,000 fl. or more, who were literate, and accustomed to sending their sons to university, and then into the church, state ser-

---

[3] G. F. Knapp, *Die Bauern-Befreiung und der Ursprung der Landarbeiter in den älteren Theilen Preussens* (Leipzig 1887).

[4] See the account of Frederick II's attempt in 1763 to abolish *Leibeigenschaft* in Pomerania, in Epstein, *The Genesis of German Conservatism*, 211–12. For Poland see Roos in Schieder (ed.), *Handbuch*, iv. 349–50 and nn.

[5] G. Franz, *Geschichte des deutschen Bauernstandes vom frühen Mittelalter bis zum 19. Jahrhundert* (2nd rev. edn., Stuttgart 1976) 232.

[6] See the excellent exposition in T. C. W. Blanning, *Reform and Revolution in Mainz 1743–1803* (CUP 1974) 87 ff.

[7] This section relies on the interesting résumé in Franz, chs. 15–16.

vice, or the learned professions. The proportion of such peasants varied from one-fifth in East Prussia or parts of north-west Germany to a tenth in Bavaria, Bohemia, or Württemberg.

However, the same researches show that 60–70% of peasants in most areas had little property, and were close to subsistence level, though literacy may have been more widespread than wealth, especially in Protestant states. More significant still, there was a growing class of cottars, garden-keepers, labourers, and other subsidiary agrarian workers, who had only a little land, and relied instead on a demand for wage labour. In Saxony, this class comprised 5% of the working population in 1550, 30% in 1750, 47% in 1843. Similar developments have been traced in Westphalia and Thuringia. Connected with this development of what may be called a rural proletariat was the increasing gap between incomes and prices from about 1760 to which Wilhelm Abel has drawn attention, which by the 1790s had created a massive general poverty of which the great subsistence crisis of 1771–2, at its worst in Central Europe, was an early manifestation.[8]

The census data examined in Ch. 3 contain a number of indications of the relevance in an Austrian context of the pattern just described. This is true of the growth of cottars and labourers in the 1780s, and also of the variation in peasant society, for example the contrast between Krain and Styria. Ancillary industrial income, especially spinning, was readily available in northern Bohemia and Moravia, little if at all in Carinthia, and so on. Before considering further evidence of such economic differences, the important question of the legal status of the peasantry must be briefly discussed. This status was concisely summed up by Lord Stormont in his despatch to the Duke of Grafton of 10 September 1765.[9] Of

---

[8] W. Abel, *Agrarkrisen und Agrarkonjunktur* (Hamburg and Berlin 1966, 3rd edn. 1978), now tr. O. Ordish, *Agricultural Fluctuations in Europe. From the Thirteenth to the Twentieth Century* (1980).

[9] See App. A. The quotation is at p. 390. The description of peasant status in the Bohemian lands in Grünberg's classic *Bauernbefreiung*, i, Introduction, has not yet been superseded. Grünberg argued, as Knapp had done for Prussia, that *Leibeigenschaft* did not exist in the Bohemian lands. However, his statement (i. 94) that the word itself only appears in the Austrian records from 1769 is dubiously correct. See the references to *Leibeigenschaft* in the documents about Bohemian peasant conditions 1698–1780 in J. Kalousek (ed.), *Řády selské* (*Archív český*, 24 (1908) 53, 156, 205, 271). It was used as an equivalent to 'Unterthänigkeit'. For a convenient account in English of peasant reforms see W. E. Wright, *Serf, Seigneur and Sovereign. Agrarian Reform in Eighteenth Century Bohemia* (Minnesota UP 1966).

Bohemia, he observed that

Another Circumstance that naturally tends to check the Growth of Affluence and Industry, is the Vassalage of the peasants. They are all according to the general Slavonick System *adscripti Glebae*. Their Servitude however is not so absolute as that of the peasants in Poland, for they are allowed to have property of their own . . .

This state of affairs prevailed also in Moravia. Stormont pointed out, however, that 'The peasants in Austria are not *Serfs* as in Bohemia and Moravia, but hold their lands subject to certain Services specified in their Lease, for which their Lord often allows them to compound.' A report procured by Stormont from John Coulston of Rumburg in Bohemia, the only British merchant in the central lands of the Monarchy at this date, also emphasized the servitude of the Bohemian peasantry.[10]

The land Estates are possessed almost entirely by the Nobility, and except in some few Instances of free Towns, the People stand, besides their Allegiance to the Queen, under a certain Servitude, Vassalage and Dependance on the Lord, upon whose Estate they are born And I apprehend it is in the Power of a Nobleman to order a Stranger when He pleases off from his Estate . . .

Coulston had in mind a commercial treaty between England and Austria. Rights of residence, and religious toleration, would be necessary for this. Even with these, however, 'the particular Constitution of Bohemia' was an obstacle.

For, as I have before observed, that State of Vassalage and Dependence they stand in to the Nobleman upon whose Estate they were born, is such as will be always an Exception in excluding them from large Credits: and besides under such Bondage are rarely found People of Honesty and integrity sufficient for that confidential Repose so necessary in the Cement of Commerce between Nation and Nation.

A few years earlier, in 1758, an indigenous account, perhaps by a German-speaking merchant, expressed similar prejudices about the Bohemian peasantry, though in terms of race, not status. The Slav

---

[10] PRO SP 80/202. Stormont to Sandwich 27 Mar. 1765 enclosing a report from John Coulston dated 15 Mar. 1765, unfoliated. Coulston acknowledged that he had 'but little of the High Dutch language'. For more about Coulston see A. Klíma, 'English Merchant Capital in Bohemia in the Eighteenth Century', *Econ. HR* 2nd ser. 12 (1959–60) 34–48.

peasant was 'lazy and stubborn, and must be held to his duties with harshness, threats and blows. If the harshness ceased, he would not perform his obligations either to the Crown or his lord'. Given this view, the author presumably regarded serfdom as a necessary constraint, though in his account of it he did not actually say so. The peasant's status under serfdom was that he had no property in his land unless he had purchased it. The lord owned the land, and gave it to the peasant to cultivate it and pay taxes from it. The peasant owed services and *robot*, which unless governed by contracts (*Urbarien*) were regulated by the royal *robot* patent of 1738, limiting it to three days in the week. The peasant could not leave his land without his lord's leave 'und daher in gewisse Maase leibeigen genennet wird'. This was perhaps equivalent to the status of *adscriptus glebae* in Roman law. However, the author observed, the Austrian peasant was worse off, even though he owned his land, since his labour services were not defined, and he must pay yearly rents as well.[11] The list of serf restrictions given here was incomplete. Serfs who had not bought the right to do so (*uneingekaufte*, as distinct from *eingekaufte*, peasants) could not sell or charge their land, or designate an heir, and were liable to be moved from their existing land to other land. All serfs were obliged to seek their lord's permission before moving or marrying or placing a child in employment.[12] Similar constraints applied to peasants in Galicia, as Count Pergen found when he became governor there in 1772. There, however, there were no restrictions on *robot*, and a full peasant was obliged to provide six days weekly in the summer, two in winter.[13]

---

[11] 'Entwurf einer Statistik von Böhmen', Riegger, *Materialien*, viii. 1–52, xii. 131 ff Riegger's surmise that the anonymous and undated account had been compiled 'about 30 years ago' is confirmed by the reference in xii. 178 to the completion of the Bohemian dominical cadastre 'two years ago', which places the report in 1758. For belief in the intrinsic idleness of the Bohemian peasant, observable 'since the days of King Wenceslas', see the representation by the Bohemian Estates of 5 July 1781, Grünberg, ii. 375. *Robot*, from Czech *robota*, labour services, Russian *rabota*, work, and German *Arbeit* are connected. In Austria, *Frondienst* was commonly used for labour service and *fronen* for its performance. *Fron* as an adjective also means 'holy', e.g. *Fronaltar*, but the idea of service to a lord seems implicit in all senses of it. *Urbarien* is one of several plurals used in this period for *Urbar*, *Urbarium*, meaning both the use of land and an agreement for this use (Ducange). *Urbar* is of old German origin; the etymology *úrbér*, in Hungarian a rent paid to a lord, suggested by Mitrofanov and others, is false.

[12] Grünberg, loc. cit. As seen in Ch. 3, the census recognized heirs.

[13] Glassl, *Einrichtungswerk*, 160, 167.

The only remedy for the Galician peasant was flight. If he evaded arrest for a year and a day, his lord lost jurisdiction over him.[14] Joseph II's 'emancipation' patent for the Bohemian lands of 1 November 1781 (5 April 1782 for Galicia) abolished *Leibeigenschaft* as a status, and allowed all peasants to marry, move, and acquire a trade, in each case with prior notification to their lord. A second patent, also on 1 November 1781, entitled Bohemian peasants to ask for 'bought in' status at a modest price. Once they acquired this, they could pledge, sell or exchange their land.[15]

In the Austrian lands, while serfdom was not a problem, labour services were. In Styria, unmeasured *robot* was a heavy burden, and the maximum of three days weekly imposed by the state in 1778 a relief.[16] In Lower Austria, 104 days yearly could be demanded, and this limit was adopted, not reduced, in the *robot* patent of 1772. However, there was much variety. In Upper Austria, *robot* was only obligatory on fourteen days in the year, and had been largely commuted to money before the start of this period.[17] In Tyrol and Further Austria, labour services were also light. The true location of *robot* labour was undoubtedly in the serf economies of the Bohemian lands and Galicia. In Moravia, the tax-register of 1750 included 10,018,377 *robot* days.[18] For Bohemia in 1756 the estimated figure is 14,693,000 days.[19] Count Pergen's table of 1773 for Galicia showed that 22,508,070 labour days were demanded, confirming that Polish conditions were the worst of all.[20] The contrasting class of a free peasantry owning allegiance only to the

---

[14] Ibid. 162.

[15] Army consent had, however to be obtained to all movement. See Grünberg, ii. 389–93 for the patents of 1781. For Galicia, see Glassl, 177.

[16] A. Mell, *Beiträge zur Geschichte des Unterthanwesens in Steiermark*, i. *Die Robot* (Graz 1892), pp. 180–95. 'Measured' (strictly defined) *robot* was small.

[17] G. Grüll, *Die Robot in Oberösterreich* (Linz 1952) 240, citing Baumann's contrast between the two provinces in 1767. For the problem whether Lower Austrian *robot* was in cash or kind see p. 97 above.

[18] Radimský–Trantírek, 229. 3,927,777 days were with horses, 1,399,954 with oxen, 4,690,646 on foot. Only 168,164 days' work was 'measured'.

[19] The number of days worked was not given in the Bohemian returns. Instead, 169,272 'robot workers' were declared. The value of *robot* labour was stated as 466,998 fl., in other versions somewhat higher, Pekař, *ČČH* xx. 414 and Table XIII. In Moravia in 1754, 10,018,377 days were valued at 318,809 fl., Radimský–Trantírek 46. Applying this to Bohemia gives a lower estimate of 14,693,560 days. This is plausible, though not definitive. In 1848 the figure was 15,172,208 days, Grünberg i. 402. The data suggest 87 *robot* days per worker in 1756.

[20] Brawer, *Galizien*, 54–5. Of the total, 3,342,613 days were served on royal estates, 19,165,457 on private ones.

Crown does not appear to be significant by this period. It certainly existed on a modest scale in Hungary. The loss of Silesia cut off a more considerable presence. A final point of note is that serfs in the Bohemian lands were typically 'rustical', that is settled on land in practice their own, though in constitutional theory ceded to them by their lords. It was these *Rustikalisten* who attracted most government attention. *Dominikalisten* were serfs settled on dominical land. They, too, could be *eingekauft* or *uneingekauft*. Their position was usually defined by a lease or other agreement with their lord. Grünberg believed them to be a minority.[21]

Against this background, some evidence for the disparate economic structure of peasant society will be considered. The pattern of Bohemian and Moravian agriculture, as shown in the tax-returns of the 1750s summarized earlier, was that peasants farmed three-quarters of arable and pasture, and lords the rest.[22] But this peasant 'ownership' was not evenly spread. In Bohemia, the returns of 1756, which are in print, of peasant cultivators of arable, show that of 215,270 heads of households, 49,888 (23.2%) owned one *Strich* (half a *Joch*) of land, or less, 27,139 (12.6%) owned one to five *Strich*, 45,364 (21%) owned five to 15 *Strich*, 43,763 (20.3%) owned 15–30 *Strich*, 37,378 (17.4%) owned 30–60 *Strich*, and 11,738 (5.5%) owned more than 60 *Strich*. According to the editors, these categories corresponded to the contemporary labels landless inhabitants and cottagers ('Landlose Inwohner und Häusler'), gardenkeepers ('Gärtner'), cottars ('Chalupner'), husbandmen ('Landwirte'), peasants ('Bauern') and large peasants ('Grosse Bauern'). As a *Strich* of land covered 0.287 ha, the holdings involved were up to 0.287 ha; up to 1.435 ha; up to 4.305 ha; up to

---

[21] *Freisassen* are discussed in *Caput* IV, *Punctum* III of the Bohemian Contribution Patent of 6 Sept. 1748, Linden, *Grundsteuerverfassung*, ii. 70 ff., but their numbers appear to have been small. A century earlier, only 426 free peasant heads of households were listed by the commissioners of the Estates, Kalousek, *Dodavek*, nos. 165–6. For *Freisassen* in Silesia see p. 87 above, and for dominical peasants Grünberg, i. 51, 69, ii. 124, 127, 141–2, 203, 265–6. Chancellor Harrach's report of 23 Oct. 1747 describes the Bohemian peasant as an 'usufructuarius', Kalousek, no. 229, para. iii. For a similar exposition by Borié in Dec. 1772 see Grünberg, ii. 207–8.

[22] See Tables 5.4, 5.9. The Bohemian Estates claimed in 1793, however, that only lords produced surpluses; the peasants farmed for subsistence, Grünberg, ii. 474. Cf. ibid. 156, Baron Unwerth's statement in 1768 that peasants produced a surplus, but only in order to pay the Contribution; they then had to buy dear corn for their own bread.

8.61 ha; up to 17.22 ha; and, in the top bracket, over this amount.[23] The translation attempted here of contemporary descriptions is inevitably Procrustean. Further, *Häusler* and *Chalupner*, the latter from Czech *chalupa*, 'cottage', are both really cottars or cottagers, and in other sources are treated as equivalent to each other.[24] The more conventional categories were 'whole', 'half-', and 'quarter'-peasants. These were applied by Joseph II's officials in 1787 during their attempt to estimate from a sample of peasant incomes the burden of royal taxes and lords' dues. A total of 1,198 cases was investigated. The results, published by Rozdolski, show that 'whole' peasants had an average holding of over 52 *Joch* (29.9 ha) in Bohemia, over 44 *Joch* in Moravia, over 34 *Joch* in Inner Austria, over 30 *Joch* (17.3 ha) in Lower Austria. These amounts were halved, and halved again, for half- and quarter-peasants. Estimated mean gross revenue for whole peasants was 401 fl. (rental peasants, *Zinsbauern*) and 361 fl. (other peasants) in Bohemia, 319 fl. in Moravia, 204 fl. in Lower Austria, 160 fl. in Inner Austria. Incomes were proportionally reduced for the other classes. Royal taxes and lords' dues, split roughly one-third and two-thirds, took an average 35% of peasant income in Moravia, 45% in Lower Austria, 50% in Inner Austria. In Bohemia, ordinary peasants paid 41% of their gross income, but rental peasants (*Zinsbauern*), cultivating crown land on the Raab system, paid only 24%, demonstrating the case for commutation of labour services.[25]

The sample taken for the inquiry was unrealistically small, and the results, which in Bohemia differ from those of 1756 given earlier, may be unrepresentative. However, the evidence presented confirms that peasant society was far from homogeneous economi-

---

[23] Chalupa *et al.* ii. 414–15. The descriptions are those assigned by the editors, without discussion, to each category, ibid. 523. Their date is 1757, but this is in effect meant 1 Nov. 1756, see ii, Ch. 7 below.

[24] Cf. Grünberg, ii. 84, analysis by the urbarial commission for Austrian Silesia 30 June 1768 of the serfs there. Those who had 30–60 Breslau *Scheffel* of arable land were equivalent to a Bohemian whole peasant. Those who had half this were called 'Grossgärtner'. Both performed *robot* services with the plough. Foot services were given by 'Dorfgärtner' with 4–8 *Scheffel* of land, by 'Häusler or Chalupner' with 0.5–3 *Scheffel*, and by 'Innleute' without land. Glassl, *Einrichtungswerk*, 159–60 has 'Bauern', 'Gärtner', 'Häusler', 'Innleute' in Galicia. However, the size of a whole peasant's holding varied capriciously, ibid. 164.

[25] R. Rozdolski, *Die grosse Steuer- und Agrarreform Josefs II.* (Warsaw 1961), app. IV. The experiment of a rent-paying peasantry free of labour-services on the Crown's ex-Jesuit and cameral estates in Bohemia from 1774, under the supervision of *Hofrat* Franz Anton von Raab, is described by Grünberg and Wright.

cally, and that the distribution of peasant wealth was skewed. In 1756, 36% of Bohemian heads of peasant households had five *Strich* of land or less, as the figures above show. The proportion of the total acreage which they controlled was probably exiguous. At the other end of the scale, 23% of heads of households each had 30 *Strich* or more, and, it is safe to assume, controlled at least half the acreage.[26] The distinction between the two groups was emphasized during the great peasant revolt of 1775 in Bohemia, 'the shame of the reign', in which, in contrast to the demands of the radical poor for emancipation from serf status, the larger peasants demanded regulation or abolition of labour services and other dues.[27]

Hungarian peasant society was also heterogeneous, not uniform. Varga shows that the urbarial inquiry initiated in 1767 returned 644,231 heads of taxpaying households, of whom 429,380 (66.6%) were *Hubner*, peasant owners of a hide (*Hube*) or part of one, 174,716 (27.1%) were housed cottars, and 40,135 (6.2%) unhoused cottars. A *Hube* or hide was on average 31.68 *Joch* (18.18 ha), but, because a *Joch* was variously interpreted, could be as little as 24, or as much as 54, *Joch*.[28] The general pattern conforms to that suggested for Hungary in Ch. 3. It is, however, general, since there was clearly much regional modification. Dr Felhő's examination of the urbarial returns in Transdanubia around 1770 gives more detail. There, 138,621 heads of peasant households were registered, of whom 90,917 (65.6%) were *Hubner*, 35,730 (25.8%) were housed cottars, and 11,974 (8.6%) were unhoused cottars. This agrees well with Varga's summary of the total returns. Of the 90,917 *Hubner*, who between them controlled 96% of the area, only 5,486 (6%) had a whole hide (*Hube*), while 34,057 (37.5%) had a quarter or less. The mean holding was just

---

[26] Chalupa *et al.*, loc. cit. The amount of land controlled by each group is not shown.

[27] *HGBL* ii. 489. The quotation is from Schlözer, *Briefwechsel*, i. 17, 'den Schandfleck Ihrer [i.e. Maria Theresia's] Regierung'. In the revolt, as Grünberg shows, it was widely believed by peasants that a decree freeing them from labour services had been drawn up in 1770–1 when army recruitment was introduced, but had been suppressed by the lords.

[28] Varga, *Typen und Probleme*, chs. 1, 5. The form *Hufe* was also used. The larger hides were in southern and south-eastern Hungary, the smaller ones in the populous north-west, see Varga's chapter in E. Molnár *et al.*, (eds.), *Magyarország története* (rev., abr. edn., Budapest 1967), map at p. 379. 'Unhoused' denoted not owning a house.

over half a hide. These general proportions in turn covered much intraregional variation. It is also justifiable to conclude that peasant farming in Hungary, though concentrated, was less so than lay lordship, examined earlier.[29]

How much land did the Hungarian peasants control? Putting together information from Czoernig, Liechtenstein, and Grellmann, the total area of Hungary proper at this time was 3,627.13 Austrian sq mil, or 36,271,300 *Joch*.[30] Of this, 31,815,124 *Joch* in 1789 were available for agricultural use, and 15,091,474 *Joch* were under the plough. Of this arable land, 4,897,217 *Joch* were peasant (urbarial) land.[31] A further 1,486,098 *Joch* comprised urbarial meadows, and 911,176 *Joch* urbarial vineyards, making a total of 6,544,059 *Joch* of peasant land.[32] The official size of a *Hube* or hide was 50 *Joch* of land. There would on this reckoning have been 130,881 *Hube* in 1789. With the actual average per *Hube* of 31.68 *Joch* found by Varga, the number would be 206,567 *Huber*.[33]

As will be apparent, the information presented here about the structure of peasant society, though suggestive, is unsatisfactorily incomplete. The further subject of government attempts to regulate peasant conditions of work and standards of life by *robot* patents (in Hungary, urbarial decrees) is too extensive to be treated in more than outline. A *robot* patent was promulgated for Bohemia in 1680, and extended to Moravia in 1713.[34] In 1717 there was a new patent for both lands, and in 1738 a revised one for Bohemia. Urbarial regulations, the equivalent measure in a Hungarian context, were

[29] Felhö, 45, 50, tables 9, 12. Cf. p. 107 above.

[30] See Table 2.1 above.

[31] *Grundlinien einer Statistik des österreichischen Kaiserthums ... betrachtet von Joseph M[arx] Freiherrn von Liechtenstern* (new edn., Vienna 1817) 82–3 (area of agricultural land) and 88 (arable in Hungary, and peasant share of this), in both cases at 1789.

[32] H. M. G. Grellmann, *Statistische Aufklärungen über wichtige Theile und Gegenstände der österreichischen Monarchie* (Göttingen 1795–1802) iii. 580–3, position in 1789. Varga, *Typen and Probleme*, 115 computes that there were 5,820,127 *Joch* of urbarial land in 1767.

[33] HHSA Nachl. Zinz., Hs. 157, notes on various provinces, unfoliated and undated but 1765, under 'Hungary'. A 'terra unius aratri' is there defined as 150 *jugera*, each 72 royal *ulnae* long and 12 wide. A *sessio colonicalis* (German *Hube*) was defined as one-third of this. Cf. Macartney, *Habsburg Empire*, 72, 'Inner Hungary ... contained ca. 1780 under 200,000 full *sessiones*, covering only 6.2 million *hold* [*Joch*].'

[34] There is a convenient summary of the *robot* legislation in Macartney, 65 n. 1. There is no general treatment, Grünberg's seminal study being confined to the Bohemian lands.

made for Slavonia in 1756, and for Hungary in 1767. The latter were applied in all Hungarian counties by the end of Maria Theresia's reign.[35] *Robot* patents were promulgated for Silesia in 1768, amended and replaced by another in 1771, for Lower Austria in 1772, and for Bohemia, and then Moravia, in 1775. A Styrian and a Carinthian patent followed in 1778.[36] A partial measure was introduced in Galicia in 1774, a more far-reaching one a decade later.[37] The patent for Krain (1782) rounded off the series. A common but not invariable feature of the Theresian patents was to limit *robot* with animals for a whole peasant's holding to a maximum of three days in the week, and to define the length and frequency of the working day. For lesser peasant holdings, and for foot *robot*, the obligations were proportionally less. In Lower Austria (1772) the maximum was two days weekly, in Hungary, under the regulations of 1767, one day a week.[38]

---

[35] Molnár et al., *M. tört.* 377–8, the last areas regulated being Croatia and the Banat of Temesvár in 1780. The account given is far from specific. The regulations for Slavonia are usually dated 1756, after disturbances in 1755. There is a good account in English in S. Guldescu, *The Croatian–Slavonian Kingdom 1526–1792* (The Hague 1970), ch. XII. The Hungarian urbarial patent was published on 23 Jan. 1767, but the written instructions for it were issued in the previous month. Cf. PRO SP 80/207, Langlois in Vienna to Rochford 13 Jan. 1770; the regulations made about three years ago in favour of the peasants in Hungary have ruined many of the lower nobility, without benefiting the peasants as much as was hoped.

[36] Macartney's statement is accepted here that a Carinthian *robot* patent appeared in the same year as the Styrian one, which is discussed by Mell, op. cit. Macartney is incorrect in stating that there was an Upper Austrian patent in 1772 as well as a Lower Austrian one. As Grüll, *Robot*, 175 points out, in Upper Austria reference was made instead to the regulation of 1597, which prescribed 14 days' *robot* a year. *HGBL* ii. 489 makes one of its rare factual errors in describing the circular of the Bohemian Government dated 7 Apr. 1774 as a *Robotpatent*. It in fact required lordships to draw up *urbaria* with their peasants, regulating *robot* according to government rules. It promised also that a *robot* patent would appear. See Grünberg, ii. 228 ff.

[37] Glassl, *Einrichtungswerk*, 175–9. Joseph II's edict of 15 Jan. 1784 for the first time restricted Galician *robot* to a maximum of three days weekly. Macartney, loc. cit. erroneously says that a provisional patent was published there in 1775 and confirmed in 1786.

[38] The Bohemian *robot* patent of 13 Aug. 1775 adopted tax payment as a measure of *robot* obligations after other measures, such as area farmed, had been rejected, Grünberg, ii. 205–17. The lower Austrian patent of 1772 has so far not been examined in depth. The account in Feigl, *Die niederösterreichische Grundherrschaft*, 325–6 is uninformative. K. Gutkas, *Gesch. des Landes Niederösterreich* (4th edn. Sankt-Pölten 1973) 342 gives a brief summary. There is a full, though not entirely clear, account of the Hungarian urbarial regulations in Johann Graf Mailath, *Das ungrische Urbarialsystem* (Pest and Leipzig 1838). A *sessio colonicalis* was obliged to render 52 days' *robot* a year with animals, or 104 days' with hand labour.

This scanty summary does little justice to legislation as complex, and as socially charged, as modern income-tax or employment law. Three features of it are selected for commentary. First, it represented a public assumption of responsibility for rules hitherto left to lords to devise. The large corpus of private *Urbarien* defining the mutual obligations of lords and peasants, which has been only partly explored by Austrian historians, shows that extended trial of voluntary agreement had occurred, over several centuries, before the state stepped in. Even so, the Austrian government only accepted with hesitation the necessity to prescribe general rules; in 1768 and 1771 in Silesia it did not restrict the days worked weekly, and laid principal emphasis on voluntary agreements between lord and tenant. In Bohemia in 1771 and 1774 it tried to compel a general conclusion of such *Urbarien*, with the government's rules as norm. Even in 1775 the *robot* patent was not mandatory. Its regulations applied only to peasants who did not choose to conclude different bargains with their lords.[39] Secondly, while it seems incontrovertible that the Theresian patents were partly a product of humanity, and ideas of natural rights, other motives were also present.[40] The patents can to some extent be regarded as forming part of the complex web of regulations affecting the peasantry woven in consequence of Haugwitz's new fiscal system of 1748–9. A constant theme of these regulations was the maintenance, and accurate recording, of peasant capacity to pay the Contribution.[41] The distinction between rustical and dominical land was essential here, and it was repeatedly insisted that it must not be blurred by lords filching rustical land and thus narrowing the tax base.[42] Similarly, lords

[39] Grünberg, ii. 88–96, 135–46 (Silesia in 1768 and 1771), 201–6, 229–36, 266, 292–303 (Bohemia in 1771, 1774, 1775). Joseph II's belief in private agreement rather than state imposition is documented ibid. 227 (1774), and his better-known hesitation about abolishing *Leibeigenschaft* in 1777, which his mother wanted, at p. 296. By Apr. 1776 127 of 991 Bohemian lordships in fact decided to stick to their old rules, ibid. 270.

[40] The strong natural-rights approach of the chancellery official Franz von Blanc, first as a member of the Silesian *robot* commission, then of those for Bohemia, is emphasized by Grünberg, especially in his first volume.

[41] The connection between peasant protection and tax capacity is correctly made by Grünberg, ii. 43 ff. Later the theme is somewhat lost, though there are references to it, e.g. Maria Theresia's assertion 29 July 1769, that the peasantry must be able to support their families and pay royal taxes in peace and war, ibid. ii. 119.

[42] Grünberg, ii. 45–6; *Sammlung*, section I, 'Kontribuzion und Robot', *Sistemalpatent* 6 Sept. 1748 § 2, allocation of tax between lords' and subjects' lands; 23 Jan. 1751 (*Hofrescript*, Bohemia), lords cannot acquire peasant land without prior investigation by the Circle office, etc.

must not burden peasants with heavy fines and interest payments, thus hampering their capacity to pay the Contribution.[43] It was repeatedly insisted that local repartition of Contribution should be equitable, and phased to take account of good months and bad months, presumably a reference to harvest and weather.[44] Lords were forbidden to make peasants buy lordship produce at fixed prices or use the lord's inns for festivities. These devices were not only unlawful, it was stated in 1770, 'but markedly weaken the Contribution'. A list of forbidden lordly practices in July 1770 included not paying peasants for fire and weather damage, deductible from the Contribution; unnecessary official fees for levying tax; obligation to buy from, and sell to, lordships at fixed prices; and excessive *robot*.[45] The last, which assumed overriding importance in the desperate conditions of 1770–5, thus formed part of a tariff of grievances which the government disapproved of partly because they weakened peasant taxpaying capacity. The same concern is clear in the discussion leading up to the Hungarian *urbarium* of 1767, in which *Hofrat* Balassa repeatedly emphasized the need to lessen lords' exactions in order to increase taxable peasant income.[46]

The third and last feature of the *robot* legislation, and other attempts to increase peasant wellbeing, to be noted is the influence on them of military thinking. This is an unexplored subject. Joseph II, describing the course of military reform to his brother Leopold in 1767, remarked that if internal population, and the stock of horses, could be increased, it would be possible to form 'an army of

---

[43] Ibid., *Hofdecret* 1 Sept. 1749, apparently for Bohemia. The same idea is expressed in the tax patent for Carinthia dated 6 Oct. 1748: lords are not to overburden peasants with robot but are to keep them 'Contributionsfähig'.

[44] For example, the Bohemian Contribution patent of 6 Sept. 1748, *Caput* II, *Punctum* II, 'Was bey der Repartition zur Beobachtung kommet', and many subsequent instances, whose repetition suggests that the problem was not solved. For the patent, see n. 21.

[45] *Sammlung*, section I, Bohemiam rescript 14 Apr. 1770, 'sondern auch zu merklichem Abbruche, und Schwächung des Kontribuzions-standes gereichen'; ibid., *Hofdecret* 14 July 1770, no area specified, but probably for Bohemia. The abuses listed were those uncovered by investigation of Prince Mansfeld's Bohemian estates, Grünberg, ii/3, ch. 2.

[46] D. Szabó (ed.), *A magyarországi úrbérrendezés története Mária Terézia korában*, i (Budapest 1933). This collection of German and Latin documents stops early in 1766; no second volume was published, despite Macartney's claim that it is in two volumes, *Habsburg Empire*, 843. Balassa was a member of the Council of Lieutenancy. For his report to Cabinet Secretary Neny of 12 Dec. 1764 arguing that lords' exactions lessened peasant tax capacity, see p. 310. There are several other examples.

cultivators and artisans'.[47] Foreign hirelings, and domestic vaga-
bonds, would be replaced, in Rousseauesque fashion, 'par de bons
citoiens ou sujets interessés, par leur propre état, a bien servir leur
Souverain'.[48] As to the Contribution, it was so heavy that all means
must be taken to render it supportable to the peasant, and to
increase his income. To do this, the grievances of peasants against
their lords were being vigorously investigated. Silesia was under
examination, but Joseph thought the main scandal had been in
Hungary, where only the peasants paid tax. The empress's Hungarian *urbarium* was 'the most glorious act of her reign, and she has at
the same time permanently consolidated the Contribution there.'[49]

The report of the president of the *Hofkriegsrat*, Count Moritz
Lacy, on conditions in Bohemia, dated 8 July 1771, exposes more
of this line of thought.[50] The army commission in Bohemia, pursuing its aim of eliciting a recruitable population, uncovered a terrible
state of affairs. In retrospect, peasant society was poised on the
brink of the catastrophic famine of 1771–2, in which, according to
Riegger, a quarter of a million died, and the starving poor ate
miller's dust and bark from the trees.[51] Peasant malnutrition, dirt,
and diseases—in some districts venereal disease brought in during
the late war—were repeatedly emphasized in the report. Peasants
were unable to meet royal taxes and lordship dues, and were
broken, and in the case of children deformed, by excessive *robot*
labour. Religious and educational provision was minimal. There
was general oppression by lordship servants. The report recommended sanitary reform, better educational and religious instruction, security of tenure for all peasants, the conversion of all
dominical land to rustical land (the mechanics of this were not disclosed), limitation of *robot*, and a procedure for complaints about it,

---

[47] HHSA FA Sammelband 88 unfoliated, end of para. 3 of section 'Militaire'.

[48] Ibid.

[49] Ibid., section entitled 'Justice, Police, et Bienêtre des Païs en General'.

[50] The report is extensively summarized by F. Mayer, 'Die volkswirtschaftlichen
Zustände Böhmens um das Jahr 1770', *Mitt. des Vereins für Gesch. der Deutschen in
Böhmen*, 14 (1876) 125 ff, and published in full by Kalousek, *Dodavek*, 491–530, in
the original German.

[51] Riegger, *Materialien*, x. 226, a series of wet summers led to a famine, in which
consumption of bad food led to general infection. The army itself was blamed in the
Staatswirtschaftsdeputation on 6 June 1771. Since 1763, grain export from Bohemia, a
principal source of peasant income, had been forbidden up to seven times because the
Hofkriegsrat wanted to fill its granaries cheaply, HHSA Nachl. Zinz., Hs. 127,
'Staatswirtschaftsdeputation', unfoliated, under date cited.

and restraints on the subdivision of rustical land. It may not be coincidence that officers taking the census were credited a little later with hinting at emancipation.[52] Lacy's, and Joseph's, approach was also consistent with the development from 1773 of the Raab system of tenure.[53]

Urban income will now be considered, taking the example of Vienna, and then incomes in general.

Vienna was the largest city in the Monarchy, and grew rapidly under Maria Theresia. Its population was on average poor. The *Schuldensteuer* payable there indicates this forcefully. This tax, introduced in 1763–64, was in effect a 1% levy on gross income.[54] It was computed in 1768 that Vienna's share would be 159,624 fl., roughly denoting a total income there of 16m. fl., more than half of Lower Austria's total.[55] It would be payable, according to this computation, by 66,984 persons in the city and suburbs. Of these, 50,690 (75.7%) were thought to have taxable incomes below 50 fl., and only 91 taxable incomes of more than 100 fl. Five persons were in the top class of taxpayers, with incomes of 80,000–100,000 fl.[56] These figures, which denote an acutely skewed distribution of income, are lent somewhat greater plausibility by the fact that taxable income was reached after deduction of other state taxes, and of interest due to creditors.[57] Some confirmation is obtained from a sample of 150 inventories at death in the period 1760–85.[58] These estates, which excluded those of nobles, ecclesiastics, and Privileged Warehousers and Wholesalers, who were subject to other courts, were distributed as shown in Table 6.1. One-fifth of the persons thus controlled 83% of the gross assets, and 65% of the persons controlled only 6.4%. The mean estate, 4,391 fl., is pulled up by the higher figures at the top. The median was only 537 fl. Too

---

[52] Schlözer, *Briefwechsel*, i. 18.

[53] See n. 25.

[54] See ii. 48, where the income scale for tax payments is discussed. The rate was 1–2% on net income after other taxes were paid. It seems justified to take this as equivalent to 1% on gross income.

[55] HKA Hs. 713, fo. 207, 'Schuldensteuer der Stadt Wien' for 1768. For total Lower Austrian income see Table 6.2.

[56] Combining the tax computations in the MS source with the income scale.

[57] Allowance for this might double the otherwise very low 50 fl. income imputed.

[58] WSLA, Herrschafts-Gerichtsakten 2/162–3, 2/190. No entries were earlier than 1760. The valuations perhaps became needed because of the *Erbsteuer* or tax on collateral inheritances introduced in 1759.

TABLE 6.1. *Analysis of 150 Viennese estates at death, 1760–85*

Category (fl.)	No.	%	Gross estate (fl.)	%
0–99	32	21.3	1,566	0.2
100–999	49	32.7	16,575	2.5
1,000–1,999	17	11.3	24,240	3.7
2,000–4,999	22	14.7	71,841	10.9
5,000–9,999	14	9.3	101,995	15.5
10,000 and over	16	10.7	442,456	67.2
Total	150	100.0	658,673	100.0

much cannot be claimed for the detail of these results. The sample is too small, and practical difficulties prevented its being more than impressionistic. It seems plausible, nevertheless, that the results point in the right direction. The gross estates, it may be noted, were quite often considerably reduced, or even eliminated, by the liabilities. Average *net* wealth was thus lower still, though its distribution was similar.

The snippets of official comment and information on the dossiers of this population of shopkeepers, artisans, minor officials, and servants and labourers often show the detail of urban poverty with unintentional poignancy.[59] Clara Winterleiter, who died on 22 January 1782 at house 160 'in the new street on the Wieden' was 'only a servant girl' ('Nur Dienstmagd'). She left 20 fl. Regina Märdl, who died on 4 February 1764 at the Hungarian Crown on the Wieden, the house of Lorenz Schuller, a married carter, was in service with the widowed toy-seller Jatschkin. She gave herself out to be a household servant ('laquai') whose husband was in Italy. She was in fact seduced and abandoned by Johann Märdl. Mother and child died in childbirth. She left 43 fl. Sigmund Weissbach 'gave himself out to be in the service of a Polish nobleman'. He died in the care of the Brothers of Mercy on 12 May 1773, leaving 19 fl. Even the better-off were exposed to much uncertainty. Christopher Millner, a sauerkraut trader, died on 30 December 1763 in Leo-

---

[59] Analysis of the 150 cases shows 38 uncertain, 4 officials, 9 professional, 9 merchants, 44 craftsmen, 9 retailers, 5 innkeepers, 5 gardeners, 17 servants, 10 other occupations. Of 150 names, 148 were German and two French. Only 81 persons left a will; 69 died intestate.

poldstadt with liabilities of 1,394 fl. and assets of 229 fl. He had
11,061 fl. due on various bonds from Joseph Jörg, master builder
(*Baumeister*) in Semmering. But Jörg went bankrupt, and compounded with his creditors. The affair dragged on until 1774. Other
examples could be cited.

The general impression of misery given by these sources is strengthened by the data for prices and wages. Wages for bricklayers,
builders, carpenters, day-labourers, and others at the bottom of the
urban labour market were very low, in the range 15–30 kr. a day,
with no expectation of a full working year. Money wages do not
seem to have changed much during the reign, at a time when the
secular price of foodstuffs was rising. Wheat, corn and barley in
Vienna fetched the following decadal average market prices in
kreuzer.[60]

	wheat	corn	barley
1720–9	74.1	48.8	39.3
1730–9	76.5	51.9	41.7
1740–9	102.7	67.0	58.6
1750–9	117.7	85.5	65.5
1760–9	120.3	79.2	68.6
1770–9	148.2	104.6	81.2
1780–9	162.2	111.0	89.8

These figures conceal much higher prices in certain years, of which
1745–6, 1755–6, 1757–9, 1765–8, 1770–5, 1780, and virtually all
Joseph II's reign, were the chief. In 1788, 1789, and 1790 the market
prices of grain exceeded even those of the terrible famine years 1771
and 1772 (Fig. 1). The annual average price of wheat reached or
exceeded 2 fl. (120 kr.) a *Metze* only once in the 1740s, three times
in the 1750s, four times in the 1760s, seven times in the 1770s, nine
times in the 1780s. It is not, however, clear how far these urban
figures can be used as a general index to the cost of living, given
probable disparity between areas, and the capacity of many peasants
to avoid market purchases altogether.

It is a presumption, but no more, that the pattern of wealth and
poverty in Vienna was reproduced in the other cities of the
Monarchy.[61] It will be seen in the next chapter that at the top of

---

[60] For prices and wages, see A. F. Pribram (ed.), *Materialien zur Geschichte der
Preise und Löhne in Österreich*, i (Vienna 1938); for annual average Vienna grain
prices see ibid. 371 ff. and for urban wages pp. 554–69. Musketeers in the infantry
were paid 48 fl. yearly 1733–68, then 42 fl., ibid. 564.

[61] See p. 51 above for the social structure of Prague in the 1780s, which appears to
resemble that of Vienna without the top tier.

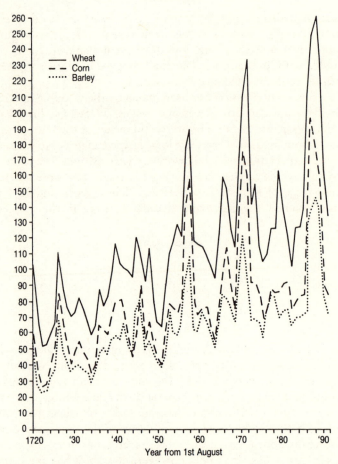

FIG. 1. Annual prices in Vienna of wheat, corn (*Korn*), and barley, in kreuzer. (*Korn* was an Austrian variant of rye.)

Viennese mercantile society the stakes were higher, for example 30,000 fl. net wealth was required for registration as a Privileged Wholesaler from 1774, though even this was small compared with the assets of the urban plutocracies of western Europe.[62] Turning to incomes not derived from trade, administrators of various kinds in Austria (government clerks, superintendents, hospital overseers,

[62] See Ch. 7.

and so on) seem, in sharp contrast to their superiors, who drew handsome sums, to have worked in the salary range 100–800 fl.[63] Councillors in the central government offices in 1763 drew 2,000–4,000 fl., heads of departments and their deputies 8,000–12,000 fl. A few salaries were higher. Kaunitz had 30,000 fl. at this date, and the ambassador in Paris, Prince Georg Starhemberg, 60,000 fl.[64] Those at the top could expect *douceurs* and bonuses as well from time to time. Army service was not a source of great fortunes, on the available evidence, but systematic investigation is needed. Baron Wachenheim, second colonel of a foot regiment, left 18,099 fl. in 1763. Countess Maria Raigecourt, widow of a *General-Feldwachtmeister*, left 18,143 fl. in 1769, partly in the form of loans at 6% to Samuel Hirschl and other Jews. *Feldmarschall-Leutnant* Christian von Wulfen, Commander of the garrison at Peterwardein, left 55,104 fl. in the same year.[65] Cesare di Gabaglio, who also died in 1769, in Pavia, left 85,278 fl., and must have been acting as a moneylender. Numerous loans to fellow Italians are noted, and one, of 12,672 fl. without interest, to Count Wied, *Feld-Zeugmeister*, dating from 1754.[66]

Summarizing, the range of incomes considered in this chapter and the previous one is from upwards of 100,000 fl. for a small class of very big landowners, a group below them which had from 10,000 fl. to 100,000 fl., supplemented for great office-holders by salaries of up to 30,000 fl.; then ranging through 1,000–10,000 fl. for middle landowners, important officials, and large merchants, 200–1,000 fl. for the bulk of the trading and professional middle classes, and 50–400 fl. for peasants, artisans, and labourers. The distribution of wealth, and also of income, was highly skewed in every social group examined, making each, in economic terms, heterogeneous, not uniform.

The sum of incomes would be a crude proxy for national income. This aggregate had already attracted the curiosity of projectors under Charles VI. A tax proposal of 1719 estimated total personal income in the Bohemian and Austrian lands as 393,385,000, or

---

[63] Pribram, 554–5.

[64] For structure of Court and *Hofstellen* salaries see K. Oberleitner, 'Die Finanzlage in den deutschen österreichischen Erbländern in Jahre 1761', *AÖG* 34 (1865) 145–209.

[65] From KA Hofkriegsrat, inventories 1770, Fsz. 26/1–89.

[66] Ibid. 26/90–188.

TABLE 6.2. *Estimated aggregate income in the Bohemian and Austrian lands, 1767–75 (m. fl.)*

	1767	%	1770	%	1775	%
Bohemia	52.1	38.4	49.061	35.7	34.791	25.1
Moravia	24.6	18.1	20.047	14.6	22.314	16.1
Silesia	4.2	3.1	4.259	3.1	3.726	2.7
Lower Austria	20.0	14.7	27.197	19.8	38.663	27.9
Upper Austria	10.7	7.9	10.929	8.0	11.333	8.2
Styria	12.6	9.3	13.492	9.8	15.581	11.3
Carinthia	4.5	3.3	6.750	4.9	5.928	4.3
Krain	6.5	4.8	4.812	3.5	5.238	3.8
Görz-Gradisca	0.5	0.4	0.687	0.5	0.800	0.6
Total	135.7	100.0	137.238	100.0	138.379	100.0

Sources: HKA Staatsschuldenakten, rote Nr. 165, fos. 79 ff., finance estimates 1767; HHSA Nachl. Zinz., Hs. 57, fo. 49ʳ, receipts 1770; HKA Kredit AA Akten, rote Nr. 1, Fsz. 1, fo. 124 ff., Final Accounts 1775.

80 fl. a head.[67] This was optimistic guesswork. So was Calzabigi's estimate in 1760 that the landed revenues of the inhabitants of the Monarchy amounted to 200m. fl.[68] A nearer proxy to income in the Hereditary Lands is afforded by the revenue derived from the *Schuldensteuer*, the tax just discussed in a Viennese context. The intended receipts for 1767, and the actual receipts for 1770 and 1775, multiplied by 100 to give a rough estimate of the income from which they derived, are shown in Table 6.2. The aggregate income derived in this way only shows a modest increase between 1767 and 1775. However, there were striking changes in its composition. The estimates of 1767 are not badly out of line with the results of 1770. In both, Bohemia had well over one-third of total income, and the Bohemian lands together one-half or more. Lower Austria appears to have been underestimated in 1767, but still only controlled a fifth of total income in 1770. In 1775, the results show that the Lower Austrian share had risen markedly, to 28%, and the Bohemian

[67] HKA Hs. 648.
[68] HHSA Hs. B. 37, 'Osservazioni sopra Lo Stato Attuale del Commercio della Monarchia Austriaca' [c.1760], iii, fo. 274ʳ. The first vol. of the memoir is missing. The probable author of the 'Observations' was the Tuscan projector Renier Calzabigi, manager from Oct. 1760 with his brother, Jean-Antoine, of the state lottery in Brussels, see G. Bigwood, 'La loterie aux Pays-Bas autrichiens', *ASRAB* 26 (1912) 85 n. 1, Kaunitz to the empress 20 May 1760.

share had fallen to 25%. The dip in the Bohemian returns must be
due to the double disruption of the famine of 1771–2 and the
peasants' revolt of 1775. The rise of Lower Austrian income by the
same date must be connected with the growth of Vienna, though
the size of the increase since 1770 is so large as to prompt caution.[69]
Are these necessarily very approximate results in the right direction? An alternative approach is to impute incomes to households,
or to social groups. If each household had a (low) 75 fl. income in
1785, a decade later than the data just examined, the aggregate
income of the Bohemian lands would have been 66.801m. fl. compared with 60.831m. fl. shown by the *Schuldensteuer* in 1775, and
that of the Austrian lands 48.338m. fl. compared with 77.543m. fl.
in 1775.[70] The first result is probably, and the second clearly, too
low. Galician income by this method was 46.114m. fl. The total in
these lands is thus 161.253m. fl. For the Hungarian lands (1787), the
same calculation gives 121.587m. fl., making a grand total of
282.840m. fl.[71] If representative incomes are assigned to members
of social groups in 1785, a technique necessarily involving even
more guesswork, 100.657m. fl. income is obtained in the Bohemian
lands, 90.165m. fl. in the Austrian lands, 35.757m. fl. in Galicia, and
168.413m. fl. in the Hungarian lands, a total of 394.992m. fl.[72]
Lastly, according to Liechtenstern, the Josephine cadastre of 1789
disclosed in the central lands of the Monarchy an *agricultural*
revenue of 363m. fl., derived from livestock, arable, meadows,
woods, and gardens.[73] Labour services, and industrial and commercial income, were not included. In a later work, he states that production in the same area from arable, meadows, woods, and gardens
in 1789 came to 252.68m. This implies that livestock production

---

[69] The abolition of the *Schuldensteuer* in Bohemia, Moravia, and Lower Austria in
1775, 1777, and 1780 respectively prevents further comparison.

[70] The numbers of *Familien* are taken from the 1785 census, HKA Hs. 735,
item *b*.

[71] The Hungarian results are based on Thirring, *M. Népessége.*

[72] *Geistliche* are assigned 200 fl., *Adelige* (reduced by two-fifths to allow for children) 5,000 fl. (Hungarian lands 100 fl.), *Beamte und Honoratiores* 500 fl., *Bürger
und Professionisten* 300 fl., *Bauern* 100 fl., *Häusler* etc. 50 fl. For Galicia, the figures
are 100 fl., 100 fl., 300 fl., 100 fl., 75 fl., 40 fl., respectively. The large element of
guesswork will be apparent.

[73] Joseph Marx Freiherr von Liechtenstern, *Skizze einer statistischen Schilderung
des Oestreichischen Staats* (Vienna 1800) 71: the central lands of the Monarchy,
excluding the recently acquired West Galicia and Venetia, have 6,625 sq. mil. of culti-
vatable land, whose produce was valued in 1789 at 363m. fl. It comprised wheat,
grass, cattle, woods, plants, and fish.

was worth 110.32m. fl. Of his 252.68m. fl., Hungary and Croatia (but not Siebenbürgen) accounted for 100.19m. fl.[74] Since Riegger gives the total of the returns for the non-Hungarian central lands at this date as 114.84m. fl., 37.65m. fl. must be ascribed to Siebenbürgen if Liechtenstern's total is reliable. The Bohemian lands, according to Riegger, accounted for 49.92m. fl. revenue, the Austrian lands for 37.67m. and Galicia for 27.25m.[75] The geographical distribution of livestock is available, but not its value.[76] The shares of each group of lands in the lower total of 252.68m. fl. were: Bohemian lands 19.76%; Austrian lands 14.91%; Galicia 10.78%; Hungary and Croatia 39.65%; Siebenbürgen 14.90%. In Table 6.3, these proportions are applied to the larger total of 363m. fl., which included livestock, to give estimated shares in total agricultural income in 1789. A figure for manufacturing output at this date is at present lacking. In Bohemia it may have been 25m. fl., and perhaps double that for the central lands as a whole.[77] The estimates for 1770, 1775 and 1785 are included in the table, and the reconstructed 1789 figures for agricultural income are reduced by 1% p.a. to procure an estimate for 1780. The most that can be said of these figures, with their uncertain statistical base and considerable variations, is that, though conjectural, they are not wholly conjectural. They point to a national income of 350–400m. fl. in the central lands around 1780. Further research, particularly at local level, is needed to test all this, and perhaps refute it. As the figures stand, they indicate that government revenue at the end of Maria Theresa's reign of about 50m. fl. took between 12 and 15% of national income, which is in line with the results of Joseph II's tax

[74] *Grundlinien*, 84, the entire worth of corn, grazing, woods, and gardens in 1789 was 252,677,260 fl., of which Hungary and Croatia produced 100,193,130 fl., Bohemia 30,057,939 fl., Lower Austria 12,932,563 fl., and Styria 8,099,452 fl. No other figures are given.

[75] Riegger, *Archiv von Böhmen*, 'Entwurf der neuen Grundsteuer' at end of vol. iii. The figure above for Siebenbürgen is logical rather than plausible.

[76] In 1787 the census registered 912,787 horses and 1,064,448 oxen in the central lands of the Monarchy, excluding the Hungarian lands. Horses: Bohemian lands 333,038 (36.5%); Austrian lands 246,211 (27.0%), Galicia 333,538 (36.5%); Oxen: Bohemian lands 307,664 (28.9%); Austrian lands 399,282 (37.5%); Galicia 357,502 (33.6%), J. V. Goehlert, 'Häuser und Volkszahl sowie Viehstand Oesterreichs in der Regierungsperiode Josef's II.', *Statistische Monatschrift*, 5 (1879) 402–5, casting corrected. There were 797,540 oxen in Hungary in 1787, Liechenstern, *Grundlinien*, 105.

[77] The figure in 1797 was 30,114,254 fl., Otruba, *Bohemia* 5 (1964) 166. Allowing for undervaluation, 25m. fl. seems plausible for 1789.

TABLE 6.3. *Estimates of Austrian national income 1770–89 (m. fl.)*

	Schuldensteuer		1780 est	1785		1789 cadastre
	1770	1775		75 fl. per household	By social groups	
Bohemian lands	73.367	60.831	65.59	66.801	100.657	71.730
Austrian lands	63.867	77.543	49.48	48.338	90.165	54.120
Galicia	—	—	35.77	46.114	35.757	39.130
Hungarian lands	—	—	181.05	121.587	168.413	198.020
Total	—	—	331.89[a]	282.840	394.992	363.0[a]

[a] Agricultural income only.

samples in 1787, Lower Austria for example showing 13.6% of peasant income taken in royal taxes, Bohemia 13.4%, Inner Austria 18.4%.[78]

This chapter ends by considering briefly some physical and behavioural characteristics of the population. Physically, the mass of men were short. A height of five feet seven inches was regarded as 'tall' for army entrants in the 1770s, and in Bohemia most recruits in that decade did not exceed five feet four inches.[79] Large quantities of alcohol were consumed. In Vienna at the end of this period daily adult consumption of wine seems to have averaged half a gallon a head.[80] Brandy was used by the Galician peasantry almost as an anaesthetic against the misery of their lot, and lords derived large sums for selling it to them.[81] The same was true of beer in Bohemia.[82] Numerous regulations against it show the prevalence of feasting and drinking in taverns (*Wirtshäuser*) in Vienna, especially on Sundays and holy days.[83] Social behaviour generally was erratic, from absconding serfs, errant journeymen, and dissipated students

[78] Rozdolski, loc. cit. (n. 25 above).

[79] Dvořáček, *Československ. statist. věstník*, 4 (1924), table 4.

[80] Schlözer, *Briefwechsel*, xlviii. 354, return of consumption of alcoholic drinks in Vienna by the *Tranksteuer-Kommission* dated 9 Aug. 1780. Wine came first with 1,752,467 *Eimer*, followed by beer with 121,613 *Eimer*. Assuming that two-thirds of the (1782) population were adults, or 133,801 persons, and that an *Eimer* represents c.14 Imperial galls., this denotes four pints per adult daily. Data to control this are at present lacking.

[81] Glassl, *Einrichtungswerk*, ch. 2(f), 'Die Bauern'.

[82] See ii, Ch. 7.

[83] *Sammlung*, section II(i), 'Polizeisachen überhaupt', numerous references.

to the duellists and idle young nobles of more elevated circles. Gambling was endemic in the capital from the top to the bottom of society, and cannot have been confined there.[84] At all levels, judging by the acerbity of government decrees, carelessness and laxity prevailed. Merchants, churches, religious houses, all failed to keep proper accounts, nobles failed to clarify and register their pedigrees, and so on.[85] No doubt the prevalence of death, which struck impartially at rich and poor, accentuated indifference to a regular style of life.

Irregularity shaded into violence. The wearing, and use, of swords, the firing of guns at weddings and festivities, the frequency of brawls and quarrels between social groups, are attested by repeated government orders forbidding them.[86] At the bottom of the social pyramid, a drifting population of beggars, casual labourers, gypsies, runaway servants, and other flotsam, caused the authorities recurrent anxiety, and was draconically controlled, partly through the operation of a criminal law whose gruesome punishments were codified in the *Constitutio Criminalis Theresiana* of 1769.[87] The accumulation of such a class in Vienna led to strengthening of police regulations there in 1776 so as to guard against

[84] The Genoa Lottery introduced on 13 Nov. 1751, ibid., shows the state tapping this propensity. The monopoly concessionaries were initially Octavio von Cataldi, subsequently Andreas Baratta & Co. The ten-year lease was renewed for eight years on 16 Jan. 1762, and again on 17 Mar. 1770 and 30 Dec. 1777. Only the Hungarian lands, Tyrol, and Further Austria were excluded from the lottery's operations. Kaunitz wrote to Cobenzl on 18 Apr. 1760 that merchants, servants, everyone, bought tickets, and lost, Bigwood, op. cit. 83. An account published in 1786 showed that 21m. fl. were placed in the lottery 1750–69, the state gaining 3.46m. fl. On a proportional basis, 20m. fl. would have been staked 1769–86, Geisler, *Skizzen*, xi. 111. The traveller J. G. Keyssler found c.1730 that the two questions asked of a foreigner were what his family was and what stakes he played for, J. G. Keyssler, *Neueste Reisen durch Deutschland* (Hanover 1751) 1214.

[85] *Sammlung*, section II(i), 14 Oct. 1772, registration of pedigrees by Lower Austrian *Herrenstand*; section IV(i), 8 Dec. 1759, chaos in church accounts; Jan. 1767, annual registration of assets of endowments (*Stiftungen*); section VI(ii) 24 Sept. 1776, proper books to be kept by Galician merchants.

[86] Numerous examples ibid., section II(i), 'Polizeisachen überhaupt'.

[87] Ibid., section II(iii), 'Armeninstitut, Ausrottung der Vagabunden, Landstreicher und Bettler'. For the forms of torture and punishment endorsed by the *Constitutio Criminalis Theresiana* published on 31 Dec. 1768, and recommended on 15 Mar. 1769 to enter into force from 1 Nov. 1769, see the extended discussion in Domin-Pet. 55 ff. Four grades of torture, starting with thumbscrews, and liberal use of the death penalty, including its application to bigamy and other moral offences, were features of the code. Cf. also P. P. Bernard, *The Limits of Enlightenment. Joseph II and the Law* (Urbana, Ill. 1979), ch. 1.

'this class of persons [who] must be considered the nursery of evil-doers and the chief source of all unrest'.[88]

The peasant masses, largely illiterate, moved to the rhythm of seedtime and harvest, as both the German and Slavonic calendars of the age, with their descriptive names for the months of the year, illustrated.[89] Both in country and town men were superstitious, believing in witches, vampires, devils, werewolves. The clergy assi-duously practised exorcism.[90] Catholicism, reflecting this, was bar-oque and ornate, appealing to the senses. Fürst noted how often the Host was ceremonially carried through the streets of Vienna, onlookers sinking to their knees before it.[91] The growing influence of asceticism in Catholic practice and doctrine associated with Jose-phinist policies, signalized by the reduction in feast-days in 1754 and 1771, and continuing through the dissolution of the Society of Jesus to the Toleration Patent and the monastic reductions, must have seemed the more bewildering to the majority. Government action and attitudes here were in conformity with the general tone of its social policy. The increasing flood of police regulations during Maria Theresia's reign aimed to ensure the decorous observation of Sundays and holy days, the elimination of debauchery, hard work by craftsmen, limitation of unnecessary wandering by peasants, journeymen, Jews, care for peasants by lordships, clarification and registration of noble titles, observance of social rank, and so on. Implicit in the whole corpus of these ordinances was a neo-puritan ethic of pure religion, industriousness, regularity, sobriety, sexual virtue, social order, which provided a fitting introduction to the reign of the virtuous emperor, Joseph II.

[88] *Sammlung* II(i) 2 Mar. 1776, police ordinance for Vienna dividing the city into 12 districts, each with a *Bezirksaufseher*, to whom all changes in the occupancy of houses were to be reported, etc.

[89] 'Hornung' for February, 'Brachmonat' for June, 'Heumonat' for July, 'Weinmo-nat' for October, 'Wintermonat' for November, were common in this period in the Austrian and Bohemian lands, as repeated examples show, and were part of general German usage, see the calendars printed in the *Gothaischer Hof-Kalender* from 1766. By 1820 every month had a special name, ibid. In the Czech calendar, *leden* (January) is related to *led* (ice); *květen* (May) to *květina* (a flower); *srpen* (August) to *srp* (a sickle); *září* (September) is 'shiny'; *listopad* (November) is 'leaf-fall'.

[90] For example, *Sammlung* section II(i), 'Polizeisachen überhaupt', 1 Mar. 1755, the celebrated Moravian case, involving burning by the clergy of corpses accused of 'magia posthuma'; ibid. 5 Nov. 1766, widespread belief in witches and wizards; 18 Nov. 1772, ban on prophecies in calendars; 3 Nov. 1779, superstitious practices of Styrian peasants at Midsummer; and so on.

[91] *Fürst (1755)* 42.

7

Merchants and bankers in Vienna

THE financial groups whose services were available to the Austrian government have been much less studied than their equivalents in England, France, or Holland in this period. It would not be difficult, for example, to infer from the secondary literature that from Leopold I to Joseph II, Austrian financiers were mainly Jewish.[1] Yet the anonymous *Almanach général des marchands de France et de l'Europe*, published in Paris in 1774, listed eleven 'Banquiers principaux de Vienne' at that date, and eight principal bankers of Prague, none of whom were Jews.[2] In this chapter it will be argued, first, that while Jewish financiers were of eminent and perhaps predominant importance under Charles VI, this importance lessened in the earlier part of Maria Theresia's reign and was not regained during it. Jewish capital, however, was dominant in Bohemian taxfarming from the 1760s, as in Bohemian trade generally, while some Jewish financiers rapidly emerged into the ranks of Viennese bankers once formal restrictions on them were relaxed in 1782. Second, it will be shown that even under Charles VI there were important Christian financial firms in Vienna whose services continued into the 1740s. Under Maria Theresia, a new generation of such financiers arose, largely drawn, as the earlier one was, from the ranks of the Vienna Warehousers, or the Wholesalers who succeeded to their position from 1774. The composition of this group

---

[1] For example, H. Schnee, *Die Hoffinanz und der moderne Staat* (Berlin 1953–67); see especially iii. 248. Cf. also Macartney, *Habsburg Empire*, 59, 'Financial fortunes, where any, were made by "privileged" Jews, chiefly by those who acted as Court moneylenders.'

[2] *Almanach général des marchands . . . de la France et de l'Europe* (Paris 1774). The bankers listed in Vienna were 'de Bender et fils'; 'Castellini et Comp.'; 'Castelmur'; 'Baron de Fries'; 'Heilmann'; 'Küner et Comp.'; Labhard et Comp.'; 'Baron de Riesch'; 'Schmidmeyr frères'; 'Segalla'; 'Stametz'. In Prague the names given are 'J. Christian Beer'; 'Paul Cassati'; 'J.-J. Koessuler'; 'Jean-Georges Pradatsch veuve'; 'Jos. Stoltz'; 'Jean-Matthias Thun'; 'Jos. Zehender, del Curto et Comp.' and 'Simon Thad. Zunterer'. Most of these are discussed below.

will be examined and its importance assessed. One of its members, the Swiss Protestant Johann Fries, quickly came to assume a leading role in government finance from 1750 when he settled in Vienna, and he remained pre-eminent until his death in 1785. Fries's strength derived partly from his excellent foreign connections. His close understanding, in particular, with the banking house of Widow Nettine & Son of Brussels was of critical importance to Austrian foreign borrowing in the period 1756–80. The Widow Nettine's firm, however, was merely the most weighty among a number of others in the Austrian Netherlands, especially those of Cogels, Dormer, and Proli, whose existence put added financial and commercial resources at Austria's disposal. These firms are described in the next chapter. The Dutch and Italian correspondents of Vienna bankers are reserved for later discussion.

Jewish finance was important for the government in Vienna in the eighteenth century, but Vienna, like Budapest and unlike Prague, was not a city of much Jewish residence.[3] About 130 Jewish families were living there in 1624 when it was decreed that they must move to a ghetto, the 'Unterer Werd', in Leopoldstadt on the north bank of the Danube. This ghetto in 1669 contained about 500 families and perhaps 2,000 inhabitants. In the following year, because of earlier anti-Jewish commotions, the entire population was expelled (order of 28 February 1670) and diffused itself through the other Habsburg lands and Germany. The expulsion had no sooner been carried through, however, than it was being reconsidered, and by 1699 twenty-five addresses for Jews in the Inner City, some of them ('Wertenheimb mit seinen Leuthen') obviously crowded, are officially noted. In 1723 only 17 'families' are listed, covering about 420 persons. The privileged head of each was licensed for himself, his relations, and his servants, the Wertheimer privilege at this date, for example, covering 100 persons. All privileges save that of Marx

---

[3] See pp. 51–2, 55. This section is based on M. Grunwald, *Samuel Oppenheimer und sein Kreis* (Vienna and Leipzig 1913) esp. pp. 170–83; id., 'Geschichte der Juden in Wien. Vom Jahre 1625 bis zum Jahre 1740' in A. Mayer *et al.* (eds.), *Geschichte der Stadt Wien* (Vienna 1897–1918), v. 65–99, which, however, adds little to the former; and, especially, A. F. Pribram's important *Urkunden und Akten zur Geschichte der Juden in Wien* (Vienna and Leipzig 1918) i. The books by Grunwald and Pribram comprise vols. 5 and 8 of the series 'Quellen und Forschungen zur Geschichte der Juden in Deutsch-Österreich.' By decree of 16 Oct. 1723 Jews in Vienna were confined to dealing in money and jewels, and forbidden to engage in general trade, Pribram, i. 310.

Schlesinger expired by the end of 1736, and it was proposed to reduce the resident 'families' to three, those of Berend Gabriel Eskeles, Löw Sinzheim, and Hirschl Spitz. This cannot have been enforced, since a further official list in 1752 shows eight 'families' (Eskeles, Manassa, Oppenheimer, Schlesinger, Simon, Sinzheim, Spitz, Wertheimer), with 452 persons, resident in Vienna. In 1777 an official census of the Jews found 99 families—a different classification must have been used—with 356 members and 263 servants. In 1782 there were 518 resident Jews. The overall Jewish population in Vienna thus remained more or less constant, and substantially below that of the seventeenth century, in line with government policy under both Charles VI and Maria Theresia. Jews were welcome for their financial services and unwelcome otherwise. At this date, just before Joseph II's Patent for Lower Austria of 2 January 1782 rather grudgingly alleviated some Jewish disabilities in the capital, Jews were obliged to wear Jewish dress, to pay special taxes, to live in designated houses; and forbidden to wear swords, to go out on Sunday mornings, to be Wholesalers, and so on.[4] Joseph's decree abolished these restrictions, reaffirmed as recently as 1764, and gave Jews the right to live anywhere in Vienna. No right to build a synagogue was conceded, however, and government policy was still that 'the number of Jewish families established here is not to be increased'. The Jewish population of Vienna was officially still only 4,296 in 1846, 6,999 in 1856.

The importance of Jewish financiers in Vienna up to the 1740s was in inverse proportion to numbers resident. The chief connection, illustrated in Fig. 2, was that of the Oppenheimer family, whose fortunes were established by Samuel Oppenheimer, probably of Heidelberg (1630–1703).[5] Oppenheimer built up a virtual

---

[4] See Joseph II's patent, Pribram, i. 494–500, tr. C. A. Macartney (ed.) *The Habsburg and Hohenzollern Dynasties in the Seventeeth and Eighteenth Centuries*. (New York 1970) 165–69, where, however, the date of 5 May 1761 for the previous regulations should be 5 May 1764.

[5] This section, and Fig. 2, are based on Grunwald; Mensi, *Die Finanzen Oesterreichs*; Pribram; Schnee, iii. 237–70, iv. 304–22; J. Taglicht, *Nachlässe der Wiener Juden im 17. und 18. Jahrhundert* (Vienna and Leipzig 1917); and S. Wininger, *Grosse Jüdische National-Biographie* (Cernăuţi 1925–36). There is new information about Oppenheimer's contracts with the government in the 1960s in Bérenger, *Finances et absolutisme*, esp. book 2, ch. V. The various Jewish relationships are frequently unclear in the literature, and Fig. 2 must be regarded as provisional. Jewish families seem at first to have adopted the suffix *er* to denote 'of' the places named but subsequently (Arnstein, Oppenheim, Sinzheim) to have eliminated it.

monopoly position in Habsburg finance and army supply from the
mid 1670s, having begun his career as army contractor to the Elector Karl Ludwig of the Palatinate. His official title from 1701 was
'Kaiserlicher Oberkriegsfaktor und Jud'. Genial, and a patron of
Jewish learning, he was none the less hated in the official circles
which could not dispense with him. At his death in May 1703 the
state owed him over 6m. fl. But he had huge foreign debts, the *Hofkammer* had counter-claims, and his firm went bankrupt in the
same year. His affairs were finally settled only in 1762. His son
Emanuel was a financier of some importance, but could not escape
the government claims against his father's estate. By 1721, when he
died, these amounted to about 8m. fl. His widow died in relative
poverty in 1738.[6] It seems, however, that marriage could save much
from the wreck. In 1725 Emanuel's son Samuel Emanuel married
Sara, the daughter of Isaac Arnsteiner, a rising Jewish financier.
Samuel Emanuel's sister Lea made a more important match still. She
married her second cousin, Wolf Wertheimer, the eldest of the three
sons of Simson Wertheimer of Worms. Simson was Samuel Oppenheimer's nephew by marriage (his sister's son-in-law), and had
come to Vienna in 1684 to work in his uncle's office. He quickly
showed as much talent, and less rapacity, in army supply and
government finance generally. In addition he was skilled in the Tal-
mud, a patron of Jewish learning and education, an honorary rabbi
in Vienna and Prague, a lover and collector of art. To the Viennese
he was 'the emperor of the Jews' ('der Juden Kaiser'). He left
1,830,660 fl. His second son Löw married a daughter of the Jewish
Court Factor at Dresden, Berend Lehmann. Simson's daughter Eva
married Bernhard (Berend) Gabriel Eskeles, another army contractor. Further Oppenheimer connections were Löw Sinzheim, originally of Mannheim, who married Samuel Oppenheimer's
granddaughter Sara Guggenheim; Lazarus Hirschl, whose daughter
married Samuel Oppenheimer's grandson, Isaac Nathan Oppenheimer; and Lemle Moses, another connection by marriage. Abraham Spitz (d. 1741), his son Hirschl Spitz (d. 1759), and Abraham

---

[6] See Mensi, 143 for Emanuel Oppenheimer's debts; Taglicht, 62–73 for Judith
Oppenheimer's assets of 11,335 fl. and liabilities of 44,327 fl. She had, however,
various 'doubtful' assets which it was hoped would close the gap, including
200,000–300,000 fl. claims on the government.

Ulm (d. 1720) were also in the Oppenheimer circle but evidently not related to it by blood.[7]

These details can be given closer reference to government finance by turning to the early part of Charles VI's reign. In the years 1714–24, Jewish firms figured in transaction after transaction with the government. The most prominent names were those of Lemle Moses, Emanuel Oppenheimer, Marx Schlesinger, Löw Sinzheim, Abraham Ulm, and Simson and Wolf Wertheimer. Most of these have been encountered already. An important addition is Marx Schlesinger (d. 1754), the son-in-law of Abraham Spitz and, like his father Benjamin Wolf Schlesinger, an army contractor and lender. The Jews who registered with the new (1717) Vienna Mercantile Court in 1725 were, unsurprisingly drawn from the families discussed: Isaac Arnsteiner, Marx Hirschl, Hertz Lehmann, Isaac Leidesdorf, Isaac Nathan Oppenheimer, Judith Oppenheimer, Marx Schlesinger, Abraham and Hirschl Spitz, Löw and Wolf Wertheimer.[8]

Of this circle, Wolf Wertheimer was still active as late as 1733, when he arranged remittance of a 300,000 fl. subsidy to the Elector of Cologne. He had previously lent millions to the Elector of Bavaria, for whom he was Court Factor, and could not get his money back. He died after 1740, the exact date being unclear. The Bavarian Court, by settling his claims at a discount in 1753, saved the credit of his house.[9] His financial position had, however, already been usurped by Löw Sinzheim, who in the 1730s was engaged in every kind of government loan, purchase of bonds, and

---

[7] The official weighting of Viennese Jewish financiers is indicated by a forced loan of 1,237,000 fl. levied in 1717. The Wertheimers had to pay 500,000 fl., Hirschl's heirs 177,000 fl., Hey Leymann, Simon Michl, Nathan Oppenheimer, Adolph Schlesinger, Löb Sinzheim, 'Spitzer' (Abraham Spitz, evidently Sinzheim's partner), and Abraham Ulm 75,000 fl. each: all other Jews 80,000 fl. between them, Mensi, 338 n.

[8] See Mensi, 483–514 for Jewish financiers after 1714. For Jewish registrations with the Mercantile Court, see WSLA Merkantil Gericht Protocoll B. 6/1, index 1725–58, fos. 920–40. All Christian and Jewish firms were ordered in 1724 to register with the court.

[9] P. C. Hartmann, *Geld als Instrument europäischer Machtpolitik im Zeitalter des Merkantilismus* (Munich 1978), esp. pp. 69, 115. In 1750 Bavaria offered 2.4m. fl. in settlement of the 7,851,963 fl. Wertheimer claims. Although Simson Wertheimer's estate is given by Taglicht, 39, as 1,830,660 fl., his son Joseph in 1745 claimed a two-ninths share of 5,030,799 fl. government debts due to his father, HKA Hoffinanz R. 1205 (1745), fo. 35.

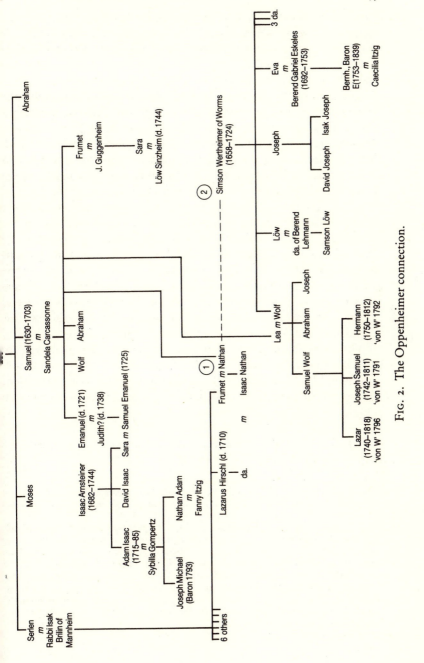

FIG. 2. The Oppenheimer connection.

foreign remittance.[10] Sinzheim appears by this period to have out-stripped all his Jewish rivals. He died in June 1744, Baron Diego de Aguilar acting as guardian of his estate.[11] The latter was contested at law for 120 years and its amount is not known.[12] He had claims on the government in 1739 of over 4m. fl.[13]

The curious figure of Sinzheim's executor Aguilar illustrates the contradictions to which financial need exposed the stiff and ortho-dox Habsburg government. Aguilar (1700–65), in Jewish sources Moses Lopes de Pereira, was a Portuguese Jew, instrumental with his father in running the Portuguese tobacco monopoly. He left Lis-bon in 1722, and via England and Holland settled in Austria, where from 1725 he first administered, then farmed until 1748, the state tobacco revenues. Unprecedentedly, he was created a baron in 1726. He left for England in 1755 to find better matches for his children.[14] Aguilar lent Maria Theresia 300,000 fl. towards the costs of building Schönbrunn.[15] The 157,000 fl. which the govern-ment owed him in 1746 may represent the balance of this.[16] In the years 1743–9 he remitted to Mathias Nettine in Brussels the inter-est due on loans floated in the Austrian Netherlands in 1738 and 1739.[17] At least as early as 1751 he was acting as cashier to the Council of the Austrian Netherlands at Vienna.[18]

The financial importance of the Oppenheimer connection, to which Aguilar's career is a kind of appendage, was undoubtedly considerable. Attempting to quantify its total contribution, Grunwald in 1913 computed that in the period 1698–1739 Jewish

---

[10] Sinzheim's activities are well documented in Mensi, see index s.n. Sinzheim was also Court Factor for Trier and the Palatinate.

[11] Taglicht, 86 and n.

[12] Ibid. 35–7.

[13] Mensi, 364 shows that in 1739 Sinzheim held government paper of about 4.5m. fl., though he was having difficulty in encashing it. Wininger simply says that Sinzheim's property in 1739 was 4.5m. fl.

[14] There are sketches of Aguilar's life in Wininger; Schnee, iii. 247; Grunwald 295–300; Taglicht, 87 n.); etc. Most of these draw on J. von Retzer, *Tabakpachtung in den österr. Ländern von 1670 bis 1783* (Vienna 1784). For Aguilar's tobacco farm see App. B. He appears to be the first ennobled Austrian Jew. It was also normal for lower titles to be conferred before a barony.

[15] Arneth, *Gesch. Mar. Ther.* iv. 142.

[16] HKA Prandau Akten, Konvolut 21, No. 12, Oct. 1746. Ibid., Konvolut 3, no 23 shows Aguilar assessed at 10,000 fl. in the *Subsidium Praesentaneum* of 1748.

[17] See p. 187; ii, Ch. 9, n. 29.

[18] AGR, Cons. des Fin. 7185, dossier for 1751.

financiers lent the government at least 78m. fl., an average of 2m. fl. a year, or a third of the annual revenue (1708–27) of 5m–7m. fl.[19] This was accepted by Schnee in 1955 without discussion.[20] From Schnee's work it has passed into the general literature.[21] It is probable that the computation makes insufficient allowance for the usurious practices of the period after 1714, at least, including loans made contingently on repayment of other paper, often bought at a discount, loans made to repay the lender himself for earlier advances, and so on. These are well documented by Mensi.[22] A more serious objection is that the figure given for state revenue is based on a misunderstanding of Mensi's data, and is too low by a factor of three. The proportion which Jewish loans comprised is therefore overestimated.[23] Despite these uncertainties, there is no reason to doubt that the scale of operations was huge by the standards of the time. Emanuel Oppenheimer's widow Judith claimed in 1723 that her husband's house had done 100m. fl. worth of business with the government over 44 years, and this does not seem implausible.[24] The whole experiment of Jewish contracting and finance, it may be surmised, impressed the authorities deeply and painfully. For while it showed that apparently bottomless Jewish purses could be tapped, it showed, too, that the state could deliver itself into the hands of financial cliques, whose usurious profits, in the eyes of hostile contemporaries, were paid 'from the subjects' sweat and blood'.[25]

Whether through reflection on her father's reign, or through her own anti-Jewish prejudices, Maria Theresia certainly used Viennese Jewish financiers less, turning to Christians instead, even if they were Protestants. This is discussed below. But Jewish traders and financiers did not disappear from the Viennese scene, and outside it continued to be important. In Bohemia, Jews dominated the textile

[19] Grunwald, 168–70. He suggests that Jewish deliveries of supplies, and services as loan-intermediaries, amounted to a further 3m.–4m. fl. a year.
[20] Schnee, iii. 248 The Spitz loans there should be dated 1706–33 not 1706–1833.
[21] See, e.g. Oestreich in Schieder (ed.) *Handbuch*, iv. 440.
[22] Mensi, 478–514.
[23] The figures taken from Mensi by Grunwald, and accepted by Schnee and Oestreich, are for cameral revenue only, and exclude military revenue and, except for 1708–10, that of the Vienna City Bank. Grunwald also takes net rather than gross revenue, thus reducing the total further still.
[24] Cit. Schnee, iii. 43. Cf. Mensi, 141; Bérenger, loc. cit.
[25] Count Gundaker Starhemberg's view dated 2 Dec. 1703, Mensi, 139–40.

trades, and the empress's abortive attempts to expel them from the kingdom in 1744–5 alarmed the Bohemian government as much as it did foreign courts, though for different reasons. In Hungary, Jews played a considerable role as moneylenders and farmers of small revenue branches, though the leading merchants there, and in Siebenbürgen, appear to have been typically German, Hungarian, Slav, or Greek, rather than Jewish.[26] In Vienna, when the Lower Austrian Mercantile Court resumed a separate existence in 1762, the following Jews registered their commercial signatures, as required by law.[27]

Adam Isaac Arnsteiner	22 January	1764
Joseph Eppinger	26 March	1766
Eva, widow of Löw Jacob Eskeles	21 March	1766
Herl Khue	13 December	1770
Wolf Joseph Lazarus	21 March	1766
Löw Isaac Leidesdorf	20 February	1764
Mandl Leidesdorf	21 March	1766
Mayer Michel	21 March	1766
Isaac Popper	26 November	1767
Hirschl Isaac Schlesinger	13 May	1770
Isaac Schlesinger, father of Hirschl Isaac S.	13 May	1768
David Joseph Wertheimer, 'Hof Jud'	20 December	1764
Isaac Joseph Wertheimer, brother of David Joseph W.	20 December	1764
Samson Löw Wertheimer	27 March	1766
Samuel Wertheimer, 'Hof Jud'	22 January	1764

[26] For the attempted expulsion of the Jews see Arneth, *Gesch. Mar. Ther.* iv. 42–9. For Maria Theresia's anti-Semitism cf. PRO SP 80/168, 27 Mar. 1745, Thomas Robinson to Lord Harrington: 'Her aversion to the sight of a Jew was too great to be concealed, when at Presburg she could not pass from the Town to her Palace, but through the very Street that was thronged by that People.' At the end of her reign she recorded 'I know of no worse plague in the State ("Pest von Statt") than this Nation, which brings people to beggary through swindling, usury, and money-lending', Pribram, i. 245, June 1777. The names of leading Hungarian merchants appear in the report of 1755–6 printed by A. Fournier, 'Handel und Verkehr in Ungarn und Polen um die Mitte des 18. Jahrhunderts', *AÖG* 69 (1887) 317–81.

[27] Merk. Gericht Prot. B. 6/2, index vol. for 1758–89, Jewish section, fos. 1–28. The Mercantile Court established in 1717 was merged with the Lower Austrian government 1749–62.

Members of these families had been on the register since its inception in 1725. (See also Fig. 2 above.) Adam Isaac Arnsteiner was the son of Isaac Arnsteiner, whose daughter Sara married Samuel Emanuel Oppenheimer in 1725. Isaac, a cousin of Simson Wertheimer, and his clerk from 1709, was the official Court Jew and supplier ('Ober Hoffaktor') of Joseph I's widow, the Empress Amalia, from 1719.[28] Tersely described as 'Jud', he appears in a *Hofkammer* document of 1742 as owed 60,000 fl., the balance of 240,000 fl. he had lent on the security of Bohemian revenues.[29] In 1746 the government owed his heirs 320,092 fl.[30] His son Adam Isaac Arnsteiner, a partner (with a 150,000 fl. share) in the tobacco farm of 1774, was a Court Factor from 1762. His wealth was partly accumulated from the Vienna banking house of Arnstein(er) & Eskeles, which he established with Simson Wertheimer's grandson Bernhard Eskeles, later Baron Eskeles, between the latter's return from Amsterdam in 1774 and his own death in 1785. The bank became one of the leading houses in Vienna until its failure in 1859. Adam Isaac Arnsteiner, who left a fortune of 777,000 fl., married Sybilla (Belle) Nymwegen Gompertz, a member of a well-known Prussian Jewish family. They had two sons. The elder, Joseph Michael, became a Catholic in 1778, and purchased the titles of 'Edler von Arnstein' in 1783, and of baron in 1793. His brother Nathan Adam (1749–1838), who remained a Jew and ran the family bank with great success, married Fanny Itzig, one of the two daughters of Frederick II's Jewish coinage contractor and financial adviser Daniel Itzig. Bernhard Eskeles married the other daughter, Cäcilia. Both sisters were philanthropists and patrons of music, and presided over brilliant salons in the Congress era.[31]

---

[28] Schnee, iii. 245 and a clearer account at iv. 329. There is no entry for Isaac Arnsteiner in Wininger. There is a short section in Grunwald, 258, where his cousinship to Wertheimer, and his clerkship, are stated, without sources. Isak Arnsteiner is 'Isaac' in official documents, and this usage is followed here.

[29] HKA Prandau Akten, Konvolut 13, no. 10.

[30] See ii, Table 10.2.

[31] Schnee, iv. 329–30; Taglicht, 146–7. There is an accurate Arnstein genealogy s.n. Fanny Arnstein in *NDB*. Berend or Bernhard Gabriel Eskeles, the son of a Cracow rabbi, made a fortune as an army contractor, and died in Vienna on 14 Mar. 1753, leaving 475,149 fl. He married Eva Wertheimer. Their son Bernhard was ennobled in 1797, made a knight in 1811, and a baron in 1822. He was a director, and subsequently vice-governor, of the Austrian National Bank. The private bank of Arnstein and Eskeles, for which no exact date is given in the literature, must have been founded after 1774 and before 1785; probably in the early years of Joseph II's reign.

Of the remaining names in the Vienna Mercantile Court list, Joseph Eppinger became a prominent member of the Jewish community, but must have been of a poor family, since when his mother died in 1773 she had no property; he had kept her for fifteen years. Wolf Lazarus may be the 'Wolf Lazaro' who was married to Hirschl Spitz's daughter Bella. Herl or Herzl Khue was an army bedding contractor who died in 1771 leaving 263,000 fl. Löw Leidesdorf was the son of Isaac Leidesdorfer from Ofen (Buda), who is in the list of 1725 referred to earlier, and who had been Samuel Oppenheimer's clerk; Isaac died in 1748. Löw was married to the daughter of Marx Schlesinger. Mandel or Mendel Leidesdorf, whose relationship to Löw is not clear, had just (1765) arrived in Vienna from Pressburg to become the partner of David Isaac Arnsteiner, brother of Adam Isaac Arnsteiner. It is possible that Leidesdorf came specifically to handle the reduction of interest on state bonds for clients, since from March 1765 to May 1766 he presented to the *Hofkammer* 500,536 fl. bonds at 6% and 5% and 639,706 fl. in cash, receiving in exchange 1,140,242 fl. 4% Vienna City Bank obligations. He died, however, in 1770, leaving assets of only 90,000 fl. Mayer Michael was the great-grandson of Simon Michael or Michl, a Jew active in Vienna finance from 1687 to 1719; Mayer died in relative poverty in 1784.[32] Leaving Isaac Popper until later, Isaac Schlesinger (d. 1771) was the son of Marx Schlesinger (d. 1754), and Hirschl Isaac was Isaac's son. The four Wertheimers, two of whom are described as 'Court Jew', were grandsons of Simson Wertheimer. Samuel was the son of Wolf Wertheimer, Samson Löw the son of Löw Wertheimer, David Joseph and Isaac Joseph were the sons of Joseph Wertheimer.[33] The sons of the eldest grandson, Samuel, were Lazar (1740–1811), financial agent to the Elector Palatine, and Hermann (1750–1812), army and coinage contractor. The three brothers were ennobled while Jews as 'von Wertheimstein' in 1796, 1791, and 1792 respectively.[34]

Isaac Popper's name in the 1764 Mercantile Court list introduces another Jewish connection, of more recent origin: the Bohemian

[32] These identifications are largely from Taglicht's scholarly monograph. For Mendel Leidesdorf's loans see HKA Geheime Bancalakten 380 B, unfoliated, under letter M.

[33] For Marx Schlesinger, father-in-law of Löw Leidesdorf and son-in-law of Abraham Spitz, see p. 144. The Wertheimers are identified in Taglicht, 113 n.

[34] Schnee, iv. 326–7.

Poppers, Dobruschkas, and Hönigs. Isaac Popper, described in the record as 'Privileged Potash-farmer', was either the son or the brother of Wolf Popper, Primator of the Jews in Prague, and an important financier there.[35] Wolf, Isaac, and Joachim Popper were all members of the fourteen-man Jewish syndicate which farmed the Austrian and Bohemian tobacco revenues for ten years from 1 January 1765.[36] Joachim was subsequently ennobled as 'Edler von Popper' in 1790 for services to industry and the state.[37] Another member, Salomon Dobruschka and his father, had long farmed tobacco revenues for the Moravian Estates. Ten of Salomon's (converted) children were ennobled wholesale, as 'von Schönfeld', in 1778.[38] The Hönig family from Kuttenplan (Planá Chovodá) in Bohemia, which provided no fewer than four members, first acquired prominence locally, but quickly came to have important interests in Vienna. Aron Moyses, Eystig Löbl, Israel Löbl, and Löbl Hönig each had one share in the farm of 1765–74. Aron Moyses and Israel Löbl retained a share in the renewed farm from 1774.[39] The brothers Abraham Löbl (subsequently 'Adam') and Lazar Löbl (subsequently 'Leopold') appear in 1777: Leopold died in 1784.[40] The relationship of these Hönigs to each other appears to be that Löbl in 1764 was the father and the others his five sons. Adam was ennobled as 'Edler von Henikstein' in 1784, his services in supplying army fodder in 1761–2 being emphasized. In 1788 he is described as 'Salt Director in Galicia'. Israel Hönig was ennobled, while Jewish, as Edler von Hönigsburg in 1789; he, too, had supplied the army during the Seven Years War. He became Director of the state tobacco monopoly in 1783 and a Lower Austrian councillor. The six sons of Aron Moyses Hönig (1730–87) were ennobled as 'von Hönigshof' in 1791.[41]

Some of these Hönigs had already sought Privileged Wholesaler

---

[35] For Wolf Popper see ibid. 325.
[36] See App. B for the tobacco farm.
[37] Schnee, loc. cit.
[38] Ibid. 319.
[39] See App. B.
[40] Merk. Gericht Prot. B. 6/2, fo. 29 in section 'Juden' and fo. 629 of main section.
[41] Schnee, iv. 321–4. Löbl Hönig is shown to have had five sons, though only Adam and Israel are named, by Ruth Kestenberg-Gladstein, *Neuere Gesch. der Juden in den böhmischen Ländern*, i. *Das Zeitalter der Aufklärung* (Tübingen 1969) 104. Aron Moyses Honig d. 27 Aug. 1787 leaving a net estate of 397,365 fl., Taglicht, 244.

status in Vienna. The first application, dated 3 May 1781, and thus many months before entry was formally conceded to Jews, was from Adam and Leopold Hönig. The Warehousers and Wholesalers had already agreed to support it, and approval was given on 16 November 1781. The brothers presumably became the first Jewish Wholesalers.[42] Similarly, Aron Moises [sic] Hönig applied for a Wholesaler's rights on 8 January 1782, two days after Joseph II's patent, and was accepted. Israel Löbl's application was agreed to on the same day.[43]

To sum up, Jewish financiers and contractors were attracted to Vienna by the wars at the turn of the seventeenth century, and became deeply involved with the government there. Huge fortunes were gained, but government reluctance to pay debts, and slowness in paying anything, ate into the profits made (Oppenheimer, Sinzheim, Wertheimer). The estates even of the richer Vienna Jews under Maria Theresia were more moderate than those during her father's reign, and modest (under £100,000) by English standards. This is connected with the fact that Jewish influence in public finance, and hence the opportunity for gain, faltered between the death of Löw Sinzheim in 1744 and the rise of Jewish houses in Vienna under Joseph II. In 1762 a government document even refers to the recent frequency of Jewish bankruptcy. But this line of argument must not be overdone. Jewish fortunes at death may not have been excessive, but were larger at the top than those of most Christian bankers, as the evidence reviewed below shows. Further, the rise of the Hönig and Popper families shows that the wars of the mid century and their fiscal aftermath gave renewed opportunities for Jewish contractors and tax-farmers. War and army supply throughout the period opened the door for Jewish financial entrepreneurs from Samuel Oppenheimer to Adam Isaac Arnsteiner.

In all Jewish business, ties of family were of great importance. The Jews of Vienna were still dominated in the 1770s by the ramifications of the Oppenheimer–Wertheimer connection. Family ties extended to the Jewish communities in Germany and Holland. There is a clear analogy with the Huguenot diaspora. Employment outside Vienna as Court Factors for other rulers followed naturally

---

[42] Merk. Gericht Prot. B. 6/2, fo. 629. The Warehousers and Wholesalers are discussed below.

[43] Ibid., fos. 631, 633. Israel showed a fund of 30,450 fl.

from these international links. From Joseph II's reign, the closeness of former Jewish connections increasingly dissolved, families like the baptized Arnsteins merging into the higher aristocracy, and entering military and government careers. A new chapter in Austrian Jewish finance was to be written by a new family, the Rothschilds. Jewish financiers at first came to Vienna from German cities (Heidelberg, Mannheim, Worms), but later the Hönigs came from Bohemia, and the Leidesdorfs from Hungary. All these families belonged to the Ashkenazi or central and eastern European Jewish community; Diego de Aguilar was a Sephardi exception. Aspects of the whole question remain obscure. While the business activities of Samuel Oppenheimer have been reconstructed in great detail by Grunwald and Bérenger, those of later financiers, for example the Arnsteiners or Hönigs, are subjects only for broad generalizations. Jewish relationships, despite the brilliant work of Grunwald, Taglicht, and others, are often uncertain, and their reconstruction is not helped by the ambiguity and duplication of Jewish names. The question of the origin of Jewish funds is largely unexplored.[44] With all these reservations, the role of Jewish finance in this period, perhaps a special case of religion and the rise of capitalism, was clearly a significant one.

Important though the Jewish contribution to government finance was, it never entirely superseded the services of Christian financiers even under Charles VI. Under Maria Theresia the balance, at least in Vienna, was reversed, with the Christians elbowing out the Jews. This subject will now be examined. The government's policy of attracting Christian capitalists to Vienna with the bait of special tax concessions and the right to conduct wholesale trade went back at least to the sixteenth century. In 1515 Maximilian I reserved the right of wholesale trade in Vienna to these Warehousers ('Niederleger'), and the practice continued.[45] The Vienna merchants

[44] For the frequency of Jewish bankruptcy see Pribram, i. 359, *Vortrag* of Boh.-Aust. Chancellery 22 Mar. 1762. On the question of funds, Taglicht, 26 asserts, without adducing evidence, that Jews acted as middlemen, in effect as bankers, rather than having big resources of their own.

[45] See K. Fajkmajer, 'Handel, Verkehr und Münzwesen' in Mayer *et al.* (eds.), *Gesch. der Stadt Wien*, iv. 524–84. Further edicts defined the position of Warehousers in 1536, 1615, 1625, 1662, 1707, 1713, and 1738, ibid. 545–6. The overlapping account of Warehousers by V. Thiel, 'Gewerbe und Industrie' (ibid. 411–523) treats the ordinances of 1662 and 1713 applying to Trading Burgesses as

('Bürgerlicher Handelstand'), who numbered 270 in 1731, were considered financially too weak to conduct operations on the scale needed. They complained frequently about the privileges of the Warehousers, who paid customs but were exempted from other taxes, and also about the activities of those licensed to supply the Court ('Hofbefreite'), who were also tax-privileged. These complaints had little effect. Under Charles VI the trading population of Vienna, leaving aside the much larger body of shopkeepers and handicraft workers, was therefore divided into the Warehousers, the Court Suppliers, and the Trading Burgesses. The first were at least in theory foreign, and sometimes Protestant. In practice, as *Hofrat* Degelmann explained in July 1770, the protective tariff of 1728 removed the need for residents to act as intermediaries for foreign houses. The Warehousers had become progressively an 'inland trading corps', composed partly of natives attracted by the tax exemptions obtainable.[46] In 1768 it was decided to name no new Court Suppliers, and, on 28 April 1774, after much discussion, to create a College of Wholesalers ('Grosshandlungs Gremium') as a substitute for the corps of Warehousers, whose members were, however, allowed to continue in business. The new body, for entry to which a trading fund of at least 30,000 fl. had to be shown, conferred nobility on its twelve members, even though they were traders, and was open to foreigners and Protestants. In 1806 the remaining Warehousers were amalgamated with it.[47]

It was in the ranks of the Privileged Warehousers and their successors the Wholesalers that the government was most likely to find alternative resources to Jewish finance. Gottfried Schreyvogel, whose services by 1700 were already so important that they

though they were for Warehousers. Helen Kuraic, 'Die Wiener Niederleger im 18. Jahrhundert' (phil. diss., Vienna 1946), completed in circumstances of great difficulty at the end of the Second World War, gives little more than an outline of government policy, without discussion of the Warehousers themselves.

[46] See Fajkmajer, 554 for the number of Trading Burgesses in 1731. They were not allowed to exercise a handicraft. Court Suppliers evidently were, Thiel, 430. Degelmann's paper on the evolution of the Warehousers, dated 6 July 1770, is summarized by Přibram, *Gewerbepolitik*, 239–40 nn.

[47] The decision to create no further *Hof-Freiheiten* was taken in July 1768, ibid. 137 and n. For the decisions of 1774 see ibid. 239–42 and Kuraic, 80–90, 108. Protestant members were to be allowed to own land and houses, but only with special permission. Existing Warehousers, 36 in number, could join the corps, but only one, Emanuel Bozenhard, seems to have done so, see App. C. The most eminent Warehouser, Johann Fries, did not become a Wholesaler.

appeared to offer release from those of Samuel Oppenheimer, belonged to this group.[48] So did Cichini & Jäger, Hilleprand & Isenflam, and Palm Brothers ('Gebrüder Palm'), all prominent in credit operations in the years 1714–24. Schreyvogel died in the mid-1730s, but Hilleprand, Isenflam, now a separate house, and Palm were still Warehousers in 1740, the firms of Hilleprand and Palm having acquired an exceptional reputation in government credit and contracting.[49] These two, and some of their prominent successors under Maria Theresia, are discussed below. It is worth while first to look at the composition and characteristics of the Warehouser and Wholesaler populations from which they were drawn. The apparent similarity in background and resources between the Wholesalers and at least the more eminent Warehousers seems to justify treating the two groups as one for the purposes of analysis.

Appendix C gives the names of the members of the Warehousers at selected dates from the *Court Calendar*, and those of the Wholesalers in 1779. This procedure may exclude firms which entered and left between those dates, but other evidence suggests that such cases are not common. As much biographical information as possible is added, the principal source being the indexes to the proceedings of the Vienna Mercantile Court for the period 1725–89. What conclusions can be reached from these admittedly incomplete and imprecise data? Numbers of Warehousers showed some interesting fluctuations. There were twenty-four in 1740, and twenty-nine in 1748. There was then a marked increase, to forty-six by 1754. This influx of new firms after the peace of 1748 is remarkable, and shows that the restrictive intention expressed by a royal ordinance of 22 December 1738 could not be enforced. Numbers then remained stable (44 in 1763, 47 in 1770), falling to thirty-six in 1774. By 1779 the twelve initial Wholesalers had increased to seventeen. In

---

[48] For Schreyvogel see Mensi, 146, and for his administration of part of the Bohemian revenues 1707–14 ibid. 120. He was still in charge in 1717, ibid. 672. He administered Hungarian copper and quicksilver revenue on behalf of Dutch creditors from 1714, H. Ritter von Srbik, *Der staatliche Exporthandel Österreichs von Leopold I. bis Maria Theresia* (Leipzig 1907) 364–5, and in May 1732 had a further contract for sale of Hungarian copper for four years, ibid. 403. Gottfried Christian and Johann Rudolph Schreyvogel of Breslau were brothers, made Bohemian knights in 1701, and imperial knights in 1706, P. Mahringer, 'Oesterreichischer Wirtschaftsadel von 1701 bis 1740' (unpub. diss., Vienna 1969).

[49] Mensi, 483–514.

1800 there were eighty-eight Wholesalers and only ten Warehousers.[50]

A minority of names of firms was French (15) and Italian (11). The late seventeenth-century prominence of Italian firms seems to have faded by this period. The solid majority was German. Origins were none the less mixed, as the cases of Fries (Mühlhausen), Kernhofer (Brünn), Labhard (Basle), Muller (Bohemia), Ochs (Basle), Paldinger (Ödenburg), Perghofer (Graz), Plattensteiner (?Nuremberg), Rieger (Switzerland), Steiner (Winterthur) and Wiesenhütter (Frankfurt am Main) demonstrate. Further genealogical research would establish whether the geographical origins of this select group resembled that of the guildmasters of the Vienna trades in 1742, 24% of whom are known to have been born in Vienna, 31% in the Austrian lands outside Vienna, 8% in the Bohemian lands, 2% in Hungary, 33% in the Empire outside the Monarchy, and 2% elsewhere in Europe.[51] The religion of Warehousers and Wholesalers is usually not noted, Gottlieb Paldinger (1765), 'a Lutheran from Ödenburg', being an exception. It is known, however, that Johann Fries was a Calvinist, and it is a fair assumption that the rest of the considerable Swiss contingent was. Similarly, while the French and Italian names in the list are not found in Lüthy's definitive monograph, it is plausible that some at least were of French or Swiss Protestant origin. The permission given in 1653 and 1664 for Protestant widows to continue the business of their husbands in Vienna implies that toleration was of long standing. As already noted, the edict creating the Wholesalers in 1774 explicitly included freedom of entry for foreigners and Protestants.[52] Christians, however, seem to have stuck together: none of the partners in the list is Jewish, though the Jewish inventories published by Taglicht show that the firms of Bender, Buiretti, Dohm, Hösslin & Falck, Küner & Co.,

---

[50] For numbers to 1779 see App. C, for 1800 see Kuraic, 114. Only one or two of the Warehousers and Wholesalers have entries in Wurzbach, *Biographisches Lexikon*. The fall in the number of Warehousers 1770–4 may be due to an increase in the bankruptcy rate, see below.

[51] The figures for 1742 are given by Thiel, 430 and n., but 'the rest of the Empire', printed as 45, must be 815.

[52] Ministerial opinion during the reduction of interest in 1766 was that the Vienna bankers were mostly foreign Protestants not inclined to the state, Beer, 'Staatsschulden', 23.

and Meyer Hey & Co. were all at one time or another creditors of Vienna Jews.

Family, as with the Jews, constituted an important business tie for the whole group, as the numerous examples of brothers and sons taken into partnership demonstrate. The Passy and Violand clans were, however, exceptional in providing six and four Warehousers respectively. More information is needed about links of marriage, at present known only in particular instances. Although only one name in the list, Count Rudiger Starhemberg, is explicitly aristocratic, the group as a whole is difficult to impugn as new men risen from low origins. The fact that at least fourteen were ennobled under Charles VI and Maria Theresia is indicative of acceptable social standing. Further, the Brentani Cimaroli, Fries, Fuchs, Hilleprand, Palm, Rieger, and Steiner families, to take names at random, were already armigerous, and in some instances of long descent. Christoph Bartenstein was a grandson of Maria Theresia's minister. Further investigation would probably confirm the hypothesis that an important minority of these financiers came from lesser landed or urban patriciate families, while others were of solid bourgeois stock and others again of artisan descent.[53]

Acquisition of a former Warehouser's business was an important means of entry to the corps, Castelmur, for example, succeeding to Dohm, Fux to Heller, Klinger to Crettier, Pappe to Castelmur, Petz to Passy. A firm's name, however, might continue when control altered, as happened when Christian Bartenstein took over the direction of Küner & Co. in 1778 and Johann Puthon the business of his deceased stepfather Johann Schuller in 1771. In the firms of Bozenhard, Fries, Ochs, and Peter, bookkeepers rose to be partners, and this may have been an important avenue to success for skilled clerks with little capital. The general impression given by the evidence is that there was a steady turnover of firms, and this was

---

[53] Georg Plattensteiner's marriage to the daughter of Johann Marci, and Johann Baptist Bouvard's marriage to the daughter of Claude Salliet, are examples of intermarriage. Johann Baptist Puthon was the stepson of Johann Georg Schuller. Count Rudiger Starhemberg must have belonged to the branch of the family which used this Christian name, though he is not identifiable in the table in Wurzbach, *Biographisches Lexikon*, xxxvii. 160. The ennobled families in the list are Bender, Dohm, Fries, Fuchs, Grosser, Hilleprand, Küner, Palm, Puthon, Riesch, Schwonasini, Smitmer, Trattner, Wiesenhütter. To these, Castelmur, Churfeld, and Falquet should probably be added. For Christian Bartenstein, see Arneth, 'Johann Christoph Bartenstein', *AÖG* 46 (1871) 69.

obviously linked to mortality. A father and son, or two brothers, were good for perhaps thirty or forty years of business life. The dominant firms in the later years of Charles VI thus differed from those under Joseph I, and both from those under Joseph II. Bankruptcy accentuated this discontinuity. Bankruptcy is known to have been frequent in Vienna, and the corps of Warehousers and of Wholesalers were not exempt from it.[54] The firms of Binnenfeld, Bozenhard, Passy (a family which almost made a profession of business failure), Peter, Petz, Starhemberg, Violand, and Weigl are all noted as having gone bankrupt, sometimes starting afresh in circumstances little short of disgraceful. The leading banking firms in Vienna by the early years of Joseph II—Arnstein & Eskeles, Brentani Cimaroli, Fries & Co., Ochs & Geymuller, Stametz, probably had larger funds and better business connections than their predecessors. It should not be overlooked, however, that only Arnstein & Eskeles and Stametz survived into the 1850s: and even Arnstein & Eskeles failed in 1859. Brentani Cimaroli went bankrupt in 1794, the great house of Fries & Co. in 1826, both Geymuller and Steiner in 1841.[55]

The financial resources of Warehousers and Wholesalers, relevant to the question of business survival, cannot be determined precisely, but some light is thrown on it by the statements of funds made to the Mercantile Court by applicants for entry to the two corps. Rules about the capital acceptable for various types of business in Vienna had been drawn up as early as 1734, when Charles VI's bankruptcy ordinance defined the capital for an exchange firm ('Wechsler') as 50,000–60,000 fl., for a Warehouser and general trader ('Universalhändler') as 30,000–40,000 fl., and for a lesser trader as 8,000–15,000 fl.[56] In the 1760s and 1770s the index to the records of the Mercantile Court shows that 8,000 fl. was accepted as the

---

[54] Between 1711 and 1731 there were 146 bankruptcies in the (relatively small) body of Trading Burgesses, Fajkmajer, 554.

[55] Leading private banks in Vienna in the 1850s included Arnstein & Eskeles, Königswarter, Perisutti, S. M. von Rothschild, Schnapper, Simon G. Sina, J. H. Stametz-Meyer, Wodianer, see E. März and K. Socher, 'Währung und Banken in Cisleithanien', in A. Brusatti (ed.), *Die Habsburgermonarchie 1848–1918*, i. *Die wirtschaftliche Entwicklung* (Vienna 1973) 330. They include Geymuller, but the firm had failed in 1841.

[56] Fajkmajer, 554.

fund for a Trading Burgess and 30,000 fl. for a Warehouser.[57] There are references to 60,000 fl. for an exchange house, but this requirement was evidently relaxed when 30,000 fl. was stipulated for entry to the College of Wholesalers in 1774.[58]

Funds are stated by 34 applicants to the Mercantile Court in App. C. Seventeen declared 30,000–39,000 fl., four 40,000–49,000 fl., seven 50,000–59,000 fl., one 60,000–69,000 fl., and five 100,000 fl. or more, but less than 200,000 fl. It seems likely that traders made application to the court as soon as their capital approached the statutory amount. Insufficient capital could be made up by persuading someone else to act as surety. Thus Augustin Castelmur in 1762 showed a fund of 55,000 fl., 30,000 fl. of which was a *Caution* from Ignaz von Böck. Wolfgang Heilmann in 1767 had 21,402 fl. of his own and 10,000 fl. *Caution* from Johann Heinrich Stametz. Franz Klinger in 1771 had 26,844 fl. property and a *Caution* from 'Mathaus' Wöss of 3,156 fl. to make 30,000 fl., and so on.[59] These statements of funds, however, do not close the question of capital resources. In 1768 Joseph von Bender, when reconstructing the firm inherited from his father in the previous year, stated that he could if necessary provide the 150,000 fl. required himself.[60] Johann Fries put a nominal 45,000 fl. into his banking partnership with Jakob Gontard in 1766, but in fact 300,000 fl. Joseph von Fuchs had 100,000 fl. invested in the Schwechat cotton-factory alone in 1769.[61] Franz Klinger, as already noted, had only 26,844 fl. in 1771, but declared trading property of 103,969 fl. in 1782.[62] Johann Puthon, whose fund was 37,218 fl. on application in 1774, had 162,738 fl. in 1780.[63] Erhard von Riesch was not only a substantial banker but a large

[57] Merk. Gericht Prot. B. 6/2, fos. 257 (Joseph Crettier, 8,000 fl. fund for a Trading Burgess, 1780); 431 (Johann von Fuchs, 30,000 fl. fund for a Warehouser, 1765); 379 (Wolfgang Heilmann adds 10,000 fl. by surety to his 21,402 fl. when applying to succeed his grandfather as a Warehouser, 1767). These are only instances: the figures 8,000 fl. and 30,000 fl. recur in this source.

[58] As explained above. Instances of a 60,000 fl. fund for an exchange-house are 'Steinmetz' (viz. Johann Stametz) in 1761, Kuraic, 39; Fries & Gontard in 1766, August Graf von Fries, *Die Grafen von Fries* (2nd edn. Dresden 1903), 128–30; and Castellini & Peter in 1772, Merk. Gericht Prot. B. 6/2, fo. 192.

[59] Merk. Gericht Prot. B. 6/2, fos. 183, 379, 219.

[60] Ibid., fo. 101.

[61] Ibid., fo. 1021 (Fuchs). For Fries, see below.

[62] Ibid., fo. 220.

[63] Ibid., fo. 134.

Saxon landowner. The widow of Johann Georg Schuller kept
120,000 fl. invested in the Sassin cotton-factory in 1770, and must
have had substantial additional resources.[64] Partnership could also
strengthen individual funds. Thus the firm of Castellini & Peter had
a trading capital of 60,000 fl. in 1772 supplied by two partnership
shares of 50,000 fl. and 10,000 fl.; Falquet & Schmuck in 1768 a
capital of 46,000 fl. (40,000 fl. and 6,000 fl.); Pappe & Gerhardi
in 1776 a capital of 30,000 fl. in two equal shares; Rieger in 1780
a capital of 160,000 fl. in two shares of 60,000 and one of
40,000 fl.[65] Such arrangements were particularly evident in factories, which are discussed next. The general impression given is none
the less that, with a handful of exceptions, the Christian financiers
of Vienna were not well off in absolute terms (100,000 fl. after all,
was only about £12,000) and certainly much poorer than, say, the
substantial bankers and merchants of Frankfurt am Main, among
whom estates at death of 200,000 fl. and over were not uncommon
from the mid eighteenth century, and estates of over 1m. fl. not
unknown by the 1780s.[66] They bear even less comparison with the
oligarchs who ran the General Farm of the French customs, the
Gores, Salvadors, and Van Necks of London, or the Cliffords and
Hopes of Amsterdam. To find Austrian equivalents to such foreign
fortunes it is necessary to look to the higher aristocracy and the
church.[67] This relative financial weakness helps to explain why taxfarming in Austria was limited in time and scope.[68] It suggests also
that there was a shortage of risk capital, and is consistent with contemporary statements that Austrian rates of interest were generally
high.[69]

Before considering some of the leading financial houses in more
detail, connections with trade and industry will be briefly discussed.
Around 1760, the firms making and receiving foreign payments for

[64] Ibid., fo. 1061. For Riesch, see below.

[65] Ibid., fos. 192, 449, 151, 971.

[66] See the chronological list of inventories at death in A. Dietz, *Frankfurter Han-
delsgeschichte* (Frankfurt am Main 1910–25) iv/2, app. I. The inventories at death of
the Vienna Warehousers and Wholesalers are not in the HHSA, the Wiener Stadt-
und Landesarchiv, or the Niederösterreichisches Landesarchiv. Their discovery
would certainly help the discussion. It must not be overlooked, however, that Fries
secured exemption from judicial inventory of his estate (see below) and others may
have done the same.

[67] See Chs. 4–5.

[68] See ii, Ch. 2.

[69] See pp. 51 and ii. 59.

the bureau of trade (*Commercien-Directorium*) included Bender, Fachiny, Heller, Küner, Erhard Riesch, Smitmer, and Stametz, all of them Vienna Warehousers. None appears amongst the fifty-six domestic and thirty-six foreign firms supplying and purchasing textiles for the bureau.[70] This implies a separation of finance from manufacture, a conclusion supported by the absence of the Warehousers, with the exception of Paul Fachiny, from a list drawn up by the council of trade in 1771 of manufacturers who had received government loans since the mid 1750s.[71] But this evidence taken alone is misleading. While it is probably true that most Warehousers and Wholesalers were primarily involved in banking and government finance, rather than being long-term investors in trade and industry, this did not preclude a minority, at least, from investing relatively substantial amounts in industry. Banking itself, in any case, could and did take the form of negotiating bills arising from manufacture, as is seen next. A hard and fast line, therefore, cannot be drawn. It is clear that the houses of Bozenhard, Fachiny, Falquet, Fries, Fuchs, Gaillard, Labhard, Müller, Puthon, Riesch, Schuller, Schwarzleithner, Steiner, and Weinbrenner all had investments of one sort or another in factories, though of varying scope and success.[72] The last firm in the list in App. C., Joseph Anton Zehendner & Co., also had connections with manufacturing industry, but of a rather different type. 'Joseph Anton Zehendner von Reisdorff' was a banker in Prague, whose firm had a branch in Vienna. In December 1767, together with two partners, one from Prague, the other from Augsburg, he was put in charge of a 'Privileged Warehouse for Hereditary Lands Manufactures'.[73] The scope of the enterprise becomes clearer from a petition which the firm made to the empress in March 1776.[74] His co-petitioner was the Prague firm

---

[70] Names taken from HKA Hs. 752, 'Commerciencassa' ledger 1758–60. The *Commercien-Directorium* operated from within the *Directorium in Publicis et Cameralibus*, see Ch. 9.

[71] HKA NÖ Kommerz, rote Nr. 48, no 105 ex Jan. 1771, one of several such schedules compiled by the *Kommerzienhofrat*.

[72] See App. C. Fries, Riesch, and Steiner are separately discussed below. Cf. Degelmann's statement that the government tried to oblige Warehousers to support factories, Přibram, *Gewerbepolitik*, 239–40 nn.

[73] Merk. Gericht Prot. B. 6/2, fo. 1195, 24 Dec. 1767. The enterprise and its failure are referred to briefly in Přibram, 192, 200. For the more successful Moravian *Lehenbank*, see App. B.

[74] This episode is reconstructed from HKA Staatsschuldenakten, rote Nr. 162, fos. 870–81, 970.

of 'Johann Georg Pradatsch Widow Son & Co.', which had evidently replaced the other two partners.[75] 'For the good of the Fatherland', they explained, they financed large commissions of cloths, glass, grain, hats, linens, stockings, wool, and so on for export. Some manufacturers fulfilled export orders of 200,000 fl. a year. But the manufacturers themselves were poor, and without the bankers' help would have to cut back production and probably starve. The bankers' activities, in turn, depended on being allowed to encash foreign bills drawn on Vienna at the bureau for cameral revenues ('Cameral Zahlamt') in Prague. This practice was at least 100 years old. But it had recently been stopped by government order, after Zunterer & Pless of Prague had encashed bills drawn on the Warehousers Schwarzleitner & Co. of Vienna. Schwarzleitners were unable to pay, and the *Hofkammer* was left holding the protested bills. Treasury resentment is perhaps understandable. But the petitioners said that unless the ban were removed they would be forced to turn from trade to speculation, with dire consequences for the manufacturers.

In stately Austrian fashion, the matter was referred to the *Hofkammer* and the Bohemian and Austrian Chancellery, which in turn consulted the *Gubernien* of Bohemia and Lower Austria and the Burgesses and Wholesalers of Vienna. In the end, after a proposal was rejected to allow only the two firms of Pradatsch and Zehender to have encashment facilities in Prague, it was decided to resume encashment for Prague houses who could find a guarantee house in Vienna to pay protested bills. Over the next months, Johann Georg Schuller & Co., who already acted as guarantor for both Pradatsch and Zehender, confirmed that they would continue to do so. Johann Heinrich Stametz of Vienna said that he would act for the two Prague firms of the widow of Simon Neustadl and her son Simka Neustadl (hence a Jewish house), and of Thum & Co. In January 1777 Küner & Co. in Vienna agreed to act for Zunterer & Pless, the original cause of the trouble. This fascinating episode in the circular flow of credit, which illustrates government revenue collection acting as a primitive banking system, and hence supplementing the weakness of private enterprise, closes on a suitably ironic note with

---

[75] This firm appears in the business legers of Charles Proli of Antwerp, who is discussed in the next chapter, in the early 1760s. It becomes 'Widow Pradatsch' in that source in 1764.

the admission as a Warehouser in 1782 of Anton Schwarzleitner, the son of the insolvent Warehouser of 1774.[76]

An important minority of these financial firms will now be considered in more detail. Their names recur in many of the following chapters. Those of Hilleprand and Palm were of especial importance under Charles VI, but continued into the early years of Maria Theresia's reign; their disappearance, it can be argued, opened the way for the spectacular career of Johann Fries. The remaining firms which will be discussed are those of Bender, Küner, Riesch, Smitmer, Steiner, and Wiesenhütter. It was shown above that in the early years of Charles VI's reign, Hillebrand & Isenflam and Palm Brothers were two of the Warehouser firms competing with Jewish houses for government financial business. Johann Jacob Isenflam's house was among the earliest registrations with the Mercantile Court, those of 1725. He was a partner with 'Bender', presumably P. J. Bender, from 1728 to 1732. He was still a Warehouser in 1740, and had connections with the banking firm of Wiesenhütter in Frankfurt.[77] Hillebrand, more correctly Hilleprand, is a family which was already in government service. Its head throughout this period was probably Peter Anton Hilleprand von Prandau (1678–1767), created a baron in 1704. He was from a family of Tyrol officials first ennobled in the sixteenth century. His father Peter, confirmed as a knight in 1674, was a councillor of the Bavarian *Hofkammer*. Peter Anton was a Councillor of the Vienna *Hofkammer*, Director of the *Universal Bancalität*, and ended his career, full of years and honour, as Vice-President of the *Hofkammer* (from 1745) and co-director of the Cameral Debts office of 1748. His brothers were probably Johann Georg Hilleprand von Prandau, created a Bohemian knight in 1730, administrator of Vienna City Bank revenues in Bohemia, and a member of the *Repraesentation und Kammer* there in 1754; the Warehouser Maximilian Emanuel Hilleprand von Prandau, also made a Bohemian knight in 1730; and Karl Ludwig Hilleprand, a judge of the *Reichsofrat* (1717), created a baron in 1734, Austrian representative at the imperial coronations

[76] Merk. Gericht Prot. B. 6/2, fo. 1135, 18 Jan. 1782. The Prague firm of Thum was not 'Thun' as in the *Alm. gén. des marchands*, see n. 2 above.

[77] For this connecton see Dietz, iv/1. 383. For Isenflam's registration, etc. see Merk. Gericht. Prot. B. 6/1, fo. 527, where 'Küner' is stated as his partner 1728–32 and fo. 209, where 'Bender' is.

of 1742 and 1745.[78] Maximilian, besides being a Warehouser, was Director (effectively liquidator) of the defunct Oriental Company from 1731, a *Hofkammer* Councillor, and an important negotiator of Habsburg loans in the closing years of Charles VI's reign.[79]

The Hilleprands were an official family with financial connections. The Palms were a financial family with official connections. The firm of Palm Brothers ('Gebrüder Palm') was perhaps the most effective rival to Jewish financial resources by 1740. Taking only its position from the 1730s, in 1734 it remitted 400,000 fl. to Frankfurt for the Austrian government and lent it 1.3m. fl. In 1735 it was appointed to administer the royal copper revenues and in 1737 handled service of the £320,000 English loan charged on them.[80] It advanced 150,000 fl. on the royal lordship of Pardubitz in Bohemia in 1740, and had lent nearly 300,000 fl. on royal estates in Hungary by 1747. It lent 490,500 fl. in anticipation of the English and Dutch subsidies in 1743. In 1746 the government owed it 343,000 fl.[81] But who were the brothers Palm? This question is difficult to answer authoritatively. The Palm genealogy is extremely confused in the secondary sources, and the firm is usually referred to in primary ones simply as 'Gebrüder Palm'. The most probable reconstruction is as follows (see also Fig. 3). Johann Heinrich I von Palm (1632–84) of the imperial city of Esslingen, who was of Swiss noble descent, had four sons: Johann David (d. 1721), Johann Heinrich II (died by 1735), Franz Johann, and Jonathan (1671–1740). The 'brothers Palm' of the later part of Charles VI's reign are probably the three sons of Johann Heinrich II: Barons

[78] Megerle von Mühlfeld; J. Siebmacher, *Grosses und allgemeines Wappenbuch. Böhmischer Adel*, rev. Count R. J. Meraviglia-Crivelli (Nuremburg 1886) s.n. Hilleprand von Prandau; Wurzbach, *Biographisches Lexikon*, xxiii. 190; and O. von Gschliesser, *Der Reichshofrat* (Vienna 1942) 389–90. *Khev.-Metsch*, 28 May 1767 records the 'able and honourable' Peter Anton's death, aged 89.

[79] See ii, Ch. 9 for his loan negotiations; *Court Cal.* 1740, 1748 for his Oriental Company position.

[80] See Mensi, 321, 363, 399, 618. He refers only to 'Gebrüder Palm'. Srbik, *Der staatliche Exporthandel*, 411 shows that Franz Gottlieb and Leopold Karl von Palm were made copper administrators on 12 Oct. 1735. They had held contracts for the sale of state copper to Germany as early as 1709, ibid.

[81] Mensi, 319 (pledge of lordship of Pardubitz for three years at 6%); HHSA Alte Kabinettsakten, Karton 6, no. 11/27, 160,000 fl. due to Franz Gottlieb von Palm on Comorn lordships and 133,000 fl. on Lipschau lordship, July 1747; HKA Prandau Akten, Konvolut 15, loans of 172,000 fl. in anticipation of the English subsidy and 318,500 fl. in anticipation of the Dutch subsidy of 1743; ibid., Konvolut 21, no. 21, 343,595 fl. due to Palm Brothers Oct. 1746.

Johann Heinrich III (d. 1744), Franz Gottlieb (d. 1749), and Leopold Carl. The concession of the copper revenue in 1735 was, however, to the last two only. The senior line of the family continued through their uncle Johann David, who distinguished himself at the siege of Vienna in 1683, was made a Lower Austrian knight in 1711, and was an important official in the War Commissariat. He must have made a huge fortune out of this, since Carl Joseph (d. 1769), the eldest of his six children, was Austrian Resident in London in the 1720s, and successively envoy in Rome, Hanover, and Regensburg; was made a baron in 1729, a count in 1750; and had revenues of over 100,000 fl. a year in Bohemia. His son Karl, in turn, was made a prince in 1783, and dissipated his inheritance. More modest lines descended through Johann David's brother.

In the earliest index to the proceedings of the Vienna Mercantile Court, 'Palm Brothers', Privileged Warehousers, are found registering their firm's name on 19 April 1725. They stated that, by a contract of 19 April 1723, Franz Gottlieb Palm had been appointed to run the business for three years, a term which must later have been extended. The contract of 1723 was made between Franz Gottlieb von Palm, Jonathan von Palm, Franz von Palm, Carl Joseph von Palm, and Johann Heinrich Palm. If the genealogy constructed above is correct, these were Franz Gottlieb's father and two uncles, and his first cousin. The only subsequent entry is dated 15 July 1751, when Palm Brothers reported the death on 4 December 1749 of Franz Gottlieb, Baron von Palm. With his brother Leopold Carl, Baron von Palm, it was stated, he had run the firm, but no dates for this are given. It was now to be administered under his own name by a new Warehouser, Johann Heinrich Stametz, with 100,000 fl. Palm capital and 20,000 fl. of his own.[82]

---

[82] Merk. Gericht Prot. B. 6/1, fo. 32. For Stametz, who was Swiss, see App. C. The Palm genealogy is reconstructed here from the same sources as for Hilleprand, supplemented by H. F. von Ehrenkrook *et al.* (eds.), *Genealogisches Handbuch des Adels* (Glücksburg and Limburg 1951–75) xvi (*Freiherrenstand*, 1957), which gives the descendants of Jonathan Palm (only). The most helpful source is Megerle von Mühlfeld, whose citation for 1735 (*Reichsfreiherren*) makes it clear that the brothers Johann Heinrich, Franz Gottlieb, and Leopold Carl von Palm were the children of the deceased Johann Heinrich von Palm, who was the brother of Johann David, Franz Johann, and Jonathan. Their father was Johann Heinrich (I). Baron Franz Gottlieb Palm d. 4 Dec. 1749; by his will dated 12 Nov. 1748 he constituted his brother Baron Leopold Carl Palm as his heir, to hold as trustee for the five children of Johann Heinrich (III). I am indebted to the Allgemeines Verwaltungsarchiv, Vienna, for sending me a microfilm of this badly burnt document. For Prince Karl Palm see p. 113 n.

The firm of Bender offers an element of continuity with one of those just discussed, since their address in 1774 was 'Kohlmarkt, dans la maison du Baron de Brandau'. The firm was started by Philipp Jacob Bender, created 'Edler von Bender und Leitha' in 1745. His son Joseph Carl was made a baron in 1770 'for encouraging trade and credit, farming the theatre, and bettering the national taste'.[83] Philipp Jacob Bender was probably the Bender who was in partnership with Johann Jacob Isenflam from 1728 to 1732, as noted above. From 1732 to 1736 he was a partner of Jacob Küner, who is discussed next. A Gaius(?) Bender was the third partner. Philipp Jacob Bender started to trade on his own as a Warehouser on 1 October 1736; he then stated that he had been running the firm of Johann Georg Helvetius, which had registered in 1725 but about which nothing further is known. The compatibility of this with the other information is unclear. Philipp Jacob Bender married Susanna Mühl in 1737. In 1751 he took in as partner his brother-in-law Johann Carl Mühl.[84] Von Bender, as he had then become, was owed 172,774 fl. by the government in 1746. In 1747 he was concerned with Küner & Co. in selling government copper. He was a correspondent in the 1750s of James Dormer of Antwerp.[85] In 1763 he was in partnership with Johann Christian Mühl, perhaps a nephew, as 'von Bender und Compagnie'. In 1765 they transferred the firm to Bender's only son Joseph Carl, but Mühl then left, and the firm became 'von Bender und Sohn'. Philipp Jacob died on 11 July 1767. His son continued the firm under the same style but in 1768 associated with it Johann Ander Kutzer and Franz, Baron Stegnere. The capital fund, they stated, could be proved by each associate showing his share, or by Bender showing that he alone could put up the whole 150,000 fl. involved. The firm is in the *Court*

---

[83] The titles of Philipp Jacob, described as royal councillor ('k.k. Rath'), in 1745 and of Joseph Carl in 1770 are given in Megerle von Mühlfeld under 'Ritter' and 'Freiherren' respectively. The firm's address in 1774 is given in the *Alm. gén. des marchands*, see n. 2 above.
[84] The details of the early partnership are given in Merk. Gericht Prot. B. 6/1, fos. 118 (Bender) and 209 (Küner).
[85] HKA Prandau Akten, Konvolut 21, no. 12, P. J. Bender was owed 172,774 fl. at the 'Schulden Cassa', Oct. 1746; HHSA Alte Kabinettsakten, Karton 6, no. 11/27, 50,000 fl. due to Küner and Bender on copper; Stad Antwerpen Archief, Ins. Boed. 1119 (James Dormer's ledger 1746–56), fo. 149, account for Bender & Co. at Vienna.

Calendar for 1779 as 'Joseph Carl, Freiherr von Bender & Comp.' but according to Ander Kutzer, who in 1778 applied to be a Wholesaler, he had run it himself for several years.[86]

The firm of Küner & Co., found more than once alongside that of Bender, was established by Jacob von Küner of the imperial city of Memmingen (in the bishopric of Augsburg), who settled in Vienna in 1732. He was a partner of Philipp Bender to 1736. From an unstated subsequent date to the end of 1747 he was in partnership with Wolfgang Riesch (see below), then from 18 May 1747 with Eberhard Friedrich Wagner and Jacob Zollikhoffer. He had an estate, Künersberg, outside Memmingen, and in 1745 established a ceramics factory there. He had a long, if relatively modest, involvement in government finance. As early as 1739 the government owed him 300,000 fl.[87] He was assessed at 6,000 fl. in the *Subsidium Praesentaneum* in 1741 and again in 1748.[88] In 1747 he was made an imperial knight as 'von Künersberg'.[89] In the same year he contracted with the government to handle the Italian copper sales until 1759. The deposit required was 330,000 fl.[90] Küner was also involved with Baron Aguilar in remittances to the Austrian Netherlands in 1747–8.[91] He died in 1765. He left two daughters, who continued the firm as 'Küner & Co.' The business was run from the 'maison du comte de Weissenwolf'. Christian Bartenstein was added as a partner on 4 July 1776. In 1778 the firm was evidently dissolved, but then

---

[86] The partnerships 1763–8 are shown in Merk. Gericht Prot. B. 6/2, fos. 44 and 101. Kutzer's application is in HKA NÖ Kommerz, rote Nr. 150 (Bender), no. 2 ex Juli 1778. It is not clear if it succeeded. I am indebted to Wirklicher Amtsrat Günter Schmidt for this reference.

[87] According to Mahringer (n. 48 above). The firm does not appear in the index to Mensi. See Merk. Gericht Prot. B. 6/1, fo. 209 for the partnerships in the text.

[88] HKA Prandau Akten, Konvolut 23, no. 3 (1741); Konvolut 3, no. 2 (1748).

[89] Megerle von Mühfeld under 'Ritter': 'Kunner von Kunnersperg, Wechsel-Negoziant'.

[90] HKA Hs. 280 under Mar. 1757, 'Künnert und Co.' have the contract for sales of Italian copper until 1759; for the deposit see HHSA Alte Kabinettsakten, Karton 6, no. 11/27. Mikoletzky, 'Schweizer Händler', 160 describes the firm as 'Kühner und Goll'. This was perhaps Jakob Goll, who died in Vienna in 1753, and was the uncle of Johann Goll of Verbrugge & Goll, Dietz, iv/2. 653. His father was Johann Goll II of Frankfurt, not (Mikoletzky) Franz Heinrich Goll, a Vienna 'Bankmann' of the later 17th c. There is no Goll in Merk. Gericht Prot.

[91] See p. 146.

continued by Bartenstein, who, however, went bankrupt in 1788.[92]

There were two Warehousers named Riesch, Erhard Riesch (1754) and Wolfgang von Riesch (1754 and 1763). In the *Court Calendar* for 1770 Wolfgang von Riesch again appears as a Warehouser, this time trading 'under the style of Erhard Riesch'.[93] The firm of Erhard Riesch was the young Count Ludwig Zinzendorf's banker in 1752. It was one of the bankers used by the bureau of trade in 1759–60, and appears again in the ledger of Charles Proli of Antwerp for 1763, making remittances for the Company of Trieste and Fiume.[94] Erhard Riesch died in May 1753. His firm was taken over by his cousin and universal heir, Wolfgang von Riesch (1712–76) from Lindau in Swabia, who had been a partner since 1747, and before that was a partner of Jacob Küner. Wolfgang was made an imperial knight in 1747 and a baron in 1766. He was a councillor of the emperor Francis Stephen. He was a Calvinist, and became a great landowner in Upper Lusatia in Saxony, where he purchased six knightly estates in 1757. He was one of a partnership of three which administered the cotton factory at Schwechat. When this partnership ended in 1769, he left 100,000 fl., subsequently reduced to 40,000 fl., invested in the factory. He was also involved from 1753 until 1768 in the royal 'privilegirte Dratzug Fabrik' in Vienna together with Bernhard von Falquet and Joseph Schwarzleitner & Son.[95]

The firm of Smitmer ('Gebrüder Smitmer') was established by Paul

---

[92] For Küner's death, notified to the Vienna Mercantile Court on 20 June 1765, and the subsequent partnership arrangements, see Merk. Gericht Prot. B. 6/2, fos. 108, 245–50. For Christian Bartenstein see p. 157, and for his bankruptcy, H. C. Peyer, *Von Handel und Bank im alten Zürich* (Zürich 1968) 155. It is not clear, however, if he was then still trading as Küner & Co.

[93] In the *Alm. gén. des marchands* of 1774 the firm is noted as 'Banquiers, Rue des Théatins'.

[94] HKA Hs. 752, fo. 58, small account for Erhard; Stad Antwerpen Archief, Ins. Boed. 1871, Charles Proli's ledger for 1763 at fo. 36; Pettenegg, *Zinzendorf*, 110. Wolfgang Riesch's partnership with Jacob Küner ended on 28 Apr. 1747, Merk. Gericht Prot. B. 6/1, fo. 209. He invested 60,000 fl. in his cousin Erhard's firm on 12 May 1747, ibid., fo. 710. He notified Erhard's death and his own succession on 18 Mary 1753, ibid., fo. 716.

[95] Megerle von Mühlfeld under 'Ritter' and 'Freiherren'; H. Schlechte, *Die Staatsreform in Kursachsen 1762–1763* (Berlin 1958) 16 n.; Merk. Gericht Prot. B. 6/2, fo. 1021, 30 March 1769. For Riesch's partnership in the wire-drawing factory see App. C, under Falquet, also W. Zorn, *Handels- und Industriegeschichte Bayerisch-Schwabens 1648–1870* (Augsburg 1961) 83. Zorn shows that Riesch came from Lindau and m. a member of the d'Orville banking family.

Smitmer of Rovereto (1663–1736), who was apprenticed as a gold-smith in Innsbruck, subsequently studied his trade in Paris, became jeweller to the Austrian Court in 1713, and was ennobled in 1719. His two sons were Franz Michael and Jacob Smitmer. The elder followed his father as Court Jeweller. He and his brother were made imperial knights in 1740 as 'Edler von Smitmer'. They appear in the *Court Calendar* for 1740 as Warehousers. In that year the Calendar lists only one Court Supplier ('Hofbefreiter'), Wenzelli & Co., whose founder, Philip Wenzell, financier for Charles VI's coronation, agent at Vienna for Genoese bankers, ennobled in 1715 as 'von Wenzelli', died in 1741. In 1748 his solitary place in the *Court Calendar* was occupied by Smitmer Brothers, who were no longer Warehousers, and it is likely that they remained Court Suppliers, though there are no further entries for them.[96] The firm was owed 10,000 fl. by the government in 1746. It acted as Vienna correspondent for Charles Proli of Antwerp from the late 1750s, and as agents for Genoa bankers raising loans for the imperial court from the 1740s to the 1780s.[97] Jacob von Smitmer, who became a Privileged Wholesaler in 1774, died in 1778. His brother Franz Michael continued the firm, associating his cousin Jakob with him. Franz Michael died in 1782, leaving three sons. The firm was still in business as Smitmer Brothers in the 1790s, though no indication of its capital resources then or earlier is available.[98]

The 'Melchior Steiner' in App. C was one of a number of Melchior Steiners from Winterthur associated with Habsburg finance in the seventeenth and eighteenth centuries. Their identical nomenclature is not helpful.[99] The first (1630–90) was involved in promoting sales of Austrian salt to Switzerland and south-west Germany. His

---

[96] For their title of 'von Smitmer' see Megerle von Mühlfeld. The firm's name is often misspelt in the sources, e.g. Smitner, Schmitmer, Schmidmeyr. Philipp Wenzell must be the Arnoldo Filippo Wenzel & Co. who were agents for Giacomo Durazzo and Giovanni Cambiaso of Genoa in 1723–7 and 1743–5, the latter date indicating continuity of the firm after Philipp Wenzell's death, see Felloni, *Gli investimenti finanziari*, 100. It acted in 1737 as agents for the sale of Prince Eugene's pictures after his death, Nicholas Henderson, *Prince Eugen of Savoy* (1964) 302.

[97] The debt is stated in HKA Prandau Akten, Konvolut 21 no. 12, Oct. 1746. For the firm's connections with Charles Proli see Ch. 8; for its agency for Genoese bankers see Felloni, 89, data for 1743–5, 1764–6, and 1784–6. In 1764–6 it acted for Merello & Carbone of Genoa, in 1784–6 for Giuseppi Negrotto there, ibid. 100.

[98] Merk. Gericht. Prot. B. 6/2, fos. 1101–4. The first volume of the index, B. 6/1, has a blank entry under 'Gebrüder Smitmer'.

[99] Mikoletzky, 'Schweizer Händler', 158, 160–3, traces the various Steiners. For the family see also Peyer, 111, 127–30, 185–6.

great-grandson was trading in Vienna at least as early as 1763, and established a swordblade-factory ('Klingen Fabrik'), which was specifically referred to when he sought, and was given, entry to the corps of Warehousers in April 1768. In September 1768 he registered a ten-year partnership with Johann Christian Schuster, as 'Melchior Steiner et Comp.'; the firm, not listed among the bankers of Vienna in 1774, was sufficiently important by 1779 to share with Fries the receipt of an important war loan raised in Holland. In June 1781 Steiner's partnership with Schuster was dissolved, and a new one established with Thadae[us] Schlosser. Melchior Steiner junior, a nephew, entered the business in September 1784; Melchior senior died in May 1786.[100] The new Melchior Steiner (1763–1837) went on to become a knight in 1811, a director of the National Bank in 1816, and a member of the inner committee 1825–37; but his firm, squeezed by government financial policies and Rothschild competition, went bankrupt (13 July 1841) shortly after his death.

The last but one of the prominent Warehouser firms discussed here, 'Wiesenhütter & Co.', appears in the *Court Calendar* for 1740, having been started in the previous year by Franz Wiesenhütter (1720–86), the eldest of four children of Johann Friedrich Wiesenhütter of Frankfurt am Main. Johann had been in business as a banker with his brother Andreas since 1719, was ennobled in 1728 as 'von Wiesenhütten', and lent his son 100,000 fl. to start a banking company in Vienna. Franz Wiesenhütter, who had certainly not arrived at years of discretion, soon got into deep water. In 1743 he became a Catholic, married Maria Elisabethe, the daughter of Baron Bartenstein, and was made a Bohemian baron as 'von Wiesenhütten'.[101] In the same year he lent in anticipation of the English subsidy. This denoted his entry to a wider field. He became a councillor of the *Hofkammer*, and on 12 December 1744, at his

---

[100] For his Warehouser status dated 11 Apr. 1768 see Merk. Gericht Prot. B. 6/2, fo. 1035; he was freed of all save registration tax on 8 Feb. 1763. The subsequent changes in partnership are given ibid. and at fos. 1037–8. His firm is not in the list of Vienna bankers in the *Alm. gén. des marchands* of 1774; for its receipt, with Fries & Co., of the load for f 5m. in 1779 see ii, Ch. 9, n. 63. Mikoletzky, 160, wrongly states that Melchior Steiner did not found his own firm until 1780.

[101] For Franz Wiesenhutter's family, see Dietz, iv/1. 383–8; for his career, Arneth, *Gesch. Mar. Ther.* iv. 81–2; Beer, 'Die Staatsschulden', 77–87. For the family titles, see Megerle von Mühlfeld, ii. 491. Wiesenhütter had two rich brothers. His sister married Johann von Olenschlager, a banker in Frankfurt.

own suggestion, was put in charge of all government credit, and of the quicksilver and copper revenues. Despite his attempt to tie the government down with a careful list of conditions, he was not able to dominate the impossible financial situation. He tried hard to do so. In 1745 he claimed to have lent 2,685,007 fl. in anticipation of military funds for 1746, and a further 1,065,116 fl. on cameral funds.[102] In 1746 he paid interest on 2.5m. fl. Bohemian debts, remitted 100,000 fl. to Deutz & Co. in Amsterdam, and so on. By December 1746 he had lent 10.7m. fl. in anticipation of the English subsidies, and was still owed 3.1m. fl. In September 1746, however, he resigned. The scale of his operations was obviously too large for either his experience or his resources. He went bankrupt in 1746, and again at Easter 1747. He was briefly *Stadthauptmann* of Trieste (1749–50), but then retired from public life, dying in 1786 with a dubious title, 'Count von Sieciechow'. He left a daughter, Baroness von Mark, and an estate of only 42,991 fl.[103] Wiesenhütter is of interest less for his somewhat comic pretensions than as epitomizing a premature attempt to introduce a 'single banker' who would do all, or most of, the government's financial business. The disastrous failure of the attempt cannot have helped his father-in-law's political standing. The next such experiment, this time a successful one, was with Johann Fries, whose patron was the shrewd and wily Kaunitz, a man accustomed to backing winners.

The firm of Johann Fries, 'Freiherr von Friess & Co. 1153 Unter Breunerstrasse' as it appears in the *Court Calendar* for 1779, was responsible for a range and scale of official finance and contracting unknown since the days of Samuel Oppenheimer.[104] Fries (1719–85) came of a Calvinist Swiss patriciate family which in vari-

---

[102] See HKA Hoffinanzakten, Protocoll 1197 (index vol.) for Wiesenhütter and the 1743 subsidy; HHSA Alte Kabinettsakten, Karton 13, 22 Dec. 1745, for his loans. In the chronological journal to the Hoffinanzakten for 1745, he is on nearly every page, as assignee. For his Instruction of 12 Dec. 1744 see ÖZV (1925) 5–11 they were based on W.'s conditions of 26 Nov. printed ibid. 1–4.

[103] HKA Prandau Akten, Konvolut 10, no. 19, Wiesenhütter pays interest on 2.5m. fl. Bohemian obligations and remits 100,000 fl. to Deutz; Beer, 'Die Staatsschulden', 85–6 for his advances against the English subsidy; Dietz, loc. cit. for his death and estate. A detailed exposition of his activities is lacking. It is clear, however that the revenues on which his repayments were assigned came in too slowly to allow him to pay his own creditors.

[104] The firm appears in the list of Privileged Warehousers in the *Court Calendar* as 'Johann Friess' (1754), 'Johann Freiherr von Friess' (1763), 'Freiherr von Friess & Co.' (1770, 1779). In his patents of nobility up to 1783 the banker's name was written Friesz, and he sometimes used this spelling himself.

ous branches was of importance in Berne, Basle, Mühlhausen, and Solothurn.[105] His father Johann Jakob (1685–1759), was the eldest son of Philipp Jakob Fries (1658–1746), burgomaster of Mühlhausen in the years 1742–46.[106] Johann in 1744 entered the 'English commissariat' charged with supplying the 'pragmatic army' of Austrian, Dutch, English, and Hanoverian troops in the Low Countries. He must quickly have made his mark, since he was asked in 1748 to go to London to negotiate for a stipulated £100,000 subsidy that the English govenment was refusing to pay. Fries's mission, which lasted a year, was successful. The English government paid up in March 1749. The empress, impressed, summoned him to Vienna. He limited himself at first to a Warehouser's privilege (1752).[107] From April 1752 he was responsible for marketing part of the state's silver thalers, and made large profits for the government, and for himself.[108] In the Seven Years War he handled receipt of French subsidies, and of Belgian and Italian loans and taxes to a total of nearly 45m. fl.[109] He undertook a secret mission

---

[105] Johann Fries, 11 May 1719–19 June 1785. There is a rather imprecise notice in Wurzbach, apparently based on the recitals in Fries's successive patents of nobility; a much fuller account by G. Otruba in *NDB*; further information in Mikoletzky, 'Schweizer Händler', 169–72. H. Matis, 'Die Grafen von Fries. Aufstieg und Untergang einer Unternehmerfamilie', *Tradition*, 4 (1967) 484–96 follows Otruba and Mikoletzky closely. All three draw, though not always with sufficient attention, on the important monograph by August Graf von Fries.

[106] Matis mistakenly assigns Philipp Jakob's dates and office to his son Johann Jakob, Johann's father. Wurzbach says that Johann Fries was burgomaster of Zürich before 1744; there was in fact no connection with the Fries family of Zürich, as August Graf von Fries, 65, points out. Lüthy, *Banque protestante*, ii. 75 makes the same error.

[107] For the subsidy, see ii, Ch. 5. The date of his settlement in Vienna is probably 1750. He was given permission to be a Warehouser on 23 Dec. 1751, August Graf von Fries, 60, 101, and registered with the Mercantile Court on 1 May 1752 as 'Johannes Friess', stating that his servant Johann Georg Haas could sign in his absence, Merk. Gericht Prot. B. 6/1, fo. 401.

[108] Fries's coinage activities, summarized by Otruba and Matis, are documented in Peez–Raudnitz, *Geschichte des Maria-Theresien-Thalers*. Fries put to Count Rudolf Chotek the project of selling silver thalers to the coinage-starved Near East, ibid. 48. Fries's instructions to sell coins at a premium to 'Turks and merchants' were dated 13 Apr. 1752, ibid. 40. From 1752 to 1763 he sold 8,027,328 thalers, just under half the total struck, providing the silver for 3m. himself, ibid. 42–4. The net profit on his sales was 1,225,049 fl., of which he took 410,093 fl. To 1767, the state realized a gain of 1,191,279 fl., August Graf von Fries, 137. The trade attracted German competitors, and became steadily less profitable. Fries's contract was renewed for ten years (30 June 1766), but at its expiry his monopoly lapsed, Peez–Raudnitz, 47, 69.

[109] See ii, Ch. 4 for Fries's payments. Otruba, followed by Matis, erroneously says that the French subsidies alone came to 45m. fl.

about subsidies to Paris and Brussels for Kaunitz during four months of 1757. He and his friends made loans to the *Directorium* during the war. He personally advanced money for Laudon's army in 1759 after the battle of Kunersdorf, and in 1760 was responsible for paying the army in Bohemia in good coin.[110] He was in charge of sales of produce from the state mines from 1759 to 1783, and claimed to have made substantial improvements there.[111] After 1763 he was responsible for most government external loans. He was a partner in the state tobacco monopoly from 1774. In 1779, Lord Stormont, minister in Vienna, observed that 'Baron Fries the first Banker here is well known in England'.[112] He was made a commercial councillor in 1752, a knight (November 1757), a baron (December 1762), a count (April 1783).[113] In 1764 he married in the Dutch chapel at Paris Anne d'Escherny, daughter of Jean d'Escherny, a burgess of Neuchâtel and consul at Lyon for the King of Poland.[114] They had four surviving children, two of whom were sons, Joseph (1765–88) and Moritz Christian (1777–1826). Johann bought the castle and lordship of Vöslau south of Vienna in 1761; the lordship of Orth in Lower Austria and the knightly estates of Dehenlohe and Oberschwaningen in Franconia in 1771.[115] In 1783–4 he built a palace in Vienna on the site of a recently dissolved convent. The architect of this symbol of mammon, Johann von Hohenberg, who had already remodelled Schloss Vöslau, was Kaunitz's protégé, and the designer of much work at Schönbrunn, including the *Gloriette* of 1775.[116]

[110] The account to this point is common, though with varying detail, to Wurzbach, Otruba, and Matis, and largely derives from Fries's memorials in Dec. 1762 and Feb. 1767. The first of these is in the Allgemeines Verwaltungsarchiv in Vienna, see Matis, 485 n. The second is printed by August Graf von Fries, 136–41.

[111] August Graf von Fries, 139, his memorial of Feb. 1767. He took ½% commission on sales. HHSA Nachl. Zinz., Hs. 136 'Mines et monneyes', fo. 159 shows that Count Hatzfeld renewed the initial three-year contracts indefinitely from 16 Jan. 1767. For the profits of the *Verschleiss-Direction* see ii, Ch. 3, n. 61.

[112] See ii, Ch. 9; App. B; PRO SP 80/208, Stormont to Rochford, 18 Aug, 1770, enclosing Fries's offer (in French) to ship 332 oaks for English naval use.

[113] 'Commerzienrat' 15 Dec. 1752; hereditary knight 25 Nov. 1757; baron 15 Dec. 1762; count 5 Apr. 1783. The last two were both imperial and Hereditary Lands titles in separate documents.

[114] Lüthy, ii. 236 n., where Anne's maternal links with the Pourtalès and Peschier families are also shown. Johann and his wife had eight children, of whom four died.

[115] August Graf von Fries, 65, 69.

[116] E. Hainisch, 'Der Architekt Johann Ferdinand Hetzendorf von Hohenberg', *Wiener Jb. für Kunstgeschichte*, 12–13 (1949) 19–90. I am indebted to Dr R. J. W. Evans for this reference.

But Fries did not live long to enjoy his sumptuous new edifice, perhaps the nearest equivalent in the Vienna of its time to those constructed or embellished in Paris by the French *Fermiers généraux*. On 19 June 1785 he was found dead in the lake of his castle at Vöslau. A man of melancholy temperament, he had probably committed suicide.

The scope of his activities was not confined to government contracting and finance. In his petitions for a barony in 1762, and for exemption from personal taxes and judicial inventory of his estate in 1767, he set out his industrial services. He had founded a fustian- and cotton-factory in 1752 on Baron Grechtler's estates of Fridau and Rabenstein.[117] He had established a brassware-factory at Weissenbach in the same year, and a woollen-factory on Baron Neffzer's lands in Bohemia in 1754.[118] Less precisely indicated are silk-ribbon and gold- and silver-lace manufactures supported by him.

so that many thousands of people have been put by me in condition to earn their bread, and in new crafts that they did not know before but learnt at my expense.[119]

In later years his firm set up a half- and whole-silk factory at Wiener Neustadt in 1781 and in 1783 took over the Kettenhof cotton-factory, started by Count Blümegen in 1765. Johann Fries's brother Philipp Jakob, made a knight in 1775 for his services to industry,

---

[117] Baron (1751) Johann Georg Grechtler, 'Ober Proviant Commissär' in the Austrian Netherlands—and hence Fries's superior—from 1746, having previously held the contracts for the army in Bavaria. See App. C for his involvement with Labhard & Co. and Meyer Hey & Co. He was named 'Armee General direktor in Commissariaticis' on 23 Feb. 1761, *Khev.-Metsch 1764–7*, app., *Staatsrat* agenda 23 Feb. 1761. He d. intestate in 1778 leaving his property, including eight lordships, to his son, Arneth, *Mar. Ther. Kinder u. Freunde*, i. 43.

[118] Johann Jacob Neffzer, cr. a baron 1749. For his Bohemian enterprise, see Klíma, *Manufakturní obdobi*, 352–8. He was a councillor of the Hungarian Chamber 1729–49. His brother Wolfgang Conrad, a councillor of the Chamber 1728–41, was cr. a baron in 1734, Megerle von Mühlfeld. Both were sons of Johann Leonhard Neffzer from the Upper Palatinate, who became a quartermaster in the imperial army and a denizen of Hungary from 1715, Nagy, *A magyar kamara*, 96–7. Johann Jacob helped Count Chotek organize the new customs tariff of 1752 and was much hated in consequence: an officer was murdered in Hungary in mistake for him, *Fürst (1755)* 29, and Fournier, 'Handel und Verkehr', 349.

[119] From the memorial of Feb. 1767, printed in August Graf von Fries, pp. 136–41; the quotation is at p. 137.

was put in to run it.[120] Philipp Jakob was created a baron in 1791. Meanwhile, Fries established a trading house in Constantinople with two Greek partners in 1774, and encouraged the Turkey trade.[121] His firm's industrial activities continued after his death. In 1790, in a petition seeking renewal of royal protection, Fries & Co. claimed that over the last thirty years it had done much to encourage national diligence ('Nationalemisgheit') and to lessen the dangerously adverse balance of Austrian trade by promoting domestic manufactures.[122]

The references to Fries in the index to the Vienna Mercantile Court are more mundane than all this. In April 1761 he applied to dissolve his existing partnership with Johann Georg Haas, and to form a new one with his cashier David Meyer. In December 1763 Meyer was given power to sign for Fries by proxy, but in April 1765 he left. This must be the same David Meyer who founded the Warehouser firm of Meyer Hey & Co. in 1770, apparently partly with capital supplied by Fries's former associate Baron Grechtler. Fries now gave his bookkeeper Johann Jacob (Jakob) Gontard a proxy. In January 1766 he was allowed to make his firm a 'Commandite . . . oder . . . ofentlichen Socium Stabiliten'. On 30 June 1766 he deposed that he had joined Gontard with him in a ten-year partnership, with Fries providing 45,000 fl. and Gontard 15,000 fl. Gontard was to get a quarter of the profits and Fries the rest. A supplementary agreement dated 20 July 1766 shows that the real capitals were much larger, Fries putting up 300,000 fl. and Gontard 35,000 fl.[123] Gontard, who came from a Frankfurt banking family of French refugee origin, became a knight in 1768 and a baron in

---

[120] Matis, 492. See also Merk. Gericht Prot. B. 6/2, fo. 217, 'Kettenhof Fabrik' founded 2 Dec. 1765 by Count Heinrich Cajetan Blümegen (20,000 fl.), *Hofrath* Peter von Simon (40,000 fl.), Ignaz Schade, burgess (20,000 fl.); 23 Feb. 1783, agreement between Blümegen, Johann von Fries, and Philipp Jacob von Fries for the last-named to direct the factory. Zorn, *Handels- und Industriegeschichte*, 54, 225, shows that Johann Fries was also an investor 1769–81, for an unstated amount, in Johann Schüle's large cotton-factory at Augsburg.

[121] Matis, 491.

[122] For the memorial, see August Graf von Fries, 176–82.

[123] Merk. Gericht Prot. B. 6/2, fos. 426–7, and August Graf von Fries, 128–33 showing the formal (26 June) and supplementary (20 July) agreements. The second is not in the Court record.

1780, and was a guardian of Fries's children after the count's death.[124]

Count Johann Fries left a substantial fortune: the two Frankish estates and two Lower Austrian lordships, his town house, and the assets of his banking and trading business. The total value was computed in 1792 as 3,636,000 fl.[125] This estate, the equivalent of about £400,000 sterling, was certainly a large one by any standards, and helps to explain the public resentment against a foreigner grown rich at the state's expense—to which Fries refers in his memorial of 1767, and consciousness of which may have driven him to suicide. It is nevertheless worth remembering that in the size, if not in the liquidity, of their assets the landed magnates easily surpassed his wealth.[126]

Johann Fries's riches, which recalled those of the earlier Jewish financiers, proved similarly impermanent. His son Moritz Christian, lover of books, paintings, and fashionable society, patron of Beethoven, married a princess, and systematically dissipated his inheritance. He died in Paris on 26 December 1826, eight months after his firm had gone bankrupt. The creditors were paid in full, and the bankruptcy was lifted in 1832, but the firm did not survive. Enough was left to provide for his heir, Count Moritz Christian II, who married Florentine Pereira-Arnstein, the daughter of Fanny Arnstein and the descendant of Baron Diego de Aguilar's nephew Heinrich Pereira. The Protestant and Jewish traditions in Habsburg finance were thus symbolically reconciled as the star of the Rothschilds rose over Vienna.

The developments examined here are consistent with contemporary statements that Austrian mercantile and banking resources were weak, and bankruptcies frequent, and that domestic entrepreneurs needed to be strengthened from outside. They perhaps confirm

---

[124] For the Gontard family see *NDB*. Johann Gontard's sister Luise was the mother of the Russian Chancellor Nesselrode (1790–1862). Otruba's incorrect statement that Gontard was already a baron in 1766 is followed by Mikoletzky and Matis.

[125] August Graf von Fries, 190, valuation of assets of Moritz Graf Fries by his trustees, 30 June 1792. Much larger estimates of the young count's inheritance when he came of age in 1801 are made ibid. 79, without documentation. Bonds are said there to have amounted to 5–6m. fl. and the count's share of the bank's profits to c. 800,000 fl. a year.

[126] The Schwarzenbergs had over 500,000 fl. of Bohemian revenue alone, see Ch. 5.

Liechtenstern's assertion in 1800 that manufacturing incompetence
and the protected internal market, made the best merchants turn
away from foreign trade to more profitable finance and agency
work. His emphasis, however, was on private dealings. He did no
comment on the profits made available for middlemen by government coinage contracts, loans, remittance and receipt of interest
revenue farms, and so on. This business greatly expanded under
Maria Theresia as a result of war and its aftermath. A number of
firms, besides that of the mighty Fries, was able to take advantage of
it, and had the resources to do so. Jewish finance was also much
more important than Liechtenstern's dismissal of it as usurious and
damaging allowed.[127] Jewish financiers were prominent under the
empress's father, and into the 1740s, and, with the Hönigs, Poppers, and others of the post-war decades of Maria Theresia's reign,
staged something of a revival, and clearly had considerable capital.
A number of references shows their importance as war contractors,
confirming Joseph II's statement in 1767 that in wartime colonels
of regiments 'threw themselves into the embrace of Jews or
others'.[128] A further aspect of the period was the willingness of the
government to tolerate Protestant finance as a means of escaping
from Jewish finance. The qualified freedom for Protestant Wholesalers conceded in 1774 was an example of this. The career of
Johann Fries demonstrated it more vividly. He was a man of
immense competence, able to build up a huge fortune partly as a
result of monopolies conceded to him by the state. He takes his
place in the interesting ranks of Maria Theresia's *Vertrauens-
männer*, whom she would support through thick and thin against
the barbed hostility which such favouritism, unfair but effective,
inevitably aroused. He thus stands with Haugwitz, Kaunitz,
Grassalkovich, Brukenthal, and others, whose varied backgrounds
and policies gave the Austrian state in this period a more mixed and
interesting character than the platitudes of its official apologists
suggested.

[127] HKA Hs. 736, no. 12, 'Mémoire sur les Manufactures de la Monarchie'
undated but apparently from 1770s (bankruptcy in Vienna); cf. Jos. Weinbrenner's
scheme of 1770 for grouping manufactures, which was intended as a remedy for the
'haüfige Fallimente', HKA NÖ Kommerz, rote Nr. 133, fo. 277, *Hofkommerzienrat* meeting of 6 Aug. 1770; Liechtenstern, *Skizze*, 121–2 (merchants), 103–6 (Jews
charge 15–20% for loans of cash or raw materials, especially in Bohemia).
[128] HHSA Sammelband 88, Joseph II's memoir for his brother Leopold. The
observation comes in the section 'Militaire'.

8

Merchants and bankers in the Austrian Netherlands

THE close, and increasing, ties of finance and trade between Austria and the Austrian Netherlands drew into government business a handful of Belgian firms: Cogels, Dormer, and Proli at Antwerp, and Nettine at Brussels. Their styles altered over time: J. B. Cogels, Widow J. B. Cogels, J. B. Cogels again; James Dormer, Dormer & Co.; Mathias Nettine, Widow Nettine, Widow Nettine Son & Co.; and Pietro Proli, a firm subsequently managed under that name by Widow Proli and Charles Proli. Several Viennese houses held accounts with them: Jacob Bender and Johann Fries with James Dormer; Diego de Aguilar with Mathias Nettine; Johann Fries with Widow Nettine, this was the largest and longest connection; Fries, Johann Georg Pradatsch of Prague, and 'Fratelli Smitmer' of Vienna with Charles Proli. The network of loans raised for Vienna in the Austrian Netherlands, and their subsequent repayment, depended on Belgian banking services. So did the supply of the English army in the 1740s, the creation of new insurance and trading companies, and to some extent the financing of domestic industry. Some attempt to examine these firms and the structure of their activities is thus necessary, even though much evidence is lacking, and much of what is available is difficult to interpret.[1] There were other banking houses in the Austrian Netherlands, as well as a much more considerable number of merchants in foreign trade, but the inference

---

[1] Of those discussed, only Pietro Proli, his sons Balthasar and Charles, and the two Walckiers have entries in the *Biog. nat. de Belgique* (Brussels 1866–1944 and supplements 1956–74); none appears in the *Nationaal Biografisch Woordenboek* (Brussels 1964–77). Cf. generally the important study by V. Janssens, *Het geldwezen der oostenrijkse Nederlanden* (Brussels 1957), esp. ch. IX. Charles Proli is the subject of a definitive monograph by Helma Houtman-de Smedt, *Charles Proli, Antwerps zakenman en bankier, 1723–1786* (Brussels 1983). I am grateful to Miss Erika Meel of the Catholic University of Louvain, who is working on James Dormer, for this reference.

from the sources is that the group discussed here was of primary importance.[2]

The bank of 'Widow J.-B. Cogels' of Antwerp acted as receiver of part of the revenue of the Hainault Estates as early as 1735, and undertook to place loans for the Belgian government in 1743, 1744, and 1755, and for the War Department in Vienna in 1755. It was receiver, with Widow Nettine, of the Belgian lottery loans of 1758.[3] Mme Cogels, who directed the bank, was one of those whom that even more powerful figure Widow Nettine declared in 1755 that she trusted most in financial matters.[4] Her husband Jean-Baptiste Cogels established a bank in Antwerp in 1720, and was cashier to the Ostend Company of 1722; he signed receipts as 'J. B. Cogels le Jeune'.[5] Cogels had died by 1735, when Widow Proli was already receiving payments from 'Widow Cogels of Antwerp'. James Dormer, also of Antwerp, used Widow Cogels as his banker from 1737. Dormer's account with her closed in 1746, however, and was not revived.[6] The last mention of 'Widow Cogels' is in a document of 1764.[7] However, the named receiver for the Belgian lotteries of 1758 was 'J. B. Cogels', not 'Widow J. B. Cogels', and it seems likely that this was a son associated with the business. In the 1780s J. B. Cogels, presumably the same man, was a marine insurer,

---

[2] Janssens, 239 gives from the *Journal de Commerce*, of 1761 the names of bankers in Brussels as François Année, Baudier & Bacon, Jean de Bay, Daniel Danoot, Joseph Menue, Widow Nettine, J. B. & A. Orion, Julien de Pester, Jean-Louis Salmon, Van Schoor & Son, C. J. Triponetty, J. B. Wouters. In Antwerp, Broëta, Cogels, Ertborn, Henssens, and Hevy, are named. The less exact data for Antwerp are reflected in the local almanac, *Geriefliche Nieuw-Jaers Gifte ofte Almanach* (Antwerp 1763 etc.) which lists Sworn Brokers and (from 1766) notaries, but not bankers.

[3] For Mme Cogels's share in the *Recette de la Linée* of Hainault see AGR Cons. des Fin. 7179 under 29 Mar. 1736, advances by Mme Proli (*sic*) to 31 Oct. and their reimbursement. For the loans of 1743–4 and 1755 see G. Bigwood, 'Les origines de la dette belge. Étude d'histoire financière', *ASRAB* 20 (1906) 15, 18, 22. For 1758 see ii, Table 9.4* and Bigwood, 'La loterie', *ASRAB* 26 (1912) 72, abortive lottery of 10 Oct. 1758. James Dormer was also named a receiver.

[4] See ii. 280 n.

[5] J. Denucé, 'James Dormer en de Keiz. & Kon. Verzekerings-Kamer te Antwerpen', *Antwerpsch Archievenblad*, 2nd ser. 4. (1929) 231. For Cogels's signature see the Ostend Company receipt reproduced in F. Donnet, *Coup d'œil sur l'histoire financière d'Anvers au cours des siècles* (Antwerp 1927) 210.

[6] See pp. 184–5 below.

[7] Rijksarchief, Antwerp, Notariaat 316 no. 41 (inventory of goods of Catherina Lunden, 1767), 8,000 fl. Hainault Estates obligation transferred to her 20 Sept. 1764 by Widow Cogels. In the same inventory a bond of 15 Jan. 1766 is paid at Cogels '& Co.', perhaps indicating that Mme Cogels died in between.

underwriting risks on ships of the new Asiatic Company. His role in the bank is not clear. Other evidence suggests that it was run in the 1760s and 1770s by Widow Cogels's son-in-law Count (1768) Julien Depestre of Brussels, 'whose family and connections are of great influence in this country'. Depestre perhaps acted as managing director under J. B. Cogels's nominal control. Depestre and Isabel-Claire Cogels had at least seven children, four girls and three boys. The eldest of these, Joseph-François, together with his mother, was speculating in French East India Company shares in Paris in the mid 1780s. His correspondents then included his uncle J. B. Cogels at Antwerp, and Jean Osy of Rotterdam.[8]

More information is available about James Dormer of Antwerp, whose business ledgers and extensive correspondence fell into official hands when his firm went bankrupt in 1771.[9] These records form an important source, which has not yet been adequately exploited, for the social and economic history of the Austrian Netherlands. Dormer (1708–58) was an English Catholic, the fourth of the eight children of Charles, Lord Dormer of Wing. He studied at the English College at St Omer, undertook a successful voyage to Canton in 1731 for the soon defunct Ostend Company, then settled in Antwerp, where he married two heiresses in quick succession. The funds so obtained were augmented by his increasing business in colonial goods and, from the late 1740s, diamonds. Dormer held part of the contracts for supplying the English troops in the Low

---

[8] L. Couvreur, 'De zeeverzekeringsmarkt der Oostenrijksche Nederlanden op het einde van de achttiende eeuw', *Ann. de la Société d'Émulation de Bruges*, 79 (1936) 61–2, 78. Couvreur's source was the 'Cogels archive at Antwerp', apparently in private hands. The letters-patent of 15 Mar. 1758 authorizing the Belgian lottery refer to 'J. B. Cogels', *Rec. des ord. des Pays-Bas autrichiens*, 3rd ser. viii (1894) 194. The 'banque Depestre et Cie', listed among the Brussels banks in 1761, acted as receiver in the Belgian lottery of 1755, Bigwood, 'La loterie', 71. For Julien Depestre and Mme Cogels, see Denucé loc. cit. Donnet, 232, incorrectly says that she m. him. The quotation is from a report by the Marquis d'Herzelles and others on the two rival insurance projects of 1754, AGR Cons. des Fin. 4331, 18 Nov. 1754. Julien-Guillain Depestre was made a count, and his estate and seignory of Seneffe a county, by letters-patent of 28 Mar. 1768, *Liste des titres de noblesse . . . accordées par Sa Majesté . . . Marie Thérèse* (Brussels [1783]), pt. ii, p. 7. For his eldest son Joseph-François, see J. Bouchary, *Les Manieurs d'argent à Paris à la fin du XVIIIᵉ siècle* (Paris 1939–43) ii. 9 ff.

[9] Stad Antwerpen Archief, Insolvente Boedelskamer. They are listed by Denucé, but the ref. nos. are now altered. There is a succinct account of Dormer's career, with a family tree, in Denucé, and a more extended account in Donnet, 227–40.

Countries in the 1740s. He was the principal director of the Imperial and Royal Insurance Company founded at Antwerp on his proposal in 1754.[10] He died suddenly in London in October 1758 during an improbable mission to float a loan there for Austria. His widow and son formed a partnership in 1759, but the father's entrepreneurial spirit was evidently not transmissible. The business failed in 1771, and James Albert Dormer died, aged only forty, five years later.

Although a full discussion of James Dormer's business activities lies outside the scope of this study, a brief indication of them from his surviving ledgers throws some light on the resources Vienna could draw upon here.[11] The accounts in Dormer's first ledger, for 1737–42, show that his correspondents were mostly in the Austrian Netherlands themselves: Antwerp (3), Brussels (1), Bruges (3), Ghent (1), Ostend (5). But he had two correspondents in Rotterdam, two in Amsterdam, no less than six in London, and one each in Bordeaux, Cadiz, Elberfeld, Gothenburg, and Paris.[12] Somewhat more surprising than this pattern, which was probably typical, is the fact that only six correspondents' names are not English. Dormer was able to draw on an extended mercantile network whose members, like him, were of English origin. It would be interesting to know how many were also Catholics. New accounts appear sub-

---

[10] The 'Chambre Impériale et Royale d'Assurance aux Pays-Bas' was established by letters-patent dated 29 Nov. 1754; it had a capital of 2m. fl. and a 25-year monopoly of corporate insurance in Brabant. There are concise amounts in Denucé and in Donnet, ch. XVII; a fuller one in L. Couvreur, 'De eerste verzekeringscompagnie te Antwerpen (1754–1793?)', *Tijdschrift voor Economie en Sociologie*, 2 (1936) 145–74.

[11] Stad Antwerpen Achief, Ins. Boed., nos. 1118, 1119, 1121, 1122, Dormer ledgers 1737–76. No. 1120, originally attributed to Mme Cogels, and reattributed by Denucé (p. 234) as Dormer's ledger 1757–64, is not Dormer's, whose ledger 1757–65 is no. 1121. The real owner has not yet been identified. Dormer kept his accounts in Dutch, and corresponded in Dutch, English, and French. His ledgers are the source for the two tables in the text.

[12] Antwerp: Martin Bladen, James Cope, Samuel Tufnell; Brussels: Melchior van Gheerdeghen; Bruges: Wm Archdeacon, Prosser & Porter, Francis Stanfield; Ghent: J. B. Grenier; Ostend: John Deane, Jean Galway, John Gould, Charles Hennessy, Thos. Ray; Rotterdam: John Archdeacon, Jean Osy & Son; Amsterdam: Aaron & David Fernandes Nunes, André Pels & Son; London: George Fitzgerald, Jos. Foster, Michael Hatton, Alexr. Hume, Francis Salvador, Stonor & Belasyse; Bordeaux: Thos. Burton; Cadiz: Cantillon & Comerford; Elberfeld: J. B. Belle; Gothenburg: Hugh Campbell; Paris: Geo. Waters.

TABLE 8.1. *Annual outlay of James Dormer's caisse, 1737–64 (fl. Brab.)*

Year	Outlay	Year	Outlay
1737	5,622	1751	152,851[b]
1738	3,126	1752	28,846
1739	2,961	1753	51,880
1740	12,201	1754	31,680
1741	7,888	1755	30,034
1742	334,863	1756	46,094
1743	551,774	1757	15,650
1744	444,944	1758	82,064
1745	765,576[a]	1759	17,741
1746	442,459	1760	78,738
1747	81,905	1761	21,177
1748	130,400	1762	11,364
1749	25,715	1763	20,522
1750	50,651	1764	8,252[c]

Sums stated are expenditure in ledger, reached by subtracting from cumulative account.

[a] Estimate from ledger accounts for ten months only; one fo. missing.

[b] Includes 90,000 fl. profits from 'ten years of London house.'

[c] Last complete year in series.

sequently. From 1746 he was dealing extensively in diamonds through George Clifford & Son of Amsterdam, evidently with Francis Salvador of London. An important account with Francis Mannock of London begins in 1746, probably for Flemish lace sold through Mannock & Ryan at Cadiz. Bender & Co. of Vienna appear in 1753.[13] Their account is credited with obligations of the Vienna City Bank sold for them by Dormer and with interest remitted, and debited with interest due. The capital sums involved seem to have been small. Payment from Vienna was partly by drafts on Cliffords in Amsterdam. This account was still open in 1763.

A rough indication of the scope of Dormer's business is afforded by the total outlay of his *caisse*, shown in Table 8.1.

The big increase in annual expenditure during the War of the

[13] Ins. Boed., no. 1119, fo. 149.

Austrian Succession was due to payments made to Dormer by Thomas Orby Hunter, whose account opens (with 60,000 ducats 'received from Amsterdam') on 29 August 1742. Hunter, whose own turnover mirrored the balance of Dormer's cash, was deputy paymaster to the English forces. These payments must have been for the troops and their supply.[14] The sums involved may be understated, since when his insurance proposals were being officially examined in 1754 it was stated that Dormer's credit was extensive, and that he had had charge 'of the considerable sums England sent into his country to pay its troops'. His account with the *caissier* Ertborn, it was claimed, did not fall below 2½–3m. fl. a year. After the capture of Brussels in 1746, Dormer had proposed to Count Kaunitz that he should receive at par the English subsidy, which was then costing Austria 11–13% loss, and advance 200,000 fl. in anticipation of it to the *Caisse de Guerre*.[15] No further details are unfortunately available from this source.

Government contracts apart, Dormer's business activity is perhaps better measured by his bank account with the 'Widow Jean-Baptiste Cogels here'. The yearly sums, in current Brabant florins, credited to her in his ledger were: 1737, 108,240; 1738, 73,949; 1739, 121,979; 1740, 195,992; 1741, 152,999; 1742, 135,505; 1743, 546,260. The jump in 1743 indicates that payments for Hunter were already affecting the figures. Before this, the account appears to be a bills one, with Mme Cogels credited with bills she paid for Dormer and debited with bills he paid to her, presumably by endorsement.[16] This suggests sales of £13,000–15,000 a year, a fairly small way of business. There is no account for Widow Cogels after 1746. Dormer subsequently used as bankers Gaspard Baudier

---

[14] Dormer's role as 'caissier des armées anglaises' is stated by Donnet, 231 without source or details. Dormer's account with Jean Osy & Son of Rotterdam shows extensive purchases of 'gold and silver' (671,763 fl. Brab. by Dec. 1744), Reuben Levy of Amsterdam being a principal supplier.

[15] See the report of 18 Nov. 1754 cit. n. 8.

[16] Typical entries in 1740 (Ins. Boed., no. 1118, fo. 76) are, on the creditor side of Mme Cogels's account, '2 March per Jean Galwey's account, to Louis van Colen'; on the debtor side, '9 Feb., to Jean Gould's account, from J. J. Moretus'. I interpret the first as an order to Dormer by Jean Galwey to pay Louis van Colen, and the second as a bill drawn in Dormer's favour on Jean Gould by J. J. Moretus. The original versions are 'pr. Jean Galwey S.R. aen Louis van Colen' and 'aen Jean Gould S.R. van J. J. Moretus'. 'S.R.' is 'sijn rekening'.

of Brussels, François van Ertborn of Antwerp, and George Clifford & Son of Amsterdam.[17]

James Dormer was a trader who diversified into government contracting, insurance, and precious stones. Mathias (or Matthias as he signed himself) Nettine, and more notably his widow after his death in 1749, were essentially bankers, making the largest share of their profits from government finance.[18] Mathias Nettine (1686–1749) was the second son of Gilles Nettine of Menin. His elder brother Jean-Godefroid Nettine helped farm the domains of Flanders. Mathias married as his second wife, in 1735, Barbe Louise Stoupy, a sister of the Vicar-General to the Cardinal Prince-Bishop of Liège.[19] At the beginning of the long regency of Charles VI's sister, the Archduchess Maria Elizabeth (October 1725–August 1741), Mathias Nettine was already Receiver of the Office of Works for the Court in Brussels, and was collecting the subsidy raised from the clergy of Flanders.[20] In 1731 he nearly cut out Pietro Proli from the latter's long-held contract for government payments to The Hague, and in the same year took over receipt of the customs

[17] This is an inference from Dormer's account with Frans van Ertborn 1751–6 (Ins. Boed., no. 1119, fos. 136, 153–5, 195) which is in the same form as that with Mme Cogels. Gaspard Baudier was credited with over 100,000 fl. by Dormer in 1755; George Clifford and Son with over 95,000 in 1756. For van Ertborn's bank see below, p. 203.

[18] This is a reasonable inference from the surviving records, but may be biased by the fact that the firm's ledgers etc., unlike those of Dormer and Charles Proli, have not survived. The relevant Nettine papers are the firm's official correspondence and accounts with the Belgian treasury, preserved in AGR Cons. des Fin. 7177–90 (1725–86). The earlier cartons are not in strict chronological order, and several concern Mme Proli.

[19] Lüthy, *Banque protestante*, ii. 658–9 says that Mathias Nettine was the son of Jean-Godefroy Nettine. Bigwood in the essays referred to above consistently adds an s to Nettine. Mathias Nettine was first married to Louise Stoupy (d. 1733), the aunt of his second wife, and required a dispensation for his second marriage. Barbe Louise Stoupy's father Sebastien was an *avocat* in Arras, see C. Bronne, *Financiers et comédiens au XVIIIe siècle: Madame de Nettine, Banquière des Pays-Bas, suivi de D'Hannetaire et ses filles* (Brussels 1969). This work is uninformative about the business of the bank Nettine, but contains useful genealogical and topographical information. My thanks to Professor Beales for the reference.

[20] AGR Cons. des Fin. 7182, statement by the Chambre des Comptes 30 Sept. 1741 of all sums paid to M. Nettine by government order 'since her late Imperial Highness's entry into these countries' [i.e. Oct. 1725]. There is an outline of the relations of Mathias Nettine, and then his widow, with the Belgian treasury in Janssens, 227–31.

revenue. In the last three months of 1733 and in 1734–5 he acted with Mme Proli as receiver for half of these revenues, and in 1736–44 as subreceiver under her.[21] From August 1744, Mme Proli having asked to withdraw, to December 1745 Nettine administered them alone. He paid government warrants of anticipation at 5%, made loans for fortifications and the artillery, and obtained cavalry forage from Holland. He also received and paid out interest on the Austrian loans of 1738 and 1739.[22] In April 1746, as the French army streamed across the Austrian Netherlands, he offered to collect at Antwerp the customs duties normally receivable at Brussels, for 1%, three times his usual commission. The Conseil des Finances refused, but in November 1748, as the Austrian authorities settled into power once more, appointed him to receive the customs, the domains revenue, and the interest on the two Austrian loans.[23] Nettine died on 28 June 1749, having greatly increased his share of government business, apparently at the expense of Mme Proli, who had done it before 1744.[24]

His widow, Barbe Nettine, continued and expanded the work of the bank. The Conseil des Finances confirmed her in the exercise of her late husband's revenue collections, and in 1750 she added those of the *Pays Rétrocédé* (the territory given back by France in 1713) and of the domains in Luxembourg.[25] In the same year, she started

[21] AGR Cons. des Fin. 7177, 4 Dec. 1731, Nettine's receipts of 1,169,080 fl. Brab. from the *droits d'entrée et sortie* in 1731. His offer about the payments to Holland, in fact misunderstood by the Conseil des Finances, is in the same carton, under 9 Jan. 1731. For his customs receipt with Mme Proli in 1733–5 see AGR Cons. des Fin. 7179, 1,111,760 fl. Brab. received by her and 1,103,700 fl. Brab. by him. According to Bronne, 22, 58, the bank Nettine was conducted until 1759 from houses in the Poldermarkt, then moved to the Rue des Longs Chariots. However, the *Almanack Nouveau* shows Mme Nettine in the Pongel-Merckt [*sic*] in 1758, 1765, 1773.

[22] His activities are documented in AGR Cons. des Fin. 7183. In 1745 he lent 495,384 fl. Brab. to the *Caisse de Guerre* at 5%. His widow claimed that he received the customs until and including Dec. 1745, ibid. 7184, her representation to the Conseil des Finances dated 24 Dec. 1749. For the interest on the 1738–9 loans see ii, Ch. 9, n. 29.

[23] AGR Cons. des Fin. 7185, 17 Apr. 1746; Cons. des Fin. 7184 under 9 June 1749, M. Nettine's receipts 20 Nov. 1748 31 May 1749.

[24] Mme Nettine's undated letter to the Conseil des Finances notifying them of her husband's death 'le 28' is enclosed with council papers dated 30 June 1749, AGR Cons. des Fin. 7184. Janssens, 227 says that Nettine died on 28 May 1749.

[25] For the council's approval of her continuation see the preceding note, and for the collections from the *Pays Retrocédé* and Luxembourg ibid., 4 Mar. 1750, also n. 49. In the letter approving the second, the council addresses Mme Nettine as 'tres chère et espéciale amie'. A portrait of Mme Nettine from a Spanish collection is in Bronne, 58.

paying into the *Caisse de Guerre* in Brussels the Dutch Barrier Subsidy, partly charged on these revenues and remitted to The Hague by Widow Proli until 1744.[26] The position of the banker as intermediary in government finance, receiving revenue and loans, making remittances abroad, paying interest at home, discharging government salaries, was already accepted by the government as a necessary one. An official report of 1740, examining the roles of Mme Proli and 'banquier Nettine' in this respect, pointed out, however, that they acted merely as 'channels of communication' supplementing the functions of the General Receivers. They were not formally accountable, and therefore should not be given letters of discharge.[27] In 1749 Mme Nettine asked to account to the Chambre des Comptes for her firm's collections in 1744/5 and 1748/9, since the scattering (*égarement*) of her books and papers at the end of the war made the previous informal method impossible.[28]

It is reasonably clear from the sources that by 1750 Mme Nettine's bank occupied the same position in government finance as Mme Proli's a decade earlier. Although the firm's ledgers have vanished, the subsequent progress of the 'banque Nettine' is partially traceable from its transactions with the Conseil des Finances, especially from the annual accounts relating to government loans, which survive as a series from 1763. An incomplete statement is available for 1748/9, and Johann Fries's special account with Mme Nettine during the Seven Years War indicate his receipts from her, though not her total receipts.[29] The relevant figures, converted in Table 8.2 into current Brabant florins from a mixture of currencies in the sources, indicate that in the Seven Years War the bank handled at least 3m. fl. to 4m. fl. Brab. Belgian revenue; in most other years it received from Vienna 2.5m.–3.5m. fl. Brab. Belgian domestic ordinary revenue during Maria Theresia's reign was between 6m. and 8m. fl. Brab., excluding interest received from Vienna.

---

[26] AGR Cons. des Fin. 7184, 30 Jan. 1751.

[27] AGR Cons. des Fin. 7180, undated report in papers for 1740, headed in French 'Systems for the moneys which pass through the hands of Madame Proli or Banker Nettine from the duties on entry and exit, subsidies, loans, assignments, or otherwise'.

[28] Ibid. 7184, 24 Dec. 1749.

[29] Mathias Nettine's account for 20 Nov. 1748 to 31 May 1749 is in AGR Cons. des Fin. 7184 under 9 Jun. 1749. It shows 864,656 fl. Brab. received from the *droits d'entrée*, 241,305 fl. from domains, 428,400 fl. from d'Aguilar and Küner at Vienna for loan interest. The figures in the text from 1764 are from ibid. 7187–90, annual statements by Nettine & Co. For Fries's account see ii, Table 4.11.

TABLE 8.2. *Receipts and expenditures by Bank Nettine,*
1748–80 (fl. Brab.)

Dec. 1748–May 1749	1,534,360		
Sept. 1757–Aug. 1759	(8,902,762)		
Sept. 1759–Apr. 1762	(10,884,503)		
Sept. 1762–Feb. 1764	(8,140,323)		
	1764	(2,556,761)	1773	3,281,482
	1765	2,366,992	1774	3,035,097
	1766	(3,603,530)	1775	2,619,810
	1767	4,329,831	1776	2,459,698
	1768	4,012,012	1777	2,584,341
	1769	2,534,952	1778	. .
	1770	3,311,667	1779	2,645,980
	1771	3,450,810	1780	4,285,757
	1772	3,401,106		

Figures in parentheses denote expenditure. Those for Sept.
1757–Feb. 1764 inclus. are sums received from Mme. Nettine
by Fries in Vienna.

During the Seven Years War revenue doubled reaching 17m. fl.
Brab. in 1762.[30] In this conflict, the Bank Nettine acted as receiver
for Belgian lotteries, subsidies, and *dons gratuits*, and also for the
French subsidies to Austria.

These subsidies were paid to Mme Nettine from 1759 by Jean-
Joseph de Laborde, *Banquier de la Cour* at Paris, who became her
son-in-law in 1760. Her two younger daughters married fashion-
ably in France in 1762. She was ennobled in 1758, and her surviving
second son André in 1762.[31] After the war ended, the bank, whose
style altered to 'Widow Nettine & Son' in 1765, and which was
officially 'Banquier de la Cour' at Brussels, continued to receive the
French subsidy to 1770, but its principal non-domestic source of
revenue was the remittances from Fries in Vienna to service Austria's Belgian loans. The Bank Nettine played a key role, negotiating
eight loans in the Seven Years War and eleven new ones between
1765 and 1779.[32] The decline in revenue handled, observable in the
table, was due to gradual repayments in the 1770s. The reward for

[30] AGR, Cons. des Fin. 7212. Cf. ii. 146 n.
[31] 'Annoblissement' on 1 Apr. 1758, with retrospective effect on her husband,
Liste des titres de noblesse pt. i, p. 21. André was cr. vicomte Nettine on 28 Sept.
1762, ibid. 26. An elder son, Dominique, d. in 1759, see Bronne, 251. For her
daughter's marriages see ii. 177 below.
[32] For the French subsidy and the Austrian loans see ii, Chs. 5, 9. Mme Nettine is
first styled 'Banquière de la Cour' in the letters-patent of 1 June 1762 establishing the
fifth royal lottery, *Rec. des ord.* viii. 470.

these activities, which by 1772 had made Mme Nettine the kingpin of government credit, can be estimated only roughly from the sources.[33] In the 1730s Mathias Nettine charged $\frac{1}{4}$–$\frac{1}{2}$% for revenue collected, and 2–2$\frac{1}{2}$% for sums remitted abroad. In 1749–50 revenue collection was resumed for $\frac{1}{2}$%. The same rate was maintained by both Mme Nettine and Fries in their payments for Kaunitz during the Seven Years War. For loans, a rate of 1% for levy and $\frac{5}{6}$% for service was standard in the 1760s.[34] It is difficult to see how this can have realized much more than 10,000–20,000 fl. a year on average over the whole period, but payments by clients receiving bond interest, and so on, probably greatly increased the total.

As noted, the accounts examined for the years after 1763 were largely confined to government credit business. General d'Ayasasa stated in 1772 that Widow Nettine, whom he referred to as a blood-sucker (*sangsue*), was also entrusted with the management of the entire Belgian revenue. If this is correct, and he was well placed to know, the conclusions reached about the firm's importance are greatly strengthened.[35] Another aspect of the bank's activities in this period, documented by Janssens, was the provision of coin and bullion for the Mint, beginning with the great recoinage of 1749, and continuing through the reign. This was a period when, after decades of inactivity, the Belgian mints were working overtime, the equivalent of over 131m. current florins being struck between 1747 and 1780. Other banks were used for this business, but Nettine and Co. had a commanding position in it. In 1769, for example the bank delivered 85% of all silver used by the Mint. According to Kaunitz, this was partly a fiction, since the bank used other bankers, paying them a share of commission. Nevertheless, its annual income from this source may have been up to 10,000 fl. annually.[36] The scope

[33] For Mme Nettine's position by 1772 see ii. 290. According to the memoirs of Count Philip Cobenzl, she was a friend and confidante of his uncle, Count Charles Cobenzl, the Austrian Minister, until his death in 1770. He saw her daily, and dined with her once a week, Arneth (ed.), 'Graf Philipp Cobenzl und seine Memoiren', *AÖG* 67 (1886), 74, 76.

[34] These rates appear from the Nettine papers, and from Bigwood, 'Les origines', 29–32.

[35] D'Ayasasa, 'Memoire Concernant les Pays bas autrichiens', misdated 1778, HHSA Nachl. Lacy, Karton I, fo. 58.

[36] Janssens, 144 for the bank's position in 1769, and Kaunitz's letter to Cobenzl of 4 Mar. 1769; ibid., app. II for coinage 1598–1789. According to Kaunitz, Widow Nettine got 1% commission from the Mint, but paid three-quarters of this to other bankers. These (ibid. and p. 231) included Anné, J. B. Cogels, Van Ertborn & Hellin, and Romberg. The computation in the text of 10,000 fl. annual commission derives from applying $\frac{1}{4}$% to the 131m. fl. struck by the Mint 1747–80.

and profitability of the bank's services for private clients would also make fascinating reading if they could be reconstructed.

The bank of 'Widow Nettine Son & Co.' continued to trade actively, under the same style, despite the death of Mme Nettine's son, André vicomte Nettine, in 1766, and her own death in December 1775. It was run by Adrien-Ange de Walckiers, (1721–99), who was made vicomte de Tronchiennes in 1786. He had married Mme Nettine's eldest daughter Dieudonnée in 1755.[37] The accession of Joseph II, coinciding with the mushroom growth of Ostend's trade in the American war, offered the prospect of a considerable augmentation of banking business.[38] In February 1782, acting on behalf of Widow Nettine & Son, Adrien-Ange's son Édouard, then aged only twenty-two, agreed with William Herries of Ostend to establish a new bank there, with a capital of 500,000 fl. ex. They claimed that scarcity of specie in Ostend, which made discounting of bills difficult, would be alleviated by the bank, which would also take deposits. The bank opened on 15 April 1782. Among the fifty-three shareholders were William Herries himself, the Bank Nettine, Édouard de Walckiers, and 'Walckiers de Gammarage'. Others included Baron Christian Bartenstein, eight English firms, the bank's secretary Walter Boyd, and John William Ker: the last two set up their own bank in Paris, Boyd, Ker & Co., later to become notorious, in 1785. In December 1782, William Herries and Édouard de Walckiers are found petitioning the Conseil des Finances in support of a larger project, a 'Banque des Pays Bas Autrichiens' with a capital of 2m. fl. ex., of which they would be the directors. In April, Herries had acquired permission to set up an insurance company for Flanders, also with a capital of 2m. fl. The pair claimed that the bank at Ostend had already succeeded beyond all hopes; formerly, merchants there had had to bring in specie from inland towns to counteract the scarcity. A larger bank would mobilize hoards, and stimulate industry. If leave for it were

---

[37] Bronne, 251. Walckiers, who has a brief notice in the *Biog. nat. de Belgique*, came of a family of government contractors and financiers. From 1762 to 1785 he was director of the Genoa Lottery in Belgium, Bigwood, 'La loterie', 94–5. He is confused with his son Édouard in W. W. Davis, *Joseph II. An Imperial Reformer for the Austrian Netherlands* (The Hague 1974) 19, who also overlooks the family's bank and insurance projects. Mme Nettine d. on 4 Dec. 1775, Bronne, 144. Dieudonnée then formally became the head of the bank.

[38] H. Houtman-de Smedt, 92 n. shows that 1,566 ships entered Ostend in 1780, 2,941 in 1781, 2,626 in 1782, 1,694 in 1783.

granted, the smaller bank would be closed.[39] This ambitious project was the latest in a series of proposals since 1720 for a public bank in the Austrian Netherlands, the most extensive previous one being by Kaunitz in November 1763. On that occasion, the Widow Nettine said that in a country accustomed to specie, such a bank would have no success. Kaunitz's plan was shelved.[40]

The necessary permission for the *Banque des Pays-Bas* does not seem to have been forthcoming, since a printed circular of the 'Banque particulière d'Ostende', dated October 1783, announced the intention of setting up branches at Bruges and Ghent; one had already been established in Brussels. It seems likely that the Ostend bank did not in any case survive the collapse of Charles Proli's Imperial Asiatic Company in 1785, to which it had lent on a substantial scale; the secession of Boyd and Ker supports this.[41] According to Bigwood, the 'banque Nettine' was asked to raise further Belgian government loans in 1787-8 and 1792-4.[42] Édouard de Walckiers meanwhile became involved with the Vonckist revolt, and withdrew to France in 1790, whence he fled to Hamburg in 1794: he went bankrupt there in 1796.[43]

The rise of the 'banque Nettine' of Brussels in this period, analogous in many ways to that of Fries & Co. in Vienna, was partly, although only partly, at the expense of the Proli family of Antwerp. Pietro Proli (1671-1733), born in Como, was the son of a Milan merchant who traced his family back to the sixteenth century. A

---

[39] AGR Cons. des Fin. 4297, 'Banques, bourses etc. 1756-1792'. For Herries's 'Compagnie d'Assurance de la Flandre Autrichienne' of 2 Apr. 1782 see Couvreur, 'De zeeverzekeringsmarkt', 66 ff. The articles of the bank of Ostend are dated 20 Feb. 1782. The list of shareholders is not dated but is from 1783. There is a brief account by Lüthy, ii. 657, but he does not refer to the project for the Banque des Pays-Bas. Janssens, 249-54 has a fuller description, including a list of all the shareholders, virtually identical with that above, and grouped by town of origin. For the Herries family, see J. M. Price, *France and the Chesapeake* (Mich. UP, 1973), esp. 620-2, 739. Jean-Joseph Walckiers de Gammerage (*sic*) was Adrien-Ange's nephew, Bronne, 149.

[40] Janssens, 244-8.

[41] The 1783 circular of the Banque d'Ostende is in AGR Cons. des Fin. 4297, cit. n. 39. The bank's Brussels branch was administered by 'Veuve Michel van Schoor et fils' and Jacques Leyniers.

[42] Bigwood, 'Les origines', 35-7.

[43] Bouchary, loc. cit. The last carton of Nettine papers in AGR Cons. des Fin. 7190 covers 1780-6 but is very scrappy after 1780. Janssens and Bronne are uninformative about the last years of the Bank Nettine.

link was claimed with the Priuli family of Venice. Pietro's father Giovanni established a trading firm at Antwerp in the late seventeenth century, associating his son with him from 1684. In 1705 Pietro married Aldegonde Pauli (1685–1761), the daughter of Florentius Pauli, an Antwerp lace-merchant from a family (originally Pauwels) of merchants, officials, and magistrates. Pietro's father gave him a wedding present of 30,000 fl. 'so that he can better exercise the calling of a merchant'. He rapidly developed his activities both as a Spanish merchant and as a banker, and was described by the Austrian governor in 1721 as 'un des premiers banquiers d'Anvers'. At his death in 1733 he left a net estate of 723,813 fl. He was one of the seven founder-directors of the Ostend Company, properly 'La Compagnie impériale et royale établie dans les Pays-Bas autrichiens,' in November 1722. Proli held 50,000 fl. of its shares. He dealt in cottons and other East India goods, and had land and houses in Antwerp and Milan.[44] His financial activities were important. He was responsible through the 1720s for payments to the United Provinces from the Belgian customs for loan-service and the Barrier Subsidy.[45] The sums charged on this branch of Belgian revenue were considerable. The debts to the Dutch, originating in the war, were nearly 10m. fl. Brab. initially, and by 1728 still nearly 7m. fl. Their service required 316,248 fl. annually.[46] In addition, from 22 December 1718 the Barrier Subsidy of 1,400,000 fl. Brab. (*f* 1,250,000) was charged as to 616,000 fl. a

---

[44] Apart from brief notices in *Biog. nat. de Belgique*, see J. Denucé, 'Charles de Proli en de Aziatische Compagnie', *Antwerpsch Archievenblad*, 2nd ser. 7 (1932) 3–63; L. Michielsen, 'De familie de Proli. Bijdrage tot de economische geschiedenis van Antwerpen in de XVIII de eeuw', *Bijdragen tot de Geschiedenis*, 26 (1935), 273–307. This literature is largely superseded by Dr Houtman-de Smedt's monograph, from which it is clear that there are numerous errors in the earlier accounts.

[45] AGR Cons. des Fin. 7177, Pietro Proli's proposals of 4 and 8 Jan. 1731. In the second of these he states that he has remitted to Holland the sums charged on the *droits d'entrée et sortie* at the ports of Lillo and Saint-Philippe for twenty years, even under the revenue-farmers Sotelet & Christiane, and Botsont. Cf. also the clear account in Janssens, 35–6.

[46] AGR Cons. des Fin. 7178, a carton largely concerned with Dutch remittances by Pietro Proli and his widow. An account of 1728 states the debts charged on Fort Saint-Philippe as initially (1692–5, 1709–12) *f* 8,052,765, with *f* 550,000 added in 1718. This would make 9,635,096 fl. Brab. Writing-down and partial repayment had reduced this to *f* 6,179,756 (or 6,921,330 fl. Brab.). Dutch loans 1690–1712 totalled 13,014,955 fl. Brab. Bigwood, 'Les origines', 7, but the balance was charged on other revenues.

year (*f* 550,000) a year on the customs revenue.[47] A further 100,000 fl. Dutch fl., or 112,000 fl. Brab., was paid annually from 1718 to 1728 to liquidate arrears.[48] These were the sums for whose remittance Proli was responsible. The remainder of the Subsidy, 700,000 Dutch fl., was met from the revenues of the *Pays Rétrocédé*.[49] When the Belgian government in 1731 resumed administration of the customs, farmed 1718–29, and entrusted their receipt to Mathias Nettine, Pietro Proli retained responsibility for his partial remittance of the Barrier Subsidy.[50] In 1732–3, when the customs were again farmed, this time to Christiaen de Sotelet, Proli acted as receiver under him.[51] In 1727 he was ennobled for his services to the government.[52] He died on 28 January 1733.[53]

His widow, apparently not weakened by the fifteen children she had borne him, at once assumed control of the firm, and continued his government contracts. For the remainder of 1733 and in 1734–5 she shared the receipt of the customs, once more administered by the government, with Mathias Nettine. From then until July 1744, when she asked to withdraw, and Nettine took over, she was formally responsible for the whole *régie*. Sotelet acted as farmer to March 1737, but then got into difficulties, and direct administration was resumed.[54] An account submitted by Widow Proli to the Conseil des Finances at the conclusion of this period summarizes her

[47] The definitive source for the Barrier Subsidy, and the negotiations leading to the Treaty of the Hague of 22 Dec. 1718, is the introduction by H. Ritter von Srbik to *Österreichische Staatsverträge. Niederslande*, i. *Bis 1722* (Veröffent. d. Kom. f. neuere Gesch. Öst. 10, Vienna 1912) 532–53. The Barrier Subsidy's total is more usually referred to in the sources as 500,000 écus or ducats (= *f* 1.25m. or 1.4m. fl. Brab.).

[48] The treaty just referred to defined arrears as *f* 500,000 to be paid at 20,000 fl. yearly, but the higher sums are stated in Cons. des Fin. 7178 under 30 July 1731.

[49] Srbik, loc. cit. The gross revenues of the *Pays Rétrocédé* in 1751 were 1,426,518 fl. Brab. or *f* 1,273,676, AGR Cons. des Fin. 7208, 'Sommier' for 1751.

[50] Cons. des Fin. 7178, 28 July 1731. It is not clear who remitted the balance of the Dutch subsidy.

[51] The vicissitudes of Belgian customs management are explained in an undated reply by the Chambre des Comptes to a letter from the Conseil des Finances dated 29 Nov. 1741, AGR Cons. des Fin. 7080.

[52] Michielsen, 277, Nov. 1727, grant of nobility to Proli and his descendants. On 1 Feb. 1730 he was allowed to continue to trade, as a noble, without derogation, ibid. 278.

[53] Michielsen, 279 erroneously says 28 Feb.

[54] See n. 51 above. According to a notarial act dated 28 June 1736 cited by Michielsen, 282, Mme Proli, while retaining overall responsibility, delegated receipt at nine of the seventeen customs bureaux to Nettine.

activities for the government during it.[55] The revenue she received from 1736 to August 1744 totalled 9,745,665 fl. Brab., an annual average of 1,133,216 fl. Expenditure was as follows, in fl. Brab. The Barrier Subsidy took 3,500,000. Sundry persons were paid 3,592,467, and the Estates of Brabant 994,154. Retention of revenue to repay short-term loans absorbed 964,241, and other accounts came to 673,985. The total was 9,724,847 fl. Brab. The first item looks tidy. The detail of the account, however, shows that this part of the Subsidy, ƒ550,000 a year, or 616,000 fl. Brab., was not met in full. The sums she paid, in fl. Brab., were: 1736, 616,000 (plus 154,000 for 1735); 1737, 308,000; 1738, 616,000; 1739, 616,000; 1740, 539,000; 1741, 539,000; 1742, 56,000; 1743, 56,000. Only half the amount due was therefore remitted in 1737, and from the outbreak of war in 1740 payments tailed off, to a chorus of Dutch and English complaints. It must be assumed that the balance, charged on the revenue of the *Pays Retrocédé*, experienced a similar fate. After the war, the resumption of the Subsidy was urgently demanded by the Maritime Powers, but it was in fact diverted to the Belgian *Caisse de Guerre* from 1750, as already noted.[56]

Mme Proli's payments 'to sundry persons' were primarily for the Civil List. Those made to the Estates of Brabant were to service loans which they made in 1729 and 1732. These were respectively for 1,366,320 fl. ex. and 5,649,853 fl. ex., and enabled the Belgian government to pay off its Dutch creditors.[57] Mme Proli explained

[55] AGR Cons. des Fin. 7181, containing Mme Proli's original account-book Jan. 1736–July 1744.

[56] See p. 186 and n. 26. Bigwood, 'Les origines', states that the Barrier Subsidy 'disappears from the budget' only in 1755. This is followed by Janssens, 36. The subsidy was in fact *transferred* at least as early as 1750, as shown in the text. It then continued as an entity within the Belgian finances, e.g. AGR Cons. des Fin. 7186 under 15 Mar. 1758, expenditure includes 'f. 95m. (i.e. 95,000 fl. ex.) à remettre mensuellement à la Caisse de Guerre Sur les fonds du Subside de la Barrière'. This would be 1,140,000 fl. Brab. instead of the original 1,400,000 fl. Brab. The subsidy is treated vaguely in E. Hubert's otherwise definitive account of the Barrier garrisons, 'Les garnisons de la Barrière dans les Pays-Bas autrichiens (1715–1782)', *Mémoires couronnés . . . publiés par l'Académie Royale des Sciences . . . de Belgique*, 9 (1901–3).

[57] The smaller loan was to repay debts of 1,366,320 fl. ex. (1,598,594 fl. Brab.) charged on the postal revenues, the larger (6,610,382 fl. Brab.) was to repay 4,243,617 fl. ex. (4,965,031 fl. Brab.) charged on the customs bureau of Fort Saint-Philippe, see an undated (?1766) report on the debts due to the Estates of Brabant, AGR Cons. des Fin. 7080. Bigwood, 'Les origines', 8 overstates the customs debt. The postal and customs revenues were ceded to the Estates. The government repaid these loans 1771–93.

later how she 'fit en 1734 aux hollandais pour le gouvernement des Pays-Bas le remboursement de leurs avances dans les guerres précédentes . . . '.[58] She was not, however, responsible for the service of further loans of 2,189,478 fl. Brab. by the Estates of Brabant in the years 1736–44 charged on the royal domains.[59] Besides managing these operations, Mme Proli provided short-term loans to the treasury, which repaid them when the customs dues came in. The details of these advances in fl. Brat. were: 1737, 250,000; 1741, 200,000; 1742, 250,000; 1743, 200,000. A further sum of 151,200 fl. Brab. was retained in 1742 and remitted to Jean Osy of Rotterdam for loan-service, making the total 1,051,200 fl., rather larger than the 964,241 fl. shown in her summary account.[60] The bank is also found in 1735 lending 1,717,805 fl. Brab. at 4% in anticipation of the Austrian loan for 2.5 fl. ex. raised through the Estates of Hainault.[61] The 'commission and interest' which form part of the remaining payments in Mme Proli's account do not, however, amount to more than 54,313 fl. Brab., a rate of 0.55% on total expenditure, including foreign remittances.

In August 1744 Mathias Nettine took over the receipt of the customs, Mme Proli declaring herself unable to continue.[62] She did not regain the official foothold then lost. But it is significant that one of the two royal Receivers under whom Nettine operated was Balthasar Proli, Mme Proli's fourteenth child and eldest surviving son (1722–1804). He acted through a deputy from 1736 till 1747 and then in person.[63] The Proli family was thus still to the fore. Its position was successfully asserted against the intrusive Nettines in the struggles in 1750 over foundation of the Privileged Company of

[58] Cited by Michielsen, 281 from an undated memoir by Mme Proli.
[59] From the MS source cit. n. 57 above. The Estates took over administration of the Brabant domains.
[60] The payment to Osy was for service of the loan authorized on 31 May 1741, of which he raised seven-twelfths, Bigwood, 'Les origines', 14. According to Bigwood, 11 n. Mme Proli lent 1,174,400 fl. Brab. 1735–45 and Mathias Nettine 634,349 fl.
[61] AGR Cons. des Fin. 7179 under 29 Mar. 1736, 'according to orders and agreements between her and Councillor Hilleprand de Prandau'.
[62] Michielsen, 281; Janssens, 226, 229.
[63] Michielsen 283. The other Receiver was François van Overstraeten. The two Receivers evidently acted in alternate years, see AGR Cons. des Fin. 7180 under 22 Dec. 1750. There are several further documents about François Jacques van Overstraeten, ibid. 7184 (1749–50). His relationship to the army contractor Nicholas van Overstraeten, who was supplying the English troops in 1744 (e.g. *Cal. T. Papers 1742–1745*, 454, 22 Feb. 1744) is not clear.

Trieste and Fiume. The *octroi* of this company, signed by the empress on 14 October 1750, showed that the Proli interests had triumphed, to the exclusion of Mme Nettine and her ally on this occasion, Mme Cogels.[64] When the company got into difficulties in 1753, it was Balthasar Proli, then in Vienna, who was asked by the directors to go to Trieste to investigate. He stayed there and in Fiume for nine months (July 1753–March 1754), reforming the bookkeeping and installing a Scottish inspector (who proved a disastrous failure).[65] In 1758 Balthasar was again in Trieste, but in 1760 returned to Brussels, where he lived (featuring in his brother Charles Proli's ledgers as 'Conseiller B. Proli à Bruxelles') until the Brabant revolution forced him to emigrate to Cologne. He died there in 1804.[66] He was made a count in 1768 and *Contrôleur de la Recette Générale* in 1784. It was his younger son Petrus who, after acquiring a fortune in India, settled in Paris as a speculator in 1783, founded the newspaper *Le Cosmopolite* in December 1791, and was executed as a suspected English agent, and channel for 'Pitt's gold', in 1794.[67]

Balthasar Proli was essentially an official and rentier, with some business interests. His younger brother Charles Melchior André (1723–86), Aldegonde Proli's fifteenth and last child, was a banker and entrepreneur, interested in trade, shipping, finance, insurance and industry. The breadth of his interests, if not their success, recalls the activities of Johann Fries. Charles Proli, however, unlike Fries, Mme Nettine, or his own mother, only sporadically acted as a government financial agent. This must be due to the virtual monopoly which the Bank Nettine had established in this sector. The scale of Proli's business engagements was large. His annual balances, laboriously reconstructed by Dr Houtman-de Smedt, show total gross assets of 530,742 fl. Brab. at the end of 1761 (part

[64] See L. Michielsen, 'De Kompagnie van Trieste en Fiume (1750–1800)', *Bijdragen tot de Geschiedenis*, 27 (1936) 70–91, 181–221. There is valuable additional information about the company's commercial activities in Houtman-de Smedt, pt. ii, ch. 3. She shows at p. 76 n. that in 1752 the 1,100 shares (each of 1,000 fl.: 900 more were not subscribed for) were held: 236 in Vienna, 16 in Prague, 12 in Trieste, 2 in Fiume, 754 in Antwerp, 12 in Brussels, 24 in Liège, 2 in Louvain, 36 in Amsterdam, 6 in Rotterdam.

[65] Michielsen, 86–9, installation of Archibald Kennedy, who absconded with company funds in 1758.

[66] Michielsen, 'De familie', 283–5.

[67] Ibid. 285–7 and refs. there. Balthasar Proli was made a count on 13 Oct. 1768, *Liste des titres* pt. ii, p. 8.

of them, however, belonged to his mother), 1,477,300 fl. at the end of 1773, 1,322,512 fl. at the end of 1779, and no less than 3,799,152 fl. at the end of 1783.[68] The greater part of these assets, which were offset by nearly equal liabilities, in fact belonged to others, for whom Proli acted; but he was responsible for the whole. From 1751 until his mother's death on 1 October 1761 he was in partnership with her, but thereafter on his own, still under his father's style of Pietro Proli & Co. His partnership with his mother preceded by a month his marriage in February 1751 to Cornelia Petronella van der Linden of Rotterdam, whose family was connected with Osy & Co., the Austrian financial agents there.[69] Living at an extravagant rate, admiring, or at least purchasing, paintings by Rubens and Van Dyck, and such French literature as the *Encyclopédie* and works by Montesquieu, Voltaire, and Rousseau, Proli seems to have systematically watered down his capital, but to have kept this deterioration in his finances concealed from prying eyes.[70] Indeed, the shakier his position became, the more ambitious he became, a not uncommon combination.

The structure of Proli's business interests can be approached by examining the items credited to his profit-and-loss account in 1772, after he had been trading on his own account for twelve years. The total credited was 64,926 fl. The chief items in this are shown in Table 8.3.[71] Proli was an original subscriber to James Dormer's 'Imperial and Royal Insurance Company' of 1754, and was named a Director of it for life in 1761. The company held its account with him (item *a*).[72] He had from 1766 a one-eighth share valued at 7,562 fl. ex., in the cottonprint-works established at Dambrugge near Antwerp in June 1753 by Jan Beerenbroeck, who was acting for an Antwerp syndicate. In the years 1776–82 this investment

[68] Houtman-de Smedt, balances on microfiche in end-pocket of the book. What follows is largely based on her learned study, but is supplemented in places by my own earlier work on Charles Proli's ledgers. These are in the Stad Antwerpen Archief, Insolvente Boedelskamer. They are listed by Denucé, 'Charles de Proli', 54–64, but the ref. nos. are now different. Proli did not leave papers or correspondence.

[69] See ii. 296 for this connection.

[70] See esp. Houtman-de Smedt, 220, where Proli's own capital, when adjusted, is shown to have risen to a peak in the early 1770s, but thereafter to have fallen to below its initial amount.

[71] Ins. Boed., no. 1882, Proli's ledger 1772–3.

[72] See Houtman-de Smedt, pt. ii, ch. 2 and refs. there.

TABLE 8.3. *Chief items credited to Charles Proli's profit-and-loss account.*
1772 (fl. Brab.)

(a) Dividend of the *Chambre d'assurances*	312
(b) Honorarium of the *Chambre d'assurances* and the cottonprint works	2,034
(c) 5% dividend on 28 shares in Company of Trieste and Fiume	3,414
(d) 1 year's interest on 100,000 fl. lent to Company of Trieste and Fiume	3,428
(e) Interest 'on the account of Urbano Arnoldt'	6,421
(f) Wulf, 1 year's interest on 23,000 fl., and commission	1,035
(g) Wulf, 1 year's life annuity and dividend on 60 shares	1,285
(h) Holtermann, 1 year's interest on 84,000 fl. in Company of Sweden	4,690
(i) Holtermann, interest on 500,000 fl.	28,000
(j) 6% dividend on shares in Company of Sweden	4,967
Total	55,586

yielded Proli between 2,000 and 3,000 fl. annually (item b).[73] In November 1750 he was chosen a Deputy (one of the Antwerp directors) of the Privileged Company of Trieste and Fiume established in the previous month (items c and d).[74] The company kept its account with him throughout this period, and insured its ships and cargoes with the Imperial Insurance Company.[75] Urbano Arnoldt (item e), a former supercargo with the Ostend Company, was the original senior Director of the Company of Trieste and Fiume, but was replaced in 1754 because of ill health. The Company was known in Vienna until 1758 as 'Urbano Arnoldt und Compagnie'. 'Wulf' (item f) must be Louis de Wulf of Ghent, in whose house Proli was interested at this time in an amount of 35,000 fl. It traded in lace to South America through Frans de Wulf Ghyselen, Morel, & Co. of Cadiz. The life annuity and sixty shares (item g) probably refer to Proli's sawmill interests with Louis de Wulf, discussed below. (Martin) Holtermann (items h–j) was Proli's correspondent in Gothenburg, and the 'Company of Sweden' was the (New) Swedish East India Company of 1766, of which Holtermann was a director. Proli's holding in the old company of 1731 was reimbursed in 1766, and he carried forward a holding valued in 1767 at 142,775 fl. The loan to Holtermann, which began as one of 200,000 fl. in 1767, must have been for trade purposes, and was presumably placed by Proli with third parties. It was cleared by the early 1780s.[76]

[73] Ibid., pt. iii, ch. 1.
[74] Ibid., pt. ii, ch. 3 and Michielsen, 'De Compagnie'.
[75] As is clear from Proli's accounts.
[76] Ibid., also refs. to Holtermann in Houtman-de Smedt.

This list does not exhaust Proli's activities, since only business which made a profit appeared in it. Proli was an unsuccessful farmer and distiller. He bought the small domain of Mishagen at Mischaat near Antwerp in 1769, and used it for animal husbandry, a brick-works, a gin distillery. All lost, the last heavily. He also built a charming house there in 1777–8, which survives.[77] He was involved in a salt refinery at Antwerp from 1762. It closed at a loss in 1768. Proli had a varying (18–60) number of 100 fl. shares in 'les Moulins d'Ostende', a sawmill company established near the port in the 1750s, in which his mother had invested. He also acted as its banker. It subsequently acquired a two-thirds interest in three further sawmills built near the Slijkpoort at Antwerp in 1764–7. Proli controlled the other third. Louis De Wulf of Ghent was a director of both these sawmill companies, which do not seem to have been very profitable.[78] In 1754 Proli entered into partnership with Jan Bastijns of Antwerp to run a sugar-refinery there. He bought Bastijns out in 1760, and took Remigius Aerts and Martinus Cels as partners, who managed the refinery in future.[79] Proli pro-vided the sugar-cane, and insured the ships which brought it with the Imperial and Royal Insurance Company.[80] In the years 1761–83 he put nearly 200,000 fl. into the refinery, which appears in his books as 'Cels, Aerts et Cie'. The evidence for its business results is lacking.[81]

In the 1770s Proli developed contacts with the government for the first time. He solicited Prince Kaunitz to form closer trading links between Austria and the Belgian provinces, a subject in which Kaunitz had been interested since the late 1760s.[82] In December 1777 Proli and Louis de Wulf, together with twenty-nine other investors, mostly from Antwerp and Ghent, took up the shares of a so-called 'Compagnie Maritime' at Bruges which was to use the town's entrepôt status to manage the Belgian end of this trade. A 'Maison de Trieste' was established at the same time, with a capital of 500,000 fl. Aust., financed equally by Fries & Co. in Vienna and the Privileged Company of Trieste and Fiume. It had faded by

---

[77] Houtman-de Smedt, pt. iii, ch. 1 (there is a photograph of the manor house at the front of her book).
[78] Ibid. for these enterprises.
[79] Ibid. The firm survived Proli's bankruptcy in 1785 but not, it appears, for long.
[80] As appears from his ledgers.
[81] Houtman-de Smedt, loc. cit.
[82] See ii. 77.

1800. The Bruges house too does not seem to have been a success.[83] Besides this, and more momentously, Proli became involved in trade to the Far East. In 1775 he helped finance the voyage from Leghorn to Africa and India of the Dutch captain Willem Bolts. The Association between Proli and his partners and Bolts was dated 28 September 1775. Bolts, whose ship, appropriately, was named the *Joseph and Theresia*, left in 1777 and did not return until 1781. In his absence, Proli organized the despatch (1779) from Lorient to China of a heavier ship, the *Prince Kaunitz*. By September 1780 she was back in Trieste, and made a large profit.[84] Proli was already a baron (1768); these new exploits won him the title of count (1779).[85] In 1780 he nearly succeeded in promoting an East India Company in Vienna, with a capital of 3m. fl. This was at first enthusiastically agreed to by Kaunitz and the empress, but Joseph II, who disliked state support for such ventures, vetoed it.[86] Proli, encouraged by the diversion of the major belligerents from the Indian market, kept pushing, and obtained royal consent (6 October 1781) to the establishment in Antwerp of the Imperial and Royal Company of Asia and Africa, known less formally as the Asiatic Company of Trieste.[87] This title is perhaps explained by the initial intention that ships should lade at Leghorn, where Bolts had just been given a monopoly right to do so, and discharge at Trieste, as the *Prince Kaunitz* did in 1780.

Bolts, despite uneasy relations with his former patrons, was able to use his Leghorn monopoly to advantage, and took 200 of the initial shares. He paid by offsetting his claims against the former Association. Proli and his associates Borrekens and Nagels subscribed for 800 more. The other half of the 2,000 shares, each of 1,000 fl. was subscribed by the public (84 persons). The Asiatic

[83] The Bruges episode is elucidated for the first time, from archival sources, by Houtman-de Smedt, pt. iii, ch. 2. The earlier acccount by Michielsen is inadequate.

[84] Houtman-de Smedt, loc. cit. Here, too, Denucé and Michielsen are unsatisfactory.

[85] Michielsen, 'De familie', 306 says Proli was made a count in 1776. The correct dates, 13 Oct. 1768 and 18 Jan. 1779, are in the *Liste des titres*, pt. ii, pp. 8, 22.

[86] See F. von Pollack-Parnau, *Eine österreichisch-ostindische Handels-Compagnie 1775–1785. Ein Beitrag zur österreichischen Wirtschaftsgeschichte unter Maria Theresia und Joseph II.* (*VSWG*, Beiheft xii (1927), pp. 108). This is largely based on the MS sources in Vienna, and is markedly weaker on the Belgian background.

[87] Houtman-de Smedt, loc. cit. Her precise and important account of the Asiatic Company supersedes those by Denucé, Michielsen, and Pollack-Parnau, which are fuzzy.

Company, it seems, was essentially a device by Proli, Bolts, and their associates to cash in on the temporary opening of the Far Eastern market. Owing to poor planning and bad luck, the gamble failed. The company's history was dismal from the start. It was undercapitalized, and relied progressively on credit. It had five ships at once in Canton harbour in 1783, hence outlay was maximized and returns were minimized. The stoppage of payments on 29 January 1785 of the Paris firm of Perrouteau Delon & Co., on which the Asiatic Company had drawn heavily, precipitated the latter's collapse. This was formally dated 10 February 1785. Proli left Antwerp for Brussels on 13 February to escape arrest by his creditors. The bankruptcy of his own firm of Pietro Proli & Co. was published on the same day. Proli did not long survive this double fiasco. He died of a stroke on 16 September 1786, leaving a widow and five children.[88] There were unfounded rumours of suicide.[89] The affairs of the Asiatic Company were not finally wound up till 1817.

The structure of Proli's assets at the close of his business career can be summarized from a balance sheet which he drew up 'from memory' in February 1785 (Table 8.4).[90] Compared with his interests in trade and insurance, his industrial portfolio, consisting of a third share in the sawmills at Antwerp and 18 shares in those of Ostend (24,000 fl.), and an eighth share in the Antwerp cotton-print-works (42,000 fl.), was small. It will also be noticed that land, houses, and goods comprised nearly half his assets. Liabilities of 650,185 fl. (miscast 2,000 fl. lower) reduced the net estate to 344,315 fl.

The pattern of his trading accounts reflects the mixture of business interests already described.[91] In his first ledger (1760–1) there are 278 accounts, in the second (1762) 217, though not all these are

[88] Houtman-de Smedt, loc. cit.

[89] Accepted by Michielsen, 'De familie' p. 305, doubted by Denucé, 'Charles de Proli', 17, and now refuted from documentary evidence by Dr. Houtman-de Smedt. W. W. Davis (see n. 37), 143, whose account of these companies is garbled, says Proli 'took his own life' in 1784 (sic).

[90] Reproduced in Denucé, 50–1. No source is given. It is not only from memory, but a series of estimates rather than anything more exact, as Michielsen, 288 points out. Neither appears to notice that its total, 948,500 fl., is miscast.

[91] Based on his ledgers, see n. 68 above. Houtman-de Smedt analyses these at length in pt. iv, chs. 2 and 3 of her book. She concludes that Proli's revenue from interest, dividends, and commissions was more important than that from any single other source.

TABLE 8.4. *Charles Proli's assets, February 1785 (fl. Brab.)*

		%
(*a*) Land and houses	328,000	32.9
(*b*) House contents	133,000	13.4
(*c*) Trade and insurance		
13 shares in the Company of Trieste and Fiume	15,600	
10,000 dollars Sw. in shares of Swedish East India Co. @ 212	136,600	
Company of Africa and Asia	210,000	
1 share in the *Maison de commerce* at Bruges	6,000	
25 shares in the (Imperial and Royal) Company of Insurance	6,500	
Total	374,700	37.7
(*d*) Industry	66,000	6.7
(*e*) Other	92,800	9.3
Total	994,500	100.0

for firms or individuals. The bulk of his correspondents were in the Austrian Netherlands, as those of James Dormer were. Outside it, they included:

Amsterdam:	Clifford & Teysett, Everard Wittert
Breslau:	Molinari & Co.
Cadiz:	Frans de Wulf
Cologne:	Martin Guaita
London:	Bartholomew Burton, Dillon & Cruise, Fonblanque & Thellusson, *et al.*
Nantes:	Dominique Deurbrœcq
Prague:	J. G. Pradatsch
Rotterdam:	Jean Osy
Stockholm:	Jennings & Finlay
Strassbourg:	Jean Dietrich
Vienna:	Smitmer Brothers, Fries & Co.

Substantial purchases of sugar in the 1760s from Jean Osy of Rotterdam, Servat Teysset & Co. of Amsterdam, and Dominique Duerbrœcq of Nantes must have been due to Proli's refining interests already noted. The accounts for Pradatsch in Prague and for Smitmer Brothers in Vienna, however, remind us of a minor, but not insignificant, part of his activities. This was the receipt of interest on Austrian bonds, and the sale and purchase of these bonds for Belgian clients. In the accounts, sales and purchases and the receipt of interest are jumbled together. The principal involved is not clearly stated except for Smitmers in 1762, when it seems to have been 163,700 fl. Brab. In subsequent years Smitmers' account is credited with sums between 28,430 fl. (1770) and 73,738 fl. (1780 and 1781). This was small beer compared to the amounts paid through Nettine's bank, but shows that the latter did not monopolize this business. J. G. Pradatsch of Prague ('Veuve Pradatsch' from 1764), who often drew on, or remitted to, Smitmers, had a smaller account. They were credited with c. 45,000 fl. Brab. 1760–1, 8,450 fl. 1766, 73 fl. 1768–70, 34,715 fl. 1780–1. They were used for purchase and service of Bohemian bonds. Both firms made payments to Antwerp by drawing on Amsterdam, and sometimes on London. Proli's other main Vienna correspondent, Fries & Co., was remitting for the Company of Trieste and Fiume from at least 1768. Earlier (1764) Erhard Riesch and Johann Stametz had done this. Fries's drafts were often discounted for Proli by François van Ertborn of Antwerp.[92] Proli's commission for this financial business, as for comparable activities, like his loans to Prince Nicholas von Salm-Salm (d. 1770), the Austrian governor of Antwerp, or his payments for the *Caisse de Guerre* (1772–3, 1779), formed a not unimportant part of his income.[93]

Charles Proli's financial stature was certainly considerable, and encouraged him to hope, though in vain, for appointment as *Banquier de la Cour* when Mme Nettine died in 1775.[94] The later sardonic comment of Joseph II, admittedly made after the collapse of the Asiatic Company in 1785, shows, nevertheless, that Proli, despite his titles and responsibilities, had a somewhat *louche* reputation:

Le comte Charles Proli a été de tous temps une mauvaise tête et un homme

---

[92] See Ch. 7 for the Austrian firms. François van Ertborn, originally of Mechelen (1715–91) was *caissier* to Proli, to the Privileged Company of Trieste and Fiume, and to the Imperial and Royal Company of Asia and Africa. In 1781 he became a director of the Prussian Emden Company. Proli paid him less than 500 fl. a year. See Houtman-de Smedt, 62 n., 238. Michielsen, 'De familie', 273, 288 surmises that he acted as a banker for Antwerp merchants, but says that his papers have disappeared. There is further information in Janssens, 258–60.

[93] Michielsen, 289–90, Prince Salm; Denucé, 7, unspecified payments for the *caisse de guerre* in 1779. Proli paid 901,185 fl. to order of the *caisse* in 1772–3, Ins. Boed., no. 1882, fo. 47. According to General d'Ayasasa, the Conseil de Guerre used Proli for remittances to Vienna and other places in place of Widow Nettine, because he charged at most 2½% commission whereas she charged 3½%. See his report, cit. n. 35 above, at fo. 58ᵛ.   [94] Denucé, 7 cites a letter of 9 June 1776.

dont la mauvaise économie domestique, le peu de bonne foi et de délicatesse dans le choix de ses moyens pour parvenir à ses buts, ne pouvoient jamais inspirer de la confiance.[95]

The exposition of Austrian society just concluded, though selective, and leaving many loose ends, shows much diversity within the Monarchy's central lands. This social differentiation underlay, and sustained, the differences in their political constitutions, upon which each insisted. Though differing between lands, society was backward, poor, and marked by polarization of rank and income. A developed entrepreneurial class was lacking, and for banking and financial services, in particular, the Crown was forced to rely on Jews and Protestants. In contrast, the Austrian Netherlands and Italy, with their greater wealth, more complex societies, and long commercial traditions, were able to provide (Catholic) bankers and businessmen, and, as appears later, substantial loans, for the government in Vienna. Social structures provided a setting for, and in important respects imposed limits on, structures of government. What was politically appropriate, and practicable, for the central lands, as they moved from the rule of Crown and Estates towards a more developed monarchical absolutism in the course of Maria Theresia's reign, was not necessarily so for the Austrian Netherlands or Lombardy. Within the central lands, Hungary always had a special position, and had to be handled cautiously. The remainder of this volume examines the pattern of government in the central lands and the reforms made in it as the Crown sought to mobilize its resources for war, and to assert its position against the powerful entrenched interests of aristocracy and church. The last two chapters examine the neglected and important subject of royal central and local councillors, and show the continued importance of the noble classes in government.

[95] Ibid. 14. The portrait of Proli in Houtman-de Smedt confirms Joseph's unfavourable views.

PART TWO
GOVERNMENT

9

Central government

EIGHTEENTH-CENTURY rulers of large states in Central and
Eastern Europe are usually credited with an Enlightened Absolutism involving, among much else, the speedy imposition on semi-
feudal societies of rational systems of administration, which facilitated deployment of political and military power. The implications
are of application of philosophic principle and adherence to a
uniform system. This view requires substantial modification if
applied to Austrian government under Maria Theresia. There was a
largely successful attempt during her reign to restructure it so as to
increase royal authority and revenue. There was much flaunting of
principle. There was an undoubtedly widespread belief in fixed,
unchanging systems. When inspected closely, however, this long
period was marked more by argument and disagreement than by a
fixed and settled administrative pattern; and change, rather than
continuity, was the norm. A running debate about the division of
business at the centre, the appropriate institutions for it, and the
provincial consequences, extended through much of the reign.
Financial issues, as will be seen in detail, were of the first importance here. Haugwitz's unitary system of 1749 was condemned and
dismantled in 1761. Yet the reforms then made at the centre, in the
name of greater efficiency, actually increased disputes about state
policy, and by 1771 it was possible for Joseph II to argue that every
organ of government fought with, and intrigued against, the others,
and that unity of control and direction was conspicuous by its
absence. The renewed changes of 1771–6, made at his suggestion but
omitting his most radical proposals, went some way to remedy this.
In Joseph's view, however, they did not go nearly far enough.
Given the emperor's impatient and perfectionist temperament, his
two decades before 1780 of exposure to government by discussion
do much to explain his pent-up irritation with it. Once the need to
defer to his mother was removed, it was therefore probable that
institutional reforms would come thick and fast. Joseph's new

system, however, only lasted as long as he did, and after his death
the process of reshuffling the central administration continued into
the Congress period.[1]

Most descriptions of Austrian central government in this period are
confined to the ministerial departments, the *Hofstellen* or *Dicasterien* in the jargon of the time. However, by 1740 the lengthy process
of displacement of the Court from the centre of Austrian politics
and administration was by no means complete; a short description
of it, and some assessment of its importance, must therefore be
attempted. The subject is one that demands a monograph of its own,
since while the outer face of Court activity is well known, the
details of Court organization and finance, and of Maria Theresia's
own work and secretariat, are much less clear. The Court was
divided formally into departments, of which the most important
were those of the 'Erster Obrist Hofmeister', the 'Zweiter Obrist
Hofmeister', the 'Obrist Kämmerer' and the 'Obrist Stallmeister'
who was in charge of the royal stables and transport. The office of
Hofmeister was senior. Its division, like other peculiarities of the
period, was the result of having two rulers, not one (though
the 'Erster Hofmeister' was clearly the more important of the two;
the merger of the two Court establishments into one after the
emperor Francis Stephen's death in August 1765 confirmed this).
The next senior officer was the 'Obrist Hofmarschall', who had
legal jurisdiction over all members of the Court, including merchants and tradesmen who supplied it, as well as over foreign
ambassadors and foreign princes and nobles. He was responsible for
security at Court. His earlier jurisdiction over the higher civil service had lapsed. ('Obrist' in these titles was South German dialect
for 'Oberst' highest, chief, which was sometimes also used.) The
holders of the leading Court offices were aristocrats. In 1762 the
'Erster Obrist Hofmeister' was Count Corfiz Ulfeld, the former
State Chancellor. The 'Zweiter Obrist Hofmeister' was Prince
Johann Trautson, *Landmarschall* of Lower Austria, and head of the
Estates there. The *Hofmarschall* was Prince Joseph Schwarzenberg.
The 'Obrist Kämmerer' was the diarist Count Johann Joseph

---

[1] For Joseph's views see Table 9.3*. Count Rudolf Chotek observed on 22 Nov.
1768 that 'one cannot refrain from observing that the frequent innovations, and the
proposed reforms of departmental arrangements, do not bring the best results with
them', cit. Beer, 'Die Finanzverwaltung', 256.

Khevenhüller-Metsch, created a prince at the end of 1763. The 'Obrist Stallmeister' was Prince Heinrich Auersperg. At this date, there were separate households for Crown Prince Joseph and Archduchess Maria Anna. The remaining royal children had a joint establishment. The further organization of the Court, with its kitchens, falconry, interpreters, guards, and elaborate arrangements for music, can be seen in detail in the accounts for 1762 printed by Oberleitner.[2]

The first function of the Court was to provide a setting for empress and emperor, to rank them in order of political importance. The affable emperor Francis Stephen, adored by his wife until his premature death in 1765, and officially co-regent with her from December 1740, was more significant in public business than has usually been realized. This was particularly true of financial matters, and his role in these is discussed in some detail in later chapters. From the start, however, it was clear that it was the empress who was the captain of the political vessel. Initially only Archduchess of Austria (1740), she progressed to Queen of Hungary (1741) then Bohemia (1743), and finally to Empress after her husband's coronation as Holy Roman Emperor in September 1745. The sequence of titles denoted her military success in asserting her contested inheritance. In her often-quoted memorial of 1750, it is clear that this ordeal by battle, and its outcome, confirmed her belief in her God-given authority, and perhaps eliminated an initial doubt whether her title was just. She set God as the origin of princely power as firmly as Frederick II, writing two years later for the edification of his successor, set the people, 'mes concitoyens'. This difference in philosophy between the two rulers did not affect their common belief in the duty of governors to rule actively for the benefit of their subjects. The empress, while retaining her grip on Court ceremonial,

---

[2] The Court has not attracted a separate monograph. There is information in ÖZV (1907); the subject is ignored in the subsequent ÖZV vols. F. Menčik, 'Beiträge zur Geschichte der kaiserlichen Hofämter', AÖG 87 (1899) 447–564 has copious appendices. The holders of leading Court offices are given there, in ÖZV (1907), pt. i (to 1749), and in Payer von Thurn's tables of 1902 and 1906. For these, and Oberleitner's article, see the Bibliography. The division of the office of *Hofmeister* into *Erster* and *Zweiter* dated from 1740. Joseph II on becoming emperor divided the office of *Erster Hofmeister* into two until Ulfeld's death on 31 Dec. 1769. Trautson, *Zweiter Hofmeister*, was not replaced when he died in 1775. See *Khev.-Metsch* (he became *Erster Hofmeister* on 3 Jan. 1770), 18 Jan. 1746, 8 Jan. 1747, 7, 11, and 14 Sept. 1765, 1 Jan. 1770, 31 Oct. 1775. The proliferation of *Hofmeister* causes much confusion in the literature.

etiquette, and rivalries, set most store on a rigorously organized pattern of work. Podewils in 1747 stated that she went to bed at ten, rose at four or five in summer, six in winter. In 1772 she described to her son Ferdinand how (by that date) she slept well for three to four hours, worked for two to three, then slept again. Her daily programme in 1770, set out to Countess Enzenberg, was: audiences on Sunday, 7 to 10.30 a.m.; ministers on Tuesdays from 8 a.m. to 5 p.m.; the *Staatsrat* on Thursdays from 9 a.m. until 4 p.m. On Monday and Wednesday she worked all day with her Cabinet Secretaries Neny and Pichler. Saturdays were reserved for personal affairs. This relentless dedication to labour and routine cannot have failed to influence and impress those who worked for her—and the public at large.[3]

The life of the Court is well described in Count, later Prince, Khevenhüller-Metsch's diaries. The religious duties of the royal couple took precedence over all others, no doubt symbolizing the public adherence of the House of Austria to the Counter-Reformation. Religion was also a natural foil to the omnipresence of death and disease. The diarist records numerous examples of child deaths, including that of his own daughter from smallpox (15 January 1746). It was no coincidence that six of Maria Theresia's 16 children, and both of Joseph II's, did not survive to their majority. Adults, too, perished like flies from smallpox, strokes, tuberculosis, and other causes. This dangerous background partly explains the Court's relentless dedication to a round of gambling, dinners, suppers, balls, theatrical performances (often by courtiers and their children), falconry, hunting expeditions, and sleigh-rides. Gallantry was practised, but the empress frowned on it, especially if it involved her husband. From 1746, when the new apartments in Schönbrunn were completed, the royal household regularly spent the summer there, and the winter in the Hofburg in Vienna. This pattern was interspersed with visits to the minor royal residences at Laxenburg and Mannersdorf near the capital, and to the emperor Francis Stephen's recently acquired estate at Holics in Hungary. He not infrequently got away there with a few cronies for the hunting

---

[3] For her memorials and their dates see ii. 3; for Frederick II's *Political Testament* of 1752, G. B. Volz, *Die politischen Testamente Friedrichs des Grossen* (Berlin 1920). For the pattern of work in 1770 and 1772 see Arneth, *Mar. Ther. Kinder und Freunde* i. 148 (2 Sept. 1772), iv. 500 (6 Oct. 1770). *Fürst (1755)* also says that the empress rose at six. *Khev.-Metsch, passim* makes it clear that Court days started early.

and hawking which he loved, leaving his regularly pregnant wife behind. Partly because of pregnancies, Maria Theresia, though an ardent horsewoman in her younger days, was no traveller, in contrast to her son. An expedition to Moravia to review the Russian troops in June 1748, to Prague for her coronation in 1743, attendance at Pressburg for the coronation Diet of 1741 and for the Diets of 1751 and 1764, the ill-fated visit to Innsbruck in 1765, marked the geographical limits of her mobility.[4]

The death of the emperor at Innsbruck on 18 August 1765 did not alter this general pattern. Khevenhüller-Metsch continues to record annual summer removal of the Court to Schönbrunn, royal residence at Laxenburg or Mannersdorf, expeditions to Schlosshof, the former palace of Prince Eugene in the Marchfeld, which the imperial couple had purchased from Eugene's heiress. But there is little doubt that the gaiety which, despite the political thunderstorms, marked the period of the empress's marriage, dispersed with her husband's death, to be replaced by melancholy and pessimism. Her black-edged writing-paper symbolized her grief for her husband, and for her son Joseph, smitten almost beyond endurance by the death of his beloved first wife, Maria Isabella of Parma, and of both children of the marriage. It perhaps also symbolized her growing belief that she was out of tune with the times, in which she saw only the growth of depravity, self-interest, cynicism, and the decline of true religion.[5]

The political importance of the Court is not easy to assess. The regular appearance of the empress and her husband in Vienna, even when in residence at Schönbrunn, and the winter sojourn of the

---

[4] *Khev.-Metsch*, index, under 'Krankheiten' and 'Ausflüge und Reisen des Hofes'; H. L. Mikoletzky, 'Holics und Sassin, die beiden Mustergüter des Kaisers Franz I. Stephan', *MÖSA* 14 (1961) 190–212. Francis Stephen acquired both estates for just over 2m. fl from the bankrupt Hungarian landowner Count Czobor (d. 1785) in 1751, though having an interest in them as creditor since the late 1730s. C. Hinrichs (ed.), *Friedrich der Grosse und Maria Theresia. Diplomatische Berichte von Otto Christoph Graf v. Podewils* (Berlin 1937) 38–54 prints Podewils's account of the empress, dated 18 Jan. 1747, which emphasizes her iron constitution, love of gambling, riding, and walking, enjoyment of harsh weather, jealous love of her husband.

[5] These attitudes frequently appear in her printed correspondence. Cf. her letter to Joseph II, cit. n. 117. In Apr. 1774, she wrote to her son Maximilian that 'le ton qui règne actuellement, est le plus mauvais pour la religion et décence . . . les jeunes gens . . . sont d'une dissolution extrême', Arneth, *Mar. Ther. Kinder u. Freunde*, ii. 318–19. Her increasing obesity and physical immobility, too, may have affected her outlook.

Court in the Hofburg, must have helped to make the monarchy familiar to—and, as a kind of exalted theatre, popular with—the residents of the capital. There is some evidence that Maria Theresia's greater seclusion as a widow was resented, though the grief at her death was marked, and genuine. In the narrower political context, Court officers, though consulted about business, as Khevenhüller-Metsch or Ulfeld continued to be, seem to have been of only peripheral importance. A repetition of the career of Prince Carl Dietrich Salm, 'Obristhofmeister' to Joseph I, and Prime Minister 1705–9, is unthinkable in this period. On the other hand, the arts of the courtier seldom harm the politically ambitious in a monarchy, and Prince Kaunitz exemplified this. Similarly, a poor performance at Court might hamper the realization of political ambitions, and so on.

The next section considers the structure of central government in the subperiod 1740–7. (See the first column of Table 9.1.) The Privy Conference was formally only an advisory council to the sovereign, not a department of state. The remaining bodies, with the exception of the Finance Conference, also advisory, and the Bank Deputation, which only acquired departmental status in 1746, comprised, under their chiefs, or 'capi', the 'Hofstellen', 'Hofmitteln', 'Dicasterien', or ministerial departments, nearly all of them with important financial responsibilities. They are fewer in number than the extended list of institutions in the *Court Calendar* at this date, all involved in government in some way or other. But this restriction is justified: in the discussions of the time, it was agreed that these were the departments which counted politically. Those concerned primarily with the German Empire, the *Reichshofkanzlei* and *Reichshofrat*, are, however, omitted here.[6]

The Privy Conference had its origins in the *Geheimer Rat* established by Ferdinand I in 1526. This, like the English Privy Council, became unwieldy in size (41 members in 1684), and a smaller body, the 'Geheime Conferenz', first appointed in 1669, took over most of its functions. After vicissitudes in the earlier part of the reign of

---

[6] For the membership of departments, see Ch. 12. A *Hofstelle* had independent existence, and the right to address the sovereign directly. The *Ministerial-Banco-Deputation* officially acquired this on 18 Nov. 1746, ÖZV (1907), pt. i, p. 109, though its absence does not seem to have cramped Count Starhemberg's style. *Dicasterium* is late Latin (from Greek) for a judicial institution. Its use in this period to mean a government department may reflect the traditional mixture of judicial and administrative business.

TABLE 9.1. *Structure of Austrian central government, 1740, 1749, and 1762*

	20 October 1740	2 May 1749	1 January 1762
(1)	Privy Conference ('Geheime Conferenz')	Privy Conference	*Staatsrat*
(2)	Austrian Chancellery ('Geheime Oesterreichische Hof-Canzley')	'Conferenz in Internis'	Bohemian and Austrian Chancellery
(3)	Austrian Netherlands Council ('Höchster Rath deren königl. österr. Niederlanden')	Austrian Netherlands Council	'Geheime Hof und Staats Canzley'
(4)	Bohemian Chancellery ('Königl. Boheimische Hof Cantzley')	'Commercien-Ober-Directorium'	'Hof Commercien-Rath'
(5)	Finance Conference ('Kaiserl. Finanz-Conferenz')	*Directorium in Publicis et Cameralibus*	*Hofkammer*
(6)	*Hofkammer* ('Kaiserliche Hofkammer')	'Geheime Hof- und Staats Canzley'	*Hofkriegsrat*
(7)	*Hofkriegsrat*	'Generalkriegscommissariat'	Hungarian Chancellery
(8)	Hungarian Chancellery ('Königl. Hungarischer Hof-Rath und Canzley')	*Hofkammer*	Italian Department
(9)	Italian Council ('k.k. Italienischer Rath')	*Hofkriegsrat*	Ministerial Bank Deputation
(10)	Ministerial Bank Deputation ('Ministerial Banco Deputation')	Hungarian Chancellery	Netherlands Department
(11)	Siebenbürgen Chancellery (Siebenburgischer Hof-Rath und Canzley')	Italian Council	*Oberste Justizstelle*
(12)	*Universal Bancalität* ('Universal Bancalitäts-Rath und Canzley')	Ministerial Bank Deputation	Siebenbürgen Chancellery
(13)		*Oberste Justizstelle*	*Ständische Credits-Deputation*
(14)		Siebenbürgen Chancellery	

Names of institutions in 1740 taken from *Court Calendar* for that year, supplemented by documents in ÖZV (1907), pts. ii–iii. 'Kaiserlich', 'königlich', were abbreviated as shown.

For 1749 the documentary sources (many mentioned in the text) are in ÖZV (1925). Formal names in *Court Calendar* are as for 1740 but with small variations: e.g. 'Ministerial-Banco-Hof-Deputation'. The *Directorium* is given as 'k. k.'

For 1762, names in quotation-marks come from *Court Calendar* for 1763; remainder from documents in ÖZV (1934). For date 1 Jan. 1762 see p. 235 n. 55. The Bohemian and Austrian Chancellery is the 'Böhemisch und Oesterreichisch Hof Canzley' in the *Court Calendar*; the Ministerial Bank Deputation 'Ministerial Banco Deputation'. The final organization of the *Hofkriegsrat* was not approved until 7 May 1762, ÖZV (1934) 417. The *Hof- und Staatskanzlei* was said to be 'der auswärtigen, niederländischen und italienischen Geschäften', emphasizing the subordinate status of the 'Italienisches Departement' and 'Niederländisches Departement' created in 1757 (see text).

Joseph I, it resumed its activities from 1709. The membership of the *Geheimer Rat* and *Geheime Conferenz* included court officers and departmental ministers. The primary function of the Conference by 1740 was to discuss foreign affairs, including such issues as royal marriages. When dealing with business of the German Empire it was called a 'Reichsconferenz'. Internal policies, or 'Provincial Angelegenheiten', were assigned to a group of ministers: the *Deputation*. This body, first constituted in November 1697 on an ad hoc basis, proved permanent. It was typically concerned with all aspects of military supply, movement and finance, especially the Contribution. Its membership overlapped, though not coinciding, with that of the Conference. Khevenhüller-Metsch, who as 'Obrist Kämmerer' from 1745 joined the Conference, records the types and numbers of meetings to which he was summoned in the years 1746–9; they are shown in Table 9.2. An Afforced Conference (a term he did not use) is defined as one with extra members, for example, the president of the Netherlands Council when Belgian business was discussed. It seems clear that foreign affairs predominated, and that discussion of internal affairs was slight, as the diarist complained. These gatherings usually occurred in a minister's house; but a minority in the presence of emperor, empress, or both, at the Hofburg or Schönbrunn. The numbers of meetings, all preceded by agenda and papers, show that councillors had no chance to be idle. But despite the press of business, the Conference was not a powerful body. Khevenhüller on 29 April 1747 recorded his belief that ministers only brought business before it when they dared not undertake responsibility themselves. The royal couple, he thought, suspected the Conference, and turned for advice elsewhere. These advisers were often half-briefed. This view is confirmed by the careful exclusion of the Conference and its ministers from the secret discussions which preceded Haugwitz's 'revolution' of 1748–9.[7]

The main *Hofstellen* or political departments in 1740 comprised the chancelleries of Austria and Bohemia; the important, but much smaller, chancelleries of Hungary and Siebenbürgen; and the finan-

---

[7] For the history of the Conference and Deputation see ÖZV (1907), pt. i, ch. 1, §§ iii–iv, also the pioneering study by H. I. Bidermann, *Geschichte der österreichischen Gesammt-Staats-Idee* (Innsbruck 1867, 1889) i. 11, 42 and nn. Initially the monarch always attended Conference meetings.

TABLE 9.2. *Conferences attended by Khevenhüller-Metsch, 1746–9*

	1746	1747	1748	1749
Conference	36	31	47	30
Afforced Conference	2	14	11	8
Deputation	4	6	1	0
Reichsconferenz	7	6	5	7
Total	49	57	64	45

cial offices: the *Hofkammer*, Ministerial Bank Deputation, and *Universal Bancalität*. (The Finance Conference, nominally only advisory, oversaw all three.) The councils (not chancelleries) of the Austrian Netherlands (1717) and Italy (1736, previously 'the Council of Spain') were organs for both supervision and representation of these newly acquired areas, Italy denoting the duchies of Milan and Mantua. The *Hofkriegsrat* (1556) was responsible for the army and, until 1753, for diplomatic relations with Russia and Turkey.[8] The other offices mostly originated in the long reign (1522–64) of Charles V's brother Ferdinand I, the first monarch faced with the problems of ruling the Bohemian and Hungarian lands, as well as those of Austria. The chancelleries will be considered first. Ferdinand established a *Hofkanzlei* or Court Chancellery in 1526, revised in 1528, responsible for all the central lands, as also for the German Empire, of which he was *Statthalter*. Secretaries were assigned to each. After Ferdinand became emperor in 1556, he reorganized the chancellery as the *Reichshofkanzlei*, and undertook with the Imperial Chancellor, the Elector of Mainz, that

---

[8] O. Schmid and J. Mayr in L. Bittner *et al.* (eds.), *Gesamtinventar des Wiener Haus-, Hof- und Staatsarchivs* (Vienna 1936–40) iv. 55 ff. 256 ff. describe the councils of the Netherlands and Italy. For the diplomatic responsibilities of the *Hofkriegsrat*, see ÖZV (1907), pt. i, p. 69 n. and K. A. Roider Jr., *Austria's Eastern Question 1700–1790* (Princeton UP 1982), who shows that they continued until at least the mid 1740s. A change in 1753, when Kauntiz became State Chancellor, is plausible. For the *Hofstellen*, see ÖZV (1907), pts. i–iii; ÖZV (1925); and ch. II of F. Walter, *Geschichte*. D'Elvert, *Verwaltungsgechichte* is more useful for local than for central developments, on which it is often unreliable. Beidtel, *Geschichte der österr. Staatsverwaltung*, is a lament about the reforms of the period, which are seldom exactly described. Haussheer, *Verwaltungseinheit und Ressorttrennung*, is an interesting exercise in comparative history, chs. III and V of which are on Austrian developments. They are largely based on the ÖZV vols.

mian and Hungarian business should in future be transacted separately.

The Austrian secretariat within the *Reichshofkanzlei* was transformed into an independent *Österreichische Hofkanzlei* in the early months of 1620, symbolizing the new emperor Ferdinand II's wish to stand on his own powers rather than his imperial rights. Shortly afterwards, and with equal symbolism, the Bohemian Chancellery returned to Vienna from Prague, where it had been located since the emperor Rudolf's removal of the main organs of government there in 1578.

The Austrian Chancellery quickly assumed a leading position. From 1665 three groups of lands looked to it: those of Upper Austria (defined as Tyrol and Further Austria); those of Inner Austria; and those of Lower Austria, defined as Austria above and below the Enns. Each regarded their department of the *Hofkanzlei* as their *Hofkanzlei*, and the Austrian *Hofkanzler* as their *Hofkanzler*. This situation reflected the rule of younger lines of the House of Austria in Inner Austria (1565–1619) and in Tyrol and Further Austria (1565–1665). Both Inner and Upper Austria retained a special status when this formal separation ended. However, the Austrian Chancellor's powerful position under Leopold I was modified by decisions of Joseph I in 1705, which placed the financial and military business of Upper and Inner Austria under the Vienna *Hofkammer* and *Hofkriegsrat* respectively, ending the patronage of the Austrian Chancellery. This change took until 1709 to complete. Joseph also divided the Austrian Chancellor's office into that of First and Second Chancellor. And from 1720 there were no longer separate departments within the Chancellery for Upper and Inner Austria.[9] Despite these vicissitudes in their power, and in the balance of power between them, the Austrian and Bohemian chancelleries were important bodies in 1740. They exercised respectively oversight of the Austrian lands and of those of the Bohemian Crown. They were responsible for both administration and justice,

---

[9] For the Austrian and Bohemian Chancelleries see *ÖZV* (1907), pt. i, chs. 3–4, also Bidermann, i. 15, 24, 43, 45; ii. 9 and n., 10, 11–12, 15. The Instruction for the Austrian Chancellery of 31 Dec. 1669 speaks of separate chancelleries for Inner, Upper, and Lower Austria, *ÖZV* (1907), pt. ii, p. 538. It seems clear, however, that these were in practice departments of one institution.

especially as courts of appeal. Much of their financial business was with the Estates, whose consent to the Contribution, the leading branch of state revenue, as Chancellor Chotek described it in 1765, was legally indispensable. The chancelleries were regularly accused until their dissolution in 1749, and after their re-creation in merged form in 1761–2, of caring more for the interests of the Estates than for those of the state itself.[10]

The two chancelleries were governed by Instructions of 1719 and 1720. By its Instruction of 26 April 1719, the Bohemian Chancellery was divided into two senates (*Senatus*), one for *judicialia*, which were badly in arrears, one for all other business, *publica*. The greater importance attached to legal matters is shown by the fact that seven councillors were assigned to them, and only three to *publica*. The Bohemian model was applied in modified form to the Instruction for the Austrian Chancellery in March 1720. This recognized the revival in 1719 of the division into two chancellors, which had lapsed in 1715. Under the Instruction, the First Chancellor, with two councillors, was to take charge of foreign and family affairs. The Second Chancellor ('Anderter kanzler'), with a vice-chancellor and seven councillors, was to look after 'judicialia' and 'provincialia'. The First Chancellor would decide on the division of incoming papers. The Second Chancellor's business, in turn, was divided into two senates, one judicial, with five councillors, one, with three councillors, for 'provincialia', i.e. everything else, including finance. The Second Chancellor could decide which senate he would attend. Combined meetings of both senates were to be held four times a week. The First Chancellor was to attend the Privy Conference and the *Reichsconferenz*, the Second Chancellor the 'Deputations' for internal business. Although, therefore, the chancelleries in 1740 dealt with both judicial and other affairs, with 'administration and justice' in the usual somewhat misleading phrase, a serious attempt was made under Charles VI to divide responsibilities within them, and in particular to have judicial business separated, and handled by experts. The effectiveness of the division, and the position in this respect of the Hungarian and

---

[10] For Chotek's statement see ÖZV (1934) 260; for Maria Theresia's analysis of the disruptive activities of the chancelleries, ii, Ch. 1.

Siebenbürgen chancelleries, which had a separate existence in Vienna from about 1690, remain obscure.[11]

The main change in the Austrian Chancellery subsequent to those of 1720 was Maria Theresia's separation from it (14 February 1742) of an independent *Hof- und Staatskanzlei* to conduct foreign affairs, leaving the Austrian Chancellor, as the Second Chancellor was now called, with internal affairs only, with a Vice-Chancellor to assist him. The creation of the separate office of 'Court and State Chancellor' formalized the arrangement of 1720. It was probably connected with a wish to block the Wittelsbach emperor Charles VII's attempt to commandeer the documents of the *Reichshofkanzlei*, an institution which the Austrian Chancellery, since its own emergence as a *Hofstelle*, was accused of oppressing.[12]

The chancelleries, including those of Hungary and Siebenbürgen, had important financial responsibilities, of which oversight of the Contribution was the chief. The central location of financial policy, however, was in the *Hofkammer*, properly in the *Hofkammer* council (*Hofkammerrat*), a numerous body with numerous enemies. The *Hofkammer*, another creation of Ferdinand I's, had had an independent existence since 1527, and is interesting for many reasons, not least because, from the start, it tried to include the revenues of all the central lands, including those of the Hungarian Crown, in its accounts, and thus, almost ex officio, paid attention to the idea of the *Gesamtstaat*. Below it in 1740 were chambers (*Kammern*) in Prague, Brünn, Breslau, Graz, Innsbruck, and Pressburg. Relations with these had initially been of 'correspondence' rather than 'dependence'. By 1740 the provincial chambers were more

---

[11] The chancellery Instructions of 26 Apr. 1719 (Bohemia) and 26 Mar. 1720 (Austria) are in *ÖZV* (1907), pt. iii, nos. 49–50. The Bohemian Chancellor was officially 'Obrister Canzler' or Chief Chancellor. In 1740 there was also a Bohemian Vice-Chancellor. The further office of 'Bohemian Chancellor' was often left vacant. A Hungarian Chancellery was operating in Vienna from at least 1690, and references to a *Landeskanzlei* go back to the mid 16th c., ibid., pp. 146–7. The number of central councillors was initially small, e.g. in 1637 three, ibid., pt. ii, pp. 224, 227. The *Diploma Leopoldinum* of 4 Dec. 1691 for Siebenbürgen, and a supplement to it of 14 May 1693, led to the creation of a chancellery for that area, distinct from that of Hungary, *Istoria Rominiei*, iii. 231, 233. Kutschera, *Landtag und Gubernium*, 147 gives 1694–5 as the date of its establishment.

[12] *ÖZV* (1907), pt. i, pp. 168–9, and documents ibid., pt. iii, no. 56. The concentration of diplomatic correspondence at the Austrian Chancellery from 1705 was a step towards the arrangements of 1720 and 1742, ibid., pt. i, pp. 162–3. The oppression of the *Reichshofkanzlei* is complained of in a memorial of 1742, ibid., pt. iii, p. 483.

definitely subordinate, except for the *Kammer* at Pressburg.[13] The *Hofkammer* suffered from several disadvantages. Despite its claims to oversight of accounts, its supervision of state revenue was only partial. The important military revenue, largely derived from the Contributions granted by the provincial Diets, was raised by the Estates under the rather nominal supervision of the local royal governments, and paid to the army. This 'Militärétat', which was of growing size, was effectively outside *Hofkammer* control, though it recorded the amount and allocation. Secondly, royal revenue from lands, customs and excise, salt, mines, and so on, the 'Cameralétat', which in the seventeenth century was the *Hofkammer*'s main concern, was increasingly withdrawn from it after 1706, and pledged to the Vienna City Bank. By 1740 about half the cameral revenue was settled on the Bank. Thirdly, the *Hofkammer* suffered from the resistance to it of other departments, especially the chancelleries, which it lacked the political weight to overcome, as Haugwitz was soon to complain. Lastly, it was too large, and was unable to organize itself properly. Under its Instruction of 1682 it was to have only ten councillors. Yet by 1704 it had forty-one, and by 1728 sixty-eight, without any comparable increase in revenue administered. In 1717, six commissions for different branches of business, in 1732 eight specialist councillors, or referendaries, preparing business for the full council, were tried. Division of work was partly by area, partly by subject. Numbers of councillors also fell, though not drastically, by 1740. By a new Instruction of 13 September 1745, Maria Theresia reduced the establishment to a president, vice-president, and fifteen councillors, and divided business into four sections, to each of which two councillors were assigned. A separate 'Collegium' was established for mines and coinage. These changes were effected only four years before Haugwitz's reforms shrank the *Hofkammer* virtually to nothing.[14]

The 'Ministerial Banco Deputation', much smaller in numbers than the *Hofkammer* Council, from which it was partly drawn,

[13] ÖZV (1907) pt. i, ch. 2; Mensi, *Die Finanzen Oesterreichs*. For the subordinate chambers see the next chapter.

[14] Sources as in the previous note. For the reform of 1745, the documents in ÖZV (1925), no. 63 are also important. These show that in 1744 Count Starhemberg accused the *Hofkammer* of having excessive staff and documentation, and no effective control of accounts. In Sept, 1748 the *Hofkammer* was again reorganized, on the eve of Haugwitz's reforms, see n. 26.

supervised the Vienna City Bank created in 1706. The Bank was nominally an independent institution of credit, legally endowed with distinct state revenues, and run from the *Rathaus* in Wipplingerstrasse by the burgomaster of Vienna. In practice, it was already an organ of government, but, throughout this period, ministers in charge of it fought to prevent its formal merger, and that of its revenues, with those under *Hofkammer* control. The *Universal Bancalität* of 1714 was originally intended as a rival to the Vienna City Bank, but was largely stripped of its powers in 1721 and 1723. It retained only its accounting and cash-keeping functions. Its cash bureau, on which payments were assigned by the *Hofkammer*, was divided into cameral and military sections. In 1742, a debts section (*Schuldencassa*) was added. In December 1744, the contract with Baron Wiesenhütten assigned the military and debts *caisses* to him. The remaining cameral *caisse* was put under Baron Prandau, created vice-president of the *Hofkammer*, in March 1745. These changes left nothing for the *Bancalität* to do, and on 24 March 1745 its dissolution was publicly announced. Lastly, the *Finanz Conferenz* (19 August 1716), comprising only four persons in 1740, was formed to define general financial policy, and settle the numerous disputes between *Hofkammer*, Bank Deputation, and *Bancalität*. Its president was Count Gundaker Starhemberg, the aged but powerful head of the Bank Deputation. Maria Theresia dissolved it on 16 February 1741, with the curt remark that 'as to the Finance Conference, I find it unnecessary'.[15]

Some further changes were made during the War of the Austrian Succession. A 'Höchstes Revisionsgericht' created in February 1745 for the Bohemian lands and Austria above and below the Enns foreshadowed the *Oberste Justizstelle* of 1749. The Austrian Chancellery protested, in vain, at this removal of its own appellate

---

[15] ÖZV (1907), pt. iii, p. 420. The treatment of the Vienna City Bank and *Universal-Bancalität* ibid., pt. i is excellent, and at some points corrects the more extended account in Mensi, *Die Finanzen Oesterreichs*. See ÖZV (1925), no. 62 for the changes of 1744–5. H. I. Bidermann, 'Die Wiener Stadt-Bank', *AKÖG* 20 (1859) 343–445, though old, and largely about the pre-1740 period, is based on MS sources and contains valuable information. The Vienna City Bank or 'Wiener Stadt Banco' was created by diploma dated 24 Dec. 1705, publ. 8 Mar. 1706. It absorbed the *Banco del Giro* created 15 June 1703 (modified 3 June 1704) see ÖZV (1907), pt. i, pp. 95–109. The patent of the *Universal-Bancalität* dated 14 Dec. 1714 was publ. 26 Jan. 1715, ibid. 116.

jurisdiction. The *Hofkriegsrat* was extensively reformed under a new Instruction (23 March 1745), and the War Commissariat given separate status as a *Hofstelle* (28 December 1746). An 'Universal-Commerciendirectorium', with ambitious aims, though few means of realizing them, was established (6 April 1746) under the new president of the Bank Deputation, Count Philipp Kinsky, with four councillors drawn from the Bank Deputation and the chancelleries, including that of Hungary. In September 1745, the business of mines and coinage was taken from the *Hofkammer* and put under a 'Münz und Bergwerks Hofcommission'. Other departments sniped at it, and in February 1747 it was made a formal *Hofstelle* as a *Münz- und Bergwerksdirections-Collegium*. Finally, in July 1745 Maria Theresia dissolved the 'Neoaquistische Commission' formed from councillors of the *Hofkammer* and *Hofkriegsrat*, and replaced it with a 'Hofdeputation in Banaticis, Transylvanicis et Illyricis'. Its tasks were supervision of the cameral revenues of the Banat of Temesvár and Siebenbürgen, liaison with the latter's *Hofkanzlei* in Vienna about other business, and protection of the Serbs (Illyrians). It was altered in 1751, and merged with the *Hofkammer* in 1755.[16] The empress thus made a serious attempt at piecemeal administrative reform in the years preceding Haugwitz's much more drastic changes of 1748–9.

The location in 1740 of some, though not all, the government departments discussed can be found in the *Court Calendar*. The *Hofkammer* was 'in the Questenberg house in Johannesgasse'. The Finance Conference probably met in the royal *Burg*, the Bank Deputation in Singerstrasse in a house next door to the Franciscan church. The 'Universal Bancalität' was 'in the Lemburch house in Herrengasse'. The Hungarian Chancellery was 'in the Zwölfer house' in Alter Fleischmarkt. The Siebenbürgen Chancellery was in Kluggerstrasse, 'at the Golden Lion'. Their modest locations perhaps indicated modest status. The Austrian and Bohemian chancelleries, with equal significance, occupied handsome buildings, put up

---

[16] The documents bearing on the *Höchstes Revisionsgericht*, which became a *Hofstelle* 30 Sept. 1746, *Hofkriegsrat*, and *Universal-Commerciendirectorium* are printed in ÖZV (1907), pt. iii, nos. 58, 55, and 60. Those for the *Münz- und Bergwerksdirection* and the *Hofdeputation in Illyricis* are in ÖZV (1925), nos. 64–5. For commentary see Fellner and Kretschmayr, ÖZV (1907), pt. i, pp. 167–73 (*Höchstes Revisionsgericht*), 264–72 (*Hofkriegsrat*); and more extensively Walter, *Geschichte*, ch. II.

for them earlier in the century. The Austrian Chancellery on the Ballplatz (present-day Ballhausplatz) was built in 1717–19 to plans of Johann Lukas von Hildebrandt. The beautiful Bohemian Chancellery between the Judenplatz and Wipplingerstrasse, facing the old *Rathaus*, was built in 1708–14 to designs by Johann Bernard Fischer von Erlach. The leading government offices were thus dotted around the centre of Vienna, outside the royal *Burg*. In most of the houses in this area, the Court had the right to use one storey, assigned as a *Hofquartier* to government ministers and officials.[17]

The revised structure of 1749 (see Table 9.1) reflects the changes carried through, almost as a *coup d'état*, at the end of the War of the Austrian Succession, by the empress and her husband, with the help of a handful of close advisers, headed by Count Friedrich Wilhelm Haugwitz. Haugwitz's 'revolution', which is discussed further in ii, Ch. 1, was intended to give permanent form to the temporary respite won by the empress's resolute defence of her inheritance. He meant to prevent the imminent collapse of the Monarchy by endowing its ruler with greater financial and military control. His central thesis was that political power, currently in the hands of the chancelleries, with their close links with the Estates, must be seized, and united with the Crown's financial claims, inadequately promoted by the *Hofkammer*. Haugwitz thought that this union of force or compulsion, *brachium*, and financial rights, *cameralia*, was exemplified by the new Prussian system in captured Silesia. A derivative of such union in an Austrian context was that judicial matters, *judicialia*, badly in arrears in most provinces, should be conducted separately from administrative and financial business, the *publica*. There should be 'a total separation of administration and justice'. This aim, however, was subordinate to, and almost an excuse for, the union of political and fiscal power. In effect, Haugwitz was arguing that the Monarchy's defective system of finance

---

[17] PRO SP 80/182, Keith to Newcastle 29 Jan. 1749. The system dated from the 16th c., and came under the *Hofmarschall*. There was a chronic shortage of quarters, as the nobility, clergy, government officers, charities, etc., claimed exemption. See J. Kallbrunner, 'Das Wiener Hofquartierwesen und die Massnahmen gegen die Quartiersnot im 17. und 18. Jahrhundert', *Mitt. des Vereines f. Gesch. der Stadt Wien*, 5 (1925) 24–36, in fact largely confined to the 16th and 17th cc. Joseph II ended the system at his accession.

and government constituted an internal enemy fully as dangerous to the Crown as the more obvious enemies without.[18]

The reforms implementing his strategy of recuperation were made initially at local level, first in Austrian Silesia (1744), of which he was governor, next in the government of Inner Austria (1746), and finally (1747) in Krain and Carinthia, two of the Inner Austrian lands. These changes, which all aimed at tighter control over military taxes, are described in the next chapter. One feature of them was Haugwitz's insistence that, to be properly effective they required supervision by a new *central* body with both political and financial authority. This idea was first, imperfectly, realized in 1747 by a *Hofcommission* to supervise the recent changes in Krain and Carinthia. Its president was the unenthusiastic Austrian Chancellor; *Hofkammer* representatives were included. This formed a precedent for a more ambitious arrangement in 1748, the cumbrously named 'Geheime Hofdeputation in Austriacis quoad militaria mixta, contributionalia et cameralia', which had jurisdiction over all the central lands outside those of the Hungarian Crown, and whose first session, according to Khevenhüller-Metsch, was on 23 August 1748. The empress and her husband presided over the *Hofdeputation*, which met every Friday, and was attended by the Bohemian and Austrian chancellors, each accompanied by a councillor, and by the president and one councillor of the War Commissariat. From November, Haugwitz prepared the business for it at an earlier meeting each week, which appears to have had the same membership, less the two rulers. The *Hofdeputation* referred its decisions, once reached, to the chancelleries for implementation. Its principal task was to receive the reports, and to govern the activities, of the local *Deputationen*. These committees, charged with oversight of military supply, marches, and quarters, with the assessment and collection of the Contribution, and with cameral revenue, were set up

---

[18] The principal documentary sources for Haugwitz's proposals and their implementation are ÖZV (1925), nos. 66, 'Aktenstücke zur Vorgeschichte der Errichtung des Directorium in Publicis et Cameralibus', and 67, 'Aktenstücke zur Errichtung des Directoriums in publicis et cameralibus und der Obersten Justizstelle'. See also Walter, *Geschichte*, ch. III. The documents printed in 1925 exposed the administrative shape of his reforms fully for the first time, all the previous literature having been to some extent defective. The 'total separation of administration and justice' is the conventional but inaccurate English rendering of such phrases as 'Total absonderung der Publicorum a Judicialibus', 30 Jan. 1751, cit. F. von Maasburg, *Geschichte der obersten Justizstelle in Wien* (2nd rev. edn. Prague 1891) 11. Separation proved only partially feasible, see below, and was restated as an objective up to 1848.

in the Bohemian and Austrian lands in the course of the year. They were important innovations. They reported directly to the *Hofdeputation*, not to the chancelleries. From 1 November 1748 the scope of their duties increased with the introduction of Haugwitz's new financial arrangements, the 'Militar-Cameral und Schulden Systemata', the leading feature of which was a greatly increased Contribution, intended to finance a standing army of 108,000 men in the central lands in peacetime. This higher Contribution was negotiated with the Bohemian and Austrian Estates in the course of the year. A further 50,000 troops were to be stationed in the Austrian Netherlands and Italy, paid for by increased budgets there.[19]

The administrative innovations of 1748, recognizably expedients rather than true reforms, proved short-lived. The obstruction encountered in the *Hofdeputation* itself, and in the chancelleries and *Hofkammer*, convinced Haugwitz, and in turn Maria Theresia, that further steps were needed. On 2 May 1749, a series of royal *Handbilletten* led to a further and more drastic recasting of central government. In contrast to the fiscal and administrative changes of the previous year, this 'revolution', as Khevenhüller called it, was made by prerogative, and without consulting the Estates, or the ministers concerned. The method was deliberate, and within the empress's rights, but was bound to cause resentment. The Bohemian and Austrian chancelleries were dissolved, and their judicial responsibilities transferred to a new High Court, or *Oberste Justizstelle*, whose presidency was offered to the aged Austrian Chancellor. He died in 1751. Their financial and administrative responsibilities were assigned to the *Hofdeputation*, renamed the *Conferenz in Internis*. This was to be serviced by a *Directorium in Publicis et Cameralibus*, under Haugwitz as President, thus formalizing the existing arrangements for the preparation of business. The *Directo-*

---

[19] The Deputations are discussed in Ch. 10. For the financial system see ii, Ch. 1. Haugwitz in Dec. 1743 suggested creation of 'ein eigenes dicasterium dahier in Wienn' for the political and cameral business of a recaptured Silesia, *ÖZV* (1925) 143–4. For the *Hofcommission* for the affairs of Carinthia and Krain, ibid. 162–8, and Walter, *Geschichte*, 125–6. The evidence for its activities is thin. Haugwitz first proposed a similar body with more general scope before 27 May 1748, returning to the subject in Aug., when he used the term 'Haupt Deputation', ibid. 208, 221–4. The membership, not clarified in the *ÖZV* vols., is given, together with its full name, in *Khev.-Metsch*, 30 Aug. 1748. Haugwitz twice proposed a separate chancellery to service this *Hofdeputation*, *ÖZV* (1925) 221–4, 225–8, late summer of 1748. On 4 Nov. 1748 he was given permission to hold weekly preliminary meetings on Wednesdays to prepare business for the Friday *Hofdeputation*, ibid. 247–8.

rium's inelegant title was unmistakably due to Haugwitz himself, and displayed some of his favourite vocabulary. The Prussian envoy Fürst in 1755 remarked that Haugwitz was imitating the General Directory in Berlin, but going even further in the concentration of power. This view, which has been generally accepted, is plausible; but there were also domestic influences on Haugwitz's thought. The awkward disappearance of the titles of Bohemian Chief Chancellor and Austrian Chancellor was temporarily met by assigning them, with limited responsibility, to *Staatskanzler* Ulfeld. They were given to Haugwitz himself in 1753.

The *Conferenz in Internis* was to deal with all 'provincialia, publica, cameralia'. In contrast to the *Oberste Justizstelle*, which, though also having common sessions, divided its business between an Austrian and a Bohemian Senate, the new *Conferenz* was deliberately given a joint Bohemian and Austrian scope. The first item on its agenda of twenty-seven articles was, significantly, 'Contributionale', emphasizing the leading importance of army finance, and the military defence of the Monarchy. But defence (which under Kaunitz's nudgings was to become offence) had to be set in the wider context of a general reform of the Austrian state. There is little doubt that Haugwitz and the empress envisaged the *Conferenz in Internis* as a forum in which the royal will, intent on reforming finance, the army, education, the law, economic life, even the church, could be deployed against the forces of conservatism and resistance, both at the centre and provincially. In this way, the reassertion of monarchical power which both of them saw as essential to Austrian survival, and revival, was meant to acquire institutional force. The provincial *Deputationen* which answered to the *Conferenz*, and oversaw financial and army affairs locally, were now restyled 'Repraesentationen und Cammern', a further instance of Haugwitz's penchant for neologism.[20] By a master-stroke of

[20] For these see Ch. 10. Haugwitz's 'system' of 1748, comprising the *Hofdeputation*, the local *Deputationen*, and the new financial arrangements, encountered bitter resistance, noted by all foreign observers. He told the empress early in 1749 that the 'capi' of the chancelleries hoped for its fall as the Jews hoped for the Messiah, ÖZV (1925) 255. For the 'revolution' of 1749 see *Khev.-Metsch* 2 May 1749, and ÖZV (1925) 270–2, 279–80. Haugwitz had earlier used 'directorium' to mean either 'control' or 'a controlling institution', e.g. ibid. 144 (1743), 209 (1748). His statement in Aug. 1748 that 'die seele des staates ist ein wohleingerichtetes finanzendirectorium' is thought by Walter, *Geschichte*, 105 to refer to the 'Finanz Kollegium' proposed in 1686 by Baron Wilhelm Schroeder in his 'Fürstliche Schatz- und Rent-Cammer'. It may only mean 'control of the finances'. The *Billetten* of 2 May 1749 were at first dated 1 May.

conciliation, the former Bohemian Chancellor, Count Friedrich
Harrach, was offered, and accepted, continuation as first councillor
of the *Conferenz in Internis*, with the right of signature in all inland
business, 'mithin in der That die Persohn eines Premier Ministre
pour les affaires du dedans vorzustellen', as Khevenhüller commented.[21] The assessment is perhaps exaggerated. The possibility
that it was not was eliminated a month later when Harrach died of
smallpox. The further history of the *Conferenz in Internis* is
obscure. Fürst in 1755 does not mention it. Bartenstein regretted
its demise in a memorial of January 1756.[22] The *Staatsrat* of
1760–1, at which the rulers were expected to attend, in some
respects denoted its revival. Meanwhile, the *Directorium* itself,
initially intended only as the chancellery of the *Conferenz in
Internis*, necessarily took on much of the latter's role. Failing the
royal presence, however, it could not play it so effectively.

The creation of the *Conferenz in Internis* effectively blocked the
pretensions of the older Privy Conference, or of some of its members, to advise on internal policy. On 26 April 1749, before the
bombshells of 2 May, Count Khevenhüller recorded the view
expressed in the Conference that the *Hofdeputation*

had begun to exclude the Conference from all knowledge of internal and
cameral affairs, whereas it ought to be the focus and rallying-point of all
government business . . .

The Conference, which had perhaps never acted in that way, continued to be of importance in foreign affairs, and the main diplomatic issues in the years leading up to the reversal of alliances of 1756
came before it. However, the Prussian envoy Fürst thought that
much foreign business was done privately by the empress and Kaunitz, and that in any case the latter and the imperial Vice-Chancellor
dominated Conference meetings. There was some revival of Con-

---

[21] *Khev.-Metsch*, loc. cit. He describes how Harrach laid down his office of Bohemian Chancellor on 2 May 1749. Harrach was so affected that he had to break off his
resignation speech and go and weep in his chamber. Walter, *Geschichte*, 177, insists
that it was Haugwitz, with his countersignature, not Harrach, who had real power
under the new arrangements.

[22] Prokeš, 'Boj', 21, Bartenstein's memorial of 31 Jan. 1756, which states the
Conferenz in Internis lapsed 'after a few years'. Maria Theresia in her memorial of
1756 says she stopped the *Conferenz* 'later' ('nach der Hand'), as everything was
proceeding smoothly. The documents in ÖZV (1925), and the account based on
them in Walter, *Geschichte*, are scantier for the period after 1749, hence less is
known about the working of the *Directorium* than about its inception.

ference business during the Seven Years War, but formal meetings seem finally to have petered out after it, only Court Conferences to discuss such matters as the coronation of Joseph II in 1764 being mentioned subsequently.[23]

Returning to the changes of 1749, it is observable that Haugwitz's intention that financial control should be unitary could not be fully realized. On 6 May 1749 he urged the empress to abolish the *Hofkammer*, and pension off its staff. She refused to do this while the aged president and vice-president lived.[24] In 1755, on the imminent death of the former, Haugwitz tried again, and was again refused.[25] The *Hofkammer* was initially drastically reduced in size, its council in 1751 having only four members; and was confined to administration of the *camerale* of Hungary and the German Empire. The latter was in fact conducted by the emperor's man of business, Baron Toussaint, and the *Directorium* itself corresponded directly with the Hungarian *Hofkammer* in Pressburg.[26] Though hanging by a thread, the *Hofkammer* nevertheless survived. From 1755 it began a partial, and, as it proved lasting, revival. The Ministerial Bank Deputation, whose president Kinsky died in January 1749, also maintained a separate existence. The view of Haugwitz's critics that the Vienna City Bank's formally independent status was a necessary condition of public credit, which, significantly, was under the emperor's direction, was difficult to refute. Until 1755 the mines and coinage were also independently administered by the Court Commission of 1745/7. Haugwitz later maintained that a 'principal defect' of the *Directorium* was the empress's refusal to

---

[23] *Fürst (1755)* 15–16; pp. 340–1 below for Conferences and councils during the war; Khev.-Metsch's diary for the post-war years. Walter, *Geschichte*, 176 and n. connects the *Conferenz in Internis* of 1749 to the *Deputation* of 1697, whose last minutes in the Hofkammerarchiv are dated 26 Oct. 1746; but it is more plausible to see it as a continuation of the *Hofdeputation* of 1748, as the empress clearly intended. See *Khev.-Metsch*, 17 March 1752, 13 Dec. 1757, for the continued existence of Deputations 'in Mixtis'.

[24] Prokeš, 15 n., Haugwitz to the empress, 6 May 1749, and her decision: 'ist noch unberürt zu lassen so lang er [Dietrichstein] lebt, Brandau auch'. This attempt is not dealt with in the ÖZV vols.

[25] *ÖZV* (1925) 340–4, same to same, 16 Feb. 1755, suggested merger of *Hofkammer* with the *Directorium*. *Fürst (1755)* 23 evidently believed this merger had occurred. D'Elvert, *Verwaltungsgeschichte*, 386 is one of numerous later authors who have also thought so.

[26] Haugwitz, loc. cit. The question is discussed further in Ch. 12. The pre-1749 *Hofkammer* was subjected to yet another reorganization of its business by a rescript of 9 Sept. 1748, *ÖZV* (1925) 235–8.

accept his advice to include within it the Bank, the Hungarian *camerale*, and the department of mines and coinage.[27]

Outside the financial departments, the *Hof- und Staatskanzlei* remained responsible for foreign affairs, and the *Hofkriegsrat* for the army, with its new, higher budget. A 'Hofkriegsrätliches Justiz-Collegium' was created (12 March 1753) for military cases, applying here, too, the principle of the separation of justice from administration.[28] The Court Chancelleries of Hungary and Sieben-bürgen were not involved in Haugwitz's reforms, which were confined to the Bohemian and Austrian lands.[29] Taken together, these factors do much to explain the surprising lack of resistance to Haugwitz's 'revolution'. The deaths of the obstructive Bank President and the former Austrian and Bohemian chancellors removed powerful critics (providentially, according to the empress). The retention of the *Hofkammer* and Bank conciliated traditionalists. As is seen in Ch. 12, assignment of key chancellery councillors to the *Oberste Justizstelle* soothed injured dignity: no one was dismissed. The thunder and lightning which would have followed any attempt to alter the Hungarian constitution were prudently avoided. Further, the system discarded, or drastically modified, in 1749, had patently failed to ward off the Prussian threat. The new one seemed likely to do so. Lastly, the prerogative of the Crown, in a primitive political system, had immense force, as the empress realized. Though many grumbled, therefore, there was no organized sabotage. It is perhaps also worth noting that the changes made were secular ones, and did not affect the spiritual or temporal structure of the Catholic church. The reforms, indeed, were explicitly intended to preserve 'die heilige Catholische religion' from the threat of Protestant Prussia. Although the empress and Kaunitz were drawing up secret plans from 1751 for ecclesiastical reform, with papal consent, these came to nothing. Haugwitz, unlike Machault d'Arnouville, did not find himself involved in a quarrel with the church, which had long before this accepted the principle

---

[27] Walter, *Geschichte*, 370, Haugwitz's *Vortrag* of 15 Mar. 1764.

[28] *ÖZV* (1925) 235–8, separation of military 'publica' from 'justitialia'. Contemporary Austrian military organization, centrally and locally, is known only in bare outline. Oskar Regele, *Der österreichische Hofkriegsrat 1556–1848 (MÖSA*, Ergänzungsband I, 1949) is less than definitive.

[29] Though obvious, this point is often omitted in the literature.

of paying taxes on its property, and, unlike the French church, did not have a central assembly with fiscal powers and the capacity to obstruct policy.[30]

Although important branches of internal government remained outside the scope of Haugwitz's reforms, both initially and subsequently, it is clear that the *Directorium* very soon showed a tendency to expand. This development was the more significant because of the cessation of the *Conferenz in Internis*. At its inception, the *Directorium* had seven councillors, in 1754 twenty-one.[31] This growth was partly at the expense of the *Oberste Justizstelle*, whose lengthy agenda initially included such 'mixed' matters as contraband and other fiscal cases, the purchase of land by religious houses, the confirmation of guild articles, and so on.[32] In January 1751, after anxious conferences, these matters, defined as 'causae summi principis', were removed to the *Directorium*, which was in future to deal with all fiscal cases in a 'judicial senate' staffed by eight new councillors, two of them from the *Oberste Justizstelle* itself. In 1749, the *Conferenz in Internis* had twenty-seven items on its agenda. After the changes referred to, the *Directorium* had forty-four.[33]

A second way in which the *Directorium* expanded was by formally absorbing other bodies, though these typically continued to operate separately from within it. After Count Philipp Kinsky's death in January 1749, the 'Universal-Commerciendirectorium' of 1746 was re-established (10 March 1749) under the more modest title of the 'Commercien-Directorium'. It was instructed to institute in each of the Bohemian and Austrian lands a committee (*consessus*)

---

[30] For taxation of the Austrian church see ii. 464. The important early stirrings of Josephinism in the early 1750s, associated with reform of clerical education and higher studies by the Archbishop of Vienna, revision of the censorship, and growing accountability of church to state, were parallel to Haugwitz's reforms rather than forming part of them. For a good review of the problem and the literature see Klingenstein, *Staatsverwaltung und kirchliche Autorität*. Cf. also ii. 33 for the plans of the empress, Kaunitz, and Bartenstein in 1753–6 to reform the parish system, and church finances.

[31] The first seven councillors, who included three previously on the *Hofdeputation*, were named in the empress's rescript of 2 May 1749, ÖZV (1925) 270–2. For the councillors of 1754 see Table 12.2*.

[32] The agenda are listed in ÖZV (1925) 279–80 nn.

[33] For these changes see ibid., no. 68, 'Directorium und Oberste Justizstelle'. The issue first arose because of a dispute about the Contribution in Moravia, of which both the *Tribunal* and *Repraesentation und Kammer* there tried to take sole charge, Walter, *Geschichte*, 199.

of two or three persons versed in trade; a kind of commercial equivalent to the *Deputationen* for finance and government. Its president was Count Rudolf Chotek, Kinsky's successor as president of the Bank Deputation. On 17 December 1753, the new body formally merged with the *Directorium*, but continued its activities, and name, within it, Chotek continuing to sign as president.[34] The mines and coinage department had an especially chequered history. The *Münz- und Bergwesendirections-Hofcollegium* of 1747 continued as a separately administered body under Count Königsegg-Erps until the death of Count Dietrichstein, the aged president of the *Hofkammer*, in February 1755. Königsegg-Erps succeeded him as president, retaining the presidency of the mines department. Day-to-day control of the latter, however, was placed in a commission under Baron Haugwitz, Count Haugwitz's cousin. In January 1757, when Königsegg-Erps resigned as mining, though not as *Hofkammer*, president, Baron Haugwitz's commission was put under the *Directorium* instead. In December it lost its status as a *Hofcommission*, but not its separate identity. In August 1758 it was taken out again, and put under the control of Count Rudolf Chotek, president of the Bank Deputation and *Commercien-Directorium*, and, after the death of Königsegg-Erps in December 1759, of the *Hofkammer* as well. Baron Haugwitz, honest but untalented, was pensioned off, and died shortly afterwards.[35] The *General-kriegskommissariat* of 1746 was similarly included within the *Directorium* (5 January 1758), but revived as a *Hofcommission*, under military control, in February 1761, then made a department of the reformed *Hofkriegsrat* in 1762.[36]

Perhaps as marked as these somewhat unsystematic tendencies to concentration were those to dispersion, caused by the creation of Court Commissions (*Hofcommissionen*) for branches of government activity. Count Kaunitz, in his *Vortrag* of 20 November

---

[34] Its continuing existence within the *Directorium* is shown by such sources as HKA NÖ Kommerz, rote Nr. 121, papers of the Lower Austrian commercial committee. The latter's reports were regularly made to the *Commercien-Directorium*, and Chotek's decisions are endorsed on them, see e.g. fo. 2ʳ, 31 May 1755.

[35] These changes are documented in *ÖZV* (1925), no. 64, 'Aktenstücke zur Geschichte des Münz- und Bergwerksdirektionskollegiums . . . 1745–1758', and also ibid. 344–51. For Königsegg-Erps, see Ch. 12 below. Baron Haugwitz's retirement, and death on 10 Oct. 1758, are shown in *Khev.-Metsch*, Aug. 1758.

[36] *ÖZV* (1925), no. 70.

1761, written during the discussions about administrative reform discussed below, asserted somewhat disingenuously that 'formerly' there had been four central government departments; the *Hofkriegsrat*, the Austrian and Bohemian chancelleries, and the *Hofkammer*. Since 1748, no less than eighteen had emerged, which he listed.[37] The date of foundation is added here where known.

(1) 'Directorium' (1749)
(2) 'Oberste Justizstelle' (1749)
(3) 'Hofkriegsrat in Publicis' (1753)
(4) 'Hofkriegsrat in Judicialibus' (1753)
(5) 'Generalkriegskommissariat' (1746–58, 1761)
(6) 'Münz- und Bergwesen Direction' (1745/7)
(7) 'Hofkammer' (1527)
(8) 'Ministerial Banco Deputation' (1706)
(9) 'Commercien Directorium' (1746/9)
(10) 'Invaliden Hofcommission' (1750)
(11) 'Militärschulden Hofcommission' (1748)
(12) 'Hauptschuldencassa Direction' (1748)
(13) 'Depositen Hofcommission' (1758)
(14) 'Studien Hofcommission' (1760)
(15) 'Sanitäts Hofcommission' [*Hofdeputation*] (1753)
(16) 'Postwesen Hofcommission' (?1753)
(17) 'Religions Hofcommission' (1751)
(18) 'Pulver und Salniter Hofcommission' (?)

Kaunitz knew perfectly well that the formation of (5) and (6) preceded 1748 and could not be imputed to Haugwitz, that the *Hofkammer* was antique, and that the Bank Deputation (8) dated from 1706. His demonstration of institutional proliferation was nevertheless difficult to reject. Two other temporary bodies, the *Hofdeputation in Banaticis et Illyricis* (1745–55) and the Court Commission for Police and Security (1749–53) had meanwhile lapsed.[38] All these developments occurred while official doctrine was in favour of the union, not the fragmentation of power.

---

[37] Kaunitz's *Vortrag* of 20 Nov. 1761 is printed in ÖZV (1934) 101–21. Some exception to his list is taken by Walter, 'Kaunitz' Eintritt in die innere Politik', *MIÖG* 46 (1932) 67 n.

[38] ÖZV (1925), no. 65 (*Hofdeputation in Banaticis*) and pp. 402–6 (police commission).

The business of the *Directorium* was conducted from the building of the former Bohemian Chancellery, doubled in size (1752–4) to plans by Matthias Gerl, and endowed with a chapel appropriately dedicated to St Theresa.[39] At the completion of this work, an inscription was inserted above the courtyard entrance from the Judenplatz, recording the royal intention that the creation of this 'Bohemiae et Austriae Gramatophylacium' (literally, a place for storing records) should ensure the correct ordering of the commonwealth, and the welfare of its subjects.[40] The *Oberste Justizstelle* was initially located here as well, then in a house in the Herrengasse, but moved back in 1760, and stayed, despite increasing overcrowding, until 1838.[41] The former Austrian Chancellery was taken over first by Ulfeld, then (1753) by Kaunitz for the *Hof- und Staatskanzlei*. The Bank Deputation continued in its location at the corner of Singerstrasse and Franziskanerplatz.[42] The *Hofkammer*, marked for destruction by Haugwitz, was installed from 1755 in Prince Eugene's magnificent palace in Himmelpfortgasse, purchased in 1753 by Count Königsegg-Erps from Eugene's heiress, Princess Victoria of Savoy. This formed an ironic link with a commander whose troops were always short of funds.[43]

✣

[39] For Gerl, see the two (variant) inscriptions on the building; for the dedication, *Khev.-Metsch*, 28 Jan. 1756, when the empress and her husband visited the *Directorium*.

[40] The inscription reads: 'Deo auspice optimi principes Franciscus et Maria Theresia Augustus et Augusta ut Republica rite ordinata subditis Populis bene sit Hoc Bohemiae et Austriae Gramatophylacium [*sic*] perenne Curarum suarum et paterni maternique affectus monumentum ff'. It is tempting to see Haugwitz's hand here, too.

[41] Maasburg, *Oberste Justizstelle*, 24 n. The Privy Conference met in the *Spiegelzimmer* in the Hofburg after Kaunitz became State Chancellor, *Khev.-Metsch*, 9 June 1753.

[42] From the *Court Calendar*, at dates up to 1780. The *Calendar* for 1754 says 'nächst denen Franciscanern'. In that year, the Hungarian Chancellery was already listed in Schenkenstrasse, where it was subsequently located. The Siebenbürgen Chancellery was 'in dem Huterischen Haus' in nearby Krautgasse. In 1763 it, too, was in Schenkenstrasse.

[43] *Khev.-Metsch*, 4 Sept. 1753 (purchase) and 14 Mar. 1755 (use for *Hofkammer* and *Kupferamt*). The reconstructed building is now the Finanzministerium. The palace was originally designed by Johann Fischer von Erlach and extended by Johann Lukas von Hildebrandt, see D. McKay, *Prince Eugene of Savoy* (1977) 191–2.

The last subperiod described in this chapter comprises the years
1761–80.[44] Haugwitz's system, compiled in haste, proved impermanent. The difficulties it encountered might have proved insuper-
able even in peacetime, for which it was intended. The Seven Years
War increased them to the point where the whole house was in
danger of collapse, as Kaunitz argued to Maria Theresia in
December 1760.[45] He was, without knowing it, using the same
metaphor as Haugwitz in 1748.[46] Haugwitz's institutional remedies were the *Hofdeputation* and the subordinate *Deputationen* in
the *Länder*, transformed in 1749 into the *Conferenz in Internis*,
Directorium, and *Repraesentationen und Kammern*. Kaunitz's
initial remedy, outlined in the document just referred to, was a
Council of State, or *Staatsrat*, to advise the sovereign about all
internal business. He had initially proposed such a body in August
1758, giving it the significant title of a *Conferenz in Internis*.[47] At
that stage, he thought its members should be the *Staatskanzler*, i.e.
himself, and the President of the *Hofkriegsrat*. The other councillors, in contrast to all previous practice, should not hold departmental office. The council's task would be to look to the general
well-being ('das allgemeine wohlseyn') of the entire monarchy, a
task at present neglected in his view. By December 1760, he had
reduced the list of office-holders to one, himself, arguing for the
need to harmonize domestic and foreign policy. The council's
scope would be wide: agriculture, commerce, credit, justice, manufactures, religion. Kaunitz rejected the notion that a prime minister
might be more effectual, remarking 'un premier ministre ne me
paroit pas pouvoir convenir à la forme du gouvernement'. He was
probably aware that he was credited with, and disliked for, aspiring

[44] The major authorities are Walter (ed.), *ÖZV* (1934) and id., *Geschichte*. A.
Beer's pioneering essay 'Die Finanzverwaltung' is still valuable, and clearly
influenced Walter, despite his disparaging comments, e.g. *ÖZV* (1934) 84 n. Arneth,
Gesch. Mar. Ther. vii, chs. 1, 7; ix, chs. 11, 12, 15, gave the first account of some of
the institutional changes but has been corrected and amplified by the latter literature.
Hock–Bidermann can only be used with caution for the period before 1780.
[45] *ÖZV* (1934) 3–10, Kaunitz to Maria Theresia, 9 Dec. 1760: government is
conducted on a day-to-day basis, and at a peace 'L'edifice ne peut gueres manquer
d'ecrouler'.
[46] *ÖZV* (1925) 210, Haugwitz to Maria Theresia [May 1748], 'sobald das gebäude
nicht auf einen rechtschaffenen grund gesetzet, solches gar bald zu boden fallen
muss'.
[47] *ÖZV* (1934) 1, Kaunitz to Maria Theresia, 6 Aug. 1758.

to be one.[48] The empress endorsed Kaunitz's analysis and remedy, approving the plan of the new council on 14 December 1760. The *Staatsrat* held its first meeting, in the presence of both rulers, on 26 January 1761.[49] It had at this stage six members: four Ministers of State (*Staatsministri*) and two State Councillors (*Staatsräte*), besides a referendary, Anton König, who prepared the business, and was himself made a State Councillor in June 1762.[50] It met frequently, and Maria Theresia and Francis Stephen attended weekly.[51] Its scope was officially 'German and inland affairs', i.e. excluding those of Hungary.[52] This was, however, merely top-dressing. From the start, it discussed Hungarian issues. The Hungarian Chancellor's protest at this (29 June 1761) met with an icy reprimand.[53]

The new council's first task was to participate in an extended official debate about the defects of existing government. This occupied most of 1761, and ended in December with the reconstruction of the central offices. The new pattern, shown in Table 9.1, was to last, with important modifications, until the end of the reign. Kaunitz's own fief, the *Hof- und Staatskanzlei*, was not affected by these changes, which concerned only internal business. His position

---

[48] Ibid. 3–10, same to same 9 Dec. 1760. For councils of executive ministers, excluding Conference members, held earlier in the war under Kaunitz's direction, see pp. 340–1 below. In his memorial of 18 Feb. 1766 Kaunitz referred to the wartime meetings of the Conference itself as resulting merely in bickering between departments; and described the *Staatsrat* as a form of corporate prime minister, which saved the situation, A. Beer, 'Denkschriften des Fürsten Wenzel Kaunitz-Rietberg', *AÖG* 48 (1872) 122–4.

[49] *ÖZV* (1934) 12, 15.

[50] Ibid. Cf. Ch. 12 below, where mistakes by Arneth about the council's initial membership are noted.

[51] See H. Schlitter's summary of the 210 sessions attended by Maria Theresia and her husband in the four years to 26 Jan. 1765, *Khev.-Metsch 1764–7*, after p. 555. There is a similar summary for 1766 ibid. nn. 166, 174. According to Schlitter, the *Protokoll*, or minutes, of these 'royal' sessions extends to 1776. Crown Prince Joseph attended from May 1761.

[52] 'teutsch- und inländischen geschäften', *ÖZV* (1934) 19.

[53] Ibid. 26–30, remonstrance of Count Nikolaus Pálffy, 29 Jun. 1761, and its 'forgiveness' (drafted by Kaunitz) by Maria Theresia. The importance attached by the *Staatsrat* to Hungarian issues is brought out in the excerpts made in the 1930s from its discussions by Gy. Ember, see his art. 'Der österreichische Staatsrat und die ungarische Verfassung 1761–1768', *Acta Historica*, 6 (1959) 105–53, 331–70; 7 (1960) 149–82. Macartney, *Habsburg Empire*, 20 implies that the *Staatsrat* did not discuss Hungarian business.

was actually strengthened by the reduction of the overstaffed Belgian and Italian councils to small departments under his control in March 1757, on the retirement of Duke Manoel Sylva-Tarouca, their former president.[54]

The institutional changes which, like those of 1749, were confined to the Austrian and Bohemian lands, were conveyed officially to *Hofmeister* Ulfeld on 29 December 1761, and took effect from 1 January 1762. Financial and commissariat business, with the important exception of the Contribution, and one or two other taxes, was taken away from the *Directorium*, which was renamed the 'Bohemian and Austrian Court Chancellery'.[55] It retained its existing location, and was provided on 21 June 1762 with an extensive and detailed Instruction, partly based on a draft of 1753, intended for the *Directorium* but never completed. The lengthy agenda were also inherited. The introduction breathed Kaunitz's views. It emphasized the necessity for completion of the union ('vereinigung') of the Bohemian and Austrian lands, a clear reference to the changes of 1749, and for each province ('provinz') to help the others in the cause of common prosperity ('wohlfarth'). Kaunitz defined agriculture, industry, mining, trade, 'and above all population', as the sources of economic strength, hence of the ruler's strength—and financial resources.

The empress insisted that Bohemian and Austrian business were to be treated as one, as they had been in the *Directorium*, not separately as in the *Oberste Justizstelle*. She ignored the passionate protests of Chancellor Chotek, who appealed (22 May 1762) to the principle of diversity, supporting himself not only on the differences between the Bohemian and Austrian lands, but with the unlikely examples of France and Prussia. Meanwhile, the *Oberste*

---

[54] See *Khev.-Metsch*, 31 Mar. 1757. In the *Court Calendar* for 1763 the *Niederländisches Departement* had a referendary, two 'Officiales', and eight other officials, the *Italienisches Departement* a referendary, a secretary, two titular secretaries, and six officials. The two referendaries were also councillors of the *Staatskanzlei*. In 1740 the Austrian Netherlands Council had a president, six councillors, and seven officials, the Italian Council a president, ten councillors, and ten officials. The remainder of this section is largely based on ÖZV (1934), no. 78, 'Aktenstücke zur Geschichte der Reform von 1761', and Walter, *Geschichte*, ch. V.

[55] ÖZV (1934) 122–4, Maria Theresia's *Handbillett* to Ulfeld, 29 Dec. 1761, sets out the changes to be made. Prokeš, 'Boj', 68 n., shows from Count Karl Zinzendorf's MS diary that Ulfeld announced the changes on 1 Jan. 1762. R. Chotek, Ludwig Zinzendorf (Karl's half-brother), Hatzfeld, and Herberstein, took their oaths of office on 27 Jan. 1762, ibid.

Justizstelle, which, like the *Directorium*, had formerly received n
Instruction, was retained and actually strengthened. Its Instruction
dated 4 February 1763, included all existing agenda, and, i
addition, restored to the court jurisdiction over the fiscal cases, th
'causae summi principis', lost to the *Directorium* in 1751. These a
once became an important part of its business.[56]

The reshaping of the *Directorium*, as drastic in its way as th
abolition of the former chancelleries in 1749, was facilitated b
Count Haugwitz's entry into the *Staatsrat* in December 176c
which obliged him to resign executive office. The caretaker head c
the *Directorium* in the ensuing year, the Vice-President and Bohe
mian and Austrian Chancellor, Count Johann Chotek, disliked i
and favoured its abolition. He was in any case more concerned wit
army supply. In February 1761 he was put in charge of a *Hof
commission* for commissariat business, and in December was nomi
nated to the revived office of General War Commissary. In Januar
1762 he became the head of the economic section of the revise
Hofkriegsrat.[57] His brother Count Rudolf was appointed Bohe
mian Chief Chancellor and Austrian First Chancellor, the titles pre
viously held by Haugwitz.[58]

The theory applied in dismantling the *Directorium* was the separ
ation of financial and political power, whose union had been th
leading principle of 1749. (In the event, the separation was nc
total, since the new Bohemian and Austrian Chancellery retaine
control of the Contribution and some other taxes. However, it wa

---

[56] For the importance of fiscal cases see Ch. 11. For the Instructions of 21 Ju
1762 and 4 Feb. 1763 see *ÖZV* (1934), nos. 79 and 85. The agenda of the chanceller
derived from the *Directorium*, began with the need to uphold the Catholic religio
and moved through *Polizei*, Jews, guilds, universities, etc., to the provinci
Landtage and the Contribution, including rectification of the cadastre. Quarterin
marches, recruits, transport, 'insofar as they concern the *Länder*', were to be adm
nistered jointly with the army and *Hofkammer*. For Chotek's protest of 22 M
1762 see J. Prokeš, 'Instrukce vydaná v r. 1762 pro českou a rakouskou dvorní ka
celář', *Věstník Král. české společnosti nauk*, tř. 1 (1926), no. V; there is a lengtl
quotation from Chotek's *Vortrag* at p. 15 n. Walter, *Geschichte*, 317 has an outli
of this episode.

[57] *ÖZV* (1934) 398–9 (Commissariat *Hofcommission*, 3 Feb. 1761); 122–
Handbillett to Ulfeld, 29 Dec. 1761 (War Commissary); 402–11, Daun's proposals
25 Jan. 1762 for a revised *Hofkriegsrat*; 412–20, the empress's approval of them. T
Hofkriegsrat had in future three divisions, military, judicial, and 'economic'. T
arrangements were approved by the *Staatsrat* on 7 May 1762, *ÖZV* (1934) 417.

[58] *ÖZV* (1934) 124–5 [Dec. 1761].

1. Count Friedrich Wilhelm Haugwitz, President of the *Directorium in Publicis et Cameralibus*, 1749–61. Bildarchiv, Österreichische Nationalbibliothek.

Wohnung des königl. ungar. Hofagenten Herrn Ludwig von Kis /
Die k. k. Hofjuweliere Pöte und Kochert,
Josephs Platz №1153

(b) Count Johann Fries's palace on Josefsplatz (now Palais Pallavicini).
Bildarchiv, Österreichische Nationalbibliothek.

2. (a) Count Johann Fries, Court Banker.
Bildarchiv, Österreichische Nationalbibliothek.

On the portrait oval border: CONS.er D'ETAT DE S. M. I. ET C. PREM.R MINIS.e ET GR.d MAITRE DE S. A. S. L'ARCHIDUC.se GOU.r GEN.des PAÏS-BAS &.c FHELD. COM.te DE HARRACH, ROHRAU ET DE THANNHAUSEN,

Quando tuos, FREDERICE, vides in imagine vultus,
Regius Ærigraphus Tibi Te, Vir Maximè, donat,
Quem patriæ Charites, populique sequuntur amores:
Ut dexter tua cœpta Deus, Curasque secundet,
Teque GUBERNATRIX, Cœlo adspirante, Ministro
Austriacos Augusta regat pro CÆSARE Belgas.

D'Krigae et Gravé par Fran.s Harrewyn, graveur de S. M. I. et C.

3. Count Karl Friedrich August Harrach (d. 1749), last sole Chancellor of Bohemia.
Bildarchiv, Österreichische Nationalbibliothek.

4. Count, later Prince, Wenzel Anton Kaunitz, *Hof- und Staatskanzler*, 1753–92.
Bildarchiv, Österreichische Nationalbibliothek.

at first intended to put these under the *Hofkammer*.) By a further application of principle, financial business was to be divided between administration, receipt and disbursement, and audit. This was first advocated by Count Ludwig Zinzendorf in October 1761, and enthusiastically adopted by his patron Kaunitz. In the event, it could not be fully implemented. The actual outcome was as follows.[59] A revived and enlarged *Hofkammer* administered all cameral revenue. The Ministerial Bank Deputation continued to supervise the Vienna City Bank, whose independent position was strengthened. The new Estates Credit Deputation was given the same president, Hatzfeld, as the Bank Deputation.[60] A new audit office, called a *Hofrechenkammer*, controlled all government accounts. Nothing was said in the *Handbillett* of 29 December 1761 of a further innovation, a *caisse générale* or *Generalkassa*, which was in fact introduced in a restricted form.[61] Count Hatzfeld was named, in his third post, as its Director.[62] Lastly, the bureau of trade of 1749 was retrieved from the *Directorium in Publicis*, in which it had merged in 1753, and changed into a 'Hof Commercien-Rath' with the status of an independent *Hofstelle*. It was intended to include some merchant councillors. This body joined the line of others which had to be consulted about policy.[63]

The administrative changes of 1749 were hatched in secrecy by Maria Theresia, her husband, and their closest advisers, and implemented with minimal consultation over the opposition of most of her ministers. Those of 1761 were, in deliberate contrast, the product of extended debate, in which courses of action alternative to those adopted were proposed, discussed and rejected. The final outcome of 29 December 1761 was itself a last-minute variant of much more ambitious proposals drafted only a week earlier. This

[59] *Handbillett* of 29 Dec. 1761, see n. 55.

[60] For the Estates Credit Deputation (*Ständische Credits-Deputation*) of June 1761 see ii. 133. For Count K. F. A. Hatzfeld see below and Ch. 12.

[61] It was at first intended that all revenue including that of the Vienna City Bank should form one fund, see below.

[62] *ÖZV* (1934) 194–6, empress's appointment of Hatzfeld as director of the 'general cassa' 23 Dec. 1761. For its subsequently restricted scope, see n. 90 below.

[63] *ÖZV* (1934), no. 84, 'Aktenstücke zur Geschichte des Kommerzienrates 1762–1776', esp. p. 344, 11 Mar. 1762, appointment of president and eight councillors, and statement that two merchants will also be named.

argument about government must now be described.[64] It was initiated by memoranda from Count Johann Chotek on 23 December 1760 and by Kaunitz in January 1761. The second was so theoretical that it had little impact. The first, which addressed itself to the organization, or reorganization, of government, was discussed by the new *Staatsrat* on 9 February 1761, the empress and her husband presiding. Haugwitz on this occasion defended his system, arguing that although everyone had said it was not possible to introduce it, he had done so, and with it control, previously lacking. Though intended for peacetime, it had lasted through the war.[65] The remainder of the council, however, agreed that things could not remain as they were, and decided to seek the views of prominent councillors in Vienna, and the heads of government in the Bohemian and Austrian lands. The questions (drafted by Kaunitz) were: how business was organized in the dissolved chancelleries; how satisfactorily it was handled by the *Directorium*; and what reforms should be made centrally and locally.[66]

Replies came in during the remainder of the year 1761, and the members of the *Staatsrat* then gave their views. Only part of this material has survived, but enough to justify some general conclusions.[67] The replies from the *Länder* were predictably conservative,

---

[64] The principal authorities are ÖZV (1934), no. 78, 'Aktenstücke zur Geschichte der Reform von 1761'; Walter, *Geschichte*, ch. V; and his essay 'Kaunitz' Eintritt in die innere Politik', which is substantially incorporated in his book. Besides these, see Prokeš, 'Boj', which has a short résumé in French. Much of the material he used was destroyed in 1927, see Walter, 'Kaunitz' Eintritt', 58. Walter's references to Prokeš (ibid. 41, 58–9 ÖZV (1934) 95–6, *Geschichte*, 292 n.) are coy and rather grudging. He does not give an exact reference to the article, and cites only its French summary. His failure to procure a full translation is perhaps ascribable to the political circumstances of the 1930s.

[65] ÖZV (1934) 91–3; Walter, *Geschichte*, 286–90. Kaunitz's memorandum 'auf was für grund-regulen das ganze systema des staats und der innerlichen verfassung zu bauen seye', apparently composed in Jan. 1761, is printed as an appendix to Walter, 'Kaunitz' Eintritt'. Kaunitz argued that increases in national income should precede increases in taxation. Government encouragement of agriculture, manufactures, and trade would procure this result.

[66] ÖZV (1934) 93–4, 15 Feb. 1761; Walter, *Geschichte*, 291. Those questioned were both Counts Chotek, Count Breuner (*Oberste Justizstelle*), Bartenstein, Cetto, Doblhof, Kannegiesser (all from the *Directorium*), and the heads of the royal governments in the Bohemian and Austrian lands, in all 20 persons.

[67] ÖZV (1934) 96–121 prints part of the *Staatsrat* votes of Borié, Blümegen, Haugwitz (out of order), Kaunitz, and Stupan; for comment, see Walter, *Geschichte*, 294–306. Prokeš summarizes the views of Bartenstein, Breuner, Cetto, both Counts Chotek, Doblhof, Kannegiesser; and, duplicating Walter, of the *Staatsrat* councillors Blümegen, Borié, Haugwitz, and Kaunitz. He only has a short summary (p. 43) of the views of the provincial governors.

condemning the *Directorium*, and asking for revival of the Bohemian and Austrian chancelleries, and the reunion of political and legal business.[68] At the centre, Bartenstein supported the *Directorium* in its initial form, but condemned its subsequent prolixity and confusion. He wanted to separate all cameral revenue from it.[69] Count Breuner, president of the *Oberste Justizstelle*, thought the restoration of the former chancelleries the best step.[70] Cetto from the *Directorium* said that the latter had worked well initially, but had deteriorated badly as its business increased. He wanted to separate all *cameralia* from it, and then to unite it with the *Oberste Justizstelle*. He condemned the separation of political and legal business.[71] Both brothers Chotek also favoured reunion of political and legal matters, separation of finance.[72] Doblhof (*Directorium*) concurred, suggesting political and legal senates in the combined central body.[73] His fellow councillor Kannegiesser drew a flattering picture of the Bohemian Chancellery, of which he had been a member, and complained that business had exploded once the *Directorium* got to work. The best remedy, in his view, was reunion of political and legal matters, and separation from them of financial ones.[74]

Those involved in, or with, the *Directorium* thus agreed, with almost suspicious unanimity, in condemning the principles of union of political and financial power, and separation of justice from administration, on which Haugwitz had proceeded. Several pointed out that the *Directorium* had never had an official Instruction, and that this had contributed to its confusion. Cetto, one of these, described how at first there were three meetings a week, and business was transacted smoothly. As the *Directorium*'s ambitions grew, more and more business flooded in, full meetings were reduced to two, then one, weekly, and most items were settled in committees. The provincial authorities, harassed from the centre, retaliated by

---

[68] Prokeš, 43.
[69] Ibid. 37–40.
[70] Ibid. 41–3. He reluctantly conceded, however, that it might be necessary to keep the existing system, purged of its faults.
[71] Ibid. 32–6.
[72] Ibid. 28–9, 40–1.
[73] Ibid. 36–7.
[74] Ibid. 29–32.

referring all decisions upwards.[75] Other criticisms agreed with this, though in less detail.

The members of the *Staatsrat* whose opinions have survived—Blümegen, Borié, Haugwitz, Kaunitz, Stupan—proved much less conservative. In particular, they rejected the view that *publica* and *judicialia* should be reunited; and wished therefore to preserve the *Oberste Justizstelle*. Haugwitz's protégé Blümegen at first seems to have wanted to retain the *Directorium* itself, or an equivalent, arguing like his master that financial and political power must be united.[76] Borié argued for one political and one financial body. All three, and also Stupan, envisaged creation of a *contrôle général* or book-keeping and audit department. Haugwitz seems otherwise to have been for the status quo.[77] Kaunitz's views, expressed in three *Vorträge*, of which that dated 20 November 1761 was the longest, exerted most influence on the empress, though not all of them proved acceptable.[78] Kaunitz argued that the hereditary lands ('die gesamte erblande') had never been formed into a full union ('vollkommene verbindung'), and that it was dangerous and difficult to do so, given that each had its own constitution ('verfassung'). Such a union could only be attempted after the existing state system had been improved. In economic terms, this meant the encouragement of agriculture, industry, population, and trade. A separate Council of Trade (*Commerzienrat*) staffed by merchants would help here. Administratively, *politica* and *judicialia* should be kept separate. The *Oberste Justizstelle* should be retained, and an 'erbländische

[75] See n. 71. Cetto admitted, however, that the Bohemian and Austrian chancelleries before 1749 had supported the Estates, and given little help to the *Hofkammer*. He argued none the less that union of financial and political power had created as many problems as the union of justice and administration before 1749. Haugwitz in 1764 contended that the assumption of war commissariat business in 1757 broke the *Directorium*'s back, Walter, *Geschichte*, 370.

[76] ÖZV (1934) 97 [Dec. 1761]; Prokeš, 46–7. Blümegen wanted an *Oberste Justizstelle*, a *Hofkriegsrat*, and a 'Stelle in publicis et cameralibus'.

[77] ÖZV (1934) 88–90 (Haugwitz), misdated ?Dec. 1760 but (Prokeš, 44–6) 5 Dec. 1761; ÖZV (1934) 96–7 and Prokeš, 47–8 (Borié). Borié argued that while union of administration and justice was harmful at the centre, it was feasible provincially, a principle applied in 1763.

[78] Prokeš, 48–64, misdated 17 Nov.; apart from the opening sections, dealing with the financial situation in 1761, the text is printed in ÖZV (1934) 101–21, and dated 20 Nov. 1761. Kaunitz's other two memoranda are referred to there, without amplification. Arneth, *Gesch. Mar. Ther.* vii. 21 ff., had previously summarized Kaunitz's major *Vortrag* at length.

cantzley' created to oversee the Contribution, education, public health, religion, the quartering of troops, and so on. The *Hofkriegs-rat* should in future be staffed with officers, not civilians. Kaunitz also emphasized the need for reform of accounts, and preparation of an annual estimate of expenditure.

This prescription coincided with much of what was carried out in December 1761. But Kaunitz also had some eccentric and impracticable financial ideas. Arguing from his general principle that at present things were united which ought to be separate, and separate which ought to be united, he condemned the virtually autonomous position of the Vienna City Bank, and the division of state revenue into different *caisses*. He proposed instead a *caisse générale*, which would unite the funds of the Vienna City Bank and the Estates Credit Deputation. The link with Vienna would be preserved by inviting the burgomaster of the city to join the board of this 'united hereditary lands bank and universal institute of credit'. The new body would soon become 'a true giro and deposit bank', with branches in the Austrian Netherlands, Italy, and the provinces.[79] A similar proposal, a *banque générale* guaranteed by the Estates, is ascribed to Blümegen.[80] It cannot be coincidence that Kaunitz's protégé, Count Ludwig Zinzendorf, president of the Estates Credit Deputation until his appointment as president of the new *Hofrechenkammer* from 1 January 1762, made very similar proposals on 7 October 1761. He wanted a *Hofkammer*, a *Rechenkammer*, and a *Generalkassa*. The last of these would unite the credit of the hereditary lands. The burgomaster of Vienna would sit on it.[81] In 1763 Zinzendorf was to develop his ideas for a state bank on these lines in much fuller form.[82]

Kaunitz, with his developing belief in the importance of economic growth, partly promoted by freer trade and cheaper credit, seems to have swallowed Zinzendorf's plans untasted. His patronage of them accounts for the initial version of financial reform, contained in a series of royal *Handbilletten* dated 23 December 1761. This envisaged a division of business between a *Hofkammer*,

---

[79] *ÖZV* (1934) 112–15; the name 'united . . . credit' is at p. 114.

[80] Ibid. 98–9, undated.

[81] Ibid. 167, 7 Oct. 1761. The 'General Kassa' was to include all credit funds, including those of the Vienna City Bank and the Estates. This was also true of the 'banque générale' ascribed by Walter to Blümegen; the similarity of the two projects suggests that this, too, was by Zinzendorf.

[82] See ii, Ch. 2.

a *caisse générale*, and a *Rechenkammer*. All credit funds (revenues pledged for debt service), including those of the Vienna City Bank, were to flow into the *caisse*; cameral and Contribution revenue was to pass through it. The *Hofkammer* was to supervise, and improve, all revenue, cameral and Contribution alike. The *Rechenkammer* was to verify all accounts, and, together with the other two departments, propose an annual budget. The text emphasized the importance of deciding correctly what should be united, or separated, in state business. This was taken directly from Kaunitz's *Votum* of 20 November, and indicates his influence.[83] In political terms, these proposals were ill judged. The statement that the *Hofkammer* would supervise the Contribution, historically under the control of chancellery and Estates, was bad enough. The proposal that the funds of the Vienna City Bank were to be poured into a new, and untried, *caisse générale* was worse. The news of it caused a panic, and the government had hastily to retreat. The final version of reform on 29 December, already noted, explicitly confined the *Hofkammer* to supervision of the Crown's cameral revenue, and said nothing about either the Contribution, in fact assigned to the chancellery, or the 'General Kassa'. The position of the Vienna City Bank was defined as follows.[84]

The existing *Stadt-Banco* is, under the terms of its first institution, to present regular accounts, and to allow the *Hofkammer* inspection of its revenue administration. In other respects, however, it is to retain its existing form. There is to be no reduction of its credit, or of the revenues settled on it for debt service. On the contrary, every care is to be taken to keep the Bank up and make it flourish.

On the same day, for good measure, the empress disingenuously published a denial that she had ever considered a union of cameral revenues with those of the Vienna City Bank, and threatened to dis-

---

[83] This version is not printed in full in *ÖZV* (1934), but is shown in the empress's *Handbillett* to Count Ludwig Zinzendorf of 23 Dec. 1761, in Pettenegg, *Zinzendorf*, 84–6. The instruction to Hatzfeld of 23 Dec., partly printed in *ÖZV* (1934) 194–6, makes clear that the 'general cassa' which he was to direct was to supervise receipt of all royal revenue, which would subsequently be used as the basis of 'a general German hereditary lands credit and bank'.

[84] Pettenegg, 88, also in *ÖZV* (1934) 123. Despite the government's modification of its plans, Count Karl Zinzendorf recorded on 1 Jan. 1762 that 'le C. Hazfeld' was to be 'le Président de la banque générale'. Prokeš, 'Boj', 68 n.

miss officials spreading rumours that this would happen.[85] Kaunitz, in short, had led her out on to a limb from which she had had to retreat.[86]

The settlement of 1760–2, devised at the climax of the Seven Years War, and at a time of acute financial difficulty, thus formed a middle ground between conservative and advanced positions. The reunion of political and judicial authority, the re-establishment of separate Bohemian and Austrian chancelleries, the separate transaction of Bohemian and Austrian business within one chancellery, were alike rejected. So too, in the opposite direction, was the pooling of all revenue in one fund, with ambitious objects. What emerged was a compromise. The dismantling of the *Directorium*, the creation from it of a conventional-sounding Bohemian and Austrian Chancellery, with responsibility for the Contribution, and for relations with the Estates, retention of the independence of the Vienna City Bank, and revival and enlargement of the *Hofkammer*, went some way to meet the views of traditionalists. The new advisory *Staatsrat*, intended to promote unity of policy, the retention of the *Oberste Justizstelle*, symbolizing the separation of justice from administration, the reconstruction of financial administration and control on new lines, the continued intention to 'unite' the Bohemian and Austrian lands, demonstrated that the reforms of 1749 would not be reversed, and that those who favoured constructive innovation still had the royal ear.

The arrangements of 1762 proved more durable than those of 1749, not least because their patron, Kaunitz, continued in power, while their opponent, Haugwitz, died in 1765. None the less, important changes soon had to be made in the way in which they operated. In particular, the division of financial business between

---

[85] Pettenegg, 197 n. According to Arneth, *Gesch. Mar. Ther.* vii 25–6 the Bohemian and Austrian Chancellery lost control over financial matters; this is repeated by O. Hintze, 'Der österreichische und der preussische Beamtenstaat im 17. und 18. Jahrhundert', *Gesammelte Abhandlungen*, ed. G. Oestreich (Göttingen 1962–7) i. 344. Beer, 'Die Finanzverwaltung', 244–5 first says that the 'Neuordnung' of 1761 was as set out in the orders of 23 Dec., then qualifies this by saying that the chancellery retained control of the Contribution.

[86] Kaunitz consoled himself that the 'absolutely independent and despotic position' of the Vienna City Bank had been ended, Beer, 'Denkschriften', 128. Walter fails to notice Kaunitz's advance, then retreat, on the issue of the Contribution and credit, which would have confirmed his view that Kaunitz was an amateur in domestic business.

'administration, money, and accounts' attempted in 1762 soon proved unworkable. Kaunitz argued that this was because his original plan of 23 December 1761 had not been fully implemented, hence division was incomplete.[87] It seems likely, however, that division itself, whether complete or not, was the real problem, since it turned ministries into rivals. This became plain in 1762–4. The *Hofkammer*, Bank Deputation, and *Hofrechenkammer* were unable to agree with each other, and were prevented by the new system from proceeding separately. Conferences, delay, acrimony, ensued. No superior institution existed able to promote accord.[88] This situation led to a prolonged discussion of possible changes, starting in February 1764 and only ending in September 1765. The reform then decided upon reasserted much of the unity of financial control shed in 1762. This result was achieved, however, by grouping existing institutions rather than demolishing them, as seemed initially probable.[89]

Between February and September 1764 the desirable structure of central government was discussed in the *Staatsrat*, but deadlock ensued between Haugwitz, Blümegen, and König, who wished to restore something like the *Directorium*, only bigger, and Kaunitz, Borié, and Stupan, who wanted to modify the existing arrangements. Kaunitz appealed to Hatzfeld and Zinzendorf, the presidents of the Bank Deputation and *Hofrechenkammer*. In their powerful joint *Vortrag* of 11 September 1764, the two ministers agreed with Kaunitz that the principles of 1762 were correct, and that their insufficient implementation was to blame for the present difficulties. The *Hofkammer* had no proper control over the Vienna City Bank. The *Generalkassa* was not general, but partial. In particular,

[87] The phrase 'verwaltung, geld und rechnung' occurs in a *Vortrag* of 11 Sept. 1764 by Hatzfeld and Zinzendorf; Kaunitz's argument that his system had been inadequately carried through in his *Vortrag* of 18 May 1764. See below for these documents. For Zinzendorf and the *Hofrechenkammer* see also ii, Ch. 3.

[88] See König's views of 1764, Walter, *Geschichte*, 374. For Hatzfeld's refusal as president of the Bank Deputation to allow *Hofkammer* attendance at his sessions, see ÖZV (1934) 172, 19 Jan. 1762; the *Staatsrat* supported him. This was one of many such examples.

[89] Walter, *Geschichte*, ch. VII, 'Die Reform von 1764/65', is one of the best in his book. It substantially reproduces the text of his article 'Der letzte grosse Versuch einer Verwaltungsreform unter Maria Theresia (1764/65)', *MIÖG* 47 (1933) 427–69. The Estates Credit Deputation of 1761 was being wound up by this date and did not figure in the government's discussions.

they attacked the growing financial power of the Bohemian and Austrian Chancellery. It was responsible not only for the Contribution, but for the recent inheritance, debts, and interest taxes, and for the provincial claims for war damages (*Supererogaten*). All these involved close relations with the Estates. The latter therefore looked to the chancellery for support, and for representation of their interests. Even the royal *Gubernien* tended to address it about all business, including financial matters. Hatzfeld and Zinzendorf proposed a restructuring of authority. The president of the *Hofkammer* should become responsible for the Bank Deputation, all cameral revenue, the *Generalkassa* and, most controversially, the Contribution and other taxes at present administered by the chancellery. The possible adverse consequences to the Vienna City Bank could be avoided by treating the union as one of the presidencies only. As for the Contribution: rectification of the cadastre, the *Postulata* to the Estates, and so on, would be left to the chancellery as a sop, while the *Hofkammer* would levy the tax.[90]

These changes implied a concentration of existing forces, but a rejection of total change. They recognizably drew on the original proposals of 1761, particularly with regard to administration of the Contribution by the *Hofkammer*. They did not command immediate assent. Discussion, stalemate, more discussion followed. At length, on 14 May 1765, the empress approved them in principle, and referred them to the *Staatsrat* and the two ministers for implementation. The anguished protests of Chancellor Chotek, who had been kept in the dark until 14 May, and who predicted the direst consequences if the provinces were in future ruled 'cameraliter' in fiscal matters, were ignored.[91] An intensive three-day conference under Kaunitz (18–20 May 1765) worked out the details. The *Hofkammer* was to be divided into four departments, the fourth being the Vienna City Bank, which, however, retained a publicly separate identity, including separate listing in the *Court Calendar*. Hatzfeld's emphasis was on making all the changes with minimum publicity. Confirmation of this scheme, with some modifications,

---

[90] Walter, *Geschichte*, 386–9. The document is summarized by Beer, 247–50, and printed in ÖZV (1934) 223–33. The *Generalkassa* was partial since the military *caisse*, and those of the Vienna City Bank, the *Schuldendirection* (under the emperor) and some others were reserved from it, ÖZV (1934) 198–200. Hatzfeld acquired control of the *Schuldendirection* on 21 Oct. 1765, after the emperor's death, Beer, 254.

[91] Walter, *Geschichte*, 405, 415.

followed in late May and early June 1765.[92] Hatzfeld, as expected
was named head of the new, enlarged *Hofkammer*. The existing
president, Herberstein, was pensioned off. On 12 June, a royal
Handbillett to Chotek confirmed the chancellery's loss of the Contribution, but made minor concessions about its levy, and about
nomination of provincial officials. Agreement on a division of
agenda between *Hofkammer* and chancellery on 26 August 1765
enabled the new arrangements to begin from 1 November, the start
of the military year 1766. They included, as a further bow to centralization, the formal subordination of the *Hofkommerzienrat* to
the chancellery, a change desired by neither.[93]

This settlement constituted a modification, not an abandon-
ment, of the arrangements of 1762. In the debate which preceded
it, Count Haugwitz, who died in September 1765, tried hard to
procure a return to those of 1749. He put up for consideration a
'Directorium in provincialibus et cameralibus' (15 March 1764)
which envisaged subordinating the *Hofkammer*, Bank Deputation, *Hofkommerzienrat* and *Hofrechenkammer* to an *Oberste
Kanzler*, conveying some marginal business to the *Oberste Justizstelle*, and then abolishing the Bohemian and Austrian Chancellery altogether. In May 1765 he was proposing union, under
Kaunitz, of a watered-down chancellery with the *Staatskanzlei*.
Even Kaunitz (18 May 1764) was prepared to abolish the existing
Hofkammer, and transfer its functions, and name, to the Bank
Deputation or *Rechenkammer*.[94] These proposals illustrated Blü-
megen's later contention that as there was no constitution
('Regierungs-Grundsätze'), the possibilities of institutional change
were boundless.[95]

---

[92] Ibid. 408–9, division of the *Hofkammer*. The other three departments covered
(1) Contribution, *Generalkassa*, Court; (2) mines and coinage; (3) cameral revenue.
Ibid. 412 for subsequent confirmation, the dating not entirely clear.

[93] ÖZV (1934) 265–6, 12 June 1765; ibid. 271–5 and Walter, *Geschichte*,
414–15, 26 Aug. 1765. Subordination of the *Hofkommerzienrat* to the chancellery,
but continuing separate identity under it, was decided in May 1765, see Walter, *Geschichte*, 416–19. The president of the council resigned.

[94] Ibid. 374, 401 (Haugwitz); 379 (Kaunitz). Haugwitz suggested that Hatzfeld
should be *Oberster Kanzler*.

[95] 30 Aug. 1773, Hock–Bidermann, 77 n. 2. However, the necessity for a royal
commission to lay the *Postulata* before the Bohemian Estates, under the *Verneuerte
Landesordnung* of 1627, and the unlikelihood that Hungary would accept commercial directions from the Bohemian and Austrian Chancellery, were mentioned in the
discussions, Walter, *Geschichte*, 409, 417.

Despite the length of the discussions of 1764–5, their outcome settled matters only temporarily. In 1768 there were further conciliar marathons about the organization of government. The *Staatsrat*, visibly wilting under a mass of business, much of it trivial, spent most of the year debating its own improvement. This time, in contrast to fruitless discussions on the same subject between September 1764 and May 1765, which had run parallel to those about the finance departments, some decisions were reached. On 16 December 1768, the émpress summed up by ordering the council to meet each Thursday at Court, and to divide its work into three classes: routine; business dealt with by circulation and a written report; and business taken to the weekly meeting. This anticipated the more elaborate reform of 1774. The Bohemian and Austrian Chancellor, chivvied by Maria Theresia (28 October 1768) about the importance of economic issues as a subject for 'political' attention, and, in particular the need for economic statistics, produced a plan for a *Staatswirtschaftsdeputation* to advise on these matters. It was to comprise members from the chancellery, the Hungarian Chancellery, the Council of Trade, and the finance departments, meeting weekly. Its brief was to study agriculture, commerce, population, tariffs. In particular, it was to supervise the new agricultural societies in the *Länder*. Manufactures, guilds etc. remained with the Council of Trade. The *Deputation* held its first session on 19 January 1769. Count Ludwig Zinzendorf's rather scrappy notes of the meetings of this new committee end in May 1775. They suggest an interesting talking-shop, immersed in detail. Agriculture, Hungary, trade with the Turks, and weights and measures, were some of the topics discussed. Lastly, the *Hofkammer* was restructured. The empress imposed on a reluctant Hatzfeld (28 October 1768) creation of two semi-independent Commissions to administer mines and coinage and the revenues of the Banat of Temesvár. Hatzfeld retained a co-signature and general oversight, but not day-to-day control. On 24 December 1768, after prolonged discussion in the *Staatsrat*, the *Hofkammer* was ordered to divide its remaining business into five commissions or divisions, each under a directing councillor. Routine matters were to be dealt with by the directors, weightier items discussed three times a week by the commissions, important business taken at full meetings of the

council twice weekly. This was recognizably analogous to the proposals for the *Staatsrat* earlier in the month.[96]

In 1771, the administrative cards were again reshuffled, twice
Early in the year, Maria Theresia sought advice from the Bohemian
and Austrian Chancellery and the *Hofkammer* about how political
and financial control (separated in 1762 and again in 1765) could be
brought under one direction, and the general flow of central business be lessened.[97] Both Chotek and Hatzfeld replied. The latter, in
his lengthy *Vortrag* of 5 February 1771, which was followed by
three later ones, put forward a plan similar to Haugwitz's of March
1764 for a revived *Directorium*. Hatzfeld argued for the union of the
presidencies of the chancellery, the *Hofkammer*, and the Bank
Deputation. This personal union, analogous to that of *Hofkammer*
and Bank Deputation in 1765, would, he argued, secure control
without needing to be made public. Business could then be grouped
in two departments. The first would contain the chancellery and the
Hofkammer, the second the Bank Deputation, the Council of
Trade, and part of the customs and salt revenues. The *Hofrechenkammer* would be abolished, and an audit department under *Hofkammer* control substituted for it. A (Bohemian) Chancellor and a
Bank Vice-President would be needed under the Finance Minister,
and would direct matters in his absence. The Minister, when
appointed (Hatzfeld did not make the mistake of assuming his own
nomination), would have to be admitted to the *Staatsrat*, partly in
order to learn about Hungarian and military business, partly (and

---

[96] *ÖZV* (1934); Walter, *Geschichte*. Pettenegg, *Zinzendorf*, 128 shows the *Hofkammer* commissions as salt and consumption taxes (Count Lamberg); customs
(Count Cobenzl); Hungarian Contribution (Count Schlick); cameral revenues
(Baron Schmidlin); domains (Baron Nefzer). Chotek proposed the *Staatswirtschaftsdeputation* on 22 Nov. 1768. His plan was approved on 28 Dec. Zinzendorf's notes
of some of its meetings are in HHSA Nachl. Zinz., Hs. 127. The reduced scope of the
Council of Trade from 1768, made clear earlier by Beer, 'Die Finanzverwaltung',
277–81, is overlooked by K. Schünemann, 'Die Wirtschaftspolitik Josefs II. in der
Zeit seiner Mitregentschaft', *MIÖG* 47 (1933) 13–56, who treats the council as the
rallying-point for protectionist interests up to 1776. For the agricultural societies, the
first, and model, of which was in Carinthia in 1765, see K. Dinklage, 'Gründung und
Aufbau der theresianischen Ackerbaugesellschaften', *Zeitschr. f. Agrargeschichte u.
Agrarsoziologie*, 13 (1965) 200–11.
[97] Beer, 'Die Finanzverwaltung', 257–8. *ÖZV* (1934) and the final chapter of
Walter, *Geschichte*, do not add to this.

significantly) in order to counter possible intrigues by his *vice-capi*.[98]

The empress named Hatzfeld *Oberster Kanzler* on 23 June 1771, in place of Chotek, who was forcibly retired and died soon after.[99] Hatzfeld thus became chancellor, and president of the Council of Trade; he was already president of the *Hofkammer* and Bank Deputation. But for the time being, at least, the *Hofrechenkammer* was retained in its existing form. The *Staatsrat* also (20 August 1771) repudiated Hatzfeld's pretensions to join it, Kaunitz's protégé Binder launching a violent attack on the great man's attempt to 'acquire the power of an uncontrolled prime minister'.[100] Like most Austrian systems, Haugwitz's in 1749, Kaunitz's in 1761, all Joseph II's before 1780, Hatzfeld's thus remained incomplete. And he only enjoyed his union of powers for six months. On 15 December 1771 the empress, following the advice of her son, who had returned from Prague in November, bristling with criticisms, promulgated a series of further changes. Hatzfeld was removed from his lofty position, and put in the *Staatsrat* as Directing Minister, a position held earlier by Prince Starhemberg. Several other changes were made in its membership. The Bohemian and Austrian Chancellery once more became an independent body, and received back the Contribution and other revenues ceded to the *Hofkammer* in 1765.[101] The personal union of the presidencies of the *Hofkammer*, Bank Deputation, and Council of Trade, which Hatzfeld had briefly enjoyed, was, however, retained; and two vice-presidents were appointed, one for trade, one for the *Hofkammer* and Bank. The commissions of 1768 within the *Hofkammer* were

---

[98] Beer, loc. cit. gives an extended summary. I have used the complete text in HKA Kredit AA Akten, rote Nr. 12, Fsz. 7 no. 8, 'Akten betreffend die Zusammenziehung Verschiedener Dikasterien nach dem Hatzfeldischen Vorschlag, 1771'. Hatzfeld's *Vortrag* of 5 Feb. 1771 is at fos. 139ʳ–285ʳ. For some of the procedural suggestions in it see Ch. 11. Hatzfeld's further *Vorträge* of 25 Feb., 5 May, and 2 Aug. 1771 are referred to in ÖZV (1934) 315.

[99] See p. 347.

[100] Beer, 262.

[101] Principally the Contribution, *Erbsteuer*, and *Schuldensteuer*. The clerical *Quindecennalcollecte*, settled to service debts incurred for building military fortresses, also went to the chancellery. The changes published on 15 Dec. 1771 were first proposed by the empress in a cleverly worded letter to Hatzfeld dated 30 Nov, but it took two weeks to induce him to give way, see p. 354.

abolished.[102] A grouping of business at personal level, was thus arrived at, while leaving institutions alone. The chancellery was actually strengthened. At least nominally, the chancellor and *Hofkammer* president were now two of the most important men in civil government.

Three comparatively restricted reforms saw the reign out. In January 1773, Zinzendorf's *Hofrechenkammer* was at last reduced to a subordinate form under control of the *Hofkammer*, as both Hatzfeld and Joseph II had proposed in 1771.[103] In April 1774, the business of the *Staatsrat* was revised on lines which took the changes of December 1768 further. In future, all inland business was to be directed to its office (*Kanzlei*), which would register it and pass it to the empress. She in turn would decide on it at once, or refer it to the *Staatsrat* or a department and record the fact. Matters referred to the *Staatsrat* would be divided into four classes: routine; business which could be decided on reading a summary; business circulated to councillors, then reported on in writing; and the weightest matters, which were to be brought to the weekly meeting. The responsible councillor (referendary) would introduce it there. The others, starting with the most junior, would then give their views. The most important task, the division of incoming business according to its importance, was intended for Joseph II himself. Because of his departure from Vienna, it fell to his mother instead.[104] Joseph II had first proposed this scheme a year earlier, as part of a much more wide-reaching change in central government. His criticism of the *Staatsrat* on this occasion was that in twelve years it had not drawn up an Instruction for itself; that through its joint sessions with executive departments it had become more like a department (*dicasterium*) than an advisory body; and that its sessions were crowded with trivial matters, while more serious ones were often dealt with only by circulation. It is not known whether

---

[102] The *Hofkommerzienrat* was under the *Hofkammer*, but its Vice-President, Baron Reischach, had semi-independence. Walter, 440, 469 has contradictory statements about this. The empress's first proposals on 30 Nov. 1771 followed Joseph II's plan of separating *Hofkammer* and Bank. Hatzfeld successfully resisted this, see *Khev.-Metsch 1770–3*, n. 124; ibid. 12 Dec. 1771.

[103] ii. 85. The model for the revised body was the Belgian *Chambre des Comptes*.

[104] ÖZV (1934) 78–84, Hatzfeld's draft of Joseph's proposals, dated 21 Apr. 1774. It was given final form on 12 May, Hock–Bidermann, 40. The empress's assumption of the task of dividing business into classes is shown in Walter, *Geschichte*, 462.

the reorganization of 1774 resolved these difficulties. From 1776 the empress and emperor appear no longer to have attended the *Staatsrat*, which remained under Hatzfeld's efficient, if conservative, direction.[105]

The final change noticed here was announced on 2 January 1776. It merged the Council of Trade, which had had a semi-independent existence under the *Hofkammer* since December 1771, in the Bohemian and Austrian Chancellery. Baron Reischach, its vice-president and effective head, was made Bohemian and Austrian Chancellor, and vice-president of the chancellery, with responsibility for commercial affairs. Three of his former councillors joined him. Reischach was Joseph II's chamberlain and protégé. His independent position under Kollowrat at the *Hofkammer* had caused friction, which the change removed. Consequential alterations were made in commercial organization. The Sanitary Commission (*Sanitäts-Hofdeputation*) of 1753, whose primary task was to administer the protective cordon against disease on the Military Frontier, was abolished. Buccari, Buccariza, Portoré, and Fiume were given to Hungary, despite protests by the *Hofstellen* that Fiume belonged to Krain, hence to the German Empire. The separate *Intendenza Commerciale* which oversaw both Trieste and Fiume, and was responsible to the Council of Trade in Vienna, was wound up; its governor, who had irritated Joseph II on his tour, was made *Landeshauptmann* of Görz instead. Two other ports, Carlopago and Zengg, were transferred to military control. The commercial business of Hungary and Siebenbürgen was transferred to the Hungarian and Siebenbürgen chancelleries. All these changes were the result of the emperor's excoriating report of 17 May 1775, written after his tour of the Croatian Military Frontier and the *Litorale*. In it, he condemned the area as poverty-stricken (Carlopago and Zengg were 'cities of beggars', everyone in Fiume was 'dying of hunger'), the Frontier Militia as totally ineffectual, the sanitary cordon as laughable and an obstacle to trade with the Turks. As usual, he proposed more than he got: on this occasion he wanted to

---

[105] Joseph's proposals dated 27 Apr. 1773 are printed in ÖZV (1934) 48–72. The subsequent discussions in the *Staatsrat* etc., are thinly documented there. The whole episode is discussed in detail in Hock–Bidermann, 29–40, which is also drawn on by Walter, *Geschichte*, 444–63. Hock–Bidermann, 101 n., states that meetings of the whole *Staatsrat* ceased from 1776. Cf. n. 51 above. *Khev.-Metsch* last records an attendance by Maria Theresia on 30 Jun. 1775.

reconstruct the Frontier Militia into a national volunteer force, serving for twelve years.[106]

The frequent institutional changes of this period were partly due to
the repeated need to resolve pressing practical difficulties. They
were partly due also to the closed system of Austrian government,
which made juggling with administrative organization more feasible
than it would have been in Holland or England, where large changes
had to be agreed to by representative bodies. The absence of a constitution, as Blümegen remarked, removed constraints on change.
The recurrent personal strife involved was also perhaps a kind of
substitute for the political disputes of more open societies. A further
factor, of increasing importance, is that Maria Theresia sometimes
disagreed with her husband as co-regent, and more frequently and
more bitterly with her son, when (17 September 1765) he became
co-regent in his father's place. As Joseph complained to his mother
(9 December 1773), dual control at the top simply created confusion. And Maria Theresia's task, he pointed out, was to decide, not
to listen to endless ministerial opinions.[107] A detailed account of
Joseph II's role during the co-regency, and of his relations with his
mother, is not relevant to exposition of the structures of government.[108] The discussion here will be limited to an outline from the

---

[106] The 'Commercien-Hofrath' appears as a separate entity in the *Court Calendar*
until 1776. The episode of its abolition is barely dealt with in ÖZV (1934), which is
confined (pp. 292–4) to printing Maria Theresia's *Handbillett* to Blümegen of 2 Jan.
1776 outlining the changes then made. There is a fuller account in Beer, 'Die Finanzverwaltung', 281 and n., and further detail in *Khev.-Metsch*, 2 Jan. 1776, also ibid. n.
112, Joseph II's report of 17 May 1775. Walter, *Geschichte*, 471–2 relies on Schünemann 'Wirtschaftpolitik', which does not mention the *Sanitäts-Hofdeputation*, but
adds the significant information (p. 55) that Joseph II ruled as emperor on 6 Feb.
1776 that his view about Fiume should be adhered to.

[107] Arneth, *Maria Ther. u. Jos.* II., no. cxc, 9 Dec. 1773. For Joseph's assumption
of the co-regency see *Khev.-Metsch*, 12 Sept. 1765 (conference on co-regency) and n.
124. The need to secure Hungarian consent, perhaps through a Diet, was raised. Paul
Festetics advised simply telling the Hungarians of the co-regency. This had occurred
on 1 Jan. 1741 in respect of Francis Stephen, ibid. The latter's co-regency was published on 7 Dec. 1740.

[108] The subject is definitively treated in the first volume of Professor Beales's life
of Joseph II, which he kindly let me read in draft. Walter, *Geschichte*, ch. VIII,
'Maria Theresia und Joseph II. 1765–1780' clearly thought the period of the co-
regency of subordinate importance. His account of the relations between the empress
and her son is based on the printed correspondence, and emphasizes Joseph's wish to
move his mother aside. Walter does not discuss the constitutional nature of, and
reasons for, the co-regency.

printed record of Joseph II's characteristically drastic views about administration and policy. Several of the institutional changes noticed in this chapter, especially those of 1771, 1774, and 1776, represent selection by Maria Theresia of the more feasible parts of Josephine plans.

The difficulties of a co-regency were already apparent during the Seven Years War. Count Khevenhüller, in a frequently cited passage from his diary (31 December 1757), noted that the Austrian defeat at Leuthen was due to the double-headed nature of Austrian government. Both emperor and empress wanted to rule, and nothing could be done in military or financial matters without the emperor's consent. Yet he was too easy-going to sustain this burden. The empress, fiery and impatient, distrusted all her ministers. They took advantage of this division of control, and confusion resulted. In Prussia, Frederick II directed everything himself. This analysis credited the emperor with more influence than other accounts have done, but is not necessarily mistaken. The importance of his financial role is examined further in ii, Chs. 1 and 2. With the young Joseph II's accession to the co-regency, however, the problems of agreement, or lack of it, between a ruler and a co-ruler became much more acute.

A selection of reform proposals made by Joseph between April 1761, when he was 20, and May 1775, when he was 34, is given in summary form in Table 9.3*. They had certain general characteristics. Joseph was disposed to unitary solutions, imposed suddenly from above. His belief in a Spartan style of leadership was joined to a conventional eighteenth-century faith in the capacity of rulers to encourage population and trade. He favoured advance by merit for merchants and officials: 'tout est au mérite personel'. He regarded inherited social rank, with claims to fiscal preference, and an easy path in government service, as harmful to the state. He regarded the state, for which the sovereign was spokesman, as an independent entity, with a good of its own, which all must seek to promote. In government organization, he showed a recurrent wish for a strong hand at the top, controlling a central chancellery or directory, merging existing departments. In 1773, this was to be done under a supreme royal Cabinet. Lastly, throughout these memoranda there is a belief that the ruler must visit his territories, and see the situation on the spot. As Joseph remarked in his report of 17 May 1775, he had formed his conclusions by personal inspection, not by reading reports of the *Commerzienrat*. His tours in the Banat and Hungary (1768, 1770), Italy (1769, 1775), Siebenbürgen (1773), Galicia (1773, 1780), Bohemia (1771, 1779) exemplified this, quite apart from his voyages to France in 1777 and Russia and Poland in 1780.

Not all the proposals of this 'first Jacobin of his time', as Lord Grenville later described him, were as draconian as those cited here.[109] His long memorandum in French for his brother Leopold, written in 1767, strikes a conservative note: maintenance of a formidable army, but avoidance of war at all costs; fostering of public credit, promotion of the wealth and well-being of subjects.[110] Other reports, on the Banat in 1768, on Siebenbürgen in 1773, were tailored to local conditions.[111] Joseph's capacity to be specific and practical is also shown in his interventions in Galician policy after 1772.[112] But the general nature of his approach to policy explains much of the evident disharmony between him and his mother. Joseph's belief in the total recasting of systems meant that he was always bitterly conscious of the limits of his own power. His plans of 1771 and 1773 would have made him a kind of dictator, under the empress's nominal supervision. His mother's awareness of her son's radical intentions, and cavalier approach to social privilege and vested rights, made her miserable. His belief in religious freedom, in destruction of the great for the sake of the majority, in 'the principle of freedom in all things' ('Freiheit in Allem'), would destroy the state if put into practice, she warned him in December 1775.[113] His resolute espousal of toleration for the Moravian Protestants, an issue which flared in 1777, showed that her views made little impression on him.[114] Much of the printed correspondence between Maria Theresia and Joseph still makes uncomfortable reading. It is

---

[109] Grenville to Henry Dundas, 27 July 1799, *HMC* Fortescue MSS, 199.

[110] HHSA Sammelband 88.

[111] His report on the Banat is described in Schünemann, 'Wirtschaftspolitik', 23–33; for Joseph's tour of, and observations on, Siebenbürgen, see G. A. Schuller, *Samuel von Brukenthal* (Munich 1967, 1969) i. 281–318.

[112] Glassl, *Einrichtungswerk, passim*.

[113] Arneth, *Mar. Ther. u. Jos. II*. no. ccxxxi [Dec. 1775]. Schünemann, 41–3 summarizes a proposal by the emperor to his mother, evidently of 13 June 1772, for a 'Diktator' who would take steps to relieve the Bohemian famine 'auf eine schier despotische Art'; the vocabulary perhaps reflected Joseph's recollection of Roman history.

[114] Arneth, nos. cclx, cclxii, cclxvi, cclxviii, cclxix, cclxx, cclxxi, June–Sept. 1777.

not surprising, given this situation, that Joseph offered to resign the co-regency, an office which he stigmatized as arduous but titular, in 1773, 1775, and 1777. In April 1773, he conceded his brother Leopold, only half in jest, the right to succeed in his place.[115] In August 1778 he wrote to him that if his mother's secret initiative in the Bavarian war led to a dishonourable peace, he would retire to Italy until she died.[116] Meanwhile, the empress expressed her wish to resign (December 1773), stating that only Joseph's unwillingness, and the critical state of affairs, stopped her.[117] The third head of state, Kaunitz, put in his resignation in 1766, 1773, 1776, and 1779.[118] This state of affairs, with the captains quarrelling on the bridge, cannot have reassured the governmental crew. It acted as a standing contradiction of the repeatedly expressed wish for system, order and unity.

It is difficult to make an accurate assessment of the division of labour between the empress and her son during the co-regency. In October 1769, the English *chargé d'affaires* in Vienna expressed the view that Joseph was 'not suffer'd to meddle as much in Politicks as Persons in His Station commonly do'.[119] Joseph, conscious of the gap between what he would like to effect, and what he could effect, consistently represented his role to his mother as otiose, and even harmful.[120] Against this, the reform of the *Staatsrat* in 1774 would, if fully implemented, have assigned Joseph a leading, and even directing, part in it. Maria Theresia, in a well-known letter to Leopold in March 1778, complained of Joseph's departure for the army as leaving her 'sans aide, l'empereur étant chargé depuis quelques années de toute la besogne, et interne'.[121] In other letters, written in

---

[115] Ibid., nos. cxc (9 Dec. 1773), ccxxxii (24 Dec. 1775), cclxviii (23 Sept. 1777), Joseph's requests to resign as co-regent; no. clxxix, Joseph to Leopold, offering to exchange places, n.d., ascribed by Arneth to Apr. 1772. Walter, *Geschichte*, 444 says this is an error for Apr. 1773.

[116] Arneth, no. ccccxiv, 8 Aug. 1778.

[117] Ibid. no. cxci, [Dec. 1773]. At this stage, she was counting on Joseph's proposals for the *Staatsrat* to pull things round, ibid.

[118] Walter, *Geschichte*, 430 (4 Jun. 1766); Arneth, nos. clxxxix (9 Dec. 1773), ccxl (29 Mar. 1776); dxxxvii (24 May 1779), all mentioned in letters by Joseph to Leopold.

[119] BL Add. MS 35500, Hardwicke Papers, Diplomatic Letter Book of Lord Stormont, i (12 Nov. 1763–1 Oct. 1771), fo. 55, Benjamin Langlois to Lord Rochford 4 Oct. 1769. Walter does not discuss the division of royal labour.

[120] See especially his letters to her of 9 Dec. 1773 and 24 Dec. 1775, Arneth, nos. cxc, ccxxxii.

[121] Arneth, *Mar. Ther. Kinder und Freunde*, i. 37–41, Maria Theresia to Archduke Leopold, 12 Mar. 1778.

1776, 1777, and later in 1778, however, she was equally emphatic about the burden of her own work.[122] In commercial matters, her detailed comments were separately registered in a series going up to March 1776.[123] In finance, which was the backbone of government business, her careful perusal of state accounts, and decisions on them, extended to the end of her reign, as many documents show. Though 'en fait de finances et d'emprunts je ne suis pas forte', a disclaimer also made by Frederick II, Maria Theresia's close and continuous attention to the subject up to 1780 cannot be doubted.[124] Her involvement with Greiner in the bizarre affair of the Lower Austrian *Getränkesteuer* in 1780 was a final demonstration of this.[125] It seems plausible to assume that the same was true in other sectors of state business. And Joseph's frequent absences from Vienna, which his mother deplored, and which were partly a device by him to avoid friction, made her work the more indispensable. On the other hand, all business was increasing in the last decade and a half of Maria Theresia's reign, and there can be little doubt that there was plenty for Joseph to do.[126] He would perhaps nevertheless have claimed that it was only in military affairs and in foreign policy (Poland, Bavaria), that the results were more than routine.

[122] Ibid. ii. 422, Maria Theresia to Archduchess Maria Christina, 15 Apr. 1776; ibid. iii. 271, same to same 31 Mar. 1777; ibid. ii. 132, Maria Theresia to Archduke Ferdinand, 6 Aug. 1778. *Khev.-Metsch*, 6 Jul. 1775 soothed the grumbling emperor by telling him that his mother consulted him on all important business.

[123] HKA Hss. 290–294, 'Maria Theresias Allerhöchste Entschliessungen zur Belebung der Industrie, des Handels, der Fabriken und Manufacturen in den k.k. österreichischen Erbstaaten 1764 bis 1776'. This source is extensively drawn on by Gustav Otruba, *Die Wirtschaftspolitik Maria Theresias* (Vienna 1963).

[124] For the empress's disclaimer to Ferdinand, see Arneth, *Mar. Ther. Kinder und Freunde*, ii. 163, 9 Dec. 1778; for Frederick II, see Arneth, *Mar. Ther. u. Jos. II.*, no. cxxix, Joseph to his mother, [Sept. 1769] at p. 309. One example of many of her attention to finance is her annotation of the final accounts for 1776, which conclude with three nearly illegible autograph lines and her signature, HKA Staatsschuldenakten, rote Nr. 165, fo. 727^r, 16 Dec. 1777. Schünemann's *ex cathedra* statement (p. 14) that the empress's comments and signature on documents provide no proof that she had really read them is not reconcilable with this and much other evidence.

[125] See ii, Ch. 8, for this episode.

[126] For the increasing volume of business after 1763 see Ch. 11.

10

The Crown's local authority

ROYAL government outside Vienna in this period has been little studied in comparison with the central administration. The Austrian and Bohemian lands will be examined first, taking the position in 1740, in 1748–9, and from 1763. Galicia (from 1772) and the Hungarian lands are considered subsequently. The next chapter discusses the Estates, whose administration overlapped with that of the Crown, and, initially at least, was only loosely subordinate to it.

The common pattern of crown authority in the Austrian and Bohemian lands in 1740 was of a royal representative (captain, lieutenant) supported by a council, and by parallel judicial, financial, and commercial bodies. This serves as a working description, though administration and justice were not clearly divided, administrative or financial councils having judicial functions and vice versa. Nor was it true that the different councils necessarily helped each other. Furthermore, royal authority depended on support from the Estates and private lordships, with their important fiscal and administrative activities. It was the officials of the Estates and lordships who, at village level, carried out royal commands, or failed to do so. This interaction of powers is symbolized by the fact that in 1740 the provincial captain, or *Landeshauptmann*, 'homo principis et homo statuum' as Count Blümegen later called him, was both the king's representative and the official head of the Estates in Bohemia, Moravia, Austria above the Enns, Carinthia, and Krain. In Silesia, the comparable position of *Oberhauptmann* had not been filled since 1718, and the *Direktor* of the royal *Oberamt* acted instead. In Lower Austria and Styria, where there was a royal lieutenant or *Statthalter*, the *Landmarschall* (Lower Austria) and the *Landeshauptmann* (Styria), not the *Statthalter*, presided over the Diet.[1]

---

[1] These areas are discussed below. Blümegen's remark of 1765 is cited by Beer, 'Die Finanzverwaltung', 270. The discussion of provincial government in chs. 5–7 of Evans, *The Making of the Habsburg Monarchy* is excellent, and though for an earlier period is relevant to most of this chapter.

The first institution discussed is the Lower Austrian *Regierung*, often also called the *Regiment*.[2] This powerful body, whose president was the royal *Statthalter* (1523), dated in its existing form from 1527, though there had been comparable arrangements since 1493. Its membership was exceptionally large. In 1740 it had twenty fully paid councillors, but thirty-eight others served unpaid in the expectation of promotion.[3] Its jurisdiction extended over Austria both below and above the Enns. 'Lower Austria' in this sense was the remainder of the larger entity of that name, which in the years 1527–65 included Inner Austria as well.[4] The *Regierung* had certain responsibilities for police and public order. Primarily, however, it was a civil and criminal court, both for appeals, and of first instance for defined categories of persons.[5] As such it was in potential competition with other courts, of which that of the *Hofmarschall* was the most eminent, and the mercantile courts of first and second instance (1717) the most recent. The court of the *Landmarschall*, who was head of the Lower Austrian Estates, was reserved for members of the nobility other than those serving at Court.[6] Financially, Lower Austria was important both because of the revenue it absorbed, and because the *Hofkammer*, Bank Deputation, and other central financial bodies were located in Vienna. Their concern was revenue from the royal domains and from indirect taxes. The Contribution, both here and in Upper Austria, was under the control of the Estates, specifically of their *Verordneten-Collegium* or finance and business committee, and this seems to

---

[2] See [A. Starzer], *Beiträge zur Geschichte der niederösterreichischen Statthalterei. Die Landeschefs und Räthe dieser Behörde von 1501 bis 1896* (Vienna 1897). As the title indicates, this work is primarily biographical. The first 125 pp. give an outline history of the council, but do not discuss its actual functions under Charles VI. The name *Statthalterei* was adopted from 1849. *Regiment* was still occasionally used in the 18th c. as an alternative to *Regierung*.

[3] For the names of councillors in 1740 see Table 13.1*. Some of those listed may not have attended, but leave had to be sought for this. For the establishment of 20 paid councillors from 1724, see Starzer, 49. He says that supernumeraries brought this to 51. Table 13.1* has 58 in 1740.

[4] See p. 20.

[5] It is not easy to get from Starzer what the *Regierung* actually did c.1740. From Domin-Pet. 7–8 it appears that it was a court of civil and criminal appeal for Upper and Lower Austria, and a court of first instance for certain categories of persons. Its administrative functions require investigation.

[6] Ibid. 7, 9–10. The *Landmarschall* had jurisdiction over the nobles of Lower Austria defined as Austria below the Enns, but those who served at Court came under the *Hofmarschall*.

have proceeded without much supervision from the Austrian Chancellery.[7]

The existence of the Lower Austrian *Statthalter* and *Regierung*, with their jurisdiction over Upper Austria, must explain why the latter in 1740 had only a *Landeshauptmannschaft*, comprising the *Landeshauptmann* and a handful of councillors. This body had (unexplored) administrative functions, but also acted as a *Landrecht* or court of first instance for the nobility.[8] A similar arrangement is observable in Inner Austria. The complex institutions of Inner Austria, whose formal head was the Inner Austrian *Statthalter*, a post created in 1625, had jurisdiction over all the Inner Austrian lands, including Trieste, Fiume, and the *Litorale*.[9] They comprised a *Geheimer Rat*, a *Regierung*, a *Hofkammer*, and a *Hofkriegsrat*, more commonly from about 1717 called a *Kriegsstelle*. These were all located in Graz, the capital of Styria, and dated from the 1560s (*Hofkriegsrat* 1578). They were a product of the separate government of Inner Austria by the Archduke Charles and his son Ferdinand of Styria, subsequently Emperor Ferdinand II, in the period 1565–1619. Similarly, Tyrol and Further Austria, which in the century 1565–1665 formed the entity 'Upper Austria', were governed by a *Geheimer Rat*, a *Regierung* or *Regiment*, and a *Hofkammer* in Innsbruck. These were created for the Archduke Ferdinand from 1565, and survived when his line died out in 1665.[10] The institutions

---

[7] See Ch. 11 and ii, Ch. 8.

[8] Domin-Pet. 14. Upper Austria (Austria above the Enns) and Inner Austria are not included in the *Court Calendar* at this date. The HKA typewritten index to the Lower Austrian *Herrschaftsakten*, 600, shows that in 1738 the *Landeshauptmannschaft* in both Carinthia and Krain consisted of the *Landeshauptmann*, eight councillors including the *Landesvizedom*, and various officials. Austria above the Enns is omitted, but it seems plausible that the position there was similar. In 1748 the 'Landeshauptmannschaftlich Judicio' in Austria above the Enns comprised the *Landeshauptmann* and six *Landräte*, HKA Hs. 220, fo. 165.

[9] V. Thiel, 'Die innerösterreichische Zentralverwaltung 1564–1749', AÖG 105 (1916) 1–210, 111 (2) (1930) 497–670 is superior to H. Pirchegger, *Gesch. der Steiermark*, iii (Graz etc. 1934), covering 1740–1919, which is useful but erratic. The government of Trieste and the *Litorale* was partly under a separate *Intendenza Litorale*, see below.

[10] H. I. Bidermann, 'Geschichte der landesfürstlichen Behörden in u. für Tyrol von 1490–1749', *Arch. f. Gesch. u. Alterthumskunde Tirols* iii (1866) 323–52 is muddled, imprecise and sometimes erroneous, but contains some interesting points. There is fuller information in J. Egger, *Geschichte Tirols von den ältesten Zeiten bis in die Neuzeit* (Innsbruck 1872–80). Egger's book, which has a defective index, is uncritical but contains a mass of facts. For the *Geheimer Rat*, etc., see Egger, ii. 252, 462, 542, though a systematic treatment is lacking there.

in Graz reduced the importance of government councils in the other Inner Austrian lands. Both Carinthia and Krain, like Upper Austria, had a *Landeshauptmannschaft*, with executive and judicial *Landrecht* functions. Görz-Gradisca, Trieste, Fiume, and Buccari each had a royal *Oberamt*.[11]

The Inner Austrian councils led a muddled and quarrelsome existence, disputing with each other as well as with the Estates. The *Geheimer Rat* was officially the channel of communication to Vienna, but the other bodies often bypassed it. It was also (until 1747) the civil and criminal appeals court for Inner Austria, and had some financial competence.[12] The *Regierung* was more important, exercising jurisdiction over religious houses and benefices, the economic life of towns, and over all royal officials and the *Landeshauptleute* throughout Inner Austria.[13] Two councillors each from Carinthia and Krain sat in it. The Inner Austrian *Hofkammer*, with up to twenty members, feuded with these bodies, with the Estates, and with the *Kriegsstelle*, which, in conjunction with the Estates, oversaw the affairs of the Military Frontier. Maria Theresia replaced the *Kriegsstelle* with a more modest 'Militär Oberdirectorium' from 1 January 1744, excluding the Estates, but expected them to keep up their Frontier payments.[14]

The responsibilities of the Vienna City Bank in Inner Austria were not large in 1740, but increased with the cession to it of the Inner Austrian customs revenue, and all cameral revenue, in March 1746 and December 1749 respectively.[15] The *Universal Bancalität*, until its dissolution in 1745, retained a *Bancalcollegium* in Graz, the only survivor of several created in 1715.[16] Mercantile courts of first

[11] HKA index, 595–9.

[12] In some criminal cases a further appeal was possible to the emperor, Thiel, ii. 523. There was overlap between councils, e.g. the presidents of the *Hofkammer* and *Kriegsstelle* sat in the *Geheimer Rat*.

[13] In Aquileia, Fiume, Flitsch, and Trieste the royal governors were styled only *Hauptleute*, ibid. 548–9. The Carinthian and Krain councillors in the *Regierung* were nominated by the local Estates, ibid. 539.

[14] Ibid. 614–15. Central oversight was provided by the Vienna *Hofkriegsrat*.

[15] HKA Hs. 280, nos. 27, 40. The earlier of these two agreements is described in Mensi, *Die Finanzen Oesterreichs*, 722.

[16] Others were established at Linz, Innsbruck, and Brünn. By 1722 only Graz was left, Mensi, 468. It had a staff of 15 in 1738, HKA index, 597. The *Bancalität* established smaller bodies called 'Bancal Repräsentanzen' in 1717–22 in Breslau, Brünn, Innsbruck, Linz, Prague, and Pressburg, consisting of a 'Bancal Oberrepräsentant' and a few helpers, Mensi, 468. Maria Theresia ordered their abolition on 27 Aug. 1745, ÖZV (1925). 20 ff. Despite their name, they had nothing to do with the Vienna City Bank.

and second instance were formed (1722) in Graz, Sankt-Veit (Carinthia), Laibaich (Krain), Trieste and Fiume.[17] The last two were declared Free Ports in 1719.[18] The 'Intendenza Commerciale' of 1730 for the *Litorale* and its ports denoted government wishes to attract Austrian and Bohemian goods there for export.[19] The *Intendenza* was in Laibach, and its president was the *Landeshauptmann* of Krain, an arrangement which lasted until 1748.[20] Central oversight of these Inner Austrian councils was divided. The *Geheimer Rat* answered to the Austrian Chancellery, the Inner Austrian *Hofkammer* to the *Hofkammer* in Vienna, the *Kriegsstelle* to the *Hofkriegsrat* there. The Ministerial Bank Deputation supervised the local officials of the Vienna City Bank. This fragmentation of control cannot have assisted the Crown's authority. The Contribution, as elsewhere, was under the control of the local Estates.[21]

In the Bohemian lands, the position of *Statthalter* is again encountered, this time collectively in the shape of the *Statthalterei* or royal council of lieutenancy (1577) in Prague.[22] Its president, the *Obrist-Burggraf* of Bohemia, was also the head of the Bohemian Estates, and, like his councillors, paid by them. This symbolized the divided allegiance of these advisers, all in theory king's men.[23] In 1740 there were fifteen, thirteen of whom were counts. They were all designated *Statthalter*. They shared between them the royal offices below that of *Burggraf*: Bohemian *Hofmeister*, *Lehenrichter*,

---

[17] Domin-Pet. 14.

[18] F. M. Mayer, *Die Anfänge des Handels und der Industrie in Oesterreich und die Orientalische Compagnie* (Innsbruck 1882) 35; L. Marini et al., *I ducati padani, Trento e Trieste* in G. Galasso (ed.), *Storia d'Italia*, xvii (Turin 1979) 652.

[19] Mayer, 108; Marini, 653.

[20] Marini, 655 shows that in 1748 a 'Provincia mercantile del Litorale' responsible to the *Commercien-Directorium* in Vienna was substituted, with an 'Intendenza Commerciale' at Trieste as a local executive body. The other ports within the 'Provincia' were Fiume, Aquileia, Buccari, and Porto Re. This organization lasted until 1776.

[21] See ii, Ch. 8.

[22] See Table 13.1* for the names of the councillors in 1740.

[23] See p. 301 for this issue. The revenue accounts for 1748 in HKA Hs. 220 show that the Crown paid the salaries of the *Appellation* in Bohemia, and the Tribunal in Moravia, but not those of the Bohemian *Statthalterei*. The Estates paid a supplementary salary to the *Appellation* councillors.

Kämmerer, and so on.[24] Those without an office were *Geheimräte* or privy councillors. The president and vice-president of the Bohemian *Kammer* (1527) were members of the *Statthalterei*, as were the president and vice-president of the *Appellation* (1548) or court of appeal, whose jurisdiction until 1753 also covered Silesia and Moravia.[25] In Moravia, the corresponding bodies were the executive and legal council, the 'hochlöblich königliche Tribunal und Gouverno' (1636), whose president is also described as *Landeshauptmann* in the *Court Calendar*, and the *Rentamt* or financial chamber (1567).[26] In both Bohemia and Moravia there were *Landrecht* courts for the nobility, in Bohemia styled a *Grösseres Landrecht*.[27] In Silesia in 1740 the royal council in Breslau was called the *Oberamt* or *Oberamtskollegium*, which in this form dated from 1629, and was part of Ferdinand II's attempt to tighten crown control in the Bohemian lands.[28] Its head was the *Oberhauptmann*, whose authority was virtually put into commission by its creation. The *Oberhauptmann*, like the *Obrist-Burggraf* in Bohemia, was both a royal official, and the head of the Estates. By law, he had to be a Silesian prince. Since 1718, the office of *Oberhauptmann* had in fact

---

[24] There were eleven such offices in 1740. Apart from those of president and vice-president of the *Appellation* and *Kammer*, they owed their origin to the existence of a Court, hence are found, in different forms, in Hungary and in Vienna too. They are not to be confused with the purely decorative hereditary offices listed in the *Court Calendar*, often with similar names, e.g. Bohemian *Obrist-Erb-Hofmeister*, Austrian *Erb-Land-Hofmister*, etc., which (Thiel part i, 28) had multiplied since the Middle Ages.

[25] J. C. Graf von Auersperg, *Geschichte des königlichen böhmischen Appellationsgerichtes* (Prague 1805), 13. This lists all the councillors and officials of the court since its establishment, and gives outline biographies of many of them. The court was often called the *Appellationskammer*. In 1783 Joseph II remodelled it as the *Appellationsgericht*.

[26] The *Rentamt* doubled with the *Bancal Repraesentation* of the *Bancalität*, and, in contrast to the *Kammern* in Silesia and Bohemia, was tiny. The standard authority in German for Moravian institutional history is still the long, confused, not always accurate, but valuable study by d'Elvert, *Verwaltungsgeschichte*, in which the Bohemian lands usually mean Moravia and Silesia. Cf. J. Radimský, *Tribunál. Sbírka normálií z let 1628–1782* (Brno 1956) and V. Vašků, *Studie o správních dějinách a písemnostech Moravského královského tribunálu z let 1636–1749* (Brno 1969), which includes photographs of the *Tribunal's* records, all kept in German.

[27] Domin-Pet. 21–2. The *Obrist-Burggraf* and other *Landesoffiziere* were judges of the Bohemian *Grösseres Landrecht*, which met three times a year, had civil and criminal jurisdiction over the nobility, with appeal only to the Crown, and survived into the 1850s, ibid.

[28] Hintze, *Behördenorganisation*, 495–556; J. R. Wolf, *Steuerpolitik im schlesischen Ständestaat. Untersuchungen zur Sozial- und Wirtschaftsstruktur Schlesiens im 17. und 18. Jahrhundert* (Marburg an der Lahn 1978) 2–12.

not been filled, and the *Direktor* of the *Oberamt* acted instead. Under him came (1737) a chancellor and fourteen councillors. These did not overlap with the eight members of the Silesian *Kammer* (1558). There were also local *Landeshauptmannschaften*, composed of a *Landeshauptmann* and three to five councillors, performing administrative and judicial duties, and answering to the *Oberamt* in Breslau.[29] This sketchy apparatus of royal power was faced by the complex institutions of the Estates, Silesia being a paradise, or nightmare, of Estates government, as the next chapter shows.

The *Statthalterei* in Prague, the Moravian *Tribunal*, the Silesian *Oberamt*, exercised a rather loose supervision of the assessment and levy of the Contribution, and ensured that the monies collected in the *Steuerämter* of the Estates were paid over to the army.[30] The Vienna *Hofkammer* and Bank Deputation, through their offices in Prague, Brünn, and Breslau, collected the Crown's cameral and domains revenues, over which the Estates had no control. The vestigial offices of the *Universal-Bancalität* have already been mentioned.[31] Lastly, the colleges of commerce in Prague (1714/24) and Breslau (1716) denoted attempts to foster local industry and trade, but mercantile courts like those in the Austrian lands were not introduced until 1763.[32] The Bohemian Chancellery and the financial offices in Vienna respectively were in charge of the local institutions described. The efficacy of *Hofkammer* control, here as elsewhere, however, is doubtful.[33]

The arrangements outlined are unimpressive if the capacity to exert power from the centre is taken as a test. They show the Crown as judge and lawgiver, its traditional medieval role, rather than as an active force. Fiscal claims were asserted through the Estates as much as through officers. The Crown's cameral revenue was damagingly

---

[29] Hintze, 542; they may have been confined to the royal principalities.
[30] See ii, Chs. 6–7.
[31] See n. 16.
[32] A. F. Pribram, *Das böhmische Kommerzkollegium und seine Tätigkeit* (Prague 1898); S. Tschierschky, *Die Wirtschaftspolitik des schlesischen Kommerzkollegs 1716–1740* (Gotha 1902). F. Facius, *Wirtschaft und Staat. Die Entwicklung der staatlichen Wirtschaftsverwaltung in Deutschland vom 17. Jahrhundert bis 1945* (Boppard am Rhein 1959), esp. 190 ff., groups and explains German and Austrian institutions for trade and industry. For the introduction of mercantile courts in the Bohemian lands in 1763 see below.
[33] See ii, Ch. 1, n. 14.

divided between the *Hofkammer* and the Vienna City Bank. Even the *Universal Bancalität* retained pretensions to its administration, though feeble ones. The local working of the whole system requires further investigation, based on the careful examination of original records. The impression of muddle and confusion conveyed by the evidence reviewed, however, suggests that some of the tensions experienced in Prussia at this date between civil and military authority, between Crown and Estates, between types of law, and types of court, must have existed also in the Austrian Monarchy.[34]

The institutional pattern described changed drastically during the next decade, under Haugwitz's propulsion. Provincial reform, at first local and piecemeal, was generalized in 1748, when small executive committees called Deputations (*Deputationen*), paid by, and reporting to, the Crown, were established in the Bohemian and Austrian lands, starting with Moravia on 27 May. The Austrian lands followed in October.[35] The task of the Deputations was to control the levy of the Contribution, check its local repartition, and ensure that it came in to the Estates chest, and out again to the army and for other uses. The Deputations were also to ensure prompt payment of quartered soldiers, provision of military supplies at current prices for cash, and prevention of military excesses.[36] In the Bohemian lands, this was to be carried out at subordinate level by the *Kreishauptmänner* or Circle Captains, who were of long standing there, and whose introduction in the Austrian lands followed in 1748–54.[37] Central control was provided from August 1748 by the *Hofdeputation* in Vienna.

The Deputations of 1748 were the culmination of a series of local

---

[34] For legal quarrels under Charles VI see Domin-Pet. 26. Special courts were formed on 24 Mar. 1753 to deal with disputes between soldiers and civilians, ibid. 40 See Hintze (ed.), Acta Borussica 6/2 (Berlin 1901) for the *Gravamina* of the Diets at the accession of Frederick II. O. Büsch, *Militärsystem und Sozialleben im alten Preussen 1713–1807* (Berlin 1962) develops the theme of jurisdictional conflict.

[35] ÖZV (1925) 210–11. Haugwitz spoke of the Deputations as the 'anzustellende directoria . . . oder repraesentationes', ibid. 209.

[36] ÖZV (1925) 211–20 nn., Instruction for the Bohemian Deputation dated 14 July 1748. It is there spoken of as an 'unsere a[ller] h[öchste] person repraesentirende instanz'. It was to be a 'militar-contributional- und cameral deputation', ibid. 214 n.

[37] See pp. 277–8.

experiments by Haugwitz, all informed by his leading idea of increasing crown control at the expense of the Estates. The latter were to be confined as much as possible to judicial tasks. An initial precedent was the Silesian *Amt* (28 January 1743), formed to rule what remained to Austria of this province; Haugwitz became its first president, with two councillors to assist him. From 12 March 1744 the three Austrian Silesian princes, and the magistrates in the towns, were left with judicial functions only.[38] Like the later Deputations, the *Amt* joined political and financial authority; but, unlike them, had no specially created central body to report to.[39] A second precedent was perhaps set by a rescript of 17 August 1746 for Inner Austria, which attempted to make the *Geheimer Rat* there 'das erste und vornehmste politische mittel', and to confine the *Regierung* to 'judicialia'. The Inner Austrian *Hofkammer* was to supervise the cameral revenues; the Contribution, so it was said, was to be directly administered from Vienna.[40] This attempt to separate administration and justice, even if effective, did not last long, for in 1747 Haugwitz was sent as royal commissary to Krain (January) and Carinthia (April), and made arrangements there which conflicted with it.[41] The occasion of his tour of inspection was the muddled and indebted condition of the Estates' finances, which was hampering payment of the Contribution. To cure this, Haugwitz established small executive committees in Krain (30 March 1747), and Carinthia (17 June 1747). With his flair for baroque nomenclature, he called these a 'Cameral-Commercial und Politische Repraesentation', the representation being of the royal presence.[42] Their main task was to assess and collect the Contribution, and see

[38] D'Elvert, *Finanz-Geschichte*, 531 (*Amt*) and 548 (nomination of Haugwitz as president, and two councillors, printed 5 Feb. 1743). See *ÖZV* (1925) 150 n. for the patent of 12 Mar. 1744 restricting the former Silesian authorities to 'lediglich die iudicialia'.

[39] Cf. Haugwitz's proposal that such a department should be created if Silesia were recaptured, Ch. 9, n. 19.

[40] For this plan see Thiel, ii. 616, 17 Aug. 1746; he does not give enough information to assess its importance.

[41] *ÖZV* (1925) 152–62 nn. The precedent for Haugwitz's despatch to Krain was Count Rudolf Chotek's similar mission in Tyrol in Feb. 1744; see Arneth, *Mar. Ther. Kinder und Freunde*, iv. 161. The members of the *Geheimer Rat* were suspended (26 Jun. 1743) for declaring inability to meet the Crown's military demands for 1743. Chotek negotiated creation of a *Landregiment*, and reforms of the Tyrol councils, implemented in 1745–6, Egger, iii. 25–34.

[42] *ÖZV* (1925) 155 n.

that it was delivered to the army.[43] In this, they closely resembled the subsequent Deputations, as also in reporting directly to a specially formed *Hofcommission* in Vienna, the 'Hofcommission in Carinthian and Krain business', rather than to the Austrian Chancellery.[44] Haugwitz also prepared a complete financial system for the Carinthian and Krain Estates, enabling the Contribution to be kept separate from their domestic chest. As a parallel step, he established judicial appeal courts (*Appellationen*) for Krain (28 April 1747) and Carinthia (29 July 1747), thus confining the jurisdiction of the Inner Austrian *Regierung* to Styria.[45]

Walter has argued that the establishment of these 'Repraesentationen' in Krain and Carinthia in 1747 marked a decisive breach with the past, and an assumption of fiscal power by the Crown at the expense of the Estates.[46] It is doubtful whether this is correct. The brief for the two committees was 'concurrently with the *Verordnete* [finance councillors] of the Estates' to supervise the assessment, levy and application of the Contribution.[47] The *Landeshauptmann*, with his dual loyalty to Crown and Estates, was their head.[48] After the introduction of Deputations in Krain and Carinthia in October 1748, the former bodies in each merged as a 'Repraesentation und Appellation'. If they had really been tough crown agencies, largely staffed with 'Silesians', as Walter claims, it would hardly have been necessary to install new Deputations as well. In fact, the members of the 'Repraesentationen und Appellationen' in 1748 look respectable and local, and not Silesian.[49] By 1752 these combined bodies, in

[43] This is made clear in the royal rescripts for both provinces dated 12 Aug. 1747, ÖZV (1925), 159–62 nn.

[44] Cf. Ch. 9, n. 19.

[45] ÖZV (1925) 156, 158–9; Thiel, ii. 617–18.

[46] Walter, *Geschichte*, 117–23, esp. 121–2, finance and political agenda were now in royal hands, and the Estates were left only with judicial business; the episode showed that the financial demands of the modern state could be enforced against them.

[47] See n. 43. The phrase used was 'concurrenter mit denen ständischen verordneten'.

[48] ÖZV (1925) 55 n. (Krain) and *Khev.-Metsch* 31 Aug. 1747, Carinthia. Walter overlooks this.

[49] Carinthia: Count Johann Anton Goes, *Landeshauptmann*; Claudius von Schneeweis, vice-president; Baron Niclas Hallerstein; Johann von Högen and Jos. Anton von Kauttelshoven. Krain: Count Joseph Auersperg, *Landeshauptmann*; Franz Carl von Hochenwarth; Niclas von Kollbnitz; Count Leopold Lamberg, *Landesverwalter*; Count Joseph Maxenstein; Baron Franz Raigersfeld; Franz von Utschan, HKA Hs. 220 (1748), fos. 219ᵛ, 239ᵛ; see also n. 48. The division between former *Repraesentation* and *Appellation* councillors is not indicated.

turn, had vanished.[50] While the evidence is not conclusive, it seems plausible that the 'Repraesentationen' of 1747 were less dramatic than Walter supposed, and represented a temporary fiscal expedient, partly in conjunction with the Estates. As such they probably failed. This must have turned Haugwitz's thinking towards the Deputations of 1748, which did mark a clear breach with existing practice. Even here, however, it should be noted that the money collected came into the chest of the Estates before being paid out to the army, and that conferences between the Deputations and the committees of the Estates were allowed 'when necessary'.[51] Further, the important principle of Estates consent to the Contribution was retained. Of equal significance is the fact that, whatever the formal regulations of 1748, confirmed and strengthened in 1749, in Lower Austria at least, and probably generally in the Austrian lands, the sub-assessment, collection, and audit of the Contribution continued in the hands of the *Verordneten-Collegium* of the Estates, not of the royal government and *Kreisämter* as it was in Bohemia.[52]

The Deputations of 1748 were primarily devices, more rigorous and more widespread than those of 1747, for assessment and collection of military revenue at a critical point in the war. Apart from the Inner Austrian *Hofkammer*, which the new Styrian Deputation replaced in October 1748, the existing institutions of local royal government were left intact. A further, and much more important, stage of innovation was reached with the *Handbilletten* of 2 May 1749 dissolving the Austrian and Bohemian chancelleries in Vienna, creating the *Oberste Justizstelle* and *Directorium in Publicis et Cameralibus*, and renaming the *Hofdeputation* the *Conferenz in Internis*. Judicial matters, the empress told Chancellor Harrach, were in future to be 'completely separated from public, provincial, and cameral business, both here and in the Länder'.[53] A series of

---

[50] This is clear from HKA Hs. 247 (1752), fos. 184ʳ, 190ʳ. One Carinthian and two Krain members of the former bodies were in 1752 in the new *Landrechte*. Thiel, ii. 621 says that in 1750 the *Appellationen* of 1747 merged with the Inner Austrian *Regierung*, but the latter's members in the 1754 *Court Calendar* in fact only show one former *Appellation* councillor.

[51] ÖZV (1925) 216 n.

[52] For the principle of consent, retained in the decennial recesses in 1748, and for the Austrian Contribution, see ii, Chs. 1, 8.

[53] ÖZV (1925) 269.

measures at local level implemented this. The Deputations were enlarged and (2 May 1749) renamed 'Repraesentationen und Cammern', the first word denoting the royal presence, as in 1747 in Krain and Carinthia, the second the subordinate *Kammern* (Tyrol and Inner Austria, *Hofkammern*) absorbed in the new bodies.[54] The older councils were abolished, or converted into judicial ones. In Bohemia, whose magnates were in a sense on probation, owing to the adherence of many to the emperor Charles VII in 1741–2, the *Statthalterei* was abolished (2 May 1749), and the *Obrist-Burggraf* and other royal officers were turned into a *Consess der obersten Landesoffiziere*, with judicial duties. The few *Statthälter* not eligible for this *Consess* were made judges of the *Grösseres Landrecht*.[55] In Moravia, the *Tribunal* was not abolished, but became purely judicial, and, in May 1753, also a court of appeal, ending its dependence on the Prague *Appellation*.[56] In Austrian Silesia, the 'separation of administration and justice' had occurred in 1744, and no further measures were necessary, but the *Amt* was renamed a *Repraesentation und Kammer* (13 May 1749).[57]

Comparable changes were made in the other lands. In Lower Austria, the office of *Statthalter* lapsed. The *Regierung* was confined to Austria below the Enns, and was divided into two. Its judicial half was named the *Regierung in Justizsachen*. Its financial and administrative half was at first called a *Regierung in Publicis*, because it was in the same place as the empress herself, hence no 'representation' was needed. However, after a year it, too, became a *Repraesentation und Kammer*'.[58] The Lower Austrian mercantile

---

[54] Ibid. 282, Maria Theresia to the Austrian Chancellor Seilern 2 May 1749, renaming of the Deputations. The 'representation of the royal person' is explained there. The interpretation of *Kammer* seems to follow from the evidence.

[55] ÖZV (1925) 282–3 nn., Maria Theresia to Harrach 2 May 1749 on the abolition of the *Statthalterei* and the treatment of the latter's councillors. The scope of the 'mixta' which the new *Consess* was to judge included fiscal cases, but is not wholly clear. According to d'Elvert *Verwaltungsgeschichte*, 346, the Bohemian *Statthalterei* was abolished on 7 May 1749, a date also given by Domin-Pet. 37.

[56] D'Elvert, *Verwaltungsgeschichte*, 346 (7 May 1749) and 358 (1 May 1753). The *Landeshauptmann* remained at the head of the (judicial) *Tribunal*.

[57] Ibid. 335–37. Despite this, HKA Hs. 247 (1752), fo. 152ᵛ still refers to it as an *Amt*.

[58] Starzer, *Beiträge*, 58–9; ÖZV (1925) 282–3, 2 May 1749. The name *Regiment in Publicis* was also used initially. It is not clear from Starzer exactly when the changes occurred. The confinement to Lower Austria was probably from Oct. 1748, and the division of function from May 1749. Court Johann Kuefstein, *Statthalter*, resigned 23 Apr. 1749, Starzer, 317.

courts, and the court of the *Hofmarschall*, were included in the *Regierung in Justizsachen*.[59] They acquired a separate existence again in 1762 and 1763 respectively.[60] Austria above the Enns, or Upper Austria, with its Deputation (20 October 1748), restyled a *Repraesentation und Kammer* from 2 May 1749, became for the first time independent of the Lower Austrian *Regierung*.[61] The court of its *Landeshauptmann* ('Landeshauptmannschaftlich Judicio'), apparently formed when the Deputation was introduced, was converted in 1749 into a *Landrecht*, at least partly paid by the Crown, with the former Upper Austrian *Landeshauptmann* as its first president.[62] The title *Landeshauptmann* then passed to the president of the *Repraesentation und Kammer*, who was a royal nominee.[63] The implied rebuff to the Upper Austrian Estates may have been deliberate. Many, though by no means all, had rendered homage to Charles of Bavaria on 2 October 1741.[64] Elsewhere, the title of *Landeshauptmann* was not again attached to the presidency of the royal local government until 1763.

The government of Inner Austria was drastically remodelled in 1748–9. The *Kriegsstelle* had already gone in 1744. The *Hofkammer* was dissolved after the introduction of the Deputations in October 1748.[65] On 15 January 1749 the *Geheimer Rat* was wound up, and its members were assigned to a *Judicium Revisorium* or court of appeal for Inner Austria.[66] The *Regierung* continued as a

---

[59] *ÖZV* (1925), loc. cit., the mercantile courts being those of first and second instance.

[60] Domin-Pet., 36.

[61] Starzer, 58 n. for the date 20 Oct. 1748.

[62] These two bodies are shown in HKA Hss. 220, fo. 165 (1748) and 247, fo. 164 (1752). It is plausible to suppose that the *Landrecht* dated from May 1749.

[63] See Table 13.2*.

[64] J. Schwerdefeger, 'Der bairisch-französische Einfall in Ober- und Nieder-Österreich (1741) und die Stände der Erzherzogthümer', *AÖG* 87 (1899) 395 and app X.

[65] Thiel, ii. 618–19. The Deputation occupied the rooms in the *Burg* previously used by the *Hofkammer*, ibid. Thiel is, however, mistaken in saying that the *Hofkammer* councillors became councillors of the Deputation, as comparison of the names shows.

[66] Ibid. 619–20. The councillors of the *Geheimer Rat* were not retired, as he states, but were transferred, see Ch. 13, n. 14. A 'Hofcommission in Publicis et Politicis' under the *Landeshauptmann* formally replaced the *Geheimer Rat* on 18 Jan. 1749. It lasted until 14 May 1749, when its agenda merged with those of the *Repraesentation und Kammer*, ibid. The last Inner Austrian *Statthalter*, Count Corbinian Saurau, was allowed to keep his title until his death in 1761, ibid. 621.

court, confined to Styria and shorn of administrative business.[67] A *Landrecht*, presided over by the *Landeshauptmann*, was formed from two older courts of the Estates.[68] In Krain and Carinthia, *Landrechte* were also created in 1749, absorbing the councillors of the 'Landeshauptmannschaftlich und Schranengericht' of 1748.[69] Tyrol, which had blotted its fiscal copybook in 1743, was also remodelled, losing its *Geheimer Rat* and *Hofkammer*, and acquiring in their place a court of appeal (*Judicium Revisorium*) and a *Repraesentation und Hofkammer* (sic). Trieste, Fiume, and the contiguous ports were subordinated to the new 'Commercien-Directorium' in Vienna.[70]

While the detail, and precise timing, of the local changes of 1748–9 need further investigation, the strategy behind them seems clear. In Contribution and army business, royal nominees, first in the Deputations, later in the *Repraesentationen und Kammern*, replaced, or were intended to replace, the councillors of the Estates. The *Repraesentationen und Kammern* also took over many executive duties hitherto performed by other local royal councils, as is shown next. Secondly, the pretensions to a looser dependence embodied in the Bohemian *Statthalterei* and in the special institutions of 'Upper Austria' (Tyrol and the *Vorlande*) and Inner Austria, buttressed centrally by the Bohemian and Austrian Chancelleries, were ended with the councils which embodied them. Kaunitz in 1763 described the abolition of the Bohemian *Statthalterei* as 'the greatest political coup' of the new system.[71] The tighter rein in Inner Austria was also significant. Tyrol, despite the disap-

---

[67] Ibid.

[68] Pirchegger, 162. He gives no details, but it seems plausible that development here was the same as in Upper Austria, Carinthia, and Krain. The 'two former courts' do not appear in the *Court Calendar* or in HKA Hs. 220 (1748). The Styrian *Landrecht* is shown in HKA Hs. 247 (1752), fo. 175, with the members each in receipt of a salary of 500 fl. The Estates may have supplemented this.

[69] This is clear from a comparison of the membership in HKA Hs. 220 (1748), fos. 219ᵛ, 240ʳ and Hs. 247 (1752), fos. 184ʳ, 190ᵛ.

[70] For Trieste and Tyrol see nn. 20, 41. In 1749 Further Austria was given a separate *Repraesentation*, but the appeals court (*Judicium Revisorium, Revisions-Stelle*) and *Regierung* covered this area and Tyrol. Egger, iii. 35 shows that the *Geheimer Rat* was abolished on 3 Sept. 1749. Its president became the head of the *Judicium Revisorium*. The *Regierung* was retained as a court. Egger does not state whether the *Repraesentation* absorbed the former *Hofkammer* councillors.

[71] Walter, *Geschichte*, 361.

pearance of its *Geheimer Rat*, and *Hofkammer*, proved more resist-
ant, and preserved various kinds of special status until the end of the
reign. Lastly, the changes made in local executive government in
1748–9 were accompanied by a generous conversion of existing
councils to judicial uses. In Bohemia with the *Consess der obersten
Landesoffiziere*, in Upper Austria, Carinthia, and Krain with the
Landrechte, the Crown actually created new bodies, or reconstructed existing ones, in order to increase the places at its disposal.
The result was that most, though admittedly not all, of the powerful
local personages affected by Haugwitz's reforms were found seats at
the royal table, in future consuming a legal instead of a mixed diet.
This clever policy alone, perhaps, stopped the bitter resentment
against the empress and her minister from getting out of hand.

The responsibilities imposed on the *Repraesentationen und Kammern* from May 1749 were the same as those assumed at the centre
by the *Conferenz in Internis*, subsequently by the *Directorium*
alone, and were more extensive that those of the Deputations of
1748.[72] They ranged from the assessment and levy of the Contribution, and reform of the tax cadastre, to supervision of crown
cameral revenue, through all matters of military supply, quarters,
marches, etc., previously handled in conjunction with the Estates,
to town finances, guilds, universities, security, and matters of *Polizei*. In 1751 an important addition was made to this already formidable list. The *mixta* hitherto taken by the *Oberste Justizstelle*,
especially fiscal and contraband cases, were transferred to the *Directorium*, and a special *consessus* was formed within it to handle them
(January 1751).[73] The corresponding committee in each province
was called a *Consessus Delegatus in Causis Summi Principis*.[74] Membership of these overlap with the *Repraesentation* and local courts
of appeal.[75] Special institutions to judge revenue and other cases in
which crown interests were involved were not new, however. The
consessus took the place of analogous courts created in Lower

---

[72] The agenda of the Bohemian Deputation are shown in the Instruction dated 14
July 1748, ÖZV (1925) 211–20 nn. The agenda of the *Repraesentationen* were to be
the same as that of the *Conferenz in Internis*, ibid. 279–80 nn. and 282.

[73] See p. 229 above.

[74] ÖZV (1925) 330. The relation of this in Bohemia to the *Consess der obersten
Landesoffiziere* of 1749, which also dealt with these matters, is unclear. The *Landesoffiziere* may have constituted an appeal court.

[75] See p. 366.

Austria in 1705, in Bohemia and Moravia in 1730, in Styria in 1746.[76] Lastly, in each province a *Consessus Commercialis* (in Lower Austria called a *Delegierte Hofkommission* from 1751) was charged with investigation and supervision of local manufactures and trade.[77] In Bohemia, a separate College of Manufactures was established in 1753, but merged with the *Consessus* in 1757.[78] In Moravia a *Manufakturenamt* (January 1751) lasted until 1763.[79] The membership of the commercial *consessus*, too, partly overlapped with that of the *Repraesentationen*.[80]

The changes in local royal government in the Bohemian and Austrian lands in 1763 are much less clearly focused in the literature than those at the centre in 1761–2 from which they derived. Walter's outline account, based on the *Protokoll* of the *Staatsrat* for 8 April and 2 May 1763, will be summarized first, then various qualifications will be developed.[81] There must have been extensive discussions before the resolutions of April and May 1763, but these are at present unstudied. The empress decided, using the colloquial vocabulary in which she expressed herself on these matters, that the 'capo' of each 'landesgouverno' should have authority over the whole 'landesregierung'. Business was then to be conducted in commissions, or *consessus*, responsible to the relevant *Hofstelle*. And 'political and judicial business is to be united' ('das politicum mit dem justitiali . . . vereiniget') as formerly.[82] The first proposition

---

[76] *ÖZV* (1925) 330, Jan. 1751, discussion by the *Directorium*. The *Consessus* replaced in Lower Austria the *Justizbancodeputation* of 1706, created to hear revenue cases involving the Vienna City Bank. In Bohemia and Moravia the bodies replaced were the 'judicia delegata in causis commissorum' created in 1730. In Inner Austria, 'judicia delegata in causis summi principis' dated from 1746, Domin-Pet. 36. The full title of the new body was to be 'consessus delegatus in causis summi principis et commissorum'. It seems plausible that the last word is the genitive plural of 'commissum', forfeiture, but this is not clear in the literature.

[77] *ÖZV* (1925) 419, 10 Mar. 1749. More detail is obtainable in Přibram, *Gewerbepolitik*, 30–2, where, however, the date of 15 Mar. 1759 for the Lower Austrian *Consess* (ibid. 31 n.) is an error for 1749. The commercial *consessus* were confined to the Austrian and Bohemian lands.

[78] Přibram, 33, 41. The name adopted in 1757 was 'consessus in commercialibus et manufacturisticis'.

[79] D'Elvert, *Verwaltungsgeschichte*, 375.

[80] In Bohemia in 1754 three of the 15 members of the *Repraesentation* also belonged to the commission for the College of Manufactures, *Court Calendar*.

[81] Walter, *Geschichte*, 358–63.

[82] Ibid. 358.

meant that the head of the local royal 'government' was also to be
Landeshauptmann, and as such head of the Estates. This change had
been made in 1748 in Upper Austria, but not elsewhere, as was seen
earlier. The reunion of justice and administration had already been
carried out in April 1759 in Lower Austria, where *Regierung* and
Repraesentation were turned back into a single *Regierung*, with separate senates for executive and judicial business, and with appellate
jurisdiction over Upper Austria. The position of Lower Austrian
Statthalter was restored.[83] This precedent may have been in Kaunitz's mind when, in his *Vortrag* of 20 November 1761 about central government, he rejected the central reunion of justice and
administration, but proposed it as a general principle at local level.[84]

In the discussions of 1763, as outlined by Walter, the position of
Bohemia appears to have caused difficulty. The local governors had
already proposed a revival of the pre-1749 *Statthalterei* in 1761.[85]
In 1763 the Bohemian and Austrian Chancellery repeated this
demand.[86] Kaunitz (1 May 1763) repudiated it, declaring his
unwillingness to support the Estates against the empress (*souve-
raine*) and the general good ('die allgeimeine wohlfahrt'). The chancellor, said Kaunitz, should be reminded that he was 'homo
principis und nicht statuum et nobilitatis'.[87] Walter argues that a
compromise was reached. As a concession to Bohemian interests,
the *Consess der obersten Landesoffiziere* created in 1749 was
retained, and plans to abolish it were abandoned.[88] In deference to
the empress, it was not incorporated in the new 'Landes-
Gouverno'. The empress believed that these officers formed 'the
principal part of the assembly of the Estates', hence could not arbi-
trate as governors.[89] The *Obrist-Burggraf* however, did become
head of the 'Gouverno'. Walter believed that the Bohemian pattern
was repeated elsewhere in the Bohemian and Austrian lands, the
essence of the change being reunion of political and judicial

---

[83] Starzer, 66. He gives no reason for the change, other than the urgings of the president of the *Oberste Justizstelle*, Count Carl Breuner.
[84] *ÖZV* (1934) 121.
[85] Prokeš, 'Boj', 43.
[86] Walter, 359, without precise formulation.
[87] Ibid. 360–1.
[88] Ibid. 359–60, 361–2 nn.; he states that he cannot go into the matter.
[89] Ibid. 359–60. Walter implies that the *Consess* continued in being, separate from
the *Gubernium*.

business, and union of the offices of 'capo' and *Landeshauptmann*; which he thought marked another decisive step forward for royal authority.[90]

This interpretation is not altogether satisfactory. The union of positions just referred to had already existed in several lands in 1740, as shown earlier. It is therefore difficult to treat it as a bold royal innovation. In fact, the reality of change in 1763 appears to be more untidy than Walter's outline of it suggests, and aspects of it remain obscure. In Bohemia, the *Repraesentation und Kammer* was indeed renamed a *Gubernium* (not 'Landes-Gouverno') (1 July 1763); but the *Consess der obersten Landesoffiziere* was merged with it (9 January 1764), the members retaining their titles.[91] This change increased the size of the *Gubernium* from eight to twenty-three members.[92] The empress must have been induced to change her mind, or at least to abandon her opposition. The Moravian *Repraesentation und Kammer* became a *Landes-Gouverno* (27 June 1763).[93] This name, selected by the empress for Bohemia, recalled the pre-1748 Moravian 'Tribunal und Gouverno'. In contrast to Bohemia, size was reduced, from twelve members to eight, several being transferred to the legal *Tribunal*. The president of the *Landes-Gouverno* became *Landeshauptmann*.[94] The Instruction for the *Landes-Gouverno* dated 15 December 1764 assigned it five divisions. These were (1) 'Publicum et Politicum', (2) Contribution, (3) Military, (4) Cameral, and (5) Commercial. The Instruction explicitly says that judicial matters are to be handled by the courts.[95] In Austrian Silesia, the name *Amt* was reverted to (16 July 1763), but the legal arrangements made in 1744 appear to have been left undisturbed.[96] An addition was the mercantile court of first and

[90] Ibid. 162–3, judicial and administrative business were to be handled by separate commissions within the *Gubernium*. Hock–Bidermann, 17 n. say that this basic pattern for provincial government was approved by the empress on 12 July 1763.

[91] Domin-Pet. 37–8; *Court Calendar*, 1765.

[92] *Court Calendar* 1765.

[93] D'Elvert, *Finanz-Geschichte*, 572, gives the date, but incorrectly says the name *Gubernium* was chosen. The *Court Calendar* shows the name adopted.

[94] Based on the lists of members in the *Court Calendar* for 1763 and 1765.

[95] D'Elvert, *Verwaltungsgeschichte*, 397–407 gives a full résumé of the Instruction. For the reference of judicial questions to the courts see p. 407. The agenda reflected those of the Bohemian and Austrian Chancellery, shown in ÖZV (1934) 133–41.

[96] D'Elvert, 335.

second instance, also introduced into the other Bohemian lands in 1763.[97]

In Lower Austria, as noted above, the *Regierung*, with its jurisdiction over both Lower and Upper Austria, was restored in 1759, divided into executive and judicial senates. The two mercantile courts in 1762, and the court of the *Hofmarschall* in 1763, again acquired separate status. The court of the *Landmarschall* of Lower Austria, which had survived the changes of 1749, was reconstructed as a *Landrecht* (1764), under a judge from the *Regierung*, reserving only an honorary presidency to the *Landmarschall*.[98] The Upper Austrian *Repraesentation und Kammer* was reconstituted in 1759 as a *Landeshauptmannschaft*, a reversion to its former name. As the *Court Calendar* shows, it combined the councillors of the former *Repraesentation* and *Landrecht*. However, there were several changes, and the new body was larger, with seventeen councillors in 1763, divided into *Herrenstand*, *Ritterstand*, and *Gelehrtenstand* members, as in the Lower Austrian *Regierung*. The *Landeshauptmann* presided, and was also the head of the Estates Committee.[99]

In Tyrol (12 December 1763), the *Repraesentation und Hofkammer* was renamed a *Gubernium*, and the *Judicium Revisorium* became a section of it. The *Collegium Revisorium*, created for fiscal appeals in March 1751, was also added to the *Gubernium*. The lower court for fiscal cases, the *Consessus in Causis Summi Principis*, was joined to the existing *Regierung*. The scope of legal business extended to Further Austria. From 1774 (only) the offices of president of the *Gubernium* and of *Landeshauptmann* were united. In Inner Austria, the arrangements made in 1763 represented a partial return to those before 1748. The separate *Repraesentationen und Kammern* in Styria, Carinthia, and Krain were replaced (29 August 1763) by an Inner Austrian *Gubernium* at Graz, whose members were partly drawn from the existing Styrian *Repraesen-*

---

[97] Ibid. 376, 22 Dec. 1763 for Moravia; the entries in the *Court Calendar* imply that this ordinance also applied to Bohemia and Silesia.

[98] Domin-Pet, 36; first session 3 Nov. 1764.

[99] Based on the entries in the *Court Calendar* for 1763 and for 1765. In 1763, a royal commissary was at the head of the *Landeshauptmannschaft*, but by 1765 this arrangement had ended. For the Estates Committee see Ch. 11.

tation.[100] As in Upper Austria, the *Landrechte* created in 1749 in Carinthia and Krain now became the judicial departments of *Landeshauptmannschaften* in those lands, the former *Repraesentationen* furnishing the other members.[101] The Inner Austrian *Regierung* was retained as a court of appeal, presumably with its pre-1747 jurisdiction. The empress, following the principle described earlier, decreed that from 1 November 1763 the president of the new Inner Austrian *Gubernium* should also be *Landeshauptmann* of Styria.[102] The Styrian Estates protested that it was impossible for him to fill both positions properly. After delaying for two years, the empress agreed (14 August 1765) to create a separate *Landeshauptmann*.[103] Joseph II, predictably, united the two offices in 1781.[104]

Summarizing, the *Länderstelle* of 1763, as they were frequently referred to collectively, were not uniform in type. The official title 'Gubernium' appears only in Bohemia, Tyrol and Inner Austria, and from 1776 in Trieste, Fiume, and Zengg. The union of the offices of royal 'capo' and *Landeshauptmann* had historical precedents rather than being a new step. Where it had not formerly existed (Lower Austria, Styria) it was avoided in 1763–5. This was initially so in Tyrol too. The 'reunion of justice and administration', meaning, if Lower Austria is an example, their union under one roof, but in different sections, with different councillors, cannot be demonstrated for Moravia or Silesia and, as shown below, is not

---

[100] For Tyrol, see Egger, iii. 38–9. The government of Further Austria was now called a *Regierung und Kammer*. For Inner Austria, F. Ilwof, 'Der ständische Landtag des Herzogtums Steiermark unter Maria Theresia und ihren Söhnen', *AÖG* 104 (1914) 166 is more specific about the changes of 1763 than Pirchegger, *Gesch. der Steiermark*, 159. Comparison of the *Court Calendar* for 1763 and 1765 shows that five of the 12 Styrian *Repraesentation* councillors of 1763, and one secretary, were among the 13 councillors and four secretaries of the Inner Austrian *Gubernium* of 1765.

[101] Pirchegger, loc. cit.; *Court Calendar* 1763, 1765. In 1770 in Krain one section of councillors is explicitly headed 'Justitial Abtheilung', but this was not done generally in the Calendar.

[102] Ilwof, 166.

[103] Ibid. 167–8.

[104] Ibid. 173. An exact date is not given. In the *Court Calendar* for 1770 a *Landeshauptmannschaft* is entered for Styria for the first time, comprising the *Landeshauptmann* and four *Verordnete*. Though having the same name as the royal councils in Carinthia, Krain, and Upper Austria, this seems to be what is there called a 'Landschaft', viz. a committee of the Estates. This is not discussed in the literature.

easy to trace in Bohemia. It may have been confined to the Austrian lands.

The local arrangements of 1763 were substantially retained until 1780. The assumption of responsibility for the Contribution by the *Hofkammer* in 1765 led to an order (26 August 1765) that finance 'senates' of two to three councillors under the governor should be created in all the Bohemian and Austrian lands.[105] This lapsed with the chancellery's resumption of the Contribution in December 1771. The commercial *consessus*, which included some members from the *Gubernien*, had separate status until 1772, then became distinct, but dependent, 'Commerzien Commissionen'. These in turn merged in the *Gubernien* in January 1776, in consequence of the final abolition of the *Hofkommerzienrat*.[106]

The commands of the local royal governments were partly addressed to, and carried out by, local lords, clerical and lay. But there were also royal officials, whose number and duties increased over the period. In 1740, the *Kreishauptmann*, or Circle Captain, was an important administrative official, with legal, fiscal, and military responsibilities, in the twelve Circles, or districts, of Bohemia and the six Circles of Moravia.[107] In Bohemia there were two such officers in each Circle, in Moravia one. In Silesia, there was a *Landeshauptmann* in each of the royal Principalities, but no Circle Captains.[108] The *Kreis* and its *Hauptmann* are not found in the Austrian lands before 1748. In Bohemia, the office of *Kreishauptmann* went back to the Middle Ages, the *kraj* or *Kreis* being originally an area around royal castles. In Moravia, the office was created in the 1630s.[109] In Bohemia, the Captain took an oath of loyalty to the Crown of Bohemia, was formally reappointed each year, and had a duty to obey the royal *Statthalterei*.[110] However,

---

[105] ÖZV (1934) 271.

[106] Přibram, *Gewerbepolitik*, 116–18. The commercial commissions within the *Gubernien* in 1772 were apparently introduced in Bohemia in May, in Lower and Inner Austria in Sept., ibid.

[107] The standard work is still the massive, repetitive, often unclear, but valuable work of Rieger, *Zřízení krajské*. The Czech word for a circle is *kruh*, not *kraj*, which means a district. The German *Kreis* has both meanings, and 'Circle' has become the standard English rendering. There were 16 Circles in Bohemia until 1714, when they were reduced to 12, Rieger, ii. 127.

[108] For the Silesian arrangements, see the HKA index to the Lower Austrian *Herrschaftsakten*. For Bohemia and Moravia see Table 13.4.*

[109] Rieger, i. 5 ff. (Bohemia) and 243 (Moravia).

[110] Ibid. 225.

since the Bohemian Estates paid the Captain's salary, and played a
large part in the business of recruitment, military supply, marches,
and lodgings, and levy of the Contribution, in which he was
involved, it was not difficult to regard him as an officer of the
Estates.[111] Under Charles VI, the Bohemian Estates proposed one
candidate for the captaincy from the *Herrenstand* and one from the
Ritterstand for each Circle, or 24 in all.[112] In Bohemia and Moravia,
the Estates appointed transport commissaries ('Führungs Commis-
särien') to help the Circle Captains with the movement and station-
ing of troops.[113]

In Silesia, with its complex structure of government, the Circle
system did not exist, and had to be invented. On Haugwitz's advice,
Maria Theresia created (21 February 1744) three officials for Austrian Silesia equivalent to *Kreishauptmänner*, but named instead
Provincial Seniors (*Landesälteste*, the German rendering of *sta-
rosty*), answering to the new royal *Amt*. They were stationed in
Teschen, Troppau, and Weidenau. Each had a Commissary to assist
him.[114] In Moravia and Bohemia, the arrangements of 1748–9
included emphasis on the duty of the Circle Captains to obey the
Deputation, then the *Repraesentation*.[115] From 1751 the Crown,
not the Estates, formally paid the Bohemian Circle Captains.[116] The
Hauptsystem introduced from 1 November 1748 in all the Bohemian and Austrian lands involved the introduction of the originally
Bohemian institution of the *Kreisamt* into the Austrian lands. This
was done in Krain on 9 November 1748, in Styria on 16 November
1748, in Carinthia on 23 January 1750, in Lower Austria on 24 July
1753, in Tyrol on 1 June 1754. The existing districts, or *Vier-*

---

[111] Ibid. ii. 187–8 for payment of the Bohemian Circle Captains by the Estates.
[112] Ibid.
[113] Ibid. ii. 209 n. (Bohemia), and D'Elvert, *Verwaltungsgeschichte*, 353–4 (Moravia). Rieger's account of these commissaries is defective. D'Elvert makes it clear that
in Moravia they went back to the 17th c. HKA Hs. 247 (1752), fo. 135ʳ shows that
there were typically two 'Durchführungs Commissarien' in each Bohemian Circle at
that date.
[114] D'Elvert, 337. *Administratoren* were appointed at the same date to supervise
the non-judicial business of the royal towns, ibid. Joseph II in 1783 renamed the
Landesälteste 'Kreishauptmänner', and reduced them to two, Rieger, ii. 134. *Landesälteste* had existed before 1740, but as councillors of the *Landeshauptmannschaften*
or local councils, Hintze 542.
[115] See n. 72.
[116] Rieger, ii. 187–8. However, the Estates continued to share the cost, paying
their half into the cameral chest, ibid. 129.

tel, in these areas decided the number of officers, for example in Lower Austria four, in Styria five, in Tyrol six. In Lower Austria, a Circle Commissary paid by the Estates was appointed to assist each *Kreishauptmann*.[117]

In Moravia, one or two Substitutes to help the Circle Captain were permitted (rescript of 20 October 1749) and were paid by the Estates, as were the six Circle Secretaries.[118] In 1770 a Moravian *Kreisamt* was described as having, under the Circle Captain, two Substitutes, a Secretary, three clerks, and two transport commissaries.[119] In Bohemia, the *locus classicus* of the Circle system, the number of Captains was reduced (23 January 1751) from twenty-four to sixteen, each in charge of one Circle. This change resulted from an inspection of the kingdom in 1750 by Count Larisch, Haugwitz's successor as governor of Silesia. His brief was to investigate the levy of the Contribution, and peasant grievances connected with this. Since the role of the Circle Captain was important for both issues, he also inspected Circle organization. Larisch initially favoured retention of two Captains in each Circle, one of them specializing in the 'Contributionale' and 'Publicum', the other in judicial affairs. The Bohemian *Repraesentation und Kammer* opposed this, on the grounds that the Circle Captains prepared cases for the courts, but were otherwise not legal experts. The typical issue coming before them was contested possession. After discussion by the *Conferenz in Internis* (14 January 1751), and by the *Directorium* with the Bohemian Estates (18 January), the upshot (23 January) was that the four largest Bohemian Circles (Bechin, Königgratz, Pilsen, Saaz) were each divided into two districts, effectively increasing the number of Circles from twelve to sixteen. The number of Captains in each was reduced from two to one, but with an *adjunctus*, the equivalent of the Moravian *substitutus*, as

---

[117] Rieger, ii. 6 n. gives these dates, thought without precise references for most of them. He has 24 June 1753 for Lower Austria; Starzer, *Statthalterei*, 64 says the patent was dated 24 July. See ibid. 66 for the Lower Austrian Circle Commissaries. Egger, iii. 36 gives 14, not 1, June 1754 for Tyrol, and emphasizes that the six Circle Captains there were named *Viertelhauptleute*, obviously a concession to Tyrolean feelings. The introduction of the *Kreisamt* into the Austrian lands has attracted much attention in the literature, but little in the way of factual information.

[118] D'Elvert, 34, *Kreissubstituten*.

[119] Ibid. In 1770, the *Neuer Brünner Titular Kalender* shows only five Moravian Circles, the former Prerau Circle having been made a division of Olmütz Circle. Each of the two divisions had a Circle Captain and two Substitutes. By 1780, 3 other Moravian Circles had 3 substitutes each, see Table 13.4*.

assistant, and two transport commissaries.[120] Prague, which was outside the Circle system until 1784, continued to be administered by the three town captains of the Old Town, New Town, and *Malá Strana* or *Kleinseite*.[121]

In 1772, the *Staatsrat* studied Joseph II's proposal, made on his Bohemian tour in 1771, that each Bohemian Circle be divided into two districts, and that each Captain have two Adjuncts, one designated as Vice-Captain.[122] Hatzfeld suggested creation of twenty-one Circles. Baron Kressel took the opportunity of asserting that the Circle Captains were so beaten down ('aviliret') that good candidates could no longer be found. The whole matter was referred to the Bohemian and Austrian Chancellery, and by it to the Bohemian *Gubernium* and Estates Committee. The latter declared that there was no discontent with the existing system, and that an increase in numbers would cause expense. The *Gubernium* concurred, stating that the real fault lay in the insufficiency and low pay of subordinate officials.[123] A further plan in March 1777 to increase the number of Bohemian Circles also came to nothing. The status quo was retained.[124]

At the Circle level of Austrian government, the distinction between fiscal, political, judicial, etc. duties appears to have been blurred. A description of 1756 shows that the *Kreisamt* in Moravia reported to the *Repraesentation und Kammer* about political and fiscal matters, but to the legal authorities about distraints, inventories, and so on.[125] Johann von Mayern's officially inspired *Einleitung zur kreisämtlichen Wissenschaft im Königreiche Böhmen* (1776) described the agenda of the Bohemian *Kreisamt* as comprising the

---

[120] Count Johann Franz Larisch was *Praeses* of the *Amt* in Austrian Silesia 1751–63, d'Elvert, *Verfassung*, 171. He was commissioned to examine the Circle organization and the Contribution in Bohemia on 22 Apr. 1750, reporting on the Contribution in July, Aug. and Nov., and on 4 June 1751 was asked to investigate further, Grünberg, *Bauernbefreiung*, ii. 55–64. Grünberg does not describe Larisch's reorganization of the Circles. This is fully dealt with by Rieger, ii. 125–9, who, however, says nothing about the Contribution. The new 'Circle districts' were in practice called 'Circles'.

[121] Rieger, ii. 143.

[122] Ibid. 131–2. Joseph's proposals formed part of the 'Anderte [second] Abtheilung' of his report of 8 Nov. 1771, which is printed in *Khev.-Metsch 1770–3*, 373–98. For this report, which emphasized the rivalries between agencies of government, see Table 9.3*.

[123] Rieger, loc. cit.

[124] Ibid. 133.

[125] D'Elvert, *Verwaltungsgeschichte*, 354.

Contribution, *Publica*, *Politica*, military business (*Militare*), the Diet (*Diaetale*), commercial matters, and legal ones (*Judiciale*).[126] Commercial issues, together with the inspectors of trade and the manufacturing commissaries, where they existed, were transferred to the *Kreisämter* in 1772; the remaining items were much the same as Larisch had found on his tour in 1751. In Lower Austria, the first instruction for the *Repraesentation und Kammer* (24 July 1753) placed much emphasis on religious business.[127]

One effect of the institutional development described was to increase the number of administrative and legal bodies at local level. To take an example, Moravia in 1765 had a *Landes-Gouverno*, a *Consessus in Causis Summi Principis* for revenue cases, a commercial *Consessus*, a *Landrecht*, the *Tribunal* or appeal court, and mercantile courts of first and second instance.[128] This was in addition to the local administration of the Vienna City Bank, the Committee of the Moravian Estates, the *Landtafel* court for disputes about noble charges on land, and the jurisdictions of the church and the army. There was thus plenty of scope for the quarrels Joseph II complained of in 1771.[129] Proliferation ironically reached a maximum in Austrian Silesia, the area at first intended to provide a model for the entire Monarchy. In 1779, Austrian Silesia had an *Amt* (eight councillors), a *Consessus in Causis Summi Principis* (five), three Provincial Seniors or *Landesälteste*, and three town administrators in Teschen, Troppau, and Jägerndorf. Besides this, the principalities of Teschen, Neisse, and Troppau-Jägerndorf each had a (judicial) *Regierung*, and the first and last a *Landrecht* court as well.[130] (The fourth principality, Bielitz, created in 1752, is not listed in the *Court Calendar*.) The Estates of Troppau-Jägerndorf, and the *Fürstentag* comprising the four princes and representatives from Troppau-Jägerndorf, added a further dimension.[131] It was no wonder

---

[126] Ibid. 357.

[127] Rieger, ii. 262, Bohemian trade inspectors and manufacturing commissaries in 1772 in future to be treated as Circle employees, consulted on all commercial agenda. Starzer, 64 rather briefly summarizes the Lower Austrian Instruction of 1753, which urged the Circle Captains to uphold the Catholic religion, seize heretics, check the use of parish funds, inspect charities, investigate guilds, visit prisons. The Contribution is not mentioned, though a fuller version might correct this.

[128] *Court Calendar 1765.*

[129] See n. 122.

[130] *Court Calendar 1779.*

[131] D'Elvert, *Verfassung*, 176.

that a merger of Silesian government with that of Moravia was proposed and nearly carried through in 1777, and was enforced by Joseph II in 1782.[132]

From such evidence, it would be easy to deduce that the government had created as much confusion as clarity by its local reforms, a view Joseph II obviously held. In qualification, it is worth noting that proliferation of offices did not denote an equal proliferation of councillors. To return to the example of Moravia in 1765, the *Gouverno* had nine members, the *Tribunal* twenty-three, the *Landrecht* fifteen, the *Consessus Summi Principis* eleven, the *Consessus Commercialis* six, or sixty-four in all. But the number of persons involved was only thirty, most of them wearing two hats, and some three or four. In particular, eight were common to the *Tribunal* and *Landrecht*, and all save one of the members of the *Consessus in Causis Summi Principis* and the *Consessus Commercialis* were drawn from one of the other bodies. Similar overlap is observable elsewhere.

The responsibilities of the *Gubernien* after 1763 were inherited from the *Repraesentationen*, and both followed the agenda set out first for the *Directorium*, then for the Bohemian and Austrian Chancellery. The latter's duties, as defined in its Instruction of 21 June 1762, extended from the preservation of 'the alone-holy-making Catholic religion' to the central question of the Contribution, with many others in between.[133] The same list appears in the Instruction for the *Landes-Gouverno* in Moravia dated 15 December 1764, and must have been generally applied.[134] The Instruction shows that in revenue cases—the *causae summi principis*—a Vienna City Bank official was to be a member of the provincial *consessus*; appeal in these cases lay to the *Oberste Justizstelle* in Vienna. The *Gouverno* was also allowed to inspect the reports (*Amtsprotokolle*) of the local Bank administration before these went forward to the Ministerial Bank Deputation, and to make comments on them if it wished. It was to see that the *Kreisämter* ensured the accurate repartition of the Contribution voted by the Estates, so that 'the peasants are not overburdened, nor oppressed by lords'

---

[132] Ibid. Reference is made there to earlier proposals for union in 1742, 1763, and 1766, without details. Joseph II's measure took effect on 30 June 1782, the *Amt* being merged with the Moravian *Tribunal*.

[133] See n. 95.

[134] D'Elvert, *Verwaltungsgeschichte*, 397–407 gives an extensive summary.

services and fees'. They were also to prosecute those in arrears with their tax payments. The *Gouverno's* military responsibilities, the *militaria mixta*, extended to quarters, marches, supply, cartage (*Vorspann*), and military excesses. But the provincial *Oberkriegs-commissarius* was no longer to attend meetings of the *Gubernium*, and the army was to handle its own recruiting.[135]

This general structure of business was reflected in that of the *Gouverno's* special commissions. The Instruction of 1764 stated that those to be retained were the *Consessus in Causis Summi Princi-pis*, the *Consessus in Commercialibus und Manufakturssachen*, and the commissions for sanitation, [charitable] foundations, police and security, studies and censorship, Jews, and the mercantile court.[136] A similar but more complex committee system is found in the *Amt* of tiny Austrian Silesia at the end of the reign. There were then no less than 16 Silesian committees ('Commissionen') for (1) the *causae summi principis*, (2) the *Erbsteuer*, (3) the *Schuldensteuer*, (4) foundations and hospitals, (5) military matters, (6) *Fideikommissen*, (7) police, (8) urbarial matters, (9) studies and schools, (10) censorship of books, (11) commercial affairs and road-building, (12) ex-Jesuit lands, (13) the wine duty, (14) appeals in mercantile cases, (15) sanitation, (16) wards ('Pupillar-commission').[137]

The arrangement of business in Bohemia was more complex still, understandably in view of its size and population. Table 10.1 shows the committees of the *Gubernium*, or its equivalents before 1763, over the whole period 1748–79. Before 1748 several of the matters listed were dealt with by separate bodies. This was true of army supply (a Bohemian 'Kriegs-Commissariat-Amt'), commerce (the 'Commercien Collegium' of 1714/24), fortifications, Jews, towns, and wards. The arrangements from 1748 subsumed all these. The number of committees moved up over the period, from eleven in 1748–9 to sixteen in 1757, twenty-two in 1763, twenty-five in 1765, to thirty in 1779. Some were clearly the product of special cir-cumstances, for example those for 'army commissariat and sup-ply', 'hospitals', 'military pensioners', 'property tax', 'salt-tax arrears', all the product of the Seven Years War. Others appear and disappear, for instance those for fortifications, charitable

---

[135] Ibid.
[136] Ibid. 406.
[137] Id., *Verfassung*, 171, without exact date.

foundations (*Stiftungen*), frontiers, roads. There is none the less much continuity, and also some development. Army business continued to be important throughout the period, the 'army' committee of 1779 presumably concerning itself with much of what was referred to individual committees earlier. Censorship of newspapers and calendars, clerical fees (the so-called *taxae stollae*), commerce and industry, Jewish business, the *causae summi principis*, chiefly revenue cases, rectification of the cadastre on which the Contribution was based, and the royal towns, were also regular objects of attention. But change of emphasis is also indicated. The supervision of agriculture (item 1 in the table) was the product of central government interest in agriculture after the peace of 1763, and took the specific form in Bohemia of the Patriotic Society established in 1769, which by 1779 had counterparts in all the other Bohemian and Austrian lands.[138] The committee for chimney sweeps (item 11) must have been collecting soot, from which saltpetre for army gunpowder could be extracted. The committee to keep track of government ordinances (item 14) is evidence of their growing profusion. The monarch, hence the *Gubernium*, was interested for obvious political reasons in entailed estates (*Fideikommissen*, item 15) and wards (item 42). The interest and inheritance taxes (item 21) were settled for service of government debts owed to the Estates. Normal schools (item 26) were those created by the ambitious plan of 1774. The scope of the committee on studies (item 37) may have overlapped with that on schools. The finances of the university of Prague were supervised by a separate committee (item 40). Police and security (item 30) were the object of increased government concern, centrally and locally, from the 1760s, though 'police' had wide connotations, and aspects of it were common to most business. The committee on sanitation presumably answered to the *Sanitätshofdeputation* (1753–76) in Vienna. The *Spinnhaus* was the workhouse, to which offenders were relegated, as numerous references show. A committee was appointed under Count Korženský in April 1748 to draft a new *Landesordnung* for Bohemia, presumably in modification of that of 1627. The work seems to have been attracted subsequently to the *Deputation*, then the *Gubernium*, explaining item 41 in the list.[139]

---

[138] They are all listed at the end of the 1779 *Court Calendar*.
[139] Maasburg, *Obersten Justizstelle*, 140 n.

TABLE 10.1. *Committees of the Bohemian Government, 1748–79*

	1748–9	1757	1763	1765	1779
(1) Agriculture and liberal arts	−	−	−	−	+
(2) Army	−	−	−	−	+
(3) Army barracks	−	+	+	−	−
(4) Army commissariat and supply	−	−	+	−	−
(5) Army quartering	−	+	+	+	−
(6) Army recruiting	−	+	+	+	−
(7) Cameral taxes	+	+	−	−	−
(8) *Causae summi principis*	−	+	+	+	+
(9) Censorship of newspapers and calendars	+	+	+	+	+
(10) Census of population and draught animals	−	−	−	−	+
(11) Chimney sweeps	−	−	−	+	+
(12) Clerical fees (*taxae stollae*)	+	+	+	+	+
(13) Commercial and industrial	+	+	+	+	+
(14) Compilation of royal ordinances	−	−	+	+	+
(15) Entailed estates (*Fideikommissen*)	−	−	+	+	+
(16) Fortifications	+	−	−	−	+
(17) Foundations	−	+	−	+	+
(18) Frontiers	+	+	+	−	+
(19) Guilds	−	+	−	−	−
(20) Hospitals	−	−	+	−	−
(21) Interest and inheritance taxes	−	−	−	+	+
(22) Jews	−	+	+	+	+
(23) Masts and ships	−	−	−	−	+
(24) Military pensioners	−	−	+	+	−
(25) Navigation	−	−	−	+	−
(26) Normal schools	−	−	−	−	+
(27) Old cameral debts	−	−	+	+	+
(28) Parish regulation	−	−	−	−	+
(29) Pawnbroking	−	+	−	+	−
(30) Police and security	−	+	+	+	+
(31) Property tax	−	−	+	−	−
(32) Rectification of the Contribution	+	−	+	+	+
(33) Roads	+	+	−	−	+
(34) Salt and drinks taxes, arrears	−	−	+	−	−
(35) Sanitation	−	−	−	+	+
(36) *Spinnhaus*	−	−	−	+	+
(37) Studies	−	−	+	−	+
(38) Tobacco taxes	+	−	−	−	+
(39) Towns	+	+	+	+	+
(40) University	−	−	+	+	+
(41) *Verneuerte Landesordnung*	+	−	−	+	−
(42) Wards	−	−	−	+	+
(43) Weights and measures	−	−	−	+	+

Sources: 1748–9, 1757, Rieger, *Zřízení krajské*, ii. 323–4 nn. For 1763–79, *Court Calendar*. The Calendar only otherwise shows committees for Austrian Silesia.

The Bohemian evidence yields no trace of the division of the *Gubernium* into executive and judicial 'senates' from 1763 observable in the Austrian lands.[140] There was a judicial aspect. Of the 25 members of the Bohemian *Gubernium* in 1779, two were also president and vice-president of the *Appellation* or court of appeal, six of the *Grösseres Landrecht* or court for the nobility, one of the appeals division of the mercantile court, and one of the *Consessus in Causis Summi Principis*. There was thus a 'judicial' section of *Gubernium* councillors, but it is not clear if this was all there was. Joseph II in 1782–3, declaring (yet again) the need for 'the greatest possible separation of administration and justice' restricted all *Gubernien* to administrative work, and created new courts for judicial business.[141]

The government of newly acquired (1772–3) Galicia created many problems. Galicia's formal style was decided as 'the kingdoms (*regna*) of Galicia and Lodomeria', allegedly principalities once belonging to the Crown of Hungary, but occupied by Poland since 1412. Austria thus created a new kingdom, the first until the equally curious Kingdom of Lombardy–Venetia in 1815. By a sinister anticipation of later history, two principalities within Galicia, Auschwitz and Zator, were separately named in the documents of annexation as formerly Silesian, and thus claimed by the empress as King of Bohemia. Kaunitz as first tried to keep Galicia as a separate fief. The Hungarian Court Chancellery was attracted by the idea of uniting it to Hungary, and Maria Theresia at first seems to have considered this. Joseph II spoke consistently for its absorption into the existing pattern of Bohemian–Austrian administration. A Galician Court Chancellery was created in Vienna (May 1774–April 1776), and at once began to 'protect' Galician interests. When it was abolished, at Joseph II's insistence, its business was transferred to a 'Galician senate' of the Bohemian and Austrian Chancellery. The relative automony of the Galician governor Count Auersperg (1774–80), however, continued, with the approval of both rulers. Austria introduced standard administrative organs into Galicia, a

---

[140] Although the *Court Calendar* rarely specifies this, it seems clear from the evidence reviewed that this double function of the *Gubernien* did exist in most of, if not all, the Austrian lands.

[141] Domin-Pet. 90 ff. The *Justizsenate* of the *Gubernien* were abolished, evidently in 1782, ibid. 91. The elusive *Justizsenate* appear also in Hintze, 'Beamtenstaat', where they are credited with responsibility for 'administrative justice', op. cit. 347.

Gubernium in Lemberg, six Circles, mercantile courts of first and second instance, a *Landtafel*. It subjected church and nobles to direct taxation, and began to register, and give titles to, the nobility, It also tried to attract the latter into government by introducing a Galician Diet. Hatzfeld's proposals for this in the *Staatsrat* in 1774 were impressive in scope, and included provision for a six-man Committee of the Diet to act between full sessions. Half of this Committee was to be re-elected triennially by secret ballot. This interesting scheme had to be deferred until 1782, owing to noble reserve. Resolute, if not wholly successful, attempts were also made to reform Galician law.[142]

The kingdom of Hungary formed an important part of what may be called Maria Theresia's system of government. This involved respecting the liberties of the Austrian Netherlands and Hungary, while keeping a firm, even autocratic, control over the German Hereditary Lands, Tyrol to some extent excepted. It was to the Hungarian nation, she told her son Maximilian in 1774, that she owed her existence on the throne of her ancestors. They had shown the greatest attachment to her during her reign, and the greatest zeal to obey her orders. She had learned of their merits, as of much else, from her late husband.[143] The empress's views on this occasion overlooked the numerous tensions between Austria and Hungary, most recently at the Diet of 1764–5, but are none the less significant. A string of concessions to Hungary during her reign shows that she meant what she said. Meanwhile, her leading ministers after the Seven Years War also devoted their attention to Hungarian problems, though with a more jaundiced eye.[144]

Hungary was a kingdom independent of the Holy Roman

---

[142] Based on Part 1, 'Staatliche Eingliederung', of Glassl's authoritative *Einrichtungswerk*. For the name 'Galicia et Lodomeria' see ibid. 54 n.; for Joseph II's wish to exclude the nobility from Galician government, and Hatzfeld's to include them, via the new Diet, ibid. 101–6. For law reform in Galicia see Domin-Pet. 45, 51–2, creation of a Tribunal (1774), an *Appellation* (1775), etc.

[143] Arneth, *Mar. Ther. Kinder und Freunde*, ii. 320, n.d., but referring to the 33 years of her reign, presumably since the coronation of 1741.

[144] Ember, 'Der östereichische Staatsrat', *passim*. Ministers wanted a fixed plan ('Haupt System') for Hungary, and to increase its wealth, education (in 'German' principles), and population. The amount of crown lands was to be increased; offices were to be filled with Germans and foreigners. A census of population, and reform of the Contribution and the law, were other projects. It was recognized that Hungary was at best an aristocratic monarchy, at worst a republic; and that Hungarian privileges needed careful handling.

Empire and papacy, and hereditary in the Habsburg line (Diet of 1687), with the vestigial concession that if the descent of Leopold I and his two sons failed, the ancient right of election would revive.[145] The succession could be in the female line (Diet of 1723, article 2), hence Maria Theresia was king of Hungary, 'Rex noster'.[146] Croatia, Dalmatia, and Slavonia, belonged to the Hungarian Crown, as did, according to Koller in 1760, Bulgaria, Cumania or *Chersonesus Tartarica*, Galicia and Lodomeria, and Transylvania or Siebenbürgen.[147] The king was obliged by the diploma of Ferdinand II in 1622 to try to obtain all these lands, if not already in possession, and to preserve Hungary's frontiers, using Hungarian troops. He was obliged to observe the laws, administer justice, keep the crown of St Stephen in Hungary, listen to the grievances of the Estates, and ensure the latter's right to choose a Palatine.[148]

The government of Hungary was adapted, below the monarch, to the kingdom's division into the four Estates of clergy, barons and magnates of the realm (*barones et magnates regni*), nobles, and Royal Free Towns.[149] The clergy, the first estate, played a role in both administration, as sheriffs, and justice, as judges of the royal central courts. The Primate of Hungary had a right to be consulted about any government changes affecting the church.[150] The *barones regni* comprised the holders of the leading secular offices of state.

[145] Marczali, *Hungary in the Eighteenth Century*, ch. V. 'The royal power and the Government of the State', has not been superseded as a general account, though more information is now available on the Council of Lieutenancy and the Chamber. Marczali is closely followed, often in exaggerated form, by Király, *Hungary in the late Eighteenth Century*, chs. VI and VII. This section draws extensively on Koller's MS for Archduke Joseph, HHSA Nachl. Zinz., Hs. 156, cf. Ch. 5, n. 79. Koller, fos. 912–4 argues for Hungarian 'independence'.

[146] This point, clear from the proceedings of the 1741 Diet, with its formula of 'Vivat Domina, et Rex noster' (Arneth, *Gesch. Mar. Ther.* i. 269) and other evidence, is not directly discussed by Koller or Marczali, Cf. also *Khev.-Metsch*, 5 May 1764; Holzmair, cit. Ch. 2, n. 3.

[147] Koller, fos. 915–16. He explains 'Cumania' as the district whence 40,000 families were settled in Hungary by Béla IV in 1240, ibid. fo. 917. This is the 'Kunság' of the Hungarian literature. The 'Jaziger' of the contiguous 'Jaszság' were other immigrants, their name recalling the Iazyges who migrated from the Lower Danube in Roman times, *ex inf.* Dr L. A. Holford-Strevens. The Hajdú towns formed a second privileged district, see below.

[148] Koller, fos. 916–17 gives this list from Ferdinand II's diploma. It overlaps, but does not coincide, with the contents of Maria Theresa's coronation oath of 1741, reproduced in Marczali, 350–1.

[149] Cf., however, Ch. 5, n. 79.

[150] Koller, fos. 929–33. The Primate was the Archbishop of Esztergom (Gran).

These offices were those of Palatine, *Judex Curiae Regiae*, Ban of Croatia, and seven others, all, save that of the Palatine, who was elected by the Diet from four royal candidates, appointed by the Crown.[151] The office of Palatine was in fact vacant 1731–41 and again 1765–90, and a royal *Locumtenens* or *Statthalter* acted instead.[152] The next section of the second estate, the magnates, who were typically counts and barons, had an exclusive right to the important position of Chief Sheriff (*Supremus Comes, Obergespann, Főispán*) in the counties.[153] The nobles, forming the third estate, had a corresponding right to the office of Deputy Sheriff (*Vice-Comes*), and were elected to it by their peers from candidates proposed by the sheriff.[154] The latter also nominated a substitute Deputy.[155] The flavour of public life in Hungary was markedly legal, appropriately in a kingdom where, according to Koller, the tenure of land was subject to such uncertainty that young nobles studied law to the exclusion of everything else.[156] The chief court, at Pest, was the *Curia Regis*, comprising two divisions, the Seven Man Table (*Tabula Septemviralis, Septemviral-Tafel*) and the Royal Table (*Tabula Regia, Königliche Tafel*).[157] The first was a supreme

---

[151] The election of a Palatine in 1741 from two Catholic and two Protestant candidates is described by Arneth, *Gesch. Mar. Ther.* i. 273. For the officers of state, see the *Court Calendar* for 1740. Apart from those mentioned, they comprised the *Agazonum Magister* (Stablemaster), *Cubiculariorum Magister* (Chamberlain), *Curiae Regiae Magister* ('Hofmeister'), *Dapiferorum Magister* (Chief Steward), *Janitorum Regalium Magister* ('Obrist Thurhütter'), *Pincernarum Magister* (Cupbearer), and *Tavernicorum Regalium Magister* ('Schatzmeister'), all held by men of high rank. Koller's exposition (section 9) does not throw much light on their functions, but provides most of the German equivalents. Two 'Cron-Hütter', or *Custodes Sacrae Coronae*, with the duty of guarding St Stephen's crown, followed in rank, ibid., fo. 944.

[152] The office of Palatine was not to remain vacant more than a year (Diet of 1741, art. 9) but this was evidently ignored from 1765. Vice-Palatines were appointed, however. The Palatine to 1731 was Count Michael Pálffy, from 1741 to 1751 Count Johann Pálffy, from 1751 to 1765 Count Lajos Batthyány.

[153] For the sheriffs see Koller, fos. 944–6. The lists of sheriffs in Lehotzky, *Stemmatographia* 108–67 show that sheriffs were typically counts, occasionally barons or bishops. A few sheriffdoms were hereditary.

[154] The noble monopoly of this office is clear from Lehotzky, 184–224. For procedure, Koller, fo. 973.

[155] Koller, loc. cit.

[156] Koller, fo. 989.

[157] Marczali, 338–9, though he was mistaken if he really said that 'the actual executive work' of Hungarian government was undertaken by the *Curia Regis*, as his translator asserts. Domin-Pet. 28 states that the Seven Man Table was a 'court of revision', i.e. a supreme, not just an appellate, court. According to Koller, fo. 930, five clerics served on the Seven Man Table and two on the *Tabula Regia*.

court, and in 1740 was presided over by Maria Theresia's husband Francis Stephen of Lorraine (*Statthalter* 1731–41). Under him came sixteen councillors.[158] The *Tabula Regia* was a court of appeal, with some first-instance jurisdiction, whose president was the *Personalis Praesentiae Regiae in Judiciis Locumtenens*.[159] This important officer, often confusingly referred to by contemporaries simply as the *Personalis*, was a noble not a magnate, and by law also presided over the lower chamber of the Hungarian Diet.[160] He counted, according to Khevenhüller-Metsch, applying the concepts of a foreign political culture, as the head of the Hungarian 'Ordo equestris'.[161] Four district courts with civil jurisdiction were established in 1723 under the *Tabula Regia* at Debreczen, Eperies, Guns, and Tyrnau.[162] Cases not reserved to these could be taken by those of the counties (*sedes judiciaria*), whose judges were, under the chief sheriff's supervision, elected by the county assemblies (of prelates, barons, magnates, nobles, towns) and nominally renewed every three years.[163] Finally, the fourth estate comprised the Royal Free Towns, which were royal peculiars supervised by the *Kamara*, and were corporately noble, though their members were not. They were typically presided over by a *Stadtrichter* (rather than *Bürgermeister*), and had a small Inner Council, a larger Outer Council (*Innerer Rat, Äusserer Rat*), and a Body of Electors (*Electa Communis*) which put up names for the councils. The members of the latter were chosen for life, but had to be renewed every two to three years.[164] This

---

[158] *Court Calendar* 1740. When there was a Palatine, he presided.

[159] Ibid. and Domin-Pet., loc. cit. The *Personalis* in 1740 (and until 1748 when he became president of the Hungarian Chamber) was Anton Grassalkovich.

[160] Koller, fos. 946–8. He also states, however (fo. 946), that the Diet of 1751, art. 6, ascribed the office the rank of *Herrenstand*, hence its holder could be considered a magnate.

[161] *Khev.-Metsch*, 12 May 1748.

[162] Domin-Pet., loc. cit. In 1780 they each had a dozen or so councillors, Marczali, App. V.

[163] Domin-Pet. 29 for the *sedes justiciaria*; Koller, fos. 973–4 for election and renewal, which he implies was sometimes deferred.

[164] See I. Kállay, 'Zur Verwaltungsgeschichte der freien königlichen ungarischen Städte im 17. und 18. Jahrhundert', *MÖSA* 15 (1962) 181–99, the best of several articles by him about aspects of Hungarian towns in this period. For legal purposes, the towns came under either the *Personalis* or the *Magister Tavernicorum*, hence were described as 'personales' or 'tavernicales', see the lists ibid. 182 n.

structure appears to have been imported from the German Empire, from which the burgesses in origin typically came.[165]

The primary instruments of royal political control in Hungary were the Royal Council of Lieutenancy (*Consilium Regium Locumtenentiale*) and the Chamber (*Camera, Kamara*), both at Pressburg until removed to Buda in 1784. Military administration overlapped with civil, however, on such matters as billeting, finance, supply. The Council of Lieutenancy was established in 1724, after approval from the Diet in the previous year.[166] In theory, it was directly responsible to the Crown. In practice, the Hungarian Court Chancellery in Vienna exercised considerable control over what was sent to the council and what came back from it for royal perusal.[167] Further influence was exercised by the *Staatsrat* from 1761.[168] In 1769 and 1776, however, new instructions allowed the council greater initiative in all ordinary business.[169]

The council's initial brief was to ensure the correct conduct of the county sheriffs, supervise the levy of the Contribution by counties and towns, promote manufactures and population, and apply royal orders in religion. This rather general instruction becomes specific in the voluminous records, all in Latin, listed by Felhő and Vörös.[170] These nearly all run through the entire period 1724–83. They include army supply and quartering, censorship of books, the Contribution, customs business, economic policy, guilds, supervision of Jews and nobles, mendicancy, public health (mostly precautions against plague), and numerous aspects of religion, including pious foundations, Protestants, and supervision of the Parish Chest created in 1733 to supplement Catholic benefices. Enforcement of the urbarial regulations from 1767 created a further

---

[165] The so-called Hajdú towns, whose inhabitants were descendants of Stephen Bocskay's forces in 1604, formed a privileged district in this period, Marczali, 169 and Koller, fos. 936–7, who shows that the *Kamara* was at odds over them with Szabolcs county, where they were located.

[166] Ember, *A M. kir. helytartótanács*, 2. The date of foundation was 20 Jan. 1724, and the opening session 21 Mar. 1724. The Diet of 1722–3 (arts. 97–102) approved the establishment of the council, ibid. Evans, *The making of the Habsburg Monarchy*, 239 is mistaken in saying that the council existed under Leopold I.

[167] Ember, 5–6, though without much in the way of evidence.

[168] See p. 234.

[169] Ember, 29 and Felhő–Vörös (eds.), *A helytartótanácsi levéltár*, 26–8.

[170] Op. cit.

mountain of work.[171] Joseph II's reorganization of the council in 1783 involved its division into a number of departments, many of which lasted until 1848.[172] Most of the existing business was retained, and other branches were added. It is not surprising that there was a marked expansion from about 1770 in the amount of paper the council had to handle.[173] Its membership also grew. When it was founded, it comprised, besides the president, twenty-two councillors, and twenty officials. In 1740 there were twenty-one councillors and twenty-eight officials; in 1754, twenty-five councillors and thirty-eight officials; in 1769, twenty-five councillors and forty-nine officials, in 1783, twenty councillors and no fewer than 107 officials. The union of the Council of Lieutenancy with the Hungarian *Hofkammer* (1785–90) led to a further increase in numbers. These did not go back to their former level when the union ended. In 1796 the council had a president, twenty-two councillors, and 170 officials.[174]

A powerful body responsible to the Council of Lieutenancy was the *Commissariatus Provincialis*, with a director, vice-director, and, in this period, one commissary for each of the eight districts into which Hungary was divided. It supervised correct levy of the Contribution, and all supply, billeting, transport, and horses for the royal troops. It acted closely with the army command on the one hand and the counties and towns on the other. The Estates were formally dispensed from responsibility for these matters by article 63 of the Diet of 1741, seven years before the decennial recesses attempted to do this in the Bohemian and Austrian lands.[175]

Financial control in Hungary before Maria Theresia's reign was fragmented, both geographically and functionally. Mines revenue, and those of the Banat of Temesvár, were separately administered,

---

[171] Ibid. 28 and 118. There were earlier precedents for the Parish Chest ('Cassa Generalis Parochorum').

[172] Ember, 85–7 lists these departments.

[173] See p. 323.

[174] From the figures in Ember, 193–7. In 1848 there was a total of 268 persons, ibid. This is misprinted as 868 in G. Barany's important chapter 'Ungarns Verwaltung: 1848–1918' in A. Wandruszka and P. Urbanitsch (eds.), *Die Habsburger Monarchie 1848–1918*, ii (Vienna 1975) 314.

[175] Koller, fos. 967, 972–3. The *Commissariatus Provincialis* is referred to in Felhő–Vörös 102–3 but its duties are not specified there. A similar body in Siebenbürgen, the *Oberlandeskommissariat*, oversaw collection of the Contribution, and the quartering, etc., of troops. Its director was a member of the *Landesgubernium*, Kutschera, *Landtag und Gubernium*, 151–2.

and were directly controlled from Vienna.[176] The *Hofkammer* in Vienna also supervised the Hungarian salt revenues directly until 1743. Distinct cameral administrations reporting to Vienna existed for the Szepes (Zips) district, for five counties comprising the Szeged Inspectorate, and for Lower Slavonia. The Chamber at Pressburg, founded in 1528, was primarily concerned before 1740 only with the Hungarian customs (thirtieths) revenue, and thus had less money under its care than, for example, the Szepes Chamber at Kassa.[177] From 1741, however, when the Diet once again emphasized the importance and independence of the Chamber, a process of financial centralization ensued. The Hungarian Chamber administered the salt revenues from 1743. The Szeged Inspectorate was subordinated to it in 1742, that of Lower Slavonia in 1746, of the Szepes chamber in 1749.[178] In line with these increased responsibilities, the head of the Hungarian Chamber was addressed from 1742 as 'Praeses', instead of the subordinate 'Praefectus', and from July 1748 the 'Chamber' became a 'Court Chamber', a *Hofkammer*.[179] By this stage, the income it supervised, derived from customs, salt, royal domains, Jewish tolerance tax, and some minor branches, was at seven times the modest level of 1740.[180] The Contribution, mining revenue and the revenues of the Banat of Temesvár (until 1778) remained outside its jurisdiction, however. The first was supervised by the Council of Lieutenancy, the second and third by bodies in Vienna. The practice, which developed from 1747, though with earlier precedents, was for the Hungarian Chamber to

---

[176] Supervision of the Banat under Maria Theresia underwent numerous changes. Locally, throughout the period 1740–78 there was a council of government (*Banater Landesadministration*) in Temesvár, comprising a president and several councillors. Centrally, the *Hofkammer* and *Hofkriegsrat* exercised control jointly 1740–5; the *Hofdeputation in Banaticis, Transylvanicis et Illyricis* 1745–55; the Vienna *Hofkammer* 1755–7; the *Directorium* 1757–9; the *Ministerial Banco Deputation* 1759–69; the *Hofkammer* again 1769–72, when the Bohemian and Austrian Chancellery took over the 'political' part. There is an outline of this tangled history in Jordan, *Die kaiserliche Wirtschaftspolitik in Banat*, 75–81.

[177] See the important and scholarly monograph by Nagy, *A magyar kamara 1686–1848*, 66–7, 86, 100, 113. In 1717 the *Kamara* controlled about 105,000 fl. revenue, the Szepes administration about 350,000 fl. Nagy is the first writer to bring out the relatively subordinate position of the Hungarian Chamber under Charles VI. 'Hungary' had expanded since the 1680s. The Chamber had not.

[178] Ibid. 122 (Diet), 113–14, 134 (revenue).

[179] Nagy, 171, 31 Mar. 1742 and 14 July 1748.

[180] Ibid. 100, 160: 359,894 fl. and 2,567,868 fl.

pay Vienna a fixed Court Quota (*Hofquota*), and to spend the rest of its funds in Hungary, a practice much disliked by Austria's financial mandarins.[181]

The official position of the Chamber was one of subordination to the *Hofkammer* in Vienna, a view expressed, for example, in 1672 and 1696. This was contested, however, by Hungarian ministers, and by the Hungarian Diet, the latter regularly asserting a relationship of 'correspondentia', not 'dependentia'. The Diet of 1741 again claimed a position of 'correspondentia' for the Chamber, and its direct access to the sovereign. Maria Theresia conceded this access, though it was more a matter of form than substance. Her concessions on 'correspondentia' were more of substance than form. In practice from 1749 the enlarged Hungarian *Hofkammer* enjoyed much freedom of action, a state of affairs partly due to the empress's trust in its talented president from 1748 to 1771, Count Anton Grassalkovich, an ennobled member of a minor gentry family.[182] His death afforded the new *Hofkammer* president in Vienna, Count Leopold Kollowrat, the chance to draft an instruction (June 1772) ending the *Hofquota* system, and withdrawing the treasury at Pressburg from the control of the Chamber there. In future, Hungary would retain a fixed sum for expenses, and pay over the surplus to Vienna, an inversion of the existing system. In face of the impassioned resistance of the president and vice-president of the Chamber, Counts János Erdődy and Pál Festetics, Maria Theresia decided against Kollowrat on both issues (July and November 1772). A new instruction for the Chamber (14 November), and the decision to create a Credit Commission in Pressburg (15 November), to some extent even increased Hungarian financial independence.[183] The latter must not be overemphasized. The *Hof-*

[181] Ibid. 163–4. Cf. ii. 27.

[182] Nagy, 68–71, 74, 78, 169–74. The older article by T. Mayer, 'Das Verhältnis der Hofkammer zur ungarischen Kammer bis zur Regierung Maria Theresias', *MIÖG* 9 (*Ergänzungsband*) (1915) 178–263 is still of value. He shows how the Hungarian Diet reasserted the (1537) principle of 'correspondentia' ten times from 1608 to 1741, ibid, 208. From 1749 to 1762 it was almost the case that the much-reduced Vienna *Hofkammer* depended on the Hungarian, rather than the other way round.

[183] This significant episode is discussed by Nagy, 178–80 and in more detail by J. Herzog, 'A m. kir. hitelfőpénztár megszervezése és működése Mária Terézia korában', *Századok*, 59–60 (1925–6) 161–5. For the Credit Commission ibid. 165–7. Its work is discussed in ii, Ch. 10.

kammer in Vienna continued to send the Chamber a mass of what amounted to instructions, from the 1770s largely in German rather than Latin, as though to underline the point.[184] None the less, the increase in standing and size of the Chamber over the period is in interesting contrast to government hostility, noted earlier, to the independent pretensions of the chambers in Innsbruck, Graz, and Prague.

The scope of the Hungarian Chamber's work partly overlapped with that of the Council of Lieutenancy. In 1750 the Chamber had six standing committees, for customs (thirtieths), economic business, grain, legal matters, supervision of the Royal Free Towns, and salt.[185] In the 1760s, committees for afforestation, pious foundations, and manufactures followed.[186] From 1772, a division of the Chamber into a number of departments, initially fourteen, replaced the committee system.[187] Instead, referendaries were required to prepare business and present it to the board, a change already introduced in the Council of Lieutenancy.[188] Joint committees of the latter and the Chamber for economic and fiscal business were still of importance in the decade before their union in 1785.[189] Like the Council, the Chamber steadily expanded in numbers, having, besides its president, thirteen councillors, and thirty-eight officials in 1746, twenty-two councillors and 107 officials in 1773, and twelve councillors and 161 officials in 1785.[190]

The Kingdom of Croatia and Slavonia comprised six counties and a further area forming part of the Military Frontier. The six counties were, giving their Hungarian names, those of Körös, Varasd, and Zágráb (Croatia) and Pozsega, Szerém, and Verőcze (Slavonia). The last three, formed in 1746, came under the Hungarian Council of Lieutenancy and *Kamara* for fiscal purposes, but otherwise under Croatia. The latter, with its Ban (*Banus*), *Vice-Banus*, Banal Council, Treasurer (*Praefectus Aerarii*), and Diet (*Sabor*), briefly (1767–79) had a council of lieutenancy of its own, the *Consilium Locumtenentiale Croaticum*, but thereafter was subordinated to the

---

[184] See p. 316.
[185] Nagy, 139.
[186] Ibid.
[187] Ibid. 180–1.
[188] Ibid. 183.
[189] Ibid. 186–7.
[190] From the figs. ibid., app. 366–7.

Hungarian Council of Lieutenancy and Chancellery. The areas within the Military Frontier were controlled from 1744 by the *Hofkriegsrat* in Vienna. Croatia has been fully discussed recently in English by Guldescu, and the Military Frontier by Rothenberg, and it would be superfluous to treat these subjects at any length.[191] Siebenbürgen or Transylvania, also historically belonging to the Crown of St Stephen, had a civil governor ('Gouverneur'), who before 1771 might also be military commander, and a council of government in Hermannstadt, in which Catholics and Calvinists were entitled to four places each, Saxons to three, Unitarians to one. A *Thesauriat* or Chamber controlled finance. The Principality (Grand Principality, *Grossfürstentum*, 2 December 1765), was purposely kept separate from Hungary, and in the 1760s and 1770s was the object of extensive, though only partly realized, plans for its economic, fiscal and social reform. Some of these are noticed elsewhere.[192]

[191] Guldescu, *The Croatian-Slavonian Kingdom 1526-1792*; Gunther E. Rothenburg, *The Austrian Military Border in Croatia 1522-1747* (Urbana, Ill. 1960); *The Military Border in Croatia 1740-1881* (Chicago UP 1966). The responsibility of the Slavonian counties to the Hungarian Council of Lieutenancy for the Contribution, and to the *Kamara* otherwise, are shown in Koller, fo. 981 and Nagy 113 respectively.

[192] Kutschera, *Landtag und Gubernium*, ch. III. Cf. p. 377 below for the councillors in 1773; ii. 259-65 for reform of the Contribution.

11

Patterns of government

THIS chapter discusses the part played in Austrian government by the provincial Estates, and then the numbers involved in government, the language and forms of administration, and the structure of policy as shown by the ever-increasing body of royal decrees.

Estates government was parallel to royal government, and partly overlapped with it. The reasons for this were primarily fiscal and military. The Contribution, the main tax for the army, was consented to by the Diets, and levied under their supervision. The revision of the cadastre, on which the Contribution was based, was carried out through the Estates in Bohemia and Silesia under Charles VI, and both there and in Moravia and the Austrian lands under his daughter. Government war taxes before 1740, for example in the years 1734–9, were normally commuted for by the Bohemian and Austrian Estates, which then stepped into the royal shoes, and levied the taxes themselves. The Estates were formally responsible until 1748, and in practice longer, for recruits for the army and their quarters. Until 1743, the Estates of Inner Austria were largely in charge of the finance and organization of the Military Frontier, and so on. In practice it was often difficult to draw the line between royal and Estates authority. Thus, in Bohemia the originally royal offices of *Obrist-Burggraf* and the rest became offices of the Estates in the sixteenth century, then, from the *Verneuerte Landesordnung* of 1627, were once again under royal control and were nominated to by the Crown, in theory for five years at a time. Despite this, however, by the 1740s the *Statthalterei* composed of these officers was acting, according to Maria Theresia, more in the interests of the Estates, and was protected in its attitudes by the Bohemian Chancellery in Vienna. The notorious confusion of royal and Estates finances, condemned by Haugwitz, further exemplified this blurring of authority. The parallel structure of royal and Estates government went back into the sixteenth century, and was in several respects confirmed by the development of a

standing army in the later seventeenth century, and the recurrence
of expensive wars in which it was deployed. This made it necessary
to seek money from the Estates cap in hand. More generally, the
entire process of building up the Monarchy on the twin bases of
magnate support and Catholic orthodoxy, so cogently described by
Dr Evans, must in many respects have confirmed and increased the
traditional powers and ambitions of the Estates, in which the
church, a major recipient of royal generosity, as Maria Theresia
complained, officially constituted the first rank. From this point of
view, the tougher policies towards the Estates in general, and the
Catholic church in particular, under the empress and her son, represented a counter-attack against a position first created by the Crown
itself.[1]

The visible focal point of royal consultation with the Estates in
this period, outside the Hungarian lands, was the annual Diet or
Landtag. Ambitions for more wide-reaching representation, in the
form of 'Ländercongresse', had faded by 1740. Such bodies were
not uncommon before 1620, but attempts to revive them for financial purposes in 1700 and 1714 failed. Instead, the Crown succeeded
in driving individual bargains with the Diets of the various lands, as
it was to do again in 1748.[2] Count Karl Zinzendorf's proposal of
1787, admittedly abortive, for an Assembly of Notables to discuss
Joseph II's fiscal programme, lay in the future.[3] The usually
accepted view of the decline of the representative principle under
Maria Theresia seems undoubtedly correct. Certain qualifications
must, however, be made. Royal indebtedness to the individual
provinces during the Seven Years War in some respects increased
their political weight.[4] The government made important use of the
combined credit of the Estates in the Estates Credit Deputation of
1761–7.[5] Count Ludwig Zinzendorf's proposals of 1767, initially

---

[1] Evans, *Making of the Habsburg Monarchy*, does not explicitly draw this conclusion, but it seems to follow from his exposition. For the royal offices in Bohemia see
HGBL ii. 256, 287. In practice after 1627 they were held for longer periods than five
years.

[2] See ii, Ch. 1, n. 53 for these precedents. According to *HGBL* ii, 250–1, thirteen
'General Landtage' of the Bohemian lands were held in the 16th c., four 1611–20,
none thereafter.

[3] Rozdolski, *Steuer- und Agrarreform*, 107, proposal for a 'Notablen Versamm-
lung', dated only Feb. The French Notables assembled on 22 Feb. 1787.

[4] See ii, Ch. 4.

[5] Ibid.

accepted, envisaged making an Estates Bank a permanent source of finance for the entire Monarchy.[6] The Estates in Bohemia, Moravia, Lower Austria, Inner Austria, proved to be far from ciphers during the revision of the tax cadastre after 1748.[7] The annual *Gravamina* of the Diets kept local grievances before royal eyes. The Hungarian Diets of 1741, 1751, and 1764–5 were recalcitrant. As already noted, the government actually tried to invent a Diet for Galicia in the 1770s. To some extent, Estates government underwent a revival from the reign of Leopold II, though outside Hungary perhaps as an adjunct of royal power rather than in the older spirit of independence.

The full Diets in the Bohemian and Austrian lands in this period comprised four Estates, the clergy (*Prälatenstand*), the nobles (*Herrenstand*), the knights (*Ritterstand*), the towns (sometimes referred to as the 'Vierter Stand'). In Styria, Carinthia, and Krain, however, the nobles and knights sat as one Estate. In Tyrol, this was also true, but there was a fourth Estate consisting of representatives from the courts (*Pflegegerichte*) with jurisdiction over the numerous royal peasants. The right to sit in the Diet was defined by law and custom. Thus, the newer religious orders, such as the Jesuits, and in practice the parish clergy, were excluded from the First Estate, which comprised archbishops, bishops and abbots.[8] In practice, archbishops and bishops seem only rarely to have attended the Diets.[9] The *Herrenstand* comprised the titles of nobility down to and including baron (*Freiherr*), the *Ritterstand* consisted of knights and noble persons (*Edelleute*). Ennobled persons could only sit after twenty to thirty years, effectively a generation.

---

[6] See ii, Ch. 2.

[7] See ii, Chs. 7–8.

[8] This section is largely based on the learned treatment by Hassinger, 'Ständische Vertretungen'; see pp. 251, 265 for the statements in the text. He correctly insists on the uncertainty of the whole subject. O. Brunner's classic *Land und Herrschaft. Grundfrage der territorialen Verfassungsgeschichte Österreichs im Mittelalter* (4th edn. rev., Vienna and Wiesbaden 1959), ch. V, 'Landesherrschaft und Ländergemeinde', is helpful on the Estates, cf. pp. 378–80 for the *Pflegegerichte* in Tyrol.

[9] Cf. ii. 238, where it is shown that the Bishop of Olmütz's presidency of the Moravian Diet of 1748 was the first attendance by a bishop since 1666. In Lower Austria, it was the heads of religious houses who attended, see above, p. 98. In Upper and Lower Austria, the archbishop of Vienna and the bishops, claiming to be *reichsunmittelbar*, were included in the (otherwise secular) *Herrenstand*, Brunner, 406, 408; Hassinger, 252. However, the bishops of Trent and Brixen sat on the *Prälatenbank* of the Tyrol Estates, Hassinger, loc. cit.

Like the superior ranks of the church, the highest secular nobles often did not attend the Diets.[10]

The situation in Silesia in 1740 was especially complex, and helps to explain why Haugwitz, who was a councillor of the royal *Oberamt*, was so antagonistic to Estates government. The Diet was summoned annually by royal commissaries as a *Fürstentag*, and twice yearly by the president of the *Oberamt* as a *Conventus Publicus*, with the same membership. The councillors of the *Oberamt* sat in the Diet. The Diet had three Chambers. The first, of Princes, comprised the seven non-royal princes and the six Free Estates Lordships, which had a collective vote. The second, of Knights, consisted of knightly representatives from the seven royal principalities, and from Breslau city. The third, of Towns, comprised representatives from the remaining royal, and some other, towns. Each Chamber had a collective vote. Between Diets, a Smaller Committee (*Engere Landeszusammenkunft*) was responsible for the administration of taxes voted, and for other business. The *Generalsteueramt* of the Estates received the taxes voted, but was supervised by the *Oberamt*. Part of this bewildering structure survived into the fragment of Silesia retained by Austria after 1742.[11]

Representation of towns was in theory wide, in practice restricted. Thus, in Bohemia the *Bürgerstand* of Prague, Budweis, Kuttenberg, and Pilsen, all royal towns, comprised the Fourth Estate of the Diet and had one vote between them.[12] In Austria, the eighteen 'royal and market towns' outside Vienna sent one representative to the Diet and Vienna two. They had one collective vote.[13] Styria, too, sent one representative, the *Städtemarschall*, to the Fourth Estate.[14] In Krain and Upper Austria, on the other hand,

---

[10] Hassinger, 255 for ennobled persons. Christian von Schierendorf complained in the early 18th c. that princes and dukes of the Empire did not take their seats in the Bohemian Diet because the clergy (from 1627) was the First Estate, A. Fischel, *Studien zur Österreichischen Reichsgeschichte* (Vienna 1906) 186. In the Lower Austrian Diet, counts and barons comprised the *Herrenstand*, see above, p. 98, though the president was a prince.

[11] D'Elvert, 'Verfassung'; Hintze, 'Behördenorganisation'; Wolf, *Steuerpolitik*. Wolf corrects earlier writers' errors, but it is difficult to master all his distinctions.

[12] 'Entwurf einer Statistik von Böhmen [1756], in Riegger, *Materialien*, viii, 39. In theory all royal towns enjoyed the right to send representatives, *HGBL* ii, 249. The *Verneuerte Landesordnung* of 1627 reduced the towns to one collective vote, ibid. 288.

[13] Hassinger, 262–3.

[14] Ibid. 263. The Marshal represented the 14 royal towns and 17 royal markets.

all the towns sent a burgess.[15] Diets were typically held annually, though in Tyrol, for reasons mentioned below, they were less frequent. The various Estates normally sat and voted separately. In Tyrol they sat together by 'Circles', of which there were thirteen.[16]

In this period, the work of the Diets was more commonly conducted by an Estates Committee (*Landes-Ausschuss*), the full Diet only assembling to hear the annual royal requirements (*Postulata*) for taxation.[17] In Bohemia, a Committee of the Diet was established in 1714, with two members from each of the four Estates, and as Director the *Obrist-Burggraf*, also head of the royal government.[18] A similar committee, with similar membership, existed in Moravia from 1686, again with the president of the royal government as its Director.[19] In both Upper and Lower Austria the Committees had twenty-four members. In Tyrol, the Committee was much larger, thirteen members from each of the four Estates, and effectively replaced the full Diet.[20]

The volume of the State Inventory of 1763 devoted to the finances of the Estates shows the membership of the Committees, which was usually not entered in the *Court Calendar*.[21] In Bohemia, no prelates are listed. Under the *Obrist-Burggraf* as Director, the Committee had four *Herrenstand* members and two each from

[15] Ibid., eight and seven representatives respectively.

[16] Ibid. 265–7. These 'Circles' were not the same as the administrative districts of the same name. In Styria, there were two Diets each year until 1748, then one.

[17] This was the procedure in Lower Austria. In Bohemia and Moravia the Diet nominally sat throughout each year, with very few exceptions, but full sessions were normally held only at the beginning and end of each. The dates of the annual sessions are in print in Z. Tobolka *et al.* (eds.), *Knihopis českých a slovenských tisků* (Prague 1939–65), s.v. 'Artikulové', i.55–196 (Bohemia), 197–267 (Moravia). I am indebted to Dr Evans for this reference. See Hassinger, 268 for the development of Committees of the Estates, which were, as he says, 'kleine Landtage'.

[18] *HGBL* ii. 437; a fuller account in English in Kerner, *Bohemia in the Eighteenth Century*, 23, 146–53.

[19] R. Flieder, 'Zemský výbor stavovský na Moravě', *Sborník věd právních a státních*, 16 (1916) 136–57. The origin of the Committee is traced to 23 Jan. 1686. In 1739, rules for the better and more methodical conduct of its business were enforced by the Crown, and a quorum of 24 was introduced for election of the members, half of whom were to retire every six (previously three) years. From several later documents quoted, it is clear Maria Theresia had difficulty in enforcing attendance for Committee business. The Committee was abolished by Joseph II on 15 Mar. 1783, and restored by Leopold II on 14 Mar. 1791; see the continuation of Flieder's article, ibid. 18 (1917/18) 193–214.

[20] Hassinger, 266 for Tyrol. For Upper and Lower Austria, see below.

[21] HHSA Nachl. Zinz. Hs. 49, 'Provinciale', fos. 7 ff. The Lower Austrian and Upper Austrian Committees sometimes appear in the *Court Calendar*.

the *Ritterstand* and *Bürgerstand*. In Moravia, there were two members from each Estate, with the *Landeshauptmann* as Director. In Lower Austria and Upper Austria, the Committee had twenty-four members, divided into three parts, a Committee, a 'Verordneten-Collegium' or finance and business committee, and a 'Rait Collegium', or accounts committee.[22] The case of Lower Austria, considered below, shows that the three parts assembled to transact business together. The Committee in Upper, but not in Lower, Austria included two townsmen. In Styria, the *Landeshauptmann* was joined by two committee-men (*Ausschussräte*) and four *Verordnete* (two of them clerics). In both Carinthia and Krain, only four *Verordnete* are listed, one of them a cleric. None of these three provinces had townsmen on its Committee. In the Bohemian Committee, three members were also in the royal *Gubernium* in 1765, apart from the Director, who was head of both bodies.[23] In Moravia, three Committee members in 1763 were also councillors of the *Tribunal*, or court of appeal. There are two cases of such overlap in Upper Austria, one in Styria. This virtual absence of mutual contact is readily explicable, since the royal governments were larger, and did not include townsmen or clergy, the latter prominent in the Estates and in the Committees of Estates. Implicit in the watered-down memberships of Committees in 1763, especially, perhaps, those of Inner Austria, was their absorption into the royal *Gubernien*, a step taken by Joseph II from 1782.[24]

In Lower Austria, the twenty-four members of the Estates Committee in 1763 were divided into twelve 'Ausschussen', six *Verordnete*, and six Accounts Councillors or 'Raitt Herren'.[25] They met under the presidency of the Lower Austrian *Landmarschall*, at first

---

[22] In Upper Austria, each body had eight members; in Lower Austria there were twelve Committee-men ['Ausschussen' (sic)] and twelve others, divided equally. 'Rait' was from Latin *ratio*, an account.

[23] Comparing the MS source with the *Court Calendar*.

[24] The decision to end the Committees and join two Estates members to each *Gubernium* seems to have been made in 1782, and implemented in 1782–3, Hock–Bidermann, 167. Count Johann Ludwig Barth-Barthenheim, *Das Ganze der österreichischen politischen Administration* (Vienna 1838–43) i. 211 states that the Lower Austrian *Verordneten-Collegium* was merged with the *Regierung* 12 Apr. 1782 and restored 7 June 1790. For Moravia see n. 19 above. Hassinger 268–9 erroneously says that Maria Theresia abolished the Estates Committees.

[25] In the *Court Calendar* for 1740 there are only 22 listed members of the 'Nieder-österreichische Land-Standen Ausschuss', the last six being designated 'Herren Verordnete'. Barth-Barthenheim calls each of the three groups a *Collegium*.

TABLE 11.1. *Meetings of and attendance at the Lower Austrian Estates Committee, 1757–80*

1758	47	1764	18	1770	4	1776	6
1759	33	1765	15	1771	7	1777	5
1760	31	1766	8	1772	5	1778	11
1761	34	1767	7	1773	4	1779	2
1762	19	1768	7	1774	7	1780	10
1763	31	1769	4	1775	6		

	Prelates	Lords	Knights	Towns	Total
4 April 1759	4	4	6	—	14
22 February 1760	2	6	7	—	15
17 September 1761	5	6	4	—	15
17 March 1762	6	6	6	2	20
12 May 1762	5	4	5	2	16
17 November 1774	2	4	4	—	10
13 November 1775	5	6	3	2	16
26 January 1780	8	25	13	—	46

Count Aloysius Harrach, then, until his death in 1775, Prince Johann Wilhelm Trautson. The president of the royal government (*Regierung*) was not the head of the Committee, as he was elsewhere. Until 1764 there were eight members each from the *Prälatenstand*, *Herrenstand*, and *Ritterstand*. However, at the end of 1763 the *Rait Collegium* or Accounts Committee was abolished, after an embarrassing deficit was exposed at the death of the Estates receiver. This presumably reduced the total membership to eighteen.[26] The number of meetings of the Committee in the years 1757–80, and specimen attendances, excluding the president (the *Landmarschall*), are shown in Table 11.1.[27] The annual full meetings of the Estates were, however, more numerously attended, for instance by 71 persons in 1762, by 82 in 1763.[28]

As the number of Committee meetings implies, during the Seven Years War and its aftermath the members were crowded with business. An apparently endless flow of 'Hof Decrete' urged attention to the minutiae of recruiting, finance, army supply, quartering.

---

[26] See Ch. 13, n. 4 for the deficit, which approached 140,000 fl.

[27] NÖLA Ständische Bücher 94–7, 1757–84. I am indebted to Oberarchivrat Dr Silvia Petrin for kindly drawing my attention to this source. The abolition of the *Rait Collegium* is not mentioned in it, though there are several references to investigation of the deficit.

[28] Ibid. no. 96 fos. 14ᵛ (11 Aug. 1762) and 68ᵛ (12 Sept. 1763).

From the mid 1760s, the number of meetings declined, though a contentious issue could reverse the trend, and lead to an influx of non-Committee men, as attendance on 26 January 1780, when the royal proposals for a new Bohemian–Moravian style tax on beer and wine were unveiled, demonstrates.[29] The fourth Estate, in the shape of two deputies from Vienna, and one from the eighteen royal towns, only attended episodically, and often left after the item which concerned them.[30] The members of the *Verordneten-Collegium*, which administered matters of finance and credit, for instance the levy of the Contribution, or reconstruction of the debts of the Estates in 1767, attended the Committee's meetings, but are always spoken of as forming a distinct body. The record of this *Collegium's* activities, if fully recovered, would presumably be fatter than that of the Committee itself in the later part of the reign.[31]

The tone of royal orders to the Lower Austrian Committee was tolerably autocratic, and the tone of the responses tolerably submissive, though allowing much grumbling and indication of grievances. The annual *Gravamina* of the fully assembled Estates also kept these in view.[32] The annual royal *Postulata*, given to representatives of the Diet at the Hofburg or Schönbrunn, seem none the less to have been agreed to without demur. The statement thrown out by the abbot of Melk in 1765 that 'we must absolutely obey when Her Majesty absolutely commands' perhaps had wide assent, no doubt with the condition that commands ought to conform with law and precedent.[33] It is difficult to avoid the impression that during this period the Estates' councillors were becoming more and more like royal civil servants, a process also observable in the army and the church.

---

[29] For this episode see ii. 199.

[30] Hassinger, 268 says that the Fourth Estate was excluded from the reign of Ferdinand I. Though this was generally true, the record shows that town members sometimes attended under Maria Theresia.

[31] There is a good deal of evidence for the business of the *Verordnete* in NÖLA Landtagshandlungen. Those for 1766–7 and 1773–6 were searched as samples. Much of the material consists of *Hofdekrete* addressed to the *Verordnete*, copies of notices by them, often printed, accounts, etc. Minutes of meetings, or other transactions, were not found there.

[32] No continuous series of Lower Austrian *Gravamina* is in print, in distinction to those for the Diets of Bohemia and Moravia. The *Gravamina* for 1768 (rough draft) and 1774 (but not 1775–6) are in the Landtagshandlungen.

[33] NÖLA Ständische Bücher 96, fo. 126ᵛ, 27 Jun. 1765, 'man müsse absolute gehorsammen, wenn S[eine]r k.k. Majt. absolute befehle'.

The contrast between Estates government in Hungary and in the Austrian and Bohemian lands of the Monarchy is striking. In the latter, the Diets or Committees of them were in frequent session, but were relatively powerless. In Hungary, the bicameral Diet, representing the clergy, magnates, nobles, and towns, was only summoned in 1741, 1751, and 1764, but on each occasion proved obstreperous and hard to control.[34] It had no difficulty in rejecting, or modifying, royal financial demands. It passed numerous laws (70 in 1741, 41 in 1751, 47 in 1765).[35] The absence of a Diet, or of its equivalent in the form of a Committee, in the intervening years, must have been made palatable to the nobility by the continued vitality of the county assemblies, which Maria Theresia, unlike Joseph II, had the sense to leave alone.[36]

The Austrian Monarchy under Maria Theresia is usually depicted as a bureaucracy, a *Beamtenstaat*.[37] This implies a pervasive official-dom organized on Weberian lines of hierarchy, regularity, defined functions, and assigned status. Although there is a good deal of

[34] The standard account of the three Diets is in Arneth, *Gesch. Mar. Ther.*, see ii. 194, below. The Hungarian Diet is discussed by the leading authority Gy. Bónis, 'Die ungarischen Stände'. The Upper House ('Table') of the Diet comprised the arch-bishops and bishops, and noble abbots and provosts, together with the magnates, including the Ban of Croatia. In 1729, 31 prelates sat; in 1741, 210 magnates sat, ibid. 296–7. The Lower House or Table met in a separate building, and consisted of the remaining abbots and provosts, representatives of the chapters, 80–90 delegates from the counties and Privileged Districts, and two members each from the Royal Free Towns. In 1741, 39 such towns were represented, ibid. 298. The Palatine presided over the Upper House, the royal *Personalis*, as head of the 'königliche Tafel', or court for the nobility, over the Lower, ibid.

[35] *Corpus Juris Hungarici*, i, p. viii summarizes the legislative record. In Sieben-bürgen (Transylvania), the unicameral Diet was composed of the 'Status et Ordines', the first comprising representatives of the three privileged nations of Saxons, Hun-garians, and Szekler, the second royal officials and directly summoned nobles ('Rega-listen'). This last group was largest. The Diet was overwhelmingly noble. The Catholic clergy were represented only by the bishop of Weissenburg. It met nearly every year from 1700 to 1761, thereupon not until 1781. The subject is definitively treated in Kutschera, *Landtag und Gubernium*, ch. 1.

[36] For her intention, subsequently reversed, to call a Hungarian Diet in 1778, see ii. 151. In the third volume (1888) of his *Magyarország története II. József korában*, 572–77, H. Marczali published an undated Latin tract 'Maximae Status Pro Regno Hungariae', evidently by Franz Grossinger, which stated that since the last Diet, Hungarian opinion had been sought through *intimata* to the counties and towns. For Grossinger, whose tract is a kind of *reductio ad absurdum* of centralist policies towards Hungary, see Beales, 'The False Joseph II'.

[37] Hinzte, 'Beamtenstaat', has been influential. The existence of 'bureaucracy' in the Theresian and Josephine period is usually accepted as a fact in the modern litera-ture.

truth in the description, the breach with older forms of rule, in which royal household servants, aides, or professional advisers exercise power centrally, while feudal lords exercise it locally, was nevertheless by no means complete. The question of the numbers and type of officials is of importance here. As so often, a clear picture is not easily obtainable from the literature. Macartney tells us that 'Charles VI's Court numbered no less than 40,000 persons'.[38] This would have approximated to the entire adult population of Vienna, and the statement is in fact apparently based on a misreading of Keyssler, who refers to 40,000 'Kammerbedienten' in Charles VI's German Hereditary Lands.[39] Keyssler, in any case, was given to round guesses.[40] A much more modest figure of 2,175 Court employees and central government officials 'under Charles VI' has been suggested by Mikoletzky from manuscript evidence.[41] The numbers of local royal officials in 1740 can be estimated by taking the total of provincial salaries and wages paid in 1749, just over 1m. fl., and dividing this by an average of 300 fl. to give 3,300 persons. The Vienna City Bank may have employed another 1,000. Total numbers of royal officials in the central lands of the Monarchy at Maria Theresia's accession, including those employed at Court, would, on this admittedly imprecise basis, have been about 6,500, or 6,000 as a round figure.[42]

[38] *Habsburg Empire*, 52 n.

[39] Keyssler, *Neueste Reisen durch Deutschland*, 1232, 'Man rechnet vierzigtausend Kammerbedienten in des Kaisers sämmtlichen deutschen Erblanden.' Macartney's statement is taken from H. Schenk's essay, cit. Ch. 5, n. 1.

[40] Thus he thought the population of Vienna was 300,000 to 350,000, more than twice its actual size.

[41] H. L. Mikoletzky, 'Der Haushalt des kaiserlichen Hofes zu Wien (vornehmlich im 18. Jahrhundert)', *Carinthia I* Jg. 146 (1956) 668, from HKA Hs 217, evidently undated. Id., 'Die "Fräulein-Steuer" (Der Haushalt Maria Theresias während ihrer letzen Regierungsjahre)', in H. Hantsch and A. Novotny (eds.), *Festschrift für Heinrich Benedikt . . . zum 70. Geburtstag* (Vienna 1957) 39–60 is intended as a sequel to the above, but in fact adds little to it.

[42] Provincial salaries are entered as 1,025,594 fl. in HKA Hs. 220, 'MilitarCameral und Schulden Systemata vom 1ten November 1748.' They are unlikely to have been substantially less in 1740. The average provincial salary of 300 fl. may be too low, since in 1761 it was 659 fl., see below; on the other hand, that may be too high. Vienna City Bank employees are estimated below as *c.* 2,000 in 1762, when the Bank's revenue had doubled. This has been halved for 1740. Division of total salary bills by average salaries strictly gives numbers of offices rather than of persons. Given the overlap in office-holding noted in Ch. 10, the totals of persons may therefore be overstated. It seems likely, however, that duplication was uncommon below the top level.

TABLE 11.2. *Officials in census of 1762*

	Royal	Estates	Lordship and Town	Total
Bohemia	557	197	3,334	4,088
Moravia	233	156	1,666	2,055
Silesia	88	32	258	378
Lower Austria	5,123	585	4,701	10,409
Upper Austria	113	43	335	491
Styria	913	260	902	2,075
Carinthia	227	114	213	554
Krain	88	83	227	398
Görz	62	13	29	104
Gradisca	17	11	4	32
Total	7,421	1,494	11,669	20,584

The census of 1762 elicited the numbers of officials (*Beamte*), for the first time. It divided them into royal ('Landesfürstlich'), Estates ('Landschaftlich') and those of lords and towns ('herschaftliche', 'städtische'). The results are shown in Table 11.2.[43] Grossmann, the first to print these figures, gives others for subsequent years in the decade which are broadly in line.[44] A return of 1764 for Lower Austria distinguishes numbers in Vienna and outside it.[45] The total number of officials is put at 10,828, of whom 5,444 were royal, 554 belonged to the Estates, and 4,830 to lordships and towns. Of this total, 4,511, 398, and 3,391 respectively, or 8,300 in all, resided in Vienna. The first apparently firm information for Hungary comes from a government return printed by Marczali, which shows 2,494 royal councillors and officials there in 1781.[46] Those of the Estates and of lords were much more numerous than this. Martin Schwartner stated that in 1780 there were 4,421 Hungarian county officials of various grades, and in 1790 4,255. For 1798 he estimated town officials at 6,411, those of lordships at 3,000. Later

---

[43] Grossmann, 'Anfänge', table XIII.
[44] Ibid. table XXI. However, Lower Austria in 1768 is clearly aberrant.
[45] HKA Hs. 713, fos. 786–7, 'N[ieder]Ö[sterreichische] Seelen-Beschreibung Ao. 1764'.
[46] Marczali, *Hungary in the Eighteenth Century*, app. V, 'Tabelle über den sämmtlichen Einnahme und die gemeinen Ausgaben der Hung. Kameral-Fond . . . für das Jahr 1781'. This also showed numbers of persons. Of the total listed, 2,106 worked 'bey dem Wirthschafts-Salz und 30. Wesen. [Customs]'.

(1806) he increased his estimate for the latter to 11,068, and for those of towns to 8,468.[47]

The pattern which these figures disclose is one of a corps of royal household servants and officials, numerous when concentrated in Vienna, dispersed elsewhere, and outnumbered by officials of the Estates and, especially, those of lordships and towns. This was most markedly true in Hungary, confirming the usual statements about the power there of the Estates generally, and the counties in particular. In the Bohemian and Austrian lands, private officials were especially numerous in Bohemia, Moravia, and Lower Austria. For the man in the village street during this period, this officialdom must have constituted typical authority. The edicts of the central government flowed through this network, but no doubt were often diluted, or dissipated, as they went.

The general pattern described is undoubtedly plausible. There are, however, some numerical difficulties. Oberleitner in 1861 computed (from the second volume of the State Inventory of 1763) that in 1761 1,478 persons were employed at Court, and a further 1,114 in the central offices, hence 2,592 in Vienna; with 1,276 more in the Bohemian and Austrian lands, or 3,868 in all. The total omits the officials of the Vienna City Bank, but is still little more than half the 7,421 listed by the census of 1762.[48] In 1768, Zinzendorf, replying to a royal enquiry about reducing the state's bill for salaries, computed that there were 4,512 persons on the books of, without distinction, the Court, most of the central offices, and the royal governments in the Bohemian and Austrian lands. The personnel of the omitted central offices came to 64 (Oberleitner), hence the total for the Bohemian–Austrian lands, at 4,576, is higher than Ober-

---

[47] M. Schwartner, *Statistik des Königreichs Ungern* (Buda 1798) 138–40; rev. edn. (Buda 1809, 1811), pt. i, pp. 196–7.

[48] Oberleitner, 'Finanzlage', correcting his miscasting. For the Court, he seems to count all employees, including the numerous domestic servants; elsewhere only officials ('Beamte'). The implication of his data is that the average Court salary was 506 fl., the average salary in the central offices, excluding ambassadors, 1,239 fl., and the average salary of royal officials in the Bohemian and Austrian lands, 659 fl. Mikoletzky, 675–6 gives figures from HKA Hs. 222, 'Status der Besoldungen', which agree in some respects, but not all, with Oberleitner's. The [?1759] MS shows 982 employees at Court (Oberleitner 1,478), 1,165 persons in the central offices (Oberleitner 1,114) and 2,809 cameral and *Landschaft* officials in the *Länder*. If, (1762 census) 1,494 were officials of the Estates, 1,315 were royal (Oberleitner 1,276). The 'royal' total is 3,462 persons (Oberleitner 3,868), omitting the Hungarian lands and the Vienna City Bank.

TABLE 11.3. *Estimated number of cameral, Vienna City Bank, and mines officials, 1762*

	Total wages and salaries	Divided by 300 fl. gives (persons)	Divided by 400 fl. (Vienna City Bank) and 250 fl. (other) gives (persons)
Camerale in Hungary and Siebenbürgen	553,273	1,844	2,213
Mines and coinage in Siebenbürgen	112,300	374	449
Mines and coinage in Bohemian–Austrian lands	133,556	445	534
Vienna City Bank outside Hungary	742,149	2,473	1,856
Vienna City Bank in Hungary	61,895	206	155
Total	1,603,173	5,342	5,207

Source: HHSA Nachl. Zinz. Hs. 50 B, accounts for 1765, showing the position in 1762.

leitner's for 1761, and probably more authentic.[49] However, it omits the tax-gathering army of the Vienna City Bank, whose revenues doubled during the war, the employees of the mines and coinage department, and the royal officials in Hungary and Sienbenbürgen. Their numbers are not recorded in the sources examined, but can be estimated by taking the total wages and salaries for 1762, and dividing by a representative salary per head. Alternatives are presented in Table 11.3. The results, if added to those given earlier, suggest 7,494 or 6,966 royal officials in the Bohemian and Austrian lands at this date, and 2,424 or 2,817 more in Hungary and Siebenbürgen. The overall totals are 9,918 and 9,783, with 10,000 as a round estimate. The estimates fit well with the results for the Austrian and Bohemian lands in the census of 1762 shown earlier. The figures for Hungary and Siebenbürgen are not implausible, but need corroboration.

The implication of these results is that a considerable increase in the numbers of officials occurred between 1740 and the end of the Seven Years War. This is not unlikely, given the doubling of royal revenue in the same period, and the qualitative evidence that Haugwitz's revolution in government greatly increased its scope. It must,

[49] Pettenegg, *Zinzendorf*, 122; his 4,512 persons were those receiving 'Besoldungen der Hofstäbe und der deutschen Erbländer Hof- und Länderstellen'.

however, be recalled that the administration of the Court itself absorbed over 1,000 persons. The position in the last part of the reign cannot be established from the new censuses since 1777, as the rubric 'civil servants and dignitaries' excluded nobles and included an unknown number of doctors, lawyers, and others who were not state officials. About 15,000 persons appear under the rubric in 1781; 4,000 can perhaps be added for the Hungarian lands.[50] The total of 19,000 represents the upper limit of an assessment. Working from the finance estimates for 1778, and assuming average salaries, as was done for 1762, numbers of officials can be computed in round numbers as 1,500 at Court, a further 1,500 in the central offices, 1,700 locally in the Bohemian and Austrian lands, 1,500 in Galicia, and 2,500 in the Hungarian lands, with perhaps 2,000 officials of the Vienna City Bank, a total of (say) 11,000 persons.[51] These results depend on a number of assumptions, and, though having partial corroboration, must be regarded as provisional. If they are of the right order of magnitude, they indicate that numbers of officials only increased slightly during the co-regency, and then largely as a result of the acquisition of Galicia. This was more or less consistent with the empress's declared intention that they should remain constant.[52] Besides those working at Court or in the government locally and centrally, there was also a growing band of persons who had done so, and had retired to draw state pensions.[53]

✳

[50] See Tables 3.2*, 3.5.

[51] HKA Kredit AA Akten, rote Nr. 1, Fsz. 1, fos. 533 ff., finance estimates for 1778. Salaries in Hungary, Croatia, the Banat, and Siebenbürgen totalling 741,028 fl. are divided by an average 300 fl. to give 2,470 persons. Salaries of 1,361,295 fl. in the Bohemian and Austrian lands are taken as 650 fl. per head (see n. 48) to give 2,094 persons. Galician salaries of 378,812 fl. are divided by a guessed 250 fl. to give 1,515 persons. The Vienna City Bank had much the same net revenue as in 1762 (above), hence is entered for 2,000 persons. The Court figure is a rounded version of that for 1761; numbers are unlikely to have been less, and were probably more. Central salaries, excluding those of ambassadors, of 1,892,226 fl. are divided by the average 1,239 fl. of 1761 to give 1,527 persons. The total is 11,106, which is rounded to 11,000 in the text.

[52] Beer, 'Die Finanzverwaltung' 293, a statement evidently made in the 1770s.

[53] From Pettenegg, loc. cit. it can be computed that in 1768 2,801 persons received 860,175 fl. in pensions, an average of 307 fl. In 1778, pensions totalled 1,199,085 fl., implying 3,905 persons if the average was unchanged. At this date, 1,752 pensions were paid by the Privy Purse (*Geheimes Kammerzahlamt*), on average 357 fl. It is likely, though not certain, that these were additional to the others. See H. Wagner, 'Royal Graces and Legal Claims', in S. B. Winter and J. Held (eds.), *Intellectual and Social Developments in the Habsburg Empire* (Boulder, Colo., 1975) 21.

The language in which state business was conducted will now be discussed. Outside the central lands of the Monarchy, French and Dutch were used in the Austrian Netherlands, with French predominant. Correspondence between Brussels and Vienna was sometimes in German, but mostly in French. In the duchies of Milan and Mantua, Italian was used, as it also was to some extent in Tyrol, Trieste, and Fiume. In Vienna, Belgian and Italian business was conducted in French and Italian, but all the main correspondence of financial departments was in German, except for that of the Hungarian and Siebenbürgen Court Chancelleries, which was in Latin.[54] Latin and Polish were from 1772 the twin official languages of Galicia.[55] German was, throughout the period, the principal language of government business in the Bohemian lands.[56] However, the Moravian 'Gouvernium' in 1748 inherited a 'Bohemian Secretary', Wenzel Trtina, from the former *Tribunal*, as well as a German Secretary. Another official, Anton Valenta, was Bohemian Registrar and 'Translator'.[57] In the same year, no less a personage than the Bohemian Chancellor, Count Friedrich Harrach, declared a knowledge of Czech to be 'extremely necessary' for councillors of the Bohemian Court Chancellery in Vienna.[58] The *Articles* of the Diet in Bohemia and Moravia were regularly printed in Czech as

---

[54] This summary is based on work in the Belgian and Austrian archives, and conforms with the statements in the literature.

[55] Examples in Glassl, *Einrichtungswerk*, 14, 26, 38, 54; *Domin-Pet.* 51. German was, however, increasingly used for ordinary government business from the mid 1770s, Glassl, 242–3.

[56] This is well documented in the literature. However, the records of the Bohemian *Statthalterei* 1577–1749, besides German series, contain a number of Latin ones, see the list of sources appended to F. Roubík, 'Místodržitelství v Čechách v letech 1577–1749', *Sborník archívních prací*, 17 (1967) 539–603. The records of the *Tribunal* in Moravia were in German from its inception, see Vašků, cit. Ch. 10, n. 26.

[57] HKA Hs. 220 (1748), fo. 107, 'Gouvernium' (i.e. *Deputation*) in Moravia. In 1752, Valenta was 'Registrator' in the Moravian *Repraesentation*, HKA Hs. 247 (1752) fo. 144^v; Trtina does not appear. He may have gone to the (now purely judicial) *Tribunal*. The *Tribunal* had a German and Bohemian secretary from 1636, and did conduct correspondence in Czech, Vašků, 55.

[58] Harrach's statement, made to block appointment of Joseph Azzoni, who had only a passing knowledge of Czech, is cited by Maasburg, *Obersten Justizstelle*, 128 n. The administrative personnel of the Bohemian Chancellery in 1740 and of the Bohemian and Austrian Chancellery in 1775, and the Agents who introduced business there, largely had German surnames. This, though inconclusive, is in contrast to the Hungarian Chancellery, whose staff, and Agents, were Hungarian throughout the period (*Court Calendar*).

well as German up to 1848.[59] The *Robot* Patent for Silesia in 1771
was printed in German, Czech, and Polish.[60] In Hungary, while the
official language of business in the public offices was Latin, the correspondence of the *Hofkammer* in Vienna with the Chamber at
Pressburg was by the 1770s predominantly in German. In August
1773, the impetuous empress actually declared that she would sign
no more Latin Chamber documents. She subsequently modified
this at the instance of the Chamber's president, Count Johannes
Erdődy, who pointed out that only one or two central councillors,
and few local officials, knew German well.[61] It seems fair to deduce
from the evidence reviewed that German was in some ways an
advancing language within the Monarchy. The success of Heinrich
Seibt as Professor of Philosophy in Prague from 1763 in promoting
German language and style perhaps symbolized this. The leading
educated men in Prague passed through his hands.[62] But currents
flowed in other directions as well. The government itself was promoting the revival of the Czech language, and allowing a newspaper
to be published in Hungarian in Pressburg (1780).[63] Given the stirrings of linguistic nationalism, the enforced promotion of German
at the expense of Latin in Hungary was likely to stimulate the
advance of the Hungarian, not the German, language—as events
proved.

Finally, at Court the use of French by the empress, her offspring,
and such favourites as Kaunitz, who 'murdered the German

---

[59] See n. 18 for the *Articles* in Czech. For those in German, see the Bibliography,
s.v.

[60] Grünberg, *Bauernbefreiung*, ii. 135–6.

[61] Nagy, *A magyar kamara* 190–1. The empress insisted, however, that salt, customs, and credit business be transacted in German in future, as well as the *Hofkammer–Kamara* correspondence. In 1782, when Joseph II put the *Kamara* under
control of the Hungarian Court Chancellery, it had to revert to Latin. This was once
more reversed with the order that all Hungarian business be in German from 1 Nov.
1784, ibid.

[62] *HGBL*, ii. 394, 406. Seibt claimed that German was the commonest language in
Bohemia. In 1767, when the question was being discussed whether the draft *Codex
Theresianus* should be translated into as many languages as the common people
spoke, it was decided that this was not necessary, since German was sufficiently
widely spread. However, it should be translated into 'Bohemian' and Italian, cit. P.
Ritter von Harrasowky, *Codex Theresianus* (Vienna 1883–4) i. 9 n.

[63] *HGBL*, ii. 395: Czech translations of religious and secular works by Friedrich
Kindermann's helpers were used in the *Normalschule* in Prague, the model school for
the entire Monarchy. The Hungarian newspaper was the *Magyar Hírmondó* or *Hungarian News Reporter*, first published on 1 Jan. 1780.

language whenever he spoke it',[64] strikingly illustrates French cultural dominance in this period, succeeding that of Italy in the previous century. The change was exemplified by the fact that Maria Theresia's pro-Italian grandfather Leopold I repudiated French as the language of the enemy.[65] Like him, however, the empress was polyglot, at home in French, Italian, and Latin, a language in which she addressed the dignitaries of Hungary, as well as German.[66]

The documentary style of government in the central lands of the Monarchy had well-marked characteristics, which seem to have been common to all departments.[67] The typical document presented to the empress was the report or *Vortrag*, signed at the end by its author but written and dated by a clerk. A 'Nota' was a less formal version. Both usually, though not invariably, began without preamble, but a cover sheet would state that the 'most submissive' ('allerunterthänigst') report was from so-and-so, or such-and-such a body, for instance the 'truly obedient' ('treugehorsam') *Hofkammer*, about a particular matter. Interdepartmentally, notes, memorials ('Erinnerungen') insinuations ('Insinuationen'), and so on, circulated. These might have a conventional starting flourish (e.g. 'in Freundschaft' or 'to show', 'Anzuzeigen') but normally were without preamble. Documents were typically written on the right-hand side of the page only, on large paper of standard size, so as to leave generous space for marginalia or royal decisions. The latter, dictated to a secretary, would be signed by Maria Theresia, sometimes by her husband or, after 1765, by Joseph II, as 'Joseph C. R.' (for Co-Regent). Royal instructions or questions would also be directed to departments in the form of a 'Hand Billet' dictated to a

---

[64] *Fürst* (*1755*) 17, who says Kaunitz did this on purpose.

[65] Bérenger, *Finances*, book I, ch. 1.

[66] See e.g. Arneth, *Gesch. Mar. Ther.* i. 270 for her address to the Hungarian deputies at Pressburg in 1741. There is much other evidence of her command of Latin, but she appears not to have known Czech or Hungarian. Joseph II was instructed in Czech, see Beales, 'Writing a life of Joseph II', 191. Joseph was also fluent in Latin, Italian, and French. Neither he nor his mother came up to Joseph I, who apparently spoke and read Czech, French, Hungarian, Italian, Latin, and Spanish, *HGBL* ii. 314 n. 26.

[67] This section is based on experience of Austrian archives. An exposition of the rules which determined what type of document was used, and how it should be drafted, has not been found, though such expositions must have existed. The subject does not appear in the literature about central government. There is a learned examination of the documentary and linguistic forms of the Moravian *Tribunal* before 1750 in Vašků, op. cit., based on careful study of its records.

secretary and signed by empress or emperor. From the death of her husband in 1765 Maria Theresia's had a heavy black border. Communications to the central departments from the various lands apparently also took the form of reports, notes, schedules, and so on. Orders to them took the forms of the 'Hof Decret', 'Verordnung' etc. discussed below.

Documents in German were written in the special German hand employed in Germany and Austria until the present century. German words occurring in a non-German text were written in a German hand, non-German words occurring in a German text were written in an Italian one; as were all communications in French, Italian, and Latin. German handwriting was still often opaque in the 1740s, but by the 1760s the best examples were much clearer, and better still by the 1780s. Even then, however, nearly illegible ones are easy to find. Penmanship flourished in the period, as official demand for writers expanded, and virtuoso flourishes and curls adorn the more important documents and accounts. Official German was peppered with un-Teutonic forms, 'practicirt', 'soldatesca' (military forces), 'differenz', 'consideriren'. Spelling, as well as forms of expression, retained a baroque flavour for much of the period. The use of *c* for *k* ('Cammer', 'Canzlist') is still observable in the 1770s. *B* still exchanged for *p*, and *t* for *d*, in the 1760s, for instance 'Partenstein's Vote', 'Teutschen Erblande', in 1763. *Steiermark* is spelt 'Steuermarkt' in official documents as late as 1775, and the Vienna City Bank's estimates were described as 'Banko Erfoderniss [for 'Erfordernis'] und Bedeckung' in 1778. The impression from the documents studied is, none the less, that by the 1780s official spelling, expression, and handwriting had become more uniform, at the centre at least, in this offering a modest parallel to political development as a whole.

Great attention was paid to filing (*Registratur*), the documents bearing multiple references to their inspection, transfer, numbering, registration, etc. The standard method of filing was to compress documents covering a given subject in a given period into a pile between stout cardboard covers. The whole would be done up with tape, and put on a shelf. The thickness of these fascicles (*Faszikeln*) varied from a few inches to two feet. Copies and 'foul drafts' inflated them. Indexes were used, for example those to the *Hoffinanzakten*, the minutes (*Protokoll*) of the *Hofkriegsrat*, or the 'Geheime Bancal Akten' of the 1760s'. The *Hoffinanzakten* to 1749 employed a subordinate form of index: a summary on the top left-hand corner of the first page of each new set of documents. The *Staatsrat* kept very careful records, with indices to the voluminous documents (*Akten*), and a *Protokoll* or digest of the decisions taken.[68] None the less, for epistolary business books and ledgers were less characteristic than in English financial government in this period, where minute-books, letter-books, contract-books, and elaborate indexes were the norm. The prolixity and confusion of Austrian records cannot have aided decision, especially as the tide of paper rose ever higher from 1750 onwards. The censuses of population, the strenuous efforts to clarify government financial accounts associated with Count Ludwig Zinzendorf and Matthias Puechberg, the impressive ledgers of the *Münz- und Bergwesen* from 1773, the consciously elaborate records of the Hungarian *Kreditkassa* from 1774, the printing of royal decrees, discussed below, to take examples, must all have been reactions to this.[69]

Government decisions took the form of a Court order: a '(Hof) Decret', 'Entschliessung', 'Patent', 'Rescript', or 'Verordnung'. Of these, only Rescripts bore the royal signature. A printed 'Patent' of the Lower Austrian *Repraesentation* about emigration, dated 15 June 1760, was addressed to 'all lords clerical and lay of whatever worth or quality in our archduchy of Lower Austria, to their judicial administrators and officials, then to the authorities of towns, markets, villages, lands'. The document was signed for the empress by the *Statthalter*, Count Franz Schrattenbach, and his chancellor, Thomas von Pöck.[70] The Court Decree '(Hof Decret', 'Hofdekret'), was a less ambitious and public document, extensively used for communication from the chancellery to such bodies as the *Repraesentationen* and their successors. A typical (handwritten) one addressed by the *Directorium* to the Lower Austrian *Repraesentation* in 1754 starts 'Von der Röm[ischen] Kays[erlichen]

---

[68] See Bittner *et al.* (eds.), *Gesamtinventar* ii, 223–30. The council's archive 1761–1848 comprised *c.* 2,000 fascicles, ibid. 229. Nearly all the *Akten* were destroyed in the Second World War, A. Coreth, 'Das Schicksal des k. k. Kabinettsarchivs seit 1945', *MÖSA* 2 (1958) 515 ff. The *Protokoll* has not been systematically used by historians. I have consulted it for a few items 1761–7.

[69] See Ch. 2 (censuses); ii, Chs. 3 (government accounts), 10 (*Kreditkassa*). The beautifully written ledgers of the *Münz- und Bergwesen* for 1773–80 comprise the *Hofkammer* series, Hss. 339–46.

[70] NÖLA Normalien 226/4470, 'Militar Aufgebotsakten 1755–71', unfoliated.

Königl[ichen] May[estät]' and ends 'Decretum per Sacram Caesareo-Regiam Mattem. in Consilio Directorii in publicis et Cameralibus', with place and date. Count Friedrich Haugwitz and three other councillors signed. Later Court Decrees were 'Decretum . . . in Consilio Cancellariae Bohemico-Austriaco Aulicae' but their format was otherwise the same.[71] The Lower Austrian *Repraesentation* responded to this flow of Court Decrees by writing an Order (*Befehl*) to the Circle offices or the City of Vienna, less often to the provincial towns, etc. In its day-to-day business, and without any prompting by Court Decree, it managed a mass of correspondence with the Vienna City Council, the *Hofkriegsrat*, the court of the *Landmarschall*, and other authorities, usually urging or insisting that the law be observed; for example on 8 February 1752 the *Repraesentation* fined the abbot of Melk 50 ducats for not keeping in repair a ford of which he was lord. This business had a marked economic emphasis.[72]

The need for an accurate record of at least the more important government orders increased as their volume expanded. This aspect of eighteenth-century Austrian practice, perhaps definable as the systematic compilation of rules and regulations, has attracted little attention compared with the better-known attempts to codify the civil law in the unfinished *Codex Theresianus*, and the criminal law in the *Constitutio Criminalis Theresiana* of 1769. It may, however, be of equal significance, since the expansion of government in the 1750s led to such proliferation of orders that there was a real risk of administrative chaos unless an accurate record could be kept. Bartenstein in 1761 informs us that Maria Theresia repeatedly requested a summary of the existing ordinances, but that no one wanted to take on this arduous task.[73] For internal use, a register of all future 'normal' financial resolutions by the empress was ordered in September 1765. It was hoped to compile a record of similar

[71] Ibid. 309/4553, 'Untertanssachen', unfoliated, *Hofdekrete* of 1754 and 1768, the latter signed by Eugenius, Count Wrbna.

[72] Based on the contents of the two cartons just cited, and on NÖLA NÖ Regierung in Publicis 1749–52, i, a typed catalogue of the *Akten* of the Lower Austrian government (called 'Repraesentation und Kammer' from May 1751). There is no second volume. The abbot of Melk's fine is recorded on p. 83. Communications by the Lower Austrian government to the Chancellery are less common, but there is a series of the 1770s in Karton 309/4553, second bundle.

[73] Prokeš, 'Boj', 38.

resolutions from 1748 to 1764.[74] The same wish for a record, in this case a public one, must lie behind the publication by Sebastian Herrenleben in 1748 and 1752 of two stout volumes of 'Austrian laws and ordinances as these have from time to time issued and been published'. They were intended as supplements to the comparable collection of 1704, the 'Codex Austriacus', also in two volumes, which mostly contained ordinances of Leopold I.[75] Herrenleben's work, however, only covered decrees up to the death of Charles VI. It had chronological and subject indexes. It was not until 1777 that a further two volumes of 'Generalien, Patenten, Satz-Ordnungen, Rescripten, Resolutionen', and so on from 1740 to the end of 1770 appeared, thanks to the labours of Baron Thomas von Pöck, Chancellor of the Lower Austrian *Regierung*.[76] He entitled these 'Supplementum Codicis Austriaci', and, like Herrenleben, included careful chronological and subject indexes. In 1787, another collection, professing to cover 'all ordinances and laws' between 1740 and 1780 which were still of validity, was published anonymously in eight volumes by J. Kropatschek as a companion to a comparable edition of the ordinances of Joseph II.[77]

In comparison with Pöck, Kropatschek is thinner before 1765, especially for the war years 1740–8 and 1756–63, but otherwise there is considerable overlap between the two collections. None of

[74] Cit. Beer, 'Die Finanzverwaltung', 290, noted as a decision of the 'Finanzstellen' on 14 Sept. 1765. *Normalresolutionen* were presumably those establishing an issue of principle. Nothing seems to have come of this project. Cf., however, the commercial series for 1764–76, Ch. 9, n. 123. According to Bittner *et al.* ii. 155, a *Protokoll* for the royal *Handbilletten* was introduced by Joseph II in 1780. This generalized the separate register of his *Handbilletten* as co-regent, which he had kept since 1 Nov. 1774, ibid. 162. A more general *Protokoll* of all his business as co-regent went back to 1766, ibid.

[75] *Codicis Austriaci ordine alphabetico compilati Pars prima . . . secunda . . .* (Vienna 1704); *Sammlung oesterreichischer Gesetze und Ordnungen wie solche von Zeit zu Zeit ergangen und publiciret worden* (Leipzig 1748, Vienna 1752). The second volume has Sebastian Gottlieb Herrenleben's name as editor. The first volume covered decrees to 1720, the second those to 1740.

[76] Thos. Ignaz Freiherr von Pöck, *Supplementum Codicis Austriaci oder Chronologische Sammlung . . . Generalien, Patenten, Satz-Ordnungen, Rescripten, Resolutionen . . .* (Vienna 1777). The whole series from 1704 is usually referred to as the *Codex Austriacus*; this is convenient rather than accurate.

[77] *Sammlung*, arranged chronologically, with an index volume; Anon., *Vollständige Sammlung aller seit dem Regierungsantritt Joseph des Zweyten f. die k k Erbländer engangenen Verordnungen u. Gesetze* (Vienna 1788–91), also arranged chronologically, with a two-volume index.

these editions extended to the Hungarian lands, and a comparable contemporary series there has not been traced. However, government business in Hungary greatly expanded in this period, as is shown below from other sources.[78]

The annual number of published decrees outside the Hungarian lands for the years 1730–89 is shown in Table 11.5, which for the years before 1771 takes Pöck's figures and from 1771 Kropatschek's.[79] With all due reservation about the nature of the sources, which must omit many decrees, it seems clear that government activity, measured by this rather crude index, increased considerably, if erratically, during Maria Theresia's reign. During its first decade, 1741–50, the annual average number of published decrees was only thirty-six, much the same as the average thirty-one of 1731–40. From 1751 to 1760, the annual average was sixty-eight, from 1761 to 1770 100, from 1771 to 1780 ninety-six. The acceleration from 1750 fits well with the unanimous criticism of the leading officers of state in 1761 that the creation of the *Directorium*, and then the Seven Years War, led to an explosion of government directives. It seems fair to assume that administrative paper increased during the war, though the number of decrees fell. The abolition of the *Directorium* in 1761, and then the peace, did not reverse this process. Growth continued during the co-regency, and by the end of the empress's reign the output of decrees was three times that of the 1740s, easily outstripping the growth of population. Perhaps the most striking feature of the table, however, is the even more marked contrast between the reign of Joseph II and that of his mother. From December 1780, the curve of legislation changes its slope almost vertically. The total number of decrees listed for 1780–9, 6,206, is more than double the 3,017 of 1741–80. The annual Josephine average is 690. These figures, even though the average decree was now shorter, dramatically confirm the received view of Joseph's

---

[78] I. Kassics, *Enchiridium seu extractus benignarum normalium ordinationum regiarum* (Budapest 1825), which is arranged alphabetically, seems to be the source for B. Grünwald's statement that 2,340 decrees were published for Hungary under Maria Theresia and 5,000 under Francis I, cit. Király, *Hungary in the Late Eighteenth Century*, 97 n. From a rough page-count in Kassics, the figures are 2,408 decrees for 1713–80 (few, in fact, before 1740), 1,253 for 1780–90, 5,054 for 1790–1823 (only).

[79] In many instances patents were published in the same form but with different places of origin and different dates. In the collections, only one text is given in such cases.

TABLE 11.4. *Number of government decrees published annually, 1730–89 (excluding Hungarian lands)*

1730	31	1740	41	1750	66	1760	55	1770	124	1780	58 + 24
1731	35	1741	25	1751	61	1761	90	1771	100	1781	402
1732	35	1742	19	1752	84	1762	91	1772	110	1782	603
1733	29	1743	36	1753	86	1763	105	1773	105	1783	601
1734	22	1744	25	1754	92	1764	93	1774	86	1784	775
1735	21	1745	34	1755	67	1765	96	1775	116	1785	846
1736	33	1746	30	1756	68	1766	140	1776	112	1786	756
1737	40	1747	27	1757	47	1767	90	1777	72	1787	735
1738	30	1748	44	1758	58	1768	103	1778	116	1788	712
1739	29	1749	55	1759	64	1769	88	1779	93	1789	752

Sources: Thomas von Pöck, *Supplementum Codicis Austriaci* [1740–70], (Vienna 1777); Kropatschek, *Sammlung* (Vienna 1787), Anon., *Vollständige Sammlung* (Vienna 1788–91).

energies. The arrangements for digesting and listing the contents of his spate of laws were also praiseworthy, if somewhat belated.[80]

A number of other pieces of evidence confirms the increase in the pace of government activity under Maria Theresia. In the early nineteenth century, it was stated that the archive of the Bohemian and Austrian Chancellery, which inherited the records of the separate Bohemian and Austrian chancelleries from 1527, comprised over 2,000 fascicles to 1748, and 7,754 to 1792, implying that roughly 5,500 fascicles of documents were compiled between 1748 and 1792.[81] Similarly, the *Hofkriegsrat* generated five fascicles a year before 1748, 20 in 1748, 40 in 1763, 70 in 1767, over 100 in 1770.[82] The *Staatsrat* was considering over 3,000 items annually in the 1760s.[83] In Hungary, the Council of Lieutenancy made a return to the Palatine in 1807 of letters it had received from outside since its inception in 1724. These were divided into royal, presumably largely consisting of instructions and questions, which statistically were quite small, and those from elsewhere, typically other organs of government. The results, which have been published by Ember,

[80] I am indebted to the staff of the *Katalogabteilung* of the Österreichische Nationalbibliothek for extracting the annual Josephine totals. The *Vollständige Sammlung* is in their view not by Kropatschek, despite its resemblance to his collection for 1740–80. The average Josephine decree covered one page, compared to two under Maria Theresia.

[81] *Inventar des allgemeinen Archivs des Ministeriums des Innern* (Inventare Österreichischer staatlicher Archive 1, Vienna 1909) 8.

[82] *Inventar des Kriegsarchivs Wien*, i (Inventare Österreichischer staatlicher Archive 8, Vienna 1953) 125.

[83] Thus in 1764 there were 3,390 items, HHSA Staatsrat Protokoll. Other years were similar.

can be summarized for this period to show the average annual number of documents received.[84] From 1741 to 1750 the annual averages were 431 royal and 1,976 other, or 2407 in all. From 1751 to 1760, the figures were 621, 3,159, and 3,780; from 1761 to 1770, 451, 4,741, and 5,192; from 1771 to 1780, 803, 9,669, and 10,472; and in 1781–3, 977, 15,202, and 16,179.[84] The almost exponential expansion of Hungarian business towards the close of Maria Theresia's reign must be accounted for by the urbarial, educational, and financial preoccupations of that decade.[85] It foreshadowed the even faster acceleration under Joseph II, 17,373 documents being received in 1783. Ember's supposition that internally generated documents exceeded these in number is confirmed by the fact that 29,155 were registered in 1790, the first year for which separate figures are available.[86]

The increase of executive business under Maria Theresia appears to have only a rather weak parallel in judicial business until the 1770s, if Maasburg's table of annually 'completed items' in the supreme court, the *Oberste Justizstelle*, is taken as an index for judicial work as a whole. The figures were 4,389 in 1749 (the first year), 3,148 in 1755, 4,241 in 1760, 4,776 in 1765, 4,388 in 1770, 5,782 in 1775, 5,696 in 1780. The annual average for 1775–83 inclusive was 5,595. It actually fell as a result of Joseph II's reconstruction of the court (an annual average of 4,584 in 1784–9). Most business was criminal, not civil. One quarter of all cases in the years 1764–74 were revenue ones. However, these data are inconclusive, since they are compatible with a vigorous expansion of work in lower courts, blocked by accumulating arrears at the top. This subject, like others, remains uninvestigated.[87]

The increase of government business put increasing pressure on the Crown, as well as on its officials. There were already bitter complaints under the *Directorium* about 'much writing' (*Vielschreiberei*).[88] The revision of government structures in 1760–2 did not

---

[84] Ember, *A M. kir. helytartótanács*, 57–8. There is a defective version of this return in Schwartner, *Statistik*, pt. iii, p. 233.

[85] Ember, 59 suggests urbarial and educational concerns. Finance seems an obvious addition. A precise definition of the difference between royal and other documents is lacking.

[86] Ibid. 128–9, statistics of the *protocolla exhibitorum* of the Council of Lieutenancy.

[87] Maasburg, *Obersten Justizstelle*, table at pp. 62–9.

[88] Prokeš, 22, Bartenstein's memorial of 21 Jan. 1756.

solve the problem, and may have accentuated it. In October 1768 the empress demanded to know how *Vielschreiberei* could be cut down, business be speeded up, more be despatched locally rather than centrally. Prince Starhemberg presided at a meeting of the *Staatsrat* on 6 December 1768 which considered the question, but no effective conclusion was reached.[89] The same subject was broached again in 1771 as part of the extended and often bitter debate about the organization of central government which took up much of the year.[90] The Bohemian and Austrian Chancellor, Count Rudolf Chotek, in his *Vortrag* of 14 January 1771, listed fifteen classes of business which resulted in reports being made to the Crown, but claimed that the main cause of the mass of paper was the division of local financial business between so many departments, all of which sent in their own statements of fact and opinion. Some of these went to more than one central department. The chancellery tried to stem the flow, but in 1770, for example, the empress had had to read 773 reports. However, Chotek pointed out, half were compiled because she had asked for information, or communicated a projector's proposals. Most of the latter were valueless, and should in future be kept at subordinate level. As President of the Council of Trade, Chotek listed a further fifteen categories of business which involved making reports to the Crown. Some of these appear quite trivial, for example nomination of clerks, charitable donations, and small loans and grants. The minutes of the chancellery and council were also sent weekly to Court. Chotek thought much of this could be delegated in future, so that the empress was not bothered with it.[91]

Similar information and arguments were deployed by the great Friedrich Anton Hatzfeld in one section of his long and ambitious paper on the restructuring of central government, dated 5 February 1771. He proposed applying generally the methods which he had already introduced successfully into the *Hofkammer* and Bank. One-third of all business there was done by circulation of papers, including extracts of minutes, to the relevant members, who approved those which were uncontroversial, and brought the remainder to meetings. These fell into two categories: routine,

---

[89] Beer, 'Die Finanzverwaltung', 256.
[90] Cf. pp. 248–9.
[91] Chotek's two *Vorträge*, dated 14 and 19 Jan. 1771, are in HKA Hs. 736 no. 4. Both show a sharp mind at work, even though Chotek had recently had a stroke.

where the president could be absent, and those involving policy, large expenditure, reports to the empress, and so on. Hatzfeld was confident that the technique of circulation, without meetings, could profitably be extended.[92]

The difficulties exposed by these discussions show that at this stage, less than a decade before Maria Theresia's death, there was already a strong tendency for the ruler to be swamped by the growing volume of state business, which clearly had marked financial emphasis. The acquisition of Galicia in 1772 cannot have helped this situation. All large-scale organization depends for its effectiveness on delegating work as fully as is consistent with retention of central control. Only in this way can those at the centre free themselves to consider policy. On the face of the record, Maria Theresia had not solved this problem, and made it worse by a compulsive interest in minutiae. The position of Joseph II before 1780 is hard to gauge. In his printed correspondence at this period he is concerned with the defective structure of government, and the personal faults of nearly everyone involved in it. His interest in the agenda of administration seems to have been confined to an obsessive concern with the procedures of the *Staatsrat*. No doubt his passion for efficiency found its true outlet in military administration.

The increasing flow of government ordinances almost inevitably led to local confusion about their meaning and interpretation. In April 1771 the recently created *Staatswirtschaftsdeputation* held a discussion on the subject.[93] This was based on reports from the localities about how royal patents could be made better known to the subjects ('Unterthanen'), and more intelligible. The Inner Austrian government stated that publication from the pulpit was contrary to treaty with Salzburg. Instead, patents should be announced with drumbeat at the five (Styrian) Circle offices, then affixed in suitable places. Upper Austria wanted merely to publish the titles of patents quarterly. Lower Austria suggested that the Circle offices tell the village officers (*Dorfrichter*) the content of patents, and

---

[92] HKA Kredit AA Akten, rote Nr. 12, Fsz. 7, no. 8, 'Akten betreffend die Zusammenziehung verschiedener Dikasterien . . . 1771'. The document referred to in the text is at fos. 139 ff., unsigned and undated, but clearly Hatzfeld's *Vortrag* of 5 Feb. Beer, 'Die Finanzverwaltung' 258 summarizes its political content, a proposed personal union of the Chancellery and finance offices, but not its procedural suggestions.

[93] HHSA Nachl. Zinz., Hs. 127, 'Staatswirtschaftsdeputation', unfoliated, under 25 Apr. 1771.

make them enforce them. Tyrol 'insisted on the customary method of lordships allowing ordinances (*Verordnungen*) to be read, and an extract made for each village, with the principal ordinances entered in the calendar'. Count Ludwig Zinzendorf, the reporter of this discussion, notes that it was agreed that 'certainly subjects must not be punished for breaking laws not properly made known to them', and that it would be best to print patents in future, and make extracts from ordinances. For Bohemia, 'where everything is done through the Circle Captains', it was ordered that each lordship keep a register of patents, which the Circle Captain could inspect during his visitation. Sworn persons briefed by the clergy would read out and explain the patents on Sundays and Holy Days. Extracts of the passages needed for the peasants should be made. In the case of the Free Peasants ('Freybauern'), these should be sent to the oldest member in each Bohemian Circle for him to make known to the others. As to ordinances, the senior peasant in each community ('Die Vorsteher der unterthänigen-Gemeinden') should collect the new ones from their lord's offices monthly. It was observed that until now in Bohemia ordinances were taken by the Circle messenger to each lordship, which made a copy but was usually dilatory in publishing the contents. In Lower Austria, too, messengers took the latest official ordinances round the various lordships. This discussion, which unfortunately is not continued in the source, indicates that the Austrian government, perhaps not surprisingly, had difficulty in communicating its increasingly complex intentions to the lower levels of administration and to the manorial peasantry. The Hobbesian characteristics of law, authenticity, clarity, communicability, proved elusive. This presumably widened the opening for uninformed rumours about government policy, such as those of emancipation which circulated among the Bohemian peasants in the early 1770s.[94]

Lastly, the general structure of the government ordinances which were the final product of the many discussions and endless *paperasserie* at both the centre and the circumference of power, should be briefly set out. Kropatschek's thoughtful inclusion of an index volume to his collection of decrees, which can be treated as a large sample of all the decrees passed, makes it possible to construct a statistical profile of government edicts under Maria Theresia. His

[94] Cf. pp. 123, 128–9.

TABLE 11.5. *Analysis of 2,674 government rules, 1740–80*

(*a*)	Police and public order	825
(*b*)	Commerce	443
(*c*)	Coinage, post, hunting, Jews, etc. ('Kameralgegenstände')	301
(*d*)	Military, including census	295
(*e*)	Contribution, labour services and connected subjects	203
(*f*)	Clergy	190
(*g*)	Legal	165
(*h*)	Education, censorship	140
(*i*)	Instructions for officials	112
	Total	2,674

Source: Kropatschek, *Sammlung*, ix, 'Hauptelenchus'.

index extracted 2,674 rules from the 2,229 decrees he listed, since several of the latter covered more than one subject (see Table 11.5). The conclusions these figures suggest are subject to reservations. The collection was of laws 'still existing or partly altered' in the 1780s, hence is short on the relatively evanescent legislation of the war years. Section (*d*) in the table is therefore understated.[95] The criteria that determined whether a government decision was published are not clear, hence the published record does not necessarily weight different categories of business correctly. Numbers are in any case not necessarily identical with importance. Leading decisions about tax, or the status of the clergy, presumably counted for more than fifty decrees about vagrancy or games of chance. Further, decrees were of varying length and complexity. Certain inferences are, however, allowable. The importance of fiscal and economic business is undoubted, given that (*a*), police and public order, included such subjects as the sale of food, markets, weights and measures, rates of interest and so on. If (*b*), commerce ('Kommerziensachen'), and the coinage decrees in (*c*), accounting for one-third of those listed, are added, together with the important body of rules (*e*) about the Contribution, something approaching half the total is accounted for. Many other decrees had economic aspects. A sense of proportion must, of course, be observed. No doubt practically any state decision can be said to have economic implications. None the less, the importance of this aspect of government is strik-

---

[95] Analysis of the contents of the *Codex Austriacus* for sample years shows the same basic pattern as Kropatschek's, but with more military business.

ing, and tends to confirm the opinion, a cliché well before Burke, that the age was one of 'sophisters, œconomists and calculators'. The reservation to this in an Austrian context is that it was fiscal and financial matters, as much as purely economic ones, which absorbed government time, and royal attention.[96]

What conclusions about Austrian government can be reached from the evidence reviewed in this and the preceding chapter? The empress's central position, her political will, and her commitment to reform, are clear. Many further examples will be found later. The shares of Joseph II as co-regent, and of Kaunitz as councillor and friend, and her own tendency to become submerged in the increasing press of state business, qualify, but do not invalidate, her leading role. But it is clear that Maria Theresia can only with difficulty be treated as an exponent of the enlightened absolutism often attributed to her. This is in distinction to many of her advisers, most notably Joseph, who often held advanced opinions, though not always consistently. As her memorials of 1750 and 1756 showed, she believed her power came from God, must be justified, and was removable. She emphasized her duty to rule as mother of her peoples, but quite evidently did not consider that her authority derived from them. She spoke of 'my House' rather than of the state. Her hostility to religious toleration, her anti-Semitism, her detestation of the French Enlightenment, were evident. Though fully prepared to reform the Catholic church, she at all stages wished to carry the papacy with her. She was ready to cut down the pretensions of the Estates, but was horrified at Joseph's hostility to social hierarchy. She strongly believed in justice in the conduct of both domestic and foreign affairs, as her coinage motto, 'Justitia et clementia', indicated. All this in some ways marks her as an active feudal monarch, rather than as a paladin of the Enlightenment. It is in obvious contrast to the position set out in Frederick II's *Political Testament* of 1752 and its later variants.

The empress's government was not politically innocent or uncalculated, however. In terms of grand strategy, the 'union' of the Bohemian and Austrian lands from 1749, and the accompanying reconstruction of Bohemian–Austrian administration, somewhat

[96] The *Staatsrat* agenda for 1761–6 summarized by Schlitter, *Khev.-Metsch 1764–7*, 555 ff., show that financial business came first, and industrial and commercial business next, with territorial and jurisdictional disputes following.

stridently insisted upon by Friedrich Walter, were a central part of
her political achievement.[97] Her refusal to allow a separate Bohemian senate within the new Bohemian and Austrian Chancellery in
1762 was significant of her intentions.[98] It will be seen in later
chapters that tougher rules for the Contribution were enforced in
the Bohemian than in the Austrian lands.[99] In general, the empress
does not seem to have forgotten, or entirely forgiven, the events of
1741–2 in Bohemia. For Hungary, in contrast, as noted above, she
had an evident inclination, also dating from that first crisis of her
reign. The Hungarian lands were excluded from the reforms of
1749. The nomination of Batthyány as *Ajo* to Crown Prince Joseph,
the greater scope of the Hungarian Chamber from 1748–9, the
establishment of the Order of St Stephen in 1764, the retrocession of
Fiume to Hungary in 1776, and of the Banat of Temesvár in 1778,
were all gestures of varying importance towards Hungarian susceptibilities. In qualification can be set the fierce struggles over taxes in
the Diets of 1751 and 1764–5, the tariff of 1754, and the refusal to
favour the development of Hungarian industry. Similarly, the
special status of the Banat and of Fiume, and the retention of Siebenbürgen as a separate concern, were important examples of the
empress's inclination not to concede too much or too quickly. A
further instance of her sense of political realities was her consistently cautious attitude to the touchy Tyrol. The separate status of
the Austrian Netherlands, 'le seul pays heureux et qui nous a fourni
tant de ressources', as she described them shortly before her death,
and of Lombardy, both areas managed by Kaunitz almost as private
fiefs, were others. The imposition of a 'German' pattern of control
on Galicia from 1772, and the creation of a Galician senate within
the chancellery in 1776, perhaps pointed in the opposite direction.[100]

Financial and military considerations dominated the institutional

[97] Walter's views of the creation of the *Kernstaat* of Austrian–Bohemian lands in
1749, and Haugwitz's abolition of the partition wall ('Scheidewand') between Austria and the Bohemian lands are expressed in the short final chapter of his *Geschichte*
(1938), and in all his subsequent publications, down to and including his posthumously published *Österreichische Verfassungs- und Verwaltungsgeschichte von
1500–1955* (Vienna 1972).

[98] See p. 235.

[99] See ii, Chs. 6–7.

[100] Maria Theresia to Joseph II, 22 July 1780, Arneth, *Mar. Ther. Kinder und
Freunde*, i. 1.

reforms described here. But reform was hampered by muddle and confusion, neat diagrams envisaged by a Haugwitz, a Kaunitz, a Hatzfeld, fragmenting under pressure into complex and untidy patterns. A trend towards concentration, symbolized by the *Directorium*, or Hatzfeld's ambitious plan of June 1771, was matched by a tendency towards proliferation, new bodies being created *ad hoc* for new branches of administration. Even when schemes for tightening control were carried through, as in May 1765 or December 1771, the result seems often to have been not to facilitate the exercise of power, but to paralyse it. The management constraints on various types of large-scale organization were discovered by trial, or, more usually, error, rather than foreseen. Argument and debate, far from diminishing as the power of the state expanded during the reign, notably increased, symbolized by the absurdly long meetings of the *Staatsrat*; and the institutional warfare of which the empress complained so bitterly in the 1740s was equally the subject of concern and inquiry two decades later.

Much of this confusion derived from the fact that the structure of civil government was collegiate, both centrally and locally, and that individually exercised authority and initiative, such as those of the French *Intendant*, or the English JP, were not characteristic of it. Royal commissaries, like Haugwitz in Carinthia and Krain in 1747, Count Rudolf Chotek in Tyrol in 1744 and Styria in 1748, Baron Larisch in Bohemia in 1750–1, Baron Brukenthal in Siebenbürgen in 1769 and 1774, Count Leopold Kollowrat in Bohemia in 1775, exercised great, but temporary, power. The initiative of Circle Captains, of town captains, was restrained by the royal *Gubernien*, which were in turn restrained by Vienna. In Vienna, the *capi* restrained, or frustrated, each other. The idea of a Prime Minister was not acceptable, and those with pretensions in this direction, like Kaunitz or Hatzfeld, were bitterly attacked. The *Staatsrat* was supposed to act as a collective Prime Minister. Business was usually conducted round a table, and policy was hammered out by consultation, or warfare, between departments. A further characteristic is that it was typically prepared and defended on paper, rather than verbally. Oral exposition in council seems mainly to have consisted in reading a set proposal or the rebuttal of one, or in monologues, rather than in the cut and thrust of debate. Oratory, a crucial dimension of English or American government in this period, was conspicuous by its absence, and was presumably reserved for the pulpit.

Discussion, or intrigue, with the sovereign or others, on the other hand, was undoubtedly of great importance, as it always is in closed political systems. These generalizations apply with less force to Hungary, since clearly the county system left much room for local discussion and initiative. The Hungarian Diets, though sparsely held, also offered a forum for argument and complaint, though the shocked attitude of the empress's ministers to these debates showed how rarely they encountered them.[101]

There was much emphasis on form and deliberation, rather than speed. 'The Austrians', Lord Stormont reported in 1770, 'are apt to be very dilatory in all Business that does not require immediate despatch.'[102] Government was also mysterious and secretive. Its results were promulgated to subjects, usually with a tincture of propaganda, but the often acrimoniously debated grounds for policy were kept hidden. This was true even within the administration. A few top people knew much, many lesser ones not much, outside their own sphere. As eminent a minister as Hatzfeld wanted to enter the *Staatsrat* in 1771 partly to be able to inform himself of military and Hungarian affairs. As for the general public, the censorship ensured regular vetting of books and newspapers; the latter were vapid and dominated by official announcements. Government statistics of revenue, trade, and population were closely guarded. Public debate on public issues was thus not to be expected; nor was the idea of it welcome to a regime which regarded government as coming from above.

All this was quite compatible with the headlong assertion of royal will, as in Maria Theresia's support of the policies of Haugwitz and Kaunitz before 1756, or in Joseph II's support of those of Lacy a decade later. It may even have required it, as a counterweight to institutional torpor and obstruction. It was compatible, too, with empire-building by a string of ambitious ministers. The structure and style of government, however, ensured that such careers, and many lesser ones, aroused enmity, and proceeded in an atmosphere of often rancorous jealousy and recrimination. This state of affairs was already well known under Charles VI, and the rivalry between Haugwitz and Harrach, between Bartenstein and Kaunitz, between

---

[101] See for example Baron Borié in 1764 on the 'stolze Licentiösität' of the Hungarian Diet, which would give a bad example to other *Länder*, Ember, 'Der österreichische Staatsrat', *Acta Hist.* 6 (1959) 367.

[102] PRO SP 80/207, Stormont to Rochford, 24 Mar. 1770.

Hatzfeld and Zinzendorf, between Brukenthal and nearly everyone, showed that it lost none of its bitterness under Maria Theresia. The steam built up in English politics could be released through debate in Parliament, however wounding and disturbing the consequences to individuals. In Austria, there was no safety-valve. Bitter memoranda, personal intrigue, were an inadequate substitute. This element of neurosis at the centre of affairs was perhaps accentuated by the narrow, dark streets of Vienna, and by the surrounding city walls. It could be dissipated by the extravagances of religion, by music, by eating and drinking too much, by amorous intrigue. The more athletic hunted, hawked, or went and dined in Pressburg.[103]

Lastly, the Estates were not the ciphers they usually appear as in the literature, and played a quite important part in government. The Seven Years War actually strengthened their position. Officials employed by them, and, in particular, by towns and lordships, were the characteristic executants of government policy. 'Bureaucracy' was thus partly manorial, as in Prussia. The extent to which absolute monarchy could convey and implement its intentions must have been restricted by this, as by the substantial illiteracy at the base of society, which necessitated verbal communication of government orders. The episodic patterns of social behaviour noted in Ch. 6 were a further constraint on effective administration. The increasing volume of royal decrees in the period after 1763 must have made the whole situation worse. As his memoranda show, Joseph II was well aware of all this; and determined to do something about it once his hands were free.

---

[103] *Fürst (1755)* 32 for the popularity of such day-trips. The ministerial rivalries are documented in later chapters.

12

Councillors of State I

AFTER the exposition of structures of government in the previous chapters, some conclusions about personnel are attempted in this and the next. The literature is free with abstractions about bureaucracy, Enlightenment, middle-class officials and so on, but usually gives biographical details only for leading men such as Bartenstein, Haugwitz, and Kaunitz. Biographical dictionaries, principally Wurzbach, also treat officialdom episodically, and often inaccurately. However, Payer von Thurn in 1902 and 1906 provided the names of court and departmental chiefs in the period 1657–1848, and there are further lists (to 1749) in the earliest volume (1907) of the series *Die österreichische Zentralverwaltung*. Pioneering work was done by Maasburg in 1891 for the *Oberste Justizstelle*, by Gschliesser in 1942 for the *Reichshofrat*, a training-ground for other departments, by Starzer in 1897 for the *Regierung* of Lower Austria, and by Thiel in 1916 and 1930 for Inner Austria, though to 1749 only. Ember in 1940 and Fallenbüchl in 1970 provided lists for the Hungarian Council of Lieutenancy and Hungarian *Hofkammer* respectively. Most recently, Dr Hassenpflug-Elzholz has reached important conclusions about Bohemian office-holding in and before 1741. As a source, the *Court Calendar* affords ample, on the whole reliable, information about the membership of government councils, and Mergerle von Mühlfeld's *Oesterreichisches Adels-Lexikon* (1822–4) is also helpful.[1] While the quality of the data is patchy, therefore, the subject is worth pursuing. The method

---

[1] For these works, see the Bibliography. Payer von Thurn's two schedules are scarce. A precursor is Auersperg, *Geschichte des königlichen böhmischen Appellationsgerichtes*, which gives the names of the councillors and officials of the court since its foundation in 1548. The *Court Calendar* has been found to be accurate whenever it can be checked against MS sources. However, it is episodic in its coverage, and imprecise about dates of office-holding. A modern biographical approach which has attracted some attention is N. von Preradovich, *Die Führungsschichten in Österreich und Preussen (1804–1918) mit einen Ausblick bis zum Jahre 1945* (Wiesbaden 1955). This also proceeds from the *Court Calendar* at selected dates, but it is not clear that it gives enough names to validate the conclusions suggested in it.

adopted in these chapters is to examine at different dates (1740, 1748–54, 1763–5, 1775–9) the councillors of the leading civil offices with financial responsibility at the centre, and locally. An attempt is then made to reach some general conclusions. The method is crude and selective, and inevitably inexact, but, it is hoped, offers a proxy for a more extensive investigation. It will be argued that the initial tone of government was aristocratic, both centrally and elsewhere. By the mid 1770s this was less true at the centre, where career officials, often with legal training, had become prominent. At a local level, the administrative revolution of 1748–9 led to the introduction of many new men, often of mixed origin. There was then a recovery, and by the end of the reign local government was once more largely in aristocratic hands. Hungarian government was controlled by magnates and, notably, the nobility throughout the period. Here, in contrast to the other lands, the Catholic church was formally conceded a role in executive business.

The first lists of office-holders (Table 12.1*) show the membership in 1740 of the Privy Conference, the four court chancelleries, and the three leading financial councils: the Finance Conference, Bank Deputation, and *Hofkammer*. The councillors of the Conference at this date, who, perhaps emphasizing the personal character of this body, are not listed in the *Court Calendar*, were a mixture of courtiers, soldiers, and administrators. Count Alois Harrach, *Landmarschall* of Lower Austria from 1715, viceroy in Naples 1728–33, Conference Minister 1734, also a member of the Finance Conference, was the father of Counts Friedrich and Ferdinand. The latter (1707–78) was *Landmarschall* in succession to his father from 1744, governor of Milan 1747–50, then, after one year as head of the *Oberste Justizstelle*, president of the *Reichshofrat* until his death. His brother Friedrich (1696–1749), after entering the *Reichshofrat*, became *Obrist-Hofmeister* (1732–45) to Charles VI's sister, Maria Elizabeth, governess of the Austrian Netherlands. In 1745 he succeeded Count Philipp Kinsky as Bohemian Chancellor, and was made a Conference Minister. His stubborn opposition as Chancellor to Haugwitz's proposals for reform is examined elsewhere. English ministers in Vienna thought him 'incontestably the Man of the best sense of this Court' (1745) and 'much the ablest Man in the Ministry' (1749). He died of smallpox on 4 June 1749. Count

Khevenhüller on this occasion recorded that he was one of the cleverest and most active of the empress's ministers. He had set his face against the present spirit of innovation. He loved argument for its own sake, and made enemies by it. Until recently he had been an intriguer with women. He married Princess Liechtenstein in 1719. She died in 1741, having presented him with 16 children. Alois Harrach's brother Joseph, the next name in the Conference list of 1740, was president of the *Hofkriegsrat* from 1738 to 30 January 1762, when he was induced to retire, aged eighty-four. Königsegg, President of the *Hofkriegsrat* to 1738, and commander, under Francis Stephen, in the recent Turkish campaigns, was the dowager empress's *Hofmeister*. He subsequently (12 January 1747) became *Erster Hofmeister*, on the death of Count Sigmund Sinzendorf, who had served since 1724. Königsegg died in office on 8 December 1751.

Another member, Starhemberg, and the Conference's secretary, Bartenstein, are considered below. The remaining Conference minister was Count Philipp Sinzendorf (1671–1742), First Austrian Chancellor, and officially responsible for foreign policy, though in practice Bartenstein also had considerable influence. Sinzendorf's name introduces the second institution listed in the table, the Austrian Chancellery. Like Gundaker Starhemberg, Königsegg-Erps, and Hatzfeld, he was at first destined for the church, but embarked on a secular career when his elder brother was killed in the Turkish wars (1687). He served in the same campaigns, was ambassador to France at 30, second Austrian Chancellor 1705–15, then senior Chancellor. He was, stated Maria Theresia in 1750, 'a great minister, but I did not trust him'. The parallels and contrasts between his career and that of Kaunitz would bear exploration.[2] Sinzendorf's Second Chancellor, responsible for internal Austrian affairs, was Count Johann Seilern II (1675–1751), the nephew and

---

[2] There is a sketch of Friedrich Harrach's career in Arneth, *Gesch. Mar. Ther.* iv. 15, a short notice in Wurzbach, a longer one in *NDB*. *Khev.-Metsch* erroneously gives 4 May 1749 for the date of his death, but supplies further biographical details. For the English ministers' comments, see PRO SP 80/171, Robinson to Harrington 20 Nov. 1745; SP 80/182, Keith to Newcastle 29 Jan. 1749. For Sinzendorf see Wurzbach, also Arneth, i. 62, 65, who argues that he was self-interested and perhaps corrupt. He was the son of Count Georg, the *Hofkammer* president dismissed for peculation by Leopold I. Maria Theresia's view is expressed in her memorial of 1750.

adopted son of Count Johann Seilern I. The latter, a converted Protestant from the Rhine Palatinate, was Austrian First Chancellor from 1705 until his death in 1715. Johann II was a diplomat (Ryswick 1697, Baden 1714), a councillor in the Austrian Chancellery, then (1733–5) president of the college of commerce at Trieste, before becoming Austrian Second Chancellor in 1735, and sole Chancellor in 1742, when the separate office of *Hof- und Staats-Kanzler* was created, and filled by Count Corfiz Ulfeld. Seilern was named the first president of the *Oberste Justizstelle* (1 May 1749), but was unsympathetic to Haugwitz's reforms, resigned almost at once (1 January 1750), and died on 18 June 1751. The Seilerns were on Count Khevenhüller's list of politicians of low extraction.[3] Of the councillors in the Austrian Chancellery under Seilern, Baron Anton Franz Buol (1699–1767), the son of *Hofrat* Johann Georg von Buol, created a baron in 1718, had entered the Lower Austrian *Regierung* in 1723 and the Austrian Chancellery in 1727. From the *Oberste Justizstelle* (1749) he moved to the *Directorium in Publicis et Cameralibus* in 1751, then returned to the *Regierung* to become *Vice-Statthalter* in 1760. He was closely concerned in the compilation of the *Codex Theresianus*, was one of the learned men of his age, and left a library of 12,000 books.[4] Carl Cetto von Kronstorf became a councillor of the *Directorium* in May 1750, then of the Bohemian and Austrian Chancellery.[5] Carl Holler von Doblhof was Johann Bartenstein's brother-in-law, and, like Buol and Cetto, became a councillor of the *Directorium*. His patent of knighthood (1757) speaks of his 'old noble descent', but it seems plausible that he was in fact the son of Franz Holler, professor of medicine at Innsbruck, who was personal physician to Joseph I and Charles VI, and was knighted as 'von Dobelhof' (*sic*) in 1706. Carl Holler von Doblhof (d. 1767) played a role of some importance in Austria's negotiations with England for a commercial treaty 1739–46. He was a trusted confidant of Maria Theresia in the early 1740s. In 1757 he inherited the property and name of another councillor of

---

[3] Maasburg, 70–1 with some corrections. The 'college of commerce' was perhaps the *Intendenza Commerciale*, which was at Laibach, not Trieste. On Seilern (d. 18 June 1751) cf. *Khev.-Metsch*, 11 Oct. 1746; for his comments on Heinrich Blümegen, Rudolf Chotek, and Antal Grassalkovich see below.

[4] Maasburg, 112–13

[5] No entry for Cetto in Wurzbach.

the *Directorium*, Carl Joseph von Dier.[6] Jodocus Caspar von Lierwald (1680–1754) came of a Westphalian noble family, entered the Inner Austrian *Regierung* in 1710, and the Austrian Chancellery, as Inner Austrian referendary, in 1730, and was knighted in 1738.[7] Johann Georg von Managetta (1668–1751) was the great nephew of the Court physician Johann Wilhelm (1588–1666), and was born in Kaumberg in Lower Austria, where his father was a master tanner. He became a doctor of law in 1701, entered the Lower Austrian *Regierung* in 1708, the Austrian Chancellery in 1711, the *Oberste Justizstelle* in 1749, when he was eighty.[8]

The Austrian Court Chancellery provided a president and three councillors for the *Oberste Justizstelle* of 1749. The Bohemian Court Chancellery was to provide a further six (Althann, Kommergansky, Rumerskirchen, Schafgotsch, Tereschau, Turba). The powerful chancellor, Count Philipp Kinsky (1699–1749), was not one of them. He became Bohemian Chancellor in 1738, and as such played a leading role in the commercial negotiations with England. He was Bartenstein's patron. He supported Maria Theresia during her early troubles, organized her coronation at Prague in 1743, exchanged his chancellorship for the presidency of the *Ministerial Banco Deputation* on Count Starhemberg's retirement in July 1744, failed to maintain himself in favour, and died prematurely in January 1749. Khevenhüller plausibly suggests that his defective gall-

---

[6] Wurzbach offers two variant Holler genealogies. Carl Holler m. Therese von Dier, whose father Carl Joseph von Dier, *Geheimer Kammerzahlmeister*, was created Edler von Dier in 1734, Megerle, 'Edle Herren'. *Khev.-Metsch*, noting his death on 19 Nov. 1756, says that Charles VI gave him 100,000 fl. and, implausibly, that he bequeathed 400,000 ducats to Maria Theresia. His successor was Johann Adam von Mayer, see Wagner, 'Royal Graces and Legal Claims', 9–10. Carl Holler's relationship with the empress appears from numerous letters in vol. iv of Arneth's *Briefe der Kaiserin Maria Theresia*. For the commercial negotiations see P. G. M. Dickson, 'English Commercial Negotiations with Austria 1737–1752', in A. Whiteman *et al.* (eds.), *Statesmen, Scholars, and Merchants* (Oxford 1973), ch. 5. Holler (d. 30 July 1767, Starzer, 453) ended his career in the *Hofkommerzienrat* of 1762, see Table 12.3*.

[7] Maasburg, 116. Haugwitz thought him wedded to Inner Austrian interests, ÖZV (1925) 156–8 nn.

[8] Maasburg, 113–14, also Wurzbach. The name is usually spelt Mannagetta in the modern literature. For his sons Johann Joseph and Philipp Joseph see p. 365. In view of the social status of the family, Wurzbach's claim that Johann Georg's father was a master tanner is curious.

bladder, which killed him, explains his notorious irascibility.[9] Of his councillors in 1740, Count Rudolf Tereschau (1688–1770) came of the Bohemian noble family of Korženský. He entered the Prague *Appellation* in 1715, and the Bohemian Chancellery in 1720, becoming Vice-Chancellor in 1736, and Vice-Chancellor of the *Oberste Justizstelle* in 1749. On Seilern's resignation, he became its president, under Count Ferdinand Bonaventura Harrach as *Oberster Präsident*, then in May 1753 was himself named to the latter office. He retired in 1760.[10] Count Michael Althann (1710–78) entered the Lower Austrian *Regierung* in 1733 and the Bohemian Chancellery in 1736. He was Vice-Chancellor of the *Oberste Justizstelle* from 1753, retiring in 1771. He was president of the Court Commissions for revision of the criminal law from 1752 and for the civil *Codex Theresianus* from 1760, and reorganized the Bohemian criminal courts in 1765.[11] Count Wenzel Schafgotsch (1702–53) studied law and philosophy in Prague, entered the Bohemian *Appellation* in 1726, and the Bohemian Chancellery in 1736. His father was Count Johann Ernst Schafgotsch, *Obrist-Burggraf* of Bohemia (1734–47).[12] Hermann Lorenz von Kannegiesser was a councillor of the Silesian *Oberamt* in 1737, when he was made a Bohemian knight, and entered the Bohemian Chancellery in 1739. He, too, played a part in the commercial negotiations with England 1739–46. He attacked Prussia's claims to Silesia (1741) and defended Austrian interests in the peace treaties of 1742. He subsequently became a councillor of the *Directorium*, and later (1762) of the Bohemian and Austrian Chancellery.[13] His colleague in the

[9] Wurzbach; Dickson, 'Commercial Negotiations'; *Khev.-Metsch*, 12 Jan. 1749. The latter's entry shows Kinsky was b. 8 Nov. 1699, not 1 May 1700 as in Wurzbach. Arneth, *Gesch. Mar. Ther.* iv. 25 says he had previously (? June 1748) to his death laid down all his offices, but this is incorrect.

[10] Maasburg, 72–4. Count Ferdinand Bonaventura Harrach served norminally 1 Oct. 1750–May 1752. However, from 11 Jan 1751 he was president of the *Reichshofrat*. Count Tereschau and Count Carl Adam Breuner were both 'presidents' of the *Oberste Justizstelle* from 2 Jan. 1750 until 14 May 1753, when Tereschau became *Oberster President*. Breuner succeeded him in 1761. Count Michael Althann, see below, was vice-president 1753–71.

[11] Ibid. 89–91. The commission for the civil code dated from 1753.

[12] Ibid. 109–10.

[13] Wurzbach (but his end-date of 1734 for Kannegiesser's service in the Silesian government cannot be correct); Dickson, art. cit. for the commercial negotiations with England. Kannegiesser was made a baron on 18 June 1765. He was b. *c.*1700; his date of death is not known. Wurzbach says he came of an old noble family in Westphalia, but this seems doubtful.

Bohemian Chancellery, Johann Heinrich von Kommergansky (1677–1755), was of Hungarian descent, had started in cameral service in Silesia in 1711, was made a Bohemian knight and a councillor of the Silesian *Oberamt* in 1735, and a councillor of the Bohemian Chancellery in 1736.[14] Ignaz von Rumerskirchen (1690–1753) studied law at Leiden, served officially in Wetzlar and Mainz, entered the Moravian *Tribunal* in 1719 and the Bohemian Chancellery in 1736. He was made a baron in 1747 and later served on the commission for the criminal code.[15] Lastly, Johann Franz von Turba (1686–1760) became a doctor of law at Prague in 1709, then served in the *Appellation* there, and from 1726 in the Bohemian Chancellery. He was an initial member (1752) of the commission on the criminal code.[16]

Of the twenty-two persons in the two chancelleries, ten thus went on to become members of the *Oberste Justizstelle* in 1749, and three to become members of the *Directorium in Publicis et Cameralibus*. Advent to the Austrian and Bohemian chancelleries for those with legal education typically came after service in the Lower Austrian *Regierung* or Bohemian *Appellation*, but Kannegiesser and Kommergansky moved from Silesian administration, and there may have been a different *cursus* for those with legal, and those with cameral, training. Councillors were officially divided into *Herrenstand* and *Ritterstand* members.[17] It is observable that several of the latter were amongst the most active, and owed their social rise to the government they served. Hereditary aristocrats, however, were apparently not devoid of ability, as is often curiously assumed.

---

[14] Maasburg, 116–17. The family had settled in Silesia in the later 17th c.

[15] Maasburg, 117–18.

[16] Ibid. 115–16. In his despatches of 1747 the Prussian minister (1746–51) in Vienna, Count Otto Podewils, gave character sketches of the leading personalities at Court: Bartenstein, Colloredo, Friedrich Harrach, Johann Khevenhüller, Philipp Kinsky, Königsegg, Ulfeld. These conform to the other evidence here, though not in every detail. Bartenstein was 'a small pedantic schoolmaster'; Colloredo, a lazy womanizer; Harrach, able, sociable, in poor health; Khevenhüller, solid rather than brilliant; Kinsky, sly, domineering and venal; Königsegg, upright and loyal; Ulfeld, honest, muddled, and slow. Baron Koch, the empress's Cabinet Secretary, is praised by Podewils, as by others, Hinrichs, *Friedrich der Grosse u. Mar. Ther.*

[17] The further cadre of 'Gelehrtenstand' members seems to have obtained only in provincial government, for instance in the Lower Austrian *Regierung*. In the *Court Calendar*, councillors of the small Siebenbürgen Court Chancellery are not divided into *Herrenstand* and *Ritterstand* members.

Biographical information is thinner for the other institutions listed for 1740. In the three overtly financial bodies (the chancelleries had mixed responsibilities), the huge size of the *Hofkammer* contrasts with the small Finance Conference and Bank Deputation. The two latter shared a common head in the aged Count Gundaker Starhemberg (1663–1745), who had been president of the Hofkammer 1703–15, but had then resigned to devote the rest of his official life to a tenacious, though not entirely successful, defence of the position of the Vienna City Bank. He was a great man, but by 1740 a spent force.[18] His principal aide was Joachim Georg Schwandner, knighted in 1738, who was a councillor of both the Bank Deputation and *Hofkammer*, and played a successful spoiling role in the commercial negotiations with England.[19] Schwandner's colleague on the Bank Deputation, Baron (1725) Bartholome Tinti, was also a *Hofkammer* councillor, as well as a member of the Lower Austrian *Regierung*. He had a commercial background, and made important loans to the state under Charles VI. In 1737 he is listed as a member of the Inner Austrian *Hofkammer*, and after 1749 became a member of the Lower Austrian *Repraesentation und Kammer*. Count Sigmund Khevenhüller (1666–1742) was *Statthalter* of Lower Austria 1711–42, and the father of the diarist prince.[20]

Turning to the *Hofkammer* council, it is sometimes stated that Count Starhemberg was still its president at Maria Theresia's accession. The office had in fact been held since 1719 by Count Johann Franz Dietrichstein. He was previously the second president (1716–19) of the *Bancalität* created in 1714. In 1740 he was sixty-eight. When he died, aged eighty-three, in February 1755, Count Khevenhüller noted that he was a dry but honourable man, who gave 10,000 fl. yearly to the poor. There is no evidence that he

---

[18] Wurzbach, though his dates of office are wrong. Starhemberg was half-brother to Count Ernst Rudiger, the 'deliverer of Vienna' in 1683. His official career is covered in great detail in Mensi, *Die Finanzen Oesterreichs*. For his supineness in 1739–40 see Dickson, 'English Commercial Negotiations', 97. He resigned 7 July 1744, and d. 8 July 1745. He had 11 children. A granddau. m. Kaunitz.

[19] Dickson, loc. cit.

[20] Numerous references in Mensi, *Die Finanzen Oesterreichs* to the 'Wechselhaus Tinti'. For his offices see Starzer, 458. He was knighted in 1707, and made a Hungarian baron in 1714, a Hereditary Lands baron in 1725. He entered the *Regierung* in 1735. For Count S. Khevenhüller see Starzer, 301–8. Leopold von Schmerling, also a councillor of the Bank Deputation, was in the Lower Austrian *Regierung* 1714–30, ibid. 452.

had financial ability.[21] The Vice-President, Baron Prandau, properly Hilleprand von Prandau (1675–1767), was probably more important, though equally advanced in years. Prandau was a member of an official and financial family. Maximilian Hilleprand von Prandau, who was director of the defunct Oriental Company, was his brother.[22] Carl von Dier was treasurer of the *Geheimes Kammerzahlamt*, and was created Edler von Dier in 1734.[23] The three Harruckerns in the list were sons of the rich army contractor, and settler in Hungary, Baron Johann Georg von Harruckern (d. 1742).[24] (David) Heinrich von Koch went on to become a councillor of the *Directorium* in 1749. He died on 30 July 1753, noted by Count Khevenhüller as 'a very capable and experienced man in all financial and cameral business'. He was the elder, and only, brother of Baron (1748) Ignaz Koch (?1697–1763), former mentor of Prince Eugene, and Cabinet Secretary to Maria Theresia from 1742, the most influential holder of this office.[25] Baron Franz Raigersfeld was a member of the commercial *Intendenza* created for Trieste and the *Litorale* in 1730, and as such played a part in the trade negotiations with England 1739–46. He ended his career as a member of the *Repraesentation und Kammer* in Krain (1752).[26]

---

[21] Friedrich Walter is surprisingly among those who have stated that Starhemberg was still president of the *Hofkammer* under Maria Theresia, *Briefe*, 30 n. For the dates in the text see Mensi, *Die Finanzen Oesterreichs*, 463–4 and 540. Dietrichstein succeeded Count Walsegg (1714–16), first president of the *Universal Bancalität*, as its second president. Walsegg served as *Hofkammer* president 1716–19.

[22] See p. 163, for this family.

[23] See n. 6.

[24] See p. 111 for their wealth. Franz Dominick in the *Hofkammer* list was a Lower Austrian *Regierung* councillor 1720–30 (d. 14 Nov. 1775 aged 78, Starzer, 454).

[25] *Khev.-Metsch*, 30 July 1753 for David Koch; M. Braubach in *NDB* for Ignaz Koch; Bittner *et al.* (eds.), *Gesamtinventar*, ii. 115–16 for the sequence of Secretaries. David and Ignaz Koch were sons of Georg Koch, an Agent of the *Hofkriegsrat*. Ignaz was secretary to Prince Eugene from at least 1723, and a councillor of the *Hofkriegsrat* in 1728. Appointed 19 Mar. 1742 to succeed Ignaz Wolffscron as Cabinet Secretary, he became an intimate adviser of Maria Theresia. Khev.-Metsch trusted Koch, who lost favour by supporting the unsuccessful Field Marshal Browne, diary, 8 May 1753, 6 Jan. 1776. In 1759, Baron (1765) Cornelius Neny, bro. of Patrick, (pres. of the Belgian *Conseil d'État*, and son of Patrick MacNeny from Ireland), was appointed to take over part of Koch's work, and on his death (18 Feb. 1763) succeeded to his position. Neny d. 6 Jan. 1776, and Baron Carl Josef Püchler then served until 8 Dec. 1786, with Georg Zephyris, formerly cabinet secretary in Milan, as his assistant, *Khev.-Metsch*, 6 Jan. 1776.

[26] See refs. to Raigersfeld or Reigersfeld in Mayer, *Die Anfänge des Handels*, though the book is far from clear. For his appearance in the commercial negotiations see Dickson, 'Commercial Negotiations', 98–9; the English envoys consistently misspelt his name. His position in Krain is shown in Table 13.2.*

Lastly, in the Hungarian Court Chancellery, *Herrenstand* members were from prominent magnate families. Patachich was Sheriff of Zágráb county in Croatia.[27] Of the *Ritterstand* members, Johann von Adelffy had sat in the Hungarian Council of Lieutenancy 1730–3.[28] The Viennese Johann Hittner (1700–87) studied law, and became a doctor of law of Vienna University in 1723, travelled abroad, entered the Lower Austrian *Regierung* in 1731, the Hungarian Court Chancellery in 1740, the Austrian Court Chancellery in 1746, the *Oberste Justizstelle* in 1749. He took part in the introduction of the Lower Austrian *Landtafel* (1754–8), and in the early work on the criminal code, and was finally ennobled as Edler von Hittner in December 1780. He left a large collection of official papers to the *Oberste Justizstelle*.[29] Joseph Koller de Nagy-Manya must be related to Franz Xaver Koller de Nagy-Manya, a councillor of the Hungarian Court Chancellery in 1754, subsequently president of the *Hofdeputationen* for Illyria and for Sanitation, created a baron in 1770 and a count in 1771, who wrote a treatise on Hungary for the Archduke Joseph in 1760.[30]

Table 12.2* shows the position in 1754, at which date the major administrative changes promoted since 1748 had had time to take root. The Privy Conference was by this stage a largely decorative body. Its senior member, and president since 1745, was Count Corfiz Ulfeld (1699–1769), the grandson of *Rigshofmester* Count Corfitz Ulfeldt (d. 1664), minister to Christian IV of Denmark, condemned for treason to his successor Frederick III. Ulfeld was the first holder (1742–53) of the office of *Hof- und Staatskanzler*. In May 1753 he ceded it to Kaunitz, and became *Erster Hofmeister*

---

[27] *Court Calendar* 1740, list of 'Supremi Comites Comitatuum'. The name is also spelt Petachich in the sources.

[28] Ember, *Helytartótanács*, 202, list of noble (viz. non-magnate) councillors.

[29] Maasburg, 90 n. and 118–19. The *Landtafel* was the register of noble land and its rights, also of debts charged on land. It existed in Bohemia by 1705, was introduced in Styria 1730–6, in Krain 1732–7, in Upper Austria 1751, in Lower Austria 1758, in place of an existing court, Maasburg loc. cit., and Bidermann, *Gesammt-Staats-Idee*, ii. 19 n. 62.

[30] See Ch. 5, n. 79. *Khev.-Metsch 1774–6*, n. 116 shows that Koller was president of the *Hof-Deputationen* 'in Illyricis' and in Sanitation (i.e. for the cordon against plague) from Bartenstein's death in 1767 until 1776 (Sanitation) and 1777 (Illyria). This modifies the dating in Benna, 'Die Kronprinzenunterricht'.

instead. He was a friend of the empress, and when he died was buried with a ceremony 'unequalled since the death of Prince Eugene'. Field Marshal Count Joseph Batthyány (1697–1772), created a prince in 1764, was a distinguished cavalry commander and, from the peace of 1748, *Hofmeister* to the Archduke Joseph. The wealthy Count Rudolf Colloredo (1706–88), also created a prince in 1764, was Vice-Chancellor of the Empire 1737–42 and from 1745, and regularly quarrelled with Kaunitz. The diarist Khevenhüller (1706–76), who married the daughter of the last Count Metsch, and adopted his name in 1751, came of an ancient family of Carinthian origin. He was the son of Count Sigmund, *Statthalter* of Lower Austria, and entered the *Reichshofrat* in 1728, then served as Austrian minister in Denmark, at Regensburg, and in Saxony (1734–41). In November 1742 he became *Hofmarschall*, in September 1745 Court Chamberlain (*Hofkämmerer*), in 1765, as a result of Joseph II's division of the office of *Erster Hofmeister* into two, 'Mitterer Hofmeister', in January 1770, on Ulfeld's death, 'Erster Hofmeister', the senior position at Court. He was named a hereditary prince in April 1764. His diary, elaborately edited by Austrian historians, is a valuable source for the period. From it, Khevenhüller emerges as intelligent, conservative, unenergetic. Fürst's unkind remark about the Conference at this date was that Khevenhüller, Batthyány, and Ulfeld were ciphers, while Kaunitz and Colloredo ruled the roost.

Khevenhüller's diaries for 1756–9 (those for 1760–3 are missing) show that there were far fewer meetings of the Privy Conference from July 1756 until December 1757, but that they resumed in 1758 and 1759, with the same core of Ministers, though frequently with additions from other departments. One or both rulers typically presided. In the period July 1756–December 1757, a series of Military Conferences, concerned with the movement and supply of troops rather than strategy, met weekly under Kaunitz, and reported to the empress, who gave ensuing orders. Membership comprised the two brothers Chotek, respectively as Vice-President of the *Directorium* and Bank President; Count Haugwitz; Field Marshall Count Wilhelm Reinhard Neipperg, Vice-President of the *Hofkriegsrat*; and Field Marshall Franz Salburg, General War Commissary, who died in June 1758. It is not clear if these meetings continued in 1758 and 1759, but it seems probable. An effort was made in these two years to include Conference Ministers when the emperor or empress presided. On 13 December 1757, a week after the battle of Leuthen on 5 December, Khevenhüller recorded that it was the first time for fourteen months that Conference Ministers had been summoned to 'Deputations or Conferences *in Mixtis*'. Kaunitz had ensured their absence 'in order to devise remedies, and arrange the operations to be performed by the various internal offices of state, *en espèce de premier ministre*'. The querulous diarist noted on 23 May 1759, after a jumbo-sized Conference had reviewed the military budget for 1760, that Conference Ministers were still regularly excluded from internal business. It was in these smaller meetings that Kaunitz, 'now so proud and overbearing that his friends shun him' (7 March 1758), first acquired expertise 'in internis', and, perhaps, the idea of a small effective body of experts to advise the sovereign.[31]

Returning to 1754, the list of members of the *Directorium in Publicis et Cameralibus* contains a number of names already referred to, but also several new ones. Members of leading Bohemian families are noticeable by absence. They had gone to the *Oberste Justizstelle* instead, as described earlier. Johann Chotek was a Bohemian, but not of magnate descent. The first and most famous name in the list is that of the fiery and energetic president, Count Friedrich Wilhelm Haugwitz (1702–65) who had the further titles of Bohemian 'Obrist-Canzler' and Austrian 'Erster Canzler'. He came of a Silesian family which took its Lutheran beliefs into Saxon service. His father, Count (1733) Karl (1674–1745) was a Saxon general, though remaining a member of the Silesian Estates. Friedrich was converted

---

[31] For the Privy Conference in 1754, and the comment about capacities, see *Fürst* (*1755*) 15–16, also Schlitter's notes to Khevenhüller. For Ulfeld, Wurzbach and *ADB* (Schlitter), the latter following the former closely, including the erroneous date of 31 Dec. 1760 for his death. For the remark about his funeral, Langlois to Rochford, 6 Jan. 1770, PRO SP 80/207. I am indebted to Dr Holford-Strevens for suggesting the connection with the *Rigshofmester*. For Batthyány and Colloredo see Wurzbach, though he confusingly says Batthyány was created a prince 'after the Treaty of Aix on 3 Jan. 1764'. For Khev.-Metsch, see introd. to *Khev.-Metsch 1742–4*, also Payer von Thurn, Wurzbach, and *NDB*; the last two are inaccurate about his offices. He was *Hofmarschall* 19 Nov. 1742–26 Sept. 1745, with the overlapping post of second ('Anderter') *Hofmeister* 1 May 1743–20 Sept. 1745. His patent as hereditary prince was dated 30 Dec. 1763, but, as the notes on his diary make clear, the list of names (Batthyány, Colloredo, and Kaunitz were the other princes) was only published on 4 Apr. 1764.

to Catholicism (1725), like Bartenstein and Zinzendorf, both councillors of the *Directorium*, and perhaps, like them, showed the zeal
of the convert in the Monarchy's service. He entered the Silesian
government (*Oberamt*), left it as a result of the Prussian wars of
1740–2, and lived in Vienna on borrowed funds. He came to the
notice of the empress through her husband, and as governor (1743)
of the Austrian remnant of Silesia, began a public career which led
to the reconstruction of Austrian central and local government from
1748. In 1754 he was living sumptuously in his apartments in the
Directorium. Fürst's description of him (1755) as always blinking,
and appearing in his manner more like a fool than a great man, has
often been cited. Fürst also tells us that Haugwitz was a keen
gardener and huntsman, that he was more feared than loved, and
that he owed his continuance in office only to the empress's
support. Many aspects of his public career, including the disap-
pointing fortunes of the *Directorium* itself, are discussed in other
chapters. Haugwitz did well out of land purchases, borrowed
money from the city of Vienna, and endured the bitterness of his
only son's death four years before his own.[32] His second-in-
command was Count Johann Chotek (1705–87), with the title of
Bohemian and Austrian Chancellor. He was a professional soldier,
created *Feldmarschall-Leutnant* in 1744, administrator of occupied
Bavaria, general war commissary in Italy in 1746. As such, he
accepted the surrender of Genoa after its revolt, and imposed a
swingeing fine on the republic (September 1746). He became
quarter-master of the army during the Seven Years War, and was
put in charge of the newly-created commissariat department of the

---

[32] Haugwitz's three brothers all died without male heirs. Basic biographical data
from Walter in *NDB*, though the article is thin on H.'s public career, which Walter
had documented extensively in earlier publications. *Fürst* (*1755*) 20–2 is partly based
on conversation with Haugwitz. In 1743 the latter bought the lordship of Bielitz in
Teschen from Count Solms for 280,000 fl., which he borrowed; and resold it as a
principality to Count Sulkowsky in 1752 for 600,000 fl., Fürst, loc. cit, and d'Elvert,
Verfassung, 154–6. His debt to the city of Vienna was 150,000 fl. in 1760, G. Zwanowetz, 'Die Finanzgebarung . . . der Stadt Wien' (phil. diss. Innsbruck 1953), 413.
Haugwitz had 50,000 fl. annual salary but could not manage on it; his housekeeping
was chaotic; he was the empress's *âme damnée*, who threw the old constitution into
confusion; but his basic nature was good, *Khev.-Metsch*, 30 Aug. 1765. His official
salary was in fact 24,000 fl., Mikoletzsky, 'Haushalt', 677. Most sources give 11 Sept.
1765 as the date of his death.

Hofkriegsrat in 1762. He was the brother of the better-known Count Rudolf Chotek.[33]

The *Directorium* had yet another commander, the Vice-Chancellor of Bohemia and Austria. This rather meaningless title was created in May 1753 for Baron Johann Christoph Bartenstein (1689–1767). Bartenstein was one of the most influential ministers of the 1730s and 1740s, but by now a disappointed man, outstripped by his juniors Haugwitz and Kaunitz. His father, a professor of philosophy at Strasburg University, was the son of a Protestant pastor. Johann Christoph studied law, history and languages at Strasburg, travelled, became a Catholic (1716) and entered state service in Vienna under the aegis of Count Gundaker Starhemberg. He served in the Lower Austrian *Regierung* and then, as secretary to the Conference (1727) and Privy State Secretary (1733), virtually as foreign minister until 1753. His chief patron in the 1740s was Count Philipp Kinsky. Kaunitz, on becoming State Chancellor in May 1753, refused to have Bartenstein under him, with the often quoted remark that two pipers in one alehouse would not do. By this date, Bartenstein's assertive style had made him detested by every foreign power. The empress persuaded him to move with 100,000 fl., an increase in salary, and places for his sons. He was knighted in 1719, and made a baron in 1732. He was learned, difficult, pertinacious, hostile to the English entanglements of the 1740s, in favour of a French alliance, a loyal servant of the Crown, but also of his own family, which he left richer than most.[34]

---

[33] Wurzbach, though he makes Chotek Second Chancellor in 1763, a confusion with his earlier appointment; also Arneth, *Gesch. Mar. Ther.* vii. 27. He resigned 16 Feb. 1766, on Lacy's appointment as *Kriegsrat* president, *Khev.-Metsch.* Maass, *Der Frühjosephinismus*, ch. II, 'Die Entlassung des Grafen Johann Chotek (1761)', shows that on 17 Dec. 1761 Maria Theresia instructed him to confine himself to his commissariat and Pensioners duties, then at Chotek's protest relented, appointing him War Commissary on 23 Dec. 1761. The occasion of this 'dismissal', according to Maass, was his less than forthcoming response to the empress's request for advice whether she could tax the Austrian clergy as a body without papal consent. The background in this account is vague.

[34] Arneth, 'Johann Christoph Bartenstein', *AÖG* 46 (1871) 3 ff. gives a biography followed by his 1762 memorandum on the Monarchy. Arneth shows, p. 70, that Bartenstein left *c.* 750,000 fl. M. Braubach in *NDB* is useful. See Dickson, 'Commercial Negotiations' for Kinsky as his patron; *Khev.-Metsch*, 13 May 1753 for Kaunitz's remark, the hatred of Bartenstein, and the empress's bargain with him. In her memorials of 1750 and 1756 she stated that he 'alone saved the Monarchy' in 1740–2, and was second only to Haugwitz in constructing the new system of 1748–9, and enduring the consequent hostility. He m. Maria Holler von Doblhoff in

Franz von Bartenstein was the second of his two sons. Anton von Buol, Carl Cetto von Kronstorf, Carl von Dier, Carl Holler von Doblhof, and Hermann von Kannegiesser have all been encountered as former members of the chancelleries or financial departments. Gröller and Thoren were former Secretaries of the *Directorium*.[35] Count Franz Eszterházy was a member of the greatest Hungarian magnate family. He went on to become Hungarian Chancellor in November 1762. His presence in the *Directorium* must have been the result of deliberate royal policy. Baron (1753) Johann Joseph Managetta vice-president of the Lower Austrian *Repraesentation und Kammer*, under the presidency of Haugwitz's cousin Heinrich, was the son of Johann Georg von Managetta.[36] Jacob Benedict von Neffzern was a Hungarian of a different type from Eszterházy. He has already been referred to in Ch. 7. In 1763 he was a councillor of the Bank Deputation, in 1775 of the Vienna *Hofkammer* as well.[37] Franz von Pistrich is probably the Franz Pistrich who was a councillor of the *Hofkammer* in 1740. Franz Anton von Saffran is either the same man as the *Hofkammer* councillor of 1740 or a son. Count Stella was president of the Commercial Commission for Lower Austria. Count Wilczek was an infantry general (*Feldzeugmeister*), and the father of Count [Johann] Joseph, a councillor of the Lower Austrian *Regierung*

1725, and had two sons, Joseph, president of the *Reichshofrat*, and Franz. *Khev.-Metsch*, 31 Oct. 1752, 12 May 1753 records his creation as Conference Minister and *Geheimrat*.

[35] Cetto, Holler, Kannegiesser, Neymeyer or Neumayr, and Saffran were five of the seven original councillors of the *Directorium*, ÖZV (1925) 290–1. The sixth, Stupan, was in the Bank Deputation in 1754; the seventh, Kranichstätten, does not appear in the 1754 lists. For the four Secretaries of May 1749, see ÖZV, loc. cit. Buol and Stupan were assigned to the new fiscal *consessus* of the *Directorium* in Jan. 1751, ibid. 323.

[36] According to *Khev.-Metsch*, 2 May 1749, 'Regierungs-Canzler Managetta', *Hofrat* Kannegiesser, and Cabinet Secretary Koch drafted the reform proposals of 1749 at the empress's instructions. Johann Joseph Managetta 'von Lerchenau': councillor of the Lower Austrian *Regierung* 1721 and its *Kanzler* in 1742; entered the *Directorium* July 1749, vice-president of the Lower Austrian *Repraesentation* 5 May 1753; baron 15 May 1753, councillor of Bohemian and Aust. Chancellery 1762; d. 1764, Starzer, 454, but omitting his erroneous statement that Managetta was *Vice-Statthalter* of Lower Austria 1759–64.

[37] See Ch. 7, n. 118, though uncertainty about Christian names makes the identification probable rather than exact. He was, hypothetically, Joh. Jacob Benedict.

1760–6.[38] Johann Bernhard von Zencker (1724–85) came from a Bohemian official family, studied law at Prague University (doctor 1750), entered the Bohemian *Appellation* 1751, the *Directorium* in 1754, the *Oberste Justizstelle* 1759–60, then (1762) the new Bohemian and Austrian Court Chancellery. He was knighted in 1754. He concerned himself from 1760 with the completion in six volumes (1766) of the civil *Codex Theresianus*, eventually rejected by the empress, and with the subsequent labour of the Compilation Commission (1772) to revise it. He also served on the committee which prepared the criminal code of 1769.[39] Lastly, Ludwig von Zinzendorf was just beginning his distinguished, if chequered, public career. Zinzendorf (1721–80) was the eldest son of Count Friedrich Christian, and the grandson of Count Georg Ludwig, both in Saxon service and, because of their Lutheran beliefs, exiles from Austria, where the Zinzendorf family had roots in the early Middle Ages. Ludwig's uncle, by his grandfather's second marriage, was Count Nikolaus Ludwig, founder of the Moravian Brethren. His half-brother, the last male Zinzendorf, was Count Karl, diarist, traveller, governor of Trieste 1776–82, President of the *Hofrechenkammer* 1782–92. Ludwig entered Saxon service in 1739; after becoming a Catholic at the end of this year, he joined the Royal Saxon Bodyguard in July 1740, and took part in the Saxon campaign against Austria in 1741. He studied law at Leipzig and Vienna 1746–7, mended his fences with the empress, went with Kaunitz on his embassy to Paris in 1750, and was appointed a councillor in the *Directorium* in August 1753, presumably at Kaunitz's suggestion. He was also made a member of the bureau of trade. His later career as president of the Estates Credit Deputation (15 April 1761), then President of the *Hofrechenkammer* (1 January 1762) until his dismissal in January 1773, is followed elsewhere.[40]

[38] For Saffran see Table 12.1*; no entry in Wurzbach. Megerle, 'Freiherren', 'Edle Herren', states that he was created both in 1739 but the first seems to be an error. Count Stella entered the Lower Austrian *Regierung* in 1726, the Lower Austrian *Repraesentation und Kammer* in July 1750, the *Directorium* in July 1751, Starzer, 455. For Count Wilczek, who was of Polish origin, and his son, see Maasburg, 142–3 and nn.

[39] Maasburg, 131–3.

[40] See ii, Chs. 2, 4. The main biographical source is Pettenegg, *Zinzendorf*, with ample genealogical tables. See p. 8 of the book for the inference that Ludwig's half-brother Karl wrote it. Ludwig was in Russia for Kaunitz Apr.-July 1755; for his long report in French on the Court there see G. B. Volz and G. Küntzel, *Public. preuss. Staatsarchivs*, 74 (1899) 678–739. Pettenegg, 61 says that he was made a

The numbers and weight of the *Directorium* demonstrated the force of Haugwitz's institutional revolution. This was also shown, in inverse form, by the derisory size of the *Hofkammer*, which in 1740 had had a president and 52 councillors. It was actually larger in 1754 than in 1751, when it had been reduced to the president, vice-president, and two councillors. Dietrichstein and Prandau (who was made vice-president in 1745) have been discussed already. The constitutionally required Hungarian connection explains the presence of Pálffy and Nagy. At Dietrichstein's death in February 1755, he was succeeded as president of the *Hofkammer* by Count Karl Königsegg-Erps (1696–1759), who retained his existing position as president of the College of Mines. Fürst in 1755 praised him as the hardest-working minister in Vienna. Unfortunately, a deficit of 19m. fl. was discovered in the mines department in January 1757, and he had to resign; but stayed in charge of the *Hofkammer* until his death on 20 December 1759. Haugwitz's ambition in this period to abolish the *Hofkammer* entirely was clearly partly frustrated by the longevity first of Dietrichstein, then of Prandau (who only d. 1767), though the empress probably used these personal facts for political reasons.[41]

The membership of the 'Ministerial-Banco-Hof-Deputation' in 1754 was smaller and less aristocratic than in 1740, but did not now include the burgomaster of Vienna. The official career of the president, Johann Chotek's brother Count Rudolf Chotek (1707–71), had been pursued under the patronage of the emperor and his brother. Chotek's father, Wenzel Anton (d. 1754), was a successful career official from a minor noble background, who was made a baron in 1702, a count in 1723, an imperial count in 1745. He was a councillor of the Bohemian *Statthalterei* in 1740. His son

councillor of the *Commercien-Directorium* and of its Lower Austrian subsidiary the 'Delegirte Hof Commission', but provides no details. A. Beer, 'Die handelspolitischen Beziehungen Österreichs zu den deutschen Staaten unter Maria Theresia' *AÖG* 79 (1892) 490 gives the members of the *Commercien-Directorium* at 24 Nov. 1754 as Doblhof, Neffzer, Kannegiesser, Stupan, Toussaint, Wrbna. Zinzendorf's omission may, however, not be conclusive. For the 'Hof Commission' see Ch. 13, n. 6.

[41] Wurzbach; *Fürst (1755)* 26; *Khev.-Metsch*, 12 Jan. 1757 for the deficit in the Mines Department. Königsegg was at first intended for an ecclesiastical career, and became a canon of Strasburg cathedral; however, in 1719 he married the only daughter of Count Franz Erps, adding the latter's name to his own. In 1742–3 he was minister in the Austrian Netherlands, and thereafter president of the Netherlands Council in Vienna.

Rudolf entered the Bohemian *Appellation* in 1733. He supported Charles VII of Bavaria, but subsequently made his peace with the Austrian Court through Charles of Lorraine, and entered the Bohemian *Statthalterei*. In January 1747 he became Bohemian Chamberlain (*Oberst-Landkämmerer*), Count Khevenhüller noting in his diary that Chotek's birth was insufficient for this. In 1744 and 1748 he was sent on financial missions to Tyrol and Inner Austria, and after 1746 was minister in Munich. In 1749, on Count Philipp Kinsky's death, he was the emperor's candidate for Bank President. He was also made president of the bureau of trade. It was rumoured that he was a mere nominee for the emperor himself. This is, however, doubtful. Fürst in 1755 found Chotek proud, able, stubborn. His financial grasp seems undoubted. From August 1758 he assumed charge of the mines department, and, from the death of Königsegg-Erps in 1759, the presidency of the *Hofkammer* as well. On 1 January 1762 he was put in charge of the new Bohemian and Austrian Chancellery, succeeding to Haugwitz's titles of Bohemian Chief Chancellor and Austrian First Chancellor, after rejecting an offer to become a founding member of the *Staatsrat*. He was unwell from the mid 1760s, had a stroke which affected his speech in November 1770, but was still amazed to be asked to resign (9 June 1771), the message being explained and driven home by his brother Count Johann. He died on 7 July 1771.[42] Of the councillors, Baron Gillern had been in the *Hofkammer* in 1740. Anton Maria Stupan von Ehrenstein became a founding member of the *Staatsrat* in 1760. Frans Bernhard Unkrechtsburg must be related to Philipp, a councillor of the *Hofkammer* in 1740, and Georg Bernhard, a Bank councillor in 1763.

The membership of the Hungarian and Siebenbürgen Court Chancelleries in 1754 shows some continuity of person or family with those of 1740. The Hungarian Court Chancellery now,

---

[42] No entry for Rudolf Chotek in Wurzbach or *NDB*; a truncated and inaccurate one in *ADB*. His family was an old knightly one, which lost much land after 1620. His father's career is sketched in, *Ottův slovník naučný*, xii (1897) 370–1. For R. Chotek's missions in Tyrol and Carinthia, Fürst's views, and the invitation to join the *Staatsrat*, see Arneth, *Maria Ther. Kinder und Freunde*, iv. 161 (Tyrol); *Gesch. Mar. Ther.* iv. 20 (Carinthia) and 73 (Fürst's views), vii. 15 (*Staatsrat*). For the rumour about the emperor, see ii. 30; he 'discovered' both Haugwitz and Chotek. *Khev.-Metsch* has entries about Chotek on 26 Jan. 1747, 30 June and 7 July 1771; he describes him as 'one of the most experienced and penetrating ministers' of the reign, 7 Jul. 1771.

however, included a (Croatian) bishop, Count Adam Patachich, who must have been related to the Count Alexander of 1740. It is noticeable, looking forward to the lists for 1763, that there was by then a considerable change in Hungarian personnel. Count Nádasdy retired as Hungarian Chancellor in March 1758. His successor Count Nicholas Pálffy was replaced in November 1762 by Count Franz Eszterházy. Count Gabriel Bethlen, a converted Calvinist, who subsequently married the daughter of Count Khevenhüller-Metsch, succeeded Count Gyulassi as Chancellor of Siebenbürgen in March 1755.[43]

The penultimate lists of holders of central office (Table 12.3*) are for 1763, and reflect the major administrative reorganization promoted by Kaunitz, with royal, and substantial ministerial, support in 1760–2. In Kaunitz's view, the most important new organ was the *Staatsrat*, in which the further changes were planned. Its initial membership (first session 26 January 1761) comprised Counts Kaunitz, Haugwitz, Blümegen, and Daun ('Ministers of State'), with Borié and Stupan as further members ('Councillors of State'), and Anton von König as referendary, or organizing secretary. Counts Rudolf Chotek and Friedrich Hatzfeld declined nomination. Ludwig Zinzendorf, 'a young theoretician who would devise good projects which his elders would have to judge', in Kaunitz's words, was considered, but rejected.[44]

The family of Count (Prince 1764) Wenzel Anton Kaunitz (1711–94), the promoter of the *Staatsrat*, was Moravian, and correctly spelt Kaunice. Wenzel's father Count Maximilian was *Landeshauptmann* in Moravia. The young Kaunitz studied law at Leipzig University, travelled in the Netherlands, Italy, Germany, and Paris, returned to Vienna in 1734 and entered the Lower Austrian *Regierung*, then, in 1735, the *Reichshofrat*. Despite straitened circumstances, he married Countess Maria Starhemberg in 1736, by

---

[43] *Khev.-Metsch*, 19 Mar. 1755. Bethlen married the diarist's dau. in Jan. 1756.
[44] Arneth, *Gesch. Mar. Ther.* vii, ch. 1 does not make it clear that König was initially a referendary, not a councillor. The empress accepted Kaunitz's suggestions that *Herrenstand* councillors be styled 'Staatsminister', *Ritterstand* councillors 'wirklicher Hof- und Staatsrat', and the referendary, 'wirklicher hofrat und referendarius', *ÖZV* (1934), 19.

whom he had six sons, and a daughter who later married Prince Metternich. Kaunitz was a minister in Turin in 1742, minister (1744) and minister plenipotentiary (1745) in Brussels, Austrian envoy at Aix-la-Chapelle in 1748, ambassador to Paris 1750–3, and *Hof- und Staatskanzler* in May 1753, in succession to Ulfeld, having previously (December 1751) declined the office. In May 1756 he implemented the alliance with France for which he had hoped from 1749. From 1756, as already noted, he took an increasing interest in domestic policy, though foreign affairs continued to absorb most of his time.[45] Field Marshal Daun (1705–66), victor at Kolin (1757), narrow loser at Torgau (1760), succeeded the aged Count Joseph Harrach as president of the *Hofkriegsrat* in January 1762, and died on 5 February 1766. Between the war and the war council, he cannot have had much time for the *Staatsrat*.[46] Among the other founding councillors, Count Heinrich Cajetan Blümegen (1715–88) is a good example of promotion on merit, and the establishment of a new family. His father Hermann Blömegen or Blümegen (1672–1733) came from Westphalia and entered, first, the *Reichskammergericht*, then (1711) the *Reichshofrat*. He was made a knight in 1708, a baron in 1724. Heinrich Blümegen became a councillor of the Moravian *Tribunal*, or government, in 1740. In 1741–2 he was War Commissary in Moravia, and, in 1744, chancellor of the *Tribunal*. In 1748 he was made president of the new Moravian *Deputation*, subsequently *Repraesentation*. From 1753 he was also Moravian *Landeshauptmann*. From May 1759 he was War Commissary in Bohemia. In December 1760 he entered the *Staatsrat*. He was made a count in 1758, an imperial count in 1761. In December 1771 he became Bohemian Chief Chancellor and Austrian First Chancellor. He resigned in June 1782 over a financial scandal in Bohemia, where his brother was head of the government,

---

[45] K. O. von Aretin in *NBD*; Arneth, *Gesch. Mar. Ther.*, *passim*. The most recent treatment of Kaunitz's earlier career is by Professor Grete Klingenstein, *Der Aufstieg des Hauses Kaunitz* (Göttingen 1975). It is usually stated in the literature that his concern with 'Innenpolitik' dates only from 1760. I owe the suggestion that in the 18th. c. the Czech 'Kounice' was spelt as in the text to Dr Holford-Strevens.

[46] Arneth, vii. 12, 28. Kaunitz protested at Daun's appointment to the *Hofkriegsrat* while retaining his position in the *Staatsrat*, ÖZV (1934) 31. The empress overruled his objection; however, Daun's successor Lacy was excluded while holding executive office. Regele, *Hofkriegsrat*, app. I, says wrongly that Daun was created a prince in 1764. (Daun was offered the title, but refused it, PRO SP 80/200, Stormont to Sandwich, 11 Apr. 1764.)

and died six years later. In 1779 he was president of the Lower Austrian Patriotic (Agricultural) Society. Khevenhüller noted in 1748 that, despite his low birth, he was 'a very capable and well-mannered person'. Joseph II observed of his appointment as chancellor in 1771 that he was 'so to speak brought up for the post and knows our lands intimately'.[47]

Borié, König, and Stupan, the remaining members of the *Staatsrat*, were able men, though perhaps of lesser mettle. Egyd Valentin Borié (? 1719–93), correctly Beaurieu, was an adviser to the prince-bishop of Würzburg from 1739 to 1754, specializing in agricultural and industrial policy. He then quarrelled with his employer, and came to Vienna, entering the *Reichshofrat*, which he was reluctant to leave (18 January 1761) for the *Staatsrat*. He was made a baron in 1759, and a Commander of the Order of St Stephen for his success in negotiating the election of Joseph II as King of the Romans in 1764. From 1770 he was Austrian minister at the Imperial Diet in Ratisbon. In the *Staatsrat* he became interested in the Hungarian lands, and an Hungarian expert.[48] Anton König von Kronburg, the council's referendary, served as a war-office clerk on the Rhine under Eugene in 1734, then in the *Hofkriegsrat*. In 1754 he was one of the Secretaries of the *Directorium*. He was presumably a specialist in military business. His initial appointment to the *Staatsrat* (December 1760) was as referendary only, but in June 1762 he was also nominated councillor, retaining his secretarial duties. His failure to perform these to the satisfaction of his colleagues led to his dismissal in August 1770, after Borié had accused him of being

---

[47] No entry in Wurzbach, *ADB*, *NDB*, *Ottův slovník*. His dates of birth and death, and his office of war commissary in 1741–2, are taken from the obituary in *SSMSGA Notizen-Blatt* (1866) 17–18. For his father see Gschliesser, *Reichshofrat*, 381. His office as war commissary from 1759 and his resignation are noted in Rieger, *Zřízení krajské*, ii. 309–10, 354. He did not, however, resign over the Toleration Patent as Rieger states, see Hock-Bidermann, 133–4. His presidency of the Agricultural Society is shown in the *Court Calendar* for 1779. *Khev.-Metsch*, 12 Jan. 1748 says that his father was of humble Swabian origin. For Joseph II's remark of 27 Nov. 1771, see Arneth, *Mar. Ther. und Joseph II.* i. 355. However, Joseph thought Blümegen exercised undue influence at the *Staatsrat*; and Blümegen was reluctant to leave it. Cf. also Ch. 13, n. 19.

[48] Wurzbach, Arneth, Gschliesser, who do not go further into his French origins. He left the *Staatsrat* in May 1770, Payer von Thurn. For the date of his reluctant entry, see *ÖZV* (1934) 15. Borié was unmarried. Anton Löhr, who entered the *Staatsrat* in 1771, was one of his nephews. Ember, 'Der österr. Staatsrat', *Acta Historica* 6 (1959) 143–4 shows Kaunitz praising him as a Hungarian expert.

despotic.[49] Anton Maria Stupan von Ehrenstein became a councillor of the Lower Austrian *Regierung*, in 1748 was made a member of the new Deputation in Krain, in 1754 was a councillor of the Bank Deputation and bureau of trade. He was made a baron in 1765. He regaled the first meeting of the *Staatsrat* with his views of its duties: to promote religion, power, prosperity, and good administration. Both he and Borié took radical positions in the financial discussions of 1763. Blümegen, König, and Stupan as Arneth notes, were all protégés of Haugwitz. The *Staatsrat* was filled with men unfriendly to its proposer, Kaunitz.[50]

The great departments of state will now be considered. In the Bohemian and Austrian Chancellery, only the Chancellor, Chotek, and Count Wrbna, were of Bohemian descent. Chotek, as his arguments in 1762 about the structure of the chancellery showed, was tenaciously Bohemian in his inclinations. Wrbna's career had been in Austrian rather than Bohemian service. The bias in favour of 'German' councillors, already noticed with the *Directorium*, must have been due to the empress's insistence on union of the Bohemian and Austrian lands and suspicion of many of the Bohemian magnate families. Continuing down the chancellery list, Johann Bartenstein was entering on the last phase of his official career. Lorenz von Carqui appears in the 1754 *Court Calendar* as one of ten Secretaries of the *Directorium*; Anton König, as just noted, was another. Carqui was also registrar ('Registrator'). Cetto, Gröller, Kannegiesser, Managetta, and Zencker were all former councillors of the *Directorium*. Tobias Gebler (1720–86) was a convert (1753) from Saxony who had studied at Göttingen, Jena, and Halle before entering the service of the States-General in The Hague (legation secretary at Berlin, 1748) then moving to Vienna as a Secretary to the bureau of trade (1753). He was knighted in 1763, and made a baron in 1766. Despite his conversion to Catholicism, he was a Freemason, didactic playwright, and correspondent of Lessing and Nicolai, with advanced views on church reform. From the chancellery (1762) he

---

[49] No entry in Wurzbach, *ADB*, *NDB*. For the statements in the text, see Arneth, vii. 17; *Court Calendar* 1754; ÖZV (1934) 32 (1 June 1762), 39–40 (despotism), and 40–1 (8 Aug. 1770, dismissal). Hock–Bidermann, 11 say that in 1760 he was the empress's Cabinet Secretary, and acted as referendary of the *Staatsrat*, rather than as a full member, until 1770.

[50] No entry for Stupan in Wurzbach, *ADB*, *NDB*. For the statements in the text, see Arneth, loc. cit.; Megerle, von Mühlfeld, 'Freiherren'; Tables 12.2*, 13.2.*.

moved to the *Staatsrat* (1768), leaving it on 27 May 1782 and returning (19 October 1782) to the chancellery as Vice-Chancellor. He has
been described as 'the most radical, the most enlightened, so to
speak the most modern' of all Joseph II's councillors.[51] Gottfried
von Koch was the son of Baron Ignaz Koch. His soldier-brother
Johann became governor of Ostend. Count Eugenius Wrbna
(1728–89) had studied at Leipzig and was president from 1756 until
1762 of the Commercial Commission for Lower Austria. From the
Chancellery he entered the *Hofkammer* (Banat Commission,
October 1768; vice-president of the *Hofkammer* and Bank Deputation, December 1771) then became president of the short-lived
Galician Chancellery in Vienna (1774–6). In 1776 he was made
Obrist Hofmarschall, serving till 30 May 1789.[52]

The enlarged *Hofkammer* exhibited the revival of that ancient
body from near-extinction. The list has a marked Hungarian
flavour, perhaps reflecting the business of the previous decade. The
inclusion of Hungarian councillors continued, as the names for 1775
show. This is not observable in 1740, the examples of Gyöngesi and
the Harrucker family apart, and must have been deliberate policy.
Of the councillors in 1763, only Stephen von Nagy survived from
1754, but Count Carl Pálffy was probably related to the Count
Johann of 1754. The president since 1 January 1762, Count Herberstein, had formerly been president of the Carinthian *Repraesentation*. In May 1765 he was retired from the *Hofkammer* in
favour of Count Friedrich Hatzfeld. The aged Vice-President,
Baron Hilleprand von Prandau, was nearing the end of his career

---

[51] G. Gugitz in *NDB*; Hock–Bidermann, 106, give Gebler's date of birth as 1726.
He entered the *Commercien-Directorium* by applying to Count Ludwig Zinzendorf
from Berlin on 21 Aug. 1753, Pettenegg 61; he was then secretary to a Count Reuss.
The quotation is from Holzknecht, *Ursprung und Herkunft*, 18. P. P. Bernard, 'The
Philosophe as Public Servant: Tobias Philip Gebler', *East Eur. Q.* 7 (1973) 41–51,
argues that he may have been a typical, rather than exceptional, reforming official.
[52] The Czech Vrbna was Germanized to Wrbna, *ex inf.* Dr R. J. W. Evans. *Khev.-
Metsch* uses 'Würben'. For Wrbna on the Lower Austrian Commercial Commission,
see Ch. 13, n. 6. For the *Hofkammer*, see *ÖZV* (1934), 304. He was in charge of one
of the two Departments into which the combined Chancellery and *Hofkammer* were
divided June–Dec. 1771, Beer, 'Die Finanzverwaltung', 259, and on 15 Dec. 1771 was
appointed vice-president of the *Hofkammer* and Bank Deputation, under Count
Leopold Kollowrat as president. He was stepson to Count Rudolf Chotek, who m.
Wrbna's mother, sister to Chancellor Philipp Kinsky, after the early death of
Wrbna's father, see *Khev.-Metsch*, 7 Jul. 1771.

and his life. Johann Baptist von Bolza is listed in 1746 as a tax-clerk in the Austrian Chancellery. In 1752, when he was an official in the *Directorium*, he was knighted, together with his two brothers, both in other government departments. One of these brothers, Johann Peter, became an important *Hofkammer* councillor.[53] Fekete and Festetics, like Nagy and Pálffy, were Hungarian. Festetics was subsequently (1772–82) vice-president of the Hungarian *Hofkammer* at Pressburg. Joseph II wanted him in the *Staatsrat* in December 1771 but was persuaded against it.[54] Philipp von Giganth is listed in 1754 as a salt official and councillor of the Lower Austrian *Repraesentation*. He served on it until 1758. Khevenhüller was the son of the diarist *Hofmeister*, and later became president of the *Hofrechen-kammer*.[55] The Bank Deputation in 1763 included Quiex, in office there in 1754, and Neffzer, transferred from the *Directorium*. The president's chair was occupied by the powerful figure of Count Karl Friedrich Anton Hatzfeld (1718–93). Hatzfeld came of an ancient family of Hessian origin, which had acquired the great lordship of Trachenberg in Lower Silesia in 1641. Owing to Frederick II's capture of Silesia, Hatzfeld's brother, Prince Franz of Trachenberg

---

[53] Payer von Thurn shows Prandau acting as vice-president of the *Hofkammer*, only to (?May) 1765, and Count Leopold Heinrich Schlik as vice-president (?May) 1766, i.e. after a year's interval, until his death, 26 Jan. 1770. Count Wrbna, 30 Nov. (effective 15 Dec.) 1771, was the next holder. See *Court Calendar*, 1746 and 1754 for J. B. Bolza's posts. See Megerle von Mühlfeld, under 'Ritter', for the knighting in 1752 of the Bolza brothers: Johann Baptist, Controller of the *Directorium-Taxamt*; Johann Nepomuk, an official in the *Hofkriegsrat*; and Johann Peter, an official in the Illyrian department. It is reasonable to infer that the latter is identical with Joseph Peter Bolza, (1721–1807), cr. a baron 1793, whose career is outlined by Wurzbach. See Table 12.4* for his councillorship of the *Hofkammer* in 1775, also App. C. s.n. 'Bolza'.

[54] *Khev.-Metsch*, 15 Dec. 1771; the Hungarian Chancellor Eszterházy objected to a Hungarian sitting in a council formally unconcerned with Hungary. The empress decided to make Festetics a count, and send him as vice-president to the Hungarian *Hofkammer*. Paul Festetics (1722–82) was *Vice-Comes* of Sopron County 1748, deputy to the Diet of 1751, councillor of the mines department in Vienna in 1756, then of the Hungarian Chancellery there in 1758. He became a councillor of the Vienna *Hofkammer* in 1762, Vice-President of the Hungarian *Hofkammer* and a member of the Council of Lieutenancy in 1772, and Sheriff of Baránya County in 1777. He was one of the Court's principal advisers on Hungary from the end of the Seven Years War. See Ember, 'Der österreichische Staatsrat', *passim*. Biographical details in *Acta Historica*, 6 (1959) 150 n.

[55] *NDB* and *Khev.-Metsch*. Count Joseph Franz Xaver Anton Khevenhüller (1737–97), the prince's fourth son; entered the *Reichshofrat* 1760, the *Hofkammer* 1764; *Landeshauptmann* of Carinthia, Dec. 1772; president of the *Hofrechenkammer*, May 1774; Govenor of Inner Austria, 1782; *Landmarschall* of Lower Austria, 1791.

(1717–79), was a Prussian subject. Friedrich Hatzfeld's mother Anna Stadion belonged to the important family which served the Electors of Mainz. Her mother was a Schönborn. Hatzfeld at first intended to enter the church, and became a canon of Mainz cathedral. He then changed his mind, and began a civil career as a councillor of the Bohemian *Appellation* in 1743. In 1748 he was appointed an assessor (councillor) of the new *Deputation* there. In 1757–9 he was President of the Bohemian *Appellation*, then in December 1761, through the emporer's influence, President of the Estates Credit Deputation. He was also put in charge of the Bank and *Generalkassa*. In May 1765 he united these offices with that of *Hofkammer* president, and in July 1771 temporarily added those of Bohemian Chief Chancellor and Austrian First Chancellor, and president of the Council of Trade. This union of powers was unprecedented, as Khevenhüller noted, and was a mistake. Hatzfeld's numerous enemies gathered against him. In December 1771 he was dismissed from all his offices, and kicked upstairs as Directing Minister of the *Staatsrat*. Such a sudden revolution in fortune is not often encountered, Khevenhüller reflected. Hatzfeld served out his term until his death. His influence in this long last phase of his career cannot be properly assessed, because of the destruction of the records of the *Staatsrat*, but it seems fair to surmise that his undoubted ability was never again fully tapped. He was married, but died childless. Frederick II named Hatzfeld and Kaunitz as Maria Theresia's ablest ministers.[56]

The President of the Council of Trade (*Hofkommerzienrat*) in 1763, Count Franz Andlern und Witte (1698–?1771) was one of Haugwitz's 'Silesians', though by birth an Austrian. He was vice-president of the Silesian *Kammer* in 1738, a councillor of the Lower Austrian *Regierung* 1723–45, president of the *Repraesentation and Kammer* in Upper Austria in 1752. He was from an Austrian family, added his stepfather's surname of von Witte to his own in

---

[56] In the foreign policy section of his *Political Testament* of 1768. For Hatzfeld see H. Wagner, *NDB*, with corrections from Auersperg, *Gesch. Appellationsg.*, also *Khev.-Metsch*, 19 May 1765, oath as president of the *Hofkammer*; 3 July 1771, oath as Bohemian *Obrist-Kanzler*, Austrian *Erster Kanzler*; 12 and 15 Dec. 1771, change of office. The empress's initial letter to Hatzfeld on 30 Nov. 1771, which he took two weeks to accept, was skilful and conciliatory, speaking of his future position as one of 'Ministre en chef' and 'erste Staats Ministre', *Khev.-Metsch 1770–3*, n. 124. He died in harness, 2 Sept. 1793.

1730, acquired the Moravian *Inkolat* in 1733, and was made an imperial count in 1736. Johann, Edler (1752) von Degelmann became a leading light of the Council of Trade. After its dissolution in 1776, he was transferred to service in Siebenbürgen. He was made a baron in 1780. Carl Holler von Doblhof had been a councillor of both the *Directorium* and the *Commercien-Directorium*, though otherwise there does not appear to be continuity of personnel between these two bodies and the new Council of Trade. Anton Holler von Doblhof-Dier was his son. The Managetta family was prominent in Lower Austria, and are encountered again in the next chapter. Baron Judas (in other sources Simon) Reischach (1728–1803), who came from an old Swabian family, was personal chamberlain to the Crown Prince Joseph, accompanying him to Frankfurt in 1764 and on several of his later journeys. He was on the Commercial Commission for Lower Austria in 1754–6. He became vice-president of the Council of Trade in 1771, and Bohemian and Austrian Chancellor in 1776. He was in the *Staatsrat* from 1782 to 1802. Lastly, Stegner, the director of the Linz woollen-factory, had also previously served on the Commercial Commission for Lower Austria. There were several changes of membership before the Council of Trade's dissolution in 1776.[57]

The final lists of central councillors (Table 12.4*), which are for 1775, show some continuity with the names already discussed, but also a number of changes. The membership of the *Staatsrat* had altered almost completely by this date. Haugwitz died in September 1765, Daun in February 1766. The experiment made in 1766–70 of appointing Prince Georg Adam Starhemberg (1724–1807), who

---

[57] In Aug. 1770 members attending the Council of Trade were Vice-Chancellor (*sic* for Chancellor) Leopold Kollowrat, acting as president [for the Chief Chancellor, Count Rudolf Chotek], Degelmann, Holler von Doblhof, [Friedrich] Eger, Managetta, [Franz Anton von] Raab, Baron Reischach, Stegner, Titlbach. In Oct. 1774 they were Reischach, vice-president [under Count Leopold Kollowrat], Doblhof-Dier, Eger, Raab, Rottenberg, Titlbach, HKA NÖ Kommerz, rote Nr. 133, fos. 277^r, 815^r. Biographical details from *SSMSGA Notizen-Blatt* (1870) 17–18 (Andlern und Witte); Megerle von Mühlfeld (Degelmann); Hock–Bidermann, 107; pp. 251, 368 (Reischach). Titlbach must be the emperor Francis Stephen's former secretary.

had distinguished himself as minister, then ambassador, in France from 1754, as 'Directing Minister in Inland Affairs', gave the *Staatsrat* a new shape, but did not answer well. Starhemberg was supposed to study foreign affairs with a view to replacing Kaunitz. The latter, however, recovered his ascendancy, the plan collapsed, and Starhemberg was sent (31 March 1770) as Minister to Brussels when Cobenzl died in January 1770. Starhemberg was subsequently *Erster Hofmeister* (1782–1807). After an interval of nearly two years, Hatzfeld succeeded to his position as Directing Minister in December 1771, as already noted. At the same time, Baron Friedrich Binder (1708–82), Kaunitz's right-hand man at the *Staatskanzlei*, returned there in 1772, having sat in the *Staatsrat*, largely to keep Kaunitz in touch, from 1766. Count Johann Anton Pergen (1725–1814), another protégé of Kaunitz, and future chief of police to Joseph II, Leopold II, and Francis II, was appointed to the *Staatsrat* at the same time as Starhemberg, with the additional position of minister at the *Staatskanzlei*. As Khevenhüller noted, Starhemberg was so busy in the *Staatsrat* that he had no time for foreign affairs; and Pergen was so busy with the latter that he had no time for the *Staatsrat*. He went to Galicia as first Austrian governor in August 1772, returning in February 1774. Blümegen was made Bohemian Chief Chancellor and Austrian First Chancellor in December 1771. Only Kaunitz, who seldom attended, and Stupan, who died in December 1776, provided continuity with the membership of 1761.[58] The new councillors were Kressel and Löhr, both of whom entered the *Staatsrat* in December 1771. Baron (1760) Franz Kressel von Qualtenberg (1720–1801) came of a Moravian noble family, studied law in Prague, was senior referendary in the juridical faculty there in 1754, and entered the Bohemian

---

[58] The account in Hock–Bidermann, 21, 26 is far from exact, and not correct in detail. Payer von Thurn is also unsatisfactory. Walter, *Geschichte*, 430–4 is vague about the appointment of Starhemberg and Pergen. For the former, see Schlitter, *ADB*. Count Johann Baptist Anton Pergen is not in *ADB*. The entry for him in Wurzbach is often confusing. Starzer, 336–45 is based on Arneth, Hock–Bidermann, etc. Pergen's career as governor of Galicia has recently been described in detail in Glassl, *Einrichtungswerk, passim*. For Starhemberg and Pergen's introduction to the *Staatsrat*, see *Khev.-Metsch*, 3–4 Sept. 1766. Binder, König, and Ignaz Koch, who d. in the following year, were all appointed *Staatsräte* on 1 June 1762, *ÖZV* (1934) 32. However Binder seems to have attended only from 1766. He took the oaths on 20 Sept. 1766, *Khev.-Metsch 1764–7, Staatsrat* agenda after p. 555.

and Austrian Chancellery after 1763. In 1773 he was put in charge of the commission to dissolve the Society of Jesus in Austria and sell its property, and of the Studies Commission which developed from it. On 27 May 1782 he left the *Staatsrat*, and on 15 June was nominated as president of Joseph II's *Geistliche Hofcommission*. He ended his career as Bohemian and Austrian Chancellor 1789–91.[59]
Baron (1772) Johann Friedrich Löhr (1735–95) was a nephew of Baron Borié. He was born at Wetzlar, studied at Heidelberg, came to Vienna in 1758 to practise before the *Reichschofrat*, entered the Bohemian *Appellation* as a councillor in 1761, and the *Oberste Justizstelle* on 6 February 1762. On 11 May 1771 he briefly entered the Bohemian and Austrian Chancellery. From December 1771 to May 1782 he was in the *Staatsrat*, then became Vice-President of the newly-created Lower Austrian *Appellation*. He ended his career as its president (1788). Besides these real new memberships, two others were honorary. Count Ludwig Zinzendorf's membership of the *Staatsrat* was a consolation prize extended when he laid down the presidency of the *Hofrechenkammer* on 24 January 1773. Though only 52, he was already broken in health and spirit, and spent much of his time until his death on 4 October 1780 either ill, or seeking cures abroad. Count Franz Moritz Lacy (1725–1801) was also a sick man when he entered the *Staatsrat* on 28 May 1774. He had effectively ended his term as President of the *Hofkriegsrat* in the previous October, in order to go to France to recover his health, and refused to take ministerial office again. Despite this, or perhaps because of it, he lived to the age of 76. The descendant of an old Irish family which had taken service in Russia after the Boyne, Lacy entered the Austrian army in 1743, and rose to the top, first as a brave regimental officer, then as administrator and planner. All evidence concurs that, then and later, he was not a successful commander in battle. His abilities were first fully tapped by his reconstruction of the Austrian army during his presidency of the *Hofkriegsrat* (1766–74) in succession to Daun. In this period, a

---

[59] 5 Feb. 1789 to 27 Jan. 1791, according to Payer von Thurn. Wurzbach is vague and unsatisfactory on Kressel. He is not in *ADB*. Hock–Bidermann, 106 add a few details, and Rieger, *Zřízení krajské*, ii. 355 n., 358 more. His family, from Iglau in Moravia, was granted arms in 1593. The variant spelling Kressl is common, and Kresl in the Czech literature.

close bond was forged between Joseph II and Lacy, who remained an intimate adviser and friend until the emperor's death.[60]

At the Bohemian and Austrian Chancellery, the tendency to German rather than Bohemian membership observable since 1749 had strengthened. The chancellery as a whole now had an expert and middle-class composition. Count Blümegen had recently (15 December 1771) succeeded Count Hatzfeld. Franz von Blanc (1734–1806) was a natural law theorist, and former army officer, of modest origins, who helped draft the *robot* patents for Silesia (1771) and Bohemia and Moravia (1775). He entered the chancellery in 1773. He quarrelled with Joseph II in 1777 and was put out to grass.[61] Anton Edler von Curti is listed as a councillor of the Styrian *Repraesentation* in the *Court Calendar* for 1763. Franz von Heinke (1726–1803) had entered the chancellery, and been ennobled, in 1767. He was the son of a senior customs officer in Prague, also ennobled in 1767. Heinke studied in Halle and Prague, where he became Doctor of Laws in 1748, and entered the *Appellation* in 1752, specializing in the law of feudal tenures. In 1764 he was made director of the juridical faculty of Prague University. In the chancellery, at the empress's orders, he specialized in ecclesiastical law, defending Kaunitz's radical reforms from the criticisms of the church establishment. From 1776 he was director of juridical studies at Vienna University. He was a leading, and hated, figure in ecclesiastical affairs until his voluntary retirement in 1793. He was knighted in 1775, and made a baron in 1790.[62] Baron Koch was a councillor of the chancellery from its inception. Joseph Koller was also one of the two Secretaries of the *Staatsrat*. His relationship, if

---

[60] See the *Court Calendar*, 1775 for the membership indicated. Zinzendorf and Lacy, though named by Hock–Bidermann, 41 as new members, are not listed, and must have been honorary, rather than effective, councillors. Kaunitz was designated 'Conferenz und Staatsminister', Hatzfeld 'Erster Staatsminister', Pergen 'Staatsminister', and the remainder 'Staatsrat'. In 1781 the *Calendar's* list included Prince Georg Starhemberg, then in Brussels as Austrian Minister, and Count Ludwig Zinzendorf, who was dead. Kaunitz, Hatzfeld, Gebler, Kressel, and Löhr were the others named. I am indebted to the Katalogabteilung of the Österreichische Nationalbibliothek for photocopies of the relevant *Calendar* entries. See *Khev.-Metsch*, 15 and 28 May 1774 for Lacy's determination to resign office and his nominations as 'Conferenz und Staatsminister'; ibid. 12 Nov. 1775 for Count Pergen's retention of 'der Staats-Ministre Praerogativen' on being made *Landmarschall* of Lower Austria. Lacy officially ceased to be President of the *Hofkriegsrat* on 5 May 1774.

[61] See ii. 210.

[62] Art. in *NDB* by F. Maass, who also devoted vol. iii of his history of Josephinism to Heinke's career.

any, to the Hungarian Kollers previously mentioned is not clear. The distinguished jurist Carl Anton von Martini (1726–1800), the son of a notary in Italian Tyrol, was professor of natural and Roman law at Vienna University from 1754, a member of the censorship commission from 1758, of the studies commission from 1760, of the *Oberste Justizstelle* 1764–74 and again from 1779. He entered the *Staatsrat* in May 1782, returning in 1788 to the *Oberste Justizstelle* as Vice-President. He was concerned with Austrian legal codification from 1771 until two years before his death. He was made knight in 1765, a baron in 1777.[63] Johann Sebastian Müller was perhaps the son of the Bohemian jurist Johann Georg Müller (1709–89) created Ritter von Müller in 1749, a councillor of the *Oberste Justizstelle* 1749–64, translator of the *Codex Theresianus* into Czech at the empress's request.[64] Florian von Perdacher (1720–86) was born in Carinthia, studied theology, then law (doctor 1750) in Vienna, and after a period as an advocate entered the Bohemian and Austrian Chancellery in 1764. He was knighted in 1769.[65] Paul Joseph Riegger (1705–75) was an influential Josephinist canon lawyer. He came from Villingen in the Breisgau, where his father was an official in the Further Austrian government. From Innsbruck (Professor of Natural Law 1733), where he taught Martini, Riegger came to Vienna (1753) to teach canon law at the *Theresianum*. His voluminous publications, directed in Latin to a learned audience, were a programme for action against the existing usages of the church.[66] Ottocar Stupan von Ehrenstein, a councillor of the *Hofkammer* in 1763, was in 1775 president of the Court Rectification Commission for the tax cadastre, with Anton von Blanc as one of his councillors.[67]

The *Hofkammer* in 1775 was larger than in 1763 (21 members compared to 15) and overlapped with the still quite sizeable Bank Deputation, the president and three councillors being common to

---

[63] Maasburg, 94–7.

[64] Ibid. 119–21.

[65] Ibid. 141–2.

[66] Wurzbach, whose Josephinist sympathies are apparent here as elsewhere. Riegger's position was pro-royal, anti-papal, in favour of the national church, for restrictions on monastic vows and other supposed abuses, against popular superstitions. Maass, *Der Frühjosephinismus*, ch. iv, 'Der Kanonist Paul Joseph von Riegger', argues that Riegger was Maria Theresia's favourite canon lawyer, and supported the right of the Crown to tax the church without papal consent.

[67] See ii. 209. It seems plausible that he was the son of Anton Stupan.

both. The presidencies had been united since 1765. Count Leopold Kollowrat (1727–1809), appointed in December 1771, added the presidency of the Council of Trade. He belonged to the Krakowsky branch of this influential Bohemian family, and was the son-in-law of the diarist Prince Khevenhüller-Mersch. His father, Count Philipp, was made *Obrist-Burggraf* of Bohemia in 1748, serving until forced to resign in June 1771. On discharge from the army in 1748, Leopold entered the Bohemian *Appellation*. He subsequently left it, and perhaps Bohemian service, since the *Court Calendar* in 1763 does not show his name in the *Appellation, Repraesentation und Kammer*, 'Consessus derer Königl. Herren Landes-Officiren', or *Consessus in Causis Summi Principis*, the four Bohemian bodies which it lists. In 1765, however, Leopold Kollowrat is shown as a councillor of the Bohemian *Gubernium*, under his father as president. In August 1767, on Baron Bartenstein's death, he became Vice-Chancellor of Bohemia and Austria, and as such presided over the Council of Trade. In July 1771, he was sworn in as Bohemian and Austrian Chancellor, under Hatzfeld as Chief Chancellor. His responsibility was for the *Hofkammer*, Banat, and mines and coinage. In the further reshuffle announced on 15 December 1771, he became president of the *Hofkammer*, Bank Deputation, and Council of Trade, with Wrbna under him as vice-president of the *Hofkammer* and Bank, and Baron Reischach as vice-president of the Council of Trade. In 1782 he reached the top rung of the chancellery ladder as Bohemian Chief Councillor and Austrian First Chancellor, combining this with the presidencies of the *Hofkammer* and Bank Deputation. He held his chancellery offices until 1796, when he succeeded to the post, left vacant since Hatzfeld's death, of Directing Minister in the *Staatsrat*. He retired in September 1808, and died on 2 November 1809, a fortnight after the Treaty of Schönbrunn of 14 October virtually dismembered the Monarchy.[68]

Johann Baptist von Bolza in the *Hofkammer* list was now joined as councillor by his brother Johann Peter (1721–1807), who had

---

[68] Payer von Thurn; Hock–Bidermann. The short and inaccurate notice in Wurzbach states that he was *Obrist-Kanzler*, then president of the Bank Deputation, and 'later' Directing State Minister. He was made Vice-Chancellor 5 Aug. 1767, and Bohemian and Austrian Chancellor. July 1771, when he was sworn in by his father-in-law Prince Khevenhüller; see diary at that date. By 1780 Joseph II did not trust his financial abilities, PRO SP 80/223, Keith to Stormont, 10 Dec. 1780. The family's name was spelt Kolovrát; 'Kollowrat' was a German attempt to reproduce the Czech pronunciation.

started his official career in the war office, and went on to become a
baron in 1793. He was also a councillor of the Bank Deputation.[69]
Carqui had transferred to the *Hofkammer* from the Bohemian and
Austrian Chancellery. Baron Jacob Benedict von Neffzern was in
the *Directorium* in 1754. Baron Conrad was probably his son. Franz
Carl von Rustenfeld was a councillor of the Hungarian *Hofkammer*
1772–4. Baron Franz Schmidlin's relationship to Baron Christoph,
a *Hofkammer* councillor in 1763, is not clear. The council in 1775
again contained five Hungarians (Mailáth, two von Neffzern,
Pálffy, Zichy). In the Bank Deputation, Philipp von Giganth had
been at the *Hofkammer* in 1763, and Baron Spiegelfeld at the
Hofrechenkammer in 1770. Two other former *Hofrechenkammer*
members, Hermann Evers and Mathias Puechberg, were councillors of the short-lived Galician Court Chancellery. Like Spiegelfeld, they were being compensated for losing their positions when
the *Rechenkammer* was reconstructed in 1773.[70] The president of
the Galician Chancellery (May 1774) Count Wrbna, became
Obrist-Hofmarschall in April 1776.[71] Count Cavriani (1739–99),
descended from a Mantuan noble family, was a councillor of the
Lower Austrian *Landrecht* to 1767, then served in the Bohemian
Gubernium, until entering the Galician Chancellery in 1774. On its
dissolution in 1776 he moved to the *Oberste Justizstelle*, and
became its vice-president in the same year.[72] The Siebenbürgen
Court Chancellery at this date was in commission. This seems to
have been the product of special circumstances. No Chancellor had
been appointed to succeed Count Bethlen, when the latter was
retired (with the Golden Fleece and a Court position) on 6
December 1765. Instead, a *Hofcommission* of three persons, nominally headed by Count Breuner, and first appointed in May 1765,
administered the province's affairs until 1774. Its leading member
was the remarkable Baron (1762) Samuel von Brukenthal
(1721–1803). He was a member of the Lutheran Saxon Nation in
Siebenbürgen. His father, Michael Brekner, a legal official in

[69] See n. 53.
[70] See ii. 85. Evers, who was Count Zinzendorf's secretary, was made a councillor of the *Hofrechenkammer* in Jan. 1770, Pettenegg, 133. There were four others.
[71] The Galician Chancellery took the form of a *Hofdeputation* 7 Jan. 1774,
changed to a chancellery 21 May 1774. It was dissolved 26 Apr. 1776, see Glassl,
74–5, 79, and 87 (Wrbna's appointment as *Obrist-Hofmarschall*).
[72] Maasburg, 93–4.

13

Councillors of State II

THE inquiry now turns to the standard-bearers of royal local authority. Who governed the Austrian, Bohemian, and Hungarian lands in the Crown's name? Tables 13.1*–13.6* provide the material for some answers to this question. The basis of selection is royal government, ignoring for convenience that the lines between royal and Estates government tended at first to be blurred in all lands, and that much 'administration' was judicial rather than executive in character. The institutions of 1740 in Table 13.1* are the Bohemian *Statthalterei*, the Moravian *Tribunal*, and the Silesian *Oberamt* and *Kammer*; and, outside the Bohemian lands, the Lower Austrian *Regierung*, the Inner Austrian *Geheimer Rat und Kanzlei* and the Inner Austrian *Hofkammer*. Full biographical analysis of all those listed would require an amount of information at present lacking. Certain identifications and remarks are, however, possible. The *Obrist-Burggraf* in Bohemia, Count Johann Schafgotsch, who held the office 1734–47, was closely involved in revision of the tax cadastre there under Charles VI. He died in July 1747. Count Philipp Kollowrat, the father of the future *Hofkammer* president, became *Burggraf* in his place and served until 1771. Baron Netolicky was named president of the new *Deputation* in 1748. The members of the *Statthalterei* belonged with some exceptions to a restricted circle of magnate families, most of them of Bohemian stock, which monopolized the great local offices, and excluded newcomers, as Dr Hassenpflug-Elzholz, confirming Maria Theresia's statements, cogently demonstrated.[1] The Moravian *Tribunal*

---

[1] See ii. 218 for Schafsgotsch and the cadastre; *Khev.-Metsch*, 15 Oct. 1748 for Philipp Kollowrat's appointment 'with general applause'; ibid. 30 June 1771 for his resignation, caused by court intrigue; ibid., 28 Mar. 1773 for his death, aged 85 years. Hassenpflug-Elzholz, *Böhmen und die böhmischen Stände*, demonstrates (pp. 65–70) that 25 *Herrenstand* families shared the highest Bohemian offices, including that of Chancellor, from the 1620s to 1741. Prominent were Czernin, Colloredo, Gallas, Kinsky, Kokorzowa, Kollowrat (two lines), Lažansky, Nostitz, Schaffgotsch,

was headed by the future Prince Kaunitz's father. Baron Blümegen was at the start of his long public career. In the Silesian *Oberamt* in 1737, Ludwig Wilhelm is presumably a misprint for Friedrich Wilhelm Haugwitz; and Kannegiesser and Kommergansky, as he is more correctly spelt, were shortly to move to the Bohemian Court Chancellery in Vienna. In the Silesian *Kammer*, Count Horns was replaced as vice-president in 1738 by Count Franz Reinhold Andlern und Witte. The size of the powerful Lower Austrian *Regierung*, with its numerous *Ritterstand* and *Gelehrtenstand*, several of the latter being doctors of law, and others no doubt with legal qualifications, is noteworthy.[2] From this body, Count Niclas Stella, Carl Cetto, and [Johann] Joseph Managetta later entered the *Directorium*, and others the Lower Austrian *Repraesentation und Kammer*. The president of the *Regierung* in 1740, Count Sigmund Khevenhüller, the diarist's father, was *Statthalter* of Lower Austria 1711–42. Count Christoph Oedt, *Vice-Statthalter* 1734–47, had been in the *Regierung* since 1703. He was made Austrian Vice-Chancellor in 1747, and in May 1748 vice-president of the *Oberste Justizstelle*, resigning, however, at the end of the year. He became president of the Lower Austrian *Repraesentation und Kammer* in January 1750, but died in the next month. Christoph Schmidt von Wayenberg had also been in the *Regierung* since 1703, and its chancellor since 1724. He died in 1742. Count Franz Theodor Andlern (served 1723–45) was a Mainz *Hofrat*, made an imperial count in 1736. He was perhaps the brother of Count Franz Reinhold Andlern und Witte. Count Breuner (1687–1762) entered the *Regierung* in 1709. He was *Vice-Statthalter* 1747–49, then the first (and only) president of the *Regierung in Justizsachen* (1749–59). Count Dietrichstein (1706–80) served 1730–47, and Count Engel (1688–1767) served 1721–45. Count Harrach (1692–1758), a councillor since 1718, was a *Verordneter* of the Lower Austrian Estates 1733–39. Count Franz Lamberg entered the *Regierung* in 1733.

Schlick, Sternberg, Trauttmannsdorf, Waldstein, Wratislaw von Mitrowitz, Wrbna, Wrtby. Maria Theresia's complaints are in her memorial of 1750. The main source for the Bohemian *Landesoffiziere* is F. Palacký, *Přehled saučasný neywyššjch dŭstognjkŭ* (Prague 1832), repr. in J. Charvát (ed.), *Dílo Františka Palackého* (Prague 1941), i. I am indebted to Dr R. J. W. Evans for the last reference.

   [2] Biographical details are mostly from Starzer's notices of *Regierung* councillors. Gall, Schick, Leopold Schmerling, and Spaun in the *Court Calendar* list for 1740 are shown by Starzer to have served to 1733 at latest; hence they may have been only nominal councillors in 1740.

His relationship to Count Carl is not clear. Marchese Montecuccoli ended his career as president of the mercantile appeals court (?1749–52). Count Johann Baptist Pergen (1646–1741, a councillor 1701–?12 and again from 1718) was the father of Count Johann Ferdinand, who had served since 1710, and was also an Estates *Verordneter*. Count Johann Ferdinand's son was the police chief, Count Johann Anton Pergen. Count Thürheim (1692–1749), educated at Louvain, was a volunteer in the Turkish campaign of 1717, a *Regierung* councillor 1720–45, president of the Estates of Austria above the Enns until 1742. Count Stella was a councillor of the *Directorium* in 1754, and Baron Tinti of the *Hofkammer* in 1740 (Tables 12.1*, 12.2*).

The information available for many of the important group of *Ritterstand* and *Gelehrtenstand* councillors is virtually confined to their years of service in the *Regierung*. This is true, with years bracketed, of Dizent (1719–1750, when he died); Gall (1717–30 (*sic*)); Gerbrand (1705–40); Kellern (1729–45); Kirchstetten (1716–46) and Pfann (1727–49), both doctors of law; Johann Carl Weber (1739–49); and Johann Jacob Weber or Wöber (1718–46). Of the others, Carl Joseph Cetto may be identical with Carl Cetto von Kronstorf, a councillor of the Austrian Chancellery (Table 12.1*); if so his membership of the *Regierung* can only have been nominal, a place there being incompatible with any other, by regulations of Joseph I. Haan, as he is properly spelt, was a distinguished jurist, who entered the *Oberste Justizstelle* in 1749, and died in 1768. [Johann] Joseph Managetta of the *Gelehrtenstand* went on to become president of the Lower Austrian *Repraesentation und Kammer*, and councillor first of the *Directorium*, then of the Bohemian and Austrian Chancellery. His brother, Philipp Joseph, entered the *Regierung* in 1734, and became a *Verordneter* of the Lower Austrian Estates in 1740. In 1753 he was appointed one of the first Lower Austrian Circle Captains.[3] Franz Christian Menshengen or Mensshengen was born in 1692 and died after 1779. He was educated at the University of Giessen, and served as legation secretary in Brunswick and London. He entered the *Regierung* in 1719, and ended his career as president of the Lower Austrian mercantile

---

[3] See Table 13.4*. His eldest son, also Philipp Joseph, was a Lower Austrian Circle Captain 1764–78, ibid. Joseph, referred to in the next note, must have been the son of Baron Johann Joseph. Baron Johann Georg, a councillor of the *Hofkommerzienrat* 1762–73, was perhaps another son.

appeals court. Johann Baptist was his brother, serving 1739–46. Johann then entered Estates service (*Obereinnehmer* 1752), returning to the *Regierung* in 1764. His son, Ignaz, became a Circle Captain in 1760, serving to 1777. He was also a *Regierung* councillor 1762–78.[4] Pichler or Püchler was secretary of the *Regierung* in 1733, its chancellor in 1744. By 1754 he was in the Lower Austrian *Repraesentation*. His relationship, if any, to Maria Theresia's Cabinet Secretary, Carl Joseph Püchler, is not known. Jacob Christoph Schmerling entered the *Regierung in Justizsachen* in 1750, transferring to the *Repraesentation* in 1753. Leopold Schmerling, who was perhaps his father, was a councillor of the Ministerial Bank Deputation in 1740, and his membership of the *Regierung* was probably only titular. Spaun was dean of the juridical faculty at Vienna University in 1732. Zwenghof, or Zwenhof, who entered the *Regierung* in 1740, was to serve there until 1778.

Table 13.2* concentrates on the *Deputationen* and *Repraesentationen und Kammern* of 1748–54, since the existing literature, while emphasizing their importance, is imprecise about them. It seems fairly clear that there was overlap (in Bohemia, initially, identity) between the personnel of the 'Deputations' and 'Representations', but that the latter quickly expanded, being larger in 1752 than in 1748, and markedly larger in 1754. This corresponded locally to the increase in size of the *Directorium* to which they reported. A factor of some importance here was the addition of the *Consessus in Causis Summi Principis* to the *Repraesentationen* in 1751. In Bohemia in 1754 six, in Moravia four, in Silesia four, in Lower Austria three, of the councillors belonged to these bodies, which were primarily responsible for crown revenue cases, especially those concerning contraband. It is a fair inference that the new customs tariffs for the Bohemian lands in 1752, and for Upper and Lower Austria in 1755, gave them plenty of work, as the numerous cases which

---

[4] As *Obereinnehmer*, Johann Baptist became involved in a deficit of 130,286 fl. left by a previous treasurer, Joseph Managetta jr., when he d. in 1762. Mensshengen himself had a smaller deficit of 8,696 fl. Baron [Johann Joseph] Managetta offered to pay his son's debt. The whole episode was investigated by Mathias Puechberg, appointed a councillor of the *Regierung* for the purpose, see Pettenegg, *Zinzendorf*, 99, where, however, the deficit is incorrectly stated as coming to light only in 1765, and NÖLA Standische Bücher, no. 96 30 Oct. 1762 (Managetta's death and his deficiency), 23 July, 20 and 29 Aug. 1763.

went to the *Oberste Justizstelle* on appeal indicate. This further fiscal aspect of the *Repraesentationen*, whose primary responsibility was the Contribution, cannot have improved their popularity. Another new entrant to the *Repraesentation* by 1754 was the war commissary. Despite Maria Theresia's statement in 1750, that 'diesen Repraesentationen sind in denen Ländern angestellte Kriegscommissarii beigegeben worden', they are only shown in the Austrian, not the Bohemian, lands in the 1754 *Court Calendar*. This seems likely, however, to be an omission on the calendar's part.[5]

Taking membership over the period 1748–54 as a whole, in Bohemia Netolicky had been a member of the *Statthalterei* in 1740; the young Hatzfeld was on the threshold of his important career; and Ignaz Textor, who by 1752 is von Textor, is shown in the 1748 *Court Calendar* as a councillor of the Bohemian College of Commerce. In Moravia, Baron Blümegen, another future minister, had been in the *Tribunal* in 1740, as had Baron Widmann. The latter is named in the 1754 *Calendar* as still a *Tribunal* councillor, as well as minister to the Bavarian Court, and to the Frankish Circle of the Empire. The Lower Austrian *Repraesentation* in 1754 denoted the administrative section of the former *Regierung*, the *Regierung in Justizsachen* of 1749 having absorbed the remainder. The vice-president (5 May 1753), Baron Johann Joseph Managetta, together with Count Franz Lamberg, Johann Gottlieb Püchler (Pichler), Johann Schick, Jacob Schmerling, Joseph Tepfern, Baron Tinti, and Paul Zwenghof, had all been in the *Regierung* in 1740. The president (1753–58), Baron Heinrich Wilhelm Haugwitz, was in the Styrian *Deputation* in 1748; he was Count Friedrich Haugwitz's cousin, and, like him, a convert to Catholicism. He died, aged only 49, in October 1758. John Paul Buol may be the son of the *Directorium* councillor, Baron Anton Buol. Johann Eger had been one of the Secretaries of the Bohemian Chancellery as early as 1740. He continued into the post-war *Regierung* (*Ritterstand* councillor 1765), and was the father of Friedrich von Eger, a prominent executant of Joseph II's land tax reforms. Victor Joseph Häring (1687–1764), from Graz, assisted Field Marshal Prince Sachsen-Hildburghausen with the thorny reorganization of the frontier

---

[5] The empress's statement is in her memorial of 1750. For the revenue cases see p. 324.

militia in 1746. He was a councillor of the Carinthian *Deputation* in 1748, as the table shows, and entered the Lower Austrian *Repraesentation* in April 1750. Joseph Holger (1706–83) was an eminent lawyer, who served in the *Oberste Justizstelle* from 1759 until his death. Pillewitz, Reichmann, Schick, and Veronese were members of the Commercial Commission for Lower Austria. Count Sigmund Khevenhüller was the diarist's son, and in 1756 went to Portugal as Austrian minister.[6] The president of the *Repraesentation* in Upper Austria, Count Andlern und Witte, in 1752 deprived of his title in the MS source, became president of the Council of Trade in 1763. His councillor of 1752, Loscani, moved to Bohemia in 1754, and became prominent in commercial business.[7]

In Styria, as just noted, the *Deputation* in 1748 included Haugwitz's cousin Baron Heinrich Wilhelm, and the *Repraesentation und Kammer* of 1752 had a hybrid look, with a Bohemian count at its head, and councillors drawn from families only two of which (Breuner, Curti) were of any local weight. This must have been doubly galling, in view of the poverty of the nobility and church subsequently noted by Bartenstein.[8] It is suggestive, though not conclusive, that Count Nostitz (Carinthia 1748) came of a Bohemian family, and Count Sobegg (1752) of a Silesian one, while Heinrich von Blumencron in the same year was a former councillor of the Silesian *Kammer*.[9] Rudolf (Moravia 1752, 1754) was perhaps his son. Baron Ernst Mittrovsky (Krain 1748) was Silesian by birth, and had moved back to the *Amt* there by 1752. He must be related to Baron Johann (Bohemia, 1754). Count Andlern und Witte in

---

[6] *Khev.-Metsch*; Maasburg, *Gersch. ob. Justizstelle*; Starzer. For Baron Haugwitz see p. 230. The membership of the 'Delegirte Hof-Commission' for Lower Austrian trade and manufactures at 17 Dec. 1754 was Count [Niclas] Stella (pres.), Baron [Gottfried] Koch, Pillewitz, Reichmann, Reischach, Schick, Stegner, Count Salm, Veronese, [Count Eugenius] Wrbna, [Count Ludwig] Zinzendorf. At 12 Jan. 1756 it was Count Wrbna (pres.), Baron Carignani, [Paul] Festetics, Grueber, Baron Lopresti, Pillewitz, Reichmann, Baron Reischach, Stegner, Veronese, HKA NÖ Kommerz, rote Nr. 121 fo. 22ʳ, rote Nr. 113, fo. 12ʳ, Christian names not given. There was a clear overlap with the *Repraesentation*. There is much about the Sicilian Lopresti and his theatrical enterprises in *Khev.-Metsch*. Stegner was the manager of the Linz woollen-factory; he and Reischach entered the *Hofkommerzienrat* in 1763.

[7] Loscani's report of 1756 on five Bohemian manufacturing circles is printed by Fournier, 'Handel und Verkehr', 366–80, where he is described as baron.

[8] See ii. 139.

[9] See Table 13.1*. Nostitz was Count Khevenhüller's brother-in-law, diary 31 Aug. 1747.

Upper Austria was a former vice-president of the Silesian *Kammer*. Some confirmation is suggested here for contemporary views that Haugwitz was using his 'Silesians' to introduce reform over local opposition, particularly in Inner Austria, the object of his tours in 1747, and where resistance to his 'System' was initially bitter.[10] Again, Netolicky and Blümegen in Bohemia and Moravia belonged only to the minor nobility, while several of those named, there and elsewhere, especially in the period 1748–52, look like middle-class officials. The new *Kreishauptmänner* also seem to have been a mixed bunch, as is seen below. Meanwhile, the established (pre-1749) governments' members were as far as possible assigned to purely legal duties, or provided for elsewhere. In Bohemia, the *Consess der obersten Landesoffiziere* created on 7 May 1749, absorbed the former councillors of the *Statthalterei*. The *Consess* merged with the *Gubernium* in 1764.[11] The Moravian *Tribunal* in 1752 largely comprised members of the former *Tribunal und Gouverno*.[12] As already noted, a section of members of the former Lower Austrian *Regierung* became in 1749 the 'Regierung in Justiz-Sachen'.[13] Four of the seven councillors of the Inner Austrian *Geheimer Rat* were assigned after 1748 to a new *Judicium Revisorium* or appeal court. Similar moves occurred in Carinthia, Krain, and Tyrol. As argued earlier, all this must have provided some antidote to the hostility created by Haugwitz's reforms.[14]

As the 'Representations' expanded, some further accommodation

---

[10] Cf. Arneth, *Gesch. Mar. Ther.* iv. 65, Venetian ambassador's report in 1756 that 'everyone condemns the new arrangements, and the Silesians who made the plan for them'. For use of Silesian 'actuaries' to check Lower Austrian tax in 1756, see ii. 248.

[11] See p. 274. The merger accounts for the increase in the number of members of the *Gubernium* from 8 in 1763 to 23 in 1765.

[12] The eight names of councillors in 1752 are given in HKA Hs. 247, fo. 145. Six, including the *Landeshauptmann* Count Heissler, were members of the 11-man 'Gouvernium' (*sic*) of 1748 shown in HKA Hs. 220, fo. 107.

[13] The names of these members have not been traced, however from Starzer's biographical notes it appears that Count Johann Joseph Breuner was president 1749–59, with Count Johann Ferdinand Pergen as vice-president. Franz Joseph Buol, Elias Engel, who subsequently moved to the *Repraesentation*, and Dr Johann Fraisel were named from 1749. Philipp Hackher zu Hart was secretary 1749–53.

[14] The seven councillors of the Inner Austrian *Geheimer Rat* in 1748 are shown in HKA Hs. 220, fo. 189ʳ and the eight members of the *Judicium Revisorium* in 1752 in HKA Hs. 247, fo. 172ᵛ. Similarly, the Styrian *Regierung* of 1748 was retained for legal business, and its membership expanded, HKA Hss. 220, fo. 189ᵛ (1748), 247 fo. 174ʳ (1752). The members of the Inner Austrian *Hofkammer*, however, HKA Hs. 220, fo. 203ʳ (1748), do not appear to have survived its abolition.

of local worthies was possible, and perhaps expedient politically. The Bohemian list for 1754 includes one of the greatest, though most recent, Bohemian magnates, Prince Fürstenberg (1729–87), later president of the *Gubernium* there, and Franz Joseph Kollowrat, a member of this prolific clan, besides Count Wieschnick, another native, and smaller men like Dohalsky and Malowetz. The Hilleprand von Prandau family, also represented in the Moravian *Repraesentation*, were powerful, though new, landowners.[15] In Styria, Counts Auersperg and Rosenberg, both additions since 1752, were landowners in Krain and Carinthia respectively, but Count Wagensperg, who had transferred from duty in Carinthia, was a Styrian. The Tyrol list of 1754 is respectable, though there were important changes in it by 1763. The argument that the 'Representations' became more 'establishment' in composition as they became larger is weaker for Lower Austria, where professional officials easily outweighed Barons Buol, Managetta, and Tinti— themselves small beer to contemporary aristocrats—and Counts Khevenhüller-Metsch, Lamberg, and Windischgrätz. Nevertheless, it appears to have substance in the post-war period (Table 13.3*) which is discussed next.

The *Gubernium* of Bohemia in 1765 contained many of the families in the *Statthalterei* of 1740: Kinsky (Chinitz), Clary, Kollowrat, Sternberg. In 1779, the longer list was short on Kollowrats, Count Leopold having become President of the *Hofkammer*, but otherwise reads like a partial roll of the higher Bohemian aristocracy. Smaller men like Astfeld, Bieschin, Hoyer, Kotz and Mayer, (a professional official who gave public lectures on cameral practice from 1773) must have been overawed by them.[16] Perhaps this was why Keith noted in December 1780 that great changes would be needed in the government of Bohemia.[17] Similarly, in the Inner Austrian *Gubernium*, the Dietrichsteins, Herbersteins, Sauers, Stubenbergs, Stürcks, Wagenspergs, Wildensteins, and Würmbrands were all

---

[15] The great Fürstenberg family was Swabian, and their Bohemian estates were those of a secondary line.

[16] For Mayer see p. 280.

[17] PRO SP 80/223, Keith to Stormont 10 Dec. 1780. The empress told her son Ferdinand on 13 Feb. 1777 that her plans for reform of peasant conditions in Bohemia had been frustrated by 'les seigneurs, qui, par parenthèse, sont tous les ministres'. Arneth, *Mar. Ther. Kinder und Freunde*, ii. 69.

from Styrian landowning families, though Count Podstatzky (1779) was not. A former head of the tax rectification committee, he was now put out to grass.[18] In Tyrol, the list of 1779 seems markedly superior socially to that of 1765, though the Trapp family, prominent in 1754, was still excluded. The Silesian and Moravian lists are perhaps more cosmopolitan in character, as they had been all along, but it is observable that by 1779 a Blümegen (the chancellor's brother) was at the head of Moravian government, and was joined by two counts Salm, and that the Silesian government at this date included a Larisch and a Sobeck, both prominent local families.[19] The Lower Austrian *Regierung*, divided from 1759 into executive and judicial senates, was not noticeably different in composition after the Seven Years War from the body of 1740, though over the period it first shrank, then expanded. The *Court Calendar* recorded for it (besides the *Statthalter*, *Vice-Statthalter*, and *Kanzler*): in 1740, 22 members from the *Herrenstand*, 23 from the *Ritterstand*, and 13 from the *Gelehrtenstand*; in 1765, respectively 14, 20 and 13; in 1779, 30, 33, and 16; making a total (with the ex-officio members) of 61 in 1740, 50 in 1765, and 82 in 1779. These figures exclude supernumerary councillors, of whom there were 20 in 1765 and 11 in 1779. However, it seems clear that only some of those who were supposed to attend actually did so.[20] Long service, and continuity of some families, are observable from the lists. Thus Franz von Gall, Franz and Johann von Mensshengen, and Paul von Zwenghof, were all councillors in both 1740 and 1765. Baron

---

[18] See ii. 209. His family was either Moravian or Bohemian.

[19] Count Christoph Blümegen concealed an irregularity in the province's accounts, with his brother's connivance, and was forced to resign in 1782, Hock–Bidermann, 133–4. Ignaz Schröfl von Mansperg (Moravia 1765, 1779) must be related to Johann Leopold Schreffl von Mannsperg, director of mining in Hungary, whose dau. m. Cabinet Secretary Ignaz Koch. The members of the *Consessus Commerciales* in the Bohemian and Austrian lands are given in the *Court Calendar* for 1770 (in 1763 and 1765 only the committees in Lower Austria and the Bohemian lands are shown). Examination of the names indicates that the Bohemian experiment was the largest, and separation of membership there between *Consessus* and *Gubernium* most marked. This explains the hostility between the two bodies complained of by Joseph II on his Bohemian tour in 1771.

[20] Starzer, 71, Instruction of 16 Apr. 1759 requiring the *Regierung* to conduct judicial business, and 'politica et mixta', in separate senates. At p. 69 he gives numbers of *Herren*, *Ritter*, and *Gelehrte* in 1759 as 16, 20, 12, in 1776 as 21, 25, 23. A total of 37 persons attended the *Regierung* meetings of 29 May 1772, 31 July 1773, 24 Aug. 1774, 12 of whom were *Herrenstand* members, list constructed from NÖLA Normalien, Karton 309/4553.

(1750) Johann Paul von Buol, the brother of the *Vice-Statthalter* (1759–67) Baron Anton Franz Buol, entered the *Regierung* in 1742 and was still there in 1779. Johann Carl Cetto von Kronstorf (1759–78), Count Franz Sigmund Engel (1752–68), Franz de Paula Fraisel (1756–75), Jacob von Pistrich (1749–78), Ferdinand von Sartori (1755–80), and Johann Ludwig von Thiell (1745–54 and 1759–79) are other examples of lengthy service. Count Johann Abensperg (list of 1740) and his son Count Rudolph Abensperg (lists of 1765 and 1779), Count Leopold Dietrichstein (1740) and Count Johann Dietrichstein (1765), Counts Franz Friedrich Engel (1740) and Franz Sigmund Engel (1765), Johann Georg Haan (1740) and his son Mathias Wilhelm Haan or Hahn (1765), Philipp Jacob Managetta (1740) and his son of the same name (1779), Joseph Anton Dominic Mayenberg (1740) and Joseph Anton Mayenberg (1765, 1779), Johann Baptist Mensshengen (1740) and his son Ignaz (1765, 1779) Carl Joseph Cetto (1740) and Johann Carl Cetto (1765, 1779), Johann Jacob Fraisel (1740) and Franz de Paula von Fraissl (1765, 1779), and Franz Anton von Spaun (1740) and Johann Thaddaeus von Spaun (1765), denote family continuity, though the relationship cannot always be documented. From the *Repraesentation* list of 1754, Eger, Reichmann, Schick, Veronese, and Vogel reappear in the *Regierung* of 1765; Koch and Managetta went to the Bohemian and Austrian Chancellery, and Count Lamberg and Carl von Pillewitz to the new (1762) Lower Austrian *Kommerzienkonsess*.[21] Between 1765 and 1779, despite the increased numbers in the latter year, a substantial continuity of the same persons or families is evident.

This was also true at the top. Count Franz Schrattenbach, a noted enemy of Gerard van Swieten, was Lower Austrian *Statthalter* from 1759 to 1770. His universally respected successor, Count Christian Seilern, the son of the last Austrian Chancellor, was *Statthalter* 1770–9, when he became president of the *Oberste Justizstelle*. Baron Anton Franz Buol, *Vice-Statthalter* 1759–67, was at the end of his distinguished legal career, noted in the previous chapter. Count Herberstein in 1779 was only a stopgap appointment; his misfortune was to be in charge when Joseph II succeeded, determined to recast the *Regierung*, as much else. The long-serving (1759–82) *Kanzler* of the *Regierung*, Thomas von Pöck, who must

---

[21] *Court Calendar*, 1763.

have provided important continuity of advice, was in the *Oberste Justizstelle* 1751–9, and returned there from 1782 until his death in 1786. He was the compiler (1777) of the major collection of government decrees drawn on in Ch. 11. *Gelehrtenstand* members of the *Regierung* in 1765 and 1779 included some distinguished legal names. Joseph Froidevo (1779) from Arlesheim in Switzerland was in the *Regierung* 1768–71 and 1774–82, before entering the *Oberste Justizstelle*, where he served continuously until 1811. Mathias Wilhelm Haan, the son of Johann Georg Haan (1740), entered the *Oberste Justizstelle* in 1775, and in 1792 became vice-president of the Lower Austrian Court of Appeal. Philipp Jakob Hackher (1765) is the same man as the Philipp 'Friedrich' of 1779. He was Secretary of the *Regierung in Justizsachen* in 1749, and served in the *Regierung* as councillor 1764–82, then entered the Lower Austrian Court of Appeal and finally (1788) the *Oberste Justizstelle*. Franz Joseph Hackher (1779) was one of his three brothers, and was a councillor of the *Regierung* from 1774 to 1807. The *Gelehrtenstand* members in 1779 also included the distinguished doctor Joseph Quarin, future (1784) Director of the *Allgemeines Krankenhaus*, and Rector of Vienna University (1788 etc); and the powerful, though perhaps not central, figure of Professor Joseph von Sonnenfels.[22] Lastly, the Galician government in 1779, which included a member of the Raigersfeld family from Krain, had a hybrid and professional appearance. One of its members, Christoph von Koranda, an ennobled Bohemian official, was particularly charged with amelioration of peasant conditions. He worked closely with Joseph II in the 1770s. The initial Austrian intention of enlisting the large Polish landowners was frustrated by their lack of co-operation.[23]

Some information about the Circle Captains in the Bohemian and

---

[22] Biographical details from Starzer, supplemented in one or two instances by Maasburg. For a recent assessment in English of Sonnenfels's influence, arguing for its progressive decline, and his progressive conservatism, see P. P. Bernard, *Jesuits and Jacobins. Enlightenment and Enlightened Despotism in Austria* (Illinois UP. 1971), ch. 2. His role in government and academic policy is studied at length by K.-H. Osterloh, *Joseph von Sonnenfels und die österreichische Reformbewegung im Zeitalter des aufgeklärten Absolutismus* (Lübeck and Hamburg 1970). However, the question whether his doctrines influenced, or were influenced by, Austrian practice, still seems an open one.
[23] Glassl, *Einrichtungswerk*, 174–5 (Koranda) and 106 (Polish landowners).

Austrian lands is shown in Table 13.4*. Data about these important personages are not readily available in the literature, except for Bohemia, where Rieger has explored the subject to 1763 with some thoroughness. Even here, however, his assertion that there was little change in Bohemian personnel in the period 1747–52 appears to be incorrect. Change in Bohemia was accentuated by the reduction of the number of Captains from twenty-four to sixteen in 1751, though there was some transfer of personnel to the four new Circles of Bidschau, Budweis, Elbogen, and Klattau then created, as the lists show. In 1763, at least eight Circle Captains were replaced. The early turnover in Moravia was also high. The available material is unsatisfactorily incomplete, but seems to justify the conclusion that while these officials included persons of the first rank, in a number of areas they included those of secondary rank, or perhaps lower, whose appointment cannot have soothed the feelings of the magnate classes. Even in Lower Austria, the Circle Captains seem a more mixed bunch than the impeccably aristocratic Commissaries appointed by the Estates. It is not clear from this evidence that the Circle Captain was typically a gentleman, in contrast to the 'professional' Prussian *Landrat*, as Hintze has argued. The reverse situation, professional Circle Captains, and gentlemanly Prussian *Landräte*, may have obtained. In Bohemia in 1762, an *Adjunctus* is shown as assisting the Captain in seven of the sixteen Circles, and was of comparable rank. There were two commissaries ('Führungs-Commissarii') in each Circle there, all of them 'von's, though not of higher title like the Circle Commissaries in Lower Austria. By 1780 (and probably earlier) all the Bohemian Circles had an *Adjunktus*, and seven had two.[24]

The memberships of the Hungarian Council of Lieutenancy and the Hungarian Chamber have been printed fully by Ember and Fallenbüchl respectively. Their work is the basis for Tables 13.5* and 13.6*, which show the councillors of these two bodies in 1754 and 1775. The Palatine of Hungary was supposed to be president of the Council of Lieutenancy, and this was observed in the periods 1723–31 and 1741–65. Francis of Lorraine (1731–41) and Prince Albert of Saxony (1765–80), however, held the office of *Locumtenens*

---

[24] Names of *Adjuncti* and commissaries in Bohemia in 1762 in HKA Hs. 243 A, fos. 24ʳ–28ʳ. For Hintze's views, see his 'Beamtenstaat', 352–53.

or *Statthalter*. The councillors, according to the founding instructions, were to be drawn from the archbishops and bishops, magnates, and nobles. A rough four–ten–eight balance was observed,
but in 1754 it was three–fourteen–eight and in 1775
two–twelve–twelve. Ember shows that nobles were of increasing
importance in the council's work.[25] In practice, the representation
of the clergy was of a rather token variety, and their turnover
noticeably quicker than that of members. In 1754 the average
length of service by magnates was 24.2 years, by nobles 18.1; in
1775 it was 23 years and 17.1 years. Turnover among officials, and
especially among clerks, was more rapid. In the Bohemian–Austrian lands, clerks in the main government offices appear typically
to have come from lower backgrounds and to have had only
limited expectation of promotion, though there were some exceptions. In contrast to this, Hungarian officials were typically drawn
from the lesser nobility. This was also true of the Chamber and of
the Szepes Chamber at Kassa, as Fallenbüchl has demonstrated.
They were often educated at the Jesuit schools in Pressburg and
Nagyszombat, and finished in legal studies. Count Grassalkovich,
himself a member of this class by origin, recommended such
employment as an antidote to noble poverty. Officials could rise
to be councillors. In the list of 1754, Barinay and György Fabiánkovics, in that of 1775, Balogh, Károly Fabiánkovics, Hlavacs,
Klobusiczky, Krassay, Sídó, had all served as Secretary. The social
composition of the council as a whole does not appear to have
changed markedly over the period, though the dominance of the
Eszterházys in 1754 had been replaced by that of the Csákys in
1775.

The members of the Hungarian Chamber (Table 13.6*) were
initially somewhat more mixed. The president, Grassalkovich
(1694–1771), was appointed in May 1748, and served until his
death in early December 1771. He came of a landless noble family,
and held the office of *Personalis* 1731–48, giving it up with reluctance to succeed Count Erdődy as president of the Chamber. His
services at the Diet of 1741 forged a bond between him and Maria
Theresia. He supported and promoted the settlement of colonists in

---

[25] Ember, *Helytartótanács*, 26.

Hungary, and procured huge supplies of grain for the armies in the Seven Years War. He purchased large estates in Pest county and the Banat of Temesvár; rising, according to Khevenhüller, from a common advocate to one of the richest men in Hungary, worth perhaps 2m. fl. Anton von König in 1761 accused him of never rendering accounts, amassing a great fortune, treating the Hungarian revenues as though they were his own, an indictment with which Joseph II agreed. Grassalkovich was created a baron in 1736, a count in 1748. His son Antal II was made a prince in 1784.[26] The remaining councillors of the Chamber in 1754 included the imperial knight from Westphalia, Antal Cotthmann, who was made a baron in 1765, and briefly became a councillor of the Council of Lieutenancy in 1766. He was related to Cabinet Secretary Koch, and through him became an adviser to the empress on Hungarian business. They also included the former army contractor and salt official János de Jean or De Jeanne, who was perhaps of French origin; Baron Pfeffershoffen, whose father had been colonel in charge of the garrison at Nagyvarad; and Xaver Ferenc Weidinger, another imperial knight. However, Amadé, Koller, Konckel, Török, Végh were all from old noble families.[27] The list of 1775 has a more establishment tone, including at least seven counts, besides members of the gentry families of Koller, Orczy, Szendrey, Török, Végh. The Chamber's social pretensions perhaps increased with its importance.[28] Count György Csáky (Chamber 1757–77, Council 1772–83), Count János

---

[26] No entry for Grassalkovich in Wurzbach. See *Khev.-Metsch*, 12 May 1748, 15 Dec. 1771; I. Nagy, *Magyarország családi czímmerekkel és nemzedékrendi táblákkal* (Pest 1857–68); Schünemann, *Bevölkerungspolitik*, 106–7, 117, 119, 133, 139, 195, 230–33 (König); Lehotzky, *Stemmatographia*, pt. i: 174, *Personalis* 1738(*sic* for 1731)–48; 134, *Supremus Comes* of Neograd County 1748; 98, *Agazonum Magister* 1759. It seems clear from these entries that he was made a count on ceasing to be *Personalis*, an office reserved for the (non-titled) nobility. For his views on noble poverty see Fallenbüchl, *Levéltári közlemények*, 41 (1970) 334.

[27] Nagy, *A magyar kamara*, 158, examining the councillors of 1764. Török was sent into Galicia with the Austrian army in 1772 to set up a civil administration, but failed and was sent home, Glassl, 20–2, 32–4. Fallenbüchl's lists of *Kamara* councillors 1675–1785 show 133 persons, 39 of whom had German names, most of the rest Hungarian ones. According to Bidermann, *Gesammt-Staats-Idee*, i, n. 43, of 62 councillors under Leopold I, 36 were 'foreign'; there was thus a revival of Magyar influence in the 18th c.

[28] Contrast Király, *Hungary in the Late Eighteenth Century*, 101 n., 'the Hungarian nobles loathed working in the Hungarian Chamber. Very seldom did they accept posts within its sphere.'

Erdődy (Chamber 1748–82, Council 1751–72) and Count Pál Festetics (Council and Chamber 1772–82) appear to be the only overlapping councillors. Festetics had previously served in the *Hofkammer* in Vienna.

Lastly, Lehotzky's lists published at the end of the eighteenth century show that the Hungarian sheriffs, the 'Supremi Comites Comitatuum', were all from magnate families, though occasionally an archbishop or bishop was in charge. Members of the same family often followed each other in office. The (elected) deputy sheriffs, the 'vice-comites', came exclusively from noble, i.e. gentry not magnate, families, and overlapped with the deputies to the Diets of 1741, 1751 and 1764.[29]

The government of Siebenbürgen is not included in the *Court Calendar*. The principality had a civil governor until 1762, but was then ruled until 1771 by a series of generals—Baron Adolf Buccow (1762–64), Count Andreas Hadik (1764–67), and Count Carl O'Donell (1767 to September 1770). It was then decided that the exercise of both military and civil power was too burdensome for one man. Baron Preiss became military commandant, until 1784, and Count Joseph Maria Auersperg, a councillor of the *Oberste Justizstelle*, was made civil governor (31 January 1771). The new arrangement did not work well. Auersperg engaged in bitter warfare against Baron Brukenthal in Vienna, whom he accused of promoting the interests of the Saxon Nation, and came to the capital in January 1773 to press his claims, in vain as it turned out. In his absence, Joseph II visited Siebenbürgen (22 May–11 July 1773), and on his return made notes on the personnel of government there. These can be summarized as follows.

Gubernium

COUNT NICOLAUS BETHLEN	President [in Auersperg's absence] A good man, has no capacity in speech or on paper. His secretary does all the work.
COUNT WOLFGANG BANFFI	Capable; a Calvinist; an intriguer, a real Jesuit. Adherent of Nemes (see below), the Saxon Nation, and Brukenthal.

[29] Lehotzhy, *Stemmatographia*, pt. i, pp. 108–67, 188–224.

SAMUEL BAUSNERN	Count of the Saxon Nation. Quite untrustworthy. Suffers from gout.
COUNT GABRIEL HALLER	No one would have heard of him, had he not married the pretty daughter of Count Grassalkovich.
MICHAEL HUTTERN	Not incompetent, but getting old; also, prejudiced in favour of the Saxon Nation.
COUNT KEMENY	A young man of talent, with a future.
COUNT KORNIS	A Catholic. Known as just and hard-working. One of the best councillors here.
BISHOP MANZADOR	Said to be under Jesuit influence. Knows nothing of Siebenbürgen.
BARON MÖHRINGER	Well-meaning, but lacks talent and energy.
COUNT JOHANNES NEMES	Sharp, witty, talented. But an intriguer and quite untrustworthy. Your Majesty must decide if such a man should be employed.
COUNT LADISLAUS TELEKI	The Pope of the Calvinists. An old man, full of prejudices. Especially hates the Saxon Nation.

Thesauriat

COUNT BETHLEN	as above.
BALO	Learned and diligent. Fanatical against the Saxons, and in matters of religion.
COUNT BANFFI	Very young. Decisive, talented, but needs guidance. Presides because of his rank—not good for him.
BEYSCHLAG	Speaks Latin and Hungarian. Only arrived two weeks ago.
EDER VON BERGWEESEN	Knows about mines. In other business, well-meaning but weak.
WINCKLER	An old man, who relies on his memory of past times. Should be pensioned off.

Upper Sheriffs of counties

COUNT DIONYSIUS BANFFI	*Colosser Comitatus* [Kolozs, Klausenburg]. Has wit, but is immoral, and health is failing.
BARON FRANCISCUS BANFFI	*Krasnaer District.* I believe he is an old man, but I did not see him.
COUNT ANTON HALLER	*Administrator of Küküllö* [Kokelburg]. Rather wild. Studied in *Theresianum*, but no trace of this shows. Diligent.
COUNT PAUL HALLER	*Albenser Comitatus* [Weissenburg]. Quite unfit to rule such a large county. Widely thought to be a lunatic.
PAUL HOLLAKI	*Zarander Comitatus* [Zaránd]. Nothing much to be said for or against him. An old man.
COUNT LUDWIG KALMOCKY	*Thordaer Comitatus* [Thorda, Thorenburg]. A young man, perhaps well-meaning, but has not the talent for this office, nor the hope of acquiring it. Everything is done by the county Notary.
COUNT ALEXI KENDEFFI	*Hunyader Comitatus* [Hunyad]. Does not appear to advantage, but sensible when spoken to on business.
COUNT ADAM TELEKI	*Kövar District.* Quite young still: not without talent and ability.
COUNT CARL TELEKI	*Interior Szolnok Comitatus.* A Catholic. Has the best reputation in Siebenbürgen. Capable and honourable. Perhaps too ascetic.
COUNT PAUL TELEKI	*Dobokaer Comitatus* [Doboka]. A good enough man, but not outstanding.
BARON WOLFGANG WESSELENYI	*Mediocris Szolnok Comitatus.* Still young, good disposition, but does not appear talented.

Szekler Stühle

BARON STEPHAN DANIEL	*Udvarhely and Bardotz.* Is ninety, son acts as Administrator and seems to have little application.
BARON ANTON DOMOKOS	*Marosser Stuhl* [Maros]. An old man, not up to the job.
BARON EMERICH MITSCHKE	*Aranyos Stuhl.* Appears more a child or a fool than an adult. Wears a big cross, and goes around distributing crosses.

Saxon Stühle

BAUSNERN	Count of the Saxon Nation. As above.
FRIEDERICH VON STRAUS-SENBURG	*Projudex* at Bistritz. Able, honourable, sick.
ANDREAS GLATZ	*Richter* in *Reps.* Quiet man, not much knowledge.
ANDREAS HANNENHEIM	Burgomaster in *Mediasch.* Not much good.
MICHAEL HANNENHEIM	*Richter* in *Schaesburg.* Old, not inexperienced.
[G. VON] HONNOMANN	Burgomaster in Hermannstadt. Said to be able and hardworking, but is frivolous and perhaps not trustworthy.
JOHANN KISSLING	*Richter* in *Löschkirch* [Leschkirch]. Young, rather fiery.
DANIEL MONTSCH	*Richter* in *Szasvaros.* Did not see him.
MARTIN RHEDER	*Richter* in *Reinmarckt.* Too addicted to innovations.
FRIEDRICH SALMEN	*Richter* in *Grossschenk.* One of the ablest here.
GEORG SCHELL	*Schaesburg.* Fat man, understands the laws but not much else.
[JOSEPH] SCHOBELN	Burgomaster in *Cronstadt.* Quite able: has able helpers in council.
ANDREAS WELTER	*Richter* in *Mühlenbach* [Mühlbach]. Able, rather heated.

These notes show the Arbiter of the Universe in good form. The local government of Siebenbürgen appears as distinctly less stately than that of Hungary, the *Thesauriat* staffed at lower social level than the *Kamara*, mixed instead of united in religion, the whole apparatus smaller in scale, and with an Irish flavour, which Maria Edgeworth would have recognized.[30]

Despite the incomplete and exploratory nature of this chapter and the preceding one, they suggest certain general conclusions. Ministerial tone in 1740 was markedly aristocratic, the Privy Conference, the chancelleries, and the financial offices being peppered with hereditary counts from establishment families, Althann, Batthyány, Harrach, Kinsky, Kuefstein, Starhemberg. This was less true by 1775. The *Staatsrat*, though containing such luminaries as Hatzfeld and Kaunitz, from its inception also included professional officials. Binder, Borié, Gebler, König, Löhr, Stupan, though formally nobles, owed little to descent, much to merit and royal favour. Similarly, the Bohemian and Austrian Chancellery in 1775 contained only one count, Blümegen, himself a member of a newly arrived family. Two of the six counts in the *Hofkammerrat* and *Banco-Deputation* at this date were Hungarian. This was perhaps significant. The Hungarian central offices appear to have retained much the same composition throughout the period, and the Hungarian Court Chancellery still formally divided its councillors into *Herrenstand* and *Ritterstand* members, a distinction abandoned in the Court Calendar entries for the other central offices.[31] The only change here was inclusion of a bishop as councillor from 1754; which rationalists could interpret as a step backwards. The flavour of the Bohemian and Austrian Chancellery in 1775 was markedly professional. Blanc, Martini, Perdacher, Riegger, and Zencker were eminent lawyers of modest origin, who had earned their places by brains and hard work. It is ironic that the chancellery was frequently accused in the two decades after the Seven Years War of

---

[30] Joseph's 'Geheime Liste uber die in Siebenbürgen angestellte Gubernial- und Thesauriats-Räthe' is printed as n. 208 to *Khev.-Metsch*, 6 May 1773. Joseph's tour of Siebenbürgen is described in detail, with more information about several of those named, in Schuller, *Samuel von Brukenthal*, i. 281–318, but the source used here is not drawn on.

[31] This was not true of local government, however, e.g. the Lower Austrian *Regierung*.

protecting the interests of the Estates and the feudal classes of society. A further characteristic of the chancellery, and of the *Directorium* before it, was a progressive absence of members of the Bohemian magnate families, who were, however, prominent in the local government of Bohemia itself. In the central financial offices, the new families of Bolza and Neffzer were well dug in, while the Galician Court Chancellery contained two former members of the *Hofrechenkammer*, one of them the inquisitor-general of accounting, Johann Puechberg.

The thesis that central government, with the exception of the Hungarian Chancellery, moved over the period away from aristocracy towards a middle-class and professional personnel steeped in legal and cameral studies, operating under a top-dressing of aristocrats, themselves professional in outlook, undoubtedly contains some truth. It is contrasted below with the continuing aristocratic tradition in provincial government. It needs, however, to be handled cautiously. A trend towards professionalism was perhaps part of the spirit of the age, rather than a class phenomenon, and affected all levels of society, Joseph II, for example, being a more professional, though not necessarily a better, ruler than his grandfather Charles VI. Equally, 'ministeriales' of modest origin were far from absent in the early part of the period, as the careers of Bartenstein, Holler, Kannegiesser, Schwandner, and others demonstrate. Indeed, a mixture of aristocracy and meritocracy, in the form of rule by coalitions of magnates and 'new men', seems to be observable at any period of Austrian history from the sixteenth century onwards. Ennoblement could in a generation or two blur the lines between established and *arriviste* families, but the play was then repeated with a different cast. An effect of this pattern, given the closed Austrian system of government, was to enable men of insignificant origin and (perhaps) radical views to arrive relatively quickly in positions of great influence over state policy, in a way which a parliamentary system, like that of England, rendered difficult. Several of the 'Silesians' and others who assisted Haugwitz locally in the reform of the tax cadastre conform to this pattern.[32] The generation of councillors which emerged to positions of influence after the Seven Years War, Blanc, Borié, Stupan, Gebler, Heinke, Kressel, in their willingness to reform the church, and redistribute its wealth,

---

[32] See ii. Chs. 6–8.

and to regulate landlord claims on the peasantry, in both cases with encouragement from above, represented a further development of the same tendency. Johann Mathias Puechberg, with his zest for reducing the Monarchy to a set of statistics, illustrated a different kind of radical approach. It was not necessarily true, however, that middle-class officials were radicals, while nobles were torpid conservatives. Haugwitz and Zinzendorf were radical in finance and government. Kaunitz extended this to foreign policy before the Seven Years War, and to the church, and economic policy in general, after it, and so on. The most radical adviser of all before 1780, Joseph II, was also the highest born. Lastly, even for men of rank, talent counted for as much as birth. Hatzfeld, Haugwitz, Kaunitz, Kollowrat, Zinzendorf, bore famous names, but were career politicians, not wealthy heads of families. Others, like Bartenstein, Blümegen, Brukenthal, the brothers Chotek, Grassalkovich, Lacy in a military context, founded families in state service, and in doing so provoked the resentment of conservatives like Khevenhüller, who thought birth a necessary, though not sufficient, condition for high office.

The numbers involved in top-level decisions on financial and allied questions shrank over the reign. In 1740 the Privy Conference, Austrian and Bohemian Chancelleries, Finance Conference, Bank Deputation and *Hofkammer* had ninety councillors, of whom fifty-three were in the *Hofkammer*. In 1775, the *Staatsrat*, Bohemian and Austrian Chancellery, Bank Deputation and *Hofkammer* had fifty-three, of whom twenty-one were in the *Hofkammer*. This process was carried much further by Joseph II, his *Staatsrat* comprising only five members, and his *Vereinigte Hofkanzlei* of 10 October 1782 only fifteen, most of them of middle-class background. This seems to mark a significant step away from government by extended counsel to government by royal decision.[33]

---

[33] *Hofräte* in the United Chancellery (*Vereinigte Hofkanzlei*), 1 Jan. 1783, in Geisler, *Skizze*, iv. 103–5: Johann Bolza (*Kassawesen*), Peter Bolza (*Taxwesen*), Dengelmann (sc. Degelmann) (*Kommerz*), Eger (Inner Austria), Greiner (religion and schools), Hertelli (excise), Müller (Tyrol and Further Austria), Count Rottenheim (*Untertanssachen*), Count Sauer (Upper and Lower Austria), Scharf (customs), Sernawitz (Galicia), Spiegelfeld (Bank), Zenker (Bohemia), with Grueber and Ungrechtsberg for liaison with the provincial governments. The United Chancellery was a combination of the Bohemian and Austrian Chancellery, *Hofkammer*, and Bank Deputation. Besides the councillors, there were an Upper Chancellor, Chancellor, and Vice-Chancellor.

However, it must not be overlooked that the fifty-three councillors of 1775 just referred to were themselves more numerous than the thirty-nine in the Privy Conference, *Directorium*, Bank Deputation, and *Hofkammer* of 1754. Haugwitz's reforms led to a degree of concentration not subsequently maintained. A further observable trend under Maria Theresia was that the ratio of officials to councillors tended to increase. Thus in 1740 the *Hofkammer* had fifty-three councillors, but only twenty-nine central officials, while in 1771 it had twenty councillors and eighty-six central officials. In 1740 and 1746, the Bohemian and Austrian chancelleries had between them twenty-one councillors and sixty-two officials, in 1775 the Bohemian and Austrian Chancellery had fourteen councillors and seventy-seven officials. There was thus a tendency for the circle of top-level advisers to diminish and that of officials to expand. No doubt at lower echelons of government, particularly in that of tax-collection, this increase was more marked, pointing the way to the bureaucratic mass of the post-Waterloo period. An early model was provided by Haugwitz's *Directorium*, which in 1754 had only twenty-two councillors, including the president, but no less than 133 officials, sixty-one of them bookkeepers.[34]

In the areas of government considered here, laymen ruled and churchmen, in contrast to the position in the sixteenth and seventeenth centuries, were excluded. They were confined to cutting a figure in the Estates, for example in the Estates of Lower Austria, where the abbots of the great religious houses were prominent. A cardinal in charge of royal policy is no longer thinkable in this period in an Austrian, as opposed to a French, context; however attractive it may be to imagine Kaunitz in the role. The Austrian church played a less important part in royal government than the Anglican church in Protestant England. The influence of Provost Ignaz Müller and Abbot Stephan Rautenstrauch on church policy from the late 1760s actually represents a revival of ecclesiastical influence, though one directed against the traditional church. Office seems from the evidence examined to have been acquired by nomination, not purchase, and dynasties of office-holders of the kind encountered in France are lacking. None the less, through patro-

---

[34] Numbers in 1740, 1746, 1754, and 1775 taken from the *Court Calendar*; those in 1771 from the detailed lists at the end of Count Friedrich Hatzfeld's *Vortrag* of Feb. 1771, HKA Kredit AA Akten, rote Nr. 12, Fsz. 7 at fos. 282 ff.

nage and lobbying relatives could be promoted, as the families of Bolza, Koch, Managetta, Mensshengen, Neffzer, demonstrated.

Continuity of personnel at the centre is more observable in the earlier than the later part of the period. The *Directorium* partly (and deliberately) inherited its councillors and officials from the Austrian and Bohemian Chancelleries, and the Bohemian and Austrian Chancellery from the *Directorium*. On the other hand, only two councillors of the Bohemian and Austrian Chancellery in 1763 (Koch, Zencker) survived to 1775, and in the *Hofkammer* only one (J. F. von Bolza). Some transfer between departments is observable at middle level (Carqui, Ottocar von Stupan), as well as more markedly at the top. A changing body of central councillors was controlled by a very long-ruling monarch, with a senior adviser, Kaunitz, who beat the record with nearly forty years' service (1753–92) as State Chancellor.

Locally, aristocratic tone was strong in 1740, seems to have slipped during the reforms from 1749, as the *novi homines* employed by Haugwitz attacked their objectives, but recovered, possibly as a result of deliberate government concession to local prejudices, from the end of the Seven Years War. The government of Bohemia, Lower and Upper Austria, Styria, or Tyrol in 1780 was firmly in noble hands, though others participated. This must have provided an unpropitious setting for the Josephine reforms about to be unleashed. In qualification of this, the Circle Captains were a mixed bunch socially, especially in Bohemia, where they were most numerous. However, this factor, in turn, may have made it harder for Circle Captains to oppose magnate views. Lastly, Hungarian government was aristocratic throughout, though nobles rather than magnates may have done the real work. The church, too, played, at least formally, a designated role in Hungarian business. Continuty of office was more marked than elsewhere. Hungarian participation in Austrian central government was confined to the Hungarian and Siebenbürgen Court Chancelleries until after the Seven Years War, when Hungarian councillors appear more frequently in the *Hofkammer* council. Hungary, in short, was different, and, as usual, generalizations applicable to the other lands cannot be applied to it.

APPENDICES

Lord Stormont's report on the Austrian Monarchy

THE dispatch printed here, sent to the Duke of Grafton on 10 September 1765 (PRO, SP 80/202), was evidently intended as a first instalment to later communications. An extensive search in the subsequent dispatches, however, has failed to discover the account of trade and manufactures, or the 'Separate Inquiry' about Hungary, which Stormont promises.

VIENNA   SEPTEMBER 10th: 1765

My Lord

Having collected some few Lights, I will now endeavour to execute the King's Orders, transmitted to me in Lord Sandwich's letter of the 22^d: of last March; but I must begin by bespeaking your Grace's Indulgence, and by begging you to consider this and the Subsequent Letters, as a first Attempt, and rough general outline, which I hope to correct and fill up hereafter, as farther Inquiry and better Information may enable me.

In this first introductory Letter I shall confine myself to a Short Description of Her Imperial Majesty's Dominions, and general Account of the present State of each Country, of it's principal Natural productions (their Trade and Manufactures I shall consider elsewhere) of the Contributions or Land-Tax which it pays, and of the Number of it's Inhabitants, as far as I have been able to ascertain it, adding occasionally some few observations, such as either arise out of the Subject, or seem to me to throw some Light upon it.

To begin then with the most northern part; The Kingdom of Bohemia is a rich, fertile, and formerly very populous Country. It is surrounded by a Chain of Mountains and immense Forests, which form a Natural Barrier, and would be a very Strong one, if it were not that the Extent of the Frontier is so Great, that no Army can be sufficient to guard it.

The Climate is reckoned healthy and the Soil in general fruitful. It produces tolerable Wine, Great Quantities of Corn (much more than the Inhabitants consume) Flax, Saffran, good Fruit and excellent Hops. The Lakes and Rivers abound with Fish of various Sorts, and Bohemia is famous for having Game of all kinds in the greatest perfection. There were formerly Salt Mines in this Country, but they are fallen in. There are still considerable Mines of Silver, Lead, Iron, Tin, Copper and Quick Silver; there are likewise large quarries of various kinds of marbles, and there are found here different sorts of precious stones, the best and most esteemed of which are the Granates and Topasses.

Notwithstanding all these Natural Advantages Bohemia is much sunk from what it was formerly. If it's Historians are to be credited, it had in the Reign of Rhodolphus the Second no less than three Millions of Inhabitants, whereas according to the Account taken in 1762 they amount only to

$$
\begin{array}{ll}
1,768,638 & \text{Christians} \\
20,000 & \text{Jews} \\
\hline
1,788,638 & \text{Total[1]}
\end{array}
$$

To say Nothing of it's later Distresses, which are fresh in evry Body's Memory, it has never recovered the Wounds it received in the famous *Guerre de trente Ans*. Besides all that fell by the Sword, and the Calamities of that cruel War, thirty thousand families are said to have left their Habitations in the Year 1622 and the three following Years. Another Circumstance that naturally tends to check the Growth of Affluence and Industry, is the Vassalage of the peasants. They are all according to the general Slavonick System *adscripti Glebae*. Their Servitude however is not so absolute as that of the peasants in Poland, for they are allowed to have property of their own, and the Lords have by an Edict of the present Empress lost the power of Life and Death, which they had over them. They still retain the power of imprisoning, and inflicting Corporal punishment for lesser Offences, but for all Capital Crimes must deliver them over to the Civil Magistrate.[2]

Whilst Bohemia was an Elective Kingdom, the privileges and Liberties of the Subject were Great; but they were all lost in that unsuccessful Struggle with Ferdinand the Second. That prince formally abolished all those privileges in 1620, after the famous Victory of Prague, and tho' he afterwards restored them, it was but in appearance. The States, which consist of four Orders viz: 1st: The Clergy. 2d. The *Herrenstand* of princes, Counts, and Barons. 3d. The *Ritterstand* or the Inferior Nobility, and 4ly: The Cities, are but a Shadow of what they were. They cannot assemble without an order from the Sovereign, and must confine their Deliberations to what is proposed by the Crown, which is generally nothing but a Demand of some new Supply. For the States of Bohemia stil enjoy one Important priviledge, and which they have in common with all the other States in the Empresses German Dominions, viz: that no *Imposition Rëelle*, that is no Tax upon

---

[1] The census figures in Stormont's report are all somewhat higher than those shown in Ch. 2.

[2] Perhaps a reference to the royal ordinance of 22 July 1765 reducing the existing 378 Bohemian courts with the right of life and death to 30, each with a qualified judge, see Domin-Pet. 38–9. A similar measure was passed in Moravia in 1752, *HGBL* ii. 456.

immoveables can be laid except by them. The Sovereign makes the Demand, and setts forth the Reasons of it. This Demand, whatever it might be formerly, is always acquiesced in now. The States to raise the Sum required, assess it upon the whole Community, according to a fixed and pretty equitable proportion, with no Exemption for any Man that has property. The Nobles pay their full Share, and what is more the Clergy too, and that without making the least Difficulty, or so much as pretending to those Immunities, which in other Roman Catholick Countries they claim as indisputable.

The Ordinary Land Tax or Contribution as it is called which Bohemia pays at present is 5,270,488 florins 44 Creutzers.[3] This is greatly above what it paid till the Year 1748, when Monsr: Haugwitz, who was then at the Head of the Finances, raised the Empresses Revenue very considerably, by a New Regulation with regard to the Land Tax, which took place thro' all her German Dominions. Till that Time the Land Tax had been paid according to an old Estimation of the Lands, and consequently much below their present Value. There were likewise many Estates in Bohemia and Moravia, which were forfeited in the Reign of Ferdinand the Second by those whom he treated as Rebels, and given by him to the Lichtenstein, and other principal Families, that adhered to him, free of all Taxes or at least taxed much below their real value. All these Estates Monsr: Haugwitz made Subject to the Land Tax, had a general Estimation made of all the Lands throughout the Empresses German Dominions, raised the Demands of the Crown accordingly, and got the States to lay on the Land Tax agreably to that Estimation, which as it is said was in many places above the real Value. However right the general principle of this Reform might be, there was great Mismanagement in the Execution, which was attended with many harsh and oppressive Circumstances, that make Haugwitz's administration a very memorable and odious Epoch in the Annals of this Country.

Besides the abovementioned ordinary Contribution, Bohemia paid during the first Years of the Late War an Extraordinary one of two Millions one hundred thousand florins per Annum, and in the Year 1763 this Supply was augmented to 2,636,482 fl. 11 Cr. notwithstand:^{g} the strongest Remonstrances from the States of the Distress and Inability of the Country; and over and above all this, it was obliged to furnish immense *Livraisons* for the Army, at a price much below their value. It is but too obvious how deep such wounds must go.[4]

I come now to Moravia; a great part of that Country is mountainous and barren, but the low lands are very fruitful, and produce not only plenty of

---

[3] Stormont's figures for the Contribution of the various lands can be checked against those presented in ii, Ch. 6. They are usually, but not always, correct.

[4] For Bohemia's payments during the Seven Years War see ii, Table 4.5*. The table does not bear out Stormont's assertion of a regular 2.1m. fl. levy. However, this amount was demanded in 1762, and 2,635,244 fl., half of a Contribution, in 1763.

fine Corn, Hemp and Flax, but likewise what is remarkable Incense and
Myrrh. There were formerly Gold Mines in this Country, and there are still
considerable Iron ones, there are too Quarries of Marbles of various Sorts.
Sulphur, Saltpetre, Alum and Vitriol are found here in great quantities, but
no Salt. Moravia has for several Centuries been annexed to Bohemia, and its
general Constitution, as for Instance the Vassalage of the peasants, Nature
and priviledges of the States &c. is nearly the Same. Its present ordinary
Contribution amounts to 1,856,490 fl. 48 Cr. and the Number of Inhabitants in 1763 was

1,015,846	Christians
8,000	Jews
1,023,846	Total

The Jesuits have been greatly favoured in this Country; they have several
most magnificent Convents particularly at Olmütz, and Estates to the
Amount of Eighteen Millions of Florins.[5] That Superstitious bigotted
prince Ferdinand the Second, who was himself a Jesuit, made them Donations to the Value of Eight Millions of Florins.

What remains to the Empress of Silesia is a mountainous, and in general a
barren Country, and has nothing very remarkable. Its present Contribution
is 245,298 fl: 56 Cr: and the Number of Inhabitants in 1762 was 147,687.

The Dutchy of Austria is divided into Upper and Lower. Upper Austria
is, except in the Mountains, a damp swampy Country. It does not grow
Corn enough for the Inhabitants, and but little Wine, but great quantities of
good Fruit. Its lakes and rivers supply it with variety of Fish. It has likewise
very considerable Woods, and two great Salt Mines. Its present Contribution is 906,228 fl: 13 Cr: and the Number of Inhabitants is computed at
about 450,000.

Lower Austria is in general a fruitful Country. It produces much more
Corn than is consumed in it. Great quantities of Saffran (much of which is
exported) and likewise very tolerable Wine, especially in that part that bor-
ders upon Hungary. There was formerly a great Demand in several parts of
Germany, particularly in Bavaria and Swabia, for this Austrian Wine,
which when old is equal to the inferior Sorts of Rhenish, and much better
than the Neckar Wine; but this Exportation, which was highly advan-
tageous to the Country, and ought to have been encouraged as such, is
greatly diminished, by the Duties that were unwisely laid upon it, and likewise by the *Droits d'Entrée*, exacted by the Elector of Bavaria in Revenge
for those exacted here, upon all the produce of his Electorate. The Consequence of all this has been, that this valuable Commodity is now left upon

---

[5] Jesuit property in Moravia was probably no more than 2½m. fl., according to
Bílek's statistics.

their Hands, and the Cellars of Vienna filled with incredible quantities of it.

The peasants in Austria are not *Serfs* as in Bohemia and Moravia, but hold their Lands subject to certain Services specified in their Lease, for which their Lord often allows them to compound.

The States are upon the same general plan with those I have already mentioned consisting of the same four Orders, and indeed this is the Case throughout all the Empresses German Dominions. Each province has its own States, the general Nature of which is pretty nearly the same (at least the Difference is too minute to enter into such an Enquiry as this) and the principal Buissness of them all is to grant the Contributions demanded by the Crown, and to assess them according to a fixed equitable proportion without any priviledge, or Exemption being allow'd to, or so much as claimed by any Man that has property, and the Clergy paying throughout their full Share. In Austria the Clergy are likewise subject to the ordinary Civil Jurisdiction in all *Temporalibus, et active et passive*.

It seems something extraordinary, that in a Country where Zeal for the Roman Catholick Religion has run so high, and where the Interests of the State have been so often sacrificed to that Zeal, the power of the Clergy should have been brought, and kept within such narrow Bounds. Whatever may have been the Cause of this (for I have not been able to meet with any Thing satisfactory upon that Head, tho' Writers agree that Things have been upon this Footing for at least three hundred Years) it is now a fixed, generally received, and uncontroverted principle, and so far are they from any Inclination to extend the priviledges of the Clergy, that it was under Deliberation during the last War, whether they should not be made Subject to a Capitation Tax.

The Land Tax in Austria is assessed upon what they call the *Dominicale and Rusticale*. The Tax on the Dominicale is that paid by the Lord for his Lands, Droits de Seigneurie &c: This amounts at present to about thirty per Cent of his Revenue; the Clergy pay rather more. The Tax upon the Rusticale is that paid by the peasants, for which however the Lord is responsible. Every *Gantze Bauer*, or whole peasant as they call it, that is evry peasant, that has a House and thirty Acres of Land, pays at present Eighteen Florins per Annum; those who have more or less pay in proportion.

The Contribution of Lower Austria, which at the beginning of this Reign amounted only to 800,000 fl: is now raised to 2,008,968 fl: 44 Cr: Besides this they had during the late War their full Share of extraordinary Contributions and *Livraisons* for the Army. The Number of Inhabitants according to an Account in 1763 amounted to 908,750.

The Brisgau and other small districts in Swabia, which go under the general Name of Anterior Austria, have nothing very remarkable. They pay, including the new Contribution, which took place in Nov:[r] last, 220,000 fl: [s] The Number of Inhabitants I have not been able to ascertain.

Stiria is divided into upper and lower. The Latter is in general a level, fruitful Country, abounding in good Wine and Corn. Upper Stiria is mountainous, cold, and barren; but the Inhabitants are industrious, and cultivate it to the utmost, and find means to raise various sorts of Fruit, and more corn than they can consume. The Lakes and Rivers abound with Fish, and the Woods and Mountains with Game, but the great Treasure of this Country is its Silver, Tin, Copper and above all its Iron Mines. Some of these, which as 'tis said, have been worked for above these thousand years, are still very rich. The immense Forests of Stiria furnish Wood in Abundance for smelting the Iron; great quantities of which both wrought and unwrought are exported evry Year, as well as of Steel, which is reckoned remarkably fine, and is much used in England. Stiria pays 1,182,845 fl: ˢ54 Cr: ˢ and the Number of Inhabitants according to an Account taken last Year is 495,514.

Carinthia is in general a mountainous barren Country. The Mountains, however, have considerable Iron Mines, and the low lands produce good Corn, but not enough for the Inhabitants. Till this Reign they lived in Ease and plenty, but their present Land Tax which amounts to 637,695 fl: ˢ10 Cr: ˢ and which is double, or rather more than double what they paid in Time of Charles the Sixth, is a Load above their Strength (and yet there is a project to increase it) and joined to the Extraordinary Contributions they paid during the War, has brought them so low, that, as I have been assured, there is now scarce a Gentleman in that Country, that can give his Daughter five hundred florins for her Marriage portion, or afford to send his Sons to School. The number of Inhabitants in 1763 was 270,643.

Carniola tho' very mountainous especially upper Carniola, is upon the whole a fruitful Country. The plains are so fertile, that after rich Crops of Corn they often bring a second Harvest of Turkey Wheat, Hemp, and Flax. This Country too produces variety of excellent Fruit, tolerable Wine, and great quantities of Olives. It has likewise Iron, Tin and Copper Mines, but is totally without Salt. The present Contribution is 363,171 fl: ˢ56 Cr: ˢ The Number of Inhabitants I do not know.

The County of Goritz produces Good Wine, Fruit, Corn and a Considerable quantity of Flax. The small County of Gradisca makes one Department with Goritz; they pay together 41,502 florins.

The small Districts of Fiume and Trieste, which go by the general Name of *il Littorale*, produce good Wine, Figgs and other Fruit. They pay no Contribution, or at least a mere trifle. In order to favour the Trade of Hungary, and facilitate the Exportation of its Commodities, the Emperor Charles the Sixth made a fine Road from Carlstadt in Croatia to Fiume, where a good Harbour might easily be made.

Trieste is chiefly remarkable for its Harbour, which is the only considerable one in the Empresses German Dominions. Immense Sums of Money have been expended upon it in this Reign, but to very little purpose. The whole was such a Series of Blunders, as is scarce to be parallelled. The principal person employed had, it is said, never so much as seen a Harbour, and the work succeeded accordingly. With Great Labour and Expence they have made a Harbour, the Entrance into which is difficult, and when you are in it, it is often very unsafe, being exposed to some Winds, which sett full into its Mouth; so that Ships are, as I am told, often in more Danger there, than they would be at Sea. Notwithstanding these Disadvantages Trieste from its Situation might and ought to be a place of considerable Trade. How far it is from being so, I shall have occasion to mention, when I come to consider the Trade and Commerce of this Country.

Tyrol tho' a mountainous is a fruitful Country, and produces good Corn, tolerable Wine, and Fruit in as great Variety and perfection as Italy. The Number of Inhabitants is computed at between three and four hundred thousand, and the annual Contribution is only 100,000 florins. However the Revenue the Crown draws from this Country is considerable, and is reckoned to amount to near a Million of Florins per annum. This Revenue arises from the Domaines, from the Sale of Timber out of the Royal Forests, from the Tax paid to the Crown, for all Timber that is sold, (the Inhabitants sell a great deal to the Venetians and float it down the Adige) from the Silver, Iron, and Copper Mines, and from the *Salines*. The Silver Mines, which were formerly rich ones, seem now to be worn out, and scarce pay for the Expence of working them. The Iron Mines are no great Matter; but those of Copper are considerable. The Salines are extremely so; one of them was reckoned to produce formerly 200,000 florins per Annum. But the Tyrolians have suffered greatly in the Sale of their Salt, from the agreement the Elector of Bavaria, and Bishop of Saltzbourg entered into some Years ago, by which they engaged to sell their Salt at a certain price; since which Time they in a great Measure supply Swabia and Franconia, which used before to draw great quantities of Salt from Tyrol.

There is more general Affluence in Tyrol, than in almost any of the Empresses German Dominions. The Court has more than once shewed a Desire of increasing their Taxes, which, as your Grace sees, are very moderate, and is supposed to have still that object in view. But the Tyrolians are a shrewd sturdy people, who are not easily dealt with, and who know very well, how to avail themselves of the advantage of their Situation, which makes them hard to be come at, and have more than once insinuated, that if they were ill used, they would throw themselves under the protection of their Friends the Swiss.

I have now gone thro' all Her Imperial Majesty's German Dominions. I have already observed, that they are all *pais d'Etat* which is an Advantage to the Sovereign, as well as to the Subject. For besides that the Land Tax is assessed by them in an equitable proportion, without any partiality or Favour, and in such a Manner as to be easily and cheaply collected, the Good Faith of these States, and the Confidence that is placed in them has established such a public Credit, as so Absolute a Government as this, could never have had without such an additional Security.

Tho' as I have mentioned already no Land Tax can be raised without these States, yet the Hands of the Sovereign are tied only in this one Respect, and are at full Liberty to lay on by an Edict Duties Excise &c and in short any other Tax whatever. Great Use has been made of this Liberty in the present Reign. However, tho' those Taxes, of which I shall give an Account when I come to speak of the Revenue, are numerous, yet still the Land Tax is, as it ought to be in a Country like this of little or no Trade, the principal Branch of the Revenue, and the Burthen, however heavy in itself, is the more supportable, from being laid in the proper place.

I have already troubled Your Grace much too long, and will only add a few Words touching Her Imperial Majesty's Italian Dominions viz: the Dutchies of Milan and Mantua, with regard to which I have not indeed the same Opportunities of Information; Besides their principal Natural productions, and their advantages of Situation &c. are so well known, as to make it needless to say anything of them.

The Revenue of the two Dutchies together, including the Farm of the Domaines, amounts to 2,050,000 florins. The Number of Inhabitants I have not yet been able to learn, and do not know that any exact Account has been taken. The population of the Dutchy of Mantua at least must in all probability have greatly diminished, as the Inhabitants of the City of Mantua, which were formerly computed at fifty thousand exclusive of the Garrison, scarce amount at present to sixteen thousand.

I have now, my Lord, carried this introductory account thro' all her Imperial Majesty's Dominions, except Flanders, which is Sr James Porter's province, and Hungary and the Countries annexed to it, which both from the Extent, and the Importance of the Subject, I purposely reserve for a Separate Inquiry.

The Desire of omitting nothing that could be of the least Use, has made me swell this Letter to an immoderate Size, and run me into tedious Details, for which I beg your Grace's pardon.

I am with the greatest Truth & Respect
My Lord
Your Graces

Most Obedient
Most Hbl Serv:^{r}

Stormont

NB. Tho' the Bankers here reckon 8 fl: ^{s}30 Cr: ^{s} (or Eight florins and a half) for the par of Exchange, yet according to the intrinsic Value, nine Florins of the present Currency are equal to a pound Sterlin.

S

His Grace the Duke of Grafton.

The farm of Austrian tobacco revenues

THE history of the farm before 1765 is complex, and by no means all the details are clear. The first substantial farmer, at least on paper, was Maximilian Hilleprand von Brandau, who offered 350,000 fl. p.a. in 1726; it is not clear how far this contract was fulfilled. From 1734 to 1748 Diego Aguilar was the chief farmer (206,000–270,000 fl. 1738–48, Austrian lands only). Joseph Pingitzer von Dornfeld gave 330,000 fl. p.a. for the same area 1748–?1758. On 28 Nov. 1758 the Vienna City Bank undertook to make a loan to the state of 6m. fl. for the current campaign, in return for which the Estates of Lower, Upper, and Inner Austria were to assume the tobacco farm, and pay the Bank from it 475,650 fl. annually for twenty years. The Estates of the Bohemian lands paid 450,000 fl. annually 1737–43, then 150,000 fl. to 1764, to avoid the central farmers. The arrangement with the Vienna City Bank cannot have lasted, for from 1 Jan. 1764 a syndicate (Dechau, von Plöchner, Purchner, and Oestreicher) took on the farm, but went bankrupt.

This opened the way to the Jewish syndicate discussed in Ch. 7. Their contract with the *Hofkammer*, dated 23 Nov. 1764, ran from 1 Jan. 1765 for ten years. It covered the Austrian and Bohemian lands, and was for 1,100,000 fl. for one year, then for 1,210,000 fl. annually. The offices were to be in Brünn, Linz, Prague, Troppau, Vienna. The contract of association of the fourteen farmers for their capital of 500,000 fl. divided into *fifteen* shares, was dated 9 Dec. 1764. Each named subscriber put up 33,333 fl.; the fifteenth share must have gone to one of the five associates listed. The named partners were Isaac Abraham, Elias and Löbl Baruch, Salomon Dobruska, Israel Simon Frankl, Aron Moyses Hönig, Eystig Löbl Hönig, Israel Löbl Hönig, Löbl Hönig, Ascher Marcus, Enoch Peruz, and Isaac, Joachim and Wolf Popper. All, under a further contract with the *Hofkammer* of 22 July 1764, were also partners in the Moravian *Lehenbank* established by the government in 1751 to encourage Moravian industry. The two were to form 'ein gemeinschaftliches werk'. In 1774, the tobacco farm was renewed at a higher figure, and with different associates. The farm was for 1,792,250 fl., the government was to have one-quarter of any profits on top, and the title was now the 'k. k. Taback Gefällen Administration'. From 1776 Galicia was added to its scope. The six partners, whose agreement was dated 14 April 1774, each put up 150,000 fl. They were Adam Isaac Arnsteiner, Johannes von Franck 'per procura Johann Friess', Johann Michael

Grosser, Aron Moyses and Israel Löbl Hönig, and the firm of J. G. Schuller & Co. The Moravian *Lehenbank* was now run (4 September 1777 signatures) by the Hönigs: Abraham Löbl, Aron Moyses, Israel Löbl, Lazar Löbl.[1]

[1] The authorities here are WSLA Merk. Gericht Prot. B 6/2, section 'Juden', fos. 12–25, 30–7, which gives the details of partnerships, and J. von Retzer, *Tabakpachtung in den österreichischen Ländern von 1670 bis 1783. Nach echten Urkunden* (Vienna 1784), which gives the details of farms. The account in J. Schreyer, *Waarenkabinet oder Niederlage der in Böhmen erzeugten Waarenartikel und Naturprodukte* (Prague and Leipzig 1799), 535–6 overlaps with this, but contains inaccuracies. For the Vienna City Bank in 1758 see HKA Hs 280, index of the Bank's advances, at fo. 55ᵛ. For the Moravian *Lehenbank* see Přibram, *Gewerbepolitik*, 82 and A. Beer, 'Die österreichische Handelspolitik unter Maria Theresia und Josef II', *AÖG* 86 (1898) n. 83, a fuller account, though ignoring the tobacco farm. The bank traded in foreign wool, cotton, and yarn and supplied domestic weavers. Its privilege was renewed for fifteen years on 30 May 1777, Beer loc. cit. The bank was started, under government supervision, by Joh. Anton Kernhofer, an official of the Vienna City Bank, ibid.

Index of Vienna Warehousers and Wholesalers, 1740–1780

THE distinction between the Free Warehousers ('Befreite Niederleger'), the title conferred on wholesale merchants until 1774, and the Wholesalers ('Grosshändler'), the corps created in 1774, is explained in Ch. 7. New Warehouser titles were not given after 1774, but the existing ones continued until the few remaining Warehousers were made Wholesalers in 1806. The index takes the name of Warehousers from the *Court Calendar* for 1740, 1748, 1754, 1763, 1770, and 1779 and the Wholesalers listed for 1779. A cross denotes an entry, a dash no entry. '1779(1)' refers to Warehousers, and '1779(2)' to Wholesalers, at that date. A few other names are also included. Biographical data are added, the principal source being the indexes to the records of the Lower Austrian Mercantile Court, WSLA Merkantil Gericht Protokoll B6/1 (1725–58) and B6/2 (1758–89, but containing later entries). This source acts as a partial check on the accuracy of the calendar entries, the dates of several of which are incorrect. However, the date of conferment of Warehouser status is not always clear in the first volume of the Protokoll. The spelling of names is as in the sources. Addresses appear in the *Court Calendar* only from the late 1770s; house numbers then are those of the Inner City as a whole, not of individual streets or squares. The following additional abbreviations are used.

Alm. gén. des March.	Anon. *Almanach général des Marchands . . . de France et de l'Europe* (Paris 1774)
Dietz	A. Dietz. *Frankfurter Handelsgeschichte* (Frankfurt am Main 1910–25)
HGA	Herrschafts-Gerichtsakten
Lüthy	H. Lüthy, *La Banque protestante en France* (1959, 1961)
Megerle	J. G. Megerle von Mühlfeld, *Österreichisches Adels-Lexikon* (Vienna 1822–4)
Mensi	F. von Mensi, *Die Finanzen Oesterreichs von 1701 bis 1740* (Vienna 1890)
MGP(1), MGP(2)	Merkantil-Gericht Protokoll 1725–58 and 1758–89 respectively
Michielsen	L. Michielsen, 'De Kompagnie van Trieste en Fiume', *Bijdragen tot de Geschiedenis*, XVII (Antwerp 1936) 70–91; 181–221
Mikoletzky, 'Franz Stephan'	H. L. Mikoletzy. 'Franz Stephan von Lothringen als Wirtschaftspolitiker', *MÖSA* 13 (1960), 331–57

Mikoletzky,
'Schweizer Händler'

NÖ
de Ponty

Srbik

Taglicht

Id., 'Schweizer Händler und Bankiers in Österreich
(vom 17 bis zur Mitte der 19. Janrhunderts)', in *Österreich u. Europa. Festgabe fur Hugo Hantsch*... (Vienna
etc. 1965) 149–81
Nieder Österreich
F. de Ponty, *Verzeichnis der in der k. k. Hauptstadt...
Wien... befindlichen Häusern* (Vienna 1779)
H. von Srbik, *Der staatliche Exporthandel Österreichs
von Leopold I. bis Maria Theresia* (Leipzig 1907)
J. Taglicht (ed.), *Nachlässe der Wiener Juden im 17. und
18. Jahrhundert* (Vienna and Leipzig 1917)

Name	1740	1748	1754	1763	1770	1779(1)	1779(2)	Sources and notes
Allius, Johann Jacob	+	−	−	−	−	−	−	Became a Warehouser 22 Aug. 1735, MGP(1), fo. 19.
Bader, Emerich Felix	−	−	+	+	+	−	−	Widow in 1779 entry.
Bahn, Johann Christoph	−	−	+	+	+	−	−	B. listed as a Warehouser 1 Sept. 1729, MGP(1), fo. 88. 1770 entry is for his widow.
Bartenstein, Christian								See Küner.
Bender & Co.	+	+	+	+	+	+	−	See Ch. 7.
Binnenfeld, Johann Adam	−	−	−	−	−	−	+	Fleischmarkt 703. Grosshändler 23 Mar. 1178, MGP(2), fo. 161; firm failed 1780.
Bolza, Johann Baptist	+	−	−	−	−	−	−	Joh. Bapt. B. and Joh. Peter B. Warehousers 25 June 1725, MGP(1), fo. 44. Joh. Bapt. B. alone 1736. Cashier Carl B. has signature to 1734. Christoph Conradi, an associate 1739. Ibid. fo. 127: Conradi and Jos. (sic) B. Warehousers Feb. 1739–May 1741, capital 90,000 fl. Cf. Bolza 'exchanger' ('Wechsler') in Milan loans in 1700s, Mensi, 406; Johann Baptist and Peter Johann von Bolza, *Hofkammer* Councillors in 1771, see Ch. 12 and Table 12.4*.

Name	1740	1748	1754	1763	1770	1779(1)	1779(2)	Sources and notes
Bouvard, Johann Baptist	–	–	–	–	+	+	–	See Crettier for Warehousers' firm of Crettier, Bouvard & Co. 1753. This was Franz B., son-in-law of Wilh. C., and perhaps Joh. B.'s brother. MGP(2), fo. 81, 26 Feb. 1768, Johann Baptist Bouvard seeks leave to continue Warehousership (*Niederlagshandlung*) of his late father-in-law Claude Salliet (q.v.). 26 July 1768, Bouvard provides funds of 45,394 fl. 1770–4 in partnership with Claude Gaillard. 1783–1805 in partnership with Johann Peter B. and Franz B. (nephews) and Jos. Merwert. Firm turned into a Wholesalership (*Grosshandlung*) 1805.
Bozenhard, Emanuel	–	–	–	–	+	–	+	Tuchlauben 569. MGP(2), fo. 55, B.'s Warehouser status conferred 7 Nov. 1766, on condition he keep up his fine *Barchent* (fustian) factory near Klosterneuberg. His trading fund 51,229 fl. *Grosshändler* 12 Feb. 1774. 1771–9 in partnership with his son, also with his

Name							Notes
Brandesky, heirs of Joseph	—	—	+	+	+	+	Firm fails 16 Apr. 1779. Petition for its cessation 3 Jan. 1785. Franz Jos. Brandegsky (*sic*) Warehouser 18 Mar. 1725, MGP(1), fo. 28. Partnership with Franz Pöttenberger 1729–40. Death of P. notified 24 Oct. 1740. Death of B. not entered.
Brentano Cimaroli, Aloysius	—	—	—	—	—	+	'Banquier' under the style B.C. 1167 Breunerstrasse. MGP(2), fos. 121–2 shows an undated (?1771) application of A.B.C. to be a privileged Warehouser and to run a firm 'here' (i.e. Vienna) in conjunction with 'the Genoese trading house of Brentano'. His business consists entirely of exchange and dispatch ('bloss auf Wechsel und speditoren'). It is noted that he must show a trading fund of 50,000 fl. and be prepared to help factories. By a subsequent decree dated 25 Oct. 1771 he is allowed Wholesaler's rights without incorporation in the Free Warehousers or the Trading Burgesses ('Bürgerlicher Handelstand') provided he shows a fund of 30,000 fl. and

Name	1740	1748	1754	1763	1770	1779(1)	1779(2)	Sources and notes
								pays 100 fl. per annum to the Council of Trade. Ibid. fo. 122 his partnership dated 24 Dec. 1772 with Franz B.C., perhaps his father. For the family see also ii, Ch. 9.
Buiretti & Co.	+	+	+	−	−	−	−	Joh. Wilh. Buirette (*sic*) Warehouser 8 May 1725; MGP(1), fo. 41; style of firm 'B. Bros.' Changes to 'B. son & Co.' Apr. 1736. *Court Calendar*, 1740: 'The late Joh. Wilh. B. Son & Co.' Firm lends 300,000 fl. to army? 1742 (HKA Prandau Akten, Konvolut 13, no. 10). Used by Cesare Sardi of Amsterdam to remit English subsidy to Vienna 1741, 1742 (ibid. Konvolut 27). B. Bros. creditors of Hirschl Spitz 1759 (Taglicht, 172).
Castellini, Philipp Marie	−	−	−	+	+	−	−	MGP(2), fo. 178. In partnership with Barthol., Fh. von Carignani 1757–65. Then with Franz Franzoni and Ignatz Ortmayr as 'Philipp Maria de C. et Comp.' 1765–70. Fund 50,000 fl. New partnership with Melchior Peter (q.v.) 1771–74 when firm wound

Name								Notes
(continued)	–	–	+	+	–	–	–	up; fund 60,000 fl., 'the statutory fund for an exchange business'. De C. & Co., 'banquiers Tuchlauben', *Alm. gén. des March.*
Castlemur, Augustin von	–	–	+	+	–	+	+	MGP(2), fos. 183–4, 5 Oct. 1762, C. seeks to take over Dohm (q.v.) business. Admitted a Warehouser on proving a fund of 55,000 fl., 30,000 fl. of this a *Caution* of Thos. von Böck, Kanzler of Lower Austrian *Regierung*. In Aug. 1764 Joh. Rud. von Dohm replaces Böck as surety C. d. Apr. 1773, widow Eliz., May 1776, cedes privilege to Christian Pape (q.v.) and Christian Gerhardi. C. 'caissier des Commerçans en gros; banquier', *Alm. gén. des March.*
Churfeld, Frans von	+	+	+	+	+	+	–	Registered as Warehouser 21 Apr. 1725, MGP(1), fo. 167. Had been partner of Stephan Knoll until latter d. 1723.
Coith, Christian Heinrich	–	+	+	+	+	–	–	MGP(2), fo. 179. C. H. Coith a (1760) Priv. Warehouser; fund 49,407 fl. (His bro. is Christian Ernst C.) From 1770–86 assoc. his son Joh. Ernst in firm; son takes over 1786. In 1754

Name	1740	1748	1754	1763	1770	1779(1)	1779(2)	Sources and notes
								calendar (only) firm is 'Coith & Korb'. This was Andreas C. (perhaps Christian's father) and Georg Korb, who registered as Warehousers 19 May 1726, MGP(1), fo. 176.
Consoni, Caspar	—	—	+	—	—	—	—	The entry in the *Court Calendar* may be defective since Angelo C. registered as a Warehouser 18 Apr. 1725 and was succ. by his nephews Gasparo (*sic*) and Franz Carl C., from 1726, MGP(1), fo. 165. It is not, however, clear if they were Warehousers.
Crettier, Johann Wilhelm	—	—	+	+	+	—	—	Prob. but not certainly Wilh. C., Warehouser under style 'C. Bros.' 30 May 1743, MGP(1), fo. 226. Son-in-law Franz Bouvard enters firm 1749, style 'C., Bouvard and Co.' 23 Feb. 1753, ibid. Wilh. C. was father of Joseph C., see below. MGP(2), fo. 189, 1 Jan. 1761, partnership of Jos. C., Melchior Peter, Johann Batt. Bouvard and Franz Parent (*sic*). Each to take ¼ of gains or losses. Parent dies 19 Dec. 1763; remaining partners

Decret, Ludwig

– + + + + – –

dissolve firm 31 Dec. 1767. 23
Jan. 1767 Jos. Maria C. registers
new firm with Franz Bassy
(Passy), Jos. Friederich, and
Franz Xavier Klinger (q.v.) for 8
years to 31 Dec. 1774: 'C. and
Co.' 14 Dec. 1769 Jos. Maria C.
seeks status as Warehouser on
death of his father Wilhelm C.
(*sic*).
Property 35,673 fl. This status
conceded 19 Feb. 1770.
See also Bouvard, Passy.

1779: Edler von D. MGP(2), fo.
35, firm of Peter, Jos. and Peter
Franz Passy and Ludwig D.
1753–9 (see Passy). Ibid., fo.
331, Ludwig D. and sons
Ludwig (II) and Peter assoc.
with him 12 Sept. 1774; 30 June
1780 also son Johann. HKA NÖ
Kommerz, rote Nr. 121,
Vortrags Protokoll 15 Apr. 1755:
Niederlieger D. to be asked if he
will wholesale flowered silks if
made a *k. k. Commercien Rat*.
Relationship of Ludwig D. to
Franz D. not clear. Franz D. in
partnership with 'Crettier'
1734–9; 'Bros. D.' 1741;
bankrupt 1763, MGP(1), fo. 285.

Name	1740	1748	1754	1763	1770	1779(1)	1779(2)	Sources and notes
Dohm, (and Ely)	+	+	+	-	-	-	-	Hermann Fried. Dohm Warehouser 12 June 1726 in partnership with Joh. Georg Ely, MGP(1), fo. 280. On 1 Oct. 1751 D. registers dissolution of this partnership. As he has no children takes as partner his bro. Joh. Ludwig Dohm von Dohmkirchen. Partnership dissolved 1763. The firm of 1727 had been orig. founded by Joh. Ander von Mayer, who left it to his dau. Renata von Palm, who was to see it contd. as Dohm and Ely, ibid. Unclear if Renata m. to Dohm or Ely. Separate entries in *Calendar* for Dohm and Ely 1754. Hermann Fried., Liborius and Ludolph D. made Bohem. knights as 'von Dohmkirchen' 1738 (Megerle). Creditors of Löw Sinzheim 1744, Taglicht p. 36. Hermann Fried. D. invests in Tyrol loans in 1740s; Dohm and Ely owed 30,650 fl. by 'Schulden Cassa' 1746 (see ii, Table 10.4).
Donon, Stephan	-	-	+	+	+	+	-	'Widow D.' from 1763. Calendar entry must be defective since

Name									Notes
(entry continued from previous page)	−	−							Stephan D. registers as Warehouser 19 Apr. 1725, MGP(1), fo. 249.
Ely, Johann Georg	−	−	−	−	+	−	−	−	See 'Dohm and Ely'.
Fachiny, Paul	−	+	+	+	−	−	−	−	MGP(2), fo. 434, 12 Nov. 1764, Paolo Fachini (*sic*) deposes his signature as Warehouser. 10 Dec. 1782, F. requests inclusion in firm of son Johann; then sells firm, 19 Sept. 1786, as Joh. F. wants to travel. HKA NÖ Kommerz, rote Nr. 48 Jan. 1771, list of loans c.1755–70, shows P.F. given 20,000 fl. interest-free loan from 'Commerziencassa', 27 May 1763.
Falck, Bartholomé or Bartholomäus									See Hösslin.
Falquet, Bernard von	−	−	−	+	+	+	+	−	Bernard (also Bernhard) F. partner of Bernhard Violland (q.v.) 1735–40, of Ludwig Puthon (q.v.) 1740–8, when he traded alone. Puthon was F.'s cousin. F. m. Maria Anna Singer 1737. The source is not clear on the date of F.'s Warehouser status: possibly 1748. F.'s capital 30,000 fl. 1746, MGP(1) fo. 377. MGP(2) fo. 315, deposition 23 Jan. 1769 that in previous year

Name	1740	1748	1754	1763	1770	1779(1)	1779(2)	Sources and notes
Fischer, Franz	–	–	–	–	–	–	+	partnership of Wolfg. Fh. von Riesch, Bernard von F., and Jos. Schwarzleuthner & Son to run 'k. k. privilegirte Dratzugs Fabrik' dissolved. Schwarzleuthner & Co. (q.v.) will continue factory. Ibid., fo. 449, 17 Mar. 1768, partnership for 6 years from 1 Jan. 1768 of Bernard F. and Mathias Schmuck as 'F. & Co.' F. puts 40,000 fl. into business @ 5%, S. 6,000 fl. without interest. S. to have keep, 600 fl. p.a., 20% of net profits.
Fohr & Wanner	+	–	–	–	–	–	–	Obere Beckerstrasse 812.
Franzoni, Joseph	–	–	–	–	–	+	–	MGP(2), fo. 473, 26 Mar. 1772, F. seeks Warehouser status with his father Franz F. Own property 17,045 fl., father gives *Caution* to make this up to 30,000 fl. 2 Sept. 1780, firm dissolved. Ibid., fos. 6, 489. Franz F. had a silk business; sold it to Appiani and Zezzi 1768 for 24,928 fl.
Fries, Johann	–	–	+	+	+	+	–	See Ch. 7.

Fuchs, Fux Johann	–	–	+	–	–	–	–
Fuchs, Fux Joseph	+	–	–	–	–	–	–

Jos. F. 1779 Hoher Markt 552. MGP(2), fo. 431, 6 Aug. 1764, Joh. Edler v. Fux, as continuer of wholesaling business of Johann Fortunat Heller (q.v.) asks to be admitted a Warehouser. His bro. Jos. Nepomuck Edler v. Fuchs (*sic*) deposes that his brother has inherited 26,928 fl. from his father and has 6,000 fl. in obligations. Joh. F. says he will support the 'gold and silver lace factory', 7 Jan. 1765 his 5-year partnership with Mich. Portelotti (*sic*) registered. Joh. F. farms Aust. Customs 1765 with Jos. Weinbrenner, see ii, Table 2.3, MGP(2), fo. 1021, Jos. Nep. v. F. has 100,000 fl. invested in Schwechat cotton-factory 1769 as sleeping partner. Jos. Nep. F. at *Goldener Hirsch*, Leopoldstadt 217 (de Ponty). Jos. Nep. and Jos. (*sic* for Joh.) Carl F. made *Edle Herren* 1765 (*sic*) 'wegen von ihren Vorälteren durch 200 Jahre getriebenen Handel' (Megerle). MGP(2), fo. 475, Jos. Nep. F. 1771 given wholesaling rights on payment of 100 fl. p.a. without

Name	1740	1748	1754	1763	1770	1779(1)	1779(2)	Sources and notes
								being obliged to enter the corps of Warehousers or Trading Burgesses. Property 34,550 fl. For his partnership with Pappe see Pappe. 7 Oct. 1789 his partnership with Franz Natoys dissolved. 9 July 1811, Jos. von F., now a Count, gives up his Wholesalership.
Gaillard	–	–	–	–	+	+	–	'Stephan and Franz Gaillard', MGP(2), fo. 498, 15 Aug. 1763, Stephan Galliard (sic) seeks Warehouser status, and partnership with his father Franz G. and Georg Passy (q.v.). His fund is 35,470 fl. The two G.s were interested in the 'Steuermann silks factory' and the 'Schneider thin-cloth factory'. Related to Claud G., see Weigl.
Geymüller, Johann Heinrich			Not a Wholesaler in this period					In partnership with Peter Ochs (q.v.) from 28 May 1781. Mikoletzky, 'Schweizer Händler', 165–66 shows J.H.G. (1754–1824) (? of Basle) works in firm of Peter Ochs from 1772. His brother Joh. Jakob G.

Name						Notes
Gontard, Jakob Friedrich	–	–	+	–	–	(1760–1834) and he become partners in firm in 1786 (*sic*) and its style now 'O. & G.' Separate firm as 'G. & Co.' on Peter Ochs's death 1804. Joh. Heinr. G. Knight 1810, Dep. Gov. of Nat. Bank 1816–20, Baron 31 Mar. 1824, d. same day. Firm bankrupt 10 July 1841. Partner of Johann Fries. See Ch. 7.
Grahl, widow of Johann Carl	–	–	–	–	–	'Grahl' warehouses Hamburg sugar for Company of Trieste and Fiume 1758–59, contract then given to Fux Brothers (Michielsen, 196). Widow Grahl marries Peter Ochs, q.v.
Grosser, Johann Michael, Edler von	+	–	–	–	–	Kohlmarkt 167. Imperial noble 1768; Hered. Lands noble 1769 (Megerle). One of the six farmers of the tobacco revenue 1774, see App. B. MGP(2), fo. 531, Joh. Mich. von G. 23 Dec. 1777 granted Wholesaler status with fund of 30,000 fl. Ibid., fo. 532 son Joh. Mich. (II), in partnership with him since 1781, notifies his death 24 Mar. 1784.
Heilman, Heylmann, Wolfgang Friedrich	–	+	+	–	–	MGP(2), fo. 379, 4 May 1767 Wolfgang Fried. Heylmann seeks Warehouser status so that

Name	1740	1748	1754	1763	1770	1779(1)	1779(2)	Sources and notes
								he can continue his grandfather's business. Has 21,402 fl. own property and *Caution* of 10,000 fl. with Joh. Heinr. Stametz, q.v. 26 Nov. 1767, petition to be granted if H. invests 2,000 fl. at 'Commerciencassa'. Ibid., fo. 580, H. transfers his business to his bookkeeper and universal heir Jakob Gemeiner, 2 Jan. 1798; H. d. 1800.
Heller, Johann Fortunatus	+	–	+		–	–	–	A big seller of Hungarian copper in the 1730s, Srbik, 404 n. No entry in 1748. See also Fux. H. registered his firm 7 July 1729. His associate was Joh. Maria Tinti, whose death is notified 17 Aug. 1733, MGP(1), fo. 491. Cf. Mensi, index s.n. for 'exchange house' of Tinti still active in late 1730s. Bartholomé Baron T. a councillor of *Hofkammer* in 1740 and earlier: in 1754 a member of the Lower Austrian *Repraesentation und Kammer*, see Tables 12.1*, 13.2*.
Hey								See Mayer.

	See Ch. 7.							Note
Hilleprand von Prandau, Maximilian Emanuel	—	—	—	—	—	+	+	
Hösslin & Falck	—	—	—	—	+	+	+	Philipp Albrecht von Hösslin and Christopher Rad depose 13 Apr. 1725 that they are assoc. with Bartholomäus Falck (q.v.). Firm with Rad ends 1736: H. and F. continue with 150,000 fl. capital, MGP(1), fo. 504. 'Rad and Hösslin' were Vienna agents for imperial army supplies and advanced 1m. fl. 1736, Mensi, 363 n. All three families were originally from Lindau in Swabia. In 1740, because of Austrian inability to repay their advances, the firm went bankrupt. A moratorium was then imposed 1740–7. In 1747 the Vienna firm had 1,706,822 fl. assets, 1,254,156 fl. of which was in government paper. Liabilities were 815,677 fl. The parent firm in Augsburg had 755,548 fl. assets and 322,458 debts. A creditors' committee was still trying to bring in moneys in 1773, W. Zorn, *Handels- und Industriegeschichte Bayerisch-Schwabens 1648–1870* (Augsburg 1961), 34–6.

Name	1740	1748	1754	1763	1770	1779(1)	1779(2)	Sources and notes
Isenflam & Co.	+	−	−	−	−	−	−	Firm of Johann Jacob I. registered 19 Apr. 1725; partnership with Küner (q.v.) 8 Apr. 1728–31 Dec. 1732. MGP(1), fo. 527. *Court Calendar*: Joh. Jac. I cashier to corps of Warehousers. Partnership with Hilleprand 1713, Mensi 77.
Kernhofer, Johann Anton	−	−	−	+	+	+	−	*Court Calendar*, 1779 shows partnership with Franz Klinger, q.v., MGP(2), fo. 180, Joh. Anton K. of Brunn. Noted that his firm comes under Moravian *Lebenbank* and Tobacco Farm Company. (See App. B.)
Klinger, Franz Xaver	−	−	−	−	−	+	−	MGP(2), fo. 219, 4 Feb. 1771, K. granted Warehouser status having acquired Crettier (q.v.) business 19 Dec. 1770, and having shown a fund of 26,844 fl. own property, 3,156 fl. *Caution* with Mathaus (*sic*) Wöss. Ibid., fo. 220, K. says he has formed 8-year partnership with Franz Dragan as 'K. and Dragan'. Ends 31 Dec. 1786. On 21 Jan. 1782 K. shows property of 103,969 fl. Partnership with Joh. Anton

Name							Notes
	−						Kernhofer (q.v.) not noted in MGP.
Kohlmann, Joseph	−	+	+	+	−	−	Registered firm 29 May 1747 as Jos. Kolman, capital 32,345 fl., associate his employee Joh. Franz Jaccoud, MGP(1), fo. 232. K 'and Jaccoud' in 1779 Calendar entry.
Krauss, Johann Paul	−	+	+	+	+	−	Not traced in MGP.
Krauss, Paul	−	+	−	−	−	−	Perhaps same as preceding.
Kreidemann, Johann Caspar	+	+	−	−	−	−	Registered as Warehouser 16 Apr. 1725, MGP(1), fo. 159. 174,220 fl. due to him for copper sales 1747, see ii, Table 10.3.
Kriner	+	−	−	−	−	−	Zacharias K. registered as Warehouser 16 Apr. 1725. Partner Joh. George Schmidt withdraws 1725, succ. by Joh. Ander Schmidt 1727. [Joh. Caspar] Scheidlin also a partner 1728–48, then 'K. and Schmidt', MGP(1), fo. 158. See also Scheidlin.
Küner & Co.	+	+	+	+	+	−	See Ch. 7.
Kutzer, Johann	−	−	−	−	−	−	See Bender in Ch. 7.
Labhard, Johann Georg	−	−	−	−	−	−	See Mayer (Meyer).
Loschenkohl, heirs of Johann Christoph	+	−	−	−	−	−	10 Apr. 1725, firm run by Georg Christoph, Hermanus and Ander L. as 'Hanns Christoph L. seel Erben', MGP(1), fo. 544.

Name	1740	1748	1754	1763	1770	1779(1)	1779(2)	Sources and notes
								Christoph. L. ran the firm in 1740. Joh. Christoph von L. councillor in *Hofkriegsrat* made baron 1758 (Megerle): a son?
Lutz, Johann	+	+	+	+	+	+	—	Joh. L. partner with Bonaventura Riesch 16 Apr. 1725, dissolved 12 Aug. 1728, MGP(1), fo. 546. L. used by Pottenstein linen-factory to make foreign payments 1759–60, HKA Hs. 752. Sources do not show a father and son, hence L. must have been nearly 80 in 1779.
Mannsrieder, Joseph	—	+	+	+	—	—	—	'Widow of Jos. M.' 1754; 'Jos. M.' 1763. Father, mother, and son?
Marci & Plattensteiner	—	—	+	+	—	—	—	Joh. Cornelius Marci Warehouser 18 May 1735; 18 Jan. 1745 Georg Wilh. Plattensteiner deposes that he is made Warehouser by NÖ *Regierung* in respect of M.'s business, inherited by his wife, M.'s da., MGP(1), fo. 620. See also Plattensteiner.
Ochs, Peter	—	—	—	—	+	+	—	MGP(2), fo. 877. Peter Ochs registers his firm 1763. It is under his sole direction. 30 May

Georg?) Fh. v. Grechtler 17 Aug. 1764 L. partner for 10 years with Daniel Hey as 'L. & Co.', Grechtler having ¼ share. But 14 Sept. 1769 L. cedes Warehouser's freedom again to Grechtler, who transfers it to David Meyer, who trades as 'Meyer Hey et Comp.' from 11 Jan. 1770. 28 Oct. 1773, son David M. (II) admitted. Ibid. fo. 807 firm dissolved 1780–81. *Alm. gén. des March.*, Labhard and Co., bankers, 'Aussi ont une fabrique . . . d'Indiennes'. The L. family was of Basle etc., see Lüthy ii, index s.n. Mikoletsky's statement, 'Schweizer Händler', 173, that on David Meyer's death in 1774 the firm of Meyer and Hey was taken over by Peter Ochs & Co. cannot be correct, since it is still in the *Court Calendar* for 1779, and was presumably run by D.M. II. The M. family was from Gottlieben in Switzerland, Mikoletzky, loc. cit.

Firm registered 18 Aug. 1735, no partners, MGP(1), fo. 618. Unclear if this is date of Warehousership.

Monath, Peter Conrad	−	−	+	+	−	−

−	−	−

Name	1740	1748	1754	1763	1770	1779(1)	1779(2)	Sources and notes
Müller, Georg Christoph	-	-	+	+	+	-		Georg Christoph M., 13 May 1748, deposes he has taken over business and Warehousership of his cousin Daniel Wohlgemut (q.v.), MGP(1), fo. 612. From 1 Jan. 1756 firm is 'M. & Co.', viz. Julius Fried. Coith is associate, ibid.
Muller, Johann Ignatz	-	-	-	-	-	-	+	Graben 591. MGP(2), fos. 793, 836, Nanzius (sic) M. 14 Nov. 1774 admitted to Wholesaler's College. Trades as 'Ignatz M.' Is a lace manufacturer and merchant in Bohemia; has helped mining town of Weippert there for 30 years. Property there 37,667 fl. Dies 1809.
Ochs, Peter	-	-	-	-	+	+	-	MGP(2), fo. 877. Peter Ochs registers his firm 1763. It is under his sole direction. 30 May 1777 he admits to a signature (only) his bookkeeper Johann Heinrich Geymuller. q.v. 28 May 1781 G. admitted to a 5-year partnership, later extended. Ibid., fo. 901, death of Peter Ochs 23 Sept. 1804, Dissolution of firm Jan. 1805, Mikoletzky, 'Schweizer

Händler', 164–5: Ochs family from Baden settle in Basle, where bros. Wilh. O. (1700–53) and Joh. Kaspar O. (1701–52) are bankers as Ochs Brothers. Joh. Kapar's son Peter O. becomes bookkeeper to Johann Fries in Vienna 1754–62. Marries in 1761 or 1762 widow Maria Theresia Grahl, q.v. Business 'Ochs and Geymüller' 1786. Peter Ochs dies as First Deputy of Corps of Warehousers 23 Sept. 1804. Lüthy, ii. 623 n. says Peter O. a cousin of Pierre O. of Basle, founder of the Helvetic Republic. But his reference (ibid.) to 'Frère Ochs et Cie' as 'banquiers de la cour de Vienne' confuses Peter Ochs with his father and uncle in Basle.

Name							Notes
Paldinger, Gottlieb Reichard	—	+	+	—	—	—	MGP(2), fo. 49, 29 May 1765, Gottlieb P. 'of the Evangelic religion, from Ödenburg [in Hungary]' buys business of Erdmann Tech dec. (q.v.) from Widow Tech, for 15,000 fl. As further fund, exhibits 300 fl. cash and 14,812 fl. due from Sinzheim heirs (viz. heirs of Löw S. d. 1744, see Ch. 7).
Palm Brothers	+	+		—	—	—	See Ch. 7.

Name	1740	1748	1754	1763	1770	1779(1)	1779(2)	Sources and notes
Pappe, Christian Heinrich	–	–	–	–	–	–	+	'banquier, P. and Gerhardi'. MGP(2), fo. 151, Christian Heinr. P. seeks succession to Kaselmur (viz. Castelmur, q.v.) business: exhibits widow Castelmur's renunciation of her Warehouser's privilege in his favour, 4 Mar. 1776. Shows fund of 30,000 fl. 9 Nov. 1776. P. (alone) granted Wholesalership, but trades with partner Christian Ludwig Gerhardi, who provides half the 30,000 fl., as 'Pappe & Gerhardi'. Ibid., fo. 152, 5 Oct. 1779, Fh. Jos. Nepom. von Fuchs and his son Ignatz join firm. 28 July 1787 Pappe carries on firm alone.
Passy, Claudius	–	–	–	–	+	–	–	Court Calendar entries are as listed. However, MGP(1), fo. 123 shows Michael P. a Warehouser 12 Oct. 1736; partner with Philibert Perinet 1736–70, capital initially 52,000 fl. See also below. MGP(2), fo. 35 says partnership of Peter Jos. Bassy (sic), Peter Franz Passy and Ludwig Decret (q.v.).
Passy, Georg	–	–	–	+	–	–	–	
Passy, Joseph	–	–	+	+	–	–	–	
Passy, Michael	–	–	+	+	+	–	–	
Passy, Peter Claudius	–	–	–	–	–	+	–	
Passy, Peter Joseph	–	–	–	–	–	+	–	

formed 2 Jan. 1753, dissolved 23 Jan. 1759. Joseph P. Warehouser 15 Feb. 1753. Peter Jos. and Mich. Bernh. P. of Augsburg register 23 Oct. 1763. Firm bankrupt 1769; pays 12%. Allowed to continue as 'Peter Jos. P. & Comp.' under Franz Franzoni and Melchior Peter (q.v.) as directors. Jos. Crettier (q.v.) a partner Feb. 1778, leaves 1779. Firm again bankrupt 6 July 1779. Georg P. trades with St. Gaillard (q.v.) 1763–9. Peter Claudius P. in partnership with cousin Peter Franz P. and Christoph de la Costa 1765. Michael P., Perinet and Co. bankrupt 1770; 78,637 fl. debts written off. Michael P. a Wholesaler (!) 1775–April 1778 when he withdraws, Mathaeus Petz (q.v.) acquiring his Wholesalership.

+

−

−

−

−

−

Perghofer, Leopold Ignatz

Tuchlauben 577. MGP(2), fo. 146, 13 March 1776, Leopold Ignatz P. of Graz, where he has run a business (unspec.) with success, admitted as Wholesaler. Shows fund of 35,093 fl., ibid., fo. 148. Dies Aug. 1811.

Name	1740	1748	1754	1763	1770	1779(1)	1779(2)	Sources and notes
Perinet, Johann Bapt	–	–	+	+	–	–	–	*Philibert P.* a partner of Michael Passy 1744. see Passy. Joh. Bapt. Perinet seems (MGP(1), fo. 33) to be J. B. P. Jr. The father (ibid.) registered as a Wholesaler 1725; his partners from 1740–6 were Bernh. Franz Violland (*sic*, see Violland), Franz V., and Jacob V. Joach. Bened. Perinet, and J. B. P. Jr. join partnership 1754.
Peter, Melchior	–	–	–	–	–	–	+	M.P. & Son, Judenplatz 238. MGP(2), fo. 141, 8 Aug. 1774, M.P. granted Wholesaler privilege for himself, his son and his son-in-law Ferd. Bock. Shows assets of 55,401 fl. Ibid., fo. 142, M.P. registers partnership for four years from 6 Nov. 1774 with his son Franz Florian P., and his bookkeeper Kaspar Ferdinand, as 'M.P. & Son'. 5 March 1778, Franz Florian P. leaves firm to travel. In 1779 firm bankrupt; 5 Oct. 1779 allowed to continue, as its cotton factory of worth to community. Ibid., fo. 176, 7 Oct. 1782 death of M.P.; firm

Name								Notes
Petz, Mathaeus				·				continues as 'M.P. seel Wittib'. WSLA HGA 2/190, M.P.'s assets at death 61,607 fl., liabilities 97,017 fl. Not in 1779 *Court Calendar*. MGP(2), fo. 167, 28 Aug. 1778 M.P. seeks leave to succeed to Wholesaler's Privilege of Michael Passy (q.v.). Shows fund of 15,000 fl. (*sic*) of which 6,974 fl. in form of *Caution* with (J.B.) Puthon (see Schuller and Comp.). Petition evid. allowed. Partnership with Jacob Franz Moret 1779–86. Petz bankrupt Jan. 1806.
Pichinini, Paul	+	−	+	−	−	+	−	MGP(1), fo. 34, Paul P. Warehouser 1725; joined by son Anton 1749, firm 'P. P. & Son'. In *Court Calendar*, 1754 a Leopold P. is an Exchange Broker ('Wechsel Sensale') and is joined 1763 by Antoni (*sic*) P. Latter only in *Court Calendar*, 1770.
Plattensteiner, heirs of Joh. Christoph	−	−	−	−	+	+	−	MGP(2), fo. 65, agreement at Nuremberg between Joh. Conrad Teuerlein and guardians of Joh. Christoph Ps. children for latter to continue Warehouser's firm of

Name	1740	1748	1754	1763	1770	1779(1)	1779(2)	Sources and notes
	+							'Plattensteiner and Marci' as 'heirs of J.C.P.' from 1 Dec. 1767. There were evidently houses at Vienna and Nuremberg; Teuerlein directs latter. Widow P. has Joh. Wöllfeld direct Vienna firm from 1772 till 1779, when son Georg Wilh. P. takes over. Firm dissolved Feb. 1801. (For Wöllfeld see also Castelmur.)
Pradatsch, Johann George of Prague			Not a Vienna merchant					See Ch. 7.
Pruner, Georg von	+	—	—	—	—	—	—	MGP(1), fo. 31, Georg P. (not von P.) Warehouser 19 Apr. 1725
Puthon, Johann Baptist Edler von	—	—	—	—	—	—	+	*Court Calendar:* trades as 'Joh. Georg Schuller & Co.' 'Edler von P.' 1777 (Megerle). MGP(2), fos. 133–4, P. given Wholesaler's Privilege 31 Jan. 1774 on showing 37,218 fl. property invested in 'Schuller Handlung'. His fund Nov. 1780 shown as 162,638 fl. In partnership for 7 years from 1 Jan. 1782 with Ludwig Rüpper as 'Joh. Georg Schuller et Comp.' Director of Sassin

Name							Notes
							cotton-factory 1770–6, see Schuller.
Rieger, Johann, Freiherr von	−	−	−	−	+	−	'R. & Schwab, am Peter 578'. MGP(2), fo. 967, 24 Mar. 1778, Joh. Heinrich R. from Switzerland (no details) granted Wholesaler's Priv. on condition he prove he really has 30,000 fl. in Hered. Lands. Ibid., fo. 968, 2 July 1778, 6-year partnership with Ignaz Schwab. Ibid., fo. 971, Anton Weigl added 1 July 1780. Shares of capital: Rieger 60,000 fl., Schwab 40,000 fl., Weigl 60,000 fl. Rieger d. 1808, firm dissolved.
Riesch, Erhard	−	+	−	+	−	!	See Ch. 7.
Riesch, Wolfgang von	+	+	+	−	−	!	See Ch. 7.
Rossino, Francesco Maria	+	−	−	−	−	−	
Rössler, heirs of Paul	−	+	+	−	−	−	MGP(1), fo. 678. P.R. d. 1725; widow thereupon runs business.
Rouard, Johann Baptist	−	+	+	+	+	+	MGP(1), fo. 711 Joh. Baptista Ruard (sic) Wholesaler 3 Dec. 1746; partner with bro. Valentin R. 1747–58, capitals 30,000 fl. Joh., 37,000 fl. Valentin. Valentin R. then continues on own.
Rouard, Valentin	−	−	+	+	+	−	MGP(2), fo. 980. 1770, J. B. Rouard's business so sunk that

Name	1740	1748	1754	1763	1770	1779(1)	1779(2)	Sources and notes
								royal permission has to be sought for a composition with creditors. Business to be continued by administrators provided annual statement submitted to mercantile court.
Salliet, Claude	—	—	+	+	—	—	—	MGP(1), fo. 818. Claudius S. and Pernat partners 1746–1753; Claudius S. then partner with bro. Michael S. In Salliet & Pernat partnership, capitals Salliet 20,000 fl., Pernat 10,000 fl. Not clear if Warehousers. MGP(2), fo. 1039, 18 Feb. 1768, Michael S. requests rights of Warehouser and succession to Claude S.'s business. Assets of firm are 58,252 fl. Claude S. father-in-law of Joh. Bapt. Bouvard, q.v. See also Weigl.
Salliet, Michael	—	—	—	—	+	—	—	
Scharno, Gottlob Friedrich	—	—	—	—	+	+	—	'G.F.S. & Co.'
Scheffler, Joseph, & Co.	—	—	—	—	+	+	—	Ignaz Franz S. in 1779 entry.
Scheidlin, Johann Caspar	—	—	+	—	—	—	—	Joh. Caspar Scheidlin partner of Zacharias Kriner (q.v.) and Johann Ander Schmidt (sic) 1728–1748, MGP(1) fo. 826. Joh. Caspar von Scheidlin (sic) is noted as style of firm 1 Dec.
Scheidlin, Johann Georg	—	—	—	+	+	+	—	
Schmid & Scheidlin	+	+	—	—	—	—	—	

1748. ?Both Schmid(t) and Kriner d. 1748 × 1754. MGP(2). fos. 995–6: Joh. Caspar S. transferred his business to his son Joh. Georg 1760. Matthaeus Thomann directs firm 1761 till 1781, when he retires and Jacob Schmid taken in. Joh. Georg S. dies June 1792.

Name							Notes
Scholz, Balthasar Sigmund	+	+	+	+	−	−	'Heirs of S.S.' in 1763 entry.
Schröck, Johann Wolfgang	+	+	−				
Schuller, Johann Georg							MGP(2), fo. 1029, 11 Jan. 1768, friendly termination of 20-year partnership of J.G.S. and Franz Michael Weigl. S. subsequently (no date given) associates with him his stepson Joh. Bapt. Buthon (*sic*, see Puthon) and Anton Wolf; dies 1770. The firm of 'J.G. Schuller & Co.' run by J.B. Puthon from 1774 were Wholesalers but J.G.S. apparently was not. He was the manager of the emperor Francis Stephen's cotton-factory at Sassin from 1746, Mikoletzky, 'Franz Stephan'. He was the son-in-law of Joseph Peisser, for whom Johann Matthias Puechberg worked in the 1750s,

Name	1740	1748	1754	1763	1770	1779(1)	1779(2)	Sources and notes
	–	–						Mikoletzky, 'Holics und Sassin', MÖSA 14 (1961) 20. This may provide a connection with Philipp 'Buchberg' below. In Oct. 1770 his widow notified the Mercantile Court that as present owner of the Sassin factory she had 120,000 fl. invested in it. Balthasar Angerer of Linz had invested a further 40,000 fl. and Philipp Anton Buchberg 40,000 fl. Its director for six years from 1 Jan. 1770 was Joh. Bapt. Buthon (Puthon q.v.). Schuller & Co. were Vienna agents of Pradatsch and Co. of Prague, see Ch. 7.
Schwartzleitner, Joseph	–	–	+	+	+	+	–	See also Falquet. MGP(1), fo. 837, Jos. S. and son Warehousers 1 Jan. 1749; 22 Aug. 1754 son Franz cont. business under father's name. Death of Jos. S. July 1752. In *Court Calendar* 1779, entry is 'S. creditors' committee'. Entry for 1770 is 'Jos. Xaverius S.' For the protest of bills in 1774 drawn from Prague on this firm, see Ch. 7. MGP(2), fo. 1135, Josepha S.

								Notes
Schwonasini, Johann Bapt.	–	–	–	–	+	+	–	(presumably Franz S.'s widow) 6 Oct. 1780 seeks continuation of Warehouser's Privilege for her son Anton: shows a fund of 33,619 fl. This is agreed to, 18 Jan. 1782, ibid., fo. 1135.
Segalla & Bigongini	–	–	–	+	+	+	+	'Edler von S.' 1748, 1754.
Segalla, Joseph Anton	–	+	+	–	–	–	–	See next entry.
								Alman. gén. des March., 'Banquier, Glosserischen Haus, Kohlmarkt'. MGP(2), fo. 997, 3 Aug. 1761, Jos. Anton Segalla seeks leave to continue Warehouser's business ceded to him by his father, Jos. Amadeus S.; agreed to 3 May 1766, Jos. Anton S. seeks to annul style of S. & Pigongini (*sic*) and to trade as 'Anton S.' Fund 48,616 fl. 21 Aug. 1766 Jos. Parisi to be assoc. with firm. Ibid., fo. 997 son Joh. Bapt. S. given signature. Johann (*sic*) Anton and Johann Franz S. from Verona made knights 1718 (Megerle). HKA Prandau Akten, Konvolut 21, no. 12, S. and Bigongini owed 12,500 fl. by *Schulden Cassa*, Oct. 1746.
Smitmer Brothers	+	–	–	–	–	–	+	See Ch. 7.
Sörgel, Johann Georg	–	+	+	+	+	+	–	'& Co.' in 1779 entry.

Name	1740	1748	1754	1763	1770	1779(1)	1779(2)	Sources and notes
Stametz, Johann Heinrich	–	–	+	+	+	+	–	'Banquier, prés St. Pierre', *Alm. gén. des March.* Makes advances to Company of Trieste and Fiume in early 1760s, Michielsen, 198. Acts as guarantee house for drafts of Thum & Co. of Prague, see Ch. 7. MGP(2), fo. 1015 Joh. Heinr. S. deposes 31 Dec. 1763 that since 1751 he has carried on his business with 100,000 fl. Palm capital and 20,000 fl. of his own. 18 Aug. 1781 S. notifies Court that his son Franz Heinr. S. has a signature. Joh. Heinr. S. d. 1783 (ibid.).
Starhemberg, Rudiger	–	–	–	–	–	–	+	'R.E.D. Starhemberg, Alte Haarmarkt 495.' MGP(2), fo. 1071, Rudiger 'Graff von Starhemberg' (*sic*) seeks 'ordinary trading freedom', with a capital of 30,000 fl. On 20 Sept. 1773 admitted a Wholesaler. Evidently subsequently bankrupt, but no date given.
Steiner, Melchior, & Co.	–	–	–	–	+	+	–	See Ch. 7.
Tech, Erdmann	–	–	+	+	–	–	–	MGP(1), fo. 288, E.T. registers firm (as Wholesaler?) 22 Sept.

							Notes
						—	1735. For Gottlieb Paldinger's purchase of this business from Tech's window in 1765 see Paldinger.
Teuerlein, Christian Wilhelm	—	—	+	+	+	—	MGP(2), fo. 305, 11 Mar. 1765, T. deposes his signature on being admitted as a Warehouser. 11 Jan. 1770, he deposes end of his former partnership with Sigmund Gottlieb Bräumiller. 14 Sept. 1789, asks to transfer his business to his son. ?Connection with Teuerlein family of Nuremberg, see Plattensteiner.
Thys, Johann	Has privileges of a Warehouser from 1762 without having to be one						A Dutchman. (?Thijs) from Eupen in Rhineland. Grant of Warehouser status 10 July 1762. To pay no taxes on his cloth factory at Klagenfurt, Carinthia. In 1765 has 10 looms. In 1775 receives state grant of 100,000 fl. Ennobled 20 Apr. 1765, as *Kanzler* of Carinthian Agric. Soc. estab. in that year. In 1766, on government commission to discuss Caratto's bank project. A. Beer, 'Die österr. Industriepolitik', *AÖG* 81 (1894) 102, 104–5; K. Dinklage, 'Gründung und Aufbau der theresianischen

Name	1740	1748	1754	1763	1770	1779(1)	1779(2)	Sources and notes
								Ackerbaugesellschaften', Zeitschr. f. Agrarges. und Agrarsoziologie 13 (1965) 201–3; id et al., Gesch. der Kärntner Landwirtschaft (Klagenfurt 1966) 149; ii. 65.
Trattnern, Joseph Anton Edler von	–	–	–	–	–	–	+	Stock am Eisenplatz 862. MGP(2), fo. 339, 7 Jan. 1777, Joh. Thomas T. seeks Wholesalership for his son Jos. Anton; latter has 30,000 fl. a maternal legacy. Father must be Joh. Thos. Edler von T. (1764) Court Printer and bookseller.
Violand, Bernard Franz	–	–	+	–	–	–	–	Ignaz V. Naglergasse 218. MGP(1), fo. 397, Bernh. Franz V. Warehouser; in partnership with Bernh. Falquet 1735–40, then with Joh. Bapt. Perinet 1740–52 when V. partner with bros. Franz and Jacob V. Bernh. Franz V. m. Maria Perinet 1741. MGP(2), fo. 423, 15 Mar. 1760, Franz V. deposes to taking over Bernh. V.'s Warehouser's business. Franz V.'s former guardian was Joh. Battiste 'Berinet' (see Perinet). 11 Mar. 1761 Franz V. conceded Warehouser status. 31 Dec.
Violand, Franz	–	–	–	+	–	–	–	
Violand, Ignaz	–	–	–	–	+	+	+	
Violand, Brothers	–	–	–	–	–	–	–	

						Notes
—	+	—	—	—	—	1764, his sons Dominique and Franz Claudius V. in firm. Ibid., fo. 447, 19 Nov. 1767 Franz Dominicus (*sic*) V. deposes that after his father's death his fund is 47,800 fl. The firm will continue as 'V. Brothers'. Firm bankrupt 1770. 11 Apr. 1771 stated that creditors satisfied extrajudicially. Ibid., fo. 485, 2 Dec. 1775, Ignaz V. seeks Wholesaler status; shows fund of 43,061 fl. Agreed to, 14 Sept. 1776. Firm dissolved 10 Jan. 1788.
Volkmar, Christoph Adam	—	—	—	—	+	—	1754 entry only. Not traced in MGP.
Weigl, Franz Anton	—	—	+	—	—	—	F.A.W. lives at Hoher Markt 526. F.M.W. 'widow' 1779. MGP(2), fo. 205, 5 Dec. 1771, Franz Anton W. and Michael Salliet are new owners of 'k. k. Erbl. Penzinger Bandfabrik' started ?1767 by Marcus Kännel. Contract of 1 May 1771 says firm's capital 100,000 fl., Salliet putting up 50,000 fl., Franz Mich. W. and his brother 50,000 fl. jointly. H. Schultz leaves 50,000 fl. in factory, which continues under Kännel. 12 Mar. 1781 dissolution of this
Weigl, Franz Michael	—	—	+	—	—	—	

Name	1740	1748	1754	1763	1770	1779(1)	1779(2)	Sources and notes
								firm: Thadaeus Berger and Claude Gaillard carry on factory.
Weinbrenner, Joseph		–	–	–	+	+	–	'Gumpersdorf, in der Hauptstrasse 15 and 16' (de Ponty). Also at Haarmarkt 756. Farms Austrian customs revenue with Joh. von Fux, q.v., 1765. Submits plan to Council of Trade 1770 for grouping production by areas, K. Přibram, *Gewerbepolitik* 204 n. *Reichsfreiherr* 1795 'wegen Emporbringung des Commerzes und Beförderung der Activhandels' (Megerle). MGP(2), fo. 1155 23 July 1764 Jos. W. smoked products dealer ('Rauchewaarenhändler') seeks Warehouser's Priv. and admitted. Fund 31,967 fl.
Wiesenhütter & Co.	+	–	–	–	–	–	–	See Ch. 7.
Wohlegemut, Daniel	–	+	–	–	–	–	–	Firm registered 19 Apr. 1725, no partner, MGP(1), fo. 847. See Müller, J.G.
Zehendner, Joseph Anton	–	–	–	–	+	+	–	See Ch. 7. J.A.Z. was of Prague but had a Vienna branch.
Totals[a]	24	29	46	44	47	36	17	

[a] In a number of earlier cases, however, the date of Warehouser status is not certain; hence the totals for 1740 and 1748 may be too large.

TABLE 2.2. *Census data for the Austrian and Bohemian lands, and Galicia, 17*

	Lower Austria	Upper Austria	Styria	Carinthia	Krain	Görz-Gradisca	Tyr
1754	929,576	430,371	696,606	271,924	344,564	102,337	384,
1761	744,817	417,726	426,365	229,614	344,554	88,921	563,
1762	777,277	317,035	495,514	259,511	220,671	79,749	..
1763	..	..	..	..	..	..	
1764	801,314	..	..	..	..	..	..
1765	..	..	..	..	..	..	..
1766	..	..	..	248,055	..	..	..
1767	..	..	..	..	..	..	..
1768	804,342	361,707	501,529	..	228,809	81,145	..
1769	..	..	..	..	..	..	..
1770	..	..	..	..	..	..	..
1771	..	..	..	..	..	..	..
1772	..	..	..	..	..	..	..
1773	..	..	..	..	..	..	..
1774	..	..	..	..	..	..	..
1775	..	..	..	..	..	..	..
1776	..	..	..	..	..	..	..
1777	..	..	..	..	..	..	..
1778	..	..	..	..	..	..	..
1779	..	..	..	..	..	..	..
1780		1,569,914	807,164	292,256	401,887	115,305	657,0
1781		1,596,088	815,985	294,852	409,133	118,078	661,8
1782		1,607,929	817,260	295,807	412,250	118,784	663,6
1783		1,611,493	819,147	294,577	412,606	117,978	666,5
1784		1,611,676	819,540	294,527	412,240	116,454	668,4
1785		1,617,416	819,755	294,029	412,141	118,342	680,5
1786		1,627,327	822,080	295,118	413,316	119,423	681,6
1787		1,646,051	829,229	297,384	419,411	122,081	684,3
1788		1,642,012	814,475	292,216	..	..	683,7
1789		1,637,153	800,500	287,944	405,526	119,974	680,2
1790	994,301	622,335	..	..	..	118,569	515,6
Trend rate of annual growth (decline) 1780–90 (%)		0.33	(0.0023)	(0.06)	0.14	0.29	

a Alternative totals 6,659,902 and 6,939,047, see notes.
e Estimate.
Italicized figures denote subtotals.
Innviertel included with Lower and Upper Austria 1780–90.

Sources

1754. AVA Hofkanzlei, Karton 497, Böhmen, 'Summarium über die eingelangte Seelen und Häuser Conscriptiones de Anno 1754'. The same figures are reproduced in the summary volume of the State Inventory of 1763, HKA Hs. 243, fos. 173–5. The total for Bohemia includes 29,094 Jews, that for Moravia 19,752 Jews, that for Silesia 575. None are shown elsewhere.

Substantially the same figures, but omitting Jews, and most of the population of Further Austria, were published in 1855, by J. Vincenz Goehlert, without stating a source, 'Ergebnisse', 66–7. Goehlert's total for Bohemian Christians is 1,235 smaller than that of the table. Besides leaving out the Jewish populations, he omits most of Further Austria, but gives 396,499 for 'Tyrol and Vorarlberg'. His overall total, 6,134,558, is therefore 338,932 smaller. Goehlert's table is reproduced by Gürtler, *Volkszählungen*, table II.

Austrian Lands	Bohemia	Moravia	Silesia	Bohemian Lands	Galicia (and Bukovina)	Total
3,460,121	1,971,613	886,974	154,782	*3,013,369*	..	6,473,490*ᵈ*
3,114,257	1,471,909	845,675	119,248	*2,436,832*	..	5,551,089
2,149,757	1,669,003	834,561	135,795	*2,639,359*	..	4,789,116*ᵇ*
..	1,803,777	883,356	..	..	..	..
..	1,971,455	..	..	..	..	..
..	1,972,154	..	..	..	..	..
..	1,966,062	..	..	..	..	..
..	1,978,193	..	..	..	..	..
3,416,145(e)	2,021,415	..	..	*3,486,347*(e)	..	6,902,492(e)
..	..	..	..	..	..	..
..	..	..	..	..	..	..
..	2,605,815e	1,232,852e	264,418e	..	..	..
..	2,314,785	1,120,637e	238,141	*3,673,563*(e)	..	..
..	2,304,577	1,138,298	238,359	*3,681,234*	2,307,973	..
..	2,343,699	1,119,374	242,380	*3,705,453*	2,665,048	..
..	2,369,104	1,134,674	246,685	*3,750,463*	..	..
..	2,401,115	1,128,829	247,858	*3,777,802*	..	..
..	..	..	..	..	..	..
..	..	..	..	..	..	..
4,184,738(e)	2,550,609	1,444,939		*3,995,548*	2,775,394	10,955,680(e)
4,239,150(e)	2,615,410	1,481,466		*4,096,876*	2,872,428	11,208,454(e)
4,260,915(e)	2,646,952	1,501,473		*4,148,425*	2,958,406	11,367,746(e)
4,269,621(e)	2,668,398	1,510,958		*4,179,356*	3,007,540	11,456,517(e)
4,272,321(e)	2,696,562	1,520,004		*4,216,566*	3,107,761	11,596,648(e)
4,293,697(e)	2,718,395	1,526,177		*4,244,572*	3,229,061	11,767,330(e)
4,312,491(e)	2,746,669	1,539,258		*4,285,927*	3,280,656	11,879,074(e)
4,354,231(e)	2,807,938	1,575,904		*4,383,842*	3,435,056	12,173,129(e)
4,316,122(e)	2,846,965	1,593,765		*4,440,730*	3,422,370	12,179,222(e)
4,291,668	2,868,478	1,595,065		*4,463,543*	3,395,847	12,151,658
4,268,458(e)	2,831,874	1,589,982		*4,421,856*	3,388,732	12,079,046(e)
0.21	1.12		0.95	1.06	2.20	1.02

ᵇ Alternative totals 5,651,286 and 6,607,487, see notes.
(e) Subtotal or total including estimate.

Grossmann, *Statistische Monatschrift*, 21 (1916) 331–423; shows that Goehlert's total for Tyrol omits Brixen and Trent. Grossmann substituted 559,823 for Tyrol, 11,544 for Vorarlberg, and puts in 299,788 for Further Austria. Adding the census figures for Moravian Jews, and estimating 25,000 Jews in Bohemia, he reached a total of 6,654,541. In the table, 6,473,490 is the MS total. The figure of 6,659,902 adopts Grossmann's data for Tyrol and Vorarlberg. The third total, 6,939,047, substitutes the clerical subtotals for Silesia and Moravia for the lay ones, and increases Bohemia by one-tenth as a proxy for the clerical figure. The clerical subtotals for Moravia and Silesia are printed by Dvořáček, 'Soupisy obyvatelstva', *Českoslov. statist. věstník*, 5 table 1.

1761. Grossmann, tables XII and XIII. However, the figures are so different, and so capriciously different, from those of 1754 as to arouse suspicion. M. Straka, working from the communicants' lists, has published population estimates for Styria which considerably increase the census figures for 1761–8. He suggests 736,250 persons in 1760, 718,126 in 1770 and 797,808 in 1782. See his article 'Die Bevölkerungsentwicklung der Steiermark von 1528 bis 1782 auf Grund der Kommunikantenzählungen', *Zeitschr. des historischen Vereines für Steiermark*, 52 (1961) 3–53.

1762. Grossmann, table XIII, which includes the clerical returns. An edited version of these results is printed by Goehlert, 68–9, and reproduced in Gürtler, table III. Grossmann shows that Goehlert mistranscribed the population of Upper Austria as 417,035 instead of 317,035, hence his total is 100,000 too large (through Grossmann does not comment on the figure for 1761, also 417,000). He adds that Goehlert failed to state that the census returns were treble: by occupational group and by age group, the subtotals only corresponding to each other in Lower Austria, Styria, and Görz-Gradisca; and by clerical count, which yielded a higher total. In the table, 4,789,116 is the MS total, 5,651,286 adds to it the 1761 figures for Tyrol and Further Austria, and 6,607,487 results from adding the *higher* totals for all lands. H. Reinalter, *Aufklärung, Absolutismus, Reaktion. Die Geschichte Tirols in der 2. Hälfte des 18. Jahrhunderts* (Vienna 1974) 43–6 prints a census return of *c*.1760 which after the author's adjustments give 584,836 for Tyrol, including 145,000 for Trent and 29,868 for Brixen.

1763. For Further Austria, Grossmann, table XXII; the census omitted Bregenz and Waldkirch. For Moravia, ibid., and table XXI. The Bohemian figures for 1762–8 are from Dvořáček, Table 2. He also gives a slightly higher series from the clerical count.

1764. Lower Austria. The figure is from HKA Hs. 713, fos. 786–7, 'N.Ö. Seelen Beschreibung Ao. 1764'.

1768. Grossmann, tables XXII, XXIII. The constructed subtotals and totals are the result of taking all adjacent figures (viz. 1766–9) as though they related to 1768, then putting in Tyrol at 600,000, Further Austria at 280,000, Moravia at 1.1m. and Silesia at 0.2m. One-tenth is added to the figures for the Austrian lands to simulate clerical returns. It is probable that in 1769 a census was only taken in Austrian Silesia, and in 1770 not at all.

1771. The results in Bohemia in this first year of the new military census are confused. Dvořáčck, table 25 prints a summary by Prince Fürstenberg and Baron Wied of the male population in 1771, which is untotalled but comes to 1,354,812. In Table 26 he prints another return, by Circles, for the same year which makes the male population 1,228,698, of whom 1,194,999 were present, 14,031 were absent, and 19,668 were 'not known where'. This return, without the absentees, was published in *Schlözer's Briefwechsel*, xxi. 176–7, and in another version, in which the male total is 1,198,755, in id., *Briefwechsel meist statistischen Inhalts*, 205. A further report (Dvořáček 260 n.) stated the Bohemian population in 1771 as 2,678,573 (*sic* for 2,678,543) persons, of whom 1,349,432 were male and 1,329,111 female. In addition, there were 39,210 Jews of both sexes. On the face of it these figures are absurd, since females exceeded males here as elsewhere. This total, 2,717,753, which includes absentees represents a maximum, and 2,493,878 a minimum. The minimum (Dvořáček, loc. cit.) derives from Schlözer's lowest estimate of the number of women, combined with the Circle returns for males, and is of actually present population. The figure in the table of 2,605,815 is an average between the maximum and minimum, and as such has only loose validity. Dvořáček's highest figure (given as 2,717,783) is used by Kárníková, *Vývoj obyvalelstva*, table 1. The figures for Moravia and Silesia in the Table are an adjusted version of those in Schlözer, which combine the two populations.

1773–6. Balanced annual summaries for the Bohemian lands in Dvořáček, table 3. This includes 31,000–32,000 Jews annually in Bohemia, 21,000–23,000 in Moravia, 800 or so in Silesia. The figures for Galicia in 1773 (first Austrian census) and in 1774 are taken from Brawer, *Galizien*, table I. Schlözer published the Galician census results of 1773 as 3,888,946, *Briefwechsel*, xvi. 240. Brawer's results for 1776 and 1780, taken from Buzek, Kratter, de Luca, *et al.*, are ignored here.

1780–9. Goehlert, 'Häuser und Volkszahl . . . in der Regierungsperiode Josefs II.', *Statist. Monatschrift*, 5 (1879) 402–5, prints the military census figures, apparently on the basis of a return to the *Hofkriegsrat* to Joseph II, though no exact reference is given. Tyrol is excluded until 1785, and Further Austria entirely. In view of Grossmann's acerbic (and justified) criticisms of Goehlert's earlier and better-known work, it is comforting that Dr Kárníková, op. cit., table 2, compared the figures for the Bohemian lands for 1782, 1785, 1786–7, and 1789 with the originals and found them correct, and that copies of those for all lands for 1781, 1783, 1784, and 1785 in HKA Hs. 735, items (*a*)–(*c*) agree with Goehlert's figures.

Dvořáček, tables 6 and 13 prints the figures for the Bohemian lands, and gives variants. These show that the military totals were normally, though not invariably, higher than the civil ones. He breaks down the Moravian–Silesian total for 1780–3 and 1787 (Silesia 269,615 in 1780, 342,189 in 1781, 347,029 in 1782, 312,527 in 1787). In tables 7 and 14 he computes the actually present, as distinct from legally registered, populations of Bohemia and Moravia-Silesia 1780–1803. The difference was greater in the former, e.g. in 1785, 2,703,139 actual population against a legal one of 2,716,084, whereas in Moravia the figures were 1,525,306 and 1,526,177. See the note below for the estimates of population in Tyrol and Further Austria.

1790. AVA Hofkanzlei, Karton 498, no. 172 ex Mai 1792, return from the *Kameral Buchhalterei* dated 7 May 1792 of the civil census for 1790, giving also the figures for 1789. The documents are usable, though badly burnt in two places. An order of 10 Mar. 1790 is included, stating that on the recommendation of the Inner Austrian government, no census would be taken in 1790 in Styria, Carinthia, or Krain. In the Table, the subtotal for the Austrian lands, and hence the grand total, include the 1789 results from those three areas and Tyrol. The return for the latter in 1790 must be defective. The figures for the 1780s must include Vorarlberg with Tyrol, since Reinalter, 49–50 gives from local MS sources Tyrol populations of only 605,600 in 1787, 604,436 in 1788, in both cases including Brixen and Trent, which had 172,000 inhabitants.

The defective series for Tyrol with Vorarlberg, and for Further Austria, necessitate recourse to estimates. The method used was to add to Reinalter's figures for Tyrol (see 1762) his data for the enclaves of Trent and Brixen in 1787–8, extrapolated back to 1780. Vorarlberg population was distributed annually from the 1780 and 1790 totals in Klein 'Die Bevölkerung Österreichs', and added to that of Tyrol. For Further Austria, the census figures for 1760, *c.* 300,000, and for 1790, *c.* 360,000, implied an annual growth-rate of 0.6%, which was used to construct the data for the 1780s.

TABLE 3.1. *Age-structure, population-density, and marriage, birth-, and death-rates*

	1 Proportion of male Christians (%)		2 Persons per sq. km 1785	3 Family size (Christians) 1785	4 Proportion of male Christians of 18 and over married 1785	5 Marriages per thousand population av. 1787–92	6 Births per thousand population av. 1787–92	7 Deaths per thousand population av. 1787–92
	a under 16 years 1754	b under 18 years 1785						
Bohemia	35.04	39.50	52.4	4.67	61.93	7.9	41.8	29.5
Moravia	37.27	40.76	55.8	4.91	64.91	8.6	44.4	34.6
Silesia	33.3		51.3	4.59	55.79	9.2	38.9	42.8
Lower Austria	34.52	32.72	36.7	5.56	54.40	8.0	33.2	27.4
Upper Austria	31.48		28.5	6.06	43.80	8.0	32.5	30.3
Styria	32.96	38.58	40.2	5.52	64.53	6.0	28.5	27.9
Carinthia	32.76	31.26						
Krain and Görz-Gradisca	39.0	43.05						
Krain						8.2	35.7	32.3
Tyrol	31.1	..	35.3	..	..	6.8	30.3	27.1
Galicia	48.28	39.6	39.6	5.28	77.28	8.9[a]	39.4[a]	32.0[a]

[a] 1795 estimate.

Col. 1a. See Table 2.2* for 1754. Goehler, 'Ergebnisse', 66–7 puts males aged 1–15 in Silesia at only 6,821; this is followed by Gürtler. The true figure is 24,517. Calculations of the population *over* 15 years in 1754 in Goehlert, 61 agree with those in the table.

Cols. 1b, 2. For 1785, the (military) census figures are taken from HKA, Hs. 735, item *b*. The totals there do not correspond precisely with those given, without a reference, by Goehlert, 'Ergebnisse', 64 as the census results for 1785, which contain some figures from the military census of 1786. Goehlert's next age-distribution figures after 1754 are for 1800. The figures in Col. 1b add to the category 'Children' (*Nach-*

wachs) in the census an estimate for children who were heirs to peasants and craftsmen; and (in Galicia) for the male children of nobles, see the notes to Col. 4. By treating the *Nachwachs* column as denoting *all* children, Kárníková, *Vývoj obyvatelstva*, table 5 gives only 36.6% for the age-group 1–17 in the Bohemian lands.

Col. 3. 'Family' was defined as a unit whose head provided for it, Gürtler, 68, and could consist of a single person employing servants, ibid. It therefore came closer to 'household', though there could be several in one house. Goehlert, 'Ergebnisse', 59–60n. gives figures of family size for '1784–5' agreeing with those here, but excluding Galicia, as in all his tables.

Col. 4. The census gives the numbers of married and unmarried Christians, and of total Christians. The male Christians of 18 years and over in this column were estimated as follows. First, females (who were entered *en bloc*) were deducted from 'total Christians', to arrive at male Christians. Second 'children', i.e. male children aged 1–17, were deducted to give male Christians less male children. Third, account had to be taken of the fact that the legitimate male children of peasants and craftsmen who were heirs to their fathers were not put in the 'children' column of the census. For each area, the number of these heirs who were male children was estimated by applying to total 'peasant and crafts-men heirs' the ratio of (male) children aged 1–17 to total male Christians. This device is perhaps admissible in view of the crudity of the data. The census category of 'children' also excluded the male children of nobles, non-noble officials, and Greek and Protestant clergy. For Galicia, 40% of the estimated 52,000 nobles in 1785 were assumed to be children. In other areas, these surplus children are ignored. For the definitions of the 1777 census rubrics, see the extended account in Gürtler, 64 ff. and especially 78 ff., largely taking the form of quotation from the original decrees. Thirring, *J. de la Soc. hong. de stat.* 9 (1931) 210–47 commented on these rubrics at length, and is the only historian who has done so. However, his contention, repeated in his publications of 1938, that only children of peasants and burgesses were put under 'children' seems contrary to the official exposition, Gürtler, 80–1.

Thirring, *Népessége*, 42n., states that 'age' was defined to the end of the stated year. Thus '1–17' meant 'up to and including 17'. This is supported by the official exposition ('Gürtler, loc. cit.) that ages meant 1–17 and 18–40, and by the use of '1–18' [sic] and '18–40' in the tables introduced in 1788, ibid. 147. Kárníková, table 5 prints the age-groups for 1786 as 1–17 and 17–40. The jump in the proportion of those aged 0–17 in 1814 (ibid.) supports her contention that before 1805 the period 0–1 was omitted; though Thirring, *M. Népessége*, loc. cit. thought it was included.

Cols. 5–7. Goehlert, 'Bevölkerungsverhältnisse', 58, where, however, the rates are mistakenly said to be per 100,000. Krain excludes Görz-Gradisca. The estimates for Galicia are from AVA Hofkanzlei, Karton 498, no. 133, return dated Oct. 1795 for the Bohemian and Austrian lands, making some adjustments, but must be treated with reserve.

TABLE 3.2. *Some social categories, 1762–1846*

	Bohemia	Moravia	Silesia	Upper Austria	Lower Austria	Styria	Carinthia	Krain	Görz-Gradisca	Galicia	Totals
Clergy											
1762	6,530	3,260	389	1,052	4,765	2,755	1,314	973	1,094	..	22,132
1781	6,474	3,781			6,918	2,801	1,017		2,291	7,629	30,911
1785	6,258	3,397			5,860	2,655	938		1,985	6,609	27,702
1790	5,392	3,081		1,338	3,830	1,929[b]	716[b]	1,002[b]	569	6,194	24,051
1846	4,377	2,403		1,534	2,249	1,583	1,280[c]			4,885	18,311
Male nobles											
1762	1,426	587	395	243	5,084	858	559	348	..	..	10,527
1781	1,601	800			3,123	661	467		938	51,341e	58,931
1785	1,675	780			3,249	677	562		967	51,766e	59,686
1790	1,655	838		391	2,934	725[b]	428[b]	414[b]	437	48,333e	56,135
1846	2,275	1,100		919	4,280	1,192	921[c]			49,631e	60,318
Officials and dignitaries											
1762[a]	4,088	2,055	378	491	10,409	2,075	554	398	136	..	20,584
1781	3,368	2,329			5,107	1,355	606		701	1,434	14,900
1785	3,074	2,312			4,817	1,234	462		675	2,019	14,593
1790	3,191	2,749		699	4,713	1,562[b]	596[b]	683[b]	285	2,820	17,298
1846	10,315	4,851		2,525	8,707	2,701	1,576[c]			6,100	36,775
Jews											
1754	29,094	19,752	575	—		—	—	—		..	49,421
1781	40,438	26,377		447		—	—	—	400	159,990	227,652
1785	42,129	26,665		652		—	—	—	425	212,002	281,873
1790	45,272	28,478		875			2[c]		393	188,002	263,020
1846	70,037	40,064		4,296					3,530	328,806	446,733

	Col 1	Col 2	Col 3	Col 3b	Col 5	Col 6	Col 7	Col 8	Col 9	Col 10
Town burgesses, craft workers in countryside										
1781	92,742	33,016	44,823		10,304	4,381	3,118		17,175	205,559
1785	88,403	33,522	46,427		11,024	4,317	3,202		19,808	206,703
1790	81,989	35,081	17,084	29,168	11,226[b]	4,780[b]	2,524[b]	1,207	20,525	203,584
Peasants (heads of households)										
1781	123,685	87,450	100,129		57,638	28,453	56,451		102,910	556,716
1785	118,662	90,228	99,072		57,595	28,743	56,644		110,962	561,906
1790	122,291	89,562	38,207	63,443	58,105[b]	28,603[b]	50,267[b]	8,971	219,005	678,454
Cottars, smallholders, etc.										
1781	357,856	192,667	247,364		121,149	42,530	44,788		457,571	1,461,925
1785	413,117	209,840	264,316		129,698	44,489	47,008		527,029	1,635,497
1790	441,991	236,139	117,113	161,776	..	..		15,939	435,294	..

e Estimate.   [a] In this year, officials (*Beamte*) only.   [b] 1794.   [c] Including Krain.

1762. The census results are printed in Grossmann, 'Anfänge', table XIII. A curtailed version, published by Goehlert, 'Ergebnisse', and repeated by Gürtler, *Volkszählungen*, omits six of the social categories of the census: officials ('Beamte'), servants ('Particular Dienstbothen'), burgesses ('Bürger'), artisans and tradesmen ('Professionisten'), and peasants ('Unterthanen'). It also omits the numbers of lordships ('Herrschaften').

1781, 1785. Census summaries for these two years in HKA Hs. 735.

1790. AVA Hofkanzlei, Karton 498, no. 172 ex Mai 1792. There was no census in Styria, Carinthia, and Krain in 1790. The nearest results found were for 1794, which are those in the table. They are from ibid. no. 120 ex Aug. 1796, badly burnt.

1846. *Tafeln zur Statistik der österreichischen Monarchie für die Jahre 1845 and 1846* (Vienna 1850), vol. i, table I, where the figures are for 1846 only. Comparable data for burgesses, peasants, and cottars are not given.

TABLE 4.1. *Statistics of the Catholic and Uniat churches on the eve of the Josephine dissolutions*

	1 Churches and chapels	2 Parishes, chaplaincies etc.	3 Brother-hoods	4 Monasteries	5 Convents	6 Valuation of total church property at 20 years' purchase	7 Denoting an annual revenue of	8 Percentage share of capital and income
Bohemia	3,176	1,437	567	123	17	61,986,040	3,099,302	16.1
Moravia and Silesia	1,844	809	437	72	11	34,994,380	1,749,719	9.1
Lower Austria	1,174	665	605	102	16	55,234,200	2,761,710	14.4
Upper Austria	728	318	239	35	5	24,810,960	1,240,548	6.4
Styria, Carinthia, Krain	3,256	1,227	868	104	23	42,916,580	2,145,829	11.2
Tyrol and Further Austria	2,105	1,182	992	119	76	25,707,800	1,285,390	6.7
Trieste and Görz-Gradisca	218	188	115	?	0	5,768,920	288,446	1.5
Subtotal	12,501	5,826	3,823	555	148	251,418,880	12,570,944	65.4
Galicia	728	2,560	701	222	32	31,591,740	1,579,587	8.2
Hungary	..	3,269	..	141	13	92,132,220	4,606,611	24.0
Dalmatia etc.	..	..	..	43	..	..	..	..
Siebenbürgen	..	..	..	33	1	9,176,320	458,816	2.4
Subtotal	..	..	..	439	46	132,900,280	6,645,014	34.6
Total	(13,229)	(12,015)	(4,524)	994	194	384,319,160	19,215,958	100.0

Source: HHSA Nachl. Zinz., Hs. 146b, 'Fondations', comprising reports and accounts of the *Hofrechenkammer* and *Geistliche Hofkommission*. Count Karl Zinzendorf was president of the former. For cols. 1–3 fo. 613 (undated); for cols. 4–5, fos. 2–3, statement of position 'at the beginning of 1782'; for col. 6, fos. 449–50 (28 Oct. 1785), 465 (6 March 1786), 501, 515, 533 (14 Dec. 1786), 553 (5 Feb. 1789), all fos. recto. In each case, the values are inclusive of dissolutions, hence the statistics can be treated, without too much distortion, as stating the position at the beginning of 1782. For the use of 20 years' purchase see, e.g., fos. 288ʳ, 449ʳ–450ʳ.

Parentheses denote incomplete totals. The heading of col. 1 is 'Pfarr [Kirchen], Filial-Kirchen und Kap[elle]', of col. 2, 'Pfarrey, Lokalkaplaneyen und Curat Beneficien'. The figure for Hungary in col. 2 is of the 'benefices with stipends' given at fo. 533ʳ. In col. 4, 'Dalmatia, Croatia, and Slavonia' are assigned 43 monasteries, no convents. In col. 7, the Hungarian valuation is stated both as in the table and as 94,700,804 fl.

Hock–Bidermann, 424n, give figures for ecclesiastical income similar to, but lower than, those in the table, from a report of the *Hofrechenkammer* and *Geistliche Hofkommission* dated 6 Mar. 1786.

TABLE 9.3. *Summary of six proposals for reform by Joseph II, 1761–75*

3 Apr. 1761

At the peace, distribute the army between the *Länder*. Make these responsible for recruits, finance. Abolish the Contribution.

Gradually exchange soldiers between provinces, until each has a 'national' force.

Give one-third of troops at any one time six months' leave.

'Tout est à l'État; ce mot là renferme tout, ainsi chacun doit concourir à son avantage.'

Rêveries (Summer 1763)

One main chancellery, and one finance department. Hung. chancellery to remain, but papers, with those of Belgium and Italy, to come to *Staatsrat*, sitting daily.

Oberste Justizstelle and *Hofkriegsrat* are satisfactory.

One Belgian–Italian chancellery, answering to *Staatsrat*.

Sovereign acts as spokesman for state. To procure by consent a 'despotisme lié' for ten years, to act for public good.

Then attack the *seigneurs* by double taxes, etc., and lessen subjects' taxes.

Austere Court, reduction in state salaries.

Rêveries (cont.)

Careers open to talent: 'tout au mérite personel [*sic*]'.

Manage Hungary, make it prosperous, attack its liberties when the moment arises.

Procure a budget surplus by forced reduction of the state debts to 3%. Repay debts over 70 years. Put surplus revenue partly into manufactures and transport, partly into accumulating over 10 years a war-reserve of 50m. fl.

End 1765

Staatsrat to be reshaped as an assembly of departmental ministers. Disputes to be settled by Joseph II.

A *Directorium*, merging the *Hofkammer* and Bank Deputation, to look after finance, under a finance minister charged with increasing revenue and credit, lightening the burden on the people.

Rechenkammer to be put under *Staatsrat*. A 'supreme council of justice' to supervise both civil and military cases.

Retain *Hofkriegsrat*.

Annual conferences in Vienna with provincial chiefs.

Population growth and increase in trade first objects of state policy.

End 1765 (cont.)

Equality of fiscal burdens.

Import ban, immigration of foreigners, honouring of able merchants.

All are in fact equal; principle of derogation to lapse.

Austere Court, abolition of gala days.

Abolition of surplus religious houses.

Canton system for regiments. Military marriage then permissible. *Kreishauptmann* to be a soldier.

Kings should travel to inform themselves of their lands.

Great things are only done at a stroke. So all these changes should be made together, or none at all.

8 Nov. 1771

All parts of government should be united for the common good ('zu dem ganzen Besten'). At present, whole system of government marked by ignorance, intrigue, lack of unity.

In each province, the political, judicial, commercial, military, clerical and financial authorities are in rivalry with each other.

In each Circle, the Circle Captain, army commandant, commercial inspector, customs director,

TABLE 9.3. *(cont.)*

8 Nov. 1771 (cont.)
divide authority.
The empress should
appoint one man as
chef with supreme
control over
*Publico-Politicum,
Commerciale,
Camerale, Bancale.*
All advancement, in
government to be
'through the ranks',
without regard to
social status.

27 Apr. 1773
Reshape empress's
secretariat as a
'Geheimes Cabinet'
with a Director—who
could be Joseph II
himself. All inland
business to come to it.
Major items to be
referred to *Staatsrat*,
meeting daily, to be
discussed in royal
presence. Reform
methods of *Staatsrat*.
All foreign despatches,
and the papers of the
Netherlands and
Italian depts., to be
registered in this
Cabinet.

27 Apr. 1773 (cont.)
A *Directorium* or
'vereinigte
hofcanzley' to be
formed under an
Ober-Direktor, or
Ober-Kanzler.
Austrian, Bohemian,
Finance and Galician
senates within it. To
control *provincialia,
politica*, finance,
mines.
Plenum of councillors to
be summoned for
important items.
Director to meet
provincial *capi*
annually.
Merge chancelleries of
Hungary and
Siebenbürgen.
These reforms must be
executed boldly. A
little-by-little
approach is useless.

17 May 1775
Inhabitants of Military
Frontier poor and
needy. Present system
does not work.
Sanitary Cordon
laughable, and

17 May 1775 (cont.)
impedes trade with
Turks.
Trieste, with a defective
harbour built at great
cost, attracts state
funds, while Fiume,
Buccari, Carlopago,
Porto Re, Zengg, are
very poor. Swarms of
officials, no trade.
Abolish 8 regiments of
Frontier Militia. Keep
those who can stand
the cost as a fighting
force, serving for
10–12 years. The
others to form a reserve.
Abolish Cordon,
Sanitäts-Deputation
which supervises it.
Retain minimal
anti-infection patrols.
Abolish
Commerzienrat,
Trieste *Intendenza*.
Give Fiume to
Hungary, the small
ports to the military.
'To achieve great things,
you must look closely
and then strike
courageously.
Piecemeal measures
are futile.'

---

3 April 1761. Crown Prince Joseph's memorandum in French printed by Arneth, *Mar. Ther. und Jos. II.* i. 1–12.

Summer 1763. Joseph's *Rêveries*, published for the first time in a full text by Professor D. E. D. Beales, *MÖSA* 33 (1980) 142–60. The editor, in his valuable introduction, convincingly dates this essay (which shocked the empress deeply, and which she suppressed) to the summer of 1763.

End 1765. Joseph II's undated memoir in French printed by Arneth, *Mar. Ther. und Jos. II.*, at end of vol. iii, dated by the editor to late 1765.

8 Oct. 1771. The 'Second Part' ('Anderte Abtheilung') of Joseph II's 'Prager Relation' or report compiled on his tour of inspection in Bohemia in the late summer and autumn of 1771. Printed *Khev.–Metsch 1770–3*, n. 94, pp. 373–98.

27 April 1773. Joseph II's proposals in German for reform of the organization of central government, drawn up at his mother's request, printed *ÖZV* (1934) 48–73.

17 May 1775. Joseph II's report in German on his tour of the Military Frontier, printed *Khev-Metsch 1774–6*, n. 112.

TABLE 12.1. *Leading central councillors, 1740*

(*a*) *Privy Conference*
Count Alois Harrach
Count Joseph Harrach
Field Marshal Count Joseph Königsegg
Count Philipp Sinzendorf
Count Gundaker Starhemberg
Baron Johann Bartenstein, Secretary

(*b*) *Austrian Court Chancellery*
Count Philipp Sinzendorf, First Chancellor
Count Johann Seilern, Second Chancellor
Count Johann Kuefstein
Baron Anton Franz Buol
Carl Cetto von Kronstorf
Carl Holler von Doblhof
Caspar von Lierwald
Johann Georg von Managetta

(*c*) *Bohemian Court Chancellery*
Count Philip Kinsky, Bohemian Chancellor
Count Rudolph Tereschau, Vice-Chancellor
Count Michael Althann
Count Adam Losy
Count Wenzel Schafgotsch
Count Franz Schlick
Johann von Jordan
Hermann von Kannegiesser
Joseph von Knichen
Johann von Kommergansky
Carl von Kunbratitz
Franz von Langer
Ignaz von Rumerskirchen
Franz von Turba

(*d*) *Finance Conference*
Count Gundaker Starhemberg, President
Count Aloysius Harrach
Count Ferd. Kollowrat
Count Leopold Windischgrätz
Ferdinand Lachemair v. Ehrenheim[a] Referendary

(*e*) *Ministerial Bank Deputation*
Count Gundaker Starhemberg, President and Director
Count Sigmund Khevenhüller, Co-Director
Edler Herr Leopold von Schmerling
Joachim George Schwandner[a]
Count Joseph Starhemberg[a]
Baron Bartholome Tinti[a]
Vienna Burgomaster Johann von Zahlheim

TABLE 12.1. (cont.)

(f) Hofkammer

Count Johann Dietrichstein, President
Baron Peter Anton Brandau
Count Carl Caraffa
Count Maximilian Cavriani
Count Anton Gaisruck
Baron Carl Gillern
Baron Johann Grueb
Baron Conrad Hardung
Count Joseph Kinsky
Count Johann Lengheim
Count Franz Poztazky
Count Philip Rosenberg
Baron Franz Schmidlin
Baron Adam Söldern
Count Joseph Starhemberg
Baron Joahnn Tavonath
Count Anton Thurn
Baron Bartholome Tinti
Baron Christoph Wertenburg
Edler Herr Carl von Dier
Johann Eitelberg
Franz Geisslitzer
Anton Grieblpauer
Gabriel Gyöngesi
Carl von Harruckern
Franz von Harruckern
Johann von Harruckern
Maximilian Hilleprand von Prandau
Heinrich Joseph Koch
Ferdinand Lachemair von Ehrenheim
Johann Ludovisi
Johann Manner
Philipp Mayrberg
Johann Offnern
Johann Peterneck
Salomon von Piazoni
Johann Pichler
Franz von Plöckner
Franz Pistrich
Franz von Raigersfeld
Edler Herr Franz Anton von Saffran
Joseph Salazar
Ferdinand Sauberer
Joseph Schmuderer
Joachim Georg Schwandner
Johann von Seitern
Edler Herr Paul von Stockhammer
Antonius, Vogt von Sumerau
Franz Thalheim

Philipp von Unkrechtsberg
Augustin Webern von Wertenau
Heinrich Wispien
Johann Zuana

(g) *Hungarian Court Chancellery*
Count Ludwig Battyan, Hungarian Chancellor
Count Ladislaus Kollonich
Count Alexander Petachich
Johann von Adelffy
Johann Hittner
Joseph Koller von Nagymanya
Carl Nedecz von Nedecze
Franz von Pallasty

(h) *Siebenbürgen Court Chancellery*
Baron Johannes Kazon, Chancellor
Sigmund Cszato von Delne
Joseph Kozma de Kezdi Szent-Lelek
Samuel Rosnyai

---

a Also *Hofkammer* Councillor.

The names are from the *Court Calendar* for 1740; however, the members of the Privy Conference, not given there, are taken from Arneth, *Gesch. Mar. Ther.* i. 70, showing the position in 1738. The *Court Calendar* does not give the names of the Austrian Court Chancellery till 1746; Sinzendorf is added here for 1740, but it is possible that there were other councillors then as well, and the list must be regarded as provisional.

For the German names of the institutions see Table 9.1.

Names of persons are spelt as in the sources, but rearranged alphabetically. *Herrenstand* members (counts and barons) are put before the remainder, who belonged to the *Ritterstand*. The particle 'von' is deleted for counts and barons.

TABLE 12.2. *Leading central councillors, 1754*

(*a*) *Privy Conference*
Count Corfiz Ulfeld
Field Marshal Count Carl Joseph Batthyány
Count Rudolph Colloredo
Count Wenzel Anton Kaunitz
Count Johann Joseph Khevenhüller-Metsch

(*b*) Directorium in Publicis et Cameralibus
Count Friedrich Wilhelm Haugwitz, President; Bohemian Chief Chancellor and
    Austrian First Chancellor
Count Johann Carl Chotek, Bohemian and Austrian Chancellor
Baron Johann Christoph Bartenstein, Bohemian and Austrian Vice-Chancellor
Baron Franz Bartenstein
Baron Anton Buol
Carl Cetto von Kronstorf
Edler Herr Carl von Dier
Count Franz Eszterházy
Dionysius Gröller
Carl Holler von Doblhof
Hermann von Kannegiesser
Baron Johann Joseph Managetta
Johann von Marck
Jacob Benedict von Neftzer
Matthaeus von Neymeyer
Edler Herr Franz von Pistrich
Edler Herr Franz Anton von Saffran
Count Niclas Stella
Theodor Thoren
Count Joseph Balthasar Wilczeck
Johann Bernhard von Zencker
Count Ludwig Zinzendorf

(*c*) *Ministerial Bank Deputation*
Count Rudolph Choteck, President
Baron Carl Joseph Gillern
Ferdinand Theodor Quiex
Anton Maria Stuppan von Ehrenstein
Franz Bernhard von Unkrechtsberg

(*d*) Hofkammer
Count [Johann] Franz Gottfried Dietrichstein, President
Baron Peter Anton Prandau, Vice-President
Count Karl Caraffa
Count Johann Pálffy
Johann von Glanz
Johann von Marburg
Stephan von Nagy

(*e*) *Hungarian Court Chancellery*
Count Leopold Nadast[y], Court Chancellor
Franz Xaver Koller von Nagy-Manya
Count Ladislaus Kollonich

Carl Nedeczky von Nedecze
Baron Adam Patachich, Bishop of Novi
Anton Somsich von Sard
Jacob Szvetics

(f) *Siebenbürgen Court Chancellery*
Count Ladislaus Gyulassi, Court Chancellor
Franz Bándi von Székely-Udvarhelly
Michael Benök von Köszeg
Count Gabriel Bethlen
Kozma von Kezdi-Szent Lelek
Martin Wanckel von Seeberg

The members of the Privy Conference are given in *Fürst (1755)* pp. 15–16. The members of the Bank Deputation, and Hungarian and Siebenbürgen Chancelleries, are taken from the *Court Calendar* for 1754; this does not, however, list the *Hofkammer*. Its councillors at 31 Oct. 1754 are taken from HKA Hs 225, fos. 123 ff. I am indebted to the Director of the Hofkammerarchiv, Hofrat Dr Walter Winkelbauer, for extracting this information and for finding that at 31 Oct. 1751, Dietrichstein, Prandau, Caraffa, and Nagy were the only councillors, HKA Kameralzahlamtsbücher, no. 47, fos. 22 ff.

Names of persons are rearranged alphabetically, observing the same conventions as in 1740, but ignoring the division into *Herrenstand* (counts and barons) and *Ritterstand* (all others), which was retained in all the institutions listed.

TABLE 12.3. *Leading central councillors, 1763*

(*a*) *Staatsrat*
Count Heinrich Cajetan Blümegen
Baron Egyd Valentin Borié
Field Marshal Count Leopold Joseph Daun
Count Friedrich Wilhelm Haugwitz
Count Wenzel Anton Kaunitz
Anton Maria Stupan von Ehrenstein
Anton König von Kronburg, Referendary

(*b*) *Bohemian and Austrian Court Chancellery*
Count Rudolph Chotek, Bohemian Chief Chancellor and Austrian First Chancellor
Baron Johann Christoph Bartenstein, Bohemian and Austrian Vice-Chancellor
Lorenz Joseph von Carqui
Carl Cetto von Kronstorf
Tobias Gebler
Dionysius Gröller
Hermann von Kannegiesser
Baron Gottfried Koch
Baron Johann Joseph Managetta
Count Eugenius Wrbna
Johann Bernhard von Zencker

(*c*) *Ministerial Bank Deputation*
Count Carl Friderich Hatzfeld zu Gleichen, President
Thaddaeus Glanz
Jacob Benedict Neftzer
Ferdinand Theodor Quiex
George Bernhard von Unkrechtsberg

(*d*) Hofkammer
Count Johann Herberstein, President
Baron Peter Anton Hilleprand [von Brandau], Vice-President
Johann Baptist von Bolza
Count Johann Fekéte
Paul Festetics von Tolna
Philipp Andre von Giganth
Count Franz Anton Khevenhüller-Metsch
Baron Ignaz Kempfen
Joseph von Marburg
Johann Adam Mayer
Stephen Nagy de Fölsöbuck
Count Carl Pálf[f]y
Edler Herr Franz von Saffran
Baron Christoph Schmidlin
Ottocar Stupan von Ehrenstein

(*e*) Hofkommerzienrat
Graf Franz Rheinhold Andlern-Witte, President
Johann Bernhard, Edler von Degelmann
Carl Holler von Doblhof
Anton Holler von Doblhof-Dier
Baron Johann Georg Managetta

Franz von Mygind
Baron Judas Thaddeus Reischach
Franz Paul von Stegner, Director of Linz woollen-factory

(f) *Hungarian Court Chancellery*
Count Franz Eszterházy von Galanth[a], Court Chancellor
Count Georg Fekéte von Galantha, Vice-Chancellor
Count Theodor Batthyán[y]
Anton von Brunszvik
Caspar Farkas von Joka
Christoph von Niczky
Count Leopold Pálffy
Jacob Svetics von Nemes-Ságód
Joseph Török von Szendrö

(g) *Siebenbürgen Court Chancellery*
Count Gabriel Bethlen, Court Chancellor
Franz Bandi von Szekely-Udvarhelly
Alexander von Horvath
Johann Joseph von Pelser
Albert Somlyai von Csik-Somlyo
Johann Georg von Vest

For the *Staatsrat*, Arneth, *Gesch. Mar. Ther.* vii, ch. 1; Hock–Bidermann, 11–12; ÖZV (1934) 10–15; and Walter, *Geschichte*, ch. V. For the division into 'ministers' and 'councillors' see text. The remaining names are taken from the *Court Calendar* for 1763, in which a formal distinction between *Herrenstand* and *Ritterstand* councillors was made only in the Hungarian and Siebenbürgen chancelleries; however, in other institutions counts and barons were listed first.

The names in the *Court Calendar* for 1763 check well against those in HKA Hs. 243 A.

TABLE 12.4. *Leading central councillors, 1775*

(*a*) Staatsrat
Count Friederich Hatzfeld
Baron Tobias Gebler
Prince Wenzel Anton Kaunitz
Baron Franz Kressel von Qualtenberg
Baron Johann Friedrich Löhr
Count Johann Anton Pergen
Baron Anton Maria Stupan von Ehrenstein

(*b*) *Bohemian and Austrian Court Chancellery*
Court Heinrich Cajetan Blümegen, Bohemian Chief Chancellor and Austrian First
  Chancellor
Franz Anton von Blanc
Edler Herr Anton Curti de Francini
Franz von Greiner
Edler Herr Franz von Heinke
Baron Gottfried Koch
Joseph Koller
Joseph von Krisch
Carl Anton von Martini
Johann von Müller
Florian Perdacher von Pergenstein
Paul von Riegger
Baron Ottocar Stupan von Ehrenstein
Bernhard von Zencker

(*c*) *Ministerial Bank Deputation*
Count Leopold Kollowrat,[a] President
Alexius von Badenthal
Johann Peter von Bolza[a]
Count Johann Philipp Cobenzl
Philipp Andre von Giganth
Franz Gruber
Johann Hertelli
Johann von Holbein
Ferdinand Kestler[a]
Baron Jacob Benedict Nefzern[a]
Edler Herr Bartholome von Riethaller
Vincent von Scharf
Baron Franz Spiegelfeld
Georg von Unkrechtsberg
Joachim von Ziegler

(*d*) Hofkammer
Count Leopold Kollowrat, President
Johann Baptist von Bolza
Johann Peter von Bolza
Laurenz Joseph von Carqui
Johann Thadaeus Glantz
Joseph von Guttenberg
Ferdinandus Kessler, Edler Herr von Rosenheim

Count Adam Kuefstein
Count Anton Lamberg
Joseph Mailath von Szekhely
Edler Herr Adam von Mayer
Baron Conrad Nefzern
Baron Jacob Benedict Nefzern
Karl Ferdinand Niess
Count Carl Pálffy de Erdöd
Johann von Reabold
Carl von Rustenfeld
Georg von Saumil
Leopold Schallhass
Baron Franz Schmidlin
Count Carl Zichi de Vásonkés

(e) *Hungarian Court Chancellery*
Count Franz Eszterházy von Galantha, Court Chancellor
Joseph von Bajzáth, Bishop in Ansara, Vice-Chancellor
Count Leopold Pálffy von Erdöd
Ladislaus Batta von Vatta
Anton Brunszvik von Korompa

(f) *Siebenbürgen Court Chancellery*
Baron Michael von Görtz, Interim President
Michael Benök
Wolfgang Cserej von Bagy-Ajta
Alexander von Horváth
Baron Joseph von der Marck
Edler Herr Franz von Reichmann

(g) *Galician Court Chancellery*
Count Eugen Wrbna, Court Chancellor
Count Ludwig Cavriani
Hermann Evers
Alexander Heiter von Schwonet
Joseph Isdenczi
Anton Koczian
Mathias Puechberg

---

[a] Also in *Hofkammer*.

The names are taken from the *Court Calendar* for 1775. Conventions as in previous years. The membership of the Bank Deputation and *Hofkammer* check well against the lists for 1771 in Count Friedrich Hatzfeld's report of 5 Feb. 1771, HKA Kredit, AA Akten, rote Nr. 12, Fsz. 7, fos. 282^r–283^r. Hatzfeld's lists divide councillors into *Hofräte* and 'Hof-Commissions Räthe', the latter (five in the Bank Deputation, six in the *Hofkammer*) being paid rather less. This distinction is not observed in the *Calendar*. Besides the councillors of the *Hofkammer* proper, Hatzfeld lists those of the mines and coinage department of it, the 'Hofkammer in monetariis et montanisticis'. Under the presidency of Count Franz Kollowrat, the councillors were Bernhard von Gerhauser, Franz von Keinz, Franz von Scharf [cf. Vincent von Scharf in the Bank Deputation], Franz von Schönne, Count Johann Stampfer, Baron Franz Sternbach, Johann Baptist von Wagner.

TABLE 13.1. *Leading local councillors, 1740*

(a) *Bohemia*, Statthalterei
Count Johann Ernst Schafgotsch, *Obrist-Burggraf*
Count Carl Joachim Breda
Count Stephan Wilhelm Kinsky von Chinitz
Count Wenzel Anton Chotek
Count Joh. Philipp Clary
Count Philipp Joseph Gallas
Johann Franz von Goltz
Count Wenzel Franz Kokoržowa
Count Carl Joseph Kollowrat
Count Philipp Kollowrat[a]
Count Franz Michael Martinitz
Baron Wenzel Casimir Netolicky
Count Franz Carl Pötting
Count Joseph Sereny
Count Franz Leopold Sternberg[b]
Count Jos. Franz Würben

(b) *Moravia*, Tribunal
Count Maximilian Ulrich Kaunitz, *Landeshauptmann*
Baron Heinrich Cajetan Blümegen
Count Franz Leopold Buquoy
Count Leopold Dietrichstein
Franz Hayeck von Waldstätten
Count Augustus Ferdinand Herberstein
Carl Adolph Hertodt von Todenfeld
Franz Emmanuel Hottowetz
Peter Ferdinand Hroch von Peschitz
Count Franz Carl Kotulinsky
Franz Philipp von Preyss
Count Ernst Wilhelm Schafgotsch
Johann Wenzel von Widmann
Count Wenzel Michael Würben

(c) *Silesia*, Oberamt[c]
Count Johann Anton Schafgotsch, Director
Baron Sebastian Schwannenberg, Chancellor
Count Philipp Arco
Count Ernst Julius Gellhorn
Count Ludwig Wilhelm Haugwitz
Johann von Kamerganzky
Hermann Lorenz von Kannegiesser
Carl Maximilian von Kranichstätten
Baron Alexander Mönnich
Count Joh. Anton Proskau
Leopold Anton von Sanning
Count Heinrich Spatgen

(d) *Silesia*, Kammer[c]
Count Joh. Anton Proskau, President
Count Horns, Vice-President

Heinrich Wilh. von Blumencron
Baron Adam Gruttschreiber
Johann Sebastian Peschl
Baron Anton Saldern
Count Joseph Schlegenberg
Carl Joseph Sturm

(e) *Inner Austria*, Geheimer Rat und Kanzlei[c]
Count Johann Joseph Wildenstein, President
Peter Anton von Ceroni
Count Franz Carl Inzaghi
Count Max Adam Lengheim
Count Franz Bernhard Saurau
Count Max Joseph Schrottenbach
Franz Wagner, *Commercien Actuarius*
Count Johann Joseph Wurmbrand

(f) *Inner Austria*, Hofkammer[c]
Count Jacob Ernst Leslie, President
Count Dismas Attems, Vice-President
Paul von Aposteln
Baron Laurenz Berlendis
Count Dismas Dietrichstein
Count Georg Gleisbach
Count Karl Heinrichsperg
Johann Lautner
Count Johann Morell
Johann von Peckh
Johann Pichl
Johann Popp
Johann Prettl
Johann Rios
Johann Sartori
Count Georg Schrattenbach
Baron Franz Sternbach
Baron Bartlme Tinti
Baron Joseph Wertenberg
Johann von Wildenstein

(g) *Lower Austria*, Regierung
Count Sigmund Friedrich Khevenhüller, *Statthalter*
Count Johann Christoph Oedt, *Vice-Statthalter*
Christoph Friedrich Schmid von Wayenberg, *Canzler*

Herrenstand *Councillors*
Count Joh. Adam Abensperg und Traun
Count Franz Theodor Andlern
Count Franz Jacob Brandis
Count Joh. Jos. Breuner
Count Leopold Dietrichstein[d]
Count Franz Fried. Engel[e]
Count Carl Anton Harrach
Count Carl Otto Hohenfeld[d]

TABLE 13.1. (*cont.*)

Count Carl Jos. Lamberg und Sprintzenstein
Count Franz Anton Lamberg und Sprintzenstein
Baron Carl Gottlieb Mansberg
Marchese Franz Reymund Montecuccoli
Count Joh. Baptist Pergen
Count Joh. Ferd. Pergen
Count Ferd. Rindsmaul
Baron Ferd. Heinr. Risenfels
Count Adam Rothal
Count Jos. St. Julian
Count Xtian Augustin Seilern
Count Niclas Stella
Count Wilhelm Thürheim*e*
Baron Bartholomoeus Tinti

Ritterstand *Councillors*
Franz Eugeni Dizent von Felsenthal
Ferdinandus Andreas Engelshofen
Franz Anton Edler von Gall
Adam Domin. Ferd. Edler von Guarient u. Raal
Jos. Ant. Edler von Hoche
Wenzel von Kellern
Adam Dominic Locherer von Lindenheim
Joh. Ferd. Edler von Löwenegg*f*
Philipp von Managetta u. Lerchenau
Jos. Ant. Dominic Edler von Mayenberg
Franz Christoph Edler von Menshengen
Joh. Baptist Edler von Menshengen
Carl Jos. von Oettel
Carl Joseph von Palm*g*
Ehrenr. Adam Augustin von Pinell
Joh. Leop. Edler Herr von Schick
Jacob Christoph Schmerling
Leop. Edler von Schmerling*d*
Jos. Edler von Schweizhardt
Franz Carl von Seitern
Jos. Joh. Edler von Tepfern
Joh. Jacob Edler von Weber
Franz Ulrich Wensern von Frayenthurn

Gelehrtenstand *Councillors*
Carl Joseph Cetto
Joh. Jacob Fraisel, *utriusque juris doctor* (UJD)
Zacharias Gerbrand
Joh. Georg Hann
Joh. Math. Kirchstettern
Jos. von Managetta u. Lerchenau
Franz Adam Pfann UJD
Joh. Gottlieb Ferd. Pichler
Joh. Jacob Rampach
Joh. Georg Saar
Franz Anton Edler von Spaun UJD

Joh. Carl Weber Edler von Fumberg
Paul Maxim Zwenghof

---

^a Vice-President of Bohemian *Kammer*.
^b President of Bohemian *Kammer*.
^c 1737.
^d 'Absent'.
^e 'At Linz'.
^f 'At present, accounts Councillor ['Rait-Herr'] in the *Landhaus*'.
^g 'Absent as ambassador at Regensburg'.

Sources: for (*a*), (*b*), and (*g*), *Court Calendar* for 1740; for (*c*)–(*f*), Hofkammerarchiv, typewritten index to Lower Austrian *Herrschaftsakten*, 595–6, 612–13. Conventions of transcription and arrangement of names as in Tables 12.1*–4*. The distinction between *Herrenstand* and *Ritterstand* councillors is preserved in the table only for the large Lower Austrian *Regierung*. Hassenpflug-Elzholz, *Böhmen und die böhmischen Stände*, 73–4 gives a list for the *Statthalterei* in 1741 from the Prague *Adalbertskalender* for 1742. This omits Carl Breda, Wenzel Chotek, Johann Clary, and Franz Martinitz, and includes Franz Leop. Buquoy, Rudolf Chotek, Franz Heinr. Schlick, and Ritter Johann Dohalsky. Only exact dates for appointments would show when these changes occurred.

TABLE 13.2. *Leading local councillors, 1748–54*

*indicates a member of the *Consessus Delegatus in Causis Summi Principis et Commissorum*

1748	1752	1754
(a) Bohemia		
'Deputation'	'Repraesentation und Cammer'	'Repraesentation und Kammer'
Baron [Wenzel] von Netolicky, President	*as 1748*	Baron Wenzel Casimir Netolicky von Eysenberg, President
Count [Friedrich Karl] von Hatzfeld		*Johan Bořek Dohalsky
Count [Franz Joseph] von Pachta		Prince Carl Egon Fürstenberg
[Joseph Philipp] von Seyffert		*Count Carl Fried. Hatzfeld
[Franz Xaver von] Textor		Joh. Georg Hilleprand von Brandau
		Count Franz Jos. Kollowrat
		Otto Edler von Loscani
		Anton Ferd. von Lutter
		*Wilh. Malowetz
		*Count Vincenz Mitrowitz
		*Baron Johann Nep. Mitrowsky
		Count Franz Jos. Pachta
		Ignaz von Textor
		Count Franz Xaver Wieschnick
		*Count Franz Wenzel Zinzendorf
(b) Moravia		
'Deputation'	'Repraesentation und Cammer'	'Repraesentation und Cammer'
Baron Heinrich Cajetan Blümegen, President	Baron Heinrich Cajetan Blümegen, President	Blümegen *ut sup.*, President
Baron Franz von Tauber	Baron Franz von Tauber	Count Michael Hermann Althann
Baron [Joh. Wenzel] Widmann	Rudolph von Blumencron	Count Adam Ignatz Berchtold
	Joh. Franz von Prandau	Rudolph Maxim. von Blumencron
	Lazarus von Weinersperg	Baron Ignatz Domin. Chorinsky
		*Johann Baptista, Edler von Grimm

(c) Silesia

'Amt'	'Amt'	
Count Friedrich Wilhelm Haugwitz, President	Count Franz Larisch, President	Joh. Caspar von Hauder
Baron Gustav Stronsky	Johann Wolfgang von Dorsch	*Count Otto Carl Haugwitz
Johann von Dorsch	Ferdinand Ignatz von Glomer	Joh. Franz Hilleprand von Brandau
	Baron Ernst Mittrowsky	*Count Aloysius Podstatzky
	Baron Max Heinrich Sobeck	Count Friedr. Sinzendorf
		Baron Franz Erdmann Tauber von Taubenfurth
		Baron Joh. Wenzel Widmann
		Lazarus von Wimmersperg

'Repraesentation und Cammer, wie auch konigl. Amt.'

Count Franz Wilh. Larisch, President
Joh. Wolfgang von Dorsch
Ferd. Ign. von Glommer
*Rudolph von Grohmann
Georg Friedr. von Lachawiz
*Ernst Joh. von Locella
*Baron Ernst Benj. Mittrowsky
*Joh. Anton Pino von Friedenthal
Baron Maxim. Heinr. Sobeck
Baron Sebast. Felix Schwanenberg

(d) Lower Austria

'Repraesentation und Cammer'

Baron Heinrich Wilhelm Haugwitz, President
Baron Joh. Paul Buol
Joh. Fried. von Eger
Elias Reichhard Engel
Philipp Andre Gigant
Victor Joseph Häring

1748	1752	1754
		Jos. Ferd. Holger UJD
		Christian Ferd. von Kessler
		Count Sigmund Khevenhüller-Metsch
		Baron Gottfried Koch
		Anton Georg Koller, 'Feld-Kriegs-Commissarius'
		Joh. Jos. Kornritter von Ehrenhalm
		Count Franz Anton Lamberg
		*Ignaz von Lauch
		Baron Joh. Jos. Managetta, Vice-President
		Carl Jos., Edler von Pillewitz
		Jacob, Edler von Pistrich
		*Franz Jacob, Edler von Plöckner
		Joh. Christoph von Püchler
		Joh. Gottlieb Püchler
		Jos. Franz, Edler von Reichmann
		Joh. Leop., Edler von Schick
		Count Leopold Schlick
		Jacob Christoph, Edler von Schmerling
		Peter von Schwachheim
		Jos. Joh., Edler von Tepfern
		Baron Bartholome Tinti
		Jos. Veronese
		Anton Domin. Vogel
		*Joh. Bapt. Wagner
		Count Gottlieb Windischgräz
		Paul Michael Zwenghof

'Repraesentation und Cammer'

Count Franz Andler und Witte, President
Count Philibert Fueger
Max, Edler von Schmerling
John. Friedr. von Schmid
Franz, Edler von Schwingheim
Baron Carl Jos. Troilo von Troiburg
Andreas Witsmann, 'Kriegscommissarius'

'Repraesentation und Cammer'

Count Ernst Wenzel Schafgotsch, President
Count Carl Thomas Breuner
Franz Anton Burmeister
Anton von Curti de Francini
Joseph von Ehrenstein
Johann Joseph Kofler
Gabriel Pessler
Johann Christoph Schutz, 'Oberkriegscommissarius'
Count Maria Joseph Auersperg
Franz von Eder
Count Vincenz Ursini und Rosenberg
Count Adolph Wagensperg

'Repraesentation und Cammer'

Count Felix Sobeck (*sic*), President
Franz Philipp von Biber
Heinr. Wilh. von Blumencron
Count Joh. Gottfr. Heister
Carl Jacob Kallhammer
Count Niclas Sebast. Lodron

(f) *Styria*

'Deputation'

Count Ernst Schafgotsch, President
Franz Anton Burmeister
Heinrich Wilhelm Haugwitz
Johann Joseph Kofler

'Repraesentation und Cammer'

Franz von Andler, President
Count Philibert Fueger
von Loscani
Franz Jos. von Schwingheim

'Repraesentation und Cammer'

Count Ernst Wenzel Schafgotsch, President
Count Carl Thomas Breuner
Franz Anton Burmeister
Anton von Curti de Francini
Joseph von Ehrenstein
Johann Joseph Kofler
Gabriel Pessler
Johann Christoph Schutz, 'Oberkriegscommissarius'

(g) *Carinthia*

'Deputation'

Count Jos. Nostiz, President
[Philipp von] Biber
Adam von Ferin
Jos. Victor Haring

'Repraesentation und Cammer'

Count Felix Sobegg, President
Philipp von Biber
Heinr. Wilh. von Blumencron
Count Joh. Gottfr. Heister
Count Niclas Lodron
Count Adolph Wagensperg

1748	1752	1754
		Anton Jos. von Müllberg, 'Feld Kriegs Commissarius' Baron Matthias Carl Rechbach
(b) Krain 'Deputation' Count Johann Seyfried Herberstein, President Baron Ernst Mittrovsky Anton Maria Stupan von Ehrenstein	'Repraesentation und Cammer' Count Joh. Seyfried Herberstein, President Count Heinrich Auersperg Max von Bechini Count Jobst Barbo von Milburg, *Kriegs Commissarius* Baron Franz Raigersfeld	'Repraesentation und Cammer' Count Johann Seyfried Herberstein, President Count Heinrich Auersperg Joh. Jos. von Hoffmann, 'Landes Rectification Director' Baron Franz Raigersfeld Joh. Andre Uhris, 'Feld Kriegs Commissarius'
(i) Tyrol		'Repraesentation und Cammer' Count Joseph Trapp, President Baron Rudolph Anton Buol Joh. Ignatz von Hormayr Count Leop. Kunigl Anton von Schullern Franz Jos. von Störzinger Count Sebastian Trapp Count Anton Wicka

Sources: for 1748 and 1752, HKA Hss. 220 and 247 respectively, except for Silesia and Styria. For Silesia, the names are those appointed on 28 Jan. 1743; d'Elvert, *Verfassung*, 149–50; there may have been subsequent changes. The Styrian *Deputation* appointed in Oct. 1748 is listed in Thiel, AÖG 111 (1930) 619. The MS sources do not give any names for Upper Austria (entered as both 'Österreich ob der Enns' and 'Ober Österreich') in 1748, nor for Lower Austria in 1748 or 1752. The list of the latter's *Repraesentation* in 1754 is taken from the *Court Calendar*, which divides councillors into *Herrenstand*, *Ritterstand* and *Gelehrtenstand* members. The other names for 1754 are also from the *Calendar*, except Tyrol, taken from HKA Hs. 248 fo. 161ᵛ.

TABLE 13.3. *Leading local councillors, 1765–79*

1765	1779

(a) Bohemia, 'Gubernium'

1765	1779
Count. Philipp Kollowrat, President	Prince Karl Egon Fürstenberg, President
Joh. Philipp Bieschin von Bieschin	Count Michael Ferd. Althann
Count Franz Leopold Buquoy	Johann Wenzel Astfeld
Count Jos. Maxim. Kinsky von Chinitz	Joh. Philipp Bieschin von Bieschin
Count Carl Ignatz Clary und Aldringen	Count Jos. Maxim. Kinsky von Chinitz
Count Joh. Christoph Dohalitz	Count Carl Ignaz Clary und Aldringen
Count Adam Franz Hartig	Count Philipp Clary und Aldringen
Marcellus von Hennet	Count Adam Franz Hartig
Wilh. Ferd. Edler von Hilmayer	Marcellus von Hennet
Count Leop. Kollowrat	Wilh. Ferd. Edler von Hilmayer
Count Procop Kollowrat	Paul von Hoyer
Franz Carl Kressel, Baron Qualtenberg	Johann Marquard Kotz, Baron Dobrz
Count Franz Anton Nostitz-Rieneck	Wenzel von Margelik
Count Jos. Wilh. Nostitz-Rieneck	Joh. Edler von Mayer
Count Franz Jos. Pachta	Count Franz Anton Nostitz-Rieneck
Christian von Peche	Count Jos. Wilh. Nostitz-Rieneck
Count Carl Gotthard Schafgotsch	Count Franz Jos. Pachta
Count Ernst Wilh. Schafgotsch	Count Karl Gotth. Schafgotsch
Count Christian Sternberg	Mathias Jos. Smitmer
Count Franz Adam Sternberg	Count Christian Sternberg
Joseph Joachim Wanczura von Rzehnitz	Count Franz Adam Sternberg
Count Franz Xaver Wieschnick	Baron Joh. Wenzel Wasmuth
Count Joh. Jos. Wrtby	Count Franz Ernst Wallis
	Count Franz Xaver Wieschnick
	Count Joh. Jos. Wrtby

(b) Moravia, 'Landes-Gouverno'

1765	1779
Count Franz Ant. Schrattenbach, President	Count Christoph Blümegen *Landeshauptmann*
Baron Christoph Blümegen	Franz von Beer
Jos. Maria von Friedenthal	Baron Joh. Nepomac Fanal
Count Leop. Franz Schlick	Joh. Maria Friedenthal
Ludwig Ferd. Procopp	Joh. Jos. von Kriegisch
Ignaz Schröfl von Mannsperg	Baron Ernest Locella
Franz Erdmann Tauber, Baron Taubenfurt	Count Joh. Bapt. Mitrowsky
Baron Jos. Widmann	Count Karl zu Salm Reifferscheid
	Count Vincenz Salm u. Neuburg
	Ignatz Schröfl von Mannsperg
	Johann Tauber, Baron Taubenfurst [*sic*]

TABLE 13.3. (cont.)

1765	1779

(c) Silesia, 'k.k. Amt'

Baron Maxim. Heinrich Sobeck, President	Count Pompejus Brigido, President
Anton von Friedenthal	Jos. Peter von Altmann
Ernst Joh. von Locella	Anton von Beer
Baron Benj. Mittrowsky	Count Joh. Larisch
Baron Sebast. Felix Schwanenberg	Baron Sebast. Felix Schwanenberg
Baron Jos. Troilo	Count Joh. Sobeck
	Ant. Jos. à Sole
	Karl Töpfer

(d) Lower Austria, 'Regierung'

Statthalter

Count Franz Ferdinand Schrattenbach	Count Christian August Seilern

Vice-Statthalter

Baron Anton Franz Buol	Count Joseph Herberstein

Kanzler

Thos. Ignatz, Edler von Pöck	as 1765

Herrenstand Councillors

Count Rudolph Abensperg und Traun	Count Rudolph Abensperg und Traun
Baron Joh. Paul Buol	Count August Auersperg
Count Franz Colloredo	Count Ludwig Bathyani
Count Joh. Nepomuc Dietrichstein	Count Heinrich Blümegen
Count Franz Sigmund Engel	Baron Joseph Ignatz Brandau
Count Joseph Herberstein	Baron Johann Paul Buol
Baron Joh. Baptist Ludwigstorf	Franz Ludwig Burkhard von der Klee
Baron Joseph von der Mark	Baron Bartholomaus Carignani
Count Friedrich von der Nath	Count Joh. Clary und Aldringen
Baron Conrad Nefzer	Count Joh. Nepomuc Eszterházy
Count Ferdinand Schullenburg-Oeynhausen	Baron Johann Gudenus
Count Guido Starhemberg	Count Joh. Bapt. Haddik
Count Joseph Wilczek	Count Anton Hartig
Baron Jacob Wöber	Count Heinrich Heissenstamm
	Count Sigmund Heissenstamm
	Count Joseph Herberstein
	Baron Franz Jos. Jungwürth
	Baron Joseph König zu Cronburg
	Baron Johann Bapt. Ludwigstorf
	Baron Konrad Nefzer
	Count Wenzel Paar

1765	1779
	Baron Joseph Penkler
	Count Prosper Sinzendorf
	Count Gundacker Franz
	Starhemberg
	Count Quido Starhemberg
	Count Franz Stockhammer
	Baron Felix Stuppan
	Count Joh. Wenzel Ugarte
	Count Stephen Wallis
	Baron Jacob Wöber

Ritterstand Councillors

1765	1779
Joseph von Carriere	Jos. Anton Baumann
Johann Carl Cetto von Kronstorf	Jos. Ferd. Bock und Pollach
Joh. Friedr., Edler von Eger	Jos. von Carriere
Jos. Ignatz von Egger	Joh. Karl Cetto von Kronstorf
Franz de Paula von Fraissl	Wilh. Ernst, Edler von Felsenberg
Carl Jos., Edler von Führenberg	Franz de Paulla von Fraissl
Franz Anton, Edler von Gall	Peregrin Adam Freytag von
Franz Berh. von Kees	Freydenfeld
Jos. Aloysius von Leporini	Ignatz Ludwig von Hagen
Johann Anton, Edler von	Franz von Haling
Mayenberg	Franz Jos. von Hess
Frans Christoph, Edler von	Joh. Kaspar von Hollbein
Mensshengen	Franz Bernh., Edler von Kees
Ignatz, Edler von Mensshengen	Ignatz Franz Krammer
Joh. Bapt., Edler von Mensshengen	Franz von Mandelli
Joh. Bernhard von Pelser	Philipp Jakob, Edler von
Jacob, Edler von Pistrich	Mannagetta und Lerchenau
Franz Jos., Edler von Reichmann	Franz von Martin
Joh. Leop., Edler von Schick	Anton Jos. von Mayenberg
Joh. Ludwig von Tiell	Jos. Anton, Edler von Mayenberg
Jos. Jacob von Veronese	Ignatz, Edler von Menshengen
Paul Michael von Zwenghof	Karl Leopold von Moser
	Joh. Bernhard von Pelser
	Franz von Persch
	Zacharias Christoph, Edler von
	Perthold
	Karl Jos., Edler von Pillewitz
	Jakob, Edler von Pistrich
	Joh. Baptist, Edler von Pranghe
	Paul Rotter
	Jakob, Edler von Schickh
	Jakob Schosulan
	Joh. Ludwig von Tiell
	Joh. Bapt., Edler von Waldstätten
	Ferd. Eberl von Wallenberg
	Christian von Wallenfeld

TABLE 13.3. *(cont.)*

1765	1779

Gelehrtenstand Councillors

1765	1779
Franz Jos. Bratsch, UJD	Franz von Aichen
Joh. Jos. von Fraissl, UJD	Joseph Froidevo
Franz Carl Gaar	Franz Grader
Philipp Jakob Hackher	Franz von Grienwalder
Mathias Wilh. Hahn	Franz Jos., Edler von Hacker zu
Jos. Martin, Edler von Hauer	Hart
Franz Pallitsch von Hartenfels	Philipp Friedr., Edler von Hacker zu
Joh. Adam Penz, UJD	Hart
Joh. Jordan, Edler von Pöck	Franz Karl Hägelin
Joseph Quarin	Bernhard von Horten
Ferd. Jos. von Sartori	Franz, Edler von Kienmayr
Joh. Thaddaeus, Edler von Spaun	Joh. von Le Fefvre
Franz Anton Vogel	Franz Pallitsch von Hartenfels
	Joseph Quarin
	Anton Roscio
	Ignatz, Edler von Rustel
	Ferd. Jos. von Sartori
	Joseph von Sonnenfels

(e) *Austria above the Enns*

'Landeshauptmannschaft'

1765	1779
Count Christoph Wilh. Thürheim, *Landeshauptmann*	Count Christoph Thürheim, *Landeshauptmann*
Herr Johann Franz von Stiebar, 'Landes-Anwald'	Herr Johann Franz von Stiebar, 'Landesanwald'
	Thaddäus, Edler von Spaun, 'Kanzleydirektor'

Herrenstand

1765	1779
Count Johann Leopold Clam	Count Johann Albert Clam
Count Joseph Weichard Engl	Count Johann Leopold Clam
Count Carl Fieger	Count Joseph Weichard Engl
Baron Carl Leopold Häcklberg	Count Karl von Fieger
Baron Johann Georg Hochenegg	Baron Karl von Fieger
Baron Franz Xaver Pöcksteiner von Wossenbach	Baron Karl Leopold Hacklberg
Count Johann Christoph Salburg	Count Franz Maria von Mayantz
	Baron Johann Baptist Pilatti
	Baron Franz Xaver Pocksteiner, *Hofkammer* and Bank representative
	Count Aloysius Spindler

Ritterstand

1765	1779
Joseph von Hammer	Ehrenreich Edler von Bartuska
Ferdinand von Mayenberg	Joseph von Kurz
Franz. Edler von Schwingheim	

1765	1779
Gelehrtenbank	*Gelehrtenstand*

Thomas Carl Baussart	Franz Xaver Hotmann,
Aloysius Krannewitter	*Protomedicus, Referendar in*
Rogerius von Ruttershausen	*Sanitätssachen*
	Joseph Pachner
	Max Gandolph von Steyerer

(f) *Inner Austria,* 'Gubernium'

Count Joh. Max Wildenstein, Interim President	Count Aloysius Podstatzky-Lichtenstein, President
Count Georg Bathyan	Count Dismas Dietrichstein
Jacob Ernst von Cerroni	Karl, Edler von Geraim
Count Gundaker Herberstein	Franz Ernst Edler von Plöckner
Joh. Jos. Edler von Kofflern	Jos. Sigmund Edler von Polan
Baron Jos. von der Marck	Baron Christoph Rottenberg
Ernst, Edler von Plöckner	Count Cajetan Sauer
Count Vincenz Ursin u. Rosenberg	Wolfgang, Herr von Stubenberg
Count Cajetan Sauer	Count Anton Stürckh
Wolf, Herr von Stubenberg	Count Gottfried Suardi
Count Gundaker Stuppach	Baron Max Christoph Waldmansdorf
Ferd. Jos. von Thunfeld	Count Gundaker Thos.
Count Adolph Wagensperg	Wurmbrand-Stuppach
Count Joseph Wurmbrand	Count Jacob Wurmbrand-Stuppach

(g) *Tyrol*

	'k.k. Gubernium in O. Oesterreich
'Landes-Gubernium' 1765[a]	Fürstenthum und Landen'
Count Cassian Ignatz Enzenberg, 'President des königl. Gubernii in denen Ober-Oesterreichischen Landen'	Count Johannes Gottfried Heister,[b] President
	Count Leopold Franz Kinigl,[b] Vicepresident
Johann Ignatz von Hormayr	Baron Joseph Ceschi[b]
Count Leopold Franz Kinigl	Joseph Conforti,[b] Tyrol *Landmann*
Joseph André Laicharting von Eichberg	Count Joseph Coreth[b]
Johann Sebastian von Miller	Count Franz Enzenberg[b]
Count Aloysius Särenthein	Count Felix Khuen[b]
Franz Ignatz Störzinger von Sigmundsried	Michael von Menghin (*Rat in Sanitätssachen*)
Franz Anton von Thurnfels	Baron Karl Hieronymus Rall
	Count Aloysius Sarentheim[b]
	Count Johann Spaur[b]
	Baron Ignatz Sternbach[b]

TABLE 13.3. (cont.)

1765	1779
(b) Galicia	'Landesgouvernium', Count Heinrich Auersperg, President Georg Adalbert von Beeckhen Count Joseph Brigido Count Sigmund Gallenberg Vincenz von Guinigi Franz Joseph von Knopp Johann Christoph von Koranda Baron Michael Gottlieb Raigersfeld Franz Paula von Scheiner Johann Georg von Urtho

a The *Revisionsstelle* (see below) was merged in the *Gubernium* from 1763 and has no separate listing. In 1779 it is again listed separately but only two members were not also in the *Gubernium*.

b Also councillor of *Ober-und Vorderösterreichische Revisionsstelle*.

The names are taken from the *Court Calendar* for 1765 and 1779, and are transcribed and rearranged as in the preceding tables.

TABLE 13.4. *Circle Captains (Kreishauptmänner) at selected dates*

(a) Bohemia

	1748	1752	1762	Circle (Czech)	1763	1770	1780
Bechin	Count Wenzel Millesimo Franz von Jungwirth	Count Wenzel Millesimo	Franz Ernst von Malowetz	Bechin (Táborský)	Count Leopold Bubna	Balthazar von Bossy	Baron Joh. Adam von Werner
Beraun	Baron Stephan Malowetz Johann Martin Bischin von B.	Baron Johann Hochberg von Hennersdorf	Count Franz Przichowsky	Beraun (Berounský)	Count Franz Przichowsky	Johann Baron Dobrsch und Wohrasenitz	Joseph de Boulles
Bidschau	— —	Johann[Wenzel] Lamotta von Frintropp	Johann Lamotta von Frintropp	Bidschau (Bydžovský)	Lt. Col. Stefan des Feignes	Franz Sadlo von Wrazny	Franz Sadlo von Wrazny
Budweis	—	Wenzel Karwinsky von Karwin	Adalbert Nettworsky von Brzezy	Budweis (Budějovický)	Leopold von Berchtold	Baron des Feigni (*sic*) la Tournelle	Joh. Jos. Otto von Otenthal
Bunzlau	Count Joseph Trautmannsdorf Joh. Bsenscky von Porubr	Count Jos. Trautmannsdorf	Joseph Raschin von Riesenburg	Bunzlau (Boleslavský)	Joseph Raschim von Riesenburg	Joseph Raschin von Riesenburg	Baron Maximilian Ehrenburg
Chrudim	Count Hyronimo Kollowrat Wenzel von Stupno	Johann von Zaruba	Johann Mladotta von Selopisk	Chrudim (Chrudimský)	Johann Mladotta von Selopisk	Johann Raschin, Baron Riesenburg	Johann Raschin, Baron Riesenburg

TABLE 13.4. *(cont.)*

(a) Bohemia

	1748	1752	1762	1763	1770	1780
Czaslau (Čáslavský)	Baron Berchtold Hustirzan Franz Wenzel von Haugwitz	Baron Johann Dobrzensky	Baron Peter Dobrzensky	Jan von Jeřabiny	Joh. Jos. Gerzabek von Gerzabina	Joh. Jos. Gerzabek von Gerzabina
Elbogen (Loketský)	—	Franz Hochberg von Hunnersdorf	Franz Wenzel Haugwitz von Bisskupitz	Balthazar von Bossi	Joh. Otto von Ottilienfeld	Johann Otto von Ottilienfeld
Kaurzim (Kouřimský)	Count Ottocar Staremberg Wenzel Zhorski von Z.	Anton von Worzikowsky	Anton von Worzikowsky	Anton von Worzikowsky	Joh. Streer von Streruwitz	Karl Jos. Biener von Bienerberg
Klattau (Klatovský)	—	Joseph Schmidtgräbner von Lustenegg	Joseph Schmidtgräbner von Lustenegg	?Count Sebastian Kinigl	Count Sebastian Kinigl	Count Sebastian Kinigl
Königgrätz (Hradecký)	Baron Wenzel Wanzura [Johann] Wenzel Lamotta von Frintropp	Count Wenzel Wanzura	Count Wenzel Wanzura	Count Wenzel Wanzura	Baron Wenzel Wanzura von Rzehnitz	Anton von Hanisch

Baron Wenzel Krangstein Johann Carl Bischin von B.	Johann Carl von Pischin		Baron Franz Reyssky von Dubnitz		Baron Franz Reyssky von Dubnitz	Franz Reysky, Baron Dubnitz	Wolfgang von Schönau
Count Wenzel Klenau Joseph Schmiedelgräbner	Baron Ferdinand Rummerskirchen	Pilsen	Count Max Joseph Laschansky	(Plzeňský)	Count Max Laschansky	Baron Carl Michna von Weitzenau	Casimir Wiedersperger von Wiedersperg
Baron Johann Riemmerskirchen Ferdinand von Malowetz	[Joh.] Martin Pischin von P.	Prachin	Johann Martin Pischin von. P.	(Pracheňský)	?Johann Martin Pischin von P.	Franz Wenzel Pergler von Perglas	Lorenz Schönpflug von Gamsenberg
Count Philipp Clarenstein Carl Hildebrand Otthausen	Count Philipp Clarenstein	Rakonitz	Count Karl Clary und Aldringen	(Rakovnický)	Baron Johann Wassmuth	Count Procop Laschansky	Baron Severin von Langendorf
Baron Franz de Fin Johann von Turba	Baron Franz de Fin	Saatz	Anton Andritzky von Andrz (sc. Oudrecký z Oudřce)	(Žatecký)	Karel von Schrollenberg	Franz Carl Schroll von Schrollenberg	Christoph Ernest (sic) von Millach

Adjunkten to Bohemian Circle Captains, 1780

Bechin 1. Franz Strer von Streruwitz; 2. Jos. Tieschowsky von Trostenberg; *Beraun* Anton Losy von Losenau; *Bidschau* Count Wenzel Cavriani; *Budweis* Ignaz von Papa; *Bunzlau* Ferd. von Papa; *Chrudim* Leop. Talatsko von Geschtietitz; *Czaslau* 1. Jos. Stransky von Stranska, 2. Ernest von Scheumann; *Elbogen* Christoph von Bigato; *Kaurzim* 1. Joh. von Launay, 2. Baron Jos. Kotz von Dobrz; *Klattau* 1. Ferd. Patzowsky von Liebin, 2. Peter Nigroni von Riefenbach; *Königgräz* 1. Wenzel Logdmann von Auen, 2. Count Anton Bredau; *Leitmeritz* 1. Baron Wenzel Reisky von Dubnitz, 2. Caspar von Albek; *Pilsen* 1. Franz Pergler von Perglas, 2. Count Rudolph Morzin; *Prachin* Franz von Brieschin; *Rakonitz* Joh. von Mayern; *Saatz* Ignaz Otto von Ottilienfeld

TABLE 13.4. (cont.)

(b) Moravia

Circle	1737	1748	1752	1762	1770	1780
Brerau (Přerovský)	..	Baron Minquitsberg	Emanuel Cajetan von Zawisch	Count Friedrich Sinzendorf	Johann Franz von Beer	Emmanuel Zebo von Brachfeld
Brünn (Brněský)	Franz von Morowetz	Baron Walldorf	Count Michael Hermann Althann	Joh. Leop. von Schmelzdorf	Count Carl Friedr. Zollern	Count Carl Friedr. Zollern
Hradisch (Hradištský)	Count Franz Carl Chorinsky	von Zialkowitz	Baron Franz Wassenberg	Baron Franz Wassenberg	Baron Franz Wassenberg	Baron Achatius Rebentisch
Iglau (Jihlavský)	Carl von Almstein	Count Althann	Joh. Leop. von Schmelzdorf	Baron Joh. Adam Werner	Baron Joh. Adam Werner	Balthasar Clement von Bossi
Olmütz (Olomucký)	Franz Campoli Baron Miniatti	Baron Schubirz	Baron Carl Gottfried Almstein	Baron Emanuel Cajetan Zawisch	Count Friedr. Sinzendorf	Maximilian Butz von Rolsperg
Znaim (Znojemský)	Count Carl Souches	Count Berchtold	Baron Wolfgang Eisenberg	Baron Wolfgang Eisenberg	Baron Wolfgang Kaltschmied von Eysenberg	Baron Wolfgang Kaltschmied von Eysenberg

Substitutes to Circle Captains in Moravia 1770, 1780

Brerau, 1770 1. Count Michael Philipp Althann, 2. Johann von Adametz auf Dambrowka, 1780 1. Baron Johann Bapt. von Forgatsch, 2. Johann von Adametz auf Dambrowka, 3. Johann Nepomuck, Edler von Salerno; *Brünn* 1770 1. Count Michael Johann Althann, 2. Sigmund von Stössl, 1780 1. Count Michael Johann Althann, 2. Baron Franz Dubsky von Tržebomislitz, 3. Ferdinand von Geissler; *Hradisch* 1770 1. Johann Řžikowsky von Dobreschitz, 2. Maximilian Butz von Rolsperg, 1780 1. Ignaz Cajetan von Bevier und Freyriedt, 2. Johann Nepomuc von Zischka, 3. Augustin Cajetan Reichmann von Hochkirchen; *Iglau* 1770 1. Baron Achatius Rebentisch 2. Emanuel Zebo von Brachfeld, 1780 1. Count Leopold Berchtold, 2. Johann Nepomuck von Ollnhausen 3. Vincenz Jos, Edler von Rosenzweig, *Olmütz* 1770 1. Baron Franz Michael Schubirž von Chobinie, 2. Carl Franz von Strachwitz, 1780 Baron Johann Zwolle and Carl Franz von Strachwitz; *Znaim* 1770

(c) Silesia

Landesältester in 1762: Principality of *Neisse*, Franz von Mykusch und Buchberg; *Teschen*, Rudolph von Bselesta; *Troppau*, Franz Ignatz von Görlich

(d) Austria below the Enns (*Lower Austria*)

Ober-Manhartsberg		Unter-Manhartsberg	
Count Johann Joseph Herberstein	1753–5	Baron Philipp Joseph Managetta	1753–64
Baron Anton Egon Alberstorf	1755–64	Baron Philipp. Jos. Managetta jr.	1764–78
Count Leopold Hoyos	1764–71	Baron Johann Michael Sala	1778–1801
Baron Johann Cristoph Gudenus	1771?–86		
Circle Commissary 1763 Count Leopold Hoyos		*Circle Commissary* 1763 Count Wenzel Sinzendorf	
Ober-Wienerwald		Unter-Wienerwald	
Joseph von Sondersleben	1753–64	Baron Anton Vincenz Pilatti	1753–60
Count Wolf Auersperg	1764–71	Ignaz, Edler von Mensshengen	1760–77
Count August Auersperg			
Circle Commissary 1763 Count Leopold Schallenberg	1771–86	*Circle Commissary* 1763 Count Carl Pergen	

(e) Austria above the Enns (*Upper Austria*)

	1752	1763	1770	1780
Hausruck	Ferd. Hannibal von Rosenfeld	Ferd. Hannibal von Rosenfeld	Ehrenreich Edler von Bartuska	Ehrenreich Edler von Bartuska
Mühl und Machland	Ehrenreich Edler von Bartuska	Ehrenreich Edler von Bartuska	Count Reichard Salzburg	Jos. Zacher von Sonnenstein
Traun	..	Johann Jos. Eckhart zum Hammer	Jos. Zacher von Sonnenstein	Ferd. Haiden von Dorf

TABLE 13.4. *(cont.)*

(f) Carinthia, Styria, Tyrol

	1752	1756	1762
Carinthia			
'Mittleres Crays Amt'	Carl Jos. Keckhammer von Rannach		Count Norbert von Aicholt
'Oberes Crayss Amt'	Rochus von Leidl		Rochus von Leidl
'Unteres Kreisamt'	—		Baron Anton Mattenclot
Styria			
Cilli	Joh. Anton von Fuhrenberg		Johann Anton von Fuhrenberg
Judenburg	Count Gottfried Zoardi		Wolf von Stubenberg
Muhr und Trau	Max Sigmund von Bendel		[Bruck] Anton Franz von Philipitsch
Merzthal	Count Franz Anton Inzaghi		[Graz] Count Gottfried von Suardi
Vorrau	Count Christoph Webersperg		[Marburg] Max Sigmund von Bendel
Tyrol			
Viertel		*Viertelhauptleute*	
Bozen		von Franzin	[Etsch und Eisack] Joh. Andreas Franzin von Zinnenberg
Hall		Baron Rost	[Unterinnthal] Baron Leopold Rost
Imst		Baron Beier	[Oberinnthal] Joh. Andreas von Lachmayr
Italian Borders ('Welsche Confinen')		Baron Ceschi	Baron Joseph Ceschi
Meran		Baron Voglmayr von Grebner	Baron Anton Vogelmayr
Pust- und Wipptal			Joseph von Grebner

1737 Moravia, Hofkammerarchiv, typewritten index to the Lower Austrian *Herrschaftsakten*, 608–9, returns of 1738 showing the position in the previous year. *Bohemia* is omitted in this source. The names given here are taken from Hassenpflug-Elzholz, *Böhmen und die böhmischen Stände*, 59–60. In Silesia, there were no Circle Captains at this date, their equivalents, the *Landesälteste*, dating from 1744.

1748. HKA Hs. 220.

1752. HKA Hs. 247, also, for Bohemia, Rieger, *Zřízení krajské v Čechách*, ii. 163 n., Bohemian Circle Captains in 1751, 1756, 1763.

1762. HKA Hs. 243A, the volume of the *Staats-Inventarium* of 1763 dealing with the Bohemian and Austrian *camerale*. I am grateful to the staff of the Hofkammerarchiv for extracting the names other than those for Bohemia.

1763. For Bohemia, Rieger *loc. cit.* For Upper Austria, *Court Calendar*, 1763. For the Lower Austrian Circle Commissaries, paid by the Estates, HHSA Nachl. Zinz. Hs. 49, fo. 39^v, Lower Austrian *Landschaft* accounts. For the Lower Austrian *Kreishauptmänner*, Starzer, *Beiträge*, 494–7, with some corrections from the *Court Calendar*.

1770, 1780. The Moravian names are taken from the *Neuer Brünner Titular Kalender*; the Bohemian names are from the *Neuer Prager Titular und Loguaments Calender . . . auf das 1770 Jahr* and the *Neuer Titular und Wirtschafts-Kalender auf das Schaltjahr 1780* respectively. I am indebted to Mr J. E. Wall, Dr Vladislav Dokoupil, and the National Museum in Prague for microfilms of the relevant entries.

The Bohemian *Kreisadjunkten* are only entered in the 1780 calendar. Besides these names, a *Führungs-Commissarius* is entered for each Circle, and 8 Circles also had a *Commerzien-Commissarius*. In addition, there were several supernumeraries.

TABLE 13.5. *Membership of the Hungarian Council of Lieutenancy,*
1754 and 1775

Years of service bracketed

1754	1775
President	*President*
Count Lajos Batthyány (1751–65)	Prince Albert of Saxony (1765–80)
Clergy	*Clergy*
Count Miklós Csáky (1751–7)	Count Ferenc Berchtold (1766–76)
János Stephenics (1753–66)	Count József Batthyány (1772–85,
Károly Zbiskó (1746–55)	1790–9)
Magnates	*Magnates*
Count György Apponyi (1747–79)	Count György Apponyi (1747–79)
Count Pál Balassa (1734–71)	Baron (1772 Count) Ferenc Balassa
Count János Csáky (1743–83)	(1756–85)
Count György Erdődy (1723–59)	Count György Csáky (1772–83)
Count János Erdődy (1751–72)	Count Imre Csáky (1759–82)
Count Miklós Erdődy (1743–57)	Count János Csáky (1743–83)
Count Daniel Eszterházy (1749–57)	Count György Fekéte (1773–83)
Count Ferenc Eszterházy (1723–54)	Count Pál Festetics (1772–82)
Count Károly Eszterházy (1750–7)	Count János Illésházy (1759–79)
Count Miklós Eszterházy (1738–44,	Count János Mednyánszky (1771–89,
1748–55)	1791–1818)
Count József Illésházy (1747–66)	Count János Sztáray (1767–82)
Count József Keglevich (1735–65)	Count János Szunyogh (1750–82)
Baron József Révay (1746–66)	Count Zsigmond Zichy (1763–82)
Count János Szunyogh (1750–82)	
	Nobles
Nobles	István Andrássy (1769–76)
László Barinay (1738–62)	József Aszalay (1770–83)
Mihály Bobok (1746–56)	János Bachó (1770–83)
Imre Csiba (1748–69)	László Balogh (1757–75)
György Fabiánkovics (1732–54)	Károly Fabiánkovics (1766–83)
István Gosztonyi (1751–70)	János Hlavacs (1769–82)
Ferenc Sauska (1730–54)	József Klobusiczky (1770–88)
Márton Szuhányi (1733–54)	József Krassay (1762–76)
József Török (1754–8)	Ferenc Radkovicz (1769–90)
	Antal Sauska (1765–82)
	Mihály Sídó (1754–81)
	Ferenc Skerlecz (1769–97)

Source: Ember, *A. M. kir. helytartótanacs*, 197ff.

TABLE 13.6. *Membership of the Hungarian Chamber* (Hofkammer),
1754 and 1775
Years of service bracketed

1754	1775
Count Antal Grassalkovich, President (1748–71)	Count Nepomuc János Erdődy, (1772–82), President
László Amade (1750–64)	Count Pál Festetics, Vice-President
Antal Cotthmann (1750–66)	(1772–82)
Count Antal Csáky (1748–63)	József Bacsák (1769–85)
Count Nepomuc János Erdődy (1748–70)	Count József Batthyány (1770–82)
János Antal Hanssen de Jean (1741–60)	Count György Csáky (1757–77)
Antal Hraboviszky (1750–60)	Count József Csáky (1772–83)
Ferenc Kákonyi (1753–60)	Count Antal Grassalkovich jr.
Engelbert Kempelen (1753–4)	(1755–80)
János Koller (1746–76)	János Hentl (1773–9)
Károly Lajos Konckel (1741–61)	Farkas Kempelen, salt official (1764–85)
Félix Mohr (1754–64)	János Koller (1746–76)
Baron József Pfeffershoffen (1754–82)	László Orczy (1775–82)
István Podhradszky (1749–64)	Baron József Pfeffershoffen (1754–82)
Adam Rajcsányi (1743–64)	Gergely Sághy (1773–80)
György Ribics (1754–69)	Ferenc Schönholz (1767–84)
Ferenc Török (1743–76)	János Schilson (1771–84)
Baron László Vajay (1749–72)	József Splényi (1772–83)
Ignác Végh (1754–83)	Benedek Szendrey (1764–77)
Xavér Ferenc Weidinger (1733–57)	Ferenc Szöllösy (1774–85)
	Pál Szlávy (1766–83)
	Ferenc Török (1743–76)
	Ignác Végh (1754–83)
	Count Ferenc Zichy (1770–85)

The names are given by Fallenbüchl, *Levéltári közlemények*, 41 (1970) 294–8. He does not state state councillors' titles, and the ascription of them in the table is probably defective.

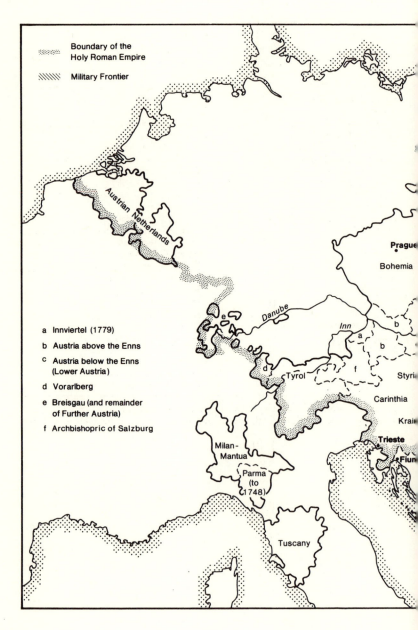

Boundary of the
Holy Roman Empire

Military Frontier

a Innviertel (1779)
b Austria above the Enns
c Austria below the Enns
  (Lower Austria)
d Vorarlberg
e Breisgau (and remainder
  of Further Austria)
f Archbishopric of Salzburg

Austrian Netherlands

Danube

Inn

Prague

Bohemia

a

b

b

f

Styria

Tyrol

Carinthia

Krain

Trieste

Fiume

Milan-
Mantua

Parma
(to
1748)

Tuscany

Outline map of the Habsbu

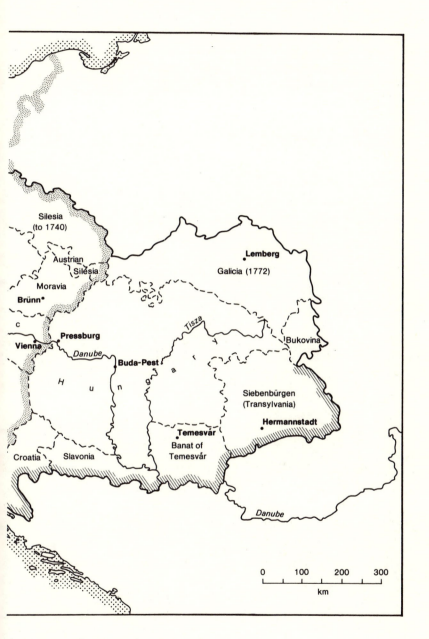

Silesia
(to 1740)

Austrian
Silesia

Moravia

Brünn•

c

Pressburg

Vienna

Danube

Buda-Pest

H   u   n   g   a

Croatia

Slavonia

•Lemberg

Galicia (1772)

Tisza

Bukovina

Siebenbürgen
(Transylvania)

•Hermannstadt

•Temesvár

Banat of
Temesvár

Danube

| 0 | 100 | 200 | 300 |
km

dominions under Maria Theresia.

INDEX

THE indexing of personal names is deliberately selective, in view of the extensive alphabetically arranged lists in the tables and App. C. Similarly, Jewish families in Vienna are not indexed by name, since many are shown in Fig. 2 and most are discussed at pp. 141–50. The page-numbers may refer to either the text or the notes.